Collectanea Augustiniana

Augustinian Historical Institute
Villanova University

General Editors

Joseph C. Schnaubelt, O.S.A.
Frederick Van Fleteren

PETER LANG
New York • San Francisco • Bern • Baltimore
Frankfurt am Main • Berlin • Wien • Paris

Collectanea Augustiniana

Augustine
Presbyter Factus Sum

Edited by
Joseph T. Lienhard, S.J.
Earl C. Muller, S.J.
Roland J. Teske, S.J.

PETER LANG
New York • San Francisco • Bern • Baltimore
Frankfurt am Main • Berlin • Wien • Paris

Library of Congress Cataloging-in-Publication Data

Augustine : presbyter factus sum / Joseph T. Lienhard, Earl C. Muller,
   Roland J. Teske.
      p. cm.
   Papers originally presented at a conference at Marquette University,
Nov. 1990.
   Includes bibliographical references and indexes.
   1. Augustine, Saint, Bishop of Hippo—Congresses.   I. Lienhard,
Joseph T.   II. Muller, Earl C.   III. Teske, Roland J.
   BR65.A9A88   1993   270.2'092—dc20   93-16709
   ISBN 0-8204-2199-5   CIP

Die Deutsche Bibliothek-CIP-Einheitsaufnahme

Augustine : Presbyter factus sum / Joseph T. Lienhard...—New York;
Berlin; Bern; Frankfurt/M.; Paris; Wien: Lang, 1993
   ISBN 0-8204-2199-5
NE: Lienhard, Joseph T. [Hrsg.]

Cover design by George Lallas.

The paper in this book meets the guidelines for permanence and
durability of the Committee on Production Guidelines for
Book Longevity of the Council on Library Resources.

CONTENTS

III God and Time

IV Human Existence

Foreword

Conceived in 1986, the *Collectanea Augustiniana* series is dedicated to advancing the understanding of various themes in Augustine's thought. The first volume was occasioned by the celebration at Villanova University in 1986–87 of the sixteenth centenary of Augustine's conversion and baptism. The occasion of this second volume, containing the best of the lectures of the conference at Marquette University in November, 1990, was the sixteenth centenary of Augustine's ordination to the priesthood. Surely, the definitive work on Augustine's theology of the priesthood has yet to be written; such a lacuna can hardly be filled by an introductory essay of this sort. Nevertheless, a few remarks on the circumstances of Augustine's ordination to the priesthood are in order.

From Augustine's baptism in the Milanese Basilica by Bishop Ambrose on Easter, 387, to his choice as the coadjutor and successor to Bishop Valerius in Hippo-Regius, much had happened. In Milan, he authored a work on the immortality of the soul, evidently notes based upon Porphyrian arguments on this topic and intended for the prospective third book of the *Soliloquia* (*Retractationes* I,v,1). At approximately the same time, the young convert embarked upon a project which he never finished, a series of works on the liberal arts which were to provide the intellectual purification, an *exercitatio animae*, necessary as a preparation for the human mind—so he thought at that time— to rise to the vision of God (*Retractationes* I,vi).

Augustine then sojourned for some six months in Rome. There, shortly after Augustine and Monica enjoyed the foretaste of eternal beatitude at Rome's port city Ostia (*Confessiones* IX,x,23–25), his mother died (*Confessiones* IX,xi,28). Of the immediate effects of this death upon Augustine we read in *Confessiones* IX,xii,29–xiii,37. Concerning the long-term effects of the death of his mother, especially a mother so influential on her son at critical junctures in his life, we can only speculate. During this same time, Augustine authored the *De moribus ecclesiae catholicae et de moribus Manichaeorum*, in which he compared the lives of those committed to the two different Weltanschauungen (*Retractationes* I,vii,1), and another work on the human soul, the *De quantitate animae*, in which he discussed the spiritual nature of the human soul (*Retractationes* I,viii,1). To some extent, this latter work, together with the *De immortalitate animae*, was Augustine's attempt to understand man's—

and therefore his own—true spiritual nature as a phase in the human mind's ascent to God. In this regard, let us not forget that the Augustinian ascent of the soul, like its Plotinian and Porphyrian predecessors, proceeds by a method of progressive interiority from material things inward to the human mind to God himself. Finally, Augustine began the *De libero arbitrio*, a work on the free choice of the human will, which he later finished in Africa after his ordination to the priesthood, circa 395 A.D. (*Retractationes* I,ix,1). In this work, destined to have great influence in the Middle Ages, Augustine successfully presented his recent formulation of the doctrine of the human free will as a coherent alternative to the Manichaean theory of the substantial nature of evil. Though Augustine's position on the relation between God's grace and the human will evolved and this evolution caused Augustine to re-evaluate many statements in this work, the references to grace and freedom of choice, as far back as the earliest works, should give us pause in evaluating the relation of Augustine to Neoplatonism. Both grace and freedom of the will are themes taken from or based upon the Bible which find little or no place in Greek or Roman thought. In our own age, in which some philosophers, following in the footsteps of the Enlightenment and more especially the German rationalists of the nineteenth century, have ignored any thought which smacks of Hebrew influence, it is well for us to remember the dominance of the biblically related themes of divine grace and freedom of the will in Augustine's thought.

Upon his return to Africa, Augustine established a community on his family estate in Tagaste. This community instantiated Augustine's intention at his conversion (*Confessiones* VIII,xii,28–30), to some extent desired ever since his reading of the *Hortensius* (*Confessiones* III,iv,7–9), to live a celibate life, apart from the world, dedicated to the pursuit of wisdom. It is altogether probable that contemplation of God was an intended goal of this "monastery." After all, it is the ascent of the soul which dominates Augustine's works and—we may presume—his life at this time. The young Augustine understood Plotinus and Porphyry, on the one hand, and the Scriptures, on the other, to be embarked to a large extent on the same project, though the doctrines of the incarnation and grace (as he understood them at the time) modified the essence of the ascent of the mind (*Contra Academicos* III,xiv,42ff). The precise nature of this communitarian enterprise has been the subject of some dispute throughout this century. Certain it is that this common life in Tagaste provided a transition from the "philosophical retreat" at Cassiciacum to the *monasterium clericorum* at Hippo. One facet of the genius of Augustine was eventually to wed the common life with its goal of contemplation to the clerical state. Throughout Augustine's own life, the tension between the two continually remained and, to some extent, this tension remains in the Augustinian tradition of religious life in the West.

During this period, Augustine wrote an allegorical exegesis of the first chapters of Genesis, the *De Genesi contra Manichaeos* (*Retractationes* I,x,1). Throughout his life and writings, to an extent unparalleled in the Christian authors before him, Augustine was occupied with the interpretation of the stories of the creation of the world and the fall of man. Further, he authored the *De musica*, the only completed extant work in the projected works on the liberal arts (*Retractationes* I,xi,1). The *De magistro*, a dialogue with his son Adeodatus on the nature of signs and teaching (*Retractationes* I,xii), and the *De uera religione*, a work promised to his patron Romanianus nearly four years previously at Cassiciacum (*Contra Academicos* II,iii,8) which details Christianity as the way of salvation, complete Augustine's theological output until his ordination.

Despite his best efforts to the contrary, the fame of Augustine and his colleagues spread across northern Africa during this period (*Sermo CCCLV* I,2). The "monks" gathered around him there and later in the *monasterium clericorum* were to provide the bishops for many of the sees in Northern Africa, a kind of seminary in late antiquity. Augustine himself, and perhaps his monks, experientially unaware of the problems and challenges endemic to the clerical life in his or any age, may have taken part in a kind of anticlericalism for a short period of time (*Epistula XXI* 2). In any event, Augustine avoided going to any village or town lacking a bishop (*Sermo CCCLV* I,2). (The task of a bishop in Northern Africa of the time may have been more comparable to that of contemporary pastor in a large parish than to that of a modern bishop of a diocese.) At the time, as many as sixty-four villages out of a total of somewhat less than five hundred may have been without a pastor. Augustine himself tells us that he misjudged the situation in Hippo-Regius, a seaport (contemporary Anaba) which already had a bishop (*Sermo CCCLV* I,2). The "monk" from Tagaste had determined to visit the city in order to meet a prospective member of his community and to found a monastery in that city (*Sermo CCCLV* I,2). But the elderly Bishop Valerius and his parishioners had different ideas. Valerius himself spoke Greek and had difficulty preaching in Latin. He was aging, and both he and his parishioners wanted someone who might succeed him as bishop. They acknowledged Augustine to be the man. However, Augustine clearly stated his intention of remaining in the common life. Astutely, Valerius offered him a garden in which he could establish his monastery (*Sermo CCCLV* I,2). Augustine reacted strongly to the enormity of the duties (*Epistula XXI* 2). Shortly after his ordination, he asked Bishop Valerius for an extended leave to study the Scriptures in preparation for his priestly duties (*Epistula XXI, passim*). Indeed, so great was Augustine's fame and so impressive his doctrinal knowledge and preaching skills that within two years he was asked to preach on the creed before the assembled bishops of Africa—an extraordinary event in view of the fact that even the ordinary preaching in the parish church was the prerogative of the bishop himself (*Retractationes* I,xvii).

Much more has been said and needs be said concerning Augustine's theology of the priesthood and his pastoral practice. However enough has been said perhaps to indicate the nature of the events in Augustine's life which has occasioned this volume. We at the Augustinian Historical Institute of Villanova University should like to congratulate the editors of this volume in the *Collectanea Augustiniana* series. It has been a pleasure for us to work with them. The essays are an evident contribution to our contemporary understanding of Augustine.

Frederick Van Fleteren
LaSalle University
September, 1992

Preface

In *Sermon CCCLV*, 2, Saint Augustine describes how he came to Hippo in 391 to visit a friend whom he thought he could win for God, "so that he might be with us in our monastery." Augustine reports that he felt safe, because Hippo had a bishop. Nonetheless, he "was seized and made a priest, and through that rank...came to the episcopate." Valerius, the bishop of Hippo, gave Augustine a garden, and there his monastery came to be. Augustine gathered there "men of good intent, my fellows in poverty, who owned nothing, just as I owned nothing, and who followed my lead...so that we might live from what we held in common. But what we held in common would be a vast and rich estate: God himself."

In November of 1990 the departments of philosophy and theology at Marquette University sponsored a conference commemorating Augustine's ordination to the presbyterate and the founding of the monastery in Hippo—events which were destined to have a profound effect upon Christianity and religious life in every century. The conference coincided with the Ignatian year and with Marquette University's celebration of the 500th anniversary of the birth of St. Ignatius of Loyola, and the 450th anniversary of the founding of the Society of Jesus. Quite appropriately, it recalled the profound debt that the Ignatian tradition owes to Augustine in philosophy, theology and spirituality.

This volume presents the papers read by the five invited speakers and a selection of the other communications given at the conference. The editors thank the scholars who accepted an invitation to deliver papers: Mary T. Clark, R.S.C.J., of Manhattanville College; George Lawless, O.S.A., of the Augustinianum; Robert J. O'Connell, S.J., of Fordham University; Tarcisius J. Van Bavel, O.S.A., of the University of Louvain; and Rowan D. Williams, of Oxford University. Communications were invited on any topic in Augustinian philosophy, theology and spirituality as well as on sources and influences of Augustine's thought. The editors are deeply grateful for all the communications that were presented and regret that limits of space prevented the publication of more of them.

The editors of this volume also gratefully acknowledge the financial support received from The Edward Simmons Religious Commitment Fund of Marquette University and the encouragement and help of the following: Francis M. Lazarus, Academic Vice President of Marquette University; Gregory F. Lucey, S.J., rector of the Marquette University Jesuit Community; Thomas C. Anderson, chair of the Department of Philosophy; Philip J. Rossi, S.J., chair of the Department of Theology; Nicholas F. Pope, S.J., of Computer Services; William Lentz, Paulette Skiba, B.V.M., and Arlene M. Gensler, graduate assistants; the many faculty members of Marquette University who assisted with the conference; and all the scholars from the United States and abroad who attended the conference and presented papers. We happily offer our special thanks to Frederick Van Fleteren and Joseph C. Schnaubelt, O.S.A., the general editors of the series *Collectanea Augustiniana*, for allowing us to edit the second volume of that series, *Augustine: Presbyter factus sum*.

Joseph T. Lienhard, S.J.
Earl C. Muller, S.J.
Roland J. Teske, S.J.

July, 1992

Abbreviations

ACW	*Ancient Christian Writers*
AS	*Augustinian Studies*
BA	*Bibliothèque Augustinienne*
CC	*Corpus Christianorum*
CSEL	*Corpus Scriptorum Ecclesiasticorum Latinorum*
FC	*Fathers of the Church*
GNO	*Gregorii Nysseni Opera*
NPNF	*A Select Library of the Nicene and Post-Nicene Fathers of the Christian Church*
PG	J. P. Migne. *Patrologiae Graecae cursus completus*
PL	J. P. Migne. *Patrologiae Latinae cursus completus*
PO	*Plotini Opera*
REA	*Revue des études augustiniennes*

Biblical Abbreviations

The apposite books in biblical order

Genesis	Gn
Exodus	Ex
Deuteronomy	Dt
Job	Jb
Psalms	Ps
Song of Songs	Sg
Wisdom	Ws
Ecclesiasticus	Si
Isaiah	Is
Jeremiah	Jr
Baruch	Br
Ezechiel	Ez
Daniel	Dn
Matthew	Mt
Mark	Mk
Luke	Lk
John	Jn
Acts	Ac
Romans	Rm
1 Corinthians	1 Co
2 Corinthians	2 Co
Galatians	Ga
Ephesians	Ep
Philippians	Ph
Colossians	Col
1 Thessalonians	1 Th
2 Thessalonians	2 Th
1 Timothy	1 Tm
Hebrews	Heb
2 Peter	2 P
1 John	1 Jn
Revelation	Rv

I

Augustine and His Critics

Augustine

Vellem quippe, si tunc ego essem Moyses—ex eadem namque massa omnes uenimus; et quid est homo, nisi memor es eius?—uellem ergo, si tunc ego essem quod ille et mihi abs te Geneseos liber scribendus adiungeretur, talem mihi eloquendi facultatem dari et eum texendi sermonis modum, ut neque illi, qui nondum queunt intellegere quemadmodum creat deus, tamquam excedentia uires suas dicta recusarent et illi, qui hoc iam possunt, in quamlibet ueram sententiam cogitando uenissent, eam non praetermissam in paucis uerbis tui famuli reperirent, et si alius aliam uidisset in luce ueritatis, nec ipsa in eisdem uerbis intellegenda deesset.

Confessiones XII,xxvi,36

Augustine of Hippo and His Critics

George Lawless, O.S.A.

During his lifetime and ever since, Augustine of Hippo has been the focus and storm center of much controversy within the Church.[1] There is irony in the fact that this could be true of a man who served God's people for more than half the span of his life, some thirty-nine years as priest and bishop. His cathedra was named "Basilica of Peace"—both he and his people possessed an intense longing for peace,—yet its bishop was seldom spared periods of dispute and criticism. His was a world of social unrest, extreme violence at times and incessant political upheaval. Titles of his works, ranging from the early *Contra Academicos* (386 A.D.) to the *Adversus Iudaeos* in the last year of his life (429/30 A.D), attest to the probing polemical character of his writings long before his ordination to the priesthood sixteen centuries ago, the event which we happily commemorate in this conference.

Controversy was perhaps congenial to Augustine's temperament; at least it seemed never to have unnerved him. How fortunate we are that Augustine was ordained a priest and, subsequently, a bishop. There is merit in Gustave Bardy's opinion that the writings of Augustine, prior to his ordination, were rather bloodless and narrowly academic.

In this paper I shall reflect upon some reasons why the Bishop of Hippo, frequently a participant in controversy, remains a subject of controversy. We shall, first of all, reflect upon some features of his writings which help explain why, in many circles, Augustine is widely misunderstood. Then, we shall listen to some jarring notes in Augustine's thought which have unsettled and alienated generations of his interpreters. Can these sounds be muted? To answer these critics adequately would require another lecture, indeed, a book-length presentation. In the third part of this lecture, we shall concentrate mainly on Augustine's personal estimate of his worth as a writer, including his own acknowledgment of shortcomings and my observations concerning the failure of later generations to take a more appreciative account of his accomplishment. Finally, in the fourth section, we shall provide a shorthand evaluation of Augustine's legacy from the perspective of those critics who classify him summarily as either a rigorist and/or a pessimist.

The Style Is the Man

The first matter for our consideration is the peculiar susceptibility to criticism inherent in Augustine's writings. Or, to put the matter in a different way: What can account for the "Augustine-bashing" that became so prominent a trademark of subsequent studies in church history and theology? The most obvious explanation, of course, is the fact that he wrote so much. The size and importance of his output subject Augustine perforce to more extensive comment and criticism.

There are 117 books extant.[2] There are, even though most of his sermons are lost, nearly 900 sermons extant. There are approximately 300 letters remaining, 26 of which were hitherto unknown until the mid-1970s and published for the first time by Johannes Divjak in 1981.[3] Among the writings of the western Fathers only those of Augustine exceed those of Jerome in sheer bulk.

For the most part, his writing was inspired by the needs of his ministry, and it made great demands on his time. Two works were written by Augustine largely for his own personal benefit: the *Soliloquies* and his fifteen books on *The Trinity*. Leaving early dialogues aside, all other writings were composed at the request of a particular individual or prompted by specific circumstances which were directly related to daily issues of Christian living. Appreciably more than ten years were required for their author to complete, respectively, *Genesis Literally Understood, The Trinity* and the *City of God*.

Each instance of his writing can provide the reader with a sense of the development of Augustine's thought. But, in an attempt to reconcile a later text with an earlier one, researchers sometimes engage (excessively?) in the elusive game of parallelomania. A similar exercise can be performed profitably by limiting the search to a single work composed over a long period of time, such as the *City of God*. Nevertheless, this tracking down of parallel texts and their subsequent critical evaluation is by no means an otiose exercise, as the studies of Anne-Marie La Bonnardière on Augustine's use of the Bible have clearly demonstrated.

With the aid of the Word-Index to Augustine's writings at the Computer Center of Würzburg University in Germany this task is lightened immeasurably. The Word-Index catalogues more than five million words. These materials are now replicated in a database at Villanova University in eastern Pennsylvania. As a result of computerized philological research, the potential for exacting scholarship in Augustinian studies is greater than ever. Yet, some pitfalls remain. First of all, Augustine's writings are so voluminous and occasional in character that it is all too easy to play off one of his utterances inappropriately against another. Secondly, research is further complicated by what has long been recognized as "the floating character of Augustine's terminology."[4] Thirdly, aiming at too much certainty in interpretation can sometimes result in attempting to find a precision which the sources refuse to yield. We can, to be sure, identify the bricks, but the edifice we build with them is another matter. Augustine never conceived of his task as creating a strict synthesis in the manner of Aquinas. Finally, there is good reason to question whether or not Augustine's thought can ever be collapsed into a system. When that happens, "[it] is," as John Burnaby has reminded us, "in great part a cruel travesty of Augustine's deepest and most vital thought."[5]

Moreover, interdisciplinary skills must be applied to linguistic findings. These skills will enable the student of late antiquity to meld historical fact with cultural environment in such a way as to decode the extent to which personal, pastoral and polemical experiences have shaped theological ideas. Dare we, for example, try to recapture Augustine's experiences and thought from a psycho-historical perspective? Such an elusive task strikes me as somewhat foolhardy in this instance, however, owing to the subjective nature of the discipline of psychology. By telling us only part of the story, such data suffer the same limitations as an historical accounting of the myriad polemical pressures which beset Augustine's pastorate.

For such reasons as these, therefore, three other considerations merit our attention: 1) the literary genre, 2) the audience, 3) the chronology. All three of these necessary elements of interpretation are required to extract from the entire corpus of the bishop's writings, for example, his mature reflections on the subject of war. More precisely, at least six literary genres form the nucleus for these reflections: an early philosophical dialogue, a polemical tract answering the Manichee, Faustus, point by point, at least three letters and assorted sermons, a commentary on the Heptateuch and, lastly, the apologetical masterpiece of all Latin literature, the *City of God*.[6]

In each of these six instances, one finds a distinctive dialectical urgency with diverse audiences. The Manichees in general and, afterwards, their inept spokesman, Faustus, comprise a particular audience at one time. The pagan *cognoscenti* and Marcellinus, to whom we owe the composition of Augustine's *City of God*, comprise an audience at another. In a biblical commentary, the bishop offers a modest slice of Old Testament exegesis. Three letters were addressed to high government officials, and at least as many sermons were preached to his Sunday congregation.

Nor is the time and duration of composition irrelevant in these matters. Nearly ten years elapsed before the completion of *Free Choice of the Will*, and thirteen years were required to complete the *City of God*. The sermons involve a longer time span.

Augustine's writing habits were constantly thwarted by myriad pastoral concerns and the administrative duties of a civil magistrate or judge, a role which he found to be utterly distasteful. The portrait of a Victorian vicar comfortably ensconced in a small country parish does not fit Augustine at all, as the publication of the new letters forcefully demonstrates.[7] By his own reckoning in one of these new letters, the bishop dictated between September 11 and December 1, 419 A.D. "about 6,000 lines" of text.[8] Here we possess a detailed inventory of several literary genres compressed within two and a half months, along with the lament that their author could not, for pastoral reasons, get on with writing the *City of God*. Even the *Confessions* were composed with haste.[9]

In the wake of all this, is it fair to impose upon the Bishop of Hippo a monochromatic approach to any subject? With such an approach, complexities and subtleties frequently elude the critic on many sides of an issue. Historians of early Christian ethics who wish to designate Augustine as "patron saint of the Just War theory," while at the same time distinguishing him from the more pacifist leanings of Origen and Tertullian, fail to appreciate the stark continuity which exists between the pre- and post-Constantinian church on these matters. The overriding emphasis in Augustine and in Christian ethics has always been to favor as little violence and force as possible and necessary in the conduct of the state. These words, written a year before he died, measure the true stature of the saint in this regard: "Greater glory lies in destroying war with human speech (*verbo*) than killing human beings with weaponry (*ferro*), in securing and maintaining peace by means of peace rather than war."[10]

There remains for our consideration still another feature of Augustine's writings which invariably elicits misunderstanding on the part of his readers. It is the unique quality of his writing style as it reflects the conventional rhetoric of his own time and place in history. Years ago Jarolav Pelikan suggested that the real "bugbear" in the "Hellenization of the Gospel" and in the development of Christian doctrine is not "speculative metaphysics" but rather "the history of Christian rhetoric, East and West."[11] I am strongly convinced that Augustine's writings provide a fertile field for validating the truth of this observation.

Parallelism, paradox and antithesis constitute such an inherent part of the bishop's thought patterns that they are able to exert a somewhat mislead-ing influence upon unwary twentieth-century interpreters.[12] Stylistically, Au-gustine perpetuates what I have elsewhere described as "the sharp contrasts of ideas and the hardened antinomies of dialectical reasoning which are indige-nous to the deliberations of ancient Graeco-Roman thought."[13]

Because of historical circumstances, the nature of rational argument, which was an Aristotelian concern, mattered less to Augustine than did the Platonic preoccupation with persuasion and the nature of rational discourse or dialogue. This is not to suggest that Augustine was unconcerned or careless in his presentation of an argument. He was scrupulously concerned with ra-tional argument, but in a dialectical or dialogical format. One should not underestimate his sensitive regard for logic and method as is clearly evident, for example, in Books 5 through 7 and in Books 9 through 14 of *The Trinity*.

The Trinity, as a matter of fact, is an essentially irenic and exploratory work which was postponed by Augustine many times and eventually pirated by impatient readers who incurred his displeasure, since at the time three and a half books were still yet unwritten.[14] It is reasonable to infer that, similarly, the bulk of Augustine's writing did not receive any more exacting treatment in their manner of composition. There was, frankly, scant opportunity available for such precision and control in the busy schedule of this man who has been, somewhat understandably, yet I should like to add extravagantly, described in his life-style as "little more than a parish priest."[15]

Such a gestalt emerges when reading our author aloud (recall that ex-cept for the *Soliloquies*, all of his oeuvre was originally dictated). The reader of Augustine regularly encounters a tensile association of ideas, replete with medial and/or terminal rhyme and *clausulae*. To cite some examples: pil-grimage/homeland, action/contemplation, reason/faith, body/soul, free choice of the will/grace, nature/grace, Adam/Christ, time/eternity, creation/sabbath.

In each of these binomials, the first term indicates subordination or limitation. There is duality without dualism; there is tension and difference. In all Augustine's writings, however, there is no rubric to suggest warring opposites. While the eschatological undergirding of his thought tends to highlight the second term of each binomial over the first, it should be pointed out that truth, for Augustine, rises above both extremes. There is, in fact, no middle term between the two extremes; nor is there any sublation or resolution in the sense of a Hegelian dialectic. Each relation has to be explained in terms of its particular *relata*.

Augustine seldom vacillates between the two extremes. Rather he oscillates by coming down on both sides of the binomial at the same time, but not in the same way, or at different times, depending upon the particular context and without self-contradiction.[16] Such a tactic is heightened by the adversarial nature of much of his writing. Secondary sources rarely take note of this stylistic mannerism and, consequently, his reasoning and argumentation are unjustly portrayed as partial, sometimes as prejudicial and frequently lopsided. In Book 22 of the *City of God*, for example, one ought not to isolate chapter 22 with its list of unrelieved human miseries, depicting sons and daughters of Adam, from chapter 23, victory in and through Jesus Christ with its sequel, chapter 24, a condensed list of blessings. These three chapters are all of a piece, possessing both an artistic and logical integrity of their own. To extrude a single thought in isolation from any one of these three chapters with no mention of the entire unit gravely distorts its meaning.

While fondness for antithesis strikes the modern reader as injudiciously overworked in some ancient writers, Augustine crafts this figure of speech skillfully and, we should add, unselfconsciously. He is more measured in this regard than, for instance, Gregory the Great. This fondness for antithesis came quite simply from Augustine's professional background. It was second nature for a former teacher of rhetoric to express himself in this antithetical mode.

Related to this matter is the charge of carelessness in composition which is sometimes leveled at Augustine by critics who maintain that he was a poor planner of books. There is no need to rehearse Henri Marrou's *retractatio* in this regard.[17] In the wake of this particular controversy, Augustine's abilities as a writer have been characterized as musical in addition to their long-recognized dramatic and narrative qualities. A musical style of composition enables us to understand better the bishop's mature thought. In this matter I acknowledge an illuminating insight from one of Augustine's more recent interpreters: "...the ancient rhetorician worked, it seems obvious on reflection, in a far more improvisational mode than we do. If music were the analogy, his idiom was jazz, not classical."[18]

Briefly put: 1) Augustine employed a style common to his day, a sort of general essay type; 2) he did not use a strictly scientific technique of prose; 3)

his books were sufficiently planned according to the mode of writing of his ·
time; and 4) whatever the style or mode of presentation, he shows himself,
throughout, a keen, relentless reasoner. The Church scene of the time offered
a wide scope for his searching, disputative mind.

Bishop and Thinker

Augustine's ministry was a long one and, quite expectedly, it involved
him in many changes of opinion. It is a great tribute to the openness of the
bishop that he changed his mind on so many issues. Because of these changes,
he himself urged us to read his works in their order of composition.[19] To expect his statements to be perfectly formed and complete without making
· allowance for chronological development is neither sensible nor realistic.
Unlike the Scholastics of the Middle Ages and many theologians of today,
Augustine was not writing for the benefit of university professors or students
of theology. Pastoral care, *cura animarum,* was foremost in his mind.

· Insufficient attention has been given to the adaptation of his technical
views to a popular audience and the shift in Augustine's mind from his intel-
lectualizing and Platonizing Christianity to the Popular Catholicism (*Vulgär-
katholizismus*) of his later years. Here, I have in mind Peter Brown's remark
apropos the Pelagian controversy: "Julian had appealed to a 'high-brow' audience. Augustine, shrewdly, will render him impotent by appealing to the
'middle-brows'."[20] Or, note the facile comment, again by Peter Brown: "Augustine had long been fascinated by babies.... The Pelagian, by contrast, was
contemptuous of babies."[21]

These observations on the Pelagian encounter are, of course, unsatisfactory. They sum it up far too easily and too cleverly. Augustine took the line
he did in the Pelagian controversy because he believed, rightly or wrongly,
that this was Catholic truth. Augustine came increasingly to respect the common faith of unlettered Christians, in contrast to the sophistries of cultured
men like Julian. To examine the reasons for this transition in Augustine's
thought would, I believe, furnish us with an extremely worthwhile piece of
research.

The Pelagian controversy created a new situation for Augustine. He
wished to make it clear that all matters of doctrine are up front; there are no

• secrets, there is no gnosis.[22] This issue is illustrated by the behavior of the apostles Peter and Paul as recounted in the second chapter of Galatians. When Peter, a Jew, lives by Gentile ways yet forces Gentiles to adopt Jewish ways, Paul publicly rebukes Peter and the Judaizers in Ga 2:11–14. Jerome followed the lead of Origen and others in interpreting this Pauline text in such a way as to suggest that the apostles were sort of play-acting in this scenario. According to Augustine, however, Paul genuinely rebuked Peter to his face on this occasion, as the Scriptures have it. Seventeen letters were required for the bishop of Hippo to convince Jerome that there is no deliberate duplicity or deception in Scripture.[23] There is no conscious falsity in doctrine, either. Paradox, irony, seeming contradiction, yes, but no double talk, no double truth, one for the masses, the other for the classes.

Augustine's resolute refusal to accept the admissibility of a lie under any circumstances is well-known. Accordingly, for him, lying is intrinsically evil. While he sometimes identifies truth with chastity, chastity is always subordinate to truth.[24] His disagreement with St. Ambrose confirms this point. Ambrose of Milan had suggested that suicide was permissible for a virgin who could find no other way to escape her assailant.[25] Not so, says Augustine! Veracity is a greater good than chastity, or wealth, self-preservation or life itself. These temporal realities can sometimes be dispensed with, but truth partakes of the eternal. Augustine argues that truthfulness, an eternal reality, can never be short-circuited for the sake of chastity or virginity, which is a temporal reality, no matter how exalted. This personal conviction lies at the heart of Augustine's deepest thought. "Wherever I found truth," he tells us, "there I found God, truth itself, and since I first learned the truth, I have not forgotten it."[26]

In a treatise entitled *Continence*, Augustine differentiates with extraordinary finesse between integrity of the *lips* and integrity of the *heart*. Apart from its biblical inspiration in the Book of Wisdom and in the Psalms, is it too farfetched to suggest that the three seals (*sigilla*) of the Manichees, the seal of the mouth, the seal of the hand or body as a whole, the seal of the bosom furnish another backdrop for the bishop's differentiation between integrity of the lips or mouth and integrity of the heart?[27] This is an artful and profound way of expressing both the catholicity of Augustine's mind (not unlike the contents of the *Reconsiderations*) and his overall intellectual integrity, which was fueled by his longing for truth. The bishop's implacable hostility towards falsehood and deceit is basic to any proper appreciation of his temperament and personality. Continence, for Augustine, always excludes a narrow biologism by embracing wholeness of mind and mouth as well as of heart and body. They were absorbed one into the other. Possible links between the *De mendacio* and the *De continentia* deserve investigation in another forum. How, for example, are we to nuance the use of *castitas animi* (6 times), *castitas mentis* and *castitas animae*, once each within a single paragraph?[28] Elaboration of this theme would presently take us too far afield.

Augustine, meanwhile, asks difficult questions regarding free choice of the will, the possibility of certitude, the origin of the human soul and the problem of evil. On these matters and many more, he wrote at length and in depth. As the bishop expounds on church doctrine in a developmental pattern, his writings reveal a continuous process of revision on a variety of issues. They include, for example, the starting point of faith (*initium fidei*), the nexus between nature and grace, original sin, religious toleration and coercion by the government, the proper understanding of the Book of Genesis, the themes of war and peace, human sexuality, embodiment and women. Subtle shades of meaning surface in his comments about these respective areas of individual and social importance.

The reality of original sin (*antiquum peccatum*), he tells us, "is better known when the preacher declares it; nothing is more of a secret when we try to understand it."[29] Deftly nuanced interpretations elevate sexuality "from the realm of the purely biological to the conflicted, compulsive, indeed uniquely human world of the psychological."[30] Paula Frederiksen concludes this assessment of Augustine's refutation of the Manichees and the Pelagians by trenchantly observing: "Sex to Julian (of Eclanum) is reproductive biology; sex to Augustine is eroticism. This is a more complex (not to mention more interesting) phenomenon."[31]

The bishop asks whether or not the way of salvation is available to all people and notes that the damned lump of humanity (*massa damnata*) exists, not because God predestined creatures to sin but because Adam sinned. Here, the Word-Index to the Würzburg collection of Augustine's writings confirms a conjecture of mine. While Augustine uses the expressions "predestination to punishment" and "predestination to damnation," he never employs the phrase "predestination to sin." A distinction of such precision may strike the reader as a niggling one, because for all practical purposes the consequences are the same. But the bishop's thinking on predestination ought not to be separated from his theology of redemption, which portrays Jesus as saying, in effect: "If you go to hell, you go there over my dead body."

At the same time, no theologian can sidestep St. Paul in this matter of predestination, and in the long run, as we shall note below, the issue is virtually insoluble. Our thoughts go to extreme lengths to preserve human freedom; Augustine's mind goes to even greater lengths to preserve God's freedom. First and foremost, he allows God to be God. "In trying to solve this question I made strenuous efforts on behalf of the preservation of the free choice of the human will," Augustine tells us, "but the grace of God defeated me."[32] His final affirmation of human freedom in the last year of his life is cryptically expressed thus: "If there is compulsion, there is no freedom."[33]

When asking difficult questions, Augustine linked the best available minds in the ancient world with the evidence of the Scriptures. In notable ways, many of these distinguished thinkers were not merely unsympathetic but indeed virulently hostile towards Christianity. For example, there could hardly have been a more acrimonious opponent of Christianity than Porphyry, whose thought Augustine nevertheless utilized both selectively and constructively by describing him as "the most renowned of the pagan philosophers."[34] It is a matter for regret that Augustine had to wait until the sunset of his life, (when so much of his talent had already been exhausted), before encountering Julian of Eclanum, his most formidable opponent in controversy.

One of his severe contemporary critics describes Augustine's thought as "a hornet's nest of contradictions."[35] How, then, to reconcile these seeming contradictions of Augustine? Can his earlier serene emphasis upon our innate desire for God be compatible with his later less enthusiastic estimate of human potential? Does not his stance on religious coercion overturn his many splendid statements advocating tolerance? Can "Augustine the libertarian" actually harmonize with "Augustine the predestinarian"? Surely, the doctrine of "a hard rather than a soft Fall"[36] is far removed from his Plotinian metaphysics of ascent. The very idea of unmerited judgment may seem to be irreconcilable with any idea of unmerited mercy. Is it any wonder, then, that the Augustine of later years has few friends?

May we enlist a comparison by asking whether the sixteen volumes of Augustine in the Migne edition fare any worse in this regard that the many volumes of Martin Luther in the Weimar edition of his writings? Augustine tells us that no author, including himself, is immune from error, much less contradiction. It is not possible, honestly, to ignore or to sidestep the ultimately insoluble conflicts in the bishop's thought. In an attempt to plot the trajectory of his mind and thought, a recent work on Augustine uses the word "continuity" in its title,[37] while another work on Augustine employs the word "disenchantment" for the same purpose.[38] Any structural approach to Augustine's writings must include this genetic model of both development (conversion) and disenchantment, as acknowledged by the bishop himself in the Prologue to his *Reconsiderations*.

On the philosophical level, the categories of being and nature are gradually overtaken and surpassed in the thought of Augustine by the biblical categories of time and history. Time and history actually complement and enlarge the perspectives of being and nature. Failure to grasp this interpretative key to understanding the bishop's thought leads the scholar into a thicket of errors.

It seems to me that the Bishop of Hippo made sound use of whatever methodology and "scientific" apparatus were available to him at the time. The net result reveals an overall coherence that is as intelligible as it is remarkable, under the circumstances. As with a tapestry, to pull a single thread threatens eventually to weaken or to tear the texture of the entire fabric. In the long haul, the lack of coherence, the compromises, the conflicts that are present effect in due course a "differentiated unity," what might be fittingly described as a sort of *coincidentia oppositorum*, in the sense that the opposing strains are reconcilable for human intelligence, however dimly we may grasp such reconciliation. We are recently given to understand that such an "ahistorical synthesis is only possible because Augustine believes that even such blatant contradictions in his writings can be ignored as long as he can solve them by additions that will modify their meaning."[39] Such an estimate requires qualification: while some contradictions are blatant at first sight, they are at the same time potentially resolvable.

Augustine on Augustine

For a better understanding of our theme, it is helpful for Augustine's readers to consider the bishop's estimate of himself as one of those authors "who writes as he makes progress and who makes progress as he writes."[40] In mid-life, he cited approvingly the warning of the Latin poet Horace: "Once a word is in print, there is no way to retrieve it."[41] In the same context, Cicero too had reminded him that the writer who refuses to take back an utterance is either a consummate fool or a perfect genius.[42]

Augustine's early treatise, *Immortality of the Soul*, was unintelligible even to himself.[43] The first of two treatises on lying he ordered to be destroyed because of its choppy style and uneven argument.[44] The brothers ignored his order. At the end of his life Augustine reviewed this book on lying and again expressed dissatisfaction with its contents. He does this in a rather unique and invaluable book entitled: *Retractationes*, in English *Retractations* or, better, *Reconsiderations*. Ninety-three books are set out and reviewed in their chronological order, which is determined by their initial date of composition. The bishop had planned to review his sermons and letters in like manner, but terminal illness and death prevented him from doing so.

The *Reconsiderations* felicitously monitor Augustine's intellectual growth by signposting the areas where he either changed his mind on a particular subject or was simply wrong. In a gloss on marriage, for example, the bishop tells us: "the good and correct use of libido is not libido."[45] This is a remarkably enlightened observation for a fifth-century bishop who had already made a more significant breakthrough, theologically, in the areas of human sexuality and marriage than any other Church Father. It is fair to ask whether there has ever been a theologian of comparable stature in the history of the Christian Churches in this area of sexual morality. When one considers the specter of Gnosticism, its fourth-century Manichean update and the Porphyrian background that Augustine had to overcome, this achievement is all the more remarkable. While few scholars fail to recognize Augustine's towering stature in this matter of sexual morality, the real controversy among his critics, of course, is whether this stature has been good or bad for the history of moral theology.[46]

Aware as he was that he was breaking new ground, the bishop's modesty is a match for his humility. Listen to his final reflection on this matter; Augustine was then seventy-four years of age:

> I wish no one to accept all my views and to follow me except in those areas where he finds that I have not been mistaken.... Were I to claim that I am perfect at this stage of my life and that my writings were free from error, I would be speaking with more arrogance than truth.[47]

To be sure, Augustine made mistakes. In the practical order of church administration, for example, he exercised extremely poor judgment in the appointment of Antoninus of Fussala, a monumental blunder with sorry pastoral consequences for which Augustine later wrote to Pope Celestine, threatening to resign as Bishop of Hippo.[48]

Thankfully, the Catholic Church never accepted Augustine's final and stringent views on predestination. Still, even in this instance, predestination does not mean, for Augustine, predetermination. John Calvin surpassed his mentor by going to the further extreme of proposing a double predestination, *gemina praedestinatio*. We recall that the Jansenist doctrine of *delectatio victrix* is a "caricature of Augustine's thought."[49]

To cite another example: the Catholic Church never accepted Augustine's opinion on the destiny of unbaptized infants, a stance so rigid, in fact, that it triggered the development of the medieval doctrine on the existence of limbo. In 415 A.D., in an anguished letter to Jerome (166,4,10), Augustine is far from indifferent to the fate of unbaptized infants. Six years later, he concedes to them "surely the mildest punishment of all."[50]

Nor has the Church ever sanctioned the bishop's gloomy outlook on the large number of the reprobate in contrast to the minuscule number of those who are saved.[51] Also there is no scriptural warrant either way to support or to deny Augustine's assertion that Mary vowed perpetual virginity.[52] Augustine's insistence upon no salvation outside the Catholic Church certainly improves upon the strictures of Cyprian of Carthage by allowing, at least in the case of adults, for the saving principle of implicit faith and conversion of heart as well as the loving inspiration of the Holy Spirit.[53]

While we are not able to rescue Augustine from his mistakes, by the same token the Bishop of Hippo ought not to be blamed for everything—or nearly everything—that went wrong in western Christianity. Some of the current objections to Augustine stem from modern prejudices that are every bit as deep as the ancient ones.

Just as Martin Luther "can only be understood as a late medieval man," and he must not be submitted to "post-Enlightenment standards of modernity,"[54] Augustine must be appreciated as a man of late antiquity. Augustine does not have an answer for every contemporary issue. Insights are plentiful, however. While further study of his stance towards politics, economics, history, sociology and religion is desirable, Augustine's thought in these areas can not be straightjacketed within the narrow compass of these single disciplines, as we understand them today.

Take one example: the over-cautious and over-circumspect posture towards politics which many interpreters attribute to Augustine bears much resemblance to Reinhold Niebuhr's reading of him. This presupposes a theological comprehension of politics that is shaped largely by a Lutheran Reformation tradition. That tradition, in turn, fails to reproduce adequately the thought of Augustine. A travel advisory of caution is indeed appropriate for anyone who attempts to canvass so vast a territory as the mind of Augustine, whether it be on the issue of politics, freedom, human sexuality, or whatever. From the early fifth to the sixteenth to the twentieth-century accuracy of understanding is frequently forfeited in translation. In a Platonic sense, the net gain constitutes an imitation (that of Reinhold Niebuhr) of an imitation (that of Martin Luther), twice removed from the original source, Augustine himself.

Similarly, there are many differences between Augustine's use of the expression *sola fides* and Luther's use of the same phrase.[55] In the same way, the richness of Augustine's multiple images of Christ is impoverished as these are portrayed in Reformation theology or conspicuously omitted from the two rival views of justification which were seeking approval during the Council of Trent.[56] As in all else, scholars must attempt to differentiate the genuine Augustine from the fictive Augustine of later ages.

(Thankfully, the Word-Index to the bishop's writings now enables us to go back to the sources to explore the subtleties of Augustine's thought. It is possible to examine the best available critical texts with an accuracy that has hitherto eluded us. Such scientific scrutiny, limited as it is, would no doubt satisfy the bishop's longing for truth.)

The selective perceptions of historians, theologians and scholars of every vintage are generally occasioned, as we have noted, by the huge bulk of Augustine's writings with the sad consequences that his expositors have produced many caricatures of his thought. By constituting, as they do, more than one-third of his oeuvre, the sermons offer a more comprehensive scope for an accurate understanding of Augustine than any other single work. That the bishop's writings have been so enormously influential aggravates the problem still further. If, as Whitehead suggested, philosophy is a "series of footnotes to Plato," then western theology is a "series of footnotes to Augustine."[57]

Consider, for example, the extent to which Augustine's writings on grace have been widely misrepresented: Gottschalk in the ninth-century, again my erstwhile Augustinian brother, Martin Luther and, subsequently, John Calvin, who exaggerated the case for Augustine when he asserted: "Augustine is entirely on our side."[58] Michel de Bay (1513–1589) boasted that he had read Augustine's treatises on grace seventy times and his complete works nine times.[59] Cornelius Jansen (1585–1638) is reputed to have read all of Augustine ten times, his anti-Pelagian treatises thirty times.[60] In the final analysis each of these interpreters presented us with a truncated Augustine and an abrasive version of the bishop's views on grace which is gravely distorted.

A contemporary critic illustrates some of these risks which beset every student of Augustine. In a bestseller which was immediately translated into French and Italian, the Harrington Spear Paine Professor of Religion at Princeton University distressingly distorts Augustine's views on politics, sexuality and freedom. This is not the forum to critique *Adam, Eve, and the Serpent* (New York: 1988), except to point out that Elaine Pagels fails to listen to Augustine's musical score.[61] The scholar's study may profitably be likened to a recording studio, where one is expected to reproduce with as much precision as possible the original melody. Otherwise, we have a solo work which ignores the incredible richness of the Augustinian ensemble. The subtlety of Augustine's thought is finely tuned. With sorry consequences some interpreters frequently tend to mute many of the original sounds while accentuating others in their endeavor to communicate the tonality or the "feel" of the original version, where tangents sometimes are not really tangents but a subtext and digressions are, in effect, footnotes.

We know far more about the interaction of Christianity with the civilization of late antiquity than the ancients themselves. In the manner of a wide-angle lens (for a zoom-lens is often unsatisfactory), the range of academic disciplines required for an intelligible grasp of the late antique world demands an expansive mindset in order to form a just appraisal, not only of Augustine, but of other ecclesiastical writers as well.

Rigorist and/or Pessimist?

Any account of Augustine and his critics must respond to two charges which assail the Bishop of Hippo from every quarter: first, rigorism and second, pessimism.

While there is some legitimacy to the charge of rigorism, on balance this criticism as it is leveled at Augustine is too severe. Oddly enough, overwhelming evidence can be marshaled to the effect that rigorism more properly belongs to the side of Augustine's adversaries. Distrust of sexual pleasure and of the body, depreciation of marriage, outright denial of human freedom, an entrenched cosmic dualism of darkness and light (which vitiates the integrity of the human person), materialism, with its pervasive presence of evil: these are the hallmarks of Manicheism. With the help of the Christian doctrines of creation, incarnation and resurrection, Augustine, in turn, repudiated each of them. Manicheism's defeat sounded the death-knell of Gnosticism, which had plagued the Church for centuries. In the matter of those critics who insist that Augustine actually failed, in the long run, to overcome his Manichean past, a seasoned scholar whose research is co-extensive with the world of late antiquity recently declared himself to be "uncertain" on the "extremely delicate issue of 'survivals' of Manichean modes of thought in Augustine."[62]

With their puritanical insistence upon a Church of saints only, the Donatists were far more rigorous than Catholics. With firm insistence on the Church as a *corpus permixtum* (an argument based upon sound theological reflection buttressed by unimpeachable biblical and historical evidence), Augustine almost single-handedly quashed both Donatist separatism and elitism. Schism, for Augustine, consisted in the failure to love in the way that love had been manifested in the truth of the incarnation. Rather than adopting a hard-line position on Catholic Church membership, one might say that Augustine went to the other extreme by lowering the standards for admission and participation in the life of the Church. Read the second longest letter in the Divjak collection, *Letter* 2, where Augustine painstakingly dismantles Firmus' arguments for resisting baptism.[63] The bishop's position stands in marked contrast to the exacting requirements of Donatist puritanism.

Against the adherents of Pelagius and Celestius, Augustine reveals a more comprehensive grasp of what it truly means to be a Christian. With keen insight, Augustine constantly inveighed against such attempts to overstate the biblical metaphor of "the athlete of Christ" and Pelagius' seriously flawed exegesis of the Pauline promise that the winner receives the prize. One can not escape hearing the anti-Donatist and the anti-Pelagian overtones deriding the pretensions of institutional and moral probity in the bishop's warning to his congregation: "It is better to be a cripple limping along (to God) than a champion athlete on the wrong track."[64]

Augustine's profound psychological perceptions of carnal habit and environment penetrate far deeper into the human psyche than either Pelagius' or Celestius' emphases upon naturalism and quasi-environmentalism. Pelagianism can be correctly construed as both a fifth-century update of ancient Stoicism and a forerunner of modern anti-supernaturalist rationalism. Pelagius was a spiritual director and reformer who was cultivating a church of super-Christians or ascetics only. If Pelagius had had his way, the world would eventually have become a monastery. Resolutely, Augustine rejects Pelagius' pursuit of perfection in the tradition of Platonic exemplarism, Plotinian individualism and, similarly, in the Stoic sense of a *cursus honorum*, a sort of "honors course" in Christianity. Here, again, the charge of rigorism is more appropriately leveled at Pelagius and his bogus asceticism than at Augustine.

African Christianity had a long history of rigorism. Augustine, on the contrary, however, loosened the tight grip of Tertullian and rejected outright the exacting measures of Cyprian regarding rebaptism. Although a horse of a different color, Donatism can, conceivably, be viewed, in institutionalized form, as a modified version of Pelagianism. Each, in its own distinctive way (the former a schism, the latter a heresy), seriously imperiled the integrity of Catholic Christianity by dropping anchor, so to speak, to the right of center. They drew the Catholic Church off course. By readmitting Donatists without rebaptism (in a manner totally at variance with the discipline of the Cyprianic Church), Augustine directed the compass to the left of center and drew the Catholic Church back on course. His unrelenting stance against Pelagius and his adherents had the same effect. Yet, no one was more conscious of the large number of nominal Christians than Augustine: "I hear the name [Christian]," he tells the newly baptized, "now let me recognize the genuine article."[65] All the while, the Church was rife with mediocre, lukewarm, à la carte Christians. By accepting such people, the Bishop of Hippo again shifted the compass to the left of center. So, the charge of rigorism aimed at Augustine must always be qualified and, generally speaking, it is wide of the mark. Augustine was a rigorist only when driven to an extreme position in the heat of controversy.

(It is worth speculating whether a Tertullianic or a Cyprianic church could have better withstood the Vandals at the gate of Hippo and, in the long run, the Arab invasions. The sudden vulnerability and decline of African Christianity remains somewhat of a puzzlement to historians. It prompts further questions about the quality and fervor of Christian life that was so completely eclipsed in the centuries immediately following Augustine's death. In this regard, some may wish to suggest that Augustine's theology of grace and the sacraments actually lowered the standards of Christian living in a significant way by not being rigorous enough.)

In like fashion, Augustine is frequently dismissed out of hand as a thoroughgoing pessimist. Such is the case, notwithstanding the study by a seasoned scholar, Vernon Bourke, who entitled his book, *Joy in Augustine's Ethics* (Villanova: Villanova University Press, 1979).

Today, not a few students of theology occasionally link the views of Joseph Cardinal Ratzinger with those of Augustine, intending, of course, a dubious compliment to both persons. Their reasoning runs as follows: Augustine is a pessimist; the Cardinal wrote his first doctoral dissertation on Augustine's views of the Church, *Volk und Haus Gottes in Augustins Lehre von der Kirche* (Munich: Karl Zink Verlag, 1954); ergo, Cardinal Ratzinger is a pessimist. According to such logic we may, therefore, attribute to Cardinal Ratzinger's doctoral thesis all those admonitory statements issuing from the Congregation for the Doctrine of the Faith.

Granted, the Bishop of Hippo reveals a pessimistic vein, or should we rather characterize it as a healthy realism, in his wholesale description of people in groups. He is deeply saddened, for example, by the spread of organized crime, terrorism and violence. One ought not to place high hopes in the tasks of local government, the judiciary, the modern "state," as we conceive of it and also the state of virginity. Augustine concurs with Plotinus on the role of the public executioner in society.[66] There is likewise a certain legitimacy to houses of prostitution as they highlight the stability of marriage and the family.[67] Augustine is credited with having coined the phrase, "there are crooks in every profession."[68] Here the bishop was describing members of the church: priests, monks, nuns and laity. Because of the radical potential for reform in human behavior, however, individuals are another matter.[69] Augustine further remarks:

> People are saying, "bad times, hard times,"
> Let us live well and the times will be well.
> Actually, we are the times;
> such as we are, such are the times.[70]

Elsewhere the bishop shrewdly asks: "Is the city to be thought of in terms of houses, and not its citizens?"[71]

At least three seasoned scholars have commented on this question of Augustine's pessimism. P. Borgomeo, *L'Eglise de ce temps* (Paris: Études Augustiniennes, 1972), p. 352, speaks of the bishop as an optimist. F. van der Meer, *Augustine the Bishop* (London, 1961), p. 578, says Augustine exhibits "a certain tendency" towards pessimism. A scholar whose competence with the history of grace and original sin is unquestioned, Henri Rondet, *Essais sur la théologie de la grâce* (Paris, 1964), pp. 36–37, says that Augustine's vaunted pessimism has been exaggerated by historians of doctrine. He states flatly that, if one speaks of the pessimism of St. Augustine, then one must by the same token speak of the pessimism of St. Thomas Aquinas and St. Thomas' contemporaries. Rondet notes further: "Augustinian pessimism, when properly understood, can thus furnish a point of departure for an optimism of grace, which takes its place alongside the optimism of the Greek Fathers."[72] The matter is by no means clear-cut, precisely because the ingredients shift so abruptly and with such varied didactic, dialectical and pastoral urgency within the huge bulk of Augustine's writings.

Augustine frequently juxtaposes *miseria* with *misericordia*: human misery alongside divine mercy. Years of reading our author convince me that God's mercy everywhere engulfs us in much the same manner as the vast deep of the ocean with its hidden undertow. The metaphor is Augustine's: "the more fast and furious misfortunes become, the sweeter will God's mercy be."[73] "Eliminate pitiful people," he observes elsewhere, "and there will be an end to works of mercy."[74] He explicitly tells us: "[God] will more easily contain his anger than his mercy."[75] Hardly the outlook of the pessimist! In his apologetical masterpiece, the *City of God* the bishop bluntly remarks: "In the long run good triumphs over evil...."[76]

If my argument for a wide-angle lens to view Augustine's legacy is valid, then one should never lose sight of the fact that divine providence played an important part in shaping the bishop's theological perspectives. Here we face an aspect of Augustine's thought which has not received from scholars the attention it deserves. Providence, accordingly, shines through his writings and mitigates much of what Augustine wrote on predestination.

One year ago, the 50th anniversary issue of *Theological Studies* described Augustine as "that most puzzling, pluralistic, and important theologian of them all."[77] But Augustine was more than a theologian. He was an author whose literary technique attempts to express again and again the drama of salvation-history. He was a speculative thinker with artistic sensibility and extraordinary human sensitivity. He was a man of letters possessed by a nonpareil power to communicate with words. And from his mid-life onward, he was a penitent, a priest, a monk and a bishop, but always the pastor and preacher.

It is indeed a marvel that Augustine's occasional writings, many of which were forged on the anvil of controversy, should furnish such solid insights into areas of common concern today. Our presence here graciously acknowledges the debt which western culture owes to both *Augustinus Magister* and *Augustinus Minister*. It is another way of saying that Augustine has buried all his undertakers.

Karl Barth, the great Swiss theologian, once remarked that, when he reached heaven, the first person he wished to meet was Wolfgang Amadeus Mozart; the second person was Ludwig van Beethoven, and the third person he wished to meet was Augustine of Hippo.[78] Personally I would reverse the order. How many of you would do the same?

Notes

[1] An earlier version of this paper was read at Immaculate Conception Seminary, the archdiocese of Newark, New Jersey, on the campus of Seton Hall University, 14 November 1989 in fulfillment of my obligations there as scholar-in-residence during the fall semester of that year. Here I wish to acknowledge the unfailing kindness of the seminary administration, faculty, and students who provided me with the opportunity to read widely in Augustine and to write in a singularly conducive atmosphere of study.

To Professor James J. O'Donnell of the Department of Classical Studies at the University of Pennsylvania and his detailed commentary on Augustine's *Confessions* (to be published by the Oxford University Press) I owe the comparison of the bishop's musical manner of composition with jazz and the reference to the Council of Trent on justification.

With the aid of the Word-Index to Augustine's writings presently housed at Villanova University, Allan D. Fitzgerald, OSA, of the Department of Theology, and editor of *Augustinian Studies*, graciously obliged me by running the search on the terms: *predestinatio ad poenam, predestinatio ad damnationem,* and *predestinatio ad peccatum.*

[2] P. Brown, *Religion and Society in the Age of Saint Augustine* (London: Faber and Faber, 1972), p. 25. There are a variety of ways to determine the number of Augustine's writings. Some of the letters, for example, can be properly classified as treatises or books. For convenience' sake I have used Peter Brown's enumeration. The actual count is higher. See the *Augustinus-Lexikon*, 1/1 (Basel/Stuttgart, 1982), pp. xxvi–xl. Augustine's preaching is reflected in 546 extant sermons, 124 tractates on the Gospel according to John, 10 homilies on the First Letter of John and more than 200 commentaries on the psalms.

[3] H. Chadwick, "New Letters of St. Augustine," *Journal of Theological Studies* n.s. 34 (1983) 425–52.

[4] H. Marrou, *Saint Augustin et la fin de la culture antique* (Paris: E. De Boccard, 1938), p. 245: "…le caractère flottant de sa terminologie."

[5] J. Burnaby, *Amor Dei: A Study of the Religion of St. Augustine* (London: Hodder and Stoughton, 1938), p. 231.

[6] D. A. Lenihan, "The Just War Theory in the Works of Saint Augustine," *AS* 19 (1988) 37–70, has furnished my listing of literary genres for illustrating Augustine's carefully nuanced approach to war.

[7] Iohannes Divjak, *Epistolae ex duobus codicibus nuper in lucem prolatae. Sancti Aurelii Augustini Opera, CSEL* LXXXVIII,2⁶.

[8] *Epistula XXIII*A* 3: *CSEL* LXXXVIII,123: *itaque dictaui ex quo ueni, id est a tertio Idus Septembris usque ad Kalendas Decembres uersuum ferme sex milia.*

[9] *Confessiones* IX,viii,17: *CC* XXVII,143.

[10] *Epistula CCXXIX* 2: *CSEL* LVII,498: *sed maioris est gloriae ipsa bella uerbo occidere quam homines ferro et adquirere uel obtinere pacem pace non bello.*

[11] J. Pelikan, ed. and intro., *The Preaching of Chrysostom. Homilies on the Sermon on the Mount* (Philadelphia: Fortress Press, 1967), p. 28.

[12] *De ciuitate dei* XI,xviii: *CC* XLVIII,337.

[13] G. Lawless, "Augustine and Human Embodiment," *Collectanea Augustiniana. Mélanges T. J. Van Bavel*, eds. B. Bruning, M. Lamberigts, J. Van Houtem (Louvain: Institut Historique Augustinien, 1990), p. 175.

[14] *Retractationes* II,xv,1: *CC* LVII,101.

[15] T. Rowe, *Saint Augustine. Pastoral Theologian* (London: Epworth Press, 1974), p. 1.

[16] G. Lawless, "On Understanding Augustine of Hippo," *The Downside Review* 100 (1982) 39–40.

[17] H. Marrou, *Saint Augustin et la fin de la culture antique. Retractatio* (Paris: E. De Boccard, 1949), pp. 623–713.

[18] J. J. O'Donnell, typescript, folio 31, n. 98.

[19] *Retractationes, Prologus* 3: *CC* LVII,6–7.

[20] P. Brown, *Augustine of Hippo* (London: Faber and Faber, 1967), p. 385.

[21] *Ibid.*, 352.

[22] At least two texts composed at an interval of more than thirty-five years reveal Augustine's basic posture in this regard: 1) *Soliloquia* I,xiii,22: *CSEL* LXXXIX,34: *Ego autem solam propter se amo sapientiam. ...Quem modum autem potest habere illius pulchritudinis amor, in qua non solum non inuideo ceteris, sed etiam plurimos quaero, qui mecum adpetant, mecum inhient, mecum teneant mecumque perfruantur, tanto mihi amiciores futuri, quanto erit nobis amata communior,* and 2) *De ciuitate dei* XIX,xix: *CC* XLVIII,686: *In otio non iners uacatio delectare debet, sed aut inquisitio aut inuentio ueritatis, ut in ea quisque proficiat et quod inuenerit ne alteri inuideat.*

[23] R. J. O'Connell, S.J., "When Saintly Fathers Feuded: The Correspondence between Augustine and Jerome," *Thought* 54 (1979) 344–64.

[24] *De mendacio* XIX,40: *CSEL* XLI,460–61. B. Ramsey, "Two Traditions of Lying and Deception in the Ancient Church," *The Thomist* 49 (1985) 510–14.

[25] *De ciuitate dei* I,xvi–xxviii: *CC* XLVII,17–30.

[26] *Confessiones* X,xxiv,35: *CC* XXVII,174: *Vbi enim inueni ueritatem, ibi inueni deum meum, ipsam ueritatem, quam ex quo didici, non sum oblitus.*

[27] *De continentia* I,1–II,5: *CSEL* XLI,141–46.

[28] See note 24 above.

[29] *De moribus ecclesiae catholicae et de moribus Manichaeorum* I,xxii,40: *PL* XXXVIII,1328: *antiquum peccatum, quo nihil est ad praedicandum notius, nihil ad intelligendum secretius.*

[30] P. Frederiksen, "Beyond the Body/Soul Dichotomy. Augustine on Paul against the Manichees and the Pelagians," *Recherches Augustiniennes* 23 (1988) 112.

[31] *Ibid.*

[32] *Retractationes* II,i,1: *CC* LVII,89–90: *In cuius quaestionis solutione laboratum est quidem pro libero arbitrio uoluntatis humanae, sed uicit dei gratia.*

[33] *Contra secundam Juliani responsionem imperfectum opus* I,ci: *PL* XLV,1117: *si enim cogitur non uult.*

[34] *De ciuitate dei* XXII,iii: *CC* XLVIII,809: *...etiam teste Porphyrio, nobilissimo philosopho paganorum.*

[35] "Das Denken Augustins ist ein Nest von Widersprüchen." K. Flasch, *Augustin: Einführung in sein Denken* (Stuttgart: Philipp Reclam jun., 1980), p. 403. See the review article by Goulven Madec, "Sur une nouvelle introduction à la pensée d'Augustin," *REA* 28 (1982) 100–111.

[36] H. Chadwick, "Providence and the Problem of Evil in Augustine," *Congresso Internazionale su S. Agostino nel XVI Centenario della Conversione*, Atti, I (Rome, 1987), p. 161.

[37] J. Pelikan, *The Mystery of Continuity. Time and History, Memory and Eternity in the Thought of Saint Augustine* (Charlottesville: The University Press of Virginia, 1986).

[38] R. A. Markus, *Conversion and Disenchantment in Augustine's Spiritual Career*. The Saint Augustine Lecture, 1984 (Villanova: Villanova University Press, 1989).

[39] A. M. Kleinberg, "De Agone Christiano: The Preacher and his Audience," *Journal of Theological Studies* n.s. 38 (1987) 31.

[40] *Epistula CXLIII* 2: *CSEL* XLIV,251: *...qui proficiendo scribunt et scribendo proficiunt.*

[41] Horace, *Epodes* II,iii,390: *nescit uox missa reuerti. Epistula CXLIII* 4: *CSEL* XLIV,254.

[42] *Epistula CXLIII* 3 and 4: *CSEL* XLIV,253 and 254.

[43] *Retractationes* I,v,1: *CC* LVII,16.

[44] *Retractationes* I,xxvii: *CC* LVII,88.

[45] *Retractationes* II,xxii,2: *CC* LVII,108: ...*quoniam libido non est bonus et rectus usus libidinis.*

[46] Further nuance is required in the otherwise splendid second chapter "The Legacy of Augustine," of John Mahoney, *The Making of Moral Theology. A Study of the Roman Catholic Tradition* (Oxford: Clarendon Press, 1987), pp. 37–71. For example, Augustine's gloss on marriage, cited in the preceding note, surely belies what Mahoney describes as: "his [Augustine's] jaundiced view of sexual desire" (p. 65).
    Some eighteen letters addressed to women (another five addressed jointly to Paulinus of Nola and his wife Therasia), and a monastic rule whose original Latin text is virtually identical for women and men offer no warrant for the following unfair observation: "Lacking, of course, from Augustine's introspective make-up was any positive appreciation of women, and he seems to have considered them as little more than sex objects" (p. 66).
    Twice (pp. 43 and 65) Mahoney fails to take into account the shift in Augustine's thought, about the time of his episcopal consecration, 395/6 A.D., from an *uti-frui* paradigm of theological discourse to an eschatological model which was immensely influenced by the pilgrimage motif as this is exemplified in the life of the Christian. For a comprehensive grasp of this matter see Oliver O'Donovan, "Usus and fruitio in Augustine's De Doctrina Christiana I," *Journal of Theological Studies* n.s. 33 (1982) 361–97.
    Finally, it is somewhat of an overstatement to conclude as Mahoney does: "And although for 1500 years [Catholic moral theology] has experienced something more than an Augustinian moment in its moral thinking, it now appears to be in the difficult process of shaking off its long Augustinian mood" (p. 71).

[47] *De dono perseverantiae* XXI,55: *BA* 24,736: *quamvis neminem velim sic amplecti omnia mea, ut me sequatur, nisi in iis in quibus me non errasse perspexerit. ...quandoquidem arrogantius loquor quam verius, si vel nunc dico me ad perfectionem sine ullo errore scribendi iam in ista aetate venisse.*

[48] *Epistulae CCIX* and *XX** (ed. Divjak): *CSEL* LVII,347–53 and LXXXVIII, 94–112.

[49] H. Rondet, *Gratia Christi. Essai d'histoire du dogme et de théologie dogmatique* (Paris: Beauchesne, 1948), p. 104: "...une caricature de la pensée d'Augustin."

[50] *Enchiridion ad Laurentium de fide et spe et caritate* XXIII,93: *CC* XLVI,99: *mitissima sane omnium poena.*

[51] *De correptione et gratia* X,28: *BA* 24,332: *Quod ergo pauci in comparatione pereuntium, in suo vero numero multi liberantur, gratia fit.*

[52] *De sancta uirginitate* IV,4: *CSEL* XLI,237–38.

[53] Among others, the following little known texts are highly instructive in this regard: *De baptismo* V,xxvii,38: *CSEL* LI,295: *namque in illa ineffabili praescientia dei multi qui foris (ecclesia) uidentur intus sunt et multi qui intus (ecclesia) uidentur foris sunt. De baptismo* V,xxviii,39: *CSEL* LI,296–97: *certe manifestum est id, quod dicitur in ecclesia intus et foris, in*

corde, non in corpore cogitandum, quandoquidem omnes, qui corde sunt intus, in arcae unitate per eandem aquam salui fiunt, per quam omnes in corde sunt foris, siue etiam corpore foris sint siue non sint, tamquam unitatis aduersarii moriuntur. In Ioannis Epistulam ad Parthos tractatus V,7: PL XXXV,2016: *Dilectio ergo sola discernit inter filios Dei et filios diaboli. Signent se omnes signo crucis Christi; respondeant omnes, Amen; cantent omnes, Alleluia; baptizentur omnes, intrent Ecclesia, faciant parietes basilicarum: non discernuntur filii Dei a filiis diaboli, nisi charitate.* In Ioannis Epistulam ad Parthos tractatus VI,13: PL XXXV, 2028: *Multi intus (Ecclesia), quasi intus sunt; nemo autem foris, nisi vere foris.*

⁵⁴ H. Obermann, *Luther: Mensch zwischen Gott und Teufel* (Berlin: Severin und Siedler, 1982; Eng. tr., New Haven: Yale University Press, 1989), cited in the *Times Literary Supplement* (March 30–April 5, 1990) 348.

⁵⁵ A. Zumkeller, "Der Terminus 'sola fides' bei Augustinus," in G. R. Evans, ed., *Christian Authority. Essays in Honour of Henry Chadwick* (Oxford: Clarendon Press, 1988), pp. 86–100.

⁵⁶ *Concilii Tridentini Actorum Nova Collectio*, t. 5, p. 2, ed., Stephanus Ehses (Freiburg im Breisgau: B. Herder, 1911), pp. 793–94.

⁵⁷ J. Pelikan, *The Mystery of Continuity*, p. 140.

⁵⁸ *Ibid.*, p. 69: "Augustinus totus noster est."

⁵⁹ H. Marrou, *Saint Augustine and his Influence through the Ages* (New York: Harper and Brothers, 1957), p. 172.

⁶⁰ J. Pelikan, *The Christian Tradition. The Emergence of the Catholic Tradition 100–600* (Chicago: University of Chicago Press, 1971), p. 331.

⁶¹ In three areas particularly Elaine Pagels puts a false construction upon Augustine's mature thought: 1) free choice of the human will, 2) for want of a better term, the bishop's "political theology" and original sin, and 3) human sexuality. By some strange alchemy, moral freedom for Augustine, so Pagels urges us, is transformed into political freedom. The author appears to be projecting a prejudice of the late twentieth-century upon her reading of fifth-century texts, while totally ignoring the fact that Augustine stalwartly refused to identify either the church or the "state" (Roman Empire) with the city of God. Pagels is heir to a long line of faulty exegetes who disregard the essentially eschatological features of the bishop's writings, in her case, by linking his theology of original sin with the politics of the time. Notwithstanding such erroneous critiques of Augustine by many subsequent interpreters, the bishop never concerned himself with formulating a theory of politics, but rather an intelligible Christian approach to political life which, most assuredly, accorded great respect to human freedom.

Among the incisive reviews of Pagels' book no one, to my knowledge, noted the egregious error where the author mistakenly identifies the Stoic theory of *rationes seminales* with male sperm (p. 109). Augustine's original text reads: *Nondum erat nobis singillatim creata et distributa forma, in qua singuli uiueremus; sed iam erat natura seminalis, ex qua propagaremur* (*De ciuitate dei* XIII,xiv: *CC* XLVIII,395).

See the following perceptive evaluations of Pagels' book: John Cavadini, *The Thomist* 53 (1989) 509–12; Goulven Madec, *REA* 35 (1989) 416–18, and M. Lamberigts, "Augustine, Julian of Aeclanum and E. Pagels," *Augustiniana* 39 (1989) 393–435.

[62] P. Brown, *The Body and Society. Men, Women, and Sexual Renunciation in Early Christianity* (New York: Columbia University Press, 1988), p. 415, n.109.

[63] *Epistula II** (ed. Divjak): *CSEL* LXXXVIII,9–21.

[64] *Sermo CLXIX* 15, 18: *PL* XXXVIII,926: *Melius it claudus in via, quam cursor praeter viam.*

[65] *Sermo CCXXVIII* 2: *PL* XXXVIII,1102: *Audio nomen, agnoscam et rem.*

[66] *De ordine* II,iv,12: *CC* XXIX,114; *Enneads* III,ii,17: *PO*, 271.

[67] *Ibid.*

[68] *Enarratio in Psalmum XCIX* 11–13 at 13: *CC* XXXIX, 1399–1402. H. Chadwick, in "The Ascetic Ideal in the History of the Church," Presidential Address to the Ecclesiastical History Society, July 1984 (*Studies in Church History*, 22 [1985] 1–23), presents an excellent account of Augustine.

[69] *De trinitate* XIV,iv,6: *CC* L/A,428–29.

[70] *Sermo LXXX* 8: *PL* XXXVIII,498:
> *Mala tempora, laboriosa tempora,*
> *hoc dicunt homines.*
> *Bene vivimus, et bona sunt tempora.*
> *Nos sumus tempora:*
> *quales sumus, talia sunt tempora.*

[71] *Sermo de excidio urbis Romae* VI,6: *CC* XLVI,258: *An putatis, fratres, ciuitatem in parietibus et non in ciuibus deputandam?*

[72] "Le pessimisme augustinien, bien compris, peut donc être le point de départ d'un optimisme de la grâce qui ne le céderait en rien à l'optimisme des Pères grecs" (H. Rondet, *Gratia Christi*, p. 139).

[73] *Enarratio in Psalmum XLI* 15: *CC* XXXVIII,472: *Quia magis crebra sunt mala, dulcior erit misericordia.*

[74] *In Ioannis Epistulam ad Parthos tractatus* VIII,5: *PL* XXXV,2038: *Tolle miseros: cessabunt opera misericordiae.*

[75] *Enarratio in Psalmum LXXVI* 11: *CC* XXXIX,1060: *Facilius ille [Deus] iram quam misericordiam continebit.*

[76] *De ciuitate dei* XIV,xi: *CC* XLVIII,432: *Vsque adeo autem mala uincuntur a bonis....*

[77] D. Tracy, "The Uneasy Alliance Reconceived: Catholic Theological Method, Modernity, and Post-Modernity," *Theological Studies* 50 (1989) 556.

[78] D. Migliore, "Centenary Harvest: A Review of Recent Books on Karl Barth," *The Princeton Seminary Bulletin* n.s. 8 (1987) 45. The author presents another line of succession by listing, after Mozart, Augustine, Aquinas, Luther, Calvin and Schleiermacher in that order.

For Specialists Only:
The Reception of Augustine and His Teachings in Fifth-Century Gaul

Ralph W. Mathisen

The role of Augustine as a theological authority in the fifth century cannot be overstated. More than anyone else, he influenced the direction of fifth-century western theological thought. His teachings, however, were not received equally well in all areas. In Gaul in particular there were serious misgivings about some, although by no means all, of his ideas. This short study will examine just how Augustine's teachings were received in Gaul, just what any reservations about them were, and what the reasons for these reservations were. First, consideration will be given to a specific case with which the Gauls were particularly concerned; attention then will turn to general Gallic perceptions of Augustine.

The aspects of Augustine's teaching that most interested the Gauls were those concerned with the doctrines of grace, free will, and original sin. Gauls had been involved in the discussion of grace since early in the fifth century, and they had been instrumental in bringing Augustine into the resultant controversies in the first place. What concerned the Gauls were some of the teachings of an expatriate Briton named Pelagius, who had settled in Rome in the years circa 400. His denial of original sin and his contention that it was possible to live without sin necessarily restricted the role of divine grace.[1]

Shortly after 410, two exiled Gallic bishops became especially involved in anti-Pelagian activities. These were Heros of Arles and Lazarus of Aix, who had lost their sees after the defeat of the usurper Constantine III and the imperial restoration in 411. After their departure from Gaul they had eventually surfaced in the Holy Land, where in 415 they dispatched a letter to the Council of Diospolis condemning Pelagianism. Despite their testimony, Pelagius was acquitted. In 416, they sent a similar letter to the Council of Carthage.[2] Initially, however, the prospects for their cause did not look good. Even the new bishop of Rome, Zosimus, elected in 417, vilified them and supported Pelagius, saying, "Is it any wonder if they wish to afflict with libelous letters a layman struggling to bear good fruit...on behalf of God?"[3]

But the African bishops, led by Augustine, did not let the matter drop. And in 418 Zosimus caved in to increasing pressure and anathematized Pelagian beliefs.[4] Shortly thereafter, Pelagianism was made a crime against the state by the emperor Honorius.[5]

In Gaul, anti-Pelagianism went on to become one of the elements that strongly united Gallic churchmen: in the fifth century, the anathematization of Pelagius became a virtual touchstone of Gallic orthodoxy. The anonymous southern Gallic author of the *Chronicle of 452*, for example, stated under the year 400, "The insane Pelagius attempts to befoul the churches with his execrable teaching."[6] And in 429, Cassian of Marseilles could say of a theological adversary who had been accused of Nestorianism, "Therefore, you see that you vomit the Pelagian poison, that you hiss with the Pelagian spirit."[7]

In 425, moreover, the imperial government went so far as to assign to the bishop of Arles the responsibility for tracking down Pelagian bishops and expelling them from "the Gallic regions."[8] In the mid 440s this authority was exercised, it seems, when bishop Germanus of Auxerre travelled to Britain and had Pelagians "expelled from the island [and] carried off to the Mediterranean regions so that they might enjoy both imperial absolution and correction."[9]

As for Augustine, some Gauls looked directly to him for guidance in related theological matters at this time. Circa 417, for example, Augustine had been consulted by Claudius Postumus Dardanus, a Gallic ex-prefect who had remained loyal to the Italian government during the Gallic revolts of 407–13, regarding the latter's uncertainties about the baptism of infants, and Augustine responded in a letter replete with his thoughts on the doctrine of grace.[10]

One also might note the case of the priest Leporius, described by Cassian as, "one of the primary or greatest assertors of the aforementioned heresy [sc. Nestorianism] in Gaul, a descendent of the teaching, or rather the depravity, of Pelagius."[11] Bishop Proculus of Marseilles, in conjunction with an otherwise unknown bishop Cillenius, responded by sending Leporius to Augustine, who later wrote back to them, "When our son Leporius, who deservedly and suitably had been rebuked for the presumption of his error by Your Sanctity, arrived in our presence, after he had been expelled, we received the confused one so that he might be soundly corrected and healed."[12] In the context of the condemnation of Pelagianism and related teachings, therefore, the Gauls and Augustine got along just fine.

Where the Gauls parted company with Augustine, however, was on the question of predestination. The aforementioned *Chronicle of 452*, which had so clearly condemned Pelagianism, also could note under the year 418, "The heresy of the predestinarians, which is said to have received its impetus from Augustine, once having arisen, creeps along."[13] The publication of Augustine's *De correptione et gratia* in 426 brought an immediate Gallic response. Book thirteen of the *Collationes* of Cassian of Marseilles attacked both Pelagianism and unconditional predestination, and stressed the need for human effort along with grace.

This Gallic denial of this aspect of Augustine's teaching brought a heated response from two of Augustine's Gallic theological partisans, Prosper of Aquitaine and a certain Hilarius. Circa 426, they wrote to Augustine himself. Hilarius reported, "These are the charges being circulated in... Gaul: that your idea that certain individuals are designated as elect according to a fixed purpose is an innovation and is useless for preaching."[14] And Prosper wrote, "Many of the servants of Christ who live in Marseilles think that, in the writings which Your Sanctity composed against the Pelagian heretics, whatever you said in them about the choice of the elect according to the fixed purpose of God is contrary to the opinion of the fathers and to ecclesiastical feeling."[15]

The method that these two Gauls chose for prosecuting their case against the Gallic theological establishment is instructive: they accused the Gallic anti-Pelagians of Pelagianism. Even though Prosper admitted that the Gallic anti-predestinarians accepted grace and original sin, the two main Augustinian tenets denied by the Pelagians, he nonetheless referred to their "spirit of Pelagianism," he claimed that "some actually fail to avoid Pelagian errors," and he described some of their teachings as the "remnants of the Pelagian depravity."[16]

But Prosper did indicate elsewhere what the main Gallic cause for complaint was: "They say that [Augustine] has eliminated free will and that in the guise of grace he preaches fatal necessity."[17] After some further exchanges in the pamphlet war in which Prosper made no discernible headway, and after the death of his patron Augustine in 430, Prosper eventually took a step favored by many disgruntled Gallic ecclesiastics and appealed to Pope Celestine in Rome. The latter, in 431, responded thus to a group of Gallic bishops, "We always have held Augustine...in our communion, nor has even the rumor of perverse suspicion tainted him.... For what reason is he opposed by such men, whom we see evilly increasing?"[18] And on just what grounds did Celestine think that Augustine was opposed? The answer to that question is suggested by the documents that he appended to his letter: an attack on Pelagian-ism. Prosper, therefore, had indicated to the pope that the Gauls who op-posed predestination were in fact Pelagians, and Celestine had been only too ready to believe him.

Meanwhile, back in Gaul the definitive Gallic response came in 434, when Vincentius of Lérins published his *Commonitorium*. Ostensibly intend-ed as a general handbook on how to distinguish heresy from orthodoxy, the book soon narrowed down its focus, stating, "The fraudulence of new heretics demands great care and attention."[19] And as to who those "new heretics" were, Vincentius referred to the recent letter of Celestine, in which the pope had rebuked the Gauls for their attacks on Augustine. Vincentius asked the question, "Someone here perhaps might wonder who these individuals might be…the supporters of tradition or the inventors of novelty? Let him [i.e. Cel-estine] speak himself…. He said, 'Let novelty cease to assault tradition.'"[20] Here, Vincentius turned Celestine's own arguments upon himself by arguing that it was Augustine's teachings that were *novitas*, and that they therefore had been condemned rightly.

Nor did the Gauls change their minds about predestination, which they continued to view as erroneous, if not downright ludicrous. At the end of the century, for example, Gennadius of Marseilles noted succinctly in his *Adversus omnes haereses* that "the predestinarians are those who say that God did not create all men so that all might be saved, but so that the earth might be adorned by a multitude of inhabitants."[21]

In the early 470s, finally, the Gauls went so far as to summon a church council at Arles to consider the case of Lucidus, who had been accused of teaching predestination. Lucidus was condemned, and bishop Faustus of Riez, the leader of the Gallic anti-predestinarians, was commissioned to lay out the Gallic position on grace. In the resultant *De gratia*, Faustus rhetorical-ly associated Pelagius with Augustine, saying, "Here, therefore, both errors contradict themselves, for, with the path and rule of truth abandoned, one [i.e. Augustine] stresses only grace and the other [i.e. Pelagius] only labor, dispa-rate by the kind of beliefs, but similar in impiety through their equally diver-gent approach, they hiss with the spirit of a single serpent, of whom one, that is the supporter of grace alone, with a distinguished facade hides his venom under the guise of piety, whereas the other, that is the assertor of labor, open-ly displays his conspicuous arrogance in his shameless elation."[22] Faustus not only accused Augustine and Pelagius of being equally wrong, but found in this wrongness an antithetical link between them. By this means, the Gauls were able to define their own intermediate position on grace and free will. And as for Augustine, Faustus elsewhere referred to him as a "destroyer of free will," who "decrees that everything has been established and defined by predestination."[23]

The Gallic opposition to predestination even extended to northern Italy, where an expatriate Gaul, the deacon Ennodius of Milan, later bishop of Pavia, wrote to his friend Constantius in 503 on the subject of predestination and the need for human labor. Regarding Augustine, he said, "I see where the poisons of the Libyan plague extend. The sandy snake not only holds these pernicious beliefs which he discloses: the matters which he confesses must be understood in the consideration of his hidden crimes. He even wishes to go so far [as to say] that no one perishes by his own sin or negligence."[24] So much, then, at least as far as the Gauls were concerned, for this particular theological doctrine of Augustine.[25]

It would appear, then, that the Gauls by no means repudiated all of Augustine's teachings. They were in full agreement with him on the anathematization of Pelagianism. But they were firmly opposed to him on the question of predestination. One problem that this stand created is that it isolated them from the theological position of Italy and the church of Rome, where it appears that Augustine's theological teachings enjoyed virtually blanket approbation, as seen above in Celestine's statement, "Nor has even the rumor of perverse suspicion tainted him...."[26]

In more recent times, too, the Gauls' unilateral stand against Augustinian predestination has borne bitter fruit. Much of the true nature of the debate, as well as the Gallic response to Augustine, has been obfuscated by nearly sixteen centuries of rhetorical posturing, misinformation, and misrepresentation. Prosper's attempts to tar his opponents with the Pelagian brush continue to bear fruit, for even now the Gallic theologians often are saddled with the misleading misnomer of "semi-Pelagians," in spite of their being virulent anti-Pelagians to a man.[27]

But this phenomenon was, in fact, only consistent with Gallic independence of action in other spheres. The Gallic revolts of 407–13 demonstrate the inclination of the Gauls to go their own ways in political matters. The same held true in the ecclesiastical, and theological, arena. The Gauls chose to make their own decisions about what was orthodox and what was heretical. In the case of Augustine, some of his teachings were accepted, others were not.

The Gauls' categorical rejection of one of Augustine's main teachings meant that Augustine never could have the status in Gaul of an unquestioned theological authority. This does not mean to say, however, that Augustine was not admired and respected. Gauls who could attack Augustine on one point could admire him and cite him as an authority on others.[28] Prosper himself, for example, in the aforementioned letter to Augustine, reported about the short-lived bishop Helladius of Arles, "Your Beatitude should know that he is an admirer and follower of your teaching in all other things, and with regard to that which he calls into question [i.e. predestination], he already wished to convey his own thoughts to Your Sanctity through correspondence...."[29] If Helladius ever did write the letter in question, no record of it survives.

Even in their condemnations of predestination, moreover, the Gauls were decidedly reluctant to cite their august opponent by name. Neither Cassian, nor Vincentius, nor Faustus attacked Augustine by name, only his teachings. In fact, Vincentius' genteel refusal to name Augustine even has led some to doubt that he was attacking him at all![30]

Furthermore, some Gallic theologians also felt comfortable citing Augustine as an authority on theological matters not related to grace and free will. The same Vincentius who condemned predestination, for example, at the same time published a collection of *Excerpta* from Augustine on the trinity and the incarnation, perhaps gathered while he was conducting his own theological evaluation of Augustine's works.[31]

Later, in the Gallic controversy over the nature of the soul in the late 460s, the Gallic priest Claudianus Mamertus of Vienne asserted in his *De statu animae*, "Aurelius Augustinus, in the acuity of his intelligence and the multitude of his topics and the mass of his work...spoke thus in his book to Jerome *On the Origin of the Soul*, 'the soul is incorporeal.'"[32] Sidonius Apollinaris, the leading Gallic littérateur of the day, even could compliment Mamertus by comparing him to Augustine.[33]

In the end, however, Mamertus' association with Augustine may have cost him, for his rival Faustus of Riez, who favored the corporealist notion of the soul, eventually won the day.[34] But if Faustus opposed the Augustinian view of the soul, not to mention predestination, even he elsewhere strongly defended Augustine's Christological views.[35]

This ambivalent attitude toward Augustine's theology is illustrated strikingly by Gennadius of Marseilles, in an entry in his *De viris inlustribus*, in which he began by describing Augustine as "a man brilliant in divine and human learning, complete in faith and pure in his life...," but then went on to say, "whence, that which the Holy Spirit said through Solomon, [that] 'in verbosity you shall not escape sin,' also happened to him, who said a great deal.... Error was incurred by his excessive speaking, was enlarged by the attack of his enemies, and not yet has escaped the accusation of heresy."[36]

A similar view was expressed by Faustus of Riez. He specified the proper attitude toward Augustine's teachings in a letter to the deacon Graecus, who in a work of his own had presumed to challenge Augustine on a Christological point. Faustus replied, "Even if some part of the works of the blessed bishop Augustine is thought to be suspect by the most learned men, you should know that there is nothing reprehensible in those sections which you thought should be condemned."[37] Faustus went on to suggest that Graecus was not sufficiently experienced to conduct such study, and advised him, "Avoid excessive reading, so that you might remove the dangerous intoxication, similar to that of wine drunken immoderately, of a spirit whose capacity is too small."[38]

With regard to his theological teachings, therefore, the Gauls clearly considered Augustine to be a topic for experts. His complexities only could be evaluated by specialists. Indeed, some Gauls, such as Faustus himself, could express surprise when they agreed with Augustine. On one of the rare occasions on which he did use Augustine as an authority, Faustus stated, "Therefore, the fact that the work of natural law was written in human hearts even the blessed priest Augustine describes in most learned speech."[39]

So much, then, for the Gallic views of Augustine's theology *per se*. One now might turn to Augustine's broader reputation in Gaul. On a more popular level, Augustine's non-controversial works were read and admired. At the end of the century, bishop Ruricius of Limoges, for example, thanked his friend Taurentius for sending him a copy of Augustine's *De ciuitate dei*; he even included a brief précis of the contents, perhaps to show that he had actually read it.[40] And the aristocrat Tonantius Ferreolus also had Augustine in his library.[41]

In this context, however, it appears that Augustine was but one of several ecclesiastical writers whose works were collected and read. Taurentius, for example, mentioned that Ruricius had returned to him works not only of Augustine, but also of Cyprian, Hilary of Poitiers, and Ambrose. And Ferreolus' library also included works of Varro, Horace, Prudentius, and Origen (translated by Turranius Rufinus).[42] In the sixth century, Augustine was cited in company with such as Athanasius, Hilary of Poitiers, Basil of Caesarea, Caesarius of Arles, Martin of Tours, Gregory of Nazianzus, and Ambrose.[43]

Furthermore, even if the Gauls had doubts about some of Augustine's theological views, there were two areas in which Augustine did make his mark upon the Gauls. One thing that amazed the Gauls was the sheer quantity of Augustine's work. At the end of the fifth century, Gennadius noted, "He wrote so many works they cannot be counted."[44] A century later, Venantius Fortunatus, in his choice of descriptive terms for famous theologians, noted, "The blessed Augustine overwhelms."[45] Even in the twelfth century, the chronicler Sigisbert could describe Augustine as "one who wrote so many things that not only could no one write so many books in his entire lifetime, no one could even read that many."[46] For some Gauls, therefore, the quantity of Augustine's work was perhaps more noteworthy than its quality. Indeed, as seen above, it was this very quantity which, in the opinion of some, got Augustine into trouble.

The second aspect of Augustine's method which seems to have made a particular impression on the erudite Gauls was his rhetorical skill. Sidonius Apollinaris, for example, cited Augustine for his dialectical ability in particular.[47] And a friend of Hilary of Arles complimented Hilary on his literary ability by exclaiming to him, "If Augustine had come after you, he would have been judged inferior."[48] Even Augustine's admirer Mamertus described him as a "spiritual sophist."[49]

Augustine's theological adversary Faustus, moreover, used him as an authority not on theological exposition but on rhetorical subtlety, noting on one occasion, "When one thing is mentioned, but not the other, the other is left unspoken but it is not denied, according to that rule which the priest Augustine insinuates, 'Not all things which are left unspoken are denied.'"[50]

For Gauls in the fifth century, therefore, Augustine the writer was to be admired for his rhetorical skill and for the sheer length of his publications list. But the Gauls were voluminous writers, and experts in rhetoric, themselves. They knew all the tricks of the trade. Their respect for Augustine's persuasive skills also would have made them wary. The evaluation of his theology, therefore, was a matter for specialists. As much as he was admired for his dialectic, he was not accepted as the final word on every theological point. The determination of proper theological opinion was something the Gauls reserved to themselves.

Notes

[1] For the Gallic view of Pelagius, see, e.g., Faustus, *Epistula II*: *CSEL* XXI,165–68 to Lucidus, and *De gratia dei* I,1; I,11: *CSEL* XXI,6–12, 36–40.

[2] Zosimus, *Epistulae* "Magnum pondus" and "Posteaquam a nobis" (*Epistulae imperatorum XLV–XLVI: CSEL* XXXV,99–108); Augustine, *De gestis Pelagii* I,2; XVI,39: *CSEL* XLII,52, 116–17; *Epistulae CLXXV* 1; *CLXXIX* 7: *CSEL* LVII,454ff. See E. Griffe, *La gaule chrétienne* (Paris: Letouzey et Ané, 1965) 2.255; and R. Mathisen, *Ecclesiastical Factionalism and Religious Controversy in Fifth-Century Gaul* (Washington, D.C.: Catholic University of America Press, 1989), pp. 37–41.

[3] Zosimus, *Epistula* "Magnum pondus": *CSEL* XXXV,100: *mirum est si laicum virum ad bonum frugem longa erga deum servitute nitentem, falsis litteris percellere voluerunt...?*

[4] In the now-lost *Epistula tractoria*; cf. his *Epistula* "Quamvis patrum": *CSEL* XXXV, 115–17, of 21 March 418.

[5] See the rescript "Ad conturbandum" of 30 April 418 (G. Haenel, *Corpus legum* [Leipzig, 1857] pp. 238–39, no. 1171).

[6] *Chronica gallica anno 452,* no. 44: *Monumenta Germaniae historica, Auctores antiquissimi* 9,650: *Pelagius vesanus doctrina execrabili ecclesias conmaculare conatur.*

[7] Cassian, *De incarnatione* V,2: *PL* L,101: *Ergo vides Pelagianum te virus vomere, Pelagiano te spiritu sibilare....*

[8] *Constitutiones Sirmondinianae* 6 (9 July 425).

[9] *Vita Germani* 27: *Sources chrétiennes* 112,172. Earlier, in 429, Germanus also had gone to Britain to combat the Pelagians; here, however, no legal action seems to have been taken. For discussion, see Mathisen, *Factionalism,* pp. 101–2, 139–40.

[10] Augustine, *Epistula CLXXXVII: CSEL* LVII,100ff. Dardanus' queries could suggest that he had Pelagian leanings; see J. Matthews, *Western Aristocracies and Imperial Court, A.D. 364–425* (Oxford: Oxford University Press, 1975), p. 323; and Mathisen, *Factionalism,* pp. 34, 40.

[11] Cassian, *De incarnatione* I,4: *PL* L,24:...*ex Pelagii, ut supra diximus, institutione, vel potius pravitate, descendens apud Gallias assertor praedictae haereseos, ut inter primos aut inter maximos....* For Nestorius, Leporius and Pelagianism, see also *De incarnatione* VII, 21: *PL* L,243–44: *Ita ergo et tu Pelagianae haereseos spinosa suboles idem ostendis in germine, quod pater tuus habuisse traditur in radice. Leporius ille enim (ut Leporius discipulus suus dixit) dominum nostrum asserebat Christum esse factum per baptismum.* Here one notes the Gallic tendency to equate all deviant beliefs with the one they all anathematized: Pelagianism.

[12] Augustine, *Epistula CCXIX* 1: *CSEL* LVII,428: *filium nostrum Leporium apud uestram sanctitatem pro sui erroris praesumptione merito idoneeque correptum, cum ad nos, posteaquam exinde exturbatus est, aduenisset, salubriter perturbatum corrigendum sanandumque suscepimus.*

[13] *Chronica gallica anno 452,* no. 81: *Monumenta Germaniae historica, Auctores antiquissimi* 9,656: *Praedestinatorum haeresis quae ab Augustino accepisse initium dicitur his temporibus serpere exorsa.*

[14] Prosper apud Augustinum, *Epistula CCXXVI: CSEL* LVII,469: *Haec sunt itaque quae Massiliae vel etiam aliquibus locis in Gallia ventilantur: novum et inutile esse praedicationi, quod quidam secundum propositum eligendi dicantur....*

[15] Prosper apud Augustinum, *Epistula CCXXV: CSEL* LVII,455: *Multi ergo servorum Christi qui in Massiliensi urbe consistunt in sanctitatis tuae scriptis, quae adversus Pelagianos haereticos condidisti, contrarium putant patrum opinioni et ecclesiastico sensui, quidquid in eis de vocatione electorum secundum dei propositum disputasti....*

[16] Prosper apud Augustinum, *Epistula CCXXV* 2–4: *CSEL* LVII,455–61.

[17] Prosper, *Epistula ad Rufinum de gratia et libero arbitrio* 3: *PL* LI,79:*...dicentes eum liberum arbitrium penitus submovere et sub gratiae nomine necessitatem praedicare fatalem....*

[18] Celestine, *Epistula XXI* II,5: *PL* L,528–37: *Augustinum sanctae recordationis virum...in nostra communione semper habuimus, nec umquam hunc sinistrae suspicionis saltem rumor aspersit.... unde resistatur talibus, quos male crescere videmus?*

[19] Vincentius, *Commonitorium* I: *CC* LXIV,147–48.

[20] Vincentius, *Commonitorium* XXXII: *CC* LXIV,193: *hic aliquis fortasse addubitet, quinam sint illi...uetustatis praedicatores an nouitatis adinuentores. Ipse dicat...sequitur enim: "desinat...incessere nouitas uetustatem."*

[21] Gennadius, *Adversus omnes haereses* 52: *PL* LXXXI,644: *Praedestinatiani sunt qui \ dicunt quod deus non omnes ad hoc creet ut omnes salventur, sed ut multitudine hominum ornetur mundus.*

[22] Faustus, *De gratia dei* I,1: *CSEL* XXI,7: *hic ergo dum altius humanam fragilitatem immemor divini timoris extollit, iudicii sui perdidit sanitatem et ita ex parte alia cecidit, dum arbitrii libertatem integram praedicat et inlaesam, sicut illi, qui eam ex toto asserunt fuisse evacuatam. hoc itaque loco gemini inter se conluctantur errores, quorum unus solam gratiam, alter solum laborem relicto tramite atque mensura veritatis insinuat. sectarum genere dispares, sed inpietate consimiles diverso quidem studio, sed spiritu unius serpentis insibilant. quorum unus, id est solius gratiae praedicator prima quidem fronte venenum suum sub specie pietatis occultat, alter, id est laboris assertor protinus extantem tumorem inproba elatione manifestat.*

[23] Faustus, *De gratia dei* I,10: *CSEL* XXI,33: *liberi interemptor arbitrii...omnia ex praedestinatione statuta et definita esse pronuntiat.*

[24] Ennodius, *Epistulae* II,xix,16: *Monumenta Germaniae historica, Auctores antiquissimi* 7,71: *video quo se toxica Libycae pestis extendant. arenosus coluber non haec sola habet perniciosa quae reserat: ad aestimationem occultorum facinorum ferenda sunt, quae fatetur. vult enim ad illud pertingere, neminem suo vitio aut neglegentia perire....* A. Lumpe, "Die konziliengeschichtliche Bedeutung des Ennodius," *Annuarium historiae conciliorum* 1 (1969) 15–36, at pp. 31–33, correctly identifies Augustine as the "Libycae pestis."

[25] It was not until the 520s that Faustus' teachings on grace were seriously questioned in the West. See A. Engelbrecht, *CSEL* XXI,xvi–xvii; A. Koch, *Der heilige Faustus, Bischof von Riez* (Stuttgart, 1895), pp. 50–55; and B. Krusch, *Monumenta Germaniae Historica, Auctores antiquissimi* 8,59. And even when they were condemned in Gaul in 529 at

the council of Orange, Caesarius of Arles and the Gallic bishops still refrained from mentioning Faustus by name, and upheld Faustus' opposition to full Augustinian predestination.

[26] This acceptance of Augustine led the Italian author (probably Arnobius Junior) of the so-called *Praedestinatus* to state, in his list of heresies (*Praedestinatus* I,90: *PL* LIII,620), *nonagesimus haeresis, quam...de nomine Augustini episcopi esse mentitam, praedestinatorum nomen accepit.* This same Arnobius, in his commentary, *In Psalmum CVIII*: *PL* LIII,495, also discussed the heresy *quae dicit Deum alios praedestinasse ad benedictionem, alios ad maledictionem.*

[27] See Mathisen, *Factionalism*, p. 129ff.

[28] Even if at times only grudgingly. Note Cassian, *De incarnatione* VII,27: *PL* L,260, where Augustine is described as *Augustinus Hipponae Regiensis oppidi magnus sacerdos*, in the same breath as Rufinus of Aquileia, the Origenist opponent of Jerome.

[29] Augustine, *Epistula CCXXV* 9: *CSEL* LVII,467: *sciat beatitudo tua admiratorem sectatoremque in aliis omnibus tuae esse doctrinae et de hoc, quod [sc. praedestinationem] in querelam trahis, iam pridem apud sanctitatem tuam sensum suum per litteras velle conferre....* By the principle of *lectio difficilior* the reading *Elladium* is to be preferred to *Hilarium* [sc. *Arelatensem*]). Helladius, even though he appears in the episcopal *fasti* of Arles, was omitted by L. Duchesne, *Fastes épiscopaux de l'ancienne Gaule* (Paris, 1907–15) 1.256. His existence was proven, however, by O. Chadwick, "Euladius of Arles," *JTS* 46 (1945) 200–205; see also Griffe, *Gaule* 2.239–41; and Mathisen, *Factionalism*, pp. 86–87.

[30] See Griffe, *Gaule* 3.379.

[31] *Excerpta Vincentii Lirinensis*: *CC* LXIV,199–231. Vincentius purported to be publishing the excerpts in refutation of the Christological views of Arius, Apollinaris, and Nestorius, who, however, are named only in the prologue, with the Nestorians (and Photinians) also cited in Book 10 (*CC* LXIV,199, 202, 231).

[32] Claudianus Mamertus, *De statu animae* II,9: *CSEL* XI,133: *Aurelius Augustinus et acumine ingenii et rerum multitudine et operis mole...libro ad Hieronymum de origine animae sic pronuntiat: incorpoream esse animam.* Mamertus' apparent citation from *De ciuitate dei* VI,ii at *De statu animae* II,8: *CSEL* XI,130, also suggests he had Augustine right before him at this point in his work.

[33] Sidonius Apollinaris, *Epistulae* IV,iii,7: *Monumenta Germaniae historica, Auctores antiquissimi* 8,55: *adstruit ut Augustinus*. Such a description, however, also could have been conventional; cf. *Epistulae* IX,ii,2: *Monumenta Germaniae historica, Auctores antiquissimi* 8,150, to Lupus, who was described as *dialecticus [ut] Augustinus*.

[34] For discussion, see Mathisen, *Factionalism*, pp. 235–44.

[35] Faustus, *Epistulae VII*: *CSEL* XXI,200–207; see below for discussion.

[36] Gennadius, *De viris inlustribus* XXXVIII: *PL* LVIII,1080:...*vir eruditione divina et humana orbi clarus, fide integer et vita purus...unde et multa loquenti accidit, quod dixit per*

Salomonem spiritus sanctus, 'in multiloquio non effugies peccatum'...error tamen illius sermone multo, ut dixi, contractus, lucta hostium exaggeratus, necdum haeresis questionem absolvit. For other potential references to Augustine as a *haereticus,* see Faustus, *De gratia dei* I,12: *CSEL* XXI,40–44, *ecce haereticus sub praetextu gratiae qualem vult hominem esse post gratiam; cum alio loco haereticus apostoli sententiam praedestinationem dei vel praefinitionem interpretetur esse.* A generous reader might translate this as "a heretic," but it would not be difficult also to take it to mean "the heretic," that is, Augustine himself. At the same time, Faustus likened predestination to Manichaeism, see *De gratia dei* I,5: *CSEL* XXI,20–21: *dum Pelagii impietatem nescis refugere, ad Manichaeorum dogma pestiferum, qui liberum arbitrium totum denegant, te intellege declinare.*

[37] Faustus, *Epistulae VII*: *CSEL* XXI,201: *in scriptis sancti pontificis Augustini etiamsi quid apud doctissimos viros putatur esse suspectum, ex his quae damnanda indicasti nihil noveris reprehensum.*

[38] Faustus, *Epistulae VII*: *CSEL* XXI,207: *cave nimiam lectionem, ut cordi parum capaci tamquam sumpti inmoderatius vini periculosam moveris ebrietatem.*

[39] Faustus, *De gratia dei* II,9: *CSEL* XXI,81: *opus itaque naturalis legis in cordibus hominum fuisse conscriptum etiam beatissimus pontifex Augustinus doctissimo sermone prosequitur ita dicens,* "utrumque simul currit...." (no reference in text to the source of this citation, but it is found in *De ciuitate dei* XXII,xxiv: *CC* XLVIII,847).

[40] Ruricius, *Epistulae* II,17: *CC* XLIV,356–58. The same work also seems to have been cited twice by Avitus of Vienne—the only work of Augustine cited by him; see *Contra Eutychianam haeresim* II: *Monumenta Germaniae historica, Auctores antiquissimi* 6,2,23 and *Contra Arianos* 7: ibid. 6,2,5, both citing Malachi 3:8, a topic also covered in *De ciuitate dei* XX,xxv: *CC* XLVIII,747–48. Ruricius even seems to have dedicated a church to Augustine, see Venantius Fortunatus, *Carmina* IV,v,11–12: *Monumenta Germaniae historica, Auctores antiquissimi* 4,1,82:

> *tempore quisque suo fundans pia templa patroni*
> *iste Augustini, condidit ille Petri.*

[41] Sidonius Apollinaris, *Epistulae* II,ix,4: *Monumenta Germaniae historica, Auctores antiquissimi* 8,31.

[42] Sidonius Apollinaris, *Epistulae* II,ix,4–5: *Monumenta Germaniae historica, Auctores antiquissimi* 8,31.

[43] Venantius Fortunatus, *Carmina* V,i,7;iii,35–40 and *Vita Martini* IV,664: *Monumenta Germaniae historica, Auctores antiquissimi* 4,1,102, 107 and 369; and *Vita Caesarii* I,54, II,46: *Monumenta Germaniae historica, Scriptores rerum merovingicarum* 3,478 and 499–500.

[44] Gennadius, *De viris inlustribus* XXXVIII: *PL* LVIII,1079: *scripsit quanta nec inveniri possunt.*

[45] Venantius Fortunatus, *Carmina* V,iii,35–40: *Monumenta Germaniae historica, Auctores antiquissimi* 4,1,107: *Augustinus inundat*; on the other hand, *Gregorius radiat....* *Basilius rutilat, Caesarius micat.*

[46] Sigisbert, *Chronica* s. a. 440: *Monumenta Germaniae historica, Scriptores* 6,308: *qui tanta scripsit, ut nullus libros eius omni tempore vitae suae non solum scribere, sed nec legere quidem valeat.*

[47] Sidonius Apollinaris, *Epistulae* IX,ii,2: *Monumenta Germaniae historica, Auctores antiquissimi* 8,150: *dialecticus Augustinus.* See also *Epistulae* II,ix,5 and IV,iii,7: *Monumenta Germaniae historica, Auctores antiquissimi* 8,31 and 55.

[48] *Vita Hilarii* 11 [14]: *PL* L,1232. *si Augustinus post te fuisset, iudicaretur inferior.*

[49] *De statu animae* II,9: *CSEL* XI,133: *spiritalis sophista.*

[50] *De gratia dei* I,5: *CSEL* XXI,20: *cum unum sine altero dicitur, tacetur alterum, non negatur secundum illam regulam, quam antistes Augustinus insinuat, "non omnia quae tacentur negantur"* (no reference in *CSEL* to the source of this citation, nor is it found in this form in any of Augustine's extant works). The aforementioned citations, it might be noted, are Faustus' only references to Augustine in the works which have come down under his name. Faustus also, however, is assigned a *Sermo in depositione s. Augustini*: *CSEL* XXI, 330–34. And a number of the sermons of "Eusebius Gallicanus" (*CC* CIA–B), which contain many references to and citations from Augustine (although, significantly, none from the works on grace and free will: *CC* CIB,1048–52), have been attributed to Faustus.

Augustine in Two Gallic Controversies: Use or Abuse?

Thomas A. Smith

St. Augustine was a figure both revered by some and deeply problematic
to other Christians in Gaul during the fifth century. Often, indeed, he was
both inspiring and vexing to the very same people.[1] The "use or abuse" of
Augustine here does not refer to the straightforward question of who styled
themselves friends and who enemies of the bishop of Hippo. Nor is our intent
to explore anything so grand as the reception of Augustinian thought in Gaul,
though this paper bears upon that inquiry. Rather, we mean to suggest that
the matter of who Augustine's allies were is not always a simple one, because
his thought was used and abused by friend and foe alike.

Perhaps the best-known use of Augustine in Gaul during the fifth century was the battle waged from c. 427–35 by Prosper of Aquitaine against the
"Massilians"—John Cassian and his followers—in the aftermath of the Pelagian controversy. This bellicose period has tended to give Gaul's fifth century
the flavor of a long-standing conflict between Augustinian and anti-Augustini-
an forces. But in fact the situation was far more complicated. After Prosper's
campaign had seen broadly anti-Pelagian sensibilities win the day, one sees a
shift from an atmosphere of overt conflict to one in which Augustine's thought
was used in quieter ways, by writers whom one would not identify with a fac-
tional Augustinianism. To illustrate one may note the use to which Augustine's thought was put—or subjected—by two influential Gallic theologians in
the latter half of the century, specifically in two theological controversies: over
the human soul and over the work of divine grace.

A Controversy Over the Soul

Sometime prior to 470, a bishop (*reuerentissime sacerdotum*) wrote a
letter to the bishop of Riez, Faustus, former abbot of Lérins and a celebrated
preacher and writer. The letter, it seems, asked three theological questions on
how to respond to Arian teaching; the last of these was the seemingly obscure
question: "Which things in matters human are to be regarded as corporeal

and which as incorporeal?"[2] The focal point of this question was the human soul. The soul had, of course, been a *locus classicus* in the philosophical schools well prior to the advent of Christianity, and the problem of its precise nature and status had occupied not a few minds. The specific problem whether the soul was corporeal or incorporeal had interested Christian writers since the first Christian treatise on the soul, the *De anima* of Tertullian. On balance, Tertullian's notion of the corporeality of the soul and its identification with the breath of life had not won wide acceptance among Christian theologians. Insofar as Christian discussions touched on the matter of the soul *per se*, incorporealist teaching, within a distinctively Christian appropriation of the Platonic tradition, became predominant by the fourth century. Not only in rather technical, abstract tractates like the *De natura hominis* of Nemesius of Emesa, but also, and supremely, in the several works of Augustine,[3] the doctrine of the incorporeality of the soul had become by the fifth century a broadly accepted facet of Christian anthropology. Broadly, but not universally: a tradition traceable to Tertullian and nurtured in certain monastic circles continued to identify soul with the senses, maintaining a passive theory of sensation wherein the soul, because it is localized within the compass of the human body and can be moved by material data, must itself partake of the corporeal realm. One finds this sort of teaching in the *Conferences* of John Cassian,[4] written in Marseilles in the early decades of the century.

The bishop who wrote Faustus seems to have held to the incorporealist doctrine, and Faustus's reply aims precisely against it: "On this matter I will say something not on behalf of the presumption of my own understanding, but on behalf of the opinion of the holy fathers."[5] Faustus goes on to explicate the doctrine of the soul's corporeality, citing Jerome by name and Cassian anonymously. Faustus's account reprises several commonplaces of the corporealist position, saying, as Cassian had, that all created reality—contingent, dependent on the creative action of God—should be considered corporeal. This is true of the natures of souls and of angels. The human soul is identified with sense and is therefore both spatially extended through and delimited by the individual human body. Alluding to Cassian, Faustus writes "nothing is incorporeal but God alone."[6]

It would seem that this letter circulated as a tract in southern Gaul, for in due time it came to the attention of Claudianus Mamertus, a priest of Vienne, who around 469/70 undertook an extensive reply to Faustus's views in his three-book work, *De statu animae*. The three books correspond roughly to the three prongs of Claudianus's attack: Book One produces a vast arsenal of incorporealist Christian authorities to discredit the claim that corporealist teaching rests on established authority; Book Two focuses on data gleaned from what Claudianus calls *philosophia*, meaning primarily pagan sources—Plato, Porphyry, and others—culled from doxographies; Book Three presents a litany of biblical prooftexts by way of illustration. Book One provides an excellent example of the use of Augustine's thought in a manner somewhat different from the zealous prooftexting employed by Prosper in an earlier generation.

Claudianus announces an important theme from the outset of Book One when, speaking of his opponents, he says "...it is no wonder that they do not think rightly either of God or of man who hold both distant from themselves by interposing hatred."[7] This is a characteristically Augustinian way of framing the problematic of the soul: the quest for self-knowledge, specifically that of the soul, is intimately bound up with the knowledge of God.[8]

After establishing the incorporeality and impassibility of God, Claudianus goes on to give detailed accounts of various theses on the corporeal soul, rejecting each in turn. Claudianus's first argument (I,v) begins from Gn 1:26–27, the creation of the human being in God's image. If, he reasons, the human soul is the *imago Dei*, it must in the nature of the case be an incorporeal image; if an incorporeal image, the soul must itself be incorporeal. As he sums it up: "Since it [the soul] is created, it is not God; since it is the image of God, it is not a body."[9] The notion that the *imago* applies strictly to the human soul is something of a commonplace in Augustine's psychology,[10] and Claudianus has clearly appropriated the logic of the position.

In chapter six of Book One Claudianus takes up another argument used by the opposition. Faustus, distancing himself from the idea that corporeality necessarily entailed coarse physicality or visibility, had asserted that corporeal things could be invisible, and that the soul was such a reality. Claudianus responds by suggesting a hierarchy: some things, he says, are invisible and incorporeal—God and the soul, for example; others are invisible and corporeal, such as the senses of hearing, touch, and so on; still others are both visible and corporeal, such as the organs of sense: ears differ from hearing, eyes from sight, and so on. The senses, as invisible and corporeal, must be distinguished from the soul. For the senses, Claudianus continues in chapter seven, are correlated with the four elements, whereas the soul is higher than the elements. He thus dismisses the thesis that the soul is made from an element like air.

At this point Claudianus is using distinctions made by Augustine in book seven of the *De Genesi ad litteram*. In *De Genesi ad littteram* VII,xx,26

Augustine had taken pains to distinguish soul from its corporeal agents, the organs of sense, and to assert its utter dissimilarity to things bodily.[11] Claudianus does not simply repeat Augustine's formulas; rather, he adapts a very well digested understanding of Augustine's incorporealist psychology to his polemic.

Claudianus next turns his attention to a prominent teaching of the Faustian tract: the notion that the soul is spatial and subject to quantity (and therefore corporeal *per definitionem*). To these—if I may say so—weighty arguments he responds again by recourse to a hierarchy of beings: some are non-spatial and non-temporal (namely God), others non-spatial and temporal, and some are both spatial and temporal. The soul belongs to the middle category. Each of the categories of being has a motion (*motus*) appropriate to it; the soul's motion is temporal rather than spatial, and so Claudianus refers to the *animam per tempus inlocaliter moveri*.[12]

Once again, Claudianus's argument is drawn directly from Augustine, whose discussion of the *motus* proper to God and to the soul occupies Book VIII, chapters 20–23 of *De Genesi ad litteram*. To cite one revealing passage:

> ...so the Spirit who is creator moves a created spirit through
> time, although he is himself unmoved in both time and space.
> But a created spirit moves itself through time and moves a
> body through time and space.[13]

After rejecting the idea that the soul is subject to quantity—here understood solely as material quantity—Claudianus speaks of the *peregrinatio* of the soul in the body and its consequent failure to know itself. This is indeed reminiscent of Augustine's account in the *Confessions* of the soul's sojourn in a *regio egestatis* or a *regio dissimilitudinis*.[14]

One could multiply examples, both in Book One and in Book Two of the *De statu animae*. We may say that this treatise does not merely show a propensity to use Augustine's words to buttress a position in theological debate. It is an Augustinian digest in the sense that it uses material from Augustine, but it is not mere slavish copying; it shows that some forty years after the death of the bishop of Hippo some in Gaul were carrying on in a lively way even the more complex insights of his theological anthropology.

Renewal of the Controversy over Grace

Not long after the pamphlet war with Claudianus broke out, the old question of divine grace, seemingly settled after Prosper's campaign of the twenties and thirties, arose yet again. Once more, Faustus of Riez found himself embroiled in controversy, this time with an obscure priest named Lucidus. Lucidus, it seems, was a predestinarian of the most radical stripe. His teaching had come to the attention of Faustus, who initially tried by letter to dissuade him from his one-sided view of the working of divine grace.[15] The views of the apparently recalcitrant Lucidus were taken up at two episcopal synods, and after Lucidus capitulated, Faustus was commissioned to compose a treatise on divine grace.[16]

This tractate *De gratia*, in two books, attempts to pursue a centrist course between the unacceptable alternatives of Pelagianism (which had been both condemned by Rome and routed in Gaul by Prosper's efforts) and predestinarianism (a more treacherous foe because it could march under the banner of Augustine). Given what appears in the battle over the soul to be Faustus's ignorance of Augustine's teaching, one might well expect the *De gratia* to be completely independent of that teaching. It is true, moreover, that Faustus regarded Augustine as suspect, or at least fallible, in some matters.[17] It is all the more remarkable, then, that Faustus makes substantial use of Augustine in the treatise.

Faustus attempts to pursue a middle course via a method of interpretation that avoids extreme, one-sided readings such as characterize the heretic, whether a Pelagian or one of the *praedestinati*.[18] This biblical hermeneutic is crystallized in the only interpretative rule set forth in the *De gratia*: "When one thing is asserted without the other, the other is unmentioned, not denied, according to that rule which bishop Augustine introduces: 'Not everything which is unmentioned is denied.'"[19] This rule seems to be a kind of summary or epitome drawn from Augustine, rather than an actual rule quoted verbatim.[20] In making use of it, Faustus lends the weight of Augustine's prestige to an enterprise that undercuts some of the more radical consequences arising from Augustine's own anti-Pelagian works. This might seem, *prima facie*, to be an abuse; it is possible, however, that Faustus was not being disingenuous, but that he saw himself as a hermeneutical ally of the bishop of Hippo, even as he questioned the exegetical support of the predestinarian position.

Faustus was also acquainted with *De ciuitate dei*. Apart from his citation of the elusive Augustinian rule just mentioned, his only other explicit attribu-

tion to Augustine is a passage from *De ciuitate dei* XXII: "Even the most
blessed pontiff Augustine agrees that the work of the natural law has been
written in human hearts when he says in a most learned discourse: 'Both run
simultaneously in the stream and current of the human race: evil, which is
handed on by the parent, and goodness, which is given by the creator.'"[21] One
finds no other explicit citations of *De ciuitate dei* in the treatise, although an
allusion to XXII,1 may occur in *De gratia* II,3,65,7–10, where Faustus speaks
of God's ability to draw good from human evil. But while this notion can be
traced back to Augustine,[22] there is no compelling textual reason to suppose
that Augustine lies behind its use here.

The first two chapters of the *De gratia* as well as a brief allusion in the
prologue provide us with the clearest and most extended dependence upon
Augustine's thought, but in a paradoxical way. On the one hand, Faustus
clearly reproduces Augustine's portrayal of, and response to, Pelagianism, as
well as his account of original sin and concupiscence. On the other hand, this
obvious dependence is not direct in the sense of being textually precise; Faustus distills rather than quotes. He certainly shares the broad perspective of
certain of Augustine's anti-Pelagian writings without entering into the intrica-
cies of their argumentation.

In the prefatory letter to Leontius, which serves as a prologue to the
treatise *De gratia*, Faustus speaks of the need to confute Pelagius's doctrine so
that Faustus's own insistence on faith and works will not be misconstrued. He
worries that someone, having been cautioned against an excessive predestina-
tionism, might mistakenly regard Pelagius's view as the catholic view: "Then,
having left the royal way by falling to the right, he might believe that we decline to the left, and in speaking of labor as the servant of grace we may seem
to place a stumbling block before the blind."[23] In adopting this metaphor,
Faustus seems to be taking up the language of Augustine's *Epistula CCXV* to
Valentinus, which accompanied the treatise *De gratia et libero arbitrio* to the
monks at Hadrumetum. With reference to the straight path to be walked by
the godly person, Augustine writes:

> Indeed, that one is understood as declining to the right, who
> wishes to assign his own good works, which pertain to the
> right-hand paths, to himself and not to God.... For which
> reason, most dearly beloved, whoever says "My will suffices
> for me to do good works" declines to the right. But on the
> other hand, those who think that a good life is to be forsaken

when they hear God's grace preached so as to believe and understand that he by himself makes human wills good from evil, and guards what he has made, and thus they say "Let us do evil, that good might come," these people decline to the left.[24]

So the attempt to tread a middle path between Pelagianism and a kind of mere "solagratianism" had already been made by Augustine in addressing the concerns of the monastic community. Faustus's use of the same metaphor, including some of the same terminology and the assigning of the "right-hand" error to Pelagius, strongly suggests a familiarity, whether at first hand or not, with this letter.

Faustus's portrait of Pelagius is certainly drawn from Augustine. The Pelagian position is adduced in its most radical formulation: "Pelagius therefore says that human nature is, in itself, sufficient for obtaining salvation. So the pestiferous doctor affirms these things, as if the makeup of our condition still remained in its unimpaired state."[25] Against such a position Faustus cites two favorite Augustinian prooftexts, Jn 15:5 and Ps 126:1. While he clearly takes this portrayal, directly or indirectly, from Augustine, it is sufficiently general as to be derivable from any of several of the anti-Pelagian works. This same phenomenon obtains through much of *De gratia* I,1–2: we find unmistakably Augustinian affirmations given in a way that suggests a familiarity but not necessarily a detailed appreciation.[26]

Faustus's second accusation against Pelagius has to do with Adam's created mortality: "Pelagius continues that Adam was made a mortal, who, whether he had sinned or not, would have been liable to death. Yet since the Apostle says, 'Therefore just as through one man sin entered this world, and through sin death,' you understand this to mean that if sin had not gone first, death would not have followed, and the bestowed immortality would have perdured."[27] In addition to the citation of Rm 5:12, Faustus invokes Gn 2:17 to show that death is not of the natural order but is the consequence of sin. Again, Faustus's discussion is redolent of Augustine's treatment. In this instance Augustine's discourse can be identified with somewhat greater certainty. Augustine confutes those who argue for Adam's original liability to death in only one place: *De peccatorum meritis et remissione* I,ii–ix. He notes that some say Adam would have died even apart from sin. These assert that Gn 2:17, "On the day you eat thereof, you will surely die," refers to the death of the soul, not bodily death. He distinguishes among the terms *mortale* ("capable of dying"), *mortuum* ("dead"), and *moriturus* ("liable to death"); Adam was created *mortale*, but not *moriturus*. His mortality was destined to be superseded by incorruption, had not sin intervened.[28] Augustine cites Rm 5:12 to underscore the physical death that results from sin. So Faustus's brief characterization of Pelagius's view here encapsulates Augustine's more extensive and detailed treatment, using some of the same Scripture references and terminology (e.g., *moriturus*). The use of Augustine is not precise or detailed, but the source is clear enough.

Faustus's treatment of Pelagius's denial of original sin could, again, have been drawn from any of a number of Augustine's works. Certain ones, however, readily suggest themselves. Pelagius's refusal to recognize original sin in infants, a defect alleged by Augustine in several places,[29] is noted, too, by Faustus, who goes on to deride Pelagius for his inability, or unwillingness, to recognize the results of original sin in the human race: "Is it any wonder that he does not recognize that tree by its fruits that he has been unwilling to recognize in its roots?"[30] This allusion to Mt 7:16 mirrors Augustine's use of the passage in precisely the same context in *De nuptiis et concupiscentia* II,xxvi,41–43.

At the beginning of *De gratia* I,2, Faustus portrays Pelagius as posing a troubling question: "Pelagius also adds: 'If through the gift of baptism original sin is removed, then those born of two baptized parents should be without this sin. How,' he asks, 'do they transmit to their offspring what they did not have at all in themselves?'"[31] For Faustus this problem is irrational and easily refutable. There are, he says, two kinds of birth, one of generation, by which the parents pass on what is of nature and proper to them, and one of regeneration, which has nothing to do with parental agency. Parents can pass on what is of nature, but not what is of grace.[32] This had already been the teaching of Augustine, employed against Pelagius in two works, *De gratia Christi et de peccato originali* and *De nuptiis et concupiscentia*: "The regenerate man does not regenerate children of the flesh but generates them.... Original sin remains in the offspring, even if in the parent the guilt of that same sin has been washed away by the remission of sins."[33]

Faustus is at one with Augustine in seeing carnal concupiscence as the mode of transmission for original sin. From parents, whether baptized or not, original sin passes on to the offspring, such that we cry out with the Prophet, "Behold, I was conceived in iniquity, and in sins my mother bore me."[34] Specifically, the bondage of sin is passed on through the desire (*ardor*) involved in sexual union:

> If you should ask whence comes the bond that drags down one's offspring, without doubt it is through the arousing ardor of cursed procreation, and through the enticing embrace of the two parents. For when you see that he alone is immune from the original contagion who was conceived not by the flesh but by the spirit...be aware that the cause of original evil comes from the delight of conceiving a child and from the sin of pleasure.[35]

Augustine's notion of the role of concupiscence may be easily recognized here;[36] Faustus's use of *ardor* to describe the culpable passion simply repeats an Augustinian commonplace.

One could marshal more evidence of an Augustinian dependence in the matter of original sin and concupiscence, e.g., Faustus's discussion of the besmirching of marriage by concupiscence. In general, we may say that the passage in *De gratia* I,1–2, from beginning to end, depends extensively on the thought of Augustine in his anti-Pelagian works, especially *De nuptiis et concupiscentia*. The broad material agreement is not matched by detailed textual dependence or a one-to-one correspondence of parallel passages, some similar vocabulary notwithstanding. The impression obtains that Augustine's works have been learned at secondhand, or, more likely, that his sensibilities have simply become a well-known backdrop to the discussion of original sin and its effects.

So Augustine's contribution to the *De gratia* was considerable. Faustus uses the anti-Pelagian corpus positively against Pelagianism; he also uses it selectively. One finds no positive use of the bipartite *De praedestinatione sanctorum* and *De dono perseverantiae*, which were addressed precisely to the monks of Gaul in 428/429; indeed, he may have regarded as suspect some of the interpretative tendencies found in these works. Further, Faustus knew at least some of *De ciuitate dei* and may have known *De doctrina christiana* and *De trinitate*.[37] Because he did not make precise and detailed citations of Augustine, we simply cannot know the exact sort of access he had to the writings of the bishop of Hippo. Nevertheless, the use of Augustine here merits attention, for it shows the bishop of Hippo being called as a witness in the mid-470s for the prosecution of theological tendencies he himself had set in motion, even as Claudianus had used him for the opposite purpose.

Conclusion

These two writers, then—Claudianus and Faustus—differ not only in their use, but in in their appropriation, of Augustine. Both have imbibed Augustine's sensibilities, but somehow they did so in a different atmosphere. Faustus was, it seems, unaware of the deep roots of Augustine's anthropology; he had absorbed certain key anti-Pelagian notions about the necessity of divine grace and the transmission of sin via concupiscence, but extracted them from Augustine's larger theological enterprise. Claudianus, however, had learned at Augustine's school; he used Augustine not with the one-sided zeal of a partisan nor with the vague familiarity of an amateur, but as one deeply engaged in the same problematics. Augustine's theological anthropology, of course, won the day; indeed, Faustus's treatise on grace shows that no one could avoid Augustine's very lively specter. Many were anxious to enlist his help, but they did so quite unevenly. J. O'Donnell has pointed out how remarkable was the rejection of the eastward-looking monasticism of the West in favor of Augustine's anthropological insights.[38] It must be added that in the course of this tide-change one cannot always see who were Augustine's legitimate heirs and who were pretenders.

Notes

[1] One thinks, for example, of Vincent of Lérins, whose *Commonitorium* seems clearly to question Augustinian theology, but whose *Excerpta* (if their attribution to Vincent by J. Madoz is correct) revere him as a figure of immense stature. Cf. J. Madoz, ed., *Excerpta Vincentii Lirinensis* in *PL* Supplementum, vol. 3, 23–45.

[2] Faustus Reiensis, *Epistula III*: *CSEL* XXI,168: *reverentissime sacerdotum*; ibid. 173: *quae in rebus humanis corporea quaeue incorporea sentienda sunt*.

[3] Augustine's treatment of the soul may be found in several works, notably: *Confessiones* (esp. II,v,10; III; IV; VII,vi,10), *Soliloquia*, *De quantitate animae*, *De immortalitate animae*, and definitively in *De Genesi ad litteram* (esp. VII, X, XII).

[4] *Conlationes* VII,13. Hilary of Poitiers, though eventually won over to the incorporealist position, began as a corporealist; in his commentary on Matthew he asserts that the soul, like everything created, is corporeal. By the *Tractatus super Psalmum CXVIII* he has changed, perhaps under the influence of Origen, whose influence on the Psalm commentary is pronounced.

[5] *Epistula III*: *CSEL* XXI,173: *ad haec aliqua non pro sensus mei praesumptione depromam, sed pro sanctorum opinione seniorum*.

[6] *Epistula III: CSEL* XXI,174:...*nihil esse incorporeum nisi solum Deum.* Cf. Cassian, *Conlatio* VII.

[7] *De statu animae* I,i: *CSEL* XI,22: *non mirandum est, si vel de Deo vel de homine probe non sentiant, qui utrumque a se odio mediante longinquant.*

[8] Cf. *Soliloquia* II,i,1: *CSEL* LXXXIX,45–47; *Confessiones* VII,i,1: *CC* XXVII,1.

[9] *De statu animae* I,v,2: *CSEL* XI,41: *Nam quia creata est, non est Deus. Quia imago Dei est, non est corpus.*

[10] E.g., *De ciuitate dei* XXII: *CC* XLVIII,805–66; *De Genesi ad litteram* VII,xxii,32: *BA* 48,552.

[11] *De Genesi ad litteram* VII,xx,26; xxi,29: *BA* 48,544–46; 548–50. Augustine remained agnostic here on the question whether the soul might have been fashioned by God from some sort of *materies* or simply created *ex nihilo.*

[12] *De statu animae* I,xviii: *CSEL* XI,65.

[13] *De Genesi ad litteram* IX,xx,39: *BA* 49,70: *ita per tempus mouet conditum spiritum ipse nec per tempus nec per locum motus conditor spiritus. sed spiritus creatus mouet se ipsum per tempus et per tempus ac locum corpus.*

[14] *Confessiones* II,x,18; VII,x,16: *CC* XXVII,26; 103–4.

[15] Faustus Reiensis *Epistula I: CSEL* XXI,161–65.

[16] The circumstances of the Lucidus affair are treated in detail by R. Mathisen, *Ecclesiastical Factionalism and Religious Controversy in Fifth-Century Gaul* (Washington: Catholic University of America, 1989), pp. 244–68.

[17] In Faustus's epistle to the deacon Graecus (*Epistula VII: CSEL* XXI,200–207), he assures his reader of Augustine's orthodoxy on the matter at hand—Christology—but mentions in passing that something in the holy bishop's writings is "regarded as suspect among very learned men" (*apud doctissimos viros putatur esse suspectum*); ibid. 201,12–13.

[18] Hence Faustus's likening in *Epistula I* 1 of heretical extremists to rash oarsmen who foolishly brave Scylla and Charybdis without a captain.

[19] *De gratia dei* I,5: *CSEL* XXI,20,11–14: *cum unum sine altero dicitur, tacetur alterum, non negatur secundum illam regulam, quam antistes Augustinus insinuat: "non omnia quae tacentur negantur."*

[20] The rule as cited does not appear to be contained among Augustine's writings. The general principle, that things concealed in one part of Scripture are manifest elsewhere, has ample attestation in Augustine. In *De doctrina christiana* II,vi,8: *CC* XXXII,36, Augustine speaks of the Holy Spirit's modulating Scripture such that open passages give access to the hungry, and obscure passages deter the proud. In *De doctrina christiana* II,ix, 14: *CC* XXXII,40–41, he counsels that one must know the whole of Scripture in order to apply what is manifest to what is obscure. Several other passages of Augustine's great hermeneutical work accord with Faustus's rule, though none matches it precisely.

[21] *De gratia dei* II,9: *CSEL* XXI,81,19–23, citing *De ciuitate dei* XXII,xxiv,1, *Opus itaque naturalis legis in cordibus hominum fuisse conscriptum etiam beatissimus pontifex Augustinus doctissimo sermone prosequitur ita dicens: "utrumque simul currit in isto alueo atque torrente generis humani, malum, quod a parente trahitur, et bonum, quod a creante tribuitur."* P. Courcelle, in "Nouveaux aspects de la culture lérinienne," *Revue des études latines* 46 (1968) 404, n. 9, has drawn attention to Faustus's substitution of *alveo* for Augustine's *fluvio*. The meaning of *malum* here for Faustus has been a matter of some contention.

[22] Besides *De ciuitate dei* XXII,i, C. Tibiletti finds the same thought expressed in *Enchiridion* VIII,27 and XXVIII,104. Cf. "Libero arbitrio e grazia in Fausto di Riez," *Augustinianum* 19 (1979) 263. Very similar terminology is found in *De peccatorum meritis et remissione* I,xxix,57: *CSEL* LX,56–57, in connection with the good use of concupiscence in marital union. The distinction between good and evil uses of things is a commonplace in Augustine's discussions of concupiscence.

[23] *De gratia dei*, Prologus: *CSEL* XXI,4,15–18:...*et omissa uia regia in dexteram cadens in sinistram declinare nos crederet, et, dum de labore seruo gratiae loquimur, offendiculum ante pedes caeci opposuisse videremur.*

[24] *Epistula CCXV* VII,7–8: *CSEL* LVII,393–94: *declinare quippe ille est intellegendus in dextram, qui bona ipsa opera, quae ad uias dextras pertinent, sibi uult adsignare non deo.* Ibid. 8: pp. 394–95: *Quapropter, dilectissimi, quicumque dicit: "Voluntas mea mihi sufficit ad facienda opera bona," declinat in dextram. sed rursus illi, qui putant bonam uitam esse deserendam, quando audiunt sic dei gratiam praedicari, ut credatur et intellegatur uoluntates hominum ipsa ex malis bonas facere, ipsa etiam, quas fecerit, custodire, et propterea dicunt: "Faciamus mala, ut veniant bona," in sinistram declinant.*

[25] *De gratia dei* I,1: *CSEL* XXI,8,23–26: *Dicit ergo Pelagius, quod ad obtinendam salutem natura hominis sibi sola sufficiat. ita haec pestifer doctor adfirmat, quasi adhuc factura conditionis nostrae in statu suo inlibata permaneat.*

[26] Among many examples, one could cite *De natura et gratia* VI,6: *CSEL* LX,236, in which Augustine speaks of those who try to show that "human nature needs no physician" (*naturam humanam neque...medico indigere*). Without directly attacking Pelagius, Augustine speaks in the same work (II,2: *CSEL* LX,234) of the notion that human nature "might be sufficient in itself" (*si potest sibi sufficere*) to fulfill the law. Cf. also *Epistula CCXV* VIII: *CSEL* LVII,395–96; *De gratia et libero arbitrio* IV,6: *PL* XLIV,885.

[27] *De gratia dei* I,1: *CSEL* XXI,9,4–9: *Prosequitur adhuc Pelagius Adam mortalem factum, qui, siue peccasset siue non peccasset, esset moriturus. sed cum dicat apostolus: "propterea," inquit, "sicut per unum hominem in hunc mundum peccatum intravit et per peccatum mors," intellegis, quia, si peccatum non praecessisset, mors secuta non esset et donata immortalitas perdurasset...*, citing Rm 5:12.

[28] *De peccatorum meritis et remissione* I,v,5: *CSEL* LX,6–7.

[29] *De natura et gratia* VIII,9: *CSEL* LX,238; *De peccatorum meritis et remissione* I,xvi, 21; xxviii,56; III,i,1; ii,4–iv,8: *CSEL* LX,20–21; 55; 128–29; 131–34. The long discussion in *De peccatorum meritis et remissione* III specifically attributes the erring view to Pelagius and refutes it in detail. Cf. also *De nuptiis et concupiscentia* II,iii,9ff: *CSEL* XLII,260ff.

[30] *De gratia dei* I,1: *CSEL* XXI,11,7–9: *quid mirum si arborem illam in fructibus non agnoscat, quam noluit in radice cognoscere?*

[31] *De gratia dei* I,2: *CSEL* XXI,12,6–9: *adtendit etiam hoc Pelagius: si per baptismi donum tollitur originale peccatum, de duobus baptizatis nati debent hoc carere peccato. quomodo, inquit, mittunt ad posteros, quod ipsi in se minime habuerunt?*

[32] *De gratia dei* I,2: *CSEL* XXI,12,9–29.

[33] *De gratia Christi et de peccato originali* II,xl,45: *CSEL* XLII,202: *regeneratus quippe non regenerat filios carnis, sed generat.* Ibid. II,xxxix,44: *CSEL* XLII,201–2: *manet quippe in prole, ita ut ream faciat originis uitium, etiam si in parente reatus eiusdem uitii remissione ablutus est peccatorum.*

[34] Faustus's reading of Ps 50:7 here is interesting. The usual Vulgate reading of the Psalm is *et in peccatis peperit me…*, but Faustus has *et in delictis peperit me….* This reading, found in Ambrose, *De poenitentia* I,ii,3, was used only once by Augustine, when quoting from Ambrose in *De gratia Christi* II,xli,47: *CSEL* XLII,159–60. Elsewhere in Augustine's citations of this verse, he has *peccatis*.

[35] *De gratia dei* I,2: *CSEL* XXI,13,2–9: *unde autem ueniat nexus iste, qui posteros trahit, si requiras: sine dubio per incentiuum maledictae generationis ardorem et per inlecebrosum utriusque parentis amplexum. nam cum illum solum uideas ab originali inmunem esse contagione, qui non carne, sed spiritu…conceptus est, agnosce causam mali originalis de oblectamento naturam conceptionis et de uitio uoluptatis.*

[36] Cf., *inter alia, De nuptiis et concupiscentia* I,xxxii,37; II,xxxiv,58: *CSEL* XLII,248–49; 316.

[37] On these see my *De Gratia: Faustus of Riez's Treatise on Grace and Its Place in the History of Theology* (Notre Dame: Univ. of Notre Dame Press, 1990), pp. 127–40.

[38] J. J. O'Donnell, "Liberius the Patrician," *Traditio* 37 (1981) 54.

Augustine as a Civil Theologian?

Michael J. Hollerich

In a recent paper on Augustine as a "Constantinian theologian," Hubert Cancik reaches the following remarkable conclusion:

> The Conference of Carthage [of 411] shows Augustine as a man of the *theologia civilis*: he knows the religion which the citizens ought to exercise, knows the laws of the rulers which govern this religion, and is vigilant about "which gods on the state's account the citizen has to venerate, and which sacred actions he has to perform." To this extent Augustine is a *theologus civilis* in the sense of Varro—except that the religion prescribed by the state is now a particular type of Christianity.... In the theoretical assertions and the practical performance of this *theologia civilis* there exists no fundamental differences between Eusebius and Constantine on the one hand, and Augustine on the other. However deep the differences in other areas may be (e.g. hamartology and soteriology), where the political dimension is concerned, there is an ecclesiastical and theological continuity.[1]

These statements fly in the face of conventional opinions of Augustine's conception of politics and the state in their religious aspect.[2] For example, Book VI of *The City of God* directly rebuts Varro's exposition of Roman civil religion; why then the claim that Augustine actually shares working assumptions with his opponent? Furthermore, *The City of God* was written precisely to show that true religion is not a "success philosophy," as Charles Norris Cochrane once characterized Eusebius' defense of Constantine's program for the church and the empire.[3] At the beginning of the book Augustine explains why Christianity should not be blamed for the sack of Rome in 410, as pagan critics were doing. God's reasons for the flourishing or decline of the wicked and the virtuous alike are unknown to us in this life: "No doubt the question will be asked, 'Why does the divine mercy extend even to the godless and ungrateful?' The only explanation is that it is the mercy of one 'who makes his sun rise on the good and the bad, and sends rain alike on the righteous and the unrighteous.'"[4] On the subject of theodicy, Augustine favored a reverent agnosticism about identifying God's purposes, as shown by his fondness for Mt 5:45.[5] Triumphalism of the type associated with Eusebius would seem to be alien to him.

This paper summarizes and evaluates Cancik's argument, first and at greater length in terms of his comparison with Varro, and then of his analysis of Augustine's "Constantinianism."

I

Varro's *Antiquitates rerum divinarum* was a lengthy compilation in sixteen books of the institutions, practices and beliefs of Roman religion.[6] The first book surveyed the subject as a whole, and developed the three-fold categorization of "theology" which Augustine made the basis for his critique of Varro in Book VI of *The City of God*. The remaining books were grouped in sets of three; they dealt respectively with *homines* (priests, augurs, *quindecimviri*), *loca* (shrines, temples, sacred places), *tempora* (holy days, circus games, stage plays), *sacra* (consecrations, private rites, public rites), and *dii* (distinguished as "certain," "uncertain," and "select").[7]

Varro distinguished three kinds (*genera*) of theology: "mythical," "physical," and "civil."[8] The first two dealt with stories about the gods, especially as told by the poets, and with the philosophers' speculations about the gods.[9] The third was concerned with the official gods of the city. This classification originated not with Varro himself but with Stoic sources.[10] The Greek origin is clear in his use of *mythicon* and *physicon* in the quotation preserved in Augustine. Despite the reference to *theologia politice* in *De ciuitate dei* VI,xii— Augustine's only use of a Greek transliteration for the third category—Varro himself seems to have used the Latin *civilis* instead.[11] This is evident from Augustine's statement to that effect, and from his citation of Latin equivalents for the other two words, *fabulare*—better *fabulosum*, Augustine notes sarcastically—and *naturale*.[12]

Varro defined *theologia civilis* in this way: "The third variety is that which the citizens in the cities, especially the priests, ought to know and administer. It includes which gods each person ought to worship officially (*publice*), and what should be done and offered in sacrifice."[13] To this account should be added the detail from Augustine's description of the similar threefold division made by Varro's older contemporary, Mucius Scaevola, who says that the third *genus* of gods—Scaevola spoke of types of gods rather than of theology—has been handed down by the leaders of the city.[14] The carriers of civil theology are thus at once the priests, the magistrates, and the mass of the citizens.

This third type drew Augustine's attention most keenly in Book VI of *The City of God*, to which we will return in a moment, because it was the blurring of civic institutions and religion which he diagnosed as the basic flaw in the system. The seriousness with which he regarded this illegitimate commingling of the political and the religious is indicated by his statement at the beginning of Book VII that *the whole* of the *Antiquitates rerum divinarum* was a *theologia civilis*.[15]

To give flesh to the skeleton of Varro's tripartite division of theology, Cancik noted typical features of Roman religious practice going back to the Republic, which Christianity later adopted:[16] 1) Regarding religious offices, he notes that the priesthood and the magistracy were distinct offices (though one person could serve in both), and that priests enjoyed special privileges and immunities. Similarly, the Christian clergy, who also assumed the nomenclature of *sacerdotes* and *pontifices*, received important exemptions from the public liturgies (such as the obligation to quarter troops, serve on town councils as decurions, and the like), which Constantine had granted almost as soon as he became sole ruler in the west. 2) Cancik notes that the *loca* and the *sacra* of Roman religion were often financed either by state endowments or direct subsidies. When the emperors became Christian, Christianity assumed the old religion's status as a ward of the state, a process evident as early as Constantine's grant of the Lateran palace to the bishop of Rome, and his grant of money to Bishop Caecilian of Carthage, as well as an unlimited line of credit to support the Christian cult. 3) As for the *tempora*, Cancik notes that the pagan *ludi magni* were organized by officials and financed by the state. Here he cites as a Christian parallel Theodosius' endorsement in the edict *Cunctos populos*[17] of the Christian faith—"the very religion handed down to the Romans [!] by the Apostle Peter"—as defined by the *pontifex* Damasus of Rome and Bishop Peter of Alexandria. He might also have mentioned Constantine's vigorous interest in a uniform date for the observance of Easter, which reveals very traditional Roman notions of the meaning of religious ritual.[18]

Cancik's argument that Augustine was a civil theologian in the sense defined by Varro turns on Augustine's association with and attitude towards this *de facto* substitution of one state religion for another. He points out that Augustine energetically defended, and never criticized, the religious partiality of the orthodox Christian emperors, who promoted the interests of Catholic Christianity against its schismatic, heretical, and pagan rivals. This unhappy record is the foundation of his case, which he develops with close attention to the repression of the Donatists, to which I will turn shortly.

The facts of Augustine's defense of religious coercion are not in dispute.[19] The question which needs to be raised is whether defending religious establishment is enough, in itself, to qualify Augustine as a Varronic "civil theologian." If we take into consideration the full meaning of *theologia civilis* as used by Varro himself, the answer plainly is no. Varro and Augustine have very little in common in the way in which they conceive the relation between the political order and religion. Here I would like to appeal to Augustine's own analysis to make the differences clear. The fundamental difference, in Augustine's view, is the transcendental character of genuine religion: Christianity offers reliable access to transcendent reality; pagan cults do not. The root inadequacy of Roman civil theology, therefore, is that it is based on a lie (*mendosum*).[20] Its deceitfulness actually makes it the worst of the three kinds of theology. As a rule, Augustine reserves his most censorious language for the obscene and debased stories about the gods which are the stock in trade of mythical or narrative theology. But on a couple of occasions he says that civil theology is even more corrupt (*etiam deterior*)[21] than mythical theology, because it promotes hypocrisy by encouraging intelligent people to profess what they know to be false, out of fear of legal penalties.[22]

In fact, Augustine argues that nothing in substance separates the two, except for the venue and the media in which they are expressed.[23] This is a point he adapted from Varro himself, who describes civil theology as, in some respects, a compromise between the other two, because the theology of the poets was inadequate to serve as a model for the people, and the writings of the philosophers were too demanding for the *vulgus* to understand.[24] Says Varro:

> These two theologies are incompatible; and yet quite a number of principles have been taken from them to form the principles of "civil theology." For that reason, where elements of civil theology coincide with elements in other categories, we shall enter them under civil theology. But we ought to cultivate the society of the philosophers more than that of the poets.[25]

Why is that? Because, as Augustine had already noted, Varro admitted that:

> ...the first type [of theology] contains a great deal of fiction which is contrary to the nature and dignity of the immortals. It is in this category that we find one god born from the head, another from the thigh, a third from drops of blood; we find stories about thefts and adulteries committed by gods, and gods enslaved to human beings. In fact we find attributed to gods not only the accidents that happen to humanity in general, but even those which befall the most contemptible of mankind.[26]

Nor is the difficulty with mythical theology limited to the stories. Augustine had pointed out in Book IV that Varro declared that the only people who have apprehended what God is are the philosophers who believe him to be the soul which governs the universe by motion and reason.[27] Furthermore, said Varro, ancient Roman religion had been free for 170 years from the worship of images, and that if that custom had survived, the worship of the gods would have been conducted with greater purity. Those who first set up the images of the gods for the people were responsible for the abolition of reverent fear (*metus*) in their cities, and for the increase of error.[28]

Therefore, concludes Augustine, if it is true both that the stories about the gods are morally offensive and that the worship of images is reprehensible, then it is hard to see how a convincing distinction can be made between mythical and civil theology. A selective critique of civil theology is impossible, because the two are bound together inseparably as one organism.

> For both civil and "fabulous" theologies are alike fabulous and civil. Anyone who intelligently examines the futile obscenities of both will conclude that both are fabulous; anyone who observes that stage shows closely related to "fabulous" theology are included in the festivals of the gods of the city and in the civic religious cult, will recognize that both theologies are, in fact, civil.[29]

In short, civil theology is a futile enterprise because the very notion is incoherent.

Not only is it an elusive and deceptive concept, it is tainted with a manipulative intention which verges on bad faith. We must be careful here to distinguish between Augustine's readiness to accuse Varro of moral cowardice—which he does, comparing him unfavorably in this respect with Seneca—and the more relevant issue of the utilitarian distortion of religion for social and political ends.[30] We will recall that the theological project behind *The City of God* was Augustine's need to purify Christianity, in the eyes of both its enemies and many of its adherents, from a mistaken concern with worldly well-being, with the notion of a divinely ordained age of Christian prosperity, the *tempora christiana*.[31] Augustine was thus quick to recognize the similar error in Roman religion. One of his keenest criticisms of Varro is that his white-washed version of "civil theology" served frankly pragmatic and political interests. Varro took his stand as a traditionalist, a spokesman not for his own judgment but for ancient customs established by the Roman state. Had he been the founder of the city, he said, he would have consecrated the gods and their names to the rule of nature (*ex naturae...formula*). But as a member of an ancient people, he was bound to defend the traditional story of their names and to encourage the common people to honor them, not to despise them. There were, he admitted, truths which it was not expedient for the general public to know, and many falsehoods which it was good for the people to believe true, which was why the Greeks kept their initiation rites veiled in silence and enclosed within walls.[32]

As an example of this pragmatism, I note a passage quoted in Book III of *The City of God*, in which Varro is reported to have held that it was useful for cities to believe stories about human descent from the gods. Men who believed they had divine ancestors were more likely to undertake bold enterprises, to be more energetic in action, and more likely to succeed because of this confidence.[33]

Thus, concludes Augustine, those experts who taught what they knew to be false did so in order to bind men more tightly to the political community, so they might bring them under control and keep them there by the same deceptive techniques.[34] Varro and his allies knew that the civic cult was a human, not a divine institution. That is why he placed the sixteen books on Roman religion after the twenty-five books on *res humanae* (actually *res romanae*, Augustine notes drily). Civil theology makes no claims on the truth; its reason for being (unlike that of natural or physical theology) is purely historical and contingent.[35] The home of the civic cult was in the city, which preceded it in the order of time and gave birth to it, as Varro explicitly stated: "The painter exists before the picture, the builder before the building. Similarly, human communities precede their institutions."[36]

To conclude: despite Cancik's contention that Augustine's support of the legal establishment of Christianity makes him to this extent a civil theologian of Varro's type, it seems that Augustine's rigorous criticism of the failure of civil theology precisely as a theology worthy of the name, makes the comparison invalid. In Augustine's thinking, the state's service of the gospel (more accurately, the Christian office-holder's service of the gospel)[37] was not part of a *quid pro quo* with God, in which divine benefaction was the payment for state support. He had nothing in common with Varro's pragmatism, a difference which Cancik glosses over in his restatement of his thesis at the end of his paper. There he rewords Varro's statement that civil theology included "which gods each citizen should worship officially" (*quos deos publice colere...quemque par sit*) to read "welche Götter *von Staats wegen* [emphasis added] der jeweilige Bürger verehren...soll."[38] While this may fairly restate Varro's thinking, it seriously distorts Augustine's. Varro appears to have found the fundamental sanction of his civil theology in the authorization of the state; it is inconceivable that Augustine could have.

II

Despite the attention I have given to Varro, the larger part of Cancik's article is devoted to Augustine's activity at the Conference of Carthage, 1–8 June 411. The conference had been convened by the emperor under the supervision of Count Marcellinus as a last attempt to reconcile the Donatists to Catholic communion. Augustine was present as the chief spokesman for the Catholic bishops, and made numerous interventions in the course of the parley. Cancik examined this event as a test case for his thesis that Augustine was a true civil theologian, because the Donatist controversy was the school in which Augustine received his education in religious coercion. The Carthage colloquy offered a convenient laboratory in which to study the skill of Augustine and his allies in working with the imperial bureaucracy—its personnel, its religious legislation, its judicial and archival routines, etc. The discussion eventually focused on the historical question of the schism's origin, which entailed the examination of numerous documents from consular, municipal, and episcopal archives. In the event, the Catholics showed themselves better prepared than their opponents. The trump card was Augustine's submission

of a report by Anulinus, proconsul of Africa, to Constantine, dated 15 April
313, which spoke of Donatist petitions to Constantine against "the crimes of
Caecilian."[39] The revelation that it was the Donatists who had first appealed
to the emperor confounded Donatist claims to pin the "Caecilianists" with
responsibility for invoking secular authority. It also undercut their insistence
at the conference that the schism was an ecclesiastical matter in which the
state should not intervene.[40]

The dramatic presentation of this document showed the careful efforts
of the Catholics to assemble a repertoire of historical and legal documentation. For Cancik, this diligence is proof of the ease with which the Catholic
bishops had become accustomed to the bureaucratic procedures of late Roman government. On the other hand, it is worth noting that Augustine told
his Donatist opponents that he would be glad to confine the discussion to
Scripture, and to refrain from archival sources, if they would drop the historical argument over the crime of *traditio*, this in reference to the Donatist bishop Petilian's protest against the replacement of "ecclesiastical custom" by
"profane custom."[41]

Cancik's assertion of Augustine's "Constantinianism" really is based on
Augustine's numerous invocations of Constantine's name as the inaugurator
of a long succession of imperial judgments against the Donatists: *Constantini
iudicium contra vos vivit* is a constant refrain in the anti-Donatist literature.
Cancik found about thirty references to Constantine's name in Augustine's
writings, in addition to those in the Carthaginian *gesta* and the brief section on
Constantine in *The City of God*. With the single exception of *De ciuitate dei*
V,xxv, every reference to Constantine is in connection with the legal status of
the Donatists. And of these fully one third are actually allusions to the *Donatists'* appeal to Constantine: they did it first, *ipsi priores*, Augustine is eager to
note.[42] For Cancik, this image of Constantine as an authoritative legislator on
religious affairs constitutes grave matter in his indictment of Augustine. He is
critical, for example, of Augustine's failure to mention any of the blemishes of
the first Christian emperor. Augustine's Constantine is a remorseless judge, a
stern and austere figure whose great accomplishment is to blaze a trail of religious coercion which leads in direct continuity from the pagan regime of Dio-
cletian into the Christian Middle Ages. Augustine is saddled with the igno-
minious responsibility for legitimating this history of religious repression.

Such a portrait appears to me to suffer from the general defect of blam-
ing Augustine for developments of which he could not have had the faintest
intimation—after all, his historical horizon ended with the Vandal siege of

Hippo—and from the more particular error of projecting a "Constantinian" fixation on Augustine which contradicts his own most deeply held convictions. In the process he passes over much of what has become scholarly *opinio communis* on the subject of Augustine's theological assessment of the state and political life.

Consider, for example, the brief section on Constantine and Christian rulership in *The City of God*. These three chapters form a unit with which Augustine ends Book V, and with it his consideration of the futility of hoping for temporal felicity from the worship of the false gods. The first chapter in the unit (*De ciuitate dei* V,xxiv) begins with a disavowal of common reasons for calling emperors *felices*: they are not happy because of the length of their reigns, their peaceful death, the stability of the dynastic succession, the defeat of their enemies or the crushing of domestic revolt. All of these are achievements which can be claimed by the worshippers of demons as well as by Christian emperors. Political well-being is due to God's mercy alone, not to membership in the kingdom of God, for God intends that those who believe in him should not demand such blessings as if they represented the highest good.

Rather, Christian rulers are *felices* if they rule with justice; if they preserve humility and avoid the pride that attends exalted rank (an important provision in Augustine's table of the virtues, if we recall the attack on the pride of the earthly city on the very first page of *The City of God*, and the critique of ancient Rome's *libido dominandi*)[43] ; if they put their office to the service of God's majesty; and a host of other attributes of humane leadership, such as mercy and self-control. Christian rulers who manifest these qualities are *felices* in this-worldly terms only in hope, and will not be happy in reality until this present life is over.

What then of Constantine? He of all rulers, Augustine admits, enjoyed worldly gifts in abundance. By all the secular indices of *felicitas*, his reign appears to have been favored by God, an observation not lost on Eusebius in his *Life of Constantine*, which cited exactly such accomplishments as proof that Constantine was of all emperors a uniquely-favored friend of God (*theôi... monos...philos*).[44] But Augustine resists the conclusion which Eusebius drew from Constantine's long life, happy death, successful campaigns, smoothly planned succession, etc. For him, their only religious value is to demonstrate that being a Christian will not disqualify an emperor from a successful reign. In no way is Constantine's secular *felicitas* an invitation to believe that being a Christian guaranteed that his successors would also have his good fortune. To prevent this erroneous deduction, declares Augustine, God removed the

Christian Jovian even more quickly than he had ended the reign of his predecessor, Julian the Apostate, and allowed the Christian Gratian to be slain by the usurper Maximus, thereby demonstating that it is only with a view to eternal life that anyone should become a Christian. It is true that Gratian was avenged by Theodosius' defeat of Maximus, but this is the kind of vindication for which pious souls should not ask.[45]

To summarize the positions taken in this paper: Constantine's cameo appearance in *The City of God*—the only time his name is mentioned—bears little resemblance to the fulsome theology of imperial election which Eusebius expounded in the *Life of Constantine*, in which Constantine is presented as a latter-day Moses come to lead God's people in a new Exodus out of slavery into freedom.[46] Augustine's guarded comments hardly qualify him as a "Constantinian theologian." Nor is he a civil theologian in the sense defined by Varro. His ready acceptance of the legal establishment of Christianity is not, in itself, sufficient to make the case, since he says emphatically that the true religion exists for no other reason than to procure eternal life for its adherents —not to provide heaven-sent political benefits for the society in which they reside, and certainly not to manipulate the citizens in the name of a religion known to rest on falsehoods. Occasionally Augustine will concede that, if the kings of the earth and all peoples were to accept Christian precepts of justice and morality, then even this present earthly life would be adorned with its own distinctive *felicitas*. But this would come to pass only because of the intrinsic superiority of Christian justice and morality, not because Christians have learned how to subordinate God's will to their own ends.[47]

Notes

[1] Hubert Cancik, "Augustinus als konstantinischer Theologe," in Jacob Taubes, ed., *Der Fürst dieser Welt. Carl Schmitt und die Folgen*, rev. ed., Religionstheorie und politische Theologie, 1 (Munich: Wilhelm Fink Verlag, 1985), p. 149.

[2] For a good overview of scholarly opinion, see the article of Klaus Thraede, "Das antike Rom in Augustins De civitate Dei," *Jahrbuch für Antike und Christentum* 20 (1977) 90–145, esp. 99–103. An excellent general presentation of the subject is P. R. L. Brown, "Political Society," in R. A. Markus, ed., *Augustine: A Collection of Critical Essays* (Garden City, N.Y.: Doubleday Anchor, 1972), pp. 311–35. I have learned most from R. A. Markus, *Saeculum: History and Society in the Theology of St. Augustine*, 2nd ed. (Cambridge: Cambridge University Press, 1988).

[3] See *De ciuitate dei* I,Praef., 8–10, 36: *CC* XLVII,1, 7–12, 34, for statements on this theme and on the purpose of the work. Cf. the contrasting assessment of Eusebius in C. N.

Cochrane, *Christianity and Classical Culture* (1940; reprint, Oxford: Oxford University Press, 1966), pp. 183–87.

[4] *De ciuitate dei* I,viii,1–4: *CC* XLVII,7: *Dicet aliquis: "Cur ergo ista diuina misericordia etiam ad impios ingratosque peruenit?" Cur putamus, nisi quia eam ille praebuit, qui cotidie "facit oriri solem suum super bonos et malos et pluit super iustos et iniustos"?* The City of God is cited in the edition of B. Dombart and A. Kalb, *Sancti Aurelii Augustini De Civitate Dei Libri* I–XXII, 2 vols., *CC* XLVII–XLVIII. English translations are taken from Augustine: *Concerning the City of God Against the Pagans*, ed. with introduction by David Knowles, tr. by Henry Bettenson (London: Penguin, 1972).

[5] Besides the citation in n. 4, cf. *De ciuitate dei* IV,ii,51; V,xvi,6–7; XXI,xxiv,82: *CC* XLVII,100; XLVII,149; XLVIII,791.

[6] Cited here by fragment number in the edition of R. Agahd, *M. Terenti Varronis Antiquitatum rerum divinarum Libri* I, XIV, XV, XVI, in *Jahrbücher für classische Philologie*, Supplementband 24 (Leipzig: Teubner, 1898), pp. 1–220, 367–81.

[7] Frag. I, 3a (ed. Agahd) = *De ciuitate dei* VI,iii,1–36: *CC* XLVII,168.

[8] Frag. I, 6 (ed. Agahd) = *De ciuitate dei* VI,v,1–10: *CC* XLVII,170–71.

[9] Frag. I, 8 and 10a (ed. Agahd) = *De ciuitate dei* VI,v,11–17, 23–29: *CC* XLVII,171.

[10] On the three-fold division of theology in Varro and other authors, see Jean Pépin, "La théologie tripartite de Varron," *REA* 2 (1956) 265–94; G. Lieberg, "Die theologia tripartita," *Aufstieg und Niedergang der römischen Welt* (Berlin and New York: Walter de Gruyter, 1973), Part I, Vol. 3, pp. 63–115; P. Boyance, "Sur la théologie de Varron," *Revue des études anciennes* 57 (1955) 57–84.

[11] Cf. *De ciuitate dei* VI,xii,12: *CC* XLVII,184. Tertullian used *gentile* (sc. *genus deorum*) in *Ad nationes* II,1, because he was thinking of the three social carriers of each type of talk about the gods: *philosophi*, *poetae*, and *populi* (cited in frag. I, 6 [ed. Agahd]). Pépin is unconvincing in his attempt to set aside Augustine's express testimony, cf. "La théologie tripartite," 273.

[12] *De ciuitate dei* VI,v,3–10: *CC* XLVII,170–71.

[13] *Tertium genus est quod in urbibus cives, maxime sacerdotes nosse atque administrare debent. In quo est, quos deos publice colere et <quae> sacra ac sacrificia facere quemque par sit.* Frag. I, 31 (ed. Agahd). The text is uncertain, though the general sense is clear; see the apparatus in Agahd's edition, and cf. the reading in Dombart and Kalb, eds., *De ciuitate dei* VI,v,56–58: *CC* XLVII,172.

[14] *De ciuitate dei* IV,xxvii,3: *CC* XLVII,121:…*a principibus ciuitatis.*

[15] *De ciuitate dei* VII,i,4–6: *CC* XLVII,185.

[16] Cf. Cancik, "Augustin," pp. 137–41, with citations.

[17] *Codex Theodosianus* XVI,i,2 (380).

68   *Augustine and His Critics*

[18] Cf. Eusebius, *De vita Constantini* III,xviii, cited according to the edition of F. Winkelmann, *Über das Leben des Kaiser Konstantins*, in *Eusebius Werke*, vol. 1, pt. 1, 2nd ed. Die griechischen christlichen Schriftsteller der ersten Jahrhunderte (Berlin: Akademie-Verlag, 1975).

[19] On this subject, see the illuminating treatment of Peter Brown, "St. Augustine's Attitude to Religious Coercion," *Journal of Roman Studies* 54 (1964) 107–16, reprinted in *Religion and Society in the Age of St. Augustine* (New York: Harper and Row, 1972), pp. 260–78.

[20] *De ciuitate dei* VI,v,50: *CC* XLVII,172.

[21] *De ciuitate dei* VI,xii,6: *CC* XLVII,184; and *De ciuitate dei* VI,x,68–69: *CC* XLVII, 182: *deteriora sunt templa...quam theatra.*

[22] Cf. the example of Seneca, *De ciuitate dei* VI,x,69–94: *CC* XLVII,182–83.

[23] See *De ciuitate dei* VI,vi–vii: *CC* XLVII,172–76.

[24] *De ciuitate dei* VI,vi,60–66: *CC* XLVII,174.

[25] *Quae sic abhorrent [inquit] ut tamen ex utroque genere ad civiles rationes adsumpta sint non pauca. Quare quae erunt communia cum populis, una cum civibus scribemus; e quibus maior societas debet esse nobis cum philosophis, quam cum poetis.* Frag. I,54a (ed. Agahd) = *De ciuitate dei* VI,vi,66–70: *CC* XLVII,174.

[26] *Primum [inquit] quod dixi, in eo sunt multa contra dignitatem et naturam immortalium ficta. In hoc enim est, ut deus alius ex capite, alius ex femore sit, alius ex guttis sanguinis natus; in hoc ut dii furati sint, ut adulterarint, ut servierint homini; denique etiam quae in contemptissimum hominem cadere possunt.* Frag. I,8 (ed. Agahd) = *De ciuitate dei* VI,v,11–17: *CC* XLVII,171.

[27] *De ciuitate dei* IV,xxxi,24–27: *CC* XLVII,125.

[28] *De ciuitate dei* IV,xxxi,33–41: *CC* XLVII,125.

[29] *De ciuitate dei* VI,viii,45–50: *CC* XLVII,177: *Nam et civilis et fabulosa ambae fabulosae sunt ambaeque civiles; ambas inveniet fabulosas qui vanitates et obscenitates ambarum prudenter inspexerit; ambas civiles, qui scaenicos ludos pertinentes ad fabulosam in deorum civilium festivitatibus et in urbium divinis rebus adverterit.*

[30] Cf. *De ciuitate dei* VI,x,1–5: *CC* XLVII,181.

[31] Announced already in *De ciuitate dei* I,i,19–20, 33: *CC* XLVII,2. The best treatment of this theme is Markus, *Saeculum*, pp. 22–44.

[32] Frag. I,10b and 55 (ed. Agahd) = *De ciuitate dei* IV,xxxi,1–19: *CC* XLVII,125.

[33] Frag. I,24 (ed. Agahd) = *De ciuitate dei* III,iv,3–8: *CC* XLVII,67.

[34] *De ciuitate dei* IV,xxxii,8–15: *CC* XLVII,126.

[35] *De ciuitate dei* VI,v,49–56: *CC* XLVII,172.

[36] *Sicut prior est [inquit] pictor quam tabula picta, prior faber quam aedificium; ita priores sunt civitates quam ea, quae a civitatibus instituta sunt*: Frag. I,4 (ed. Agahd) = *De ciuitate dei* VI,iv,22–24: *CC* XLVII,169.

[37] Cf. Markus, *Saeculum*, pp. 146–53.

[38] Cancik, "Augustin als konstantinischer Theologe," p. 149.

[39] No. 10 in the collection edited by H. von Soden, *Urkunden zur Entstehungsgeschichte des Donatismus*, Kleine Texte für Vorlesungen und Übungen, no. 122 (Bonn: A. Marcus and E. Weber's Verlag, 1913), pp. 12–13.

[40] For the discussion leading up to the introduction of the report of Anulinus, cf. the *gesta* of the third session, *Collatio Carthaginiensis* III,176–220, especially the Donatist reaction and the question of authenticity and date in III,216–20. Cited according to the edition of S. Lancel, *Actes de la conférence de Carthage en 411*, 3 vols., *Sources chrétiennes*, 194, 195, and 224 (Paris: Editions du Cerf, 1972, 1975), in 224,1122–62.

[41] *Collatio Carthaginiensis* III,155, 185–87: *SC* 224,1105–6, 1130–34.

[42] Citations in Cancik, "Augustin," pp. 142–43.

[43] *De ciuitate dei* I,Praef.,9–23: *CC* XLVII,1.

[44] Eusebius, *De vita Constantini* I,iii,4: *Eusebius Werke* 1, pt. 1, pp. 16–17. The prologue to the *vita* (I,i–xi) gives the conventional catalogue of secular accomplishments, though Eusebius stresses his intention to write chiefly about characteristics which pertain to Constantine's godly life (*tou tês prokeimenês hymin pragmateias skopou mona ta pros ton theophilê synteinonta bion legein te kai graphein hypoballontos*), *De vita Constantini* I,xi,1: *Eusebius Werke* 1, pt.1, p. 20.

[45] *De ciuitate dei* V,xxv,1–24: *CC* XLVII,160–61.

[46] Cf. Eusebius, *De vita Constantini* I,vii–viii and xii: *Eusebius Werke* 1, pt.1, pp. 17–18, 21. On these texts and the Moses-Constantine comparison, see M. Hollerich, "Myth and History in Eusebius' *De vita Constantini*: *Vit. Const.* 1.12 in Its Contemporary Setting," *Harvard Theological Review* 82 (1989) 421-45.

[47] Cf. *De ciuitate dei* II,xix,22–29: *CC* XLVII,51.

II

The Triune God

Augustine

"Non est similis tibi in diis, Domine"; quantum autem sit dissimilis Deus, non dixit, quia dici non potest. Intendat Caritas uestra: Deus ineffabilis est; facilius dicimus quid non sit, quam quid sit...Et quid est? Hoc solum potui dicere, quid non sit. Quaeris quid sit? Quod oculus non uidit, nec auris audiuit, nec in cor hominis adscendit. Quid quaeris ut adscendat in linguam, quod in cor non adscendit?

Enarratio in Psalmum LXXXV 12

God in between Affirmation and Negation
According to Augustine

T. J. van Bavel, O.S.A.

Many scholars have been puzzled by the following paradox in Augustine's writings: On the one hand, we find many affirmative propositions about God and, on the other hand, many texts stressing God's ineffability and incomprehensibility. Some authors qualify Augustine's approach to God as "negative theology." Pierre Hadot, however, considers this an ill-chosen designation, for, logically speaking, it would lead to the denial of the divine character of the subject-matter of theology. Hadot makes a distinction between aphaireticism and apophaticism. Both terms mean negation, but each in a different way. Plato's aphairetic method consists in making abstraction of all sensorially perceptible or corporeal determinations and additions, in order to attain to the most simple, spiritual, absolute being, of which we have some knowledge. Making abstraction from all corporeality in our idea of God is a kind of negation. The apophatic Neoplatonic method, in particular that of Plotinus, consists in negating any determination or predicate of the divine transcendent One, for they constitute a denial of its real transcendence. The One or the Good is beyond Being and Intelligence. The absolute can never be an object of knowledge. Because our thinking is based on subject and predicate, the attribution of being to the One amounts to the introduction of duality into the One. Our intellect is reduced to silence here. Only through mystical and transrational experience can we come into contact with the transcendent One.[1] Hadot thinks that Christian apophatic theology is based upon Neoplatonism.[2] A. H. Armstrong, on the contrary, regrets that some possibilities of Neoplatonic apophaticism are imperfectly realized in the Christian West. Whereas Plotinus asserts radically that to enquire whether the One is intelligent or unintelligent is to ask a silly question, and that if the One tried to formulate propositions about itself, it could only talk nonsense, we find in Christian theology a mixture of negation and affirmation in order to preserve something of the mystery of God. The strong prejudice against Neoplatonic apophaticism sometimes found in Christian writers is due to the fear of a false God. Augustine's attempt to explain the Trinity makes acceptance of the full apophatic theology impossible. Armstrong concludes as follows: Many people are looking for an unorganized and unorganizable Good as the only true object of worship, the source of value as the goal of desire, whose light shines everywhere in this ever-changing world.[3]

The problem we wish to clarify is: Where do we situate Augustine: on the side of Plato or on that of Neoplatonism? I will follow the same method as Roland Teske in his publications, namely, Augustine's distinction between speaking about God, thinking about God, and the being of God, or in Augustine's wording, "God is more truly thought than He is spoken of, and is more truly than He is thought." *Dicere—cogitare—esse* form three different levels on which we try to express our relationship with God.[4]

1. Affirmative Speech about God

Augustine remarks at the beginning of his *De trinitate* that Holy Scripture uses all kinds of words in speaking about God: words taken from material objects, e.g., "Protect me under the shadow of your wings"; words which are borrowed from human psychology, e.g., "Our God is a jealous God," or "God is angry."[5] Augustine does not hesitate to use the metaphorical language of the Bible. He asserts that we "may call God honey, gold or wine—speak as we may of that which cannot be spoken. Whatever we wish to say, we are naming God. But what do we say when we say 'God'? All that we can say is beneath him."[6] God is everything for us: bread, water, fountain, light, clothing, a house. Everything can be said about God, but nothing is said worthily. Nothing is more comprehensive than this deficiency (*inopia*). You look for a suitable name; you do not find it.[7] God can be called Father as well as Mother.[8]

Augustine remarks in the same text of *De trinitate* that Divine Scripture rarely mentions concepts that are properly ascribed to God and which are not found in any creature, as, for example, "I am who am," or "He who is sent me to you." With regard to these "metaphysical" concepts Augustine declares: Through a purification of our mind we are able to see the ineffable in an ineffable way.[9] This category of concepts is of special interest for our topic, for it played an important part in the evolution of his thinking about God.

He never had doubts about the existence of God, but the crucial question for him was: Who is this God? Retracing Augustine's conception of God, we see that it passed through three phases. As a Manichaean he could not think of God as the Creator of evil things, and he adopted a dualistic view of

God, believing that there were two eternal substances, a good one and an evil one. He thought of God as the good principle imprisoned in the human being and, therefore, greater in this and smaller in that being; he saw God as a kind of material extension.[10] When he began to distance himself from Manichaeism, he adhered to a more Stoic view, imagining God as a spatial infinity, an immense corporeal mass; this world is permeated by God in a pantheistic way. If God were not spatial, He would coincide with nothing.[11] A third phase started with the reading of some Neoplatonic writings, in which he discovered a strictly spiritual view of God. It enabled him to reject any materialistic representation of God. There also he found his doctrine of participation and learned that our ideas about God are not the result of rational demonstration but the end point of an ascent. Nevertheless, he criticizes the Neoplatonists for not knowing the way to God, which is found only in Jesus Christ. From the very moment of his conversion he identified Christ with Wisdom.[12]

After having discovered God as a spiritual substance, he describes Him as great, good, just, wise, merciful, happy, true, omnipresent, everlasting, unchangeable, immortal, incorruptible, eternal, living, powerful, beautiful, as person, spirit, substance and essence. All these properties of God are, however, subordinated to, or consequences of, the mysterious name that God revealed to Moses, *"Ego sum qui sum"* (Ex 3:14), which can be translated as "I am who am" or "I am He who is."[13] We read in the same passage: "You shall say to the children of Israel: He who is sent me to you." Therefore, according to Augustine, "Being," or better "To Be," is God's proper and highest name; it applies only to God. "All other names by which God could be called and named are set aside; God answered that He is *ipsum esse*..., He is true being, immutable being, and He alone is that."[14] God is the great "Is" and no one is able to grasp this.[15] Although Augustine uses also the noun "essence," he seems to prefer the use of the verb *"esse"* or *"est."* What he is searching for is that simple "Is," that true "Is," that pure "Is."[16] He explains the biblical term *"idipsum,"* the selfsame, i.e., God is always identical with Himself, in the same sense, that is to say, as indicating the mystery of God's immutable Being.[17]

Because God is simple Being, we have to break down all the idols in our heart.[18] Augustine interprets "idols" as more than corporeal or psychological representations of God (such as God's wings, his jealousy or anger); all our attributions must be purified from human limitations: "Let us think of God, if we are able, and insofar as we are able, in the following way: as good without quality, as great without quantity, as creator without need, as presiding without posture, as containing all things without possession, as whole everywhere without place, as eternal without time, as making mutable things without any change of Himself and undergoing nothing."[19] "Therefore, since we doubtless prefer the Creator to created things, we must confess that He lives in the highest sense, that He perceives and understands all things, that it is impossible for Him to die, to be corrupted, or to be changed; that He is not a body, but the most powerful, the most just, the most beautiful, the best, and the most blessed spirit of all."[20] This statement implies that we must also transcend ourselves, for God is above our souls.[21]

Consequently, there is a last step: goodness, truth, wisdom, love, etc. may not be considered as accidents in God, for God *is* goodness, truth, wisdom, love, etc., whereas we *have* these qualities as attributes only. Thus Augustine declares that he can say nothing better than that God is good, but he relates this affirmation immediately to "I am who am," i.e., God is good beyond all the goods we know, good in Himself. Whereas we know only particular goods, this or that good thing, to be good is for God "*ipsum esse.*"[22] The same applies to truth: "Behold and see if you can...that God is truth....Do not ask 'What is truth?' For at once the mists of bodily images and the clouds of phantasms will obstruct your view, and obscure the brightness which shone upon you."[23] All such affirmations coincide with God's being: "Whatever in that ineffable and simple nature seems to be said according to qualities, must be understood according to substance and essence."[24] This way of thinking about God has clearly a negative character as is stressed by the following text: "Whoever so thinks of God, even though he does not yet discover fully what God is, nevertheless, by his pious attitude of mind avoids, as far as is possible, thinking about Him what He is not."[25]

2. God Is Ineffable

In spite of the many affirmations made about God by Augustine, he never ceases to stress the inaccessibility of God to human comprehension and the inadequacy of human language to speak truly about Him.[26] Does Augustine see his affirmations as expressions of authentic knowledge, or only as tentative statements? How can we reconcile his affirmative statements with his frequent declarations that God is ineffable? If it is true that our words fail to express our thoughts in daily speech, this is incomparably more the case in speaking about God: "First of all, pay attention to this: The Creator transcends in an inexpressible way all that we can bring together through our bodily senses or mental thinking."[27] Even in his early works, Augustine emphasizes God's ineffability: "How great a good is God! In what manner should we proclaim and honor the Creator of all, ineffable in any language, ineffable in any thought."[28] In another text dating from the beginning of his episcopate, we read:

> Since God's eternal power and divinity transcend in a wonderful and unhesitating way all the words of which human discourse is composed, all that we say of God in a human way —even that which seems contemptible to people—warns our human weakness that even the biblical expressions about God which one considers as said suitably, are more adapted to our human capacity than to God's sublimity. Therefore, we must transcend them by a purer understanding.[29]

Explaining the words of Psalm 86:8, "Among the gods not one is like thee, O Lord," Augustine remarks: "The psalmist did not say how much God is unlike, because he could not express it. Take care: God is ineffable. It is easier to say what He is not than what He is...I was only able to say what He is not. Do you seek what He is?...Why do you wish that there may enter into speech that which did not enter into the heart?"[30] Of course, ineffability applies especially to the mystery of the Trinity which Augustine calls "wonderfully ineffable, and ineffably wonderful."[31] God's ineffability goes so far that, strictly speaking, we cannot even say that God is ineffable:

> Have we spoken or announced something worthy of God? I feel rather that I have done nothing but wish to speak. If I have spoken, I have not said what I wished to say. Whence do I know this, except because God is ineffable? If, however, what I have said were ineffable, it would not have been said. And for this reason God should not even be said to be ineffable, for when this is said something is said. Thus a certain battle of words arises, since if that is ineffable which cannot be spoken, then that is not ineffable which with certainty can be called ineffable. This battle of words is to be avoided by silence rather than resolved by words. Nevertheless, God, although nothing worthy may be spoken of Him, has accepted the worship of the human voice and wished us to take joy

in praising Him with our words. Therefore, He is called God. Indeed, He is not really known through the noise of this one syllable. When, however,...this sound reaches the ears, it incites us to think of a most excellent and immortal nature.[32]

In Sermon 117 Augustine exclaims: "What are we doing? Will we keep silent? If only that would be permitted!" and he continues: "All that we say is not ineffable, whereas God remains ineffable."[33] God's ineffable sublimity surpasses the power of any language; consequently, respectful silence would be more fitting than any human words,[34] but it is not permitted. At the end of *De trinitate* he formulates it in this way: "I venture to acknowledge openly that I have said nothing worthy of that ineffable highest Trinity among all the many things that I have already said, but confess rather that your knowledge, after having become wonderful from my personal experience, is too great: I cannot reach it."[35] Augustine refers here to an old Latin translation of Ps. 138 (139):6, "*Scientia tua mirificata est ex me*," and he explains this "*ex me*" as follows: from the experience that we do not even know ourselves, we can gather how incomprehensible God is.[36] Hence, this paradoxical statement about saying something by silence: "Who would be able, with untroubled and pure mind, to contemplate this Totality about which I have tried to speak by not speaking, and not to speak about it by speaking?"[37]

The first reason why God is ineffable is that God has never spoken in His substance, not even to Moses, but always through the mediation of creatures.[38] The second reason is that nothing similar to God's immutable essence can be found here on earth: all our words relate to time and space.[39]

3. God Is Incomprehensible

As we have seen, God is more truly thought than He is spoken of, but there is something more: He *is* also more truly than He is thought.[40] It is possible that in his earliest writings Augustine was more optimistic concerning the comprehensibility of God, at least if we have to interpret his expression, "*Deus intelligibilis*," in this sense.[41] His later texts are more radical: We are unable to understand fully God's name as revealed to Moses, "I am who am"; rarely we can understand a very little fraction of it (*ex quantulacumque particula rara*).[42] It is not only difficult to understand something of it, it is also too much for our understanding and apprehension.[43] "Behold a great 'Is,' a great 'Is.' What is a human being compared to it?...Who is able to grasp that 'to be'? Who can become a sharer in it? Who may grasp after it? Who long for it? Who presume that he can be there?"[44] In whatever way we exert the power of our mind, we can only touch it with our mind, but not attain to it.[45]

Sometimes Augustine leaves open the possibility that Moses understood better than we do, "I am who am," but they to whom he was sent certainly could not understand it, and in particular the little ones, that is, the common believer. Augustine counts himself as one of these: "We are little ones. I speak to you what God is not; I do not show what He is. Therefore, what shall we do that we may grasp what He is? Will you be able to by me, through me? I shall say this to the little ones, to you and to myself; there is only One (= the Lord) through whom we may be able."[46]

God's Being is an object of faith. Explaining Jesus' words, "If you do not believe that I am, you will die in yours sins" (Jn 8:24) in this sense: "If you do not believe that I am God," Augustine thanks Jesus for having said, "If you do not believe," and not, "If you do not grasp it," for who is able to do that?[47] He feels happy that after the words of Ex 3:14, "I am who am," we hear those of Ex 3:15, "I am the God of Abraham, the God of Isaac, and the God of Jacob." This last text expresses what God is for us, His relationship with us. "I am who am" indicates what God is in Himself, or as Augustine says, "what belongs to God alone," and what we will never fully understand, for even Moses was frightened at hearing God's proper name.[48] This makes it all the more important for us to know God at least as revealed in salvation history: the God for us.[49]

The reason why God remains incomprehensible is that all created things are mortal and changeable.[50] Regarding his *"Est,"* we cannot stay firm, for our thoughts are fleeting and our heart is unstable.[51] How then would flesh and blood understand *"Ego sum qui sum"*?[52] If we take into account that a human person does not even know who he or she is, then it is not surprising that God's being remains incomprehensible to us: "When do I understand myself in myself? How, then, can I understand that which is above me?"[53] More than that, we are also ignorant regarding the process of human knowing, and can barely explain how memory shows to thought what it has taken from the world outside; how much less will we be able to grasp the relationship between the Father and the Son?[54] "For with what understanding does a human being grasp God, who does not yet grasp his or her own understanding itself, through which one desires to grasp Him?"[55]

All that is said about the incomprehensibility of God as pure and simple Being applies also to Him as the highest good, truth, love, etc. No matter how much the human mind amplifies God's attributes, they will remain very much beneath the reality they seek to express.[56] In this light, we can easily understand Augustine's statement that it is not an inconsiderable beginning in the task of knowing God to understand what He is *not*: "If you cannot now comprehend what God is, at least comprehend what He is not. You will have made much progress if you do not think of God something other than He is. As yet you cannot attain to what He is; attain to what He is not."[57] Even more radical is his remark made in one of his earliest works: "We know God better by not knowing [Him].... About the Maker himself of the universe, the soul has no knowledge except to know how it does not know Him."[58] Augustine held to this conviction for the rest of his life. He continues to emphasize that, "Since we are speaking about God, such an ignorance is more pious than a presumed science.... Speaking about God, what wonder if you do not understand? If you do understand, it is not God.... To come in contact mentally —be it poorly—with God, means great happiness, but to understand God is absolutely impossible."[59]

If we think we have understood God, we may be sure that we have understood something else instead of God and that we deceived ourselves by our thoughts.[60] "Reject all from your mind; negate all that has presented itself there; be aware of the weakness of your heart. Precisely because something presents itself that you could think of, say: It is not this, for if it were this, it would not have presented itself to me."[61] Augustine warns not only against phantasms or fictitious assumptions, but also against the reasoning power itself: "Whatever you imagine, it is not God; whatever you understand by thinking, it is not He."[62] Notice how Augustine calls this kind of ignorance *"pia ignorantia, docta ignorantia."*[63]

4. Now We See through a Mirror

God's incomprehensibility can be illustrated also by Augustine's view of the relationship between belief and understanding, sometimes called his hermeneutical circle. We should understand in order to believe and believe in order to understand.[64] A human being would never seek something if it were not already known in some way or other; seeking, however, would not be necessary if we had perfect knowledge without any uncertainty or darkness.[65] After this life, we will see God, but even then we will not comprehend God fully; we will rather participate in His divinity.[66] Here on earth we have to live by faith,[67] as expressed in 1 Co 13:12: "Now we see through a mirror and in an enigma, but then we shall see face to face. Now I know in part, but then I shall know even as I am known." If such a great man as Paul admits that he sees God only through a dark mirror, how much more must our mind be aware of the unlikeness between itself and God, and of its inability to grasp Him![68] "Let no one wonder, therefore, that we must toil to see anything at all, even in this manner of seeing which has been granted in this life, namely, through a mirror in an enigma."[69] Augustine realizes that his theological reflections are beyond the comprehension of the little ones; the stronger ones perhaps can understand something, but only *"in enigmate"*.[70] According to him, an enigma is something which neither reveals nor conceals completely the truth.[71] In spite of its ambiguity, its function is to show the right direction.

1 Co 8:2–3 is another text to which Augustine refers: "If anyone thinks that he knows anything, he does not yet know as he ought to know. But if anyone loves God, this person is known by God," and Augustine comments: Paul does not say, "This person knows God," for that would be a dangerous presumption, but "This person is known by God."[72] His commentary on Ph 3:13: "I myself do not think to have apprehended," is interpreted along the same lines: "What? When I see that which I could not see, and grasp what I could not grasp previously, will I then be safe? Will I then be perfect? The answer must be, 'no,' as long as you live here…. Who ventures to say that he understands? Behold, even Paul did not understand."[73]

Our life in faith is an ongoing process as Ps 105:4 expresses it: "Seek His face evermore." Faith and reason have a part to play in this process. Both faith and intellect will lead us deeper and deeper into the one truth: "Our intellect helps us to understand what we believe, and belief helps us to believe what we understand. The mind progresses in understanding in order to get an ever deepening insight."[74] With regard to incomprehensible things, this interaction between seeking and finding will never come to an end, since God is not only a concealed mystery but also immeasurable.[75] Therefore:

> Is God still to be sought, even when He is found? For so
> ought a person to seek incomprehensible realities, lest he

should think that he has found nothing, who could find how incomprehensible is the reality which he is seeking. Why, then, does he so intensely seek if he comprehends that what he seeks is incomprehensible, unless because he knows that he must not cease as long as he is making progress in the search itself of incomprehensible things, and is becoming better and better by seeking so great a good, which is sought in order to be found, and is found in order to be sought.[76]

"Inventus quaerendus est," i.e., we have to seek God even when found. Seeking is hoping for that which we do not see, and expecting it with patience.[77] We have begun to know in some way through faith, but our knowledge will be perfected only later. What matters is the desire to seek, not the presumption to know unknown things. Let us, therefore, so seek as about to find, and so find as about to seek.[78] When the Lord comes and brings to light the things hidden in darkness, we shall contemplate the "I am who am."[79]

Conscious that his own heart is but a human heart in which many *"figmenta,"* that is, representations in thought, imaginations, and fictions are born,[80] Augustine concludes his *De trinitate* with the following prayer:

Many are my thoughts, such as You know. They are the thoughts of a human being, since they are vain (Ps 94:11). Grant me that I may not consent to them, and if at any time they delight me, grant that I may nevertheless reject them, and may not, as though slumbering, dwell upon them.... When we will have come to You, the many things which we say (Si 43:29) without having attained You shall cease; and You as One shall remain.[81]

5. Why Do We Speak about the Ineffable?

We can ask one last question regarding God's ineffability: if He is ineffable, why then do we speak at all? Augustine felt this to be an obligation; as he expressed it in *De trinitate*, "Due to the fact that we have to speak about ineffable things, and in order to be able to speak in some way about things which in no way we can speak out, it is said by the Greeks: one essence, three substances."[82] This obligation can be looked at from four angles.

a) The first reason is that we ourselves have to avoid a false representation of God. The opening lines of the *Confessions* refer in all probability to Augustine's own experience: "For it would seem clear that no one can call upon Thee without knowing Thee, for if he did he might invoke another than Thee."[83] Some knowledge, then, is needed, for it is possible to hope for and love a false God: "Therefore, even He who is not known, but in whom one believes, is already loved. Care must, of course, be taken lest the mind, in believing what it does not see, picture it to itself as something which it is not, and so hope for and love that which is false."[84]

b) The second reason is that we should assist souls of our own kind who have gone astray and struggle in error.[85] There are also loquacious, silly, or cunning people, and willy-nilly we have to answer these adversaries, in particular those who are in error; otherwise they would remain convinced of being right, if we cannot answer them.[86]

c) The third reason for naming, speaking, and thinking about God is that we have to proclaim, to honor, to admire and to praise God's ineffable greatness and goodness.[87] The praise of Him should be a joy for us: "When you have learned that you cannot say what you feel about God, will you keep silent and not praise Him?"[88]

d) The last reason is that all the efforts of our speaking and thinking are meant to open us for the mystery of the radical Other. Armstrong's remark concerning the view of Plotinus that there are some privileged terms used by the Neoplatonists in speaking about the One and the Good, and that those terms are used in order to keep our mind pointed in the right direction and to help us to remember Him as the goal of our desire, applies also to Augustine.[89]

6. Conclusion

Is our ignorance about God here on earth only a passing stage on the way to a positive knowledge of God? In other words, can we overcome ignorance already in this life? I do not think that this is the view of Augustine. Isabelle Bochet's statement: "This negative way is only a stage; Augustine affirms the possibility of a positive apprehension of God,"[90] is to my mind ambiguous. The word *apprehensio*, which means "to grasp" or "to understand," seems to me inappropriate in this context, for Augustine always denies that we can apprehend God; he uses the term *attingere* (to touch, or to come in contact with) which expresses, rather, a real relationship between the human person and God. I consider it important to respect the Augustinian paradox: on the one hand, his attempts to speak about God in every possible way with rhetorical figures, with metaphors, playing on words, crying and shouting, or with the whole arsenal of his philosophical knowledge,—and on the other hand, his constant declaration that God is beyond our knowledge and language. God reveals Himself precisely as unknowable; therefore, the order of positive language has to be changed into a positivity of ignorance. God has the initiative in a knowledge of which the human being is not the master. What does matter is to learn how one does not know. It is not permitted to let God disappear in our human representations.[91] Augustine wished to do nothing other than to pave the way to the revealed Unknowable, and this requires at the same time an emptying out of every kind of representation. He describes our seeking intellect as *conjiciens*, i.e., seeing by conjecturing that which we now see only through an image; such is our knowledge in the interim.[92] He describes it also as *palpans*, i.e., seeking one's way by touch; in order to attain some knowledge of the highest Being we seek gropingly without seeing.[93]

We encounter two traditions in Augustine: Greek philosophical thinking based upon intellectual concepts and the Jewish-Christian tradition based upon salvation narratives. E. König defends the opinion that Augustine had to make a choice between these two traditions, and chose the Greek philosophical way to God.[94] E. Feldmann, however, remarks rightly that philosophy and theology were never considered as opposites by Augustine.[95] E. Jüngel defends another extreme opinion; from the Augustinian texts declaring it impossible for us to comprehend God, he concludes that Augustine declined to think about God. Jüngel considers such an attitude dangerous to faith.[96] But as we have seen Augustine did not refrain from speaking and thinking about God.

I agree rather with R. Lorenz, who stresses the interconnection of knowledge and grace in Augustine; our knowledge also is a divine gift.[97] Augustine could never subscribe to Plotinus's statement that any self-expression or self-manifestation of the unknowable first principle is nonsense; Augustine's belief in the Bible as God's address to us is too strong for that. God is not beyond being and intelligence in the radical sense meant by Plotinus; Augustine would not agree with the latter's assertion that neither can we speak meaningfully about God, nor can God about Himself. We can at least make statements which point in the right direction and build a way of preparing our mind for the awareness of the transcendent God. Augustine lets his insights end in the mystery of the Infinite, so that our *conjicere* and *palpare* are not meaningless. Consequently, I consider Augustine's thought more in keeping with that of Plato than with that of Plotinus. Augustine's God-talk has more points in common with aphaireticism than with apophaticism.[98] In this way Augustine asks, in the concluding prayer of *De trinitate*: "Deliver me, O God, from the multitude of words," for in the multitude of words, as in a void, something inaudible presents itself to be listened to, namely, the divine Word which transcends all speech and thought.[99]

Notes

[1] P. Hadot, "Apophatisme et théologie négative," *Exercises spirituels et philosophie antique* (Paris: Études Augustiniennes, 1981), pp. 185–93 and "Dieu comme acte d'être dans le Néoplatonisme. A propos des théories d'E. Gilson sur la métaphysique de l'Exode," *Dieu et l'Etre* (Paris: Études Augustiniennes, 1978), pp. 57–63.

[2] This is also the opinion of P. Agaësse and A. Solignac, "Paradoxe de la connaissance de Dieu," *BA* 48,674–75.

[3] A. H. Armstrong, "The Escape of the One. An Investigation of some Possibilities of Apophatic Theology Imperfectly Realised in the West," *Studia Patristica* XIII (Berlin: Akademie-Verlag, 1975), pp. 77–89; "Negative Theology," *The Downside Review* 95 (1977) 176–89; and "Neoplatonic Valuations of Nature, Body and Intellect," *AS* 3 (1972) 35–59. J. Trouillard, "Théologie négative et autoconstitution psychique chez les néoplatoniciens," *Savoir, faire, espérer: les limites de la raison.* I (Bruxelles: Facultés universitaires de Saint-Louis, 1976), pp. 307–21; "Raison et mystique chez Plotin," *REA* 20 (1974) 3–14; "Valeur critique de la mystique plotinienne," *Revue philosophique de Louvain* 59 (1961) 431–44. A. J. Festugière, "La transcendance de l'Un - Bien - Beau chez Platon," *La révélation d'Hermès Trismégiste* IV (Paris: Lecoffre, 1953), pp. 79–140. J. Hochstaffl, *Negative Theologie. Ein Versuch zur Vermittlung des patristischen Begriffs* (München: Kosel, 1976).

The following text of Plotinus (*Ennead* V,iii,13–14: *PO* II,324) illustrates very well his thinking: "The One does not think and we cannot think of it. How can we find words to describe the One? It is true, we apply some words to it, but we cannot express it properly, and we have no knowledge and thought of it. How can we speak about it, if we do not possess it? Yet, if we do not possess it through knowledge, are we then deprived of it completely? No, we possess it in such a way that we speak about it, without ever expressing its real nature. We say what it is not, but what it really is, we do not say. Consequently, we speak about it with the help of concepts which came into existence later. Nothing, however, prevents us from possessing it—even though we do not express it really—like people who are in ecstasy or are obsessed know that they possess something greater in themselves, although they do not know what it is." "Possession" means here the obscure understanding of the unspeakable through mystical and transrational experience.

[4] *De trinitate* VII,iv,7: *CC* L,255: *Verius enim cogitatur deus quam dicitur, et uerius est quam cogitatur.* Cf. R. J. Teske, "Properties of God and the Predicaments in *De trinitate* V," *The Modern Schoolman* 59 (1981/2) 1–19, and "Augustine's Use of 'Substantia' in Speaking about God," *The Modern Schoolman* 62 (1985/6) 147–63.

[5] *De trinitate* I,i,2–3: *CC* L,28–31. *Tractatus in Euangelium Ioannis* XCIX,4: *CC* XXXVI,584: *Nec mireris quod ineffabilis Dei scientia, qua nouit omnia, per uarios humanae locutionis modos, omnium istorum corporalium sensuum nominibus nuncupatur....* See also the beautiful paradoxical approach to God in *Confessiones* I,iv,4: *CC* XXVII,2–3.

[6] *In Ioannis Epistulam ad Parthos tractatus* IV,6: *PL* XXXV,2009: *Melle dicamus, aurum dicamus, vinum dicamus: quidquid dicimus quod dici non potest, quidquid volumus dicere, Deus vocatur. Et quod dicimus Deus, quid diximus? Duae istae syllabae sunt tantum quod expectamus? Quidquid ergo dicere valuimus, infra est.*

[7] *Tractatus in Euangelium Ioannis* XIII,5: *CC* XXXVI,133: *Totum tibi fit Deus.... Omnia possunt dici de Deo, et nihil digne dicitur de Deo. Nihil latius hac inopia. Quaeris congruum nomen, non inuenis; quaeris quoquo modo dicere, omnia inuenis.* See also Augustine's answer to the question: "What do I love when I love Thee?" in *Confessiones* X,vi,8: *CC* XXVII,159.

[8] *Enarratio in Psalmum XXVI, Sermo II* 18: *CC* XXXVIII,164: *Pater est quia condidit, quia uocat, quia iubet, quia regit; mater, quia fouet, quia nutrit, quia lactat, quia continet.*

[9] *De trinitate* I,i,2–3: *CC* L,29–30. *Quae uero proprie de deo dicuntur, quae in nulla creatura, raro ponit scriptura diuina, sicut illud quod dictum est ad Moysen: "Ego sum qui sum," et: "Qui est misit me ad uos."...Et ideo est necessaria purgatio mentis nostrae qua illud ineffabile ineffabiliter uideri possit....*

[10] *Confessiones* VII,xiv,20: *CC* XXVII,106 and VI,iii,4: *CC* XXVII,76. See E. Feldmann, "'Et inde rediens fecerat sibi Deum' (Conf. 7,20). Beobachtungen zur Genese des augustinischen Gottesbegriffes und zu dessen Funktion in den Confessiones," *Mélanges T. J. Van Bavel* II,881–904 (= *Augustiniana* 41 [1991]).

[11] *Confessiones* VII,i,1–2: *CC* XXVII,92–93. See Ch. Baguette, "Une période stoïcienne dans l'évolution de la pensée de saint Augustin," *REA* 16 (1970) 47–77.

[12] *Confessiones* V,xiv,25: *CC* XXVII,71–72 and VII,x,16: *CC* XXVII,103–4. *De ciuitate dei* X,xxix: *CC* XLVII,304: *Ubi, etsi uerbis indisciplinatis utimini, uidetis tamen qualitercumque et quasi per quaedam tenuis imaginationis umbracula, quo nitendum sit; sed incarnationem incommutabilis Filii Dei, qua saluamur, ut ad illa, quae credimus uel ex quantulacumque parte intellegimus, uenire possimus, non uultis agnoscere.* See R. J. Teske, "Divine Immutability in Saint Augustine," *The Modern Schoolman* 63 (1985/6) 233–49; G. Madec, "Notes sur l'intelligence augustinienne de la foi," *REA* 17 (1971) 119–42, and "Connaissance de Dieu et action de grâces. Essai sur les citations de l'Ep. aux Romains I, 18–25 dans l'oeuvre de saint Augustin," *Recherches Augustiniennes* II (1962) 273–309.

[13] The last translation is preferred by G. Madec, "'Ego sum qui sum' de Tertullien à Jérôme," *Dieu et l'Etre*, pp. 121–39. See further: E. Zum Brunn, "L'exégèse augustinienne de 'Ego sum qui sum' et la métaphysique de l'Exode," *Dieu et l'Etre* (Paris: Études Augustiniennes, 1978), pp. 141–64; E. Gilson, "Notes sur l'être et le temps chez saint Augustin," *Recherches Augustiniennes* II (1962) 205–23.

[14] *Enarratio in Psalmum CXXXIV* 4: *CC* XL,1940: *Sublatis de medio omnibus quibus appellari posset et dici Deus, ipsum esse se uocari respondit; et tamquam hoc esset ei nomen: "Hoc dices eis," inquit, "Qui est, misit me"…. uerum esse, incommutabile esse est, quod ille solus est.*

[15] *Enarratio in Psalmum CI, Sermo II* 10: *CC* XL,1445: *…magnum "Est"…Quis apprehendat illud esse?*

[16] *Enarratio in Psalmum XXXVIII* 7: *CC* XXXVIII,409: *"Est" illud simplex quaero, "Est" uerum quaero, "Est" germanum quaero.*

[17] *Enarratio in Psalmum CXXI* 5: *CC* XL,1805: *Quid est "idipsum"? Quod semper eodem modo est; quod non modo aliud, et modo aliud est. Quid est ergo "idipsum," nisi, quod est? Quid est quod est? Quod aeternum est.* See R. J. Teske, "Augustine's Use of Substantia," 156–57.

[18] *Sermo Denis II* 5: *MA* I,16: *Frangite idola in cordibus vestris; attendite quod dictum est ad Moysen, cum dei nomen inquireret: "Ego sum qui sum."*

[19] *De trinitate* V,i,2: *CC* L,207: *…ut sic intellegamus deum si possumus, quantum possumus, sine qualitate bonum, sine quantitate magnum, sine indigentia creatorem, sine situ praesentem, sine habitu omnia continentem, sine loco ubique totum, sine tempore sempiternum, sine ulla sui mutatione mutabilia facientem nihilque patientem.*

[20] *De trinitate* XV,iv,6: *CC* L/A, 468: *Ac per hoc quoniam rebus creatis creatorem sine dubitatione praeponimus, oportet ut eum et summe uiuere et cuncta sentire atque intellegere, et mori, corrumpi mutarique non posse; nec corpus esse sed spiritum omnium potentissimum, iustissimum, speciosissimum, optimum, beatissimumque fateamur.*

[21] *Sermo Denis II* 3: *MA* I,14: *Totum transcende, te ipsum transcende. Enarratio in Psalmum XLI* 8: *CC* XXXVIII,465: *Quaerens eius substantiam in meipso quasi sit aliquid quasi ego sum, neque hoc inueniens; aliquid super animam esse sentio Deum meum.*

[22] *Enarratio in Psalmum CXXXIV* 4: *CC* XL,1940: *Est enim est, sicut bonorum bonum, bonum est. De perfectione iustitiae hominis* XIV,32: *CSEL* XLII,33: *…cui bonum esse hoc est ipsum esse. De trinitate* VIII,iii,4: *CC* L,272: *Bonum hoc et bonum illud. Tolle hoc et illud, et uide ipsum bonum si potes; ita deum uidebis…. ipsum bonum.*

[23] *De trinitate* VIII,ii,3: *CC* L,271: *Noli quaerere quid sit ueritas; statim enim se opponent caligines imaginum corporalium et nubilia phantasmatum et perturbabunt serenitatem quae primo ictu diluxit tibi cum dicerem, ueritas….*

[24] *De trinitate* XV,v,8: *CC* L/A,470: *…sed non ita est in illa ineffabili simplicique natura. Quidquid enim secundum qualitates illic dici uidetur secundum substantiam uel essentiam est intellegendum.* See M. Smallbrugge, *La nature trinitaire de l'intelligence augustinienne de la foi* (Amsterdam: Rodopi, 1988).

[25] *De trinitate* V,i,2: *CC* L,207: *Quisquis deum ita cogitat etsi nondum potest omni modo inuenire quid sit, pie tamen cauet quantum potest aliquid de illo sentire quod non sit.*

[26] R. A. Markus, "Marius Victorinus and Augustine," in A. H. Armstrong, *The Cambridge History of Later Greek and Early Medieval Philosophy* (London: Cambridge University Press, 1970), p. 397.

[27] *Sermo CXVII* x,15: *PL* XXXVIII,670: *Ante omnia tamen servate hoc, quidquid de creatura potuimus colligere, aut sensu corporis, aut cogitatione animi, inerrabiliter transcendere creatorem.*

[28] *De libero arbitrio* III,xiii,37: *CC* XXIX,297: *Quantum ergo bonum et quam uel ineffabiliter linguibus omnibus uel ineffabiliter cogitationibus omnibus praedicandus et honorandus est creator omnium deus....*

[29] *De diuersis quaestionibus ad Simplicianum* II,q. 2,1: *CC* XLIV,75: *Cum uero uerba omnia quibus humana conloquia conseruntur, illius sempiterna uirtus et diuinitas mirabiliter atque incunctanter excedat, quidquid de illo humaniter dicitur, quod etiam hominibus aspernabile uideatur, ipsa humana ammonetur infirmitas etiam illa quae congruenter in scripturis sanctis de deo dicta existimat humanae capacitati aptiora esse quam diuinae sublimitati, ac per hoc etiam ipsa esse transcendenda sereniore intellectu.*

[30] *Enarratio in Psalmum LXXXV* 12: *CC* XXXIX,1186: *"Non est similis tibi in diis, Domine"; quantum autem sit dissimilis Deus, non dixit, quia dici non potest. Intendat Caritas uestra: Deus ineffabilis est; facilius dicimus quid non sit, quam quid sit.... Et quid est? Hoc solum potui dicere, quid non sit. Quaeris quid sit? Quod oculus non uidit, nec auris audiuit, nec in cor hominis adscendit. Quid quaeris ut adscendat in linguam, quod in cor non adscendit?*

[31] *De trinitate* XV,xxiii,43: *CC* L/A,521: *Quod sane mirabiliter ineffabile est uel ineffabiliter mirabile.... Tractatus in Euangelium Ioannis* XXI,14: *CC* XXXVI,220–21: *Magna enim illa forma ubi adhuc aequalitas Patris et Filii cognoscitur: ineffabilis, incomprehensibilis, maxime paruulis.*

[32] *De doctrina christiana* I,vi,6: *CC* XXXII,9–10: *Diximus aliquid et sonuimus aliquid dignum deo? Immo uero nihil me aliud quam dicere uoluisse sentio; si autem dixi, non hoc est quod dicere uolui. Hoc unde scio, nisi quia deus ineffabilis est? quod autem a me dictum est, si ineffabile esset, dictum non esset. Ac per hoc ne ineffabilis quidem dicendus est deus, quia et hoc cum dicitur, aliquid dicitur et fit nescio quae pugna uerborum, quoniam si illud est ineffabile, quod dici non potest, non est ineffabile, quod uel ineffabile dici potest. Quae pugna uerborum silentio cauenda potius quam uoce pacanda est. Et tamen deus, cum de illo nihil digne dici possit, admisit humanae uocis obsequium.... Nam inde est et quod dicitur deus. Non enim re uera in strepitu istarum duarum syllabarum ipse cognoscitur, sed tamen...cum aures ...sonus iste tetigerit, mouet ad cogitandum excellentissimam quandam inmortalemque naturam.* One is tempted to compare this text with a statement of the Neoplatonist Damascius (sixth century!): "We show our ignorance and our incapacity to speak about him (*aphasia*)." *Dubitationes et solutiones de primis principiis*, par. 7, ed. Ch. Ruelle (Paris, 1889), I, pp. 11, 20. Damascius's viewpoint, however, is more radical than that of Augustine. Damascius holds that the One is absolutely indescribable, whether in terms of immanence—transcen-

dence, identity—otherness, or any others. P. Hadot, "Théologie négative," 190, writes: "Damascius analyse avec une lucidité parfaite les apories de l'inconnaissable: il est également impossible de dire que le principe est inconnaissable et qu'il est connaissable. 'Notre ignorance à son sujet est complète.'"

[33] *Sermo CXVII* v,7: *PL* XXXVIII,665: *Et quid facimus nos? Silebimus? Utinam liceret. Forsitan enim silendo aliquid dignum de re ineffabili cogitaretur. Nam quidquid potest fari, non est ineffabile. Ineffabilis est autem Deus.*

[34] *Contra Adimantum* VII,4: *CSEL* XXV/1,129: *Sancta enim scriptura verbis nostris loquens etiam per haec verba demonstrat nihil digne de deo posse dici. Cur enim non etiam ista verba dicantur de illa maiestate de qua quicquid dictum fuerit, indigne dicitur, quia omnes opes linguarum omnium ineffabili sublimitate praecedit?* Ibid. 11: *CSEL* XXV/1,136: *Illi enim haec verba exhorrescunt, qui nondum viderunt ineffabili maiestati dei nulla verba congruere....* Sanctus enim spiritus hoc ipsum hominibus intellegentibus insinuans, quam sint ineffabilia summa divina, his etiam verbis uti voluit, quae apud homines in vitio poni solent, ut inde admonerentur etiam illa, quae cum aliqua dignitate dei se putant homines dicere, indigna esse illius maiestate, cui honorificum potius silentium quam ulla vox humana conpeteret.*

[35] *De trinitate* XV,xxvii,50: *CC* L/A,531: *Verum inter haec quae multa iam dixi et nihil illius summae trinitatis ineffabilitate dignum me dixisse audeo profiteri, sed confiteri potius mirificatam scientiam eius ex me inualuisse nec potuisse me ad illam.*

[36] *De trinitate* XV,vii,13: *CC* L/A,479: *"Mirificata est scientia tua ex me; inualuit et non potero ad illam." Ex me quippe intellego quam sit mirabilis et incomprehensibilis scientia tua qua me fecisti, quando nec me ipsum comprehendere ualeo quem fecisti.... De natura et origine animae* IV,viii,12: *CSEL* LX,391: *Cur enim adiecit 'ex me' nisi quia ex se ipso quam incomprehensibilis esset dei scientia coniciebat, quando quidem se ipsum comprehendere non valebat? Enarratio in Psalmum CXXXVIII* 9: *CC* XL,1997: *Veluti posuisti super me manum tuam, mirus mihi factus es; non te comprehendo cum quo eram. Enarratio in Psalmum CIII, Sermo I* 3: *CC* XL,1475: *"Mirificata est scientia tua ex me," mira enim facta est ex me. Ego illam miror conversus ad illam.*

[37] *Epistula CCXXXII* 5: *CSEL* LVII,514–15: *Est quiddam invisibile...summum, aeternum, incommutabile et nulli effabile nisi tantum sibi.... Quis autem hoc totum, quod non dicendo dicere conatus sum et dicendo non dicere, quis hoc possit serenissima et sincerissima mente contueri...?*

[38] *Enarratio in Psalmum CXXXVIII* 8: *CC* XL,1994: *Moyses sanctus Dei famulus, cum quo loquebatur Deus per nubem, quia temporaliter loquens utique per assumptam creaturam loquebatur seruo suo; id est non per substantiam suam. Epistula CXLVII* VIII,20: *CSEL* XLIV,294: *Ipse ergo erat in ea specie, qua apparere voluerat, non autem ipse apparebat in natura propria, quam Moyses videre cupiebat; ea quippe promittitur sanctis in alia vita.*

[39] *Sermo CXVII* vi,9–10: *PL* XXXVIII,666: *Et sic forsitan non invenitur aliqua similitudo nativitatis ejus, quomodo non invenitur et substantiae ejus, et immutabilitatis, divinitatis, majestatis ejus. Quid enim simile hic inveniri potest?...Et revera, fratres, non sum inventurus temporales similitudines, quas aeternitati possim comparare. De Genesi ad litteram* V,xvi,34:

CSEL XXVIII/1,159: *Quamvis, inquam, illa substantia ineffabilis sit nec dici utcumque homini per hominem possit nisi usurpatis quibusdam locorum ac temporum verbis, cum sit ante omnia tempora et ante omnes locos, tamen propinquior nobis est….*

[40] *De trinitate* VII,iv,7: *CC* L,255: *…uerius est quam cogitatur.*

[41] *Soliloquia* I,viii,15: *CSEL* LXXXIX,23: *Intelligibilis nempe Deus est.*

[42] *Enarratio in Psalmum CIV* 4: *CC* XL,1537: *"Ego sum qui sum," et: "Dices filiis Israel: Qui est, misit me ad uos," quod ex quantulacumque particula rara mens capit.*

[43] *Enarratio in Psalmum CXXI* 5: *CC* XL,1805: *"Ego sum qui sum"…. Non potes capere; multum est intellegere, multum est adprehendere.* Notice that 'multum' can have the meaning 'too much.'

[44] *Enarratio in Psalmum CI, Sermo II* 10: *CC* XL,1445: *Magnum ecce Est, magnum Est! Ad hoc quid homo est? Ad illud tam magnum Est, homo quid est, quidquid est? Quis apprehendat illud esse? quis eius particeps fiat? quis anhelet? quis adspiret? quis ibi se esse posse praesumat?*

[45] *Tractatus in Euangelium Ioannis* II,2: *CC* XXXVI,12: *Aut quis, quomodocumque intenderit uires mentis suae, ut adtingat quomodo potest id quod est, ad id quod utcumque mente adtigerit, possit peruenire?*

[46] *Tractatus in Euangelium Ioannis* XXXVIII,8: *CC* XXXVI,342: *"Ego sum qui sum." Quis digne eloquatur quid sit: sum?…Forte multum erat et ad ipsum Moysen, sicut multum est et ad nos, et multo magis ad nos, intellegere quid dictum sit: "Ego sum qui sum."…Et si forte caperet Moyses, illi ad quos mittebatur quando caperent? Distulit ergo Dominus quod capere homo non posset, et addidit quod capere posset; adiunxit enim et ait: "Ego sum Deus Abraham, et Deus Isaac, et Deus Iacob." Hoc potes capere; nam "Ego sum qui sum," quae mens potest capere? Tractatus in Euangelium Ioannis* XXIII,11: *CC* XXXVI,241: *Paruuli sumus; loquor uobis quid non sit Deus, non ostendo quid sit; ergo ut capiamus quid sit, quid faciemus? Numquid a me, numquid per me poteritis? Dicam hoc paruulis, et uobis et mihi: est per quem possimus; modo cantauimus…"Iacta in Dominum curam tuam, et ipse te enutriet." Tractatus in Euangelium Ioannis* XVIII,7: *CC* XXXVI,184: *Non sum tam audax, tam temerarius, ut hoc explicare pollicear et me et uos; utcumque suspicor modulum uestrum, noui tamen meum. Sermo Denis II* 5: *MA* I,16–17: *Sed Moyses homo erat…. Nam illud quod dictum est "Ego sum qui sum" quando capiebat?…illo non ualente comprehendere quid sit "Ego sum qui sum" et "Qui est misit me ad uos," aut forte, si ipse comprehendebat, nobis legendum erat, qui comprehendere non ualemus, continuo post nomen substantiae dixit nomen misericordiae. Tamquam diceret Moysi: Quod dixi "Ego sum qui sum" non capis; non stat cor tuum, non es immutabilis mecum, nec incommutabilis mens tua…. Non potes capere nomen substantiae meae; cape nomen misericordiae meae.* Regarding "the little ones," see: R. J. Teske, "A Decisive Admonition for St. Augustine?" *AS* 19 (1988) 85–92.

[47] *Tractatus in Euangelium Ioannis* XXXVIII,10: *CC* XXXVI,344: *Bene, Deo gratias, quia dixit: "Nisi credideritis"; non dixit: Nisi ceperitis. Quis enim hoc capiat? Aut uere, quia ausus sum dicere, et uisi estis intellegere, aliquid de tanta ineffabilitate cepistis? Si ergo non capis, fides te liberat.*

[48] *Enarratio in Psalmum CXXI* 5: *CC* XL,1806: *Qui est, uoluit esse homo, ut tu es; et ideo secutus ait Moysi quasi expauescenti nomen. Quod nomen? Quod est: "Est".... "Ego sum Deus Abraham, et Deus Isaac, et Deus Iacob."*

[49] *Enarratio in Psalmum CXXI* 5: *CC* XL,1805: *Retine quod pro te factus est, quem non posses capere. Retine carnem Christi. Enarratio in Psalmum CX, Sermo II* 10: *CC* XL, 1445: *Audisti quid sim apud me, audi et quid sim propter te. Sermo VII* 7: *CC* XLI,75–76: *Esse, nomen est incommutabilitatis.... Cum ergo sit hoc nomen aeternitatis, plus est quod est dignatus habere nomen misericordiae: "Ego sum deus Abraham, et deus Isaac, et deus Iacob." Illud in se, hoc ad nos. Si enim hoc solum esse uellet quod est in se, quid essemus nos? Enarratio in Psalmum CXXXIV* 6: *CC* XL,1942: *Quia ipsum proprie esse menti humanae difficile erat capere...continuo Deus temperauit laudem suam, et hoc de se dixit quod capi dulciter posset.... Quod enim "Ego sum qui sum" ad me pertinet; quod autem "Deus Abraham, et Deus Isaac, et Deus Iacob" ad te pertinet; et si deficis in eo quod mihi sum, cape quod tibi sum.*

[50] *Tractatus in Euangelium Ioannis* II,2: *CC* XXXVI,12: *Quod nomen suum dixit famulo suo Moysi: "Ego sum qui sum"; et: "Misit me qui est." Quis ergo hoc capiet, cum uideatis omnia mortalia mutabilia...?* *Enarratio in Psalmum* CXXI,5: *CC* XL,1806: *Noli de te desperare, quia dixi: "Ego sum qui sum"...quia tu modo fluctuas, et mutabilitate rerum et uarietate mortalitatis humanae percipere non potes quod est idipsum.*

[51] *Sermo Denis II* 5: *MA* I,16: *Cogitate, si potestis, "Ego sum qui sum".... State ad Est, state ad ipsum Est. Quo itis? State, ut et vos esse possitis. Sed quando tenemus volaticam cogitationem, et ad id quod manet affigimus?*

[52] *Enarratio in Psalmum CI, Sermo II* 14: *CC* XL,1449: *Et quomodo intellegi a carne et sanguine potest: "Ego sum qui sum"?*

[53] *Enarratio in Psalmum XCIX* 5: *CC* XXXIX,1395: *Et quando comprehendo me in me? Unde ergo possum quod supra me?*

[54] *Tractatus in Euangelium Ioannis* XXIII,11: *CC* XXXVI,241: *Sed si uix hoc cepimus, uix explicare potuimus, quomodo memoria quod cepit extrinsecus, ostendat cogitationi, quanto minus capere aut explicare poterimus quomodo Pater Deus demonstrat Filio...?* There is nothing in our understanding that enables us to have access to the mystery of the Trinity through the law of similarity: *De trinitate* VIII,v,8: *CC* L,279: *Sed ex qua rerum notarum similitudine uel comparatione credamus quo etiam nondum notum deum diligamus, hoc quaeritur.*

[55] *De trinitate* V,i,2: *CC* L,206: *Nam quo intellectu homo deum capit qui ipsum intellectum suum quo eum uult capere nondum capit?*

[56] *Sermo XXI* 1: *CC* XLI,277: *Quantumcumque enim sibi humana mens exaggerauerit bonum quod deus est, minus agit et ualde infra est, et necesse est plus inueniat adeptio quam formabat cogitatio. Tractatus in Euangelium Ioannis* CX,6: *CC* XXXVI,626: *Quapropter incomprehensibilis est dilectio qua diligit Deus, neque mutabilis.*

[57] *Tractatus in Euangelium Ioannis* XXIII,9: *CC* XXXVI,238: *Nuncsi non potestis comprehendere quid sit Deus, uel hoc comprehendite quid non sit Deus; multum profeceritis, si*

non aliud quam est, de Deo senseritis. Nondum potes peruenire ad quid sit, perueni ad quid non sit. De trinitate VIII,ii,3: *CC* L,270: *Non enim paruae notitiae pars est cum de profundo isto in illam summitatem respiramus si antequam scire possimus quid sit deus, possumus iam scire quid non sit. Epistula CXX* III,13: *CSEL* XXXIV/2,715–16: *Et quidquid tibi, cum ista cogitas, corporeae similitudinis occurrerit, abnue, nega, respue, abice, fuge; non enim parua inchoatio est cogitationis dei, si ante quam possimus nosse, quid sit, incipiamus iam nosse, quid non sit.*

[58] *De ordine* II,xvi,44: *CC* XXIX,131: *Quisquis ergo ista nesciens, non dico de summo illo deo, qui scitur melius nesciendo…. De ordine* II,xviii,47: *CC* XXIX,133: *…ad dinoscendos duos mundos et ipsum parentem uniuersitatis, cuius nulla scientia est in anima nisi scire, quomodo eum nesciat.* P. Agaësse and A. Solignac, art. cit., refer to this text of Porphyry, *Aphormai* XXV, ed. B. Mommert (Leipzig, 1907), p. 11,4: "About the *nous* who is beyond everything many things are said according to our thought, but one understands him better by un-knowing than by knowing."

[59] *Sermo CXVII* iii,5: *PL* XXXVIII,663: *Magis pia est talis ignorantia, quam praesumpta scientia. Loquimur enim de Deo…. De Deo loquimur, quid mirum si non comprehendis? Si enim comprehendis, non est Deus. Sit pia confessio ignorantiae magis, quam temeraria professio scientiae. Attingere aliquantum mente Deum, magna beatitudo est; comprehendere autem, omnino impossibile.*

[60] *Sermo LII* 16: ed. P. Verbraken, *Revue Bénédictine* 74 (1964) 27: *Quid ergo dicamus, fratres, de deo? Si enim quod uis dicere, si cepisti, non est deus. Si comprehendere potuisti, aliud pro deo comprehendisti. Si quasi comprehendere potuisti, cogitatione tua te decepisti. Hoc ergo non est, si comprehendisti; si autem hoc est, non comprehendisti. Quid ergo uis loqui, quod comprehendere non potuisti?*

[61] *Enarratio in Psalmum XXVI, Sermo II* 8: *CC* XXXVIII,158: *Totum ab animo reicite, quidquid occurrerit negate; cognoscite infirmitatem cordis uestri, et quia uel occurrit quod cogitare possetis, dicite: Non est illud; non enim si illud esset, mihi iam occurrisset. Tractatus in Euangelium Ioannis* CXI,3: *CC* XXXVI,631: *Non tamen parum proficitur, si saltem quidquid tale oculo cordis occurrit, negatur, respuitur, improbatur; et lux quaedam in qua ista neganda, respuenda, improbanda cernuntur, sicut potuerit, cogitatur…quae cum penetrare mens inualida…patienter ferat quamdiu fide mundatur.*

[62] *Sermo XXI* 2: *CC* XLI,278: *Quid longe lateque uolitant fantasmata cogitationis tuae, et dicis tibi: "Putas quid est deus? Putas qualis est deus." Quicquid finxeris, non est; quicquid cogitatione comprehenderis, non est. Si enim ipse esset, cogitatione comprehendi non posset.*

[63] *Sermo CXVII* iii,5; see note 59. *Epistula CXXX* XV,28: *CSEL* XLIV,72: *Est ergo in nobis quaedam, ut ita dicam docta ignorantia, sed docta spiritu dei, qui adiuuat infirmitatem nostram.*

[64] *Sermo XLIII* 9: *CC* XLI,512: *Ergo intellege ut credas, crede ut intellegas;* cf. the whole sermon. In this process both faith and reason have to play a part: G. Madec, "Notes sur l'intelligence augustinienne."

⁶⁵ A. Vergote, *Interprétation du langage religieux* (Paris: Seuil, 1974), p. 28: "L'homme ne chercherait jamais ce qui ne lui serait pas déjà connu de quelque manière. Mais s'il le cherche, c'est qu'il ne le connaît que dans l'incertitude et dans l'errement."

⁶⁶ *Enarratio in Psalmum CXLVI* 11: *CC* XL,2130: *Ergo: Intelligentiae eius non est numerus. Conticescant humanae uoces, requiescant humanae cogitationes; ad incomprehensibilia non se extendant quasi comprehensuri, sed tamquam participaturi; participes enim erimus. Non hoc quod capimus erimus, nec totum capiemus; sed participes erimus. Sermo LII 23*: ed. P. Verbraken, *Revue Bénédictine* 74 (1964) 35: *Et tamen cum poteris, numquid sic poteris tu nosse deum quomodo se novit deus? Enarratio in Psalmum CXLIV 6: CC XL,2091: Verumtamen, quia magnitudinis eius non est finis, et eum quem non capimus, laudare debemus.... Deum tamen totum capere non possumus. De trinitate IX,xi,16: CC L,307: Quocirca inquantum deum nouimus similes sumus, sed non ad aequalitatem similes quia nec tantum eum nouimus, quantum ipse se…ita cum deum nouimus, quamuis meliores efficiamur quam eramus antequam nossemus…fitque aliqua dei similitudo illa notitia, tamen inferior est quia in inferiore natura est. Epistula CXLVII XV,36: CSEL XLIV,309: Hanc plenitudinem dei quidam in sermone apostoli sic intellexerunt, ut putarent nos hoc futuros omnino, quod deus est…auersaris istum utique et detestaris humanae mentis errorem, scio. Epistula CXLVII XXIII,53: CSEL XLIV,329–30: Beati enim mundo corde, quia ipsi deum uidebunt…cum uenerit ad eos et mansionem fecerit apud eos, quoniam sic implebuntur in omnem plenitudinem dei, non cum fuerint et ipsi plenus deus, sed cum perfecte fuerint pleni deo.*

⁶⁷ *Sermo XXI* 1: *CC* XLI,276: *Quid iubetur? Quid datur? Ut iocundemur in domino. Quis iocundabitur in ea re quam non uidet? An forte uidemus dominum?…Nunc autem "per fidem ambulamus"....*

⁶⁸ *De trinitate* V,i,1: *CC* L,206: *…quamuis et ipsa nostra cogitatio cum de deo trinitate cogitamus longe se illi de quo cogitat imparem sentiat neque ut est eum capiat sed, ut scriptum est etiam a tantis quantus Paulus apostolus hic erat, "per speculum in aenigmate uideatur."*

⁶⁹ *De trinitate* XV,ix,16: *CC* L/A,482: *Nemo itaque miretur etiam in isto uidendi modo qui concessus est huic uitae, "per speculum" scilicet "in aenigmate," laborare nos ut quomodocumque uideamus.*

⁷⁰ *Sermo CXVII* v,8: *PL* XXXVIII,665–66: *Tamen servata illius majestatis ineffabilitate, cum aliquas similitudines contra illos dederimus, putet nos aliquis per istas similitudines jam pervenisse ad id quod nec dici nec cogitari a parvulis potest (certe et si potest ab aliquibus majoribus, potest ex parte, potest in aenigmate, potest per speculum; nondum autem facie ad faciem); demus et nos aliquas similitudines adversus illos, unde illi refellantur, non unde illud capiatur. Enarratio in Psalmum XCIX 6: CC XXXIX,1396–97: Ante enim quam sentires, dicere te putabas Deum; incipis sentire, et ibi sentis dici non posse quod sentis…. Quomodo, inquis, laudabo? Modicum ipsum quod sentire possum ex parte in aenigmate per speculum, iam explicare non possum.*

⁷¹ *De diuersis quaestionibus ad Simplicianum* II, praef.: *CC* XLIV,57: *Aenigma uero tamquam per speculum, sicut idem apostolus ait: Vidimus nunc per speculum in enigmate, nec euidentissimam detegit speciem nec prorsus obtegit ueritatem.*

[72] *De trinitate* IX,i,1: *CC* L,292: "*Si quis se*," *inquit (Paulus), "putat aliquid scire, nondum scit quemadmodum scire oporteat. Quisquis autem diligit deum, hic cognitus est ab illo." Nec sic quidem dixit "cognouit illum," quae periculosa praesumptio est, sed "cognitus est ab illo."*

[73] *Enarratio in Psalmum CXXX* 14: *CC* XL,1909–10: *Quid ergo? cum uidero quae non poteram uidere, et cepero quae non poteram capere, iam securus ero? perfectus ero? Non, quamdiu hic uiuis…. Quis audet dicere quia comprehendit? Ecce Paulus non adprehendit.*

[74] *Enarratio in Psalmum CXVIII, Sermo XVIII* 3: *CC* XL,1724–25: *Proficit ergo noster intellectus ad intellegenda quae credat, et fides proficit ad credenda quae intellegat; et eadem ipsa ut magis magisque intellegantur, in ipso intellectu proficit mens.*

[75] *Tractatus in Euangelium Ioannis* LXIII,1: *CC* XXXVI,485–86: "*Quaerite Deum, et uiuet anima uestra." Quaeramus inueniendum, quaeramus inuentum. Ut inueniendus quaeratur, occultus est; ut inuentus quaeratur, immensus est…. Hic autem semper quaeramus, et fructus inuentionis non sit finis inquisitionis.*

[76] *De trinitate* XV,ii,2: *CC* L/A,461: *An et inuentus forte quaerendus est? Sic enim sunt incomprehensibilia requirenda ne se existimet nihil inuenisse qui quam sit incomprehensibile quod quaerebat potuerit inuenire. Cur ergo sic quaerit si incomprehensibile comprehendit esse quod quaerit nisi quia cessandum non est quamdiu in ipsa incomprehensibilium rerum inquisitione proficitur, et melior meliorque fit quaerens tam magnum bonum quod et inueniendum quaeritur et quaerendum inuenitur?*

[77] *Enarratio in Psalmum CIV* 3: *CC* XL,1537: *Item si fide inuentus, non adhuc esset perquirendus, non diceretur: Si enim quod non uidemus, speramus, per patientiam exspectamus.*

[78] *De trinitate* IX,i,1: *CC* L,293: *Hoc ergo sapiamus ut nouerimus tutiorem esse affectum uera quaerendi quam incognita pro cognitis praesumendi. Sic ergo quaeramus tanquam inuenturi, et sic inueniamus tanquam quaesituri.*

[79] *De trinitate* I,viii,17: *CC* L,50: *Quod enim dicit famulo suo Moysi "Ego sum qui sum"…contemplabimur cum uiuemus in aeternum…. Hoc fiet cum uenerit dominus et inluminauerit occulta tenebrarum. Epistula CXXX* XIV,27: *CSEL* XLIV,72: *Quod enim, sicuti est, cogitare non possumus, utique nescimus, sed, quicquid cogitanti occurrerit abicimus, respuimus, inprobamus, non hoc esse, quod quaerimus, novimus, quamvis illud nondum quale sit, noverimus.*

[80] *De trinitate* IV,i,1: *CC* L,160: *Ego certe sentio quam multa figmenta pariat cor humanum. Et quid est cor meum nisi cor humanum?*

[81] *De trinitate* XV,xxviii,51: *CC* L/A,535: *Sed multae sunt cogitationes meae tales quales nosti "cogitationes hominum quoniam uanae sunt." Dona mihi non eis consentire, et si quando me delectant, eas nihilominus improbare nec in eis uelut dormitando immorari…. Cum ergo peruenerimus ad te, cessabunt "multa" ista quae "dicimus et non peruenimus," et manebis unus "omnia in omnibus."*

[82] *De trinitate* VII,iv,7: *CC* L,255: *Itaque loquendi causa de ineffabilibus ut fari aliquo modo possemus quod effari nullo modo possumus, dictum est a nostris graecis "una essentia, tres substantiae."*

[83] *Confessiones* I,i,1: *CC* XXVII,1: *Sed quis te inuocat nesciens te? Aliud enim pro alio potest inuocare nesciens.* See also the first pages of this article. Even in Plotinian apophaticism the task of the intellect remains important: we cannot apply to God any metaphor; one cannot say that God is a thing like the air or a stone, that he is satan or a tyrant, a criminal or a drunkard. See J. Trouillard, "Valeur critique." A. H. Armstrong, "Negative Theology," p. 185, writes: "…resisting the temptation to what I call 'black mysticism,' the feeling that in the circumstances one might as well say anything as anything else about God." A. Vergote, *Interprétation du langage religieux*, p. 65: "La coïncidence des opposés en Dieu ne signifie pas la cohabitation des contraires. Briser à ce point le langage, c'est lui enlever toute signifiance, et c'est désarticuler les symboles et les abîmer dans le non-sens."

[84] *De trinitate* VIII,iv,6: *CC* L,275: *Amatur ergo et quod ignoratur sed tamen creditur. Nimirum autem cavendum est ne credens animus id quod non uidet fingat sibi aliquid quod non est et speret diligatque quod falsum est.*

[85] *De quantitate animae* XXXIV,78: *CSEL* LXXXIX,227: *Errantibus vero cognatis animis et laborantibus, quantum licet atque praeceptum est, opem ferendam esse sciamus ita, ut hoc ipsum, cum bene agitur, deum per nos agere intellegamus.*

[86] *De libero arbitrio* III,xii,35: *CC* XXIX,296: *Postremo, ut relinquamus contemplationem pulchritudinis rerum his, qui eam diuino munere uidere possunt, nec eos ad ineffabilia contuenda uerbis conemur adducere et tamen propter loquaces aut infirmos aut insidiosos homines tantam quaestionem brevissima complexione peragamus.* *Sermo CXVII* v,7: *PL* XXXVIII,665: *O si haberet quod diceret, diceret mihi! Deficienti ista excusatio est. Victus est veris, qui respondere non vult.* *Epistula CXX* III,13: *CSEL* XXXIV/2,716: *…et ipsae scripturae sanctae, quae magnarum rerum ante intelligentiam suadent fidem, nisi eas recte intellegas, utiles tibi esse non possunt. Omnes enim haeretici…ipsas sibi uidentur sectari, cum suos potius sectentur errores.*

[87] *De doctrina christiana* I,vi,6: *CC* XXXII,10: *Et tamen deus, cum de illo nihil digne dici possit, admisit humanae uocis obsequium, et uerbis nostris in laude sua gaudere nos uoluit.* *Enarratio in Psalmum XXXII, Sermo II* 1,8: *CC* XXXVIII,254: *Et quem decet ista iubilatio, nisi ineffabilem Deum? Ineffabilis enim est, quem fari non potes; et si eum fari non potes, et tacere non debes, quid restat nisi ut iubiles?* *De libero arbitrio* III,xiii,37: *CC* XXIX,297 (see under note 28).

[88] *Enarratio in Psalmum XCIX* 6: *CC* XXXIX,1396: *Cum autem ibi didiceris dici non posse quod sentis, tacebis, non laudabis? Ergo mutus eris in laudibus Dei, et gratiarum actionem non reddes ei qui uoluit se notum tibi facere?…Debetur honor, debetur reuerentia, debetur magna laudatio.*

[89] A. H. Armstrong, "The Escape," p. 82.

[90] Isabelle Bochet, *Saint Augustin et le désir de Dieu* (Paris: Études Augustiniennes, 1982), p. 188: "Cette voie négative n'est cependant qu'une étape; Augustin affirme la possibilité d'une appréhension positive de Dieu."

[91] R. Dragonetti, "L'image et l'irrépresentable dans l'écriture de saint Augustin," *Qu'est-ce que Dieu* (Bruxelles: Facultés universitaires Saint-Louis, 1985), pp. 393–413. See also V. Lossky, "Les éléments de 'Théologie négative' dans la pensée de saint Augustin," *Augustinus Magister* (Paris: Études Augustiniennes, 1954), I, pp. 575–81, who holds that Augustine did not consider God as the One beyond being, but the fullness of being; in his conclusion he calls Augustine's view "une sombre lueur de l'apophase mystique." About the relationship between Augustine and Gregory of Nyssa in this regard, see Maria-Barbara von Stritzky, "Beobachtungen zur Verbindung zwischen Gregor von Nyssa und Augustin," *Vigiliae Christianae* 28 (1974) 176–85.

[92] *De trinitate* XV,xxiii,44: *CC* L/A,522: *"Per" quod tamen "speculum" et "in" quo "aenigmate" qui uident sicut in hac uita uidere concessum est...illi (sunt) qui eam tamquam imaginem uident ut possint ad eum cuius imago est quomodocumque referre quod uident et per imaginem quam conspiciendo uident etiam illud uidere coniciendo quoniam nondum possunt "facie ad faciem."* De natura et origine animae IV,viii,12: *CSEL* LX,391: *...quam inconprehensibilis esset dei scientia coniciebat, quando quidem se ipsum comprehendere non ualebat?* Cf. *Enarratio in Psalmum* CXXXIV 6: *CC* XL,1942: *Tendebatis uos ut uideretis, et forte in extendenda acie mentis uestrae deficiebatis. Hoc enim ex me conicio; sic patior.*

[93] *De moribus ecclesiae catholicae et de moribus Manichaeorum* II,i,1: *PL* XXXII, 1345: *Id enim est quod esse verissime dicitur...conemur, quantum possumus, ad qualemcumque tantae rei notitiam pervenire pedetentim atque caute, non ut videntes, sed ut palpantes solent quaerere.*

[94] E. König, *Augustinus Philosophus. Christlicher Glaube und philosophisches Denken in den Frühschriften Augustins* (München: W. Fink, 1970), p. 16.

[95] E. Feldmann, "Et inde rediens," pp. 883–84.

[96] E. Jüngel, *Gott als Geheimnis der Welt.* 2nd ed. (Tübingen: Mohr, 1977), pp. 7–8.

[97] R. Lorenz, "Gnade und Erkenntnis bei Augustinus," *Zum Augustin-Gespräch der Gegenwart*, ed. C. Andresen (Darmstadt: Wissenschaftliche Buchgesellschaft, 1981), II, pp. 43–125. Lorenz rejects the opinion of Barbara Aland, "Cogitare Deum in den Confessiones," in *Pietas.* Festschrift B. Kötting (Münster, Westfalen: Aschendorff, 1980), pp. 93–104, who holds that there is a radical distinction in Augustine between grace and nature and that knowledge of God is due to grace only.

[98] The difference between Augustine and the Neoplatonists is well described by J. Trouillard, "Théologie négative": According to Augustine, God is not wise in the way human beings are wise; He is the fullness of wisdom, an incomprehensible, dazzling light. According to a Neoplatonist, God is beyond wisdom; darkness, negation and emptiness characterize all our thinking of God. I admit that it is not easy to grasp the view of Plato. A. J. Festugière states, "Nous croyons avoir prouvé qu'il existe chez Platon une doctrine de la connaissance du Premier Principe ineffable" and "Dieu n'est pas connaissable positivement, on ne peut dire que ce qu'il n'est pas" ("La transcendance de l'Un," pp. 92 and 79). The later Neoplatonists are more radical than Plato; this is at least the opinion of P. Hadot who quotes the following text of Porphyry: "Et ainsi on ne pourra ni tomber dans le vide, ni oser non plus Lui attribuer quelque chose, mais on ne pourra que demeurer dans une com-

préhension non compréhensive et dans une conception qui ne conçoit rien" (*Porphyre et Victorinus* II [Paris: Études Augustiniennes, 1968], pp. 68–71).

⁹⁹ *De trinitate* XV,xxviii,51: *CC* L/A, 534: *Libera me, deus meus, a multiloquio quod patior intus in anima mea misera in conspectu tuo.* See also R. Dragonetti, "L'image et l'irrépresentable," p. 412.

Augustine on Person: Divine and Human

Mary T. Clark, R.S.C.J.

In English we have a formal noun to refer to an individual human being who is unique in the sense of being irreplaceable by another human being. That noun is "person." The concept it expresses is complex. By conceptual analysis one may try to arrive at what it means to be called a person. Since words stand for concepts, the history of a word can often trace the gradual enrichment of a concept. Since we are heirs to Greco-Roman culture, it may prove useful to review the history of the Greek and Latin formal nouns which came to be used to denote human individuals and which are now translated into English as "person," and useful to accent their origin and their evolving reference within those cultures.

Since individual human beings have been present in all cultures and are readily distinguishable, at least in appearance, from non-human beings, it is quite likely that there were some words used in every culture which expressed the difference. Most languages made use of what we have come to call personal pronouns: I-you-he-she instead of the "it" standing for a non-human being. Some languages used nouns already being used to denote a part of a human being or human-nature-itself to signify also an individual human being. This is surely the case in early Greek literature. It is erroneous, therefore, to claim that antiquity had no notion of personhood, a notion which came to light, it is said, with Christianity and was delivered to the modern world by medieval thinkers, of whom Boethius was the first representative.

Several points have to be made to clarify the situation. First of all, the absence in other cultures of a word that we are familiar with to refer to the special importance or value of human beings does not mean an absence of any notion of their uniqueness. A pre-philosophical awareness of the uniqueness of the human being manifests itself in Greek drama and poetry, in Herodotus and Plutarch.[1] But it is also true that identifying a concept as such is distinct from using it implicitly. Gilson has claimed that this identification did not occur before Boethius.[2] He admits, however, that because "they never denied the reality of the individual, the Greeks opened the way for the Christian recognition of the eminent worth of the person; not only did they not prevent it …they did a great deal to forward its success."[3]

I want to argue that ancient philosophers not only did a great deal to ensure the future recognition of the value of personhood but they also recognized this value. I shall give evidence for the philosophical distinction of person from nature by a Stoic thinker in the second century B.C., by the non-Christian thinker, Plotinus, in the third century A.D., and by Augustine in the fourth century—all of them prior to Boethius.

II

There is no general agreement as to the precise history of the Greek word πρόσωπον and the Latin word *persona* from which our English word "person" derives. One notable authority claims that the Latins derived *persona* from πρόσωπον.[4] Maurice Nédoncelle disputes this and reports that *persona* was thought to have derived from the Etruscan *phersu* which meant "masked" and appeared on a monument depicting a ritual scene where the dancer is masked—in 550 B.C.[5] Nédoncelle suggests that this does not explain the presence of the suffix "ona" nor the femininity of the word *persona*. He thinks that *persona* is a transcription of the name of a goddess—Phersipnai, Persephone, and finally appearing at Corfinum as Persepona. On the feast of this goddess Persepona, people used masks, and so the name of the goddess came to signify mask. The change from proper names to common names was usual in Rome, as, for example, "calepin" from the name, Calepino, *vulcanus*, to signify fire.

Therefore *persona* originates either from the proper name Persepona or from an archaic adjective relative to Phersu. Although the word *persona* originated with the Etruscan rites, it was laicized around 364 B.C. to become a technical theatre term. The ritual masks were then no longer called *personae* but *oscillae, larvae, maniae*. *Persona* was then detached from *Persepona* or *Phersu*.

Although the Greeks were the first to relate their formal noun πρόσωπον to certain interior characteristics of human beings, characteristics signifying dignity and value, the Romans were the first to universalize their equivalent formal noun, *persona*, by referring it to every individual human being (except slaves). And so, just before the Christian era, *persona* was already expressing the idea of human individuality, and more frequently than was πρόσωπον.

III

Although it can be shown that the classical philosophers implicitly used a notion of person especially in their ethical thought, is there any evidence that ancient philosophers identified the concept as such? When a concept is identified as such, it tends to be given a new name. This was done in the second century B.C. by Panaetius in his work *On Duties*, where he must have used the word πρόσωπον which Cicero quoted and translated by *persona*. This word, *persona*, is used by Cicero, relying on Panaetius, a Greek Stoic, to distinguish a human individual from human nature and to denote the individual's spiritual uniqueness. In his *De officiis* I,xxx,107 Cicero says:

> We must realize that we are invested by Nature with two characters, as it were: One of these is universal arising from the fact that we are all alike endowed with reason and with that superiority which lifts us above the brute. From this fact all morality is derived and upon it depends the rational method of ascertaining our duty. The other character is the one that is assigned to individuals in particular.[6]

He goes on to say that just as there are great differences in the matter of physical endowment, diversities of character are still greater. Words which had been used to refer to the individual human being in Greek and Latin—σῶμα (this body), ψυχή (this soul), ἄνθρωπος (this man)—*corpus, anima, homo, caput*—have been replaced by πρόσωπον and *persona*.

Without using the Greek term, πρόσωπον, Plotinus dealt explicitly with the spiritual differences between human individuals. Unlike his predecessors, he searched for the metaphysical foundation of such differences. This represents an important shift in the evolution of the notion of person; it originates an attempt at conceptual analysis through philosophical reflection on individual realities. His explanation entails a metaphysics of the Transcendent. Among the Plotinian triad of the One, the Νοῦς, and All-Soul the Platonic forms were placed in the Νοῦς. For Plato, of course, all Forms were universal. Plotinus taught that the archetype of every individual human being was in the Νοῦς.

> No, there cannot be the same forming principle for different individuals, and one man will not serve as model for several

men differing from each other not only by reason of their
matter but with a vast number of special differences of form.
Men are not related to their form as portraits of Socrates are
to their original, but their different structures must result
from different forming principles.[7]

The human individual is a knower and a lover of the intelligible but not
all do this in the same way, and so each must participate in an individual form.
Although Plotinus does not use the word πρόσωπον he notes the difference
between universality and uniqueness in a human soul. There is a formal difference between one human individual and another. The fact that there is a
Form for each individual human being indicates its value and irreplaceability.
To transcend oneself by identifying with this higher self which is an intelligence open to truth is an opportunity offered only to human individuals for
eventual union with the One. The ascent to the One occurs through ἔρως for
the Absolute Good, an ἔρως which characterizes human reality but which must
be consented to by the human individual (or person).[8] The person is affirmed
here as not only intellectual but as affective and free.[9]

Of all the ancient philosophers Plotinus had the most to say about human individuality or personhood. He never ignored the contributions to the
human personality made by heredity and environment but he would consider
this to be the empirical personality. Socrates as a person in his metaphysical
reality "would only begin to appear and be fully operative when he began to
make something of what his country and city and period and parents and
bodily nature had given him, to use his circumstances as material for free and
responsible moral decisions and to find in them the way back to self-realiza-
tion and self-transcendence."[10]

Plotinus, without ever using the term πρόσωπον (his substitute for that
is ψυχή or this soul) has retained aspects of the person to which Plato, Aristotle and the Stoics already pointed and has deeply enriched the notion through
relating the individual human ψυχή to the Transcendent as the source of its
existence and of the love which draws it to return to its homeland by becoming
aware of its dignity as related to the One. Plotinus' notion of the human ψυχή
explicitly includes moral responsibility by reason of its capacity for true
thought and free decision for arriving at a personal union with its Transcendent Source. In this union the human soul becomes with the three Divine
Hypostases a Providence for all reality. This early attempt to analyze the

metaphysics of personhood shows that the latter does not entail subjectivism in the pejorative sense of individualism.

IV

As Augustine sought to give to the educated pagans of his day some clue as to the non-absurdity of the doctrine that Christ was both God and man, he declared in Letter 138.1 that he would use the authorities the pagans would find acceptable. These authorities were Porphyry and Plotinus. He also used the pedagogical device of beginning with experience, the human experience of being body and soul. He would have to make sense of this human experience before discussing the Incarnation of Christ. The Neoplatonic theory of human reality was the prevailing one in the fourth century, A.D.

Plotinus had rejected the Stoic interpretation of human reality as material, as well as the matter-form theory of Aristotle. In welcoming the Platonic view of soul and body as two substances, Plotinus had given an original version of their union. He said:

> ...none of the ways of a thing's being in anything which are currently spoken of fits the relationship of the soul to the body, but it is also said that the soul is in the body as the steersman is in the ship; this is a good comparison as far as the soul's ability to be separate from the body goes, but would not supply very satisfactorily the manner of its presence, which is what we ourselves are investigating.[11]

After mentioning all the insufficiencies of the Platonic metaphor to explain the union of body and soul, Plotinus asks if we may say that the soul is present to the body as fire [or light] is present to air? For light

> ...like soul...is present throughout the whole and mixed with none of it, and stays still itself while the air flows past; and when the air goes outside the space where the light is, it departs without retaining anything of it, but while it is under the light, it is illuminated, so that one can rightly say here too that the air is in the light rather than the light in the air.[12]

Then in typical fashion Plotinus puts this under the authority of Plato by saying:

> That is why Plato (Tim 36D9–E3) rightly does not put the soul in the body when he is speaking of the universe, but the body in the soul, and says also that there is a part of the soul in which body is and part in which there is no body, clearly the powers of the soul of which the body has no need. And the same principle clearly applies to the other souls.[13]

This explanation, whether he learned of it directly from Plotinus or through Porphyry, gave Augustine the wherewithal to maintain that the coming together of the divine and human natures did not, like ordinary mixtures, lead to the diminishment of either nature. It was a union without confusion. The simplicity of the divine nature would mean that it could lose nothing of its reality in being joined to human nature.[14] Human nature would thus remain human but become unusually enriched in dignity through the divine Incarnation of Christ.

Plotinus seems to have recognized a personal unity in the human being without using the word πρόσωπον, as can be seen from his remarks immediately after describing the union of body and soul in the Fourth Ennead where he says that αὐτός (i.e. he) will be punished by reincarnation into a lower body as a result of certain actions on earth. Responsibility is thus attributed to this human reality which Plotinus refers to as αὐτός.

Although Augustine would not have met the term *persona* in the Latin translation of the Neoplatonic texts he read, it is highly unlikely that he had not read Tertullian's work *Against Praxeas* XXVII,1 where he speaks of *una persona*.[15] Augustine's understanding of what the term *persona* signified shows a certain evolution. We first find him using this term in *De agone christiano* where it signifies "the revealing form of a thing."[16] Around A.D. 412 he uses the word *persona* to signify the possessor of natures, distinct from nature but not separated from nature. This distinction is explicitly made in the *De trinitate*, probably written between A.D. 399 and 419. Nature is something which is had in common; person, on the other hand, is *aliquid singulare atque individuum*.[17]

We have not encountered such a philosophically explicit distinction of person from nature since Cicero's report of the statements of Panaetius. One wonders whether Augustine, who knew his Cicero so well, was here in conscious dependence upon him. We find this distinction being used in Augustine's Letter 137:

> For as the soul makes use of the body in a single person to
> form a man, so God makes use of man in a single Person to
> form Christ. In the former person there is a mingling of soul
> and body; in the latter Person there is a mingling of God and
> man; but the hearer must abstract from the property of mate-
> rial substance by which two liquids are usually so mingled
> that neither retains its special character although among such
> substances, light mingled with air remains unchanged.
> Therefore the person of man is a mingling of soul and body,
> but the Person of Christ is a mingling of God and man, for,
> when the Word of God is joined to a soul which has a body, it
> takes on both the soul and body at once. The one process
> happens daily in order to beget men; the other happened
> once to set man free.[18]

This echo of Plotinus is strongly articulated in Sermon 186 where Augustine sums up his Incarnation-theory: "*Idem Deus qui homo, et qui Deus idem, Homo: non confusione naturae, sed unitate personae.*"[19]

The personal union of God and man in Christ was to be defined at Chalcedon in like manner and called the hypostatic union. The union gives power to act divinely and humanly. Through his reflection on the Incarnation of Christ Augustine came to see every human person as a close union of body and soul, able to act materially and spiritually. He admitted this union to be natural but confessed that he knew no adequate philosophical explanation of it. Indeed, he complained:

> But there are some who request an explanation of how God
> is joined to man so as to become the single person of Christ
> as if they themselves could explain something that happens
> every day, namely, how the soul is joined to the body so as to
> form the single person of a man.[20]

In trying to understand the Incarnation of God Augustine's notion of person evolved from meaning the revealing form of a thing to meaning a unified whole, including nature, but accenting the responsible agent of all natural operations. Under the influence of Christology the word "person" came to be applied to all human beings, signifying them as responsible centers of their natural activities.

V

From the Neoplatonists Augustine received not only a way to conceive the union of the divine and human natures of Christ but also certain insights which enabled him to experience his own human personhood.

The first of these was the insight into human interiority where contact with Transcendence becomes possible. God was both within and beyond.[21] For the Neoplatonists it sufficed to purify the eye of the mind to become aware of one's affinity with the divine and so enter into union. Augustine, as he recounts in *Confessions*, Book VII, tried to act out this conviction but fell back into his outward way of life, far removed from divinity. Courcelle believes that this experience of failure stimulated Augustine to compare the Johannine Prologue with the Platonic books just read. In that Prologue he discovered that the Logos had entered history, had become embodied. He then searched the epistles of Paul where he found expressed the human need for God's healing. Paul taught Augustine the creaturely aspect of the human person, its non-affinity with God. Not by finding oneself does one find God, but by transcending oneself. Not even self-transcendence, however, enables one to reach the transcendent God. The very mind which the Platonists used as the power to unite with the One was neither reliable nor powerful in the eyes of Paul. The body is not sinful; the mind of man corrupts the body. The mind needs to be liberated from slavery to the flesh and for this a Mediator-Savior is needed. Not only is creation a divine initiative, initiating existence, but a conversion—from unlikeness to likeness to God. Some have said that Augustine, unlike the other Fathers, did not distinguish between image and likeness. Can this be maintained when one remembers how he described in Book VII his failure to ascend to God for any satisfying union because he was far from God in the region of unlikeness? And in the *De trinitate*, he wrote that the human image of God will only be perfect, that is, obtain a perfect likeness, in the beatific vision.[22] The contemplation of God, he came to realize, resulted from the will's surrender in love for God; and such *caritas* is God's own gift. Therefore, the Trinitarian analogy of memory-knowledge-will represents the natural image of the Trinity, but this image is a capacity for union with God. The final analogy of remembering God, understanding God, and loving God is the actualization of this capacity, and is achieved by the cooperation of created nature and grace as it was when Adam and Eve were created to the image and likeness of God.

It is precisely in this image-doctrine that Augustine makes his original contribution to the notion of human personhood, thereby enriching it. By reflection upon creation, Augustine came to appreciate the religiousness of the human person, that is, the necessary and intimate relation between the creature and the Creator. As a creature of God, the human person therefore is himself or herself, that is, becomes truly self-possessive only insofar as the relation to God becomes a conscious one. By reflection upon the incarnation and resurrection of Christ, he grew to appreciate the intimate relation of the body to the soul which was made in the image of God. In listening to Ambrose's sermons on the *Hexameron* he learned that entrance into Trinitarian life which enables the human being to be a true image comes through Christ. Christ is the exemplar of a perfect image of the Father and He is the way to personal perfection. This perfection of reflecting God will come not merely through knowledge but through the will's choices.[23] If the initiative of the grace of *caritas* which increases the human image's likeness to God is from God, there is nevertheless the human reality of freedom which consents to grace and in prayer asks for more.

The insight into interiority as essential to human personhood was a valuable gift from Plotinus. But Augustine did not leave it as he found it. He viewed it not as a proof of affinity to God but as corroboration of the revelation that the human being was made to the image of God. The very notion of image entails a relationship of origin. In choosing image as the most fundamental aspect of human persons, Augustine accented their relationship to the Trinitarian God as fundamentally a call to a growing union with the divine Persons by a continual growth in the relationship of love. His preferred image and likeness of God within the soul was the action of remembering, understanding, loving God.

This maintains the distinction between God and the soul (not strongly accented by Plotinus) and ratifies in the psychological order the person's ontological relationship to God.

Faith is the condition for the actualization of the image to a more perfect likeness to the Trinity through *caritas*. Faith precedes the understanding that being an image gives a capacity for union with God. This union which is achieved through likeness requires an education in love.

The doctrine of illumination and the doctrine of the image are complementary aspects of "interiority" as God's presence within. As image of God, the soul can be illuminated.[24]

Augustinian interiority is constituted of memory, understanding, and will which are subsumed under *ratio sapientiae* and *ratio scientiae*. The latter is the link between knowledge of the ideas and knowledge of the sensible world. This inferior reason exercises the role of the will. It has a twofold function: it orders sensible knowledge and initiates action—supposedly in relation to the *ratio* of wisdom.

As for the memory, it maintains interior unity and constitutes the logical structure of the mind to allow for a knowledge of first principles and the most fundamental notions. It also contains an implicit self-knowledge. All of the, so-to-speak, parts of the soul mentioned by Augustine are considered by him to be merely aspects, not parts, not faculties. *Intellectus, ratio, mens, memoria, voluntas, sensus, imaginatio, consilium*—all designate only functions of the one human soul.[25] This is specified when he speaks of the higher reason which contemplates and of the lower reason which directs action:

> And therefore a certain aspect of our reason, not separated so as to sever unity, but diverted, as it were, so as to help fellowship, is set aside for the performing of its own proper work...so, the one nature of the mind embraces our intellect and action,...or our reason and reasonable appetite....[26]

He goes on to insist: "We are therefore discussing only a single thing when we discuss the human mind; nor do we double it into these two things that I have mentioned, except in regard to its functions."[27]

Only in the whole mind to which belongs the contemplation of eternal realities is there a trinity that is also an image of God. Guided by St. Paul in Colossians 3:9–10, Augustine asserts that no one can doubt that man has been made to the image of him who created him, not according to the body, nor according to any part of the mind, but according to the rational mind where the knowledge of God can reside.

Since this knowledge is actualized through baptism and the acceptance of God's self-communication, the image of God is perfected not only in men but also in women.

> Who is it then that would exclude women from this fellow-
> ship, since they are with us co-heirs of grace, and since the
> same Apostle says in another place: "For you are all children
> of God through faith in Christ Jesus. For whoever have been
> baptized in Christ have put on Christ. There is neither Jew
> nor Greek, there is neither slave nor free, there is neither
> male nor female. For you are all one in Christ Jesus."[28]

St. Paul therefore has to be taken out of context if he is used to witness
against the spiritual equality of men and women. For, indeed, all persons are
created to the image of God. Who is the Image? Only Christ is the natural
image of the Father. But by baptism, all persons begin their assimilation to
Christ the perfect image.

In being perfected as an image of God one needs to integrate *sapientia*
and *scientia* in the knowledge of God. Only then will the mind as a whole
become an image-likeness of God.

> It is obvious that when we live according to God, our mind,
> intent on his invisible things, must be formed continuously by
> his eternity, truth, and love; yet a part of our reasonable at-
> tention, that is, an aspect of this same mind must be directed
> to the use of changeable and corporeal things, without which
> this life does not continue, not in order that we may be con-
> formed to this world by placing our final end in such goods
> and in directing our desire for happiness towards them, but
> that whatever we do in the use of temporal things under the
> guidance of reason, we do it with our gaze fixed on the eter-
> nal realities which we are to obtain, passing quickly by the
> former, but clinging to the latter.[29]

And so no classification of men as *mens* and women as *ratio* can eliminate the
fact that women as well as men can contemplate eternal reasons and that men
as well as women can lose the vision of eternal realities and thereby deform
themselves as images of God. This happened with both Adam and Eve.

Indeed, Augustine is fond of saying that there is a perverse way of trying
to become like God—that of power-grabbing.

> For the true honor of man is to be the image and likeness of
> God which is preserved only in relation to him by whom it is
> impressed. Hence he clings to God so much the more, the
> less he loves what is his own. But through the desire of prov-
> ing his own power, man by his own will falls down into him-
> self, as into a sort of center. Since he therefore wishes to be
> like God under no one, as a punishment he is also driven
> from the center, which he himself is, into the depths, that is,
> into those things wherein the beasts delight; and thus, since
> the likeness to God is his honor, the likeness to the beasts is
> his dishonor.[30]

As we begin to examine Augustine's use of the word "person" in his *De
trinitate*, it is well to remember his hesitations in saying anything at all about
God. He is acutely aware that whatever we say or think about God, the divine
reality is greater. He affirmed often that the divine reality cannot be put into
language as it is understood in our thought and it cannot be understood in our
thought as it really is.[31] While not a theological agnostic, he never forgot that
God is ineffable. He is a cataphatic theologian with respect to the mysterious
Trinity only because Arianism and Sabellianism required the use of basic ontological language. He wrote:

> But just as the Arians accuse us of being Sabellians although
> we do not say that the Father, Son and Holy Spirit are one
> and the same, as the Sabellians say, but we say that there is
> one and the same nature of Father, and of Son, and of Holy
> Spirit, as the Catholics say.... But just as the Arians, while
> they reject the Sabellians, fall into something worse, because
> they have not dared to discern persons of the Trinity, but
> natures....[32]

Augustine in his *De trinitate* certainly distinguished person from nature as the
text proves. But does the notion of person in the trinitarian theology of Augustine play the role "that one too often imagines"? "Augustine," says Pierre
Hadot, "who bases the distinction between Father, Son, and Holy Spirit on
their mutual relations, sees no connection between 'person' and 'relation.'"[33]
To support his position, Hadot quotes from *De trinitate*:

...in God to be is not one thing, and to be a person another thing, but it is wholly and entirely one and the same.... For he is called a person in respect to Himself, not in relation to the Son or to the Holy Spirit, just as he is called in respect to himself, God, great, good, just, and other like terms.[34]

Compare this with a quotation from the *City of God*:

And this Trinity is one God, and nonetheless simple because a Trinity. For we do not say that the nature of the good is simple, because the Father alone possesses it, or the Son alone, or the Holy Spirit alone; nor do we say, with the Sabellian heretics, that it is only nominally a Trinity, and has no real distinction of persons; but we say it is simple because it is what it has, with the exception of the relation of the persons to one another.[35]

Do these two passages give evidence of a change of mind, or was Augustine trying to say in the first instance that "person" used of Father, Son, and Holy Spirit, although it pertains to what is distinctive, namely, relationship, yet as a true hypostasis, it includes the shared consciousness and will belonging to the divine substance? In other words, to refer to persons is to speak of primary substance in the Aristotelian sense, i.e., concrete subjects; but the divine persons share the one same primary substance. And so Augustine says: "When we speak of the person of the Father, we speak of the substance of the Father."[36] Surely one would not want to exclude the substance of divinity from the Father's personhood. Augustine never says three substances or essences, yet he is willing to say three persons. Thus he continues: "And this Trinity, although having the property and subsistence of singular persons, nevertheless on account of its individual and inseparable essence or nature of eternity, of truth, of goodness, there are not three Gods but one God."[37]

In the light of all this, he formulated a rule concerning God-language: "whatever is spoken of God in respect to Himself and of each single person is to be predicated in the singular of each divine person and not in the plural."[38] He does not really want to say "three persons," because there is no common word to indicate the three: each relationship is different.

In Book VII of the *De trinitate* Augustine expresses his opinion that both the word *persona* and the word ὑπόστασις are inappropriate for referring to

Father, Son, and Holy Spirit. In the early Christian period the word *persona* was used by Tertullian to distinguish the speakers in the Bible: "There is the one who speaks, the Spirit; there is the Father to whom he speaks; there is the Son, of whom he speaks."[39] The word *persona* is used here much as the Latin grammarians used it, i.e., in the first, second, and third persons of a verb. Tertullian, it is said, was influenced by Hippolytus who used the word πρόσωπον when he interpreted the plural form in the Scriptural statement: "The Father and I are one" as implying two persons. The word ὑπόστασις was used by Origen of the Son and the Holy Spirit to assert against theological monarchians, who downplayed them, that they really existed. But ὑπόστασις was not sufficiently distinguished from οὐσία which the Latins translated as *substantia*. Hence the one *substantia* of the Latin could too easily be interpreted as one ὑπόστασις. Thus the word ὑπόστασις could result in modalism or Sabellianism. But the word *persona* as used of human beings already had, as we have noted, a conceptual content which could move the Christian doctrine of God in the direction of tritheism if it were not given a restricted theological meaning. Augustine warned his readers not to think of the ordinary meaning of person as a center of individual consciousness and will under pain of being misled concerning God's reality. We use the word "person," said Augustine, simply to have a word whereby to answer, "Three what?" He has not, therefore, committed the fault attributed by Karl Rahner to most theologians of the Trinity, namely, using a philosophical analysis of the human person with its emphasis upon individually distinct consciousness and will when referring to the three divine persons.

"When it is asked what the three or who the three are," said Augustine, "we seek to find a generic or a specific name which may include the three together. But we come across none, because the supereminent excellence of the divinity transcends all the limits of our accustomed manner of speaking."[40] He reluctantly uses the term "persons" while admitting that "three persons are spoken of—not to tell something but lest one be silent."[41] Is it really correct to use a plural form like "persons" to refer to a divine Three having one same divine substance and each having its own incommunicable property?

> What remains then but to admit that these words were born out of necessity, since there was need of a thorough explanation of the Trinity against the snares and errors of the heretics? And when human feebleness sought to express in words the doctrine about the Lord God its Creator, to which it held

fast according to its capacity, in the inner recesses of the mind, whether by its pious faith or by any reflections of its own, it feared to say three essences lest a diversity of any kind should be understood in that highest equality. But on the other hand it could not say that they were not three somethings since, by denying this, Sabellius fell into heresy....

When asked to explain what these three were, the answer given was substances or persons...so that not only would the unity be understood there, because they were called one essence, but the Trinity also, because they were called three substances or persons.[42]

With Augustine we have to acknowledge that the term "person" as it is applied to each member of the Trinity is emptied of some of the content belonging to the term as applied to human beings. But is this so different from the term "Father" and the term "Son"? The terms "Father" and "Son" have to be emptied of some of the content they have when applied to human beings. The generation of the divine Son from the divine Father is unlike the transmission of life among human beings. And yet the relation of the divine Father to the divine Son warrants the use of the word "generation." We have here analogical terms. Likewise, the distinctness of Father, Son, and Holy Spirit acting out of knowledge and love warrants the use of the term "person" in a way that bears an analogy to its use with reference to human beings.

At the time of Augustine the conceptual analysis of the term "person" had not brought forth the many constituents of that term as it is used today by contemporary philosophers. In his day it was generally applicable to a singular and individual intellectual being, as shown in his texts. He stated that "person" is not a relative term and hence he found it inappropriate for referring to the Divine Three who although they subsisted relationally are consubstantial. The theological use of the term person, however, to refer to Father, Son, and Spirit who subsisted relationally contributed a new element to the concept person, that of relationality, one that has been accented in the contemporary analysis of personhood. It seems to be a case of its having become explicit through Trinitarian theology, although it was implicit in many of the discussions on friendship among the ancients.

VII

Does it seem reasonable that Augustine who emphasized the fact that human beings are created to the image of the Trinity and likewise emphasized that to be Trinity is to be in relation would have passed over the responsibility of "relating" as intrinsic to human persons as images of God?

A. C. Lloyd recognizes that Augustine's concept of a divine person as a relational concept implies that for a human being to be a person is for him to stand in certain relations.[43] He believes that this is philosophically promising because it makes a person logically dependent for existence as a person on others or at least on one other. "Only then," says Lloyd, "can social roles, or functions which are relational because they imply interaction, be recognized as essential attributes." But, concludes Lloyd, Augustine "did not accept the opportunity of making an analogy between the interior relationships of the Trinity and *exterior* or mutual relationships of human persons. The only object to which these persons have a necessary relation is God himself, who is of course to be found within us. Consequently the love, the understanding, the knowledge that chiefly interest Augustine are each man's self-love, self-understanding, and self-knowledge."[44]

In this same vein, Cardinal Ratzinger has recently asserted that Augustine failed to pass on the relationality aspects of the Trinity to human persons. Augustine, he said, "projected the divine persons into the interior life of the human person and affirmed that intra-psychic processes correspond to these persons. The person as a whole, by contrast, corresponds to the divine substance. As a result," said he, "the trinitarian concept of person was no longer transferred to the human person in all its immediate impact."[45]

Both critics fail to see that the interior faculties chosen as analogies by Augustine are not merely mutually related but are the source for all human relating. Moreover, Augustine explicitly exhorted human persons to image the relational character of God by individually relating by love to the Trinity and to one another. Consider the passage in *De trinitate* where he says that through the Holy Spirit, Father and Son are joined together and

> through him the begotten is loved by the begetter, and in turn loves him who begot him; in him they preserve the unity of Spirit through the bond of peace. And we are commanded by grace to imitate this unity, *both in our relations with God as well as among ourselves.* On these two commandments de-

pend the whole Law and the Prophets. Thus the Three are
the One, the only, the great, the wise, the holy, and the blessed God. But we are blessed by Him, through Him, and in
Him because by his Gift we are one among ourselves.[46]

Conclusion

In focusing upon the human being as an image of God Augustine highlighted the value of every person.

But it is above all in his *Confessions* that one finds the earliest exploration of that unique subjectivity which has become central to the modern concept of person. The Greeks had spoken of the human being in the third person. Augustine wrote an autobiography. He used the "I." "Who am I and
what am I?" said he in *Confessions* IX,i,1, thereby distinguishing between person and nature. Socrates had advised the anthropological turn: Augustine
took the turn.

And men go abroad, to wonder at the heights of the moun-
tains, the huge waves of the sea, the broad streams of rivers,
the vastness of the ocean, the turnings of the stars—and they
do not notice themselves.[47]

Augustine took notice and declared: "I became for myself a great question."[48]
He sought the answer within, in the historicity of his memory. He recalls the
historical facts of his past, his present grasp of their meaning, that is to say, the
body-mind aspect of personhood, and the presence of the Transcendent God
as source of judgment and conversion. His subjectivity did not merely provide
an encounter of self with self but brought an encounter with God. As Josef
Pieper has said, the spirit has "the power and capacity to relate itself to the
totality of being....the greater the power of establishing relations, the greater
the degree of inwardness."[49]

If the concept of "person" denotes a thinking, loving, free being, the
concept can refer to beings other than human. In that case the term "person"
is an analogical term. As a term that in our experience distinguishes human
individuals from non-human ones, it is a value-term. It refers to those aspects
of ourselves which enable us and require us to take responsibility for our actions. There is something ethically normative in possessing the psychological

capacities of knowing and willing. Responsibility involves actual decisions by a unique agent and such responsibility cannot be shared.

The use of the word person for a human being, rather than being a value-judgment in the sense of an attribution of value to human beings, is a value-recognition, a recognition that grew gradually through the centuries beginning with the insight of the classical Greek philosophers and the patristic writers. Civilization rises or falls with this recognition of the value of persons as responsible agents who are therefore the locus of rights. As Augustine had emphasized the interiority of human personhood, so as a priest he never let go of the interior divine dimension of the Church. For him life in the Church was a certain reproduction of the missions of the Son and of the Spirit and of their union with the Father. By his faith in the mystery of the kenosis of Christ (as described in Philippians 2:6 and in the Passion) he found the model for the priestly life of humility and charity and for his understanding of the high vocation of all persons as created to the image and likeness of the Trinity to show forth the love that unites Father, Son and Spirit, a love that is shared with human persons through creation and salvation.

Notes

[1] C. J. De Vogel, "The Concept of Personality in Greek and Christian Thought," *Studies in Philosophy and the History of Philosophy*, ed. J. K. Ryan (Washington, D.C.: Catholic University of America Press, 1963).

[2] E. Gilson, *Spirit of Medieval Philosophy* (New York: Scribners, 1940), pp. 189–208, especially p. 204.

[3] E. Gilson, *Spirit of Medieval Philosophy*, p. 189.

[4] S. Schlossmann, *Persona und Πρόσωπον im Recht und im christlichen Dogma* (Kiel and Leipzig: Lipsius and Tischer, 1906).

[5] M. Nédoncelle, "Prosopon et persona dans l'antiquité classique," *Revue des sciences religieuses* XXVIII (1948) 277–99.

[6] M. T. Cicero, *De Officiis* I,xxx,107 (London: William Heinemann, 1928), p. 108: *intellegendum etiam est duabus quasi nos a natura indutos esse personis; quarum una communis est ex eo, quod omnes participes sumus rationis praestantiaeque eius, qua antecellimus bestiis, a qua omne honestum decorumque trahitur, et ex qua ratio inveniendi officii exquiritur, altera autem, quae proprie singulis est tributa.*

[7] Plotinus, *Ennead* V,vii,1,19–23, tr. A. H. Armstrong (Cambridge, MA: Harvard University Press, 1984), V,224: ἢ τῶν διαφόρων οὐκ ἔστιν εἶναι τὸν αὐτὸν λόγον, οὐδὲ ἀρκεῖ ἄνθρωπος πρὸς παράδειγμα τῶν τινῶν ἀνθρώπων διαφερόντων ἀλλήλων οὐ τῇ

ὕλη μόνον, ἀλλὰ καὶ ἰδικαῖς διαφοραῖς μυρίαις· οὐ γὰρ ὡς αἱ εἰκόνες Σωκράτους πρὸς τὸ ἀρχέτυπον, ἀλλὰ δεῖ τὴν διάφορον ποίησιν ἐκ διαφόρων λόγων.

[8] Plotinus, *Ennead* VI,vii,35.

[9] Plotinus, *Ennead* I,iv,6, 11; III,ii,10; V,v,12; VI,iv,14; VI,ix,4.

[10] A. H. Armstrong, "Form, Individual and Person in Plotinus," *Dionysius* I (1977) 49–69.

[11] Plotinus, *Ennead* IV,iii,21,4–9; tr. Armstrong IV,100: ἐπεὶ τοίνυν τῶν νῦν λεγομένων τρόπων τοῦ ἕν τινι οὐδεὶς φαίνεται ἐπὶ τῆς ψυχῆς πρὸς τὸ σῶμα ἁρμόττων, λέγεται δὲ οὕτως ἐν τῷ σώματι εἶναι ἡ ψυχή, ὡς ὁ κυβερνήτης ἐν τῇ νηΐ, πρὸς μὲν τὸ χωριστὴν δύνασθαι εἶναι τὴν ψυχὴν καλῶς εἴρηται, τὸν μέντοι τρόπον, ὡς νῦν ἡμεῖς ζητοῦμεν, οὐκ ἂν πάνυ παραστήσειεν.

[12] Plotinus, *Ennead* IV,iii,22,1–8; tr. Armstrong IV,102: Ἆρ' οὖν οὕτω φατέον, ὅταν ψυχὴ σώματι παρῇ, παρεῖναι αὐτὴν ὡς τὸ πῦρ πάρεστι τῷ ἀέρι; καὶ γὰρ αὖ καὶ τοῦτο παρὸν οὐ πάρεστι καὶ δι' ὅλου παρὸν οὐδενὶ μίγνυται καὶ ἕστηκε μὲν αὐτό, τὸ δὲ παραρρεῖ· καὶ ὅταν ἔξω γένηται τοῦ ἐν ᾧ τὸ φῶς, ἀπῆλθεν οὐδὲν ἔχων, ἕως δέ ἐστιν ὑπὸ τὸ φῶς, πεφώτισται, ὥστ' ὀρθῶς ἔχειν καὶ ἐνταῦθα λέγειν, ὡς ὁ ἀὴρ ἐν τῷ φωτί, ἤπερ τὸ φῶς ἐν τῷ ἀέρι.

[13] Ibid., lines 8–13: διὸ καὶ Πλάτων καλῶς τὴν ψυχὴν οὐ θεὶς ἐν τῷ σώματι ἐπὶ τοῦ παντός, ἀλλὰ τὸ σῶμα ἐν τῇ ψυχῇ, καί φησι τὸ μέν τι εἶναι τῆς ψυχῆς ἐν ᾧ τὸ σῶμα, τὸ δὲ ἐν ᾧ σῶμα μηδέν, ὧν δηλονότι δυνάμεων οὐ δεῖται τῆς ψυχῆς τὸ σῶμα. καὶ δὴ καὶ ἐπὶ τῶν ἄλλων ψυχῶν ὁ αὐτὸς λόγος.

[14] Plotinus, *Ennead* I,i,7 and Augustine, *De trinitate* I,vii,14: *CC* L,44–46.

[15] Cf. Tertullian, *Adversus Praxean* XXVII,1: *CC* II,1198.

[16] Cf. Augustine, *De agone christiano* XX,22: *CSEL* XLI,122–23.

[17] Augustine, *De trinitate* VII,vi,11: *CC* L, 263.

[18] Augustine, *Epistula CXXXVII ad Volusianum* III,11: *CSEL* XLIV,520: *Nam sicut in unitate personae anima utitur corpore, ut homo sit, ita in unitate personae deus utitur homine, ut Christus sit. in illa ergo persona mixtura est animae et corporis, in hac persona mixtura est dei et hominis, si tamen recedat auditor a consuetudine corporum, qua solent duo liquores ita misceri, ut neutum seruet integritatem suam, quamquam et in ipsis corporibus aeri lux incorrupta misceatur. ergo persona hominis mixtura est animae et corporis, persona autem Christi mixtura est dei et hominis; cum enim uerbum dei permixtum est animae habenti corpus, simul et animam suscepit et corpus. illud cotidie fit ad procreandos homines, hoc semel factum est ad liberandos homines.*

[19] Augustine, *Sermo CLXXXVI* I,1: *PL* XXXVIII,999.

[20] Augustine, *Epistula CXXXVII ad Volusianum* III,11: *CSEL* XLIV,109: *Sic autem quidam reddi sibi rationem flagitant, quo modo deus homini permixtus sit, ut una fieret perso-*

na Christi, cum hoc semel fieri oportuerit, quasi rationem ipsi reddant de re, quae cotidie fit, quo modo misceatur anima corpori, ut una persona fiat hominis.

[21] Augustine, *Confessiones* X,xvii,26: *CC* XXVII,168–69.

[22] Augustine, *De trinitate* I,viii,16: *CC* L,49–50.

[23] Augustine, *Sermo LII* VIII,20: *PL* XXXVIII,362–63.

[24] Augustine, *De diuersis quaestionibus LXXXIII* XLVI,2: *CC* XLIV/A,73: *Sed anima rationalis inter eas res, quae sunt a deo conditae, omnia superat et deo proxima est, quando pura est; eique in quantum caritate cohaeserit, in tantum ab eo lumine illo intelligibili perfusa quodammodo et inlustrata cernit non per corporeos oculos, sed per ipsius sui principale quo excellit, id est per intellegentiam suam, istas rationes, quarum uisione fit beatissima. Quas rationes, ut dictum est, siue ideas siue formas siue species siue rationes licet uocare, et multis conceditur appellare quod libet, sed paucissimis uidere quod uerum est.*

[25] Augustine, *De trinitate* X,xi,18: *CC* L,330–31.

[26] Augustine, *De trinitate* XII,iii,3: *CC* L,358: *Et ideo quiddam rationale nostrum non ad unitatis diuortium separatum sed in auxilium societatis quasi deriuatum in sui operis dispertitur officio…. sic intellectum nostrum et actionem, uel consilium et exsecutionem, uel rationem et appetitum rationalem, uel si quo alio modo significatius dici possunt, una mentis natura complectitur….*

[27] Augustine, *De trinitate* XII,iv,4: *CC* L,358: *Cum igitur disserimus de natura mentis humanae, de una quadam re disserimus, nec eam in haec duo quae commemoraui nisi per officia geminamus.*

[28] Augustine, *De trinitate* XII,vii,12: *CC* L,367: *Quis est ergo qui ab hoc consortio feminas alienet cum sint nobiscum gratiae cohaeredes et alio loco idem apostolus dicat: "Omnes enim filii dei estis per fidem in Christo Iesu. Quicumque enim in Christo baptizati estis Christum induistis. Non est iudaeus neque graecus, non est seruus neque liber, non est masculus et femina; omnes enim uos unum estis in Christo Iesu."*

[29] Augustine, *De trinitate* XII,xiii,21: *CC* L,374: *Sed siue isto siue illo siue aliquo alio modo accipiendum sit quod apostolus uirum dixit imaginem et gloriam dei, mulierum autem gloriam uiri, apparet tamen cum secundum deum uiuimus, mentem nostram in inuisibilia eius intentam ex eius aeternitate, ueritate, caritate proficienter debere formari, quiddam uero rationalis intentionis nostrae, hoc est eiusdem mentis, in usum mutabilium corporalium rerum sine quo haec uita non agitur dirigendum, non ut conformetur "huic saeculo" finem constituendo in bonis talibus et in ea detorquendo beatudinis appetitum, sed ut quidquid in usu temporalium rationabiliter facimus aeternorum adipiscendorum contemplatione faciamus per ista transeuntes, illis inhaerentes.*

[30] Augustine, *De trinitate* XII,xi,16: *CC* L,370: *Honor enim hominis uerus est "imago et similitudo dei" quae non custoditur nisi ad ipsum a quo imprimitur. Tanto magis itaque inhaeretur deo quanto minus diligitur proprium. Cupiditate uero experiendae potestatis suae quoddam nutu suo ad se ipsum tamquam ad medium pronuit. Ita cum uult esse sicut ille sub nullo, et ab ipsa sui medietate poenaliter ad ima propellitur, id est ad ea quibus pecora laetantur; atque ita cum sit honor eius similitudo dei, dedecus autem eius similitudo pecoris….*

[31] Augustine, *De trinitate* V,iii,4: *CC* L,208–9.

[32] Augustine, *De nuptiis et concupiscentia* II,xxiii,38: *CSEL* XLII,292–93: *sed sicuti Ariani Sabellianos nos esse criminantur, quamuis non dicamus unum eundemque esse patrem et filium et spiritum sanctum, quod Sabelliani dicunt, sed dicamus unam eandemque esse naturam patris et filii et spiritus sancti, quod catholici dicunt…. sed sicut Ariani, dum Sabellianos fugiunt, in peius aliquid inciderunt, quia trinitatis ausi sunt non personas discernere, sed naturas….*

[33] P. Hadot, "De Tertullien à Boèce: Le developpement de la notion de personne dans les controverses théologiques," in *Problèmes de la personne* (Paris: Mouton, 1973), p. 132.

[34] Augustine, *De trinitate* VII,vi,11: *CC* L,261–62: *non enim aliud est deo esse, aliud personam esse sed omnino idem. Nam si esse ad se dicitur, persona uero relatiue…. Ad se quippe dicitur persona, non ad filium uel spiritum sanctum; sicut ad se dicitur deus et magnus et bonus et iustus et si quid aliud huiusmodi.*

[35] Augustine, *De ciuitate Dei* XI,x: *CC* XLVIII,330: *Et haec trinitas unus est deus; nec ideo non simplex quia trinitas. Neque enim propter hoc naturam istam boni simplicem dicimus, quia Pater in ea solus aut solus Filius aut solus Spiritus sanctus, aut uero sola est ista nominis trinitas sine subsistentia personarum, sicut Sabelliani haeretici putauerunt; sed ideo simplex dicitur, quoniam quod habet hoc est, excepto quod relatiue quaeque persona ad alteram dicitur.*

[36] Augustine, *De trinitate* VII,vi,11: *CC* L,262: *cum dicimus personam patris aliud dicimus quam substantiam patris.*

[37] Augustine, *Sermo LXXI* 18: *RB* 75 (1965) 82: *Et hanc trinitatem, quamuis seruata singularum proprietate et substantia personarum tamen propter ipsam indiuiduam et inseparabilem aeternitatis, ueritatis, bonitatis essentiam uel naturam, non esse tres deos, sed unum deum.*

[38] Augustine, *De trinitate* V,viii,9: *CC* L,216: *Quidquid ergo ad se ipsum dicitur deus et de singulis personis ter dicitur patre et filio et spiritu sancto, et simul de ipsa trinitate non pluraliter sed singulariter dicitur.*

[39] Tertullian, *Aduersus Praxean* XI,10: *CC* II,1172: *Est enim ipse qui pronuntiat spiritus et pater ad quem pronuntiat et filius de quo pronuntiat.*

[40] Augustine, *De trinitate* VII,iv,7: *CC* L,255: *Cum ergo quaeritur quid tria uel quid tres, conferimus nos ad inueniendum aliquod speciale uel generale nomen quo complectamur haec tria, neque occurrit animo quia excedit supereminentia diuinitatis usitati eloquii facultatem.*

[41] Augustine, *De trinitate* V,ix,10: *CC* L,217: *Dictum est tamen "tres personae" non ut illud diceretur sed ne taceretur.*

[42] Augustine, *De trinitate* VII,iv,9: *CC* L,259: *Quid igitur restat? An ut fateamur loquendi necessitate parta haec uocabula cum opus esset copiosa disputatione aduersus insidias uel errores haereticorum? Cum enim conaretur humana inopia loquendo proferre ad homi-*

*num sensus quod in secretario mentis pro captu tenet de domino deo creatore suo siue per
piam fidem siue per qualemcumque intellegentiam, timuit dicere tres essentias ne intellegeretur
in illa summa aequalitate ulla diuersitas.   Rursus non esse tria quaedam non poterat dicere,
quod Sabellius quia dixit in haeresim lapsus est…. Quaesiuit quid tria diceret et dixit substan-
tias siue personas, quibus nominibus non diuersitatem intellegi uoluit sed singularitatem noluit
ut non solum ibi unitas intellegatur ex eo quod dicitur una essentia, sed et trinitas ex eo quod
dicuntur tres substantiae uel personae.*

⁴³ A.C. Lloyd, "On Augustine's Concept of a Person," *Augustine*, ed. R. A. Markus
(New York: Doubleday, 1972), pp. 191–204.

⁴⁴ Lloyd, "On Augustine's Concept of a Person," pp. 203–4.

⁴⁵ J. Ratzinger, "Concerning the Notion of Person in Theology," *Communio* 17
(1990) 439–54, here 447.

⁴⁶ Augustine, *De trinitate* VI,v,7: *CC* L,235: *Siue enim sit unitas amborum siue sanctitas siue caritas, siue ideo unitas quia caritas et ideo caritas, quia sanctitas, manifestum est
quod non aliquis duorum est quo uterque coniungitur, quo genitus a gignente diligatur genera-
toremque suum diligat, sintque non participatione sed essentia sua neque dono superioris alicu-
ius sed suo proprio "seruantes unitatem spiritus in uinculo pacis." Quod imitari per gratiam et
ad deum et ad nos ipsos iubemur, "in quibus duobus praeceptis tota lex pendet et prophetae."
Ita sunt illa tria deus unus, solus, magnus, sapiens, sanctus, beatus. Nos autem "ex ipso et per
ipsum et in ipso" beati quia ipsius munere inter nos unum ….*

⁴⁷ Augustine, *Confessiones* X,viii,15: *CC* XXVII,162–63: *Et eunt homines mirari alta
montium et ingentes fluctus maris et latissimos lapsus fluminum et Oceani ambitum et gyros
siderum et relinquunt se ipsos nec mirantur….*

⁴⁸ Augustine, *Confessiones* IV,iv,9: *CC* XXVII,44: *Factus eram ipse mihi magna
quaestio….*

⁴⁹ J. Pieper, *Leisure, the Basis of Culture* (New York: Pantheon Books, 1952), p. 114
and pp. 117–18.

The Paradoxes of Self-Knowledge in the *De trinitate*

Rowan Williams

I

Augustine's treatment of knowledge and certainty in *De trinitate* X has frequently been compared with Descartes' *Second Meditation*.[1] The mind's awareness of its own reality is presented as the paradigm of certitude, the decisive refutation of radical scepticism, in a way that, on first reading, unmistakably evokes the *cogito*. What the present essay sets out to show is that we ought not to stop at the first reading: what Augustine has to say about *self-*knowledge here is only intelligible in the light of a fuller reading of *De trinitate* VIII and IX, and a grasp of where the argument is heading after Book X. Even in his comparable treatments of scepticism and certitude elsewhere, it may be questioned whether anything like the Cartesian agenda is in evidence. Descartes seeks for an irreducible assurance that *all* our thoughts and impressions are not deceits; his goal is to establish that the thinking subject's thought of its own activity is the single foundational principle of all intellectual operations, the most simple and directly accessible and invulnerable epistemological datum we possess.[2] Augustine's aim is something less radical and programmatic. He wants to refute 'Academic' scepticism, which is based specifically on the fallibility of sense-perception: no impression of the senses carries with it an assurance of its own veracity, and so no such perception can be received as certain. Therefore, we never have unquestionably valid premises on which to base inferences; we can never advance beyond probability. This, it should be clear, is something distinct from Cartesian doubt; and Augustine's various responses accordingly do not set out to establish an infallible touchstone for all knowledge, a single foundation, but rather attempt to show that, since there are things we know quite independent of *inference*, programmatic scepticism cannot in fact be intelligibly stated.

The parallels and the gulfs between Augustine and Descartes would need several more papers to explicate; but the main point for our present purposes is to note that Augustine's discussion of the certitude of self-knowledge is better described as an analysis of the grammar of the 'subject' (not simply the intellect) than as a quest for assurance against the possibility of global error. And this is why the discussion is an integral part of the argument of the final books of *De trinitate*, not simply a tiresome digression. Ultimately, what these observations contribute towards is the full articulation of that theological anthropology which the *De trinitate* displays, the analysis of how the structures of being human speak to us of the life of God even in their very difference from the divine life.[3]

Back then to Book VIII, where the trajectory begins that leads to Book X's treatment of self-knowledge. Books V to VII have arrived at an impasse; they have served to clarify something of the *structure* of trinitarian language, but the clarification of formulae is not enough for authentic understanding. We must proceed *modo interiore* if we are to arrive at an understanding of the essence or definition of the truth that God is. To know or acknowledge that God is truth is at least to grasp that the divine persons cannot be portions or subdivisions of a primordial substance, and that there can be no inequality as between the way in which the persons possess or manifest or exemplify divinity. But having drawn this anti-materialist conclusion, we cannot go any further positively: the mind cannot form an abiding concept of final truth, being weighed down with particular and material impressions. It can have momentary and unthematizable contact, but no more (VIII,ii).

Thus, at the very beginning of the long and massively complicated argument of these last books, Augustine signals his refusal to concentrate on the mind's capacity for abstraction; and here we encounter a first paradox. The last eight books of *De trinitate* are usually and rightly seen as a gradual purification of our understanding of the image of God from all that is 'lower,' material and contingent: the mind is only God's image when all trace of worldly impression is absent and it is open wholly to what is immaterial and eternal. Yet here Augustine dismisses—almost casually—the possibility of the mind conceiving eternal truth, *succeeding* in the effort of abstraction. What gradually becomes plain in these books is that the mind cannot contemplate eternal truth as an object in itself: it can encounter it only through a particular kind of self-reflection. And this self-reflection likewise cannot be the perception of mind itself as object; it exists only as an awareness of the mind's working, the mind's movement. This movement in turn is only intelligible as the movement of desire. It is—as we shall see in Book IX—the fact that the mind knows truth in and only in knowing itself as knowing and loving that constitutes the mind an image of God, so that the understanding of mind at its most radically distinctive opens the door to some understanding of the unity in diverse articulation of the divine life of *sapientia*.[4]

This still lies ahead from the viewpoint of Book VIII, but helps to explain why Augustine so summarily turns away from discussion of truth in isolation, and begins to treat the question of the good (VIII,iii). Our mental life involves not only the effort for conceptual possession but the element of judgment, the taking of attitudes, positive or negative, to what we perceive. We approve, we love—or we want to avoid. By what inner criterion do we monitor our wanting and our wanting to avoid? The activity of the reasoning self entails that that self is both moving and moving intelligibly or purposefully; it trusts itself to make judgments about negative and positive goals. Therefore, Augustine argues, it presupposes an orientation to what is comprehensively, non-contingently good. We might spell out the argument like this. Human desire can be set out phenomenologically, as Augustine more or less does at the beginning of VIII,iii—here are the sorts of thing people like, enjoy, approve of, *want to experience*. But such an analysis would leave out the rational element in approbation—connecting this desirable thing with that, recognizing this as analogous to that and so as comparably desirable; and, as so often elsewhere in Augustine,[5] this analogical skill or capacity for recognition is held to presuppose a capacity to abstract from this particular and that particular so as to identify what, as desirable, they have in common. Yet, as we have seen, this identification cannot issue in an *object* for the mind: to see the reasoning self advancing through a *history* of affective and attitudinal responses, a series that has some cohesion and consistency to it, *is* to see what the non-contingent Good is. It is that to which the maximally consistent rational self is tending.

The notion of analogical skill, however, is severely tested by certain cases. What does it mean to love justice, to love just persons *as* just? We are not here dealing with objects of perception that we can classify in the ordinary way; we do not learn to recognize justice by recognizing material features in common between objects. The ordinary structure of recognition involves first of all a strategy of classifying perceptions (the capacity to assign to genus and species): we recognize this as being like that, and this is the ground for our ability to say that they are coherently or reasonably desirable—our ability to make the higher order judgment that they both participate in what I treat as good. But when I recognize a person as just and am positively affected towards that person because justice is desirable, what is going on? Justice is not a feature of someone—like brown hair—which can be recognized by the simple identification of learned and agreed material signs: it is not to be understood, in fact, except by a practitioner (just as a tone-deaf person couldn't be expected to recognize, to have affective attitudes towards, the different levels of musical performance; she might know what material acts counted as 'performing music,' but could not operate any specifically musical categories). However, people who are not saints love people who are, and love them for their holiness; and *quis diligit quod ignorat?*[6] Augustine's discussion of how the holy can be loved rightly or intelligently by the not-so-holy is in fact an attempt to find a way into the more far-reaching problem of how the human mind can love God; but we shall return to this in a moment.

If I am not a practitioner of justice, I do not know what the word means; yet I love or desire or approve of just persons precisely because of what distinguishes them as just. I must then have some inbuilt skill at recognizing justice —not like the skill involved in ordinary analogical judgments. I recognize not by comparing one object with another, but by comparing the perceivable pattern of life in another person with my own aspiration. In other words, the love of a righteous person is intelligible because the pattern I perceive is what I want to realize in myself (VIII,vi). I know what I want to be: which is a slightly odd kind of knowledge, undoubtedly, but one which gives us the recognitional skills ordinarily associated with knowing. Augustine's emphasis on the fact that the meaning of *iustitia* is not to be learned *nisi apud me ipsum*[7] simply states that our induction into the use of moral concepts depends on the presupposition that what is proposed as a pattern of behaviour is something we can reasonably be expected to find *attractive*; or, in other terms, moral knowledge, skill in moral judgment, cannot properly be ascribed to anyone who has no sense of what it might be to *want* to be thus-and-not-otherwise in their behaviour. Moral knowledge is no more constituted by an ability to classify certain patterns of behaviour as generally the objects of moral people's approbation than musical knowledge is reducible to the ability to classify certain activities as what musical people count as making music. Moral knowledge involves a particular kind of alertness to motivation (desire once again) inaccessible to the person for whom the critique or refinement of motivation is not a problem because they have no moral wants. It might be said in passing that a society unclear about what moral wants it should nurture in its citizens will produce minds largely incapable of understanding moral crisis and moral tragedy: how many good productions of *Macbeth* or *Measure for Measure* have you seen in the last ten or fifteen years?

I have been paraphrasing Augustine fairly freely; but my aim is, I hope, a legitimate one—to query the common assumption that, when Augustine appeals to an 'inner' source or criterion for knowledge, he is appealing simply and rather crudely to innate data, notions that can be uncovered by introspection. As I hope to show further, the introspection of *De trinitate* (and other works) is not a search for epistemological buried treasure but something more like an invitation to observe what we can't but take for granted in speaking about mental life at all, as distinct from speaking about the process of registering external impressions. And the discussion in *De trinitate* VIII of loving justice and just persons is a significant example of his method in this respect. We do in fact talk about loving justice, and we admire the saints; by what logic do we suppose that there is a cognitive and rational dimension to this, given the distinctive nature of what counts as 'knowledge' in the moral sphere? And the issue of this discussion is to bring into focus the centrality of *dilectio* or *caritas* in the understanding of God. Once more, we are directed *away* from a solitary knowing ego as the doorway to theological insight. When we have grasped that we have a fundamental orientation towards the good, we are able to see the centrality of wanting in our human constitution. When we see how this wanting helps us make sense of the partial, often muddled, always mobile business of moral knowledge, we see how closely our love of the morally advanced is bound to our own aspiration. We love the saints because they show us the form of life we recognize ourselves as desiring; and that self-recognition is awakened in us by the attractiveness of others. Justice itself *is* loving, since it wills the good of all, not only its own fruition: the righteous person's righteousness is an active will to diffuse the good, to make others loving. Hence, Augustine is able to complete the first cycle of his argumentation in VIII,viii: what our moral longing longs for, loves, is love, in that it is directed to persons who are loving (for just people are loving people). This is why love of God and love of neighbour are not really to be distinguished: love of the neighbour is love of the actual or possible presence of loving generosity in him (either we see it and approve it or don't see it and long for it to be there); but to love loving generosity as the goal and standard of our humanity is to love it as the good, *simpliciter*—which is to love it as God.

So far, then, Augustine has moved from observing the centrality of appetition in human rational activity to an analysis of moral self-recognition in terms of understanding the self's directedness towards *iustitia*, and thence to the conclusion that our moral and intellectual nature is to love loving—and so to love God, who is *caritas*. So far from being directed towards a solipsistic interiority, we are given an account of mental life in which the fundamental category is lack of and quest for an other to love: the moral will is realized only in and as will for another's good. Outside this, it is wholly void.

II

Book IX is the first serious attempt to apply the framework thus elaborated to the divine life as explicated in the trinitarian dogma. Revelation tells us that God is trinity and that we are in God's image; the discussion of Book VIII has elucidated something of what it means to say that God is love, and that we are oriented to loving the reality of love. So how does the structure of our finite loving minds correspond to that of the infinite loving agency of God? What Augustine essentially has to do here is to display the proper differentiation between self-knowing and self-loving. Book VIII has insisted that to know oneself one must see oneself as loving: my subjectivity is thus engaged in a threefold pattern, the self, its 'other' and the action of loving which binds the two. But this is to take the self as related to something external; as Augustine will elaborate in due course, this cannot be a satisfactory image of God. Yet the self as loving itself yields only two, not three terms (IX,ii); so we must go back and refine our model a bit further. I do not love myself without knowing myself as loving, and that self-knowledge is not the same act as my self-love: *mens enim amare se ipsam non potest nisi etiam nouerit se. nam quomodo amat quod nescit?*[8] The self is other to itself in two ways, as what is known and as what is loved, and because true and rational love is grounded in recognition of love *in* what is loved, it presupposes a knowledge of love's object. Perfect self-awareness would mean wholly to know the self as loving because the self is wholly in love with itself (IX,ii, iv, and v). Self-knowledge and love thus exist in inseparable interconnection: there is no self that is not knowing and loving, no self that can claim to be whole or truthful that is not knowledge of a loving self, no self-loving without the *acknowledgement* or awareness that love is what the self is engaged in.

The trinitarian pattern is slowly coming to light, as is a second and profoundly theological paradox about self-knowledge: it arises out of love, yet it is presupposed by love. The mind generates its inner word, the *verbum* famously discussed in IX,viii, because behind all knowing lies intention and appetition, hopeful wanting directed to what is strange and other.[9] The moral issue for finite minds is whether this appetition is *caritas* or *cupiditas* (the desire simply to possess, to overcome the other's otherness). So for the mind to know itself as a knower, it must know that its cognitive efforts arise out of love, true or false: and in turn, full self-love depends on fully grasping the lack and desire out of which we live; it cannot flourish without knowing. And when the mind is in this way fully attuned to itself, its knowledge is a perfect 'image' of itself. The mind has 'begotten' a *verbum* reflecting its own reality (IX,xi). The paradoxical relation of knowledge and love here sketched should alert us (though it has often been missed by commentators) to the paradoxical character of the relation between Son and Spirit set out in the later sections of *De trinitate*, where it is by *no* means to be concluded that the Spirit is in some way subordinated to the Son; but that is another and longer story, which would involve teasing out how Augustine suggests something like a mutual dependence of Son and Spirit.[10] Enough for now to note how he so defines self-knowing and self-loving as to make each unintelligible without the other, and how his means of doing this is the reiterated pointing to the radical incompleteness and other-directedness of created selfhood.

Perhaps we should pause for a moment here, in the hope of a little more clarity—even if it is only the clarity of a further turn of the paradoxical rack. The finite self's perfect self-correspondence is, on Augustine's account, conceptually very odd indeed. It fully knows itself as a reality that is *not* 'full,' not a finished and determinate object: it knows itself as loving, and, the more loving it is, the more perfectly in love with itself it is. But perfect self-love can only exist on the basis of perfect other-directedness. When the self becomes a perfectly adequate and proper object for its own love, it has become perfected in the love of God and neighbour; it is never a true or adequate term of knowledge if preoccupied with its own 'individual' identity. When it stands in the relations it ought to stand in, it displays its knowledge of unchanging truth, its knowledge of what the good is, of what constitutes *iustitia*. Simply to display a knowledge of the contents of an individual consciousness is something quite different, a showing of what is essentially changeable and contingent: to show true self-knowledge is to show what can be authoritatively recognized by another, because it works in precisely the same way as the recognition of goodness in others (IX,ix). Thus, on the one hand, true self-knowledge is knowledge of what is timeless—the nature of love and justice; while on the other hand this can only occur within the temporal world in which the love of God and neighbour is learned and exercised.

III

Here, I think, we touch one of the central themes in Augustinian anthropology; and with this in mind, it should become a lot harder to read *De trinitate* X as a proto-Cartesian essay. Book IX ends with the distinction (IX,xii) between knowledge as 'product,' something that can be spoken of as *partum uel repertum*,[11] a *proles* or 'progeny' of sorts, and love as the quest which precedes or grounds this bringing-forth. Book X explores further the potential strangeness, already noted more than once by Augustine, of saying that we love what we don't yet know. X,ii enumerates the four senses in which we might take a claim to love what is not known, and reduce this claim to intelligible form, but Augustine at the end of this section, observes that all this fails to give us any real help in the case of *self*-knowledge, which does not fit any of the four interpretations offered, as he proceeds to show in X,iii. We have to face the central paradox of this entire discussion, Books VII to X, at the end of X,iii: if the self loves the idea of knowing itself, even when still in search of and thus in some measure ignorant of itself, it must at least know what knowing is: but that means that it *does* know itself, because it knows itself as, in general, a knowing subject. You cannot imagine anything that could be called a conscious life that failed to register that what it was engaged in was what was commonly called knowing. Thus, in Augustine's own words here,

> How can it [the mind] know that it knows at all without knowing itself? It's not that it knows some other subject than itself as the subject of its knowing; so it *does* know itself. So when it seeks for itself so as to know itself, it already knows itself as seeking—and so it already knows itself. Thus it can't be in complete ignorance of itself, because in knowing its own lack of knowing, it is to that extent aware of itself. If it was *not* aware of its lack of knowing, it wouldn't be seeking to know itself in the first place. So it is in virtue precisely of itself seeking that it can be shown to be more aware of itself than not. While it seeks to know, it knows itself as seeking, it knows itself as not knowing.[12]

What follows in X,iv, is an attempt to block any crude conclusion that the mind as thus characterized could be divided into a knowing part and a known or knowable part. If the mind knows itself, *what* it knows is the activity of seeking and discovering, not a static object; any other conclusion would be nonsensical, as Augustine has no difficulty in showing. If it knows itself, 'it knows itself entire,' *totam se scit*.[13] In this way, Augustine is able to distinguish self-knowledge from the possession of more or less information: the paradox he presses upon us is that a mind intrinsically incomplete, desirous and mobile, intrinsically incapable of possessing a definitive and unrevisable account of its contents and specific workings, can rightly and intelligibly be said to know itself completely. Self-knowledge is being defined, not as cognition of a spiritual substance, but as awareness of the conditions of finitude and the ability to live and act within them. Hence the further point in X,v that to know oneself is to live reflectively according to one's nature, to live in one's proper place in the universe: as a creature (below God), but a reasoning creature (above the animals). So when we say that someone lacks self-knowledge, we don't mean that she lacks information, or even that she is not given to thinking about herself (the well-known and useful Augustinian distinction of *nosse*, being aware of and *cogitare*, reasoning about, is here deployed). Lack of self-knowledge is a failure in moral and spiritual *habit*, a deficiency in the skills of living according to nature. It is inseparable from failure in love, in the sense that mind misconceives its own nature when it loves (and so identifies with) objects that do not correspond to its most true and fundamental aspirations (X,vi–viii). Of this mainstream Augustinian theme, little needs to be said here, except to underline the way in which Augustine holds together the moral skills of truthful, un-self-regarding love with the capacity for authentic self-awareness—a point, once again, not always adequately weighed by commentators.

All of this is the background to the discussion of the certainty or immediacy of self-knowledge in X,viii–x. Asking how or where the mind is to look for itself is a surprising, a baffling (*mirabilis*) question: there is no alien object to seek, nothing at a distance from the mind itself. The 'quest' is rather for the mind's clear discernment of its own activity—which is possible only through the purification of its loving. When it loves something other than its own loving action (towards God and neighbour), when it is so attached to particular objects and their remembered images that it can no longer distinguish itself, its fundamental orientation to love, from the succession of transient impressions, it fails in self-knowledge (X,viii). Part of the process of re-

discovering itself is the kind of self-catechesis described in X,ix–x. We understand what 'know yourself' means, to the extent at least that we know how to
use the two words intelligibly; press this further, press the notion of *presence* to
self, and you move closer to understanding what it is to exercise mental activity. Augustine's argument here could be very broadly paraphrased in this way.
"Do I know what I'm doing?" is a question wholly unlike "Do I know (recall,
have the ability now to bring to mind) Newton's laws of motion, the date of
Augustine's ordination, that man's name?" It is not a search for a possibly
mislaid item of information. The answer 'No' might be appropriate as a moment of moral reflection, but it is logically incapable of being a denial of cognition. We cannot intelligibly deny that we are alive, capable of remembering
(because we are, in posing a question to ourselves, employing concepts we
have learned) and of responding to what is given, forming attitudes and policies (asking a question means *wanting* to know). Augustine is not here, I believe, appealing to some luminous intuition of our spiritual essence, though he
is quite capable at times of using language that comes close to this: he is attempting to show us what we cannot pretend not to 'know'—in the sense that
we cannot articulate its contrary without self-subverting nonsense. Remember
that he is spelling out what *nosse* of the self or mind is, the habit of unthema-
tized awareness, rather than fixing a concept in our intellectual sights. The act
of articulating questions to myself, even questions of the most radically scepti-
cal kind, should show me what I can't but assume; and since I cannot (again,
logically cannot) think of my mind as one of my mind's objects, I can be shown
that—whatever I *think* I am saying—I cannot in fact believe that my mind is a
piece of stuff. There is no sane way of behaving that would display such a
habit.

Seeing Augustine's argument in this way should, I have suggested, make
us very wary indeed of a 'Cartesian' reading of these pages. What is at issue is
not the search for an indubitable element in cognition, but a clarification of
what can and can't be sensibly said about mental activity, of the necessary difference between knowing oneself and knowing some piece of information or
receiving the impression of some object. In this respect—if anachronistic
philosophical comparisons may be ventured at all—he stands closer to the
Wittgenstein of *On Certainty* than to the Cartesian problematic: Wittgenstein's
demonstration of the oddity of using 'This is my hand' as a paradigm of a fact
that I'm sure of has some striking points of contact with Augustine's *nosse-
cogitare* distinction, in that it reminds us that what I cannot help assuming is
not to be assimilated to what I *come to know*. The process of justification and

explication involved in discussing the latter are inappropriate in respect of the former, not because 'This is my hand,' or whatever, is a supremely good example of something I know, but because we cannot begin to talk intelligibly about *learning* or giving reasons for holding it true.[14]

The end of Book X sketches rather briefly how what has so far been discussed can be summarized by saying that the life of mind is equally, simultaneously and irreducibly memory, understanding and will; and a new phase in the argument opens. What has Augustine so far established? He has, above all, laid the foundations for his later conclusion that the *image* of God in us, properly so called, is not 'the mind' in and to itself (whatever that is—he will effectively dismiss such a notion in the final stages of his argument) but the mind of the saint—the awareness of someone reflectively living out the life of justice and charity. Our interest must be not in introspection as such but in what the saint 'knows,' takes for granted as the rationale for and ground of the habits of justice. The saint's mind images God because its attitude to its own life has become indistinguishable from its commitment to the eternal good; when it looks at itself, it sees the active presence of unreserved charity. Its action is transparent to its divine source. Augustine arrives here by dismantling the idea that we could *observe* the self or mind in a neutral way: because what we see when we look at ourselves is desire, we cannot look at ourselves without 'owning' (or refusing to own) that desire, we cannot pretend it is something else. The paradoxes of self-knowledge—loving before we know, yet needing to know before we love, knowing completely that we have no complete knowledge—are meant to reinforce this upon us, to show us the impossibility of stating any theory of the self as determinate object. We are to know and to love ourselves as questing, as seeking to love with something of God's freedom (in the sense of a love not glued to specific objects of satisfaction) and seeking so to grasp this as our nature and our destiny that we continue to grow in the skills of loving relation and away from *cupiditas*, the possessive immobilizing of what is loved. *En route*, Augustine has provided a number of tough exercises for our philosophical wits, at least some of which still have philosophical interest: particularly in a context where debates over the 'mental' status of artificial intelligence are being pursued, Augustine's challenge as to whether we can intelligibly assimilate our thinking about our thinking to thinking about a material object or process remains a serious one, in that it does not simply appeal to intuitions of immaterial substance but questions what we can and do actually say. His thoughts on learning moral concepts and on the emotion-cognition frontier are also of lasting interest, however, impenetrable their idiom may seem at first glance to the twentieth-century philosophical reader.

His focal achievement in the whole treatise is something very like the opposite of what its critics have often read there. It is an affirmation of the need at least to begin with the mind's involvement, in time and in other selves. But this should not surprise us; if we are misled by reading only fragments of *De trinitate*, extracting passages or even phrases that seem to present an individualist and crudely dualist anthropology, then we must acknowledge that the same distortion can be caused by reading *De trinitate* in abstraction from the context of Augustine's whole work at the time of writing this particular treatise. He has only lately emerged from the Donatist controversy; and this should remind us that *caritas*, for him, has a strongly 'public,' even institutional dimension. It is concretely the bond of peace in the Catholic Church, and we should not fall into the trap of unduly individualizing and privatizing it. The discussions of *De trinitate* VIII to X may not turn explicitly to the work of Christ and the reality of the Church (for which we must look back to IV and VI, and forward to XV), but this does not mean that the love here enjoined is not the fruit of Christ's grace, or that we can break through over habitual untruthfulness merely by a decision to engage in introspection. Again, the *De trinitate* is reaching completion as the early stages of the Pelagian controversy are nearing the crisis points of 417 and 418; the inability of created spirit to save itself, the fragile interdependence, in sin and grace, of human persons, the reality of penitence and growth, are all in Augustine's mind as he completes the work. Or take the word *iustitia*; the explicit allusion in VIII,vi to Cicero's definition of the word should bring to mind yet another more or less contemporaneous work, the *De civitate dei*, especially the account of justice and *pax* in Book XIX, in the content of a critique of Cicero.[15] Justice, like charity, is a public matter. If the *De trinitate* does not always present us clearly with anything like these conceptual cross-references, that is no excuse for reading the work as if it were sealed off from the rest of Augustine's intellectual labours of the period.

For the treatise is not a belated Cassiciacum dialogue; even where it echoes idioms and arguments of Augustine's most overtly Neoplatonic phase, these allusions are woven into a web of very different texture. As has more than once been remarked Augustine is not the first to conceive the will to know God in strongly affective or erotic terms: Plotinus bequeathed to him the language of *eros* towards the One, and the earlier Augustine had frequently taken this language, as a Neoplatonist well might, to entail the rejection of goods other than the One, and a desire to leave behind time, body and passion. Already in the *Enarrationes*,[16] in *De doctrina christiana*[17] and most eloquently, in *Confessiones* VII,[18] this entailment is (at least implicitly) challenged; but only in *De trinitate* does the challenge find anything like a full theoretical rationale (although it is important not to forget how strongly the doctrine of the incarnation works in this direction in *De doctrina christiana* and *Confessiones*). In this mature reworking of the whole theme of 'entering into oneself' to find God, the Plotinian *eros* for the One is transformed into an *eros* directed to the understanding of *eros* itself. God cannot be sought without the seeker seeking and finding, wanting and holding to, the creaturely incompleteness, the exigence and expectancy, that *eros* represents. Before we can rightly want God, we must know and want our wanting nature. To desire the creator, we must first desire to be creatures; by recognizing our openness to, dependence upon, and sharing in the *caritas* of God, we present, we 'image' that *caritas*. Because this recognition involves seeing ourselves as complex beings, articulating our own unity in a tightly-knit manifold of activities, it brings with it some clue about the unity in self-relation that is God, some *vestigium*; but only in the awareness ('self-awareness' if you will, but it is a misleading term for us who identify it as being *interested* in the self) of the saint, the habit of acting in the light of God's charity, do we recognize the image.

If, as has been said, everything Augustine wrote is really a treatise *De beata vita*, we should hardly expect the *De trinitate* to be a Cartesian meditation. Ultimately, for Augustine, the problem of self-knowledge is the problem of true conversion; which is difficult, but not *conceptually* difficult. The teases and convolutions of his treatment have the (paradoxical) goal of letting us know that what we lack in tackling the problem is not information or clarity but the truthful love of God.

Notes

[1] *The Philosophical Writings of Descartes*, tr. by John Cottingham, Robert Stoothoff and Dugald Murdoch (Cambridge: Cambridge University Press, 1984) vol. II, pp. 16–23. The parallels were noted by Arnauld in his objections to Descartes (ibid., p. 139, referring to *De libero arbitrio* II,iii,7), and Descartes (ibid., p. 154) acknowledged and welcomed the comparison.

[2] See J. A. Mourant, "The *Cogitos*: Augustinian and Cartesian," *AS* 10 (1979) 27–42; E. Booth, *Saint Augustine and the Western Tradition of Self-Knowing*, The St. Augustine Lecture 1986 (Villanova: Villanova University Press, 1989); Gerard O'Daly, *Augustine's Philosophy of Mind* (Berkeley and Los Angeles: University of California Press, 1987), pp. 162–71.

[3] Cf. Rowan Williams, "Language, Reality and Desire in Augustine's *de doctrina*," *Journal of Literature and Theology* 3 (1989) 138–50, esp. 144–47, and "*Sapientia* and the Trinity. Reflections on the *de trinitate*," *Collectanea Augustiniana*. Mélanges T. J. van Bavel, ed. B. Bruning, M. Lamberigts, J. van Houtem (Leuven: Institut Historique Augustinien, 1990), pp. 317–32, esp. p. 326.

[4] Cf. "*Sapientia* and the Trinity," passim, esp. pp. 319–21.

[5] E.g., *De libero arbitrio* II,viii,22–x,28 and *Confessiones* VII,17, etc.

[6] *De trinitate* VIII,iv,6: *CC* L,275.

[7] *De trinitate* VIII,vi,9: *CC* L,281.

[8] *De trinitate* IX,iii,3: *CC* L, 295–96.

[9] Cf. *De trinitate* XI,ii and vii; *De musica* VI; etc.

[10] See, e.g., *De trinitate* XV,xvii,29: the Spirit is bestowed on the Son by the Father in the act of begetting.

[11] *De trinitate* IX,xii,18: *CC* L,309.

[12] *De trinitate* X,iii,5: *CC* L,318: *Quo pacto igitur se aliquid scientem scit quae se ipsam nescit? Neque enim alteram mentem scientem scit sed se ipsam. Scit igitur se ipsam. Deinde cum se quaerit ut nouerit, quaerentem se iam nouit. Iam se ergo nouit. Quapropter non potest omnino nescire se quae dum se nescientem scit se utique scit. Si autem se nescientem nesciat, non se quaeret ut sciat. Quapropter eo ipso quo se quaerit magis se sibi notam quam ignotam esse conuincitur. Nouit enim se quaerentem atque nescientem dum se quaerit ut nouerit.*

[13] *De trinitate* X,iii,6: *CC* L,319.

[14] Wittgenstein, *On Certainty*, ed. G. E. M. Anscombe and G. H. von Wright, tr. Denis Paul and G. E. M. Anscombe (Oxford: Basil Blackwell, 1969), paragraphs 36, 44–46, 84, 94, 140, 192, 341–44, 369–75, 476, etc.

[15] XIX,xxi–xxiv, taking up the earlier and inconclusive discussion at II,xxi.

[16] See, e.g., *Enarratio in Psalmum LV* 6 and *Enarratio in Psalmum LXXVI* 14 (on not seeking to avoid *affectus* or *affectiones*); *Enarratio in Psalmum CXIX* 1 (on the need for humble acceptance of the conditions of our present life, in imitation of the incarnate Christ's humility).

[17] I,xiv,13 on the right use of mortality, following Christ's example.

[18] VII,18 and 20, insisting on beginning with the flesh in which the Word is incarnate and walking in a specific path through human history.

The Priesthood of Christ in Book IV of the *De trinitate*

Earl C. Muller, S.J.

For Augustine the success of the project of the *De trinitate* pivots on the ability of the Christian to mount the sort of contemplative ascent which governs the latter half of this work. That ascent is threatened by human sinfulness which cuts us off from God and renders the sort of contemplative union with the One envisioned by Neoplatonic philosophy impossible. If Augustine is to attempt the ascent nonetheless, he must arm himself and his reader with the appropriate medicine necessary to purify one enmeshed in sin. It is in this spirit in part that he turns to a discussion of the salvation accomplished by the Incarnation and by the death of the incarnate Lord in book four.

Augustine's account of how Christ accomplishes our salvation in becoming human follows from his overall philosophical approach—Christ mediates between irreconcilable extremes. "For we are not God by nature," says Augustine,

> by nature we are men, and by sin we are not just. God, there-
> fore, having been made a just man, intercedes for sinful man.
> For there is no harmony between the sinner and the just but
> between man and man. Accordingly, by uniting the likeness
> of His own humanity with us, He has taken away the unlike-
> ness of our iniquity, and having been made a sharer of our
> mortality, He has made us a sharer of His divinity.[1]

Augustine's argument here, of course, modifies the notion of mediation found in his Neoplatonic background.[2] Within Middle and Neoplatonism there is no direct contact between the utterly transcendent and temporal earthly realities. This immediately says too much. Plotinus did achieve mystical union with the One according to Porphyry, but this union involved contemplatively working his way through the several mediating levels between his individual contemplating mind and the One. The great temptation earlier in the Christian appropriation of Middle Platonic thought was to consider Christ as a mediating reality as Platonism conceived this. This, of course, led to that subordination of the Son to the Father which denied their equality. What is of interest in Augustine is that Christ does not in this way ontologically mediate between God and humanity. The mediation is ontologically grounded, but of itself is a moral mediation between the Just One and sinners, not between God and humanity essentially understood.[3]

These points are more or less explicitly discussed by Augustine in the *City of God*, book nine, chapter seventeen. Toward the end he notes that

> it is unthinkable that God, who is incapable of defilement, should be afraid of contamination by the human nature in which he was clothed. For by his incarnation he showed us ...that the true divine nature cannot be polluted by the flesh, and that demons are not to be reckoned our superiors because they are not creatures of the flesh.[4]

There is more at stake here than the immutability of God. Jesus is not some third sort of reality hovering between the divine and the human. He is at once both.[5] It is this which allows Him to mediate between the Just One and sinners. The Just One, Jesus, is one with the Father; the Man, Jesus, is in union with sinful humanity. The incongruity is thus not between human flesh and divine reality but between justness and sinfulness.[6] This lack of incongruity between flesh and divine reality is grounded in the goodness of creation. If the contemplative ascent is theoretically possible this is nonetheless concretely demonstrated not through the pride and optimism of the pagan contemplative ascent but by the humility of a God who chose to unite Himself to a mortal body received from a virgin and who poured out His blood for our purification.

Christ does not mediate merely between a just and holy God and sinful humanity. There is a mediation also between a humanity that is sinful and a humanity that has been justified. Again, the extremes are between sinfulness and justification. If the ontological ground for the possibility of union with God lay in the lack of incongruity between God and the good creation, which is to say, sinless flesh; the ontological ground for the possibility of "harmonizing" the human extremes of sinfulness and justification is shared humanity.[7] The problem of salvation could be expressed in terms of the gulf that exists between human mortality, at once physical and spiritual, and human immortality. Humanity is sinful and therefore mortal—even now spiritually dead because of sin and subject to physical death. We are cut off from that immortal life of the spirit which is true justice; we are cut off from the physical immortality which is the reward of true justice. The gulf is bridged through

Christ, whose single death corresponds to our double death and whose single resurrection has brought us two resurrections.[8]

There are, then, four linked realities: our double death occasioned by our sinfulness, Christ's single death, Christ's single resurrection, our double resurrection which is salvation and justification. With four linked realities there are three connecting links. It is to these links we now turn. Before doing so, however, it will be useful first to summarize briefly the three fundamental ways in which Augustine conceives oneness, since all of these come into play in his understanding of the way Christ mediates.

Simply stated there is the oneness of individual substance, the oneness of two diverse realities, the oneness of multiple similar realities. Anthropologically this gives us these three: the individual human being, marriage, the community.[9] Augustine, however, uses these fundamental conceptions of oneness on a variety of levels. Most relevant for the discussion in book four of the *De trinitate*, he sees God as an instance of individual substantial oneness;[10] in contrast, creation is the realm of a multiplicity that is nonetheless held in unity, ultimately by the action of God's Spirit; and Christ, who joins God and creation, is often depicted by Augustine as doing so in marital terms.

One sees these sorts of oneness coming into play when Augustine describes the links between our double death and Christ's single death and our double resurrection and Christ's single resurrection. "Hence our Savior applied his own single death to this double death of ours, and to bring about our resurrection in both he proposed beforehand and offered His one Resurrection both as a mystery and as a type" (*in sacramento et exemplo*).[11] The former sacramental relationship is an example of a union of diverse realities, the latter exemplary relationship of multiple similar realities.[12]

Both of the concepts indicated here have roots deep within Augustinian thought and have been commented on extensively in the literature.[13] The latter term, *exemplum*, has a root meaning similar to the English term "example," but one finds in Augustine's time and in his own usage more causal connotations.[14] Christ's physical resurrection is not simply one example of many possible examples of physical resurrection. It is the prototype, indeed, it is causally effective in our own resurrection.

In book four both terms are most often used in conjunction with the relation of Christ's single resurrection to our double resurrection. Augustine does not use the same terms to link our own double death to Christ's single death—there would be, for example, an awkwardness in speaking of Christ's physical death as being causally effective in our own double death. He reserves such direct causality to Satan, the mediator of death.[15] One must none-theless insist that Augustine's argument hinges on the unification of our dou-ble death with Christ's single death every bit as much as on the unification of our double resurrection with Christ's single resurrection. In this regard one notes his willingness on more than one occasion to lump Christ's death and resurrection together as the sacrament and example of our own. One can take this one step further. Christ's death, as a sacrifice offered to God, functions with causal efficacy in our own capacity to offer acceptable sacrifices to God. In this sense Christ's physical death is not merely similar to our physical death; it is prototypical of the death of the saint.

This is to jump ahead, however. Augustine wants to establish a closer unity between our physical death and Christ's even under the perspective of death as punishment for sin. He must do so if Christ is to function as a media-tor between, not the saint, but the sinner and the holy God. There, of course, can be no "harmony" between sinfulness and justice but there is "between man and man."[16] More specifically "the Son of God has deigned to become our friend in the fellowship (*consortio*) of death."[17] We are united with Christ not only in our common humanity which He has taken on but in our sin-caused death. This Christ has freely taken on since, being without sin, He did not need to suffer the punishment for sin. He could not share the sin; He chose to share the death for the sake of friendship.[18]

The notions of friendship and fellowship themselves are not unimpor-tant terms in Augustine.[19] Indeed, the reality they signify figures quite cen-trally in the argumentation of book four.

> For they could not be one in themselves, since they were separated from one another by conflicting inclinations, de-sires, and uncleannesses of sin. They are, therefore, purified through the Mediator, in order that they may be one in Him, and indeed not only through the same nature in which all mortal men become equal to the angels, but also by the same will working together most harmoniously towards the same blessedness, and fused together in some way by the fire of charity into one spirit.[20]

The first moment in the unification of us who are separated from one another by sin is the love by which God humbles Himself and enters into fellowship with us precisely in a humanity that is condemned to death because of sin. It is a communal unity that is envisioned here but one that goes beyond commonality of nature or even commonality of fate. It is a unity grounded in the love of God breathed out in the sending of the Son, breathed out in Christ's sacrificial death. If this spiritual fusing by the love of God be the sort of unity between Christ's physical death and our own double death in sin, then what is the unity between Christ's physical resurrection and our own double resurrection?

The second moment of our unification is that unity breathed out in the Gift which is the Spirit who fuses us together and makes us one as Jesus and the Father are one. This is the focus of Christ's prayer: "That they may be one, even as we are one." This second moment, especially, Augustine describes as a unity "in sacrament and in example."

The latter term has already been touched on. A few brief comments on the former must suffice. *Sacramentum* is used in a great variety of contexts throughout his writings.[21] The general sense, however, is that which one finds in *De cathechizandis rudibus*.[22] Here there is a visible reality which signifies beyond itself to some invisible reality that is holy, divine. The visible reality itself, by its union with the divine, is itself holy. In the case of the resurrection, Christ's physical resurrection is linked to our spiritual resurrection as visible to invisible. The reality is holy. It is the presence of both of these aspects which leads Augustine to describe the relationship as sacramental.

What is curious in the *De trinitate* is the rather circumscribed use of the term *sacramentum* in contrast to the wide variety of uses elsewhere. Here it occurs twenty-one times. The first and the last two uses are unspecified. Every use in book three is in reference to the Eucharist. Eight or nine of the uses in book four are of the sort discussed in the preceding paragraphs and refer to the relationship of Christ's physical death and resurrection to our double death and resurrection. He expatiates on the numerical characteristics of the "sacramental" principle he has just enunciated; then, immediately after he finishes exploring these numerical qualities of sacramentality, he throws the entire discussion into a sacrificial, ultimately Eucharistic, context—*Hoc sacramentum, hoc sacrificium, hic sacerdos, hic deus antequam missus ueniret factus ex femina*.[23] This will later be seen to be crucial to the third connecting link—that between Christ's death and resurrection. The term *sacramentum* is used four other times. Three times it is a reference to the Incarnation. The fourth time it is a reference to that reality pointed to by the marriage relationship. All of these uses ultimately figure into the unification achieved through Christ that is set out in book four.

The final connecting link to consider is that between Christ's death and His resurrection. The structure of that union has distinctive characteristics in Augustine's thought which become evident as soon as one reflects on his characterization of the first half of this relationship. Christ's death is a sacrifice. The connecting link between Christ's death and His resurrection is thus an act of worship. We turn first to an examination of that sacrificial death.

"The Son of God has deigned to become our friend in the fellowship of death." But in joining Himself to the fellowship of death Christ has transformed death. The principle involved, although Augustine does not explicitly bring it to bear on this point, is that enunciated in book six: "In spiritual things, however, when the lesser adheres to the greater, as the creature to the Creator, the former becomes greater than it was, not the latter."[24] Our double death is brought about by the mediator of death whose single death corresponds to our double. Our spiritual death is the abandonment of God in sin and God's abandonment of us: "Those words… 'My God, my God, why hast thou forsaken me?' refer to the mystery of the inner man and signify the death of our soul."[25] Physical death followed as a "just condemnation" by God "for He Himself was not the cause of death, but yet death was inflicted on the sinner as His most just retribution."[26] It is into this latter death that Christ enters into fellowship. "The Lord has handed him over for our sins."[27] But because it is Christ who is punished, cursed by God for our sake, that fellowship of physical death is made greater than it was. Before it was condemnation, punishment for sin; now it is a perfect sacrifice offered to God. Physical death has been transformed. Christ is not simply an instance of a human being condemned to death because of sin. In transforming death He becomes the causal *exemplum* of our death. His physical death is sacramentally linked to our spiritual death and that too is transformed from the death to God that is sin to the death to God that is true interior worship. We have been thereby purified.[28]

At the heart of Christ's mediation, therefore, is Christ's priesthood.[29] The sacrificial character of Christ's death forces us to look at Augustine's understanding of worship and the relationship of sacrifices to worship. The latter question has a point to the extent that sacrifice is seen as one form of worship and thus not to be identified with worship as such. All worship has at least two purposes—adoration of God and unification with God.[30] Indeed, for Augustine the two are inseparable—union with God is achieved through loving adoration. An additional purpose can be discerned with reference to the worshipper him- or herself—some good such as happiness is sought.

Within this all manner of petitionary prayer will be included. In this regard Augustine does not always distinguish worship and sacrifice—"Thus the true sacrifice is offered in every act which is designed to unite us to God in a holy fellowship (*societate*), every act, that is, which is directed to that final Good which makes possible our true felicity."[31]

This ambiguity on the part of Augustine provided material for both sides of a controversy in the first half of this century among Catholic theologians. The question at issue was whether the destruction of the offering in a sacrifice was an essential part of the act.[32] Those who argued against this position stressed the unitive dimension of worship as the true core of sacrifice, proposing a "banquet" model of sacrifice. The other position stressed the destructive, or at least transformative, dimension that concretely characterizes all sacrifices.

On the one hand, self-destruction as part of the act of worship (and a destructive sacrificial immolation ultimately symbolizes the offering of oneself) is problematic. How can the destruction of life possibly honor the God of life? Augustine senses this problem when he argues that Satan rather than God is the cause of death or that it is only as punishment for sin that God wills death. The element of immolation, whether one understands this as destructive or as transformative, of course must enter the act of worship insofar as a purification or a transformative conversion is needed. "To see him as he can be seen and to cleave to him, we purify ourselves from every stain of sin and evil desire and we consecrate ourselves in his name."[33] The death which God decrees for the sinner cannot be avoided; it can, however, be transformed. But this conversion cannot take place from within the individual as such. The individual cannot purify him- or herself. Christ's death must be "applied" to one's own double death. As is the case with Christ's mediation, so also with our purification through His immolation. Both of these are necessitated by human sinfulness, not by the essential structure of the relationship between God and humanity either ontologically considered or as actualized in the act of worship.

On the other hand, the God of life has dominion over life and the act of worship will acknowledge that dominion. Undergirding both the banquet and destruction understandings of sacrifice is the act of offering.[34] As an act of worship it is an offering of that which is most precious, of that which is most total. It is, in short, an offering of one's life. Within the banquet approach to sacrifice the life offered is not as such destroyed but is nonetheless handed over to God. This does not preclude future use of what is offered by the one doing the offering. Within the immolation approach this handing over is concretely effected through the destruction of the offering. All future use of the offering is precluded. Sin precludes a banquet, that is to say, any harmony with the Just God, without prior purification.[35] Our worship must take the form of offering to God our sinful lives—truly handing them and the sin over to God to be destroyed, to be transformed. The act of worship in both cases is ratified by God by a return gift of life. It is this mutual handing over of life which provides the unity of the act of worship and serves in the case of Christ to unite His gift of life offered to God on the cross with God's return gift in the resurrection.

The life given in return is invariably greater than the life offered. Again, the lesser is made greater in the union with the greater. Our resurrection is made better by the union with Christ's resurrection. If our death in sin is transformed into that death which is true worship of God, then our rising to life will not be to a mere human life but to divine life. Christ, in mediating between sinful humanity and redeemed humanity, at the same time mediates between humanity and God.

Since the act of worship unites humans directly with God and the only pure sacrifice is Christ's, one finds that the Incarnation provides the paradigm for that act of worship, for that sacrifice.[36] Augustine virtually identifies Christ's taking on of flesh in the Incarnation with His union with His body, the Church. One finds this set out in the *Enarratio in Psalmum XVIII* (Ps 19:4–5):

> *He hath set His tabernacle in the sun*, by establishing His Church in broad daylight.... *And He, as a bridegroom coming out of his bride chamber.... He* Himself *hath set His tabernacle in the sun*. In other terms, when the Word was made flesh, He found as a bridegroom His nuptial chamber in the Virgin's womb. Thence He came forth, united to a human nature, as from a chamber of surpassing purity.... This same bridegroom who accomplished all these things, He it is who has set His tabernacle, the Church, in the sun, in full view of all men.[37]

Mary's womb is the bride chamber; the bride is at once His human nature and the Church. There are these three then: the act of worship uniting redeemed humanity with God, the incarnational union of the Son with human nature which is maritally understood, the ecclesial union of the Church with Christ which is likewise maritally understood.

In Sermon 213, after referring to this interpretation of Ps 19, Augustine goes on—"And what shall I say? Great and unique is the condescension of her Spouse; He found her a courtesan and made her a virgin.... She is a virgin in faith."[38] This last theme is found also in the *De trinitate*—"Wherefore, that woman whom infirmity, through the binding of Satan, had bent over, and who was healed and made erect by the Lord is understood to be a type of the Church."[39] In the *De civitate dei* it is clear that Augustine identifies the Church even with the Israel of the Old Testament. It is this Church that is infirm, that was a courtesan. Christ comes, and, uniting flesh to Himself, unites Himself to His bride. In spiritual matters where the greater is joined to the lesser the lesser is made greater. The courtesan becomes a virgin; the infirm woman is healed; and we who were dead in our sins are enabled to offer acceptable sacrifices to God. "This being so," Augustine will write in the *De civitate dei*, "it immediately follows that the whole redeemed community...is offered to God as a universal sacrifice, through the great Priest who offered himself in his suffering for us."[40] In book four of the *De trinitate* he will say,

> Four things are to be considered in every sacrifice: by whom it is offered, to whom it is offered, what is offered, and for whom it is offered. Therefore, the same one and true Mediator Himself reconciled us with God by the sacrifice of peace, in order that we might remain one with Him to whom it was offered, in order to make those for whom it was offered one in Himself, and in order that He Himself might be both the One who offered, and the One who was offered.[41]

The sacrifice of Christ is the sacrifice of His flesh, of His body. It is the sacrifice of the Church, "a sacrament well-known to the faithful where it is shown to the Church that she herself is offered in the offering which she presents to God."[42]

We can, then, briefly summarize the mediational and purificatory characteristics of the priesthood of Christ. Both of these aspects have to do with our sinful condition, a condition which cuts us off from the just God. There is no harmony between justice and sinfulness but only between man and man. In becoming human and freely taking on that death which is the punishment for sin, Christ provides the harmonizing mediation that unites us to God. This mediation is sacrificial; it is an act of worship. In reestablishing through sacramental linkage our union with God *even in our sinfulness*, Christ's sacrificial death, his fellowship in our death, releases the power of God's Spirit to purify us. Thus purified, our individual interior worship, our "contemplative ascent," is enabled to achieve its goal, union with God. Thus purified, we as individuals are conflated by the action of the Spirit into one sacrificial offering, the offering of Christ Himself. This is the sacrifice of Christians. This is the sacrifice which the Church continually celebrates in the sacrament of the altar.

Notes

[1] The translations throughout are taken from Stephen McKenna, C.SS.R., *Saint Augustine: The Trinity*, FC 45. The key phrase of McKenna's translation, "between the sinner and the just man," has been modified here. The "just one" Augustine has in view at this point is not a human as such but God. This point will be taken up shortly. Edmund Hill, O.P. gives a better translation at this point in the New City Press version of the *De Trinitate*. This translation, unfortunately, came out after this article was substantially completed. *De trinitate* IV,ii,4: CC L,164: *Deus enim natura non sumus; homines natura sumus; iusti peccato non sumus. Deus itaque factus homo iustus intercessit deo pro homine peccatore. Non enim congruit peccator iusto, sed congruit homini homo. Adiungens ergo nobis similitudinem humanitatis suae abstulit dissimilitudinem iniquitatis nostrae, et factus particeps mortalitatis nostrae fecit participes diuinitatis suae.*

[2] Axel Dahl, *Augustin und Plotin: Philosophische Untersuchungen zum Trinitätsproblem und zur Nuslehre* (Lund: Håkan Ohlssons Koklryckeir, 1945), pp. 34–40.

[3] This latter needs to be stressed. Augustine does follow a Neoplatonic scheme in his Christology to this extent: the Word is not directly united with the body but through the mediation of the human soul of Christ. The Word is, however, directly united to that soul and as such is directly united with Christ's humanity. The thought is already found in Origen and Gregory of Nazianzus. Cf. Brian E. Daley, S.J., "A Humble Mediator: The Distinctive Elements in Saint Augustine's Christology," *Word and Spirit* 9 (1987) 104.

[4] The translations are taken from Henry Bettenson, *Augustine: Concerning the City of God against the Pagans* (New York: Penguin Classics, 1984). *De civitate dei* IX,xvii: CC XLVII,266,21–27: *Qui profecto incontaminabilis Deus absit ut contaminationem timeret ex homine quo indutus est, aut ex hominibus inter quos in homine conuersatus est. Non enim parua sunt haec interim duo, quae salubriter sua incarnatione monstrauit, nec carne posse contaminari ueram diuinitatem, nec ideo putandos daemones nobis esse meliores, quia non habent carnem.*

[5] Wilhelm Geerlings, *Christus Exemplum: Studien zur Christologie und Christusverkündigung Augustins*, Tübinger theologische Studien, Band 13 (Mainz: Matthias-Grünewald, 1978), pp. 111–18. Arthur F. Krueger, *Synthesis of Sacrifice According to Saint Augustine: A Study of the Sacramentality of Sacrifice*, Dissertationes ad Lauream 19 (Mundelein, IL: Seminarii Sanctae Mariae ad Lacum, 1950), p. 72 almost verges on a monophysite interpretation of Augustine here. Christ's "just humanity" is found "between God and fallen

man" not, as Krueger argues, because the Mediator is God but because humanity in falling becomes less than, further from God than, "just humanity."

[6] See, for instance, Émile Bailleux, "La Christologie de saint Augustin dans le *De Trinitate*," *Recherches augustiniennes* 7 (1971) 228–29, 234.

[7] In this regard Christ is a mediator more specifically in his humanity than in the fact that He is God-man. Krueger, *Synthesis*, pp. 71–72.

[8] *De trinitate* IV,ii,4; iii,6: *CC* L,166–67.

[9] These points have been developed in more detail in a paper given at the 1990 North American Patristics Society convention entitled "The Individual, the Community, Marriage: Three Sorts of Human Oneness in Augustine."

[10] The Trinity is individual in the sense that there is only one God. But, of course, there is immediately the problem that there are Three who are God. Are they individuals? For Augustine they are not individuals in the sense that three humans are three individuals. One way of illustrating this aspect of Augustine's thought is to point out that Augustine sees a proper image of God only in the mind of the individual. Augustine is not completely satisfactory at this point.

[11] *De trinitate* IV,iii,6: *CC* L,166–67: *Huic ergo duplae morti nostrae saluator impendit simplam suam, et ad faciendam utramque resuscitationem nostram in sacramento et exemplo praeposuit et proposuit unam suam.*

[12] Basil Studer, O.S.B., "'Sacramentum et exemplum' chez Saint Augustin," *Studia Patristica* Vol. XVI (Berlin: Akademie, 1985), pp. 578–83, argues, correctly I judge, that this conjunction of terms must be seen against the background of Augustine's exegetical practice. *Exemplum*, therefore, corresponds to the literal reading, *sacramentum* to the allegorical or spiritual. Thus, Christ can be both an *exemplum* to the angels in the form of God in *De trinitate* VII,iii,5 and an *exemplum* to humans in the form of a slave. *Exemplum* is the proper word in each case because of the substantial similarity which supports a "literal" rather than a metaphorical comparison. This obviates the problems created by an antipelagian reading of this terminological pair such as found in Geerlings' work, *Christus Exemplum*. Geerlings insists throughout that this pair is to be understood primarily in terms of the distinction between the inner and the outer, between grace and example. His methodology, however, skews his understanding of the relationship between *exemplum* and *sacramentum* insofar as he conflates many terms with *exemplum*, many of which at times should be more closely linked to *sacramentum*. This is true especially of the terms *figura* and *signum* (cf. pp. 173–78). *Exemplum* thus takes over many of the functions of *sacramentum* in this approach.

[13] Geerlings, *Christus Exemplum* does provide quite helpful material on the background and Augustinian framework for the *exemplum* concept. Studer's work has already been mentioned. Krueger, *Synthesis*, pp. 12–18, provides a better treatment of *sacramentum*.

[14] Geerlings, *Christus Exemplum*, pp. 153–55, explores the shift from the pedagogical use of *exemplum* to the metaphysical and causal use via Plato's cave analogy.

[15] *De trinitate* IV,xii,15; xiii,17: *CC* L,183. Indeed, one could argue the obverse—our double death caused Christ's single death. Temporally, Christ's crucifixion was at the hands of sinners; teleologically, our sinfulness was the purposive occasion for Christ's death —he died for our sins.

[16] *De trinitate* IV,ii,4: *CC* L,164.

[17] *De trinitate* IV,xiii,17: *CC* L,184: *Sic in mortis consortio filius dei nobis fieri dignatus est amicus.*

[18] Christ's sinlessness, as Studer ("'Sacramentum et exemplum'," p. 578) points out, necessitates that the relationship between Christ's death and our sinfulness be sacramental rather than exemplary.

[19] Cf. Joseph T. Lienhard, S.J., "The Glue Itself Is Charity," in this volume of the *Collectanea Augustiniana* for more on this subject.

[20] *De trinitate* IV,ix,12: *CC* L,177: *...quia in se ipsis non possent dissociati ab inuicem per diuersas uoluntates et cupiditates et immunditiam peccatorum; unde mundantur per mediatorem ut sint in illo unum non tantum per eandem naturam qua omnes ex hominibus mortalibus aequales angelis fiunt sed etiam per eandem in eandem beatitudinem conspirantem concordissimam uoluntatem in unum spiritum quodam modo caritatis igne conflatam.* He continues: *CC* L,177–78: *...Vt sint unum sicut et nos unum sumus, ut quemadmodum pater et filius non tantum aequalitate substantiae sed etiam uoluntate unum sunt, ita et hi inter quos et deum mediator est filius non tantum per id quod eiusdem naturae sunt sed etiam per eandem dilectionis societatem unum sint.* In this double sameness they mirror the Trinity, since Father and Son are the same nature and have the same Spirit.

[21] I am grateful to Villanova University and to Allan Fitzgerald, O.S.A., editor of *Augustinian Studies*, for providing me with the results of an electronic search of the *Augustine Concordance* of the Würzburg collection of Augustine's works on this term.

[22] *De cathechizandis rudibus* XXVI,50: *CC* XLVI,173,4–10: *De sacramento sane quod accipit, cum ei bene commendatum fuerit, signacula quidem rerum diuinarum esse uisibilia, sed res ipsas inuisibiles in eis honorari; nec sic habendam esse illam speciem benedictione sanctificatam, quemadmodum habetur in usu quolibet: dicendum etiam quid significet et sermo ille quem audiuit, quid in illo condiat, cuius illa res similitudinem gerit.*

[23] *De trinitate* IV,vii,11: *CC* L,175. Geerlings, *Christus Exemplum*, pp. 220–22, passes over this Eucharistic context in judging Augustine's references to *sacramentum* and *exemplum* to be realized primarily in Baptism.

[24] *De trinitate* VI,viii,9: *CC* L,238: *In rebus autem spiritalibus cum minor maiori adhaeret sicut creatura creatori, illa fit maior quam erat, non ille.*

[25] *De trinitate* IV,iii,6: *CC* L,167: *Interioris enim hominis nostri sacramento data est illa vox pertinens ad mortem animae nostrae. ...Deus meus, deus meus, ut quid me dereliquisti?* Cf. *De trinitate* IV,vii,11: *CC* L,175–76.

[26] *De trinitate* IV,xii,15: *CC* L,181: *...quia causa mortis ipse non fuit; sed tamen per eius retributionem iustissima mors inrogata est peccatori.*

[27] *De civitate dei* XVIII,xxix: *CC* XLVIII,620: *...et Dominus tradidit illum pro peccatis nostris.*

[28] Krueger, *Synthesis*, pp. 81–82, 90, inappropriately argues for a vicarious or substitutory understanding of Christ's death rather than the unitive and transformative one. Augustine's argument, however, is rather of the sort: humans merited death because of sin; God has chosen to save precisely through that punishment. The same sort of logic is found in *De trinitate* IV,vii,11: *CC* L 175–76: *Quia enim ab uno deo summo et uero per impietatis iniquitatem resilientes et dissonantes defluxeramus et euanueramus in multa...oportebat nutu et imperio dei miserantis ut ipsa multa uenturum conclamarent unum.* What Krueger is, with considerable justification, intent on is the "objective" versus merely "moral" or exemplary value of Christ's sacrifice. One can do this without a substitution, however. We continue to suffer the punishment for our sins. We do still physically die. But because of Christ it is no longer merely "punishment for sin," but also the "death of the saint," which itself has salvific value for Augustine insofar as the immolation of the individual Christian is conflated into the one sacrifice of Christ.

[29] Krueger, *Synthesis*, pp. 74–78.

[30] Krueger, *Synthesis*, pp. 20, 32.

[31] *De civitate dei* X,vi: *CC* XLVII,278,1–3: *Proinde uerum sacrificium est omne opus, quo agitur, ut sancta societate inhaereamus Deo, relatum scilicet ad illum finem boni, quo ueraciter beati esse possimus.*

[32] It seems the dispute was to some measure initiated by Bishop James Bellord in two articles, "The Notion of Sacrifice" and "The Sacrifice of the New Law," in *The Ecclesiastical Review* 33 (1905) 1–14, 258–73. He notes at the beginning of the second article that "the great bulk of theologians have considered sacrifice to be essentially a destruction of life in honor of God, for the purpose of expressing latreutic worship, or repentance for sin and atonement. This may be termed for present convenience the Destruction-theory. It is now alleged on serious grounds that sacrifice is of the nature of a meal, and that its object is to assert a bond of union between the partakers and the Deity. We may call this the Banquet-theory." The articles were published posthumously and immediately attacked in two articles, "The Other View of Sacrifice" and "The Sacrifice of the Cross," in the same volume of the journal (pp. 378–94, 457–68) the same year by Charles J. Cronin. Emmanuel Doronzo, O.M.I., *De Eucharistia*, Tom. II *De Sacrificio*, Tractatus Dogmaticus Vol. 4 (Milwaukee: Bruce, 1948), pp. 793–819, provides a survey of the course of the debate. Krueger, *Synthesis*, pp. 34–37, offers a briefer survey and then goes on to argue that taking immolation as essential to sacrifice is most consistent with Augustine's thought (p. 40).

[33] *De civitate dei* X,iii: *CC* XLVII,275,23–26: *Ad hunc uidendum, sicut uideri poterit, eique cohaerendum ab omni peccatorum et cupiditatum malarum labe mundamur et eius nomine consecramur.*

[34] It is at this level that love coincides with submission and with union and with immolation. Krueger's solution to the controversy is basically sound. *Synthesis*, pp. 42–43.

[35] This, in essence, is Krueger's objection to the approach of De la Taille and others who argue that the essence of sacrifice lies only in the oblation. This is fine in the ideal order; Augustine, however, is speaking in the context of the actual, fallen condition of humanity. *Synthesis*, p. 40.

[36] Augustine is fairly explicit in paralleling Christ's Incarnation with his death on the cross. Thus he writes in *De trinitate* IV,v,9: *CC* L,172: *Octauo enim kalendas apriles conceptus creditur quo et passus; ita monumento nouo quo sepultus est ubi nullus erat positus mortuorum nec ante nec postea congruit uterus uirginis quo conceptus est ubi nullus seminatus est mortalium.* Krueger's central thesis is that Augustine's thought on sacrifice is essentially sacramental in structure. In *Synthesis*, pp. 19–24, he sets out the general systematic utility of the sacramental perspective in understanding Augustine's thought; on pp. 65–66 he indicates a variety of correlations that come under this structure: visible-invisible, Old-New, interior-exterior, ideal-historical which joins Platonic interiority with a Christologically shaped history. On p. 68 he explores the sacramental character of Christ's death at Calvary itself. The approach is fruitful. One can also understand the Incarnation itself as sacramental in structure. At this point one can ask a fundamental question—which, in Augustine's view, is more important to his thought: the dyadic sacramental structure of reality which can, in part at least, be seen as an unfolding of his Platonism or his belief in the Incarnation? Stating the issue in these terms, of course, stacks the deck in favor of seeing the Incarnation as providing the central paradigm for Augustinian theology.

[37] This translation is taken from Dame Scholastica Hebgin and Dame Felicitas Corrigan, *St. Augustine on the Psalms*, Ancient Christian Writers, vol. 29-30 (Westminster, MD: Newman Press, 1961). *Enarratio in Psalmum XVIII Sermo II* 6: *CC* XXXVIII,109–10: *In sole posuit tabernaculum suum, in manifestatione ecclesiam suam…. Et ipse tamquam sponsus procedens de thalamo suo.…ipse in sole posuit tabernaculum suum; hoc est, ille tamquam sponsus, cum Verbum caro factum est, in utero uirginali thalamum inuenit; atque inde naturae coniunctus humanae, tamquam de castissimo procedens cubili…. Idem ipse ergo sponsus qui haec fecit, ipse posuit in sole, hoc est in manifestatione, tabernaculum suum, hoc est sanctam ecclesiam suam.* Strictly speaking Augustine does not name the Church here as Christ's spouse. The reason has to do with the concrete wording of the Psalm at this point. The bridegroom "rejoiced as a giant to run the way" is identified by Augustine with the course of Christ's human life. Cf. Brian E. Daley, S.J., "The Giant's Twin Substances" in this volume of the *Collectanea Augustiniana* for more on this subject. The bridegroom's tabernacle, then, is the Church. The spousal character of the Church, however, is a point Augustine frequently makes as in *Sermo CXCI* 2-3: *PL* XXXVIII,1010: *et sponsus infans de thalamo suo, hoc est utero virginali, illaesa matris virginitate procederet…ut sibi capiti immaculato immaculatam consociaret Ecclesiam*; or *Sermo CCXIII* 7: *PL* XXXVIII,1063: *Sic se habet Ecclesia catholica mater nostra vera, vera illius sponsi conjux. Honoremus eam, quia tanti Domini matrona est.* The citations can be multiplied. This use of Ps 19 recurs throughout Augustine's sermons.

[38] *Sermo CCXIII* 7: *PL* XXXVIII,1063: *Et quid dicam? Magna est sponsi et singularis dignatio; meretricem invenit, virginem fecit.…In fide virgo est.*

[39] *De trinitate* IV,iv,7: *CC* L,170: *Unde intellegitur illa mulier in typo ecclesiae a domino sanata et erecta quam curuauerat infirmitas alligante satana.*

[40] *De civitate dei* X,vi: *CC* XLVII,279,33–36: ...*profecto efficitur, ut tota ipsa redempta ciuitas, hoc est congregatio societasque sanctorum, uniuersale sacrificium offeratur Deo per sacerdotem magnum, qui etiam se ipsum obtulit in passione pro nobis.*

[41] *De trinitate* IV,xiv,19: *CC* L,186–87: *Ut quoniam quattuor considerantur in omni sacrificio: cui offeratur, a quo offeratur, quid offeratur, pro quibus offeratur; idem ipse unus uerusque mediator per sacrificium pacis reconcilians nos deo unum cum illo maneret cui offerebat, unum in se faceret pro quibus offerebat, unus ipse esset qui offerebat et quod offerebat.*

[42] *De civitate dei* X,vi: *CC* XLVII,279,52–55: *Quod etiam sacramento altaris fidelibus noto frequentat ecclesia, ubi ei demonstratur, quod in ea re, quam offert, ipsa offeratur.* Cf. Krueger, *Synthesis*, pp. 147–49.

Augustine's Trinitology and the Theory of Groups

Thomas Ryba

Introduction

Augustine's trinitology has, at various times, been characterized as implicitly—if not explicitly—modalistic.[1] One of the earliest to make this charge was Adolph Harnack who, in his *History of Dogma*, characterized Augustine's trinitology as the product of a powerful mind which tended to revel in incomprehensibles, so that Augustine's arguments could be said to have swung between "the poles of a *docta ignorantia* and a knowledge...replete with contradictions."[2] He further claimed that Augustine's "attempts to conserve the most immanent of immanent Trinities and to sublimate the Trinity into a unity" resulted in his discarding "everything in the way of a basis in historical religion."[3] Augustine lost himself "in paradoxical distinctions and speculations," because he was not able "to give clear expression to...[his] new and valuable thought."[4] The substance of this last indictment is supposedly demonstrated by the fact that Augustine was "not afraid of the paradox that two persons are equal to three, and again that one is equal to three."[5] On the basis of these charges, and others like them, Harnack telegraphs his final conclusion that "Augustine only gets beyond Modalism by the mere assertion that he does not wish to be a Modalist, and by the aid of ingenious distinctions between different ideas."[6] A theologian of the stature of Paul Tillich accepted the characterization of Harnack and, though maintaining Augustine's orthodoxy, suggested that Augustine, like the Western theological tradition as a whole, leaned toward Modalistic Monarchianism.[7]

The problem with the characterizations of Harnack and Tillich is that they amount to little more than claims which, if persuasive at all, are so rhetorically, and not because they represent any deep attempt to come to terms with the relevant trinitological texts. In the case of Harnack, his rhetorical argument is a crazy quilt of passages drawn from many of Augustine's works with little regard for his trinitological maturation evident in the sequence from the letter to Nebridius to *De trinitate*. This is doubly peculiar because Harnack claims theological development as his *métier* while apparently ignoring the historical development of Augustine's theology.[8] In the case of Tillich, his characterization of Augustine is little more than a throw-away line, uncritically tossed off, I suspect, because he was not a historian of theology himself, but studied his theological history in the penumbra of Harnack's monolithic *History of Dogma*.

Lloyd's Logical Critique of Augustine's Ontology

If the criticisms that Hanack and Tillich represent are illustrious but somewhat suspect, the classic article of Lloyd, "On Augustine's Concept of a Person," is another matter.[9] While not quite as well known as Harnack's and Tillich's, Lloyd's criticism of the Augustinian trinitology possesses more persuasive force, if only because he attempts to cast it in strict argumentative form. Indeed, Lloyd's argument goes straight to the heart of classical ontology in a way that Harnack's and Tillich's criticisms do not. In fact, Lloyd's argument is an attempt to demonstrate that Augustine could not consistently sustain his notion of the Trinity either on its own terms or on the basis of the classical ontology upon which it was parasitic. Lloyd begins his critique by distinguishing the semantic component of Augustine's argument in *De trinitate* from that component which has reference to logic and ontology. He describes the semantic distinction between relations and substantial attributes as follows:

> The way in which…relative though non-accidental attributes are properly applied to God…is not the way in which the substantial attributes are applied to God. "Son" cannot be said of the Trinity at all, and "Father" only in a more or less analogical way by reference to God's adoption of his creatures.[10]

But it is fundamental to Lloyd's critique to demonstrate that this semantic theory and its accompanying ontology contain a contradiction.

> He [Augustine] has not managed to make this…claim consistent with his starting point in the earlier chapters. In fact it entails a contradiction. Not only can God be said of the Son but the Son is identical with God; for according to Augustine

himself, diversity of substance implies plurality of gods; from this it follows that singleness of gods implies sameness of substance; singleness of gods is also, according to Augustine, a necessary fact, so that God is at least (i.e., if he is not a species) a member of a necessary one-member class; and whatever has the same substance as such an object must be identical with that object. Since therefore God is identical with the Son, *a fortiori*, Son can be said of God. The attempt to have three persons entails a non-symmetric identity.[11]

Lloyd's argument easily lends itself to something like the following logical analysis:

(1)   Diversity of substance implies plurality of things. (*Premise*)
(2)   Diversity of substance implies a plurality of gods. (From 1 by *Substitution*)
(3)   Singleness (identity) of gods implies identity of substance. (*Modus Tollens* to 1)
(4)   The singleness of God is indisputable since there is only one God. (*Premise*)
(5)   Therefore, in God there is an identity of substance. (From 3 by *Modus Ponens* and *Universal Instantiation*)
(6)   Whatever has the same (unitary) substance is identical with that substance. (*Premise*)
(7)   The relations in God have the same (unitary) substance. (*Premise*)
(8)   Therefore, the relations in God are identical with their substance. (From 6 and 7 by *Universal Instantiation* and *Modus Ponens*)
(9)   Or alternatively, if Augustine denies that the trinitarian relations are identical they must have different substances. (*Modus Tollens* to 6)
(10) Therefore, in the Trinity there is a plurality of gods. (By 2 and *Modus Ponens* to 9)

Thus, according to Lloyd, Augustine is gored on the horns of a dilemma. By Augustine's own reasoning, presumably only two, equally unacceptable, interpretations of the Augustinian trinitology are possible: either Augustine is a modalist (steps 1 through 8) or he is a tritheist (steps 1 through 5, 7, 9 and 10). It is clear that this formulation of Lloyd's argument is inferentially consistent, given his premises. But has he correctly framed his premises? Let us examine the relevant propositions:

(1)   Diversity of substance implies a plurality of things.
(4)   The singleness of God is indisputable, since there is only one God.
(6)   Whatever has the same (unitary) substance is identical with that substance.
(7)   The relations in God have the same (unitary) substance.

It would seem that premises 1 and 4 are beyond reproach, at least from Augustine's own perspective—the former as a premise of the ontology he inherited, the latter as a premise based upon divine revelation and (perhaps) natural proofs. In the case of 6 and 7, on the other hand, Lloyd's accuracy in representing Augustine's position is more questionable. The difficulty hinges on the meaning of the operative phrase "to have." Lloyd employs premise 6 to make the argument that what Augustine has done is to maintain a "non-symmetric theory of identity." This is a somewhat unhappy choice of words because it does not precisely vent Lloyd's full criticism of the Augustinian trinitology. Lloyd actually intends two criticisms of the Augustinian notion of identity which he apparently conflates in this phrase. He means to say that Augustine inconsistently proposes both a non-symmetric theory of identity and a non-transitive theory of identity.

According to Lloyd, Augustine is first trapped by his own ontological premises into maintaining that the Father, Son and Holy Spirit are each identical to God but that God is not identical to each of them taken individually. The supposed violation is a violation of the law of the symmetry (or commutativity) of identity: if **A** is identical to **X**, then **X** is identical to **A**. Second, Augustine is also supposedly trapped into maintaining that the Father and God are identical, that the Son and God are identical and that the Holy Spirit and God are identical even though the Father, Son and Holy Spirit are not identical. This supposed violation is a violation of the law of transitivity of identity: if **A** is identical to **X** and **B** is identical to **X** and **C** is identical to **X**, then **A** is identical to **B** which is identical to **C**. Therefore, in Lloyd's reckoning, Augustine's denial of these laws make him logically inconsistent.

But does Augustine actually deny these principles? Has Lloyd correctly construed Augustine's argument in *De trinitate*? In my estimation the answer is no to both questions. Even so, the simple refutation of Lloyd's argument does not advance the cause or lucidity of the Augustinian trinitology except by demolishing a barrier to it. For this reason, I propose to accomplish two things. First, I intend to demonstrate why Lloyd's arguments against the consistency of the Augustinian trinitology do not have sharp teeth. Second, I intend to demonstrate how a few felicities borrowed from the elementary theory of groups can serve to make the logic of the Augustinian trinitology clearer, though perhaps not easier to understand. I do not intend to take up Lloyd's other criticisms of Augustine's theory of trinitarian personality. My only concern, here, will be with Lloyd's critique of Augustine's theory of relations.

Difficulties in Lloyd's Interpretation of the Augustinian Ontology

It is my contention that Lloyd misconstrues Augustine's formulation of the Trinity in a perversely equivocal way when he argues that Augustine understood the relation between accidents (necessary or otherwise) and necessary non-accidental relations and their respective (unitary) substance(s) as that of identity.

Three pieces of textual evidence are useful in establishing that Augustine was not likely to maintain premise 6. First—as far as I can tell—nowhere in *De trinitate* does Augustine argue that "to have the same (unitary) substance means to be identical with that substance." Even if Lloyd believes this to be the position to which Augustine is driven by abandoning a characterization of the personal distinctions which makes them accidental, to present this as Augustine's only alternative is to damn Augustine's modification of the category of relation before one has sympathetically examined it.

Second, there is textual evidence to indicate that Augustine was well aware of the profound logical and ontological consequences that such a modification would entail. One of the Aristotelian texts that apparently was part of the antecedent textual horizon of *De trinitate*—the *Categories*—makes it clear that accidents stand in relationship to substance as adscititious additions.[12] Their inherence in the substances which they qualify closely resembles the modern notion of unnecessary set inclusion. Of all of the categories of accident, relation has a most attenuated form of existence. As Bertrand de Margerie has happily put it: as classically conceived, "relation has the weakest being among all accidents. It is more remote from substance than all the others.

Hence its 'ecstatic' character."[13] Even in the case of the much discussed necessary accidents—the first inkling of which was apparently introduced into the
Western philosophical tradition by Porphyry in the *Isagoge* and, later, employed by Augustine advantageously against the Pelagians to defend the accidental but necessary nature of original sin—these necessary accidents are not
construed as being identical with substance.[14] Given the elevation of the category of relation to an eternal, necessary category, it does not follow that a
reflexive relationship on some substance means that it must be identical to
that substance.

Third, if the report given by Augustine in his *Confessiones* is veracious
and not a romanticized memory of his college days, then the one book of Aristotle he, perhaps, understood better than all others was the *Categories*.[15]
Were this the case, it is unlikely that Augustine would maintain an interpretation of the *Categories* which put the consistency of his description of the Trinity in question. Mind you, I say "consistency of his description." I am not
maintaining that Augustine did not modify the ontology which the *Categories*
expresses. Exactly how profoundly that ontology was modified, I hope to
make clear later. For now, let me simply say that my position is that Augustine changed the notion of the category of relation in the spirit of a good "em-
piricist."[16] Because he knew of a reality which demanded its revision (the
Trinity), he did not hesitate to revise it. But—and this is a very important
'but'—he did so consistently, *contra* Lloyd.

Fourth, Augustine is aware of how greatly he stretches the limits of language in describing the structure of the Trinity. But instead of letting conventional semantic categories straightjacket his theological insights, he allows the
realities to determine the structure of linguistic usage and not the other way
around. This explains why his descriptions of the philosophical complexities
involved are so hard to follow at points.[17]

The Logic of Augustine's Trinitology and Group Theory

Thus far, my attempts to dull the sharpness of Lloyd's critique of Augustine have been based upon the inductive evidence surrounding the composition of *De trinitate*. However, it seems to me that if we are to take Augustine's
formulation seriously, on its own terms, something more is demanded. We
must show that there is no logical inconsistency in Augustine's trinitology as
Lloyd claims there is. It seems to me that the formal resemblance between

what Augustine claimed about the Trinity and some of the definitions of the mathematical theory of groups provides us with a set of appropriate tools for arguing there need not be a logical inconsistency in that interpretation of Augustine's trinitology which makes it a fundamental modification of the classical ontology.

The definitions of the mathematical theory of groups are useful because they lend formal clarity to ideas which Augustine managed somewhat less abstractly. In applying these tools, however, I ought to be clear about what I am doing. *I am not* suggesting that Augustine consciously anticipated the modern notions of relations, mappings, or groups in his formulation of the Trinity but, rather, that the notions he described are susceptible to an interpretation under these formal descriptions. In other words, the Augustinian trinitology instantiates what we might call a model of a portion of the mathematical theory of groups. Another way of putting the relation between the formal description provided here and Augustine's trinitology is that the latter is a formally isomorphic interpretation of a portion of the theory of groups.[18]

Before attempting a final mathematical reformulation of the Augustinian trinitology, a few preliminary notions are required. Aside from the notion of a set—which may be defined as a collection of at least one thing which is said to have membership in it or to belong to it—we also require the notions of a Cartesian product, a relation and a mapping. The notions of relations and mappings presuppose the notion of a Cartesian product. A Cartesian product is a pairing of set members described in the following definition:

(Def. 1)   A Cartesian product A × B is the set of all ordered pairs (x, y) such that $x \in A$ and $y \in B$, where A and B need not be different sets and x and y need not be different elements.[19]

From this definition, it is possible to define both the notion of relation and mapping.

(Def. 2)   A relation C between sets A and B is a subset of A × B. If A = B, then C is said to be a relation on A. The *domain* of a relation is defined by $\mathcal{D}(C) = \{x \mid y \in B \ni (x,y) \in C\}$ and the *range* or image of C is defined by $\mathcal{R}(C) = \{y \mid x \in A \ni (x,y) \in C\}$

Because every set is a subset of itself, a relation can exist on a single set and/or a single member of some set(s).

In the broadest sense, a mapping is an abstract operation which is used to establish connections, trace certain sorts of relations or describe functions between either elements of different sets or the elements of the same set. It should not be confused with the relation itself. Rather, it is a logical device useful for describing the formal properties of some sorts of relations. Thus, we may take the notion of a mapping, in the broadest sense, as follows:

(Def. 3)   There is a mapping $\bar{G}$ of F into S iff there is a formula (F $\times$ S) which assigns to each element of x of F an element y of S (which is called "the image of x under $\bar{G}$") and (i) for each element x $\in$ F there is a y $\in$ S such that (x,y) $\in$ $\bar{G}$ and (ii) if (x,y) $\in$ $\bar{G}$ and (u,v) $\in$ $\bar{G}$ and if x = u then y = v.

What distinguishes a mapping (or function) from a relation is the precise way a mapping assigns pairs across sets. From definitions two and three, one can see that all mappings are relations but not all relations are mappings. However, in the (trivial) case of mappings from a single member to itself, the notion of mapping perfectly coincides with the notion of relation.

(Def. 4)   A relation R is reflexive if it is a relation of x to itself.

In the Augustinian trinitology all of the relations which define the trinitarian persons are reflexive because they take the substance as their source and terminus.[20] Yet the source and terminus of the relations of generation and spiration serve to define three distinct sets which correspond to the properties of personality. Thus x, as the first member of the relation of generation (the domain of $\bar{G}$), is a member of the Father set, though as the second member of the relation of generation (the range of $\bar{G}$) it is a member of the Son (or Logos) set. Likewise, x when it stands in the first place of the relation of spiration (the domain of $\bar{S}$) it is a member of either the Father or the Son set, but when it stands in the second place of the relation of spiration (the range of $\bar{S}$) it is a member of the Spirit set. Note that the distinction between these sets would not be possible were not the relations or functions directional.

(Def. 5)   A relation is symmetric if for any elements x and
            y if xRy then yRx.

Although taking the substance as their source and terminus, the trinitarian
relations are not symmetric because x (representing the substance) stands in
the domains and ranges of the different relations (mappings) and defines
different sets.[21]

(Def. 6)   A relation is transitive if for any elements x, y, z
            xRy, yRz then xRz.

Neither are the trinitarian relations transitive. The relation of generation
does not transfer equally to the Holy Spirit, nor does the relation of spiration
transfer equally to the Son.[22]

(Def. 7)   A relation is an equivalence relation if it is re-
            flexive, symmetric and transitive.

Although reflexive, the Augustinian trinitarian relations are not symmetric or transitive. Therefore, none of these relations can be considered
equivalence relations. A related notion is that of the identity of two mappings.

(Def. 8)   A mapping $\vec{G}$ is said to be identical to a mapping
            $\vec{X}$ iff (1) $\vec{G}$ and $\vec{X}$ have the same domain, (2) $\vec{G}$
            and $\vec{X}$ have the same range, and (3) $\vec{G} = \vec{X}$ for
            each element of the domain.

The relation of generation would be formally identical to some other
relation iff they both fulfilled the set of conditions described above. In the
case of the trinitarian persons there are no two relations which satisfy all of
the above conditions, and thus there are no two relations which are identical.
This is so because though the substance occupies the ranges and domains of
the relations it does so by virtue of the three different sets to which it belongs.
(Or, put another way, the origin of the relation of generation defines the personality of the Father, the terminus of the relation of generation defines the
personality of the Son, the origin(s) of the relation of spiration constitute the

property of being the senders or breathers of the Spirit and the terminus of the relation of spiration constitutes the personality of the Spirit.) Thus, the substance only by virtue of being a member of the Father set is related to the Son set and only by being a member of the Father and Son sets is related to the Spirit set. The Father set, Son set, and Holy Spirit set are different sets to which the substance belongs and it is only as member of each that the substance can be related to the others. Put simply, the Father set—though having only a single member—is different from the Son set, and the Holy Spirit set is different from both. They represent different domains and ranges because they function to demarcate different personal properties of the substance.

(Def. 9)   A mapping $\bar{G}$ of F into S is said to be *injective* if (1) whenever x and x′ of F are distinct elements then y and y′ are distinct elements of S or (2) if the elements of the domain of the mapping $\bar{G}$ are identical to one another and the elements of the range are identical to one another.

Only the relation of generation is injective according to the above definition because spiration is a relation which takes both Father and Son sets as its domains and maps these both to the one member of its set. Although the same substance is the origin of the relation of spiration, it has membership in two different sets as the origins of the relation of spiration. In other words, there is no single one-to-one mapping which establishes the origin of the relation of spiration. It requires two. One traces its origin to the Father set, and one traces its origin to the Son set.[23]

(Def. 10)   A mapping $\bar{G}$ of F into S is said to be surjective if for each element y of S there is at least one element of F such that $\bar{G}$ maps x to y.

Both the relations of generation and spiration are surjective according to the above definition.

(Def. 11)   A mapping is said to be bijective if it is both injective and surjective; two sets are termed similar if there is a bijective mapping between them.

Because the relation of generation is both injective and surjective, it is bijective. But the relation of spiration is not bijective because it fails the criteria of injection.

(Def. 12)   A mapping is said to be the inverse of another mapping Θ (1) if Θ is bijective and (2) if Θ^{-1} from B into A is x.

Augustine allows no *real* inverse relations in the Trinity. However, the notion of an inverse *mapping* can be used to make the notion of bijection clearer. The relation of generation must act like a bijective mapping because it takes one element from the Father set and maps it onto one element of the Son set, but the relationship of spiration would apparently not be so since spiration (according to the Western definition) entails the mapping of one element from the Father set and one element from the Son set to an element of the Spirit set. This suggests that there is no unique inverse mapping of the range of the Spirit set as there is in the case of the Son set because an inverse mapping demands that the original mapping be bijective. This observation is particularly interesting given the fact that we can define the relation of spiration as the product of a mapping. The product of a mapping can be described as follows:

(Def. 13)   Given the sets F, S and H and the mappings $\overline{G}$ and $\overline{S}$ ($\overline{G}$ from F into S and $\overline{S}$ from S into H), there is a third mapping which maps F directly into H and it is called the product or composite.

Another way of viewing this mapping is to consider the Western definition of spiration which makes the spiration of the Holy Spirit relative to the Son, first, a matter of the mapping of the Father set into the Son set and then, of the Son set into the Spirit set. On the other hand, the relation of spiration relative to the Father maps the Father set directly into the Spirit set. The spiration of the Holy Spirit from the Father may, thus, be considered the product or composite of the mapping of the Father into the Son and, then, of the Son into the Spirit.

Now we are in a position to define a relationship which will be of great importance in demonstrating the consistency of the Augustinian trinitology. This is the notion of identity mapping. Given the product of some mappings, identity mappings behave something like the number 1 in arithmetic multiplication. We can define the identity mapping as:

(Def. 14)   A mapping I'A is an identity mapping if it is (1) bijective and if (2) for any element x in a set A, I'A(x) = x and for any mapping Θ, I'A(Θ) = Θ and Θ(I' B) = Θ; moreover, for any mapping Θ which is bijective, then $\Theta(\Theta^{-1})$ = I'A and $\Theta^{-1}(\Theta)$ = I'B.

In other words, the identity mapping leaves unchanged the elements of any set and the mappings between any set so long as those mappings are bijective. In the case of the Augustinian trinitology, the identity mapping operates on any individual element or relation but not across relations. This follows from definition 6 which described the conditions for the identity of relations.

(Def. 15)   A binary operation $\oplus$ on some set, is a mapping A $\times$ A into A which maps each pair (x,y) of the elements of A to an element x $\oplus$ y of A.

(Def. 16)   A groupoid is a pair (G, $\oplus$) where G is a non-empty set, and $\oplus$ is a binary operation on G.

Augustine describes only one operation which qualifies the Trinity as for consideration under definitions 15 and 16; this is the addition of substantial powers. He suggests that the addition of the powers of any two or three trinitarian members does nothing to increase them.[24] The significance of this statement will be seen below.

(Def. 17)   A semigroup is a groupoid (G, $\oplus$) whose operation is associative: (x $\oplus$ y) $\oplus$ z = x $\oplus$ (y $\oplus$ z).

From what Augustine says about the addition of trinitarian powers, the Trinity can be considered to be a semigroup—as well as a group with a single element as the definition below indicates—because the addition of the substance as it appears under inclusion in the Father set, the Son set and the Holy Spirit set does not increase its associated powers. It retains its absolute value or magnitude because the substance functions as a unit element and its own inverse.

> (Def. 18)   A group is a semigroup (G, ⊕) which satisfies two additional conditions: (1) it must possess a unit element e such that e ⊕ x = x ⊕ e = x for all x in G and (2) it must possess an inverse element such that a ⊕ â = â ⊕ a = e.

Since the trinitarian substance functions like a unit element, the trinitarian substance functions like a one member group. A one member group (by definitions 15 through 18) must necessarily be a group whose single member is the unit element. And under any binary operation ⊕ the two conditions for a group are equivalent because (e ⊕ x = x ⊕ e) = (a ⊕ â = â ⊕ a) = e.[25]

Pictorially, we can convey something of what Augustine intends by the following diagram:

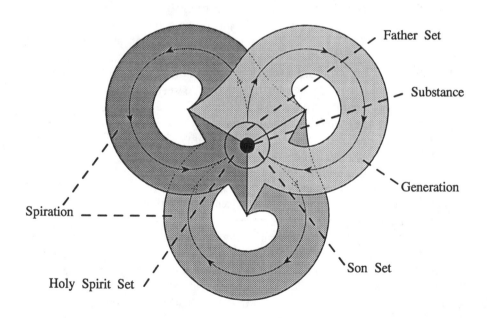

Summary and Conclusion

Now where exactly does this all lead us with respect to Lloyd's original point? I think it is clear that Lloyd's arguments that Augustine (1) is forced to maintain a theory of relation which forces him to accept proposition 6 and (2) that Augustine is forced otherwise to maintain a non-symmetric theory of identity both stem from a singular lack of imagination. To paraphrase Maritain, Lloyd has confused what was unimaginable, for him, with what is logically impossible, for everyone.[26]

How then do we describe the Augustinian trinitology in a way which clarifies the consistency of his thinking? The following expresses the above formulations in a nutshell. Augustine is maintaining that the trinitarian relations themselves define the personal properties. These relations are reflexive with respect to the substance but they are directional. Put in modern logical terms this means that the substance standing as the one element of the domain of the relation of generation defines the property of Fatherhood but standing as it also does in the range of that same relation it defines the property of Sonship. But this identification of Fatherhood with the range of the relation of generation is absolute as is Sonship with the domain of the same relation. Sonship cannot be associated with the domain (or point of origin) of the relationship any more than Fatherhood could be associated with the range of the same relation. The order which the direction of the relation of generation imposes on the substance defines a simple serial order. Because this order is formally absolute, the property of being in the domain of the relation of generation is not identical to the property of being in the range of the relation of generation—in the language of the Trinity, the Father is not the Son. In fact, there is only one thing which stands in each of these places—the substance,— but it does so uniquely in each place, thus, making the relation of generation bijective (as described above). In the case of spiration, the logical relations are a bit more involved, owing to the fact that Augustine accepted the classical *filioque* formulation of spiration.

The spirating of the Holy Spirit may be logically described as two relations: spiration as taking both the range of the relation of generation as its domain as well as the domain of the relation of generation. The range of the relation of spiration again takes the substance to produce the personality of the Holy Spirit. What this suggests is that the relation of spiration relative to the Father is the product of the relations of generation and spiration while the relation of spiration relative to the Son is a simple relation. If considered the same relation, this relation cannot be considered bijective since it is not injective but merely surjective. Finally, the substance of the Trinity may be construed as an automorphic one member group under all binary operations.

What all of this means to Lloyd's analysis is the following. Lloyd is mistaken in arguing that Augustine is forced to maintain "a non-symmetric theory of identity." He is mistaken because a singular lack of imagination does not allow him to see a way out of the dichotomy between tritheism or modalism. But there is a way out, and Augustine has found it by revising the categories of classical ontology to allow relations to operate reflexively upon substances to define new necessary properties. Put another way, the words "Father," "Son," and "Holy Spirit" are properly applied to the substance as it takes either the domains or ranges of the various trinitarian relations but *only as it does so.* There is no question of identifying the properly substantial properties with the-properties-of-being-in-the-domain-and-range of either trinitarian relation since three such properties belong to the substance only inasmuch as it is related to itself according to the relations of generation and spiration. To identify the trinitarian persons—as Lloyd does—is to identify relationally derived substantial properties with proper substantial properties of the Trinity. To attempt to fragment the Trinity into three substances—Lloyd's other alternative—is to make the relational properties accidental differences which differentiate substances. As the theory of groups shows us, Augustine can consistently allow neither.

Moreover, inasmuch as the substance behaves like a unit set, operations over the results of the various relations would consistently yield the same result: the unit set. Thus, there is no paradox in the powers of the Son added to the powers of the Father not being any greater than the powers of the Father taken alone, contrary to the assertions of Harnack.

The above provides some idea of how Augustine's descriptions of the Trinity may be conceptualized through the use of a mathematical analogy. Such a conceptualization reveals a logically consistent and subtle structure though it may not be one which is particularly easy to understand, especially when described orally. For this reason, I leave you with a final visual analogy which bears a number of formal resemblances to the mathematical description I have constructed above. Imagine you have a bipolar bar magnet and you place it on a white flat surface. Then, you spill iron filings around it. The iron filings will line up in concentric arcs whose end points are the poles of the magnet. Now imagine you could pare the magnet down almost to a point source. The shapes of the arcs would change to form two circles with a commonly shared point (the fragment of the magnet). The area atop the point source would be one pole of the magnet and the area below the point source would be its opposite. If you let the magnet stand for the trinitarian substance, the arcs of magnetic force for the relations of generation and spiration and the poles for the trinitarian persons, then you have a rough idea of the structures Augustine was describing. Of course, in Augustine's Trinity there are three poles, two relations and one substance, all of which are metaphysical and beyond physical categories of space, time and force as we understand them. Nevertheless, they do have formal similarities to things we do understand, like sets, relations and groups.

Notes

[1] The idea of providing an interpretation of the Augustinian trinitology on the basis of the theory of groups occurred when I was an assistant professor of Religious Studies at Michigan State University. One day, while lecturing on the development of Christian thought, I shared with my students some of the content of an unpublished paper I had been working on in which I demonstrated that Augustine's trinitology could be described within the logical theory of relations formulated by Carnap. One of my students, Daniel Kirkwood (a very bright mathematics major now at the University of Michigan) was quite surprised that a theologian would be making use of such tools. Immediately, he suggested that the analysis might be extended to mathematical group theory. Daniel's suggestion was the germ of this paper, though he can be held responsible for contributing neither to its material development nor its shortcomings. As is well known, the theory of groups, itself, can be given a purely logical formulation.

[2] Adolf Harnack, *History of Dogma*, vol 4, tr. by N. Buchanan (repr. Gloucester: Peter Smith, 1976), p. 130.

[3] Ibid., 129.

[4] Ibid.

[5] Ibid., 130.

[6] Ibid., 131.

[7] P. Tillich, *A History of Christian Thought* (New York: Simon and Schuster, 1968), pp. 116–17.

[8] To be fair to Harnack, he obviously does recognize that Augustine had written earlier works of trinitological significance—Letters 11 and 120, in particular—but even with respect to the earliest of these, Harnack maintains that "it nevertheless already contained his [Augustine's] fundamental thought..." (*History of Dogma* 4, 130, n. 1). It is this claim that I dispute in an unpublished historical study of Augustine's trinitological development, where I argue that Augustine's earlier conceptions of the Trinity—on the surface of

things—are much more modalistic than his later thought, thus evidencing considerable development.

[9] A. C. Lloyd, "On Augustine's Concept of a Person," in *Augustine: A Collection of Critical Essays*, ed. R. A. Markus (New York: Anchor Books, 1972), pp. 191–205.

[10] Lloyd, "On Augustine's Concept of a Person," p. 195.

[11] Ibid.

[12] *Categories* 2a19–2b6; *Prior Analytics* 43b1–43b39; *Metaphysics* 1025a14–1025a34.

[13] Bertrand de Margerie, *The Christian Trinity in History*, tr. Edmund Fortman (Still River: St. Bede's Publications, 1982), pp. 133–34.

[14] Porphry the Phoenician, *Isagoge*, tr. Edward Warren (Toronto: The Pontifical Institute of Medieval Studies, 1975), pp. 61–62.

[15] *Confessiones* IV,xvi,28–31: *CC* XXVII,54–56.

[16] I take it that Augustine's trinitological formulations are founded upon first-hand contemplative experience and are not merely a matter of a fertile theological imagination. This is especially clear in the later books of *De trinitate*.

[17] Augustine explains how reality drives theological discourse in a number of places throughout *De trinitate*. See, for example: V,i,1; V,iii,4, and V,vii,8: *CC* L,206; 208–9; 212–15, where Augustine succinctly summarizes his method. In the last passage he says: "*Quamobrem non est in rebus considerandum quid uel sinat uel non sinat dici usus sermonis nostri sed quis rerum ipsarum intellectus eluceat.*" Also, the discussion contained in Book VII (*CC* L,244–67), as a whole, shows the distinctive marks of Augustine's moving from realities to the structuring of appropriate language.

[18] The notions of "model" and "interpretation of a model" are given various meanings in the literature. What I am maintaining is that the logical structure of Augustine's description of the Trinity and the logical structure of portions of the theory of groups are identical, the differentiating material being the interpretation assigned to the predicates in each set of descriptions. I am arguing that there is a formal isomorphism between Augustine's trinitology and the mathematical description of a group with a single member. In other words, Augustine's trinitology and the elementary theory of groups are formally analogous according to the description of *proportionaliter eadem* provided by I. M. Bochenski in his article "On Analogy," in *Logico-Philosophical Studies*, ed. by A. Menne (Dordrecht: Reidel, 1962), pp. 97–117.

[19] These definitions I have borrowed and modified freely from two works: J. A. Green, *Sets and Groups* (London: Routledge & Kegan Paul, 1971) and J. Landin, *An Introduction to Algebraic Structures* (New York: Dover, 1989).

[20] *De trinitate*: V,xiv,15: *CC* L,222–23; VI,v,7: *CC* L,235–36; VI,vii,9: *CC* L,237–38; VII,i,2: *CC* L,245–49; VII,ii,3: *CC* L,249–50. Of course, Augustine does not make use of a Latin synonym of the English word "reflexive," but the notion of the reflexivity of the trinitarian relations is implicit in his notion that all of the persons are of the substance and yet

related to one another. Lacking the definition of reflexivity (the major premise), Augustine provides the minor premise.

[21] *De trinitate* V,vi,7: *CC* L,211–12; VIII,iv,7: *CC* L,275–76.

[22] This follows from there being two different relations. See *De trinitate* V,xii,13: *CC* L,220; VIII,iv,7: *CC* L,275–76; VIII,viii,12: *CC* L,286–89.

[23] I take it that in *De trinitate* V,xiv,15: *CC* L,222–23, Augustine's reference to the one source of the Spirit is a reference to this source under the description of substance since the properties he describes are substantial properties and are not properties produced by the relations.

[24] *De trinitate*: V,vi,7: *CC* L,211–12; V,viii,9: *CC* L,215–16; VI,viii,9: *CC* L,238; VI,x, 12: *CC* L,242–43.

[25] The isomorphism expressed, here, between the theory of groups and the Augustinian trinitology is also susceptible to a description using symbolic logic, a description I have already completed in an unpublished paper. Moreover, Augustine's trinitology would also seem susceptible to description in terms of mereology according to the method of double (diatomic) pairing developed by J. P. Burgess and presented in the appendix to D. Lewis, *Parts of Classes* (Oxford: Blackwell, 1991), pp. 121–27.

[26] J. Maritain admirably summarizes the dangers of confusing imaginative, logical and metaphysical necessity in *The Degrees of Knowledge* (New York: Charles Scribner's Sons, 1959) n. 2, pp. 106–7, by way of a critique of the Husserlian "*epochê*": "By making the object of various intentional functions freely vary, by way of imagination, so as to keep only the *eidos* of those functions, a *de jure* necessity grasped in an essence is not thereby set free before the mind; only *de facto* necessity of intentional life is thereby stated and it is but a substitute for true intelligible necessity." Lloyd's attempt to eliminate a *tertium quid* and to allow only the alternatives of modalism or tritheism is possible only under a peculiarly unimaginative interpretation of what Augustine is up to. As soon as one understands that Lloyd's interpretation is not the only one possible, recourse to a description like mine becomes a live option. See also: G. E. Hughes and M. J. Cresswell, *Introduction to Modal Logic* (London: Methuen, 1973), pp. 75–80.

III

God and Time

Augustine

Promittitur autem nobis uita aeterna per ueritatem a cuius perspecuitate rursus tantum distat fides nostra quantum ab aeternitate mortalitas. Nunc ergo adhibemus fidem rebus temporaliter gestis propter nos et per ipsam mundamur ut cum ad speciem uenerimus quemadmodum succedit fidei ueritas ita mortalitati succedat aeternitas.

De trinitate IV,xviii,24

Time and Ascent in *Confessions* XI[1]

John C. Cavadini

What is time? Timeless and interesting as that question may be, it is not the subject of this paper, nor, I would argue, of Book XI of Augustine's *Confessions*. Augustine does of course raise the question,[2] and reflection on it and related questions occupies a large, although not the whole, bulk of the book. Yet this need not mean that Book XI is the equivalent of a treatise *peri aiônos kai chronou* ("On Eternity and Time") like that of Plotinus in *Ennead* III.vii.[3] Nor is it clear that Augustine ever gives a completely self-consistent and unequivocal answer to the question of what time is,[4] the many helpful summaries of Augustine's views on the subject notwithstanding.[5] Rather than add to their roster, I will propose the desirability of asking the more modest question of how the discussion of time in Book XI functions in its context in that book. What is, in fact, its context? In the course of the discussion it will become evident, I hope, that Augustine is much more interested in exploring questions regarding our awareness of time, rather than precisely settling the question regarding time itself.

Let us begin *in medias res*, where the question: What is time? first comes up, as in Plotinus' discussion, after an initial consideration of eternity.[6] To our immediate chagrin, we learn that time can only be said to exist insofar as it tends to non-existence.[7] This is, in a way, the sum and substance of Augustine's answer, sufficient for his purposes as far as its content goes. But Augustine, happy to show he can trade in philosophical *epigramata*, is usually not satisfied with them, no matter how arresting. One senses an uneasiness with them, especially here, where the very complexity of the puzzle is a kind of pleasure which permits us to think we know more than we do, to distance ourselves falsely from the impact of the problem at hand. What does this mean for *us*?

Augustine will interpret his epigram, then, not by taking it as an entrance into a fuller, more specific philosophical description of time itself, but by shifting the focus to a consideration of our *awareness* of time.[8] He addresses the soul, telling her that "she is gifted with the ability to be aware of and to measure intervals of time."[9] Our measurement of time is based on our awareness of what we call a "long time" or a "short time," phrases which we use to describe a past or future time,[10] but what does this awareness actually represent? The past exists no longer and the future does not yet exist:[11] thus, they cannot be either long or short.[12] As for the present, it can't be "long" because it is always passing from future to past in such a way that its duration has no length.[13] Yet, for all that, "we are aware of intervals of time, and we do compare them, saying some are longer, some are shorter."[14] We measure them "by our awareness,"[15] even if our awareness is not an awareness of "times that are past" (*tempora praeterita*) or "times that are future" (*tempora futura*), but of times "as they pass" (*praetereuntia tempora*), that is, of the passing of time.

This doesn't mean that there is no past or future, i.e., that there are no past or future *events*[16] —that we have no past or future. Augustine adduces his own childhood, discussed in Book I, as an example. There are, therefore, future and past events, but these are not the same as independently existing "times past" or "times future"—the only awareness of time is of time *passing*. Any other construct placed on our awareness is an illusion. One begins to suspect, as well, that it is not an entirely disinterested illusion. Augustine's unraveling of his epigrammatic statement in terms of what it means to be aware of something which exists only in virtue of its tendency to non-existence is coming closer to home. If all our awareness of time is actually of time passing, then it is a continual awareness of our own ephemerality. It may be that we find it convenient to shield ourselves from that.

At any rate, if future and past do exist, they exist—"wherever and whatever they are"—as *praesentia*,[17] as "presents," as things present. Specifically, things past, like Augustine's childhood, no longer exist, but images of those things do presently exist in the memory. Our awareness of things past is thus an awareness of their images present in the memory.[18] This means that our awareness of things past is actually a kind of awareness of the *present*, and, in particular, awareness of the mind remembering. Similarly, with regard to the future, it is not future actions or events which are present to our awareness—since they are, precisely, *future*—but rather our own *praemeditationes* or *imaginatio* about the future, our "plans" or expectations, based upon our own intentions and/or observations of signs and causes.[19] As with the case of past events, awareness of future events is actually a kind of awareness of the *present*, and, in particular, of the mind imagining or expecting. If one feels one must still talk about "three times," one should not refer absolutely to past, present, and future as though these had being, but rather "the present of things past, the present of things present, and the present of things future,"[20] keeping in mind, however, that the present of things past is memory, the present of things present is attention (*contuitus*), and the present of things future is expectation.[21]

But what does this mean for measuring time? Measuring time involves, as already noted, awareness of extension,[22] but the extension we are aware of when we are measuring time is not an extension of a body into movement,[23] or of the voice into speech,[24] but rather of the mind[25] in remembering, attending, or expecting. At this point, Augustine interposes an invocation to his own mind bravely to press on, reminding himself that God is his helper and that "God made us—we did not make ourselves."[26] This is not idle rhetorical flourish.[27] He is steeling himself to face the truth, "which lightens now in the East,"[28] instead of a customary illusion, and that is the difficult truth of what awareness of time ultimately is: an awareness of our own ephemerality, an awareness that "we" in fact "did not make ourselves," that God made us, and that we have no control over our passing away. Our awareness of time is ultimately a species of *self-awareness*, and as such is an awareness, with the Ambrosian verse he is about to consider, that "God is the Creator of all" (*Deus creator omnium*).

Augustine continues: Since, when we are measuring time, we are measuring the *affectiones* which things make in the mind as they pass,[29] our awareness of time passing is our awareness of a change in the way our mind is "affected" by something, or is extended in its consideration of something which moves from being expected, through being attended to, into being remembered.[30] The present time lacks extension because it vanishes into a point, but attention perdures: so a long future and a long past are, respectively, a long expectation of the future, and a long memory of the past.[31] Everything passes from expectation to memory, until it is all memory, that is, a present awareness of ourselves having somehow "passed away"—not an awareness of ourselves somehow still existing "in the past." And this is true not only of psalm passages and hymn verses, but of our own actions, lives, and of the whole *saeculum*—the "parts" of which are nothing more than the lives of human beings.[32] Our actions are extended, but not "in time," where that is some sort of realm where these actions still exist, even though past—our actions are extended[33] from expectation to memory, and our awareness of their extension, i.e. of time, is in the first instance an awareness of our own mind's expecting and remembering. We need God's help to face this because it means the renunciation of a comfortable illusion, that of a "time" in which our acts even if they are past, still retain some anchor in existence, and in which we, therefore, have a claim on some kind of eternity, however shadowy, and with it the implicit denial that "God created us, we did not create ourselves"—*Deus creator omnium*.

We may wonder now if Augustine has come to the same conclusion as Plotinus in his treatise on time and eternity, and to some extent we are entitled to claim that he has. Like Plotinus, Augustine denies the existence of a temporal realm or "time" apart from the life of the mind or soul. But in order to make the comparison with Plotinus' treatise and his conclusions more precise, we must first give further consideration to the character and context of Augustine's discussion. In focusing the discussion on our *awareness* of time and the way in which our awareness of time is at once an awareness of or an implicit claim about God, Augustine's discussion is revealed not as a *treatise* on time but, in good Neoplatonic tradition, as an "ascent" of the soul in which consideration of created things leads one to contemplation of God. Augustine has recast Plotinus' treatise into an ascent crafted by his rhetoric. Augustine has taken us all, Plotinus included, on an introspective ascent patterned after the "ascents" which Augustine learned to make from the "Platonist books" and described at other places in the *Confessions*, most notably at VII,x, VII,xvii, and IX,x. These have been amply discussed by Courcelle and others,[34] and the links to these reports are numerous.

This particular ascent begins early in Book XI, in an effort to understand the first verse of Genesis. "I would hear and understand, how *In the Beginning*, you *made heaven and earth*."[35] Augustine starts not by opening a treatise-like, explicit dialogue with the positions of other philosophers (as does Plotinus) or exegetes, but by considering the heavens and the earth themselves, the air and the waters, who "proclaim that they did not make themselves."[36] Their beauty or goodness is but an occasion and even exigence for the consideration of the greater beauty towards which they point.[37] We move further, and take a characteristic inward turn, when it is considered that God created the heavens and earth by speaking.[38] Consideration of what God's speaking might be like occurs coincident with, as a consideration of, our own words; we are prompted to an awareness of the eternal character of God's Word by contrast with the ephemeral character of our own.[39] The link with the ascent at Ostia is clear here.[40]

The terminus of the ascent, finally, is described in terms very reminiscent both of the ascents in Book VII and Book IX (Ostia). We come to a consideration of the "Beginning" in which God created, that is, the eternity of God's Word, God's Wisdom:[41]

> What is that light whose gentle beams now and again strike through to my heart, causing me to shudder in awe yet firing me with their warmth? I shudder to feel how different I am from it: yet insofar as I am like it, I am aglow with its fire. It is the light of Wisdom, Wisdom itself, which at times shines upon me, parting my clouds. But when I weakly fall away from its light, those clouds envelop me again in the dense mantle of darkness which I bear for my punishment.... And so I shall remain until you, 0 Lord, who *have pardoned all my sins*, also *heal all my mortal ills*.[42]

The ascent is successful, to an extent, but in its very success, in fact *because of its success*, it fails; *because* the "light" is glimpsed, Augustine "falls away." It is too bright for Augustine's weakness, and, as in the visions in Book VII and at Ostia, Augustine is left with longing, not fulfillment. What is this weakness? Augustine suggests that it involves the way in which this vision is predicated upon, is in fact coincident with, an awareness of his "unlikeness" (as at VII, x).[43] That is what causes him to "shudder." Awareness of God's eternity is coincident with the painful awareness that we are not eternal, and we resist that awareness.[44]

More specifically, the problem is that there is no past or future in eternity, which is always "still," that is, always wholly present, never past or future.[45] We resist having our minds "seized" and "held" in the awareness of God's eternity, and the long subsequent discussion of time shows us why—it is awareness of the present which we most resist, because awareness of the present is awareness of our own ephemerality, of the way in which we are always verging on and vulnerable to non-existence. We prefer, like the Manichee (and others) who ask, "What was God doing before God created the world,"[46] to imagine that eternity is an endless succession of times, an infinity of past and future, to which even God is subject. That makes God more like us, and us less "unlike" God. But Augustine proposes that he will in fact "seize" our heart and "hold" it,

> that it may be settled for a short while, and for that short while glimpse the brilliance of eternity, standing, as always,

> still, and compare it with times and the way they never stand
> still, and see that it is not comparable.[47]

Augustine's discussion of time will be a way of "holding" our minds at the
moment of the terminus of the ascent, where not only the "brilliance" of eternity and our "unlikeness" or "incomparability" to it may be glimpsed, but
where something else may be glimpsed for analysis, namely, the very way in
which our hearts resist being "held" and "fixed" in the awareness of God's
eternity.

We can see now that Augustine's discussion of time, which begins as an
answer to the Manichaean question, has functioned not only to evoke an
awareness of God by evoking self-awareness, like all good ascents, but has also
served as an analysis of our habitual and continuing resistance to this awareness. We are led to a self-awareness which includes not only an awareness of
our unlikeness to God, but a new recognition of our resistance to this awareness. It is in this sense that it shows us, finally, that our life itself has been a
"distention," a *diastasis* in Plotinus' language,[48] but not in Plotinus' sense.[49]
We are led to see and to say with Augustine, *ecce distentio est uita mea*,[50] "Behold, my whole life has been a *diastasis*!" I am continually attempting to
"stretch" myself out into an eternity by displacing my awareness of time—in
the first instance an awareness of self—onto an illusory realm of past, present,
and future in which, once it is established as objective, I may then take some
scant assurance of a claim about my own immortality. The very structure of
my consciousness is infected by pride! We are led here to a new self-awareness, one which has the precise character, finally, of *confession*—a confession,
that is, of sin.

But Plotinus himself is not exempt from this confession. After all, he
has not been able to say without qualification *deus creator omnium*, for the
diastasis of the soul of which he speaks creates not only time but engenders
the world as well.[51] The notion of the distention or fall of a world-soul from
primal contemplation as itself a creation of time and an engendering of the
world is thus revealed as an ideology of pride, a kind of mythos of pride, spun
out of our common and sinful reluctance to accept our own non-divine status.[52] If in some sense Plotinus' spirituality of ascent was itself polemically
articulated as an attempt to demythologize the Gnostic doctrine of ascent, it is
Augustine's business to demythologize, so to speak, Plotinus' myth of the pri-

mordial fall,[53] and the doctrine of ascent predicated upon it. The ascent on which Augustine conducts us in Book XI is a polemical one, meant not only to follow but to recontextualize Plotinus' treatise, and with it all of his language. We do not "fall" into time; we "fall"[54] by trying to escape time into eternity, by claiming that time is more than our own remembering, attending, and expecting as historical subjects defined by that remembering, attending, and expecting.

How can we avoid this? Not by engaging in philosophical ascents. Augustine has shown that these are essentially attempts to escape time. The more successful these are, the more we are tempted to fall back, to shield ourselves from our awareness of ephemerality by constructing ourselves as creators. We can only avoid this by, with Augustine at the end of Book X, bearing in mind our "price," the price of our redemption which is the blood of Christ.[55] Insofar as we hold this in our memories in faith, our very consciousness of our own ephemerality becomes the obverse side of a consciousness of the love[56] of God which "sought us when we sought him not,"[57] which bridged the gap between God's eternity and our unlikeness. In faith, as Augustine points out at the end of his discussion on time, we "forget" the "old days" of our sin, "'forgetting what we have left behind,' and...'press on, eager for the prize'" (Ph 3:12–14),[58] a goal which is truly eternal. In faith, our remembering becomes "confession," and our expectation, "hope." We stop trying to escape time because Christ has made time the place we find God's gracious love.

It is to bring us to this point that Augustine has written Book XI, which he began by repeating that he writes his *Confessions* "for the love of God's love," in an effort to bring others to the same:

> Why then do I recount so many things for you? Not, certainly, that you may know them from me. Rather, I am stirring up my love and that of those who read this, so that we might all of us say, "The Lord is great and greatly to be praised!" (Ps 47:2; 95:4; 144:3). I have already said and I will still say, I am doing this for the love of your love.[59]

The discussion of time in Book XI is thus at the service of the agenda of the *Confessions* as a whole, and that is to bring its readers to be able to confess, with the first line of the whole work repeated here, "The Lord is great and greatly to be praised!," or, to put it another way, *Deus creator omnium*.[60]

Notes

[1] I would like to thank the following, from whose conversation, criticism, and/or advice regarding this paper I have benefitted: Professors Barbara Agnew, Celia Chazelle, Anthony Godzieba, Kathryn Johnson, J. J. O'Donnell, Roland Teske, S.J., Joseph Wawrykow, and many students.

[2] *Confessiones* XI,xiv,17,lines 3–4, cf. line 8: *CC* XXVII,202: *Quid est enim tempus?* Cf. also *Confessiones* XI,xxiii,30,line 15: *CC* XXVII,209: *Ego scire cupio uim naturamque temporis....*

[3] E. P. Meijering, *Augustin über Schöpfung. Ewigkeit und Zeit: Das elfte Buch der Bekenntnisse* (Leiden: E. J. Brill, 1979), notes: "Das elfte Buch der Bekenntnisse ist nicht in erster Linie eine systematische Abhandlung zum viel verhandelten Thema: 'Schöpfung, Ewigkeit und Zeit'" (p. 115). To some extent, Augustine is following the order of thought in *Ennead* III,vii, as suggested by R. J. O'Connell, *St. Augustine's Confessions: The Odyssey of Soul* (Cambridge: Belknap, 1969), pp. 139–42 (although one would wish for more, and more specific, references to Plotinus' text). When Augustine remarks (*Confessiones* XI,xiv, 17,lines 4–9: *CC* XXVII,202) that it is easy enough to know what time is until someone asks us what time is, he seems to be faintly echoing Plotinus' comment at *Ennead* III,vii,1,lines 4–9: *PO* I,337 (all translations of Plotinus from A. H. Armstrong, tr., Loeb Classical Library, vol. 442). Also, following Plotinus, Augustine raises the question of eternity before he treats time, and, again following Plotinus, he refutes the views of others. Some of the language Augustine uses is also similar. Yet this does not in itself mean that Augustine is arguing a Plotinian agenda (just as one cannot say that Plotinus is simply re-arguing Plato's positions, despite his acknowledged indebtedness). In fact, *Confessions* XI seems to be a different sort of project than *Ennead* III,vii, which has the unmistakable "scholastic" tone of a treatise. Plotinus turns immediately, when considering both eternity and time, to expositions and discussions of the positions of the "blessed philosophers" (*Ennead* III,vii,1,lines 13–14: *PO* I,337; "blessed ancients," *Ennead* III,vii,7,lines 11–12: *PO* I,347). These discussions are quite lengthy—the discussion of previous theories of time occupies all of III,vii,7–10 (about half of the discussion of time), and reflection continues on these positions and others (Plato's in particular) in the sections that follow. Augustine, by contrast, raises only one of the positions which Plotinus discusses, and that very briefly (time is the movement of a body: *Confessiones* XI,xxiii–xxiv: *CC* XXVII,208–10; Plotinus, time is movement: *Ennead* III,vii,7,1ine 19; 8,lines 1–22: *PO* I,347–48—both argue that motion can stop but time does not). For other theories of influence on Augustine's treatment of time, see J. F. Callahan, *Augustine and the Greek Philosophers* (Villanova: Villanova University Press, 1967), pp. 74–93 and the literature there cited connecting Augustine's views to Basil of Caesarea and Gregory of Nyssa, and G. O'Daly, *Augustine's Philosophy of Mind* (Berkeley: University of California Press, 1987), pp. 152–61, who advances the theory of Stoic influence.

⁴ As, e.g., O'Daly notes (p. 153): "[Augustine] does not give an answer to this question."

⁵ In addition to literature already cited above, the most helpful are: J. Guitton, *Le temps et l'éternité chez Plotin et saint Augustin* (Paris: Boivin et Cie., 1933); J. F. Callahan, *Four Views of Time in Ancient Philosophy* (Cambridge: Harvard University Press, 1948), pp. 149–87; R. Jordan, "Time and Contingency in St. Augustine," *Review of Metaphysics* 8 (1954–55) 394–417; A. Solignac, S.J., in *Les Confessions de Saint Augustin; Livres VIII–XIII*, BA 14,581–91. See also the discussions in: R. Sorabji, *Time, Creation and the Continuum* (Ithaca, NY: Cornell University Press, 1983), pp. 29–32; 157–73. All of these works (except Jordan's) discuss Augustine's relation to Plotinus. See also the interesting suggestion of R. A. Markus, *Saeculum*, rev. ed. (Cambridge: Cambridge University Press, 1989), p. 10.

⁶ *Confessiones* XI,xiv,17,lines 3–4: *CC* XXVII,202. Plotinus' discussion of time begins at *Ennead* III,vii,7: *PO* I,346. O'Connell points out that both treatises consider eternity first (pp. 138–39).

⁷ *Confessiones* XI,xiv,17,lines 18–19: *CC* XXVII,203:...*scilicet non uere dicamus tempus esse, nisi quia tendit non esse.*

⁸ Note that I am not proposing that Augustine offers a "psychological" or subjectivist model of time, a model often attributed to him in the literature, and especially in critical assessments of Augustine's views, as, e.g., in Bertrand Russell, *Human Knowledge: Its Scope and Limits* (New York: Simon and Schuster, 1948), p. 212. I am proposing, instead, that Augustine is much more interested in analyzing our awareness of time as itself a phenomenon worthy of investigation, rather than in settling questions about time itself in a definitive way. One might say that metaphysically, Augustine's epigram is as much as he will say regarding time itself: the rest is an analysis of what it means for us to have awareness of time as existence tending towards non-existence. I am not assuming, then, that Augustine is even interested in speculating definitively about time itself, an assumption which goes unrecognized as such in almost all of the literature on Book XI (including such treatments as R. Suter, "Augustine on Time with Some Criticisms from Wittgenstein," *Revue internationale de philosophie* 16 [1962] 387–94; C. W. K. Mundle, "Augustine's Pervasive Error concerning Time," *Philosophy* 41 [1966] 165–68; J. McEvoy, "St. Augustine's Account of Time and Wittgenstein's Criticisms," *Review of Metaphysics* 38 [1984] 547–77; and O'Daly, p. 152, who talks about Augustine's "speculative freedom," and points this out as the basis of the critique in the last three articles cited).

⁹ *Confessiones* XI,xv,19,lines 22–23: *CC* XXVII,203: *Videamus ergo, anima humana, utrum praesens tempus possit esse longum: datum enim tibi est sentire moras atque metiri.*

¹⁰ *Confessiones* XI,xv,18,lines 1–2: *CC* XXVII,203: *Et tamen dicimus longum tempus et breue tempus neque hoc nisi de praeterito aut futuro dicimus.*

¹¹ *Confessiones* XI,xiv,17,lines 12–14: *CC* XXVII,203: *Duo ergo illa tempora, praeteritum et futurum, quomodo sunt, quando et praeteritum iam non est et futurum nondum est?* Note that this is not derived from Plotinus. In fact, Plotinus seems to want to admit some appropriate and objective sense in which the past exists: "So the spreading out of life (*diastasis zôês*) involves time; life's continual progress involves continuity of time, and life which

is past involves past time. So would it make sense to say that time is the life of soul in a movement of passage from one way of life to another? Yes, for if eternity is life at rest, unchanging and identical and already unbounded, and time must exist as an image of eternity...then we must say that there is...an image of unity, that which is one in continuity; and instead of a complete unbounded whole, a continuous unbounded succession" (*Ennead* III,vii,11,lines 41–56: *PO* I,356). It is true that time would be "abolished" (*anêirêtai chronos, Ennead* III,vii,12,line 20: *PO* I,357) should the soul return to union with the One in contemplation, and that there would then be no "before," "after," or "future" (lines 12–13), but these are characteristics of eternity (line 11), not time. At any rate, since this is the World-Soul of which Plotinus is speaking, whose *diastasis* engenders not only time but the universe (*to pan*, line 24; cf. III,vii,13,line 28: *PO* I,360, "one life produces both heaven and time"), the time thus engendered is as objective as the universe and the heavens. Plotinus goes on to note, "But if someone were to take the 'before' and 'after' of this movement [of the heavenly sphere] and call it time—on the ground that this is something real—but though the truer movement [of soul] has a 'before' and 'after,' were to deny this any reality, he would be quite unreasonable..." (III,vii,13,lines 30–34, 49–52: *PO* I,360–61). If anything, Augustine seems critical of this view. O'Daly's citation of a Stoic distinction on this point (p. 157; see the texts actually quoted by Sorabji, p. 22) seems more striking, although it is difficult to know how Augustine would have known these texts.

[12] *Confessiones* XI,xv,18,lines 6–9, 13–14, 53–56: *CC* XXVII,203–4.

[13] *Confessiones* XI,xv,20,lines 48–53: *CC* XXVII,204. O'Daly compares this to Stoic positions (p. 154).

[14] *Confessiones* XI,xvi,21,lines 1–2: *CC* XXVII,204.

[15] *Confessiones* XI,xvi,21,lines 5–6: *CC* XXVII,205:...*sentiendo metimur.*

[16] *Confessiones* XI,xvii,22,lines 10–11: *CC* XXVII,205: *Sunt ergo futura et praeterita*; the neuter plural here referring generically to things or events (as the prophet truly sees *futura* in line 7) as opposed to, simply, "the past" and "the future" (*praeteritum, futurum,* lines 3–4).

[17] *Confessiones* XI,xviii,23,lines 4–6: *CC* XXVII,205.

[18] *Confessiones* XI,xviii,23,lines 10–13: *CC* XXVII,205: *Pueritia quippe mea, quae iam non est, in tempore praeterito est, quod iam non est; imaginem uero eius, cum eam recolo et narro, in praesenti tempore intueor, quia est adhuc in memoria mea.* Note that this is a link not only to the events narrated in Book I, but it relates Augustine's reflections on our awareness of time to his work of telling his own story, a story, furthermore, contained in his memory (thus linking Book XI to Book X).

[19] *Confessiones* XI,xviii,23,lines 16–18; 24,line 36: *CC* XXVII,206.

[20] *Confessiones* XI,xx,26,lines 4–5: *CC* XXVII,207: *praesens de praeteritis, praesens de praesentibus, praesens de futuris.*

[21] *Confessiones* XI,xx,26,lines 6–7: *CC* XXVII,207.

[22] *Confessiones* XI,xxiii,30,line 43: *CC* XXVII,209: here, *distentio*.

[23] *Confessiones* XI,xxiii–xxiv: *CC* XXVII,208–10.

[24] *Confessiones* XI,xxvi,33: *CC* XXVII,211. This example does not come from *Ennead* III,vii.

[25] *Confessiones* XI,xxvi,33,lines 20–21: *CC* XXVII,211: *distentionem…ipsius animi*.

[26] *Confessiones* XI,xxvii,34,lines 1–2: *CC* XXVII,211: *Deus adiutor noster; ipse fecit nos, et non nos*, a link to Gn 1:1, the subject for exegesis in Book XI, and another link to Book I, at I,vi,10,lines 54–55: *CC* XXVII,5: *An quisquam se faciendi erit artifex?* connected immediately to considerations of time and eternity (I,vi,10,lines 58–66: *CC* XXVII,5).

[27] It is important to point this out. Passages such as this are often disregarded, or (worse) regarded cynically, as though present only for emphasis or to prepare for what the reader might regard as an unorthodox "plunge." For example, O'Connell notes of XI,xix, "Augustine breaks into prayer for light on all these difficulties. It alerts us we may have come to a crucial turning in the *exercitatio*." He is equally dismissive of XI,xxv ("And I confess to you, Lord, that I still do not know what time is…."): "Another fervent plea for light, and he is ready to take a decisive step forward" (pp. 140–45). But Augustine's voice has never left prayer so that it could "break into" prayer. He never leaves the voice of confession (as O'Connell implies when he notes that at XI,xxix,39 Augustine is presented as "encasing that formula in a *confessio*" [p. 142]. Thus O'Connell too treats Book XI essentially as a treatise on time, even if somewhat artfully done, so that such outbursts must always be seen as incidental or pragmatic waverings from the speculative work at hand. Instead one should be asking how the course of argument in Book XI is used to help the reader understand the character and genesis of the very voice that is able to make all utterances a confession, such that discussion of time and prayer for light are not heard as two different voices.

[28] *Confessiones* XI,xxvii,34,lines 2–3: *CC* XXVII,211: *Attende, ubi albescit ueritas*. I translated "whitens now in the East"—is there a hint of Plotinus' analogy that we can only wait for the One, who will come into our contemplation as the sunrise?

[29] *Confessiones* XI,xxvii,36,lines 49–50: *CC* XXVII,213.

[30] *Confessiones* XI,xxviii,37,lines 3–5: *CC* XXVII,213: *Nam expectat [animus] et attendit et meminit, ut id quod expectat per id quod attendit transeat in id quod meminerit*.

[31] *Confessiones* XI,xxviii,37,lines 8–13: *CC* XXVII,214: *Et quis negat praesens tempus carere spatio, quia in puncto praeterit? Sed tamen perdurat attentio, per quam pergat abesse quod aderit. Non igitur longum tempus futurum, quod non est, sed longum futurum longa expectatio futuri est, neque longum praeteritum tempus, quod non est, sed longum praeteritum longa memoria praeteriti est*.

[32] *Confessiones* XI,xxviii,38,lines 23–27: *CC* XXVII,214.

[33] With regard to singing or reciting the verse of a song, cf. *Confessiones* XI,xxviii, 38,lines 17–20: *CC* XXVII,214:…*distenditur uita huius actionis meae in memoriam propter quod dixi et in expectationem propter quod dicturus sum: praesens tamen adest attentio mea, per quam traicitur quod erat futurum, ut fiat praeteritum*.

[34] P. Courcelle, *Recherches sur les Confessions de Saint Augustin* (Paris: E. de Boccard, 1950), especially pp. 157–74, 222–26; see also F. E. Van Fleteren, "Augustine's Ascent of the Soul in Book VII of the *Confessions*: A Reconsideration," *AS* 5 (1974) 29–72, and the literature cited therein.

[35] *Confessiones* XI,iii,5,lines 1–2: *CC* XXVII,196: *Audiam et intellegam quomodo in principio fecisti caelum et terram.*

[36] *Confessiones* XI,iv,6,lines 1–7: *CC* XXVII,197.

[37] *Confessiones* XI,iv,6,lines 7–10: *CC* XXVII,197, echoing similar themes from the similar guided ascent in Book X.

[38] *Confessiones* XI,v,7,lines 21–22: *CC* XXVII,198, *Ergo dixisti et facta sunt atque in uerbo tuo fecisti ea.*

[39] *Confessiones* XI,vi,8,lines 7–13: *CC* XXVII,198: note the characteristic themes associated with the ascent—themes of the interior consideration of the mind, comparing the words sounding in time, which are "below" (*infra*) the mind, to the silent and eternal Word, which is above (*supra*) the mind.

[40] See, e.g., *Confessiones* IX,x,24,lines 28–32: *CC* XXVII,147–48, and the way in which the whole of the next section (IX,x,25: *CC* XXVII,148) is predicated on the image of all created things "falling silent" so that we might hear the Word of the Creator, not spoken with tongue or angel voice or any other created thing. Note too that it is in Book IX, in connection with the death of his mother, that Augustine first recites the Ambrosian hymn which appears like a refrain in Book XI, *Deus creator omnium* (IX,xii,32,line 59: *CC* XXVII,151; see also IX,x,24,lines 23–27: *CC* XXVII,147, where there is an explicit reference to time).

[41] Augustine seems here to be echoing Plotinus, who, at what might be considered a parallel point in their two works, seems to want to distinguish eternity from the One *per se*, identifying it with *nous* (following Armstrong's translation and interpretation at *Ennead* III,vii,5, note 1, p. 310).

[42] *Confessiones* XI,ix,11,lines 4–12: *CC* XXVII,199–200: *Quid est illud, quod interlucet mihi et percutit cor meum sine laesione? Et inhorresco et inardesco: inhorresco, in quantum dissimilis ei sum, inardesco, in quantum similis ei sum. Sapientia, sapientia ipsa est, quae interlucet mihi, discindens nubilum meum, quod me rursus cooperit deficientem ab ea caligine atque aggere poenarum mearum.... donec tu, domine, qui propitius factus es omnibus iniquitatibus meis, etiam sanes omnes languores meos....* I have followed here Pine-Coffin's translation (Saint Augustine, *Confessions*, tr. R. S. Pine-Coffin (New York: Penguin, 1961), p. 260.

[43] *Confessiones* XI,ix,11,line 6: *CC* XXVII,200: *dissimilis ei sum*; *Confessiones* VII,x, 16,line 17: *CC* XXVII,103, *et inueni longe me esse a te in regione dissimilitudinis.* Note that, by contrast, Plotinus' work in *Ennead* III,vii seems predicated on awareness of the likeness between soul and eternity. See e.g. *Ennead* III,vii,7,lines 3–5: *PO* I,346 ("...For what understanding could there be [of eternity] if we were not in contact with it? But how could we be in contact with what was not our own? We too, then, must have a share in eternity").

Actually, it is tempting to imagine that Augustine takes Plotinus, as it were, on just such an ascent as Plotinus describes at *Ennead* III,vii,1,lines 20–24: *PO* I,337–38 ("But if someone, before contemplating eternity, should form a picture in his mind of what time is, it would be possible for him, too, to go from this world to the other by recollection and contemplate that of which time is a likeness, if time really has a likeness to eternity"). Augustine shows that what happens if we undertake such an ascent is that we founder on the unlikeness of time (which for Plotinus is the image of eternity) to eternity. Augustine seems to be replying to Plotinus' conjecture at *Ennead* III,vii,5,lines 7–12: *PO* I,343: "What, then, if one does not depart at all from one's contemplation of it [the eternal] but stays in its company, wondering at its nature, and able to do so by a natural power which never fails? Surely one would be…oneself on the move towards eternity and never falling away from it at all, that one might be like it and eternal, contemplating eternity and the eternal by the eternal in oneself." Augustine, in *Confessiones* XI,ix: *CC* XXVII,199–200, shows what happens if one tries to make such an ascent, thinking to proceed to eternity from one's likeness to it, identifying our resistance to this and then going on to hold this resistance up for analysis. Augustine's ascent shows what, in his view, actually happens should one attempt to contemplate eternity: one glimpses it as the obverse side of a glimpse of one's own unlikeness, not one's likeness. Such an ascent, Augustine is arguing, is programmed to fail.

⁴⁴ Note that the awareness considered here is not the conceptual, philosophical knowledge of the mind's "contingency" (Jordan's term, from his title and *passim*), but the mind's own immediate awareness of itself, like that spoken of in the ascent at e.g. *Confessiones* VII,xvii: *CC* XXVII,107, where the mind becomes aware of its own operations in reasoning and judging, and of the principles (the "light") upon which those operations are predicated.

⁴⁵ *Confessiones* XI,xi,13: *CC* XXVII,200–201; cf. *Ennead* III,vii,3: *PO* I,339–40.

⁴⁶ *Confessiones* XI,x,12,line 2: *CC* XXVII,200; XI,xii,14,lines 1–2: *CC* XXVII,201; XI,xxx,40,lines 3–4: *CC* XXVII,215. That this is a Manichaean question is universally recognized because Augustine elsewhere reports it as such, but it could also come from other quarters, more broadly philosophical, including the Neoplatonists and Epicureans. See Solignac, p. 581, and Meijering, pp. 40–41.

⁴⁷ *Confessiones* XI,xi,13,lines 5–8: *CC* XXVII,201:…*ut paululum stet et paululum rapiat splendorem semper stantis aeternitatis et comparet cum temporibus numquam stantibus et uideat esse incomparabilem*….

⁴⁸ As O'Connell points out, p. 142, referring to *Ennead* III,vii,11.

⁴⁹ Also O'Connell's position (i.e., that Augustine is arguing an essentially Plotinian agenda): "The implication [of Augustine's exclamation *ecce distentio via mea* and its location in Augustine's text at a place analogous to the location of *diastasis* in *Ennead* III,vii] is clear: the soul's existence in time, its immersion in 'action,' is evidence of its 'fallen' state" (p. 142).

⁵⁰ *Confessiones* XI,xxix,39,line 2: *CC* XXVII,214.

⁵¹ *Ennead* III,vii,12,lines 22–25: *PO* I,357; cf. *Ennead* III,vii,13,lines 26–28: *PO* I,360.

[52] Nor do I think that O'Connell's hypothesis can be rescued by simply claiming that Augustine preserves the world-soul but renders it non-divine. Those who take this position (the most convincing articulation of it is by R. Teske, "The World-Soul and Time in St. Augustine," *AS* 14 [1983] 75–92) make the claim that the universe apart from the soul is still engendered by the distention or fall of the soul, but that that is the way in which God wills to create (Teske, p. 84). Part of the defense of the position is that Augustine's "definition" (pp. 88, 89) of time as a *distentio animi* would involve him in a hopelessly subjective view of time, one which in any event is inconsistent with other statements made by Augustine, if "soul" were not a larger reality in which time could have some "objective" reality apart from the mind. But this assumes, essentially, that Book XI is a treatise on time, that it does intend to "define" time (instead of, e.g., to analyze our awareness of time and/or the ascent of the soul itself), that because of Augustine's particular "definition" he is boxed into accepting Plotinus' position, and that Plotinus' problems are therefore Augustine's too. With regard to the latter, Teske notes: "Could Augustine who was very familiar with [*Ennead* III,vii] and who is otherwise so sensitive to the nuances of Plotinus' thought have failed to spot Plotinus' concern with the unity and objectivity of time and also have failed to realize that the Plotinian solution rested upon the doctrine of the universal soul with which individual souls are one?" (p. 85). But this assumes that Augustine is trying to solve a Plotinian problem instead of bringing up the problem as a critique of Plotinus. It is Augustine, after all, not Plotinus, who is uncomfortable with a "past time" with objective existence. Plotinus points out that there is no past or future in eternity, but Augustine's point is that there is no past or future *time*—i.e., the world soul, in which it resides, is a myth, and what is left, if one insists on writing treatises like Plotinus instead of examining time as the definitive posing of the question of self-awareness, is reduced to solipsism.

And, in any event, as Teske recognizes (p. 92, n. 49), his position is equivalent to saying that creation necessitated the fall (for an interesting approach to this problem see E. Zum Brunn, *Augustine: Being and Nothingness*, tr. Ruth Namad, 2nd ed. [New York: Paragon House, 1988]. Also, the description in *Confessiones* XI,xxxi of the mind which would know all ages past and future as a person knows a psalm, cannot actually be the description of the *unfallen* portion of a world-soul (Teske, p. 90), since the knowledge of the world it is assigned by Augustine is sequential, exactly analogous to our temporal knowledge, and thus it must be in time (fallen there, unless there is another way). Actually, there is no indication that Augustine meant the discussion in XI,xxxi to be anything but a return to the question which he raised in the opening lines of XI,i, regarding the way in which God knows temporal things. His discussion of time has enabled him to show, at least, that this description is wrong. In fact, it is what the Manichaean questioner from XI,x, to which Augustine returns in XI,xxx, would think the answer to the question was. Thus it is a foil to the correct answer, given in the last chapter (XI,xxxi).

[53] See Guitton, pp. 38–54.

[54] *Confessiones* XI,ix,12, line 8: *CC* XXVII,200: *deficientem*.

[55] *Confessiones* X,xliii,70,lines 34–39: *CC* XXVII,193, the last two sentences before Book XI begins.

[56] *Confessiones* X,xliii,69,lines 13–15: *CC* XXVII,192–93: *Quomodo nos amasti, pater bone, qui filio tuo unico non pepercisti, sed pro nobis impiis tradidisti eum! Quomodo nos amasti....* This is echoed in *Confessiones* XI,i,1,line 6: *CC* XXVII,194, where Augustine says that he writes *amore amoris tui* (a *verbatim* echo of *Confessiones* II,i,1,line 3: *CC* XXVII,18) for the love of God's love, which is not thus "God's love" in the abstract, but as revealed in the Incarnation. Should we not hear overtones of this at *Confessiones* XI,xxix, 39,line 14: *CC* XXVII,215 as well?

[57] *Confessiones* XI,ii,4,lines 49–50: *CC* XXVII,196, actually in the second person, addressed to God:...*per quem [Iesum Christum] nos quaesisti non quaerentes te, quaesisti autem, ut quaereremus te.*

[58] *Confessiones* XI,xxix,39,lines 5–9: *CC* XXVII,214: *et a ueteribus diebus conligar sequens unum, praeterita oblitus, non in ea quae futura et transitura sunt. sed in ea quae ante sunt non distentus, sed extentus, non secundum distentionem, sed secundum intentionem sequor ad palmam supernae uocationis....* Note that we do not escape the extension which characterizes time, but instead of being *distentus* into illusion, we are *extentus* (using a Scriptural word) with the "intent" extension of expectation which we may call hope. The citation of Ph 3:13 is another link between Book XI and the Vision at Ostia, at *Confessiones* IX,x,23,lines 7–8: *CC* XXVII,147, where the verse is cited at the beginning of the account of the vision.

[59] *Confessiones* XI,i,1,lines 2–6: *CC* XXVII,194: *Cur ergo tibi tot rerum narrationes digero? Non utique ut per me noueris ea, sed affectum meum excito in te et eorum, qui haec legunt, ut dicamus omnes: magnus dominus et laudabilis ualde. Iam dixi et dicam: amore amoris tui facio istuc.*

[60] Again, it is also possible to see the discussion of time in Book XI as part of Augustine's justifying and characterizing the voice of confession. The reader learns that the Neoplatonic ascent as an attempt to escape time fails and must fail because it is the avoidance ultimately of oneself. It is the denial that one *has* a story, that one's identity is constituted by a history. Thus Augustine's critique of what he sees as escapist ideologies or spiritualities is his prescription for a return to oneself and to the possibility of telling one's story. Faith enables us to stop embracing promises of escape from time. Thus returned to ourselves, we are enabled to tell our stories; we speak with the voice of confession. And, after all, Book XI begins with Augustine asking why he is telling God so many stories: *Cur ergo tibi tot rerum narrationes dirigo?* (*Confessiones* XI,i,1,lines 2–3: *CC* XXVII,194) and connects that question to God's eternal knowledge of temporal events. Book XI gives an answer to this question.

The Theological Dimension of Time in *Confessiones* XI

Christopher J. Thompson

It is true that Augustine's analysis of time in Book XI of the *Confessiones* has provided much reflection for centuries. And among related truths is the general thesis that what we are given in these passages is a psychological account of time. John F. Callahan has contributed much to this appellation "psychological" in his *Four Views of Time in Ancient Philosophy*, and has among other things contrasted the Augustinian approach to time with an Aristotelian account. Aristotle, according to Callahan, focuses on the physical aspects of time with its apparent connection to the problems of motion, while Augustine develops "a full-fledged psychological view."[1]

I propose that the Augustinian analysis of time in Book XI of his *Confessiones* is more properly a *theological* than psychological analysis, and that the genuine theological dimensions of the discussion have not always been fully appreciated—perhaps due to an overzealous interest in comparative analysis.

In more recent times, Paul Ricoeur has embarked on a similar kind of comparative venture in his three-volume *Time and Narrative*, and while his reading of Augustine is the more profound of the two, he also presents a particularly un-theological account of Book XI and thereby also produces an inadequate reading.[2] The common link between Callahan's and Ricoeur's approaches lies in their assumption that the Augustinian analysis of time is wedded only to Book XI, and, moreover, that it only begins to be substantively formulated around Chapter 17.[3] The effect of this approach is to wrench the discussion out of its proper context and this, in turn, sows the seeds for many subsequent distortions.[4] In other words, part of the problem in not adequately recognizing the theological aspects of Augustine's analysis stems largely from the tendency to ignore the broader context of the discussion.[5]

Sensitivity to the broader context would have illustrated that Augustine's primary concern in Book XI is not merely to provide an analysis—psychological or otherwise—of the character of time. Rather, the primary concern of Book XI is to situate the doctrine of creation and the created order within the doctrine of the Word, and to maintain this primacy of the Word in spite of our "fallen" tendencies to do otherwise. Why the question of time begins to emerge at all in the latter chapters of Book XI is the simple fact that to claim, among other things, that creation took place "in time" would suggest that there is a primordial category which underwrites creation of the world. And thus the notion developed in the early phases of Book XI concerning creation in the Word, the Word who is "creator of all ages,"[6] would become null and void.

In Book XI, it is the Word which is the first principle of all creation. By this the Word is not subject to time as those who wonder what God was doing before the creation of the world might suggest. To wonder what God was doing before the creation of the world is to invite the notion that the utterly creative activity of the Word is subject to time—thereby negating its primacy. This, in my opinion, is what fuels the discussion about time and its characteristics in Book XI. And it is in this sense that the discussion of time is more properly a theological account. In other words, Augustine's preoccupation with the arguments about the measurement of time stems from his interests in preserving the primacy of the Word in creating and sustaining all things. Book XI opens specifically with the question of his relationship to God, in that Augustine wonders if his efforts in recounting his deeds are of any merit. He concludes that they are because others may be inspired from reading them. In Chapter 2 he begins lamenting the limited amount of time he has in contemplating all God has done, and appeals to Christ, the Word "through whom you have made all things," to help him understand the creation of the world as it is given in Genesis.

In Chapter 3 the discussion of the meaning of the first lines of Genesis is formally introduced—a theme which is extensively investigated in the remaining Books XII and XIII. The material contingency (and therefore temporality)[7] of the created order is taken up in Chapter 4, largely as an introduction to the discussion of creation taken up in Chapter 5. In that chapter Augustine suggests that creation did not occur in the manner of an artist who fashions a product out of some pre-existent material. Indeed, creation of the world did not occur in some place at all, but proceeded from the Word. From this position of the creative Word, Augustine contrasts the spoken *verba* of creaturely communication with the creative *Verbum* of God, a contrast that is established specifically on the grounds of temporality. He concludes that because there was no bodily thing, no creature before the creation of the world, the creative command "Let heaven and earth be made" could not have been a temporal utterance, since creaturely communication is extended over time. In Chapters 7 and 8 he proposes that the creative command is once and forever given in the creative, eternal Word—the second person of the Trinity—and that it is this same creative Word who is the true teacher of all, the Christ who speaks the truth to our "inner" ear and is our true beginning. Chapter 9 is a kind of summary of the previous insights and culminates the discussion by declaring, "In the beginning, O God, you made heaven and earth in your Word, in your Son, in your Power, in your Wisdom, in your Truth, speaking in a wondrous way and working in a wondrous way."[8]

This simple synopsis of the early chapters in no way does justice to the subtlety of Augustine's thought, but it is sufficient to demonstrate that the discussion of time which follows and which has been the focus of so much discussion among scholars ever since is situated in the much broader and more profound considerations of the creative Word. It is Augustine's insistence on the primacy of the Word which serves as the backdrop for the more overt discussions about time and its characteristics.

After the subtle reflections about the Word, Chapter X finally discusses the specific question of what God was doing before the creation of the world.[9] From this point, the reflections of Book XI do in fact become more focused on the subject of time. But, as already indicated, the questions emerge only in light of Augustine's previous reflections. The question as to what God was doing "before" the creation of the world raises the very real possibility that time is a kind of primordial container in which events (now specifically creation) must unfold. It raises the possibility that time is in the order of a first principle alongside—so to speak—the creative Word. Thus, unless the question is addressed, Augustine's previous remarks about the primacy of the Word must be dismissed.

His answer is direct: the Word is above time, and is indeed the maker of all times; and, therefore, prior to creation there was no "before."[10] Time, then, is not in the order of a first principle, but is itself the product of the creative Word. Understood in its proper light as created, then, time is not something that the Word is subject to, and hence cannot be said to provide a schema for understanding the free activity of the Word. The answer is terse, but we have been given clues to his position earlier in the text.[11] In having cited the contingent character of the created order, Augustine indirectly tells us of its temporal quality. Yet, in having contrasted the creaturely voice with the Divine Word,[12] (a contrast established on the grounds of temporality) we are given clues to the unique, non-temporal dimension of the creative act.

Finally, it is only in Chapter 14 that Augustine takes up the direct question: What, then, is time? Here the full weight of his theological reflections is brought to bear. And it is here that his theological reflections must be maintained if we are to avoid profoundly distorting the text.

Augustine's opening thesis in this chapter: that the past and future do not exist as extra-mental entities, and that the present itself has the character of tending towards non-being—is the position from which Augustine develops the rest his discussion. We know this is his operative thesis because he has already indicated that time itself is not in the order of a first principle. He has refuted this cosmology on the grounds of the primacy of the creative Word. The failure to grasp this results in failing to recognize that if Augustine were to be sympathetic to any view, it would be one that does not allow time to become more than it is, especially a primordial principle in which all events unfold. In other words, by beginning in the Word and not the cosmos, Augustine is inclined to speak first of the unreality of time and only then reviews the problems associated with our claims about its measurement. It is the primacy of the Word which fuels the subsequent discussion on time.

One of the effects of ignoring the theological context is to read the subsequent discussion (i.e., from Chapter 14 on) upside down, that is, taking the thesis for the antithesis and vice versa. Callahan misses the broader context and thus initially interprets the arguments which follow in Chapter 15 about the "length of time" as *positively* contributing to Augustine's thesis, and views the previous discussion about the unreality of the present as a kind of paradoxical stumbling block.[13]

As a matter of fact, Augustine never abandons the initial thesis that the past and future do *not* exist as extra-mental entities, nor does he ever explicitly deny that the present is unextended. He cites the arguments about the measurement and length of time in Chapter 15 not in an effort to illustrate his position, but in an effort to show how ordinary language provides too many uncritical barriers to grasping the more profound insight into the primacy of the Word.[14] Augustine never significantly deviates from this initial hypothesis, and from this position systematically challenges any competing assumptions.

The upside down reading of the discussion is even clearer in Ricoeur's analysis when he at several points indicates that it is ordinary language that spares us from Augustine's initially "skeptical" conclusions about time.[15] This is a rather remarkable interpretation of Augustine's development since it is "experience, articulated by language" that is precisely dismissed for its general inadequacy. In fact, Augustine's thesis about the non-existent character of time is prefaced with the remark: "I state confidently that I know this."[16]

In other words, *despite* our habitual manner of speaking about times as "long or short" (Chapter 15), or of measuring time (Chapters 16 and 21), or of prediction and prophecy (Chapters 17 and 18), or of time as related to the motion of heavenly bodies (Chapter 23), such habits of ordinary speech eventually *distort* the more profound character of the creative Word. In short, ordinary language is the source of the confusion not the solution.[17]

However, Chapter 15 does signal a unique shift in the analysis, but this newest development in no way negates the previous reflections about time and the primacy of the Word. The difference in these latest developments lies in the fact that Augustine begins to direct his analysis from the perspective of our fallenness, our creatureliness. Thus the questions of longer and shorter times, prophecy and the historical past, motions of heavenly bodies, measurements of time and longer and shorter syllables are all questions about the character of time not any longer from the perspective of the creative Word, but now from the perspective of the fallen creature. The force of his discussion is to show that from this perspective the deeper theological dimensions concerning the primacy of the Word as above time are largely distorted by our habitual, fallen methods of reflection.

Finally, the discussion of *distentio* ought to be interpreted in this light. For in that discussion we are given an account of the experience of measuring time which at the same time prevents us from collapsing the entire question of time, creation, and the Word to this one dimension. In other words, the notion of *distentio* answers much more than the question, "How do we measure intervals of time?" It answers the more profound questions, "How is it that we speak of measuring 'lengths' of time, when we know that time is not in the order of a first principle, when we know that time is not some primordial container in which events unfold, when we know that the created order is sustained in the Word?" Without the broader theological context firmly established, the function of *distentio* as closing that gap between our fallen experience and the primacy of the Word is entirely lost.

Moreover, we know that *distentio* does not exhaust all the dimensions of creaturely experience because we know that in Book 12[18] there are creatures who, because they are created, are temporally/historically bound but which themselves do not experience *distentio*. These are the citizens of the heavenly Jerusalem who, because of their free, loving union to the creative Word, do not experience distention. *Distentio* cannot be interpreted, then, as encompassing Augustine's entire reflections on time, since there is more to time and history than what you and I, as fallen creatures, experience in our distended ways.

From here it should become obvious, then, that the claim that Augustine provides a psychological account of time is simply misleading. It fails to draw into the discussion the theological components which underwrite the project. Time is far more profound in its theological ramifications than the psychology of *distentio*, despite its brilliance, is designed to address. From the vantage point of the Word, we see that time is an element of creation, *distentio* is an element of the fall. And the temptation to see all of creation from the prism of *distentio* is to miss the primacy of the Word. The more profound reading is impossible to discern when the discussion of time is wrenched from the broader context. A more fruitful analysis lies in a more faithful reading.

Notes

[1] J. F. Callahan, *Four Views of Time in Ancient Philosophy* (Cambridge: Harvard University Press, 1948), p. 200.

[2] P. Ricoeur, *Time and Narrative*, 3 vols., tr. Kathleen McLaughlin and David Pellauer (Chicago: University of Chicago Press, 1984). My criticism of Ricoeur is limited to his treatment of Augustine's analysis of time in *Confessiones* XI. I am referring specifically to the opening chapters of Volume 1 and 3.

[3] Callahan begins at Chapter 14.

[4] In fairness to Ricoeur I should mention that he is conscious of reading the text out of sequence. On the other hand, I think it is also fair to say that despite this awareness, Ricoeur's analysis of the early passages in Book XI do not substantially alter his interpretation. In Volume 3, especially, he seems to have left aside Augustine's earlier remarks.

[5] R. Jordan, "Time and Contingency in St. Augustine," *Review of Metaphysics* 8 (1954–55) 394–417; reprinted in R. A. Markus, ed., *Augustine: A Collection of Critical Essays* (New York: Doubleday and Company, Inc., 1972), pp. 255–79. Jordan also argues that the discussion has often been distorted due to insensitivity to the broader context.

[6] *Confessiones* XI,xiii,15: *CC* XXVII,202: *Nam unde poterant innumerabilia saecula praeterire, quae ipse non feceras, cum sis omnium saeculorum auctor et conditor?* All English citations are from *The Confessions of St. Augustine*, tr. John K. Ryan (New York: Doubleday and Company, Inc., 1960).

[7] *Confessiones* XII,viii,8: *CC* XXVII,220.

[8] *Confessiones* XI,ix,11: *CC* XXVII,199: *In hoc principio, deus, fecisti caelum et terram in uerbo tuo, in filio tuo, in uirtute tua, in sapientia tua, in ueritate tua miro modo dicens et miro modo faciens.*

[9] This question of what God was doing before the creation of the world is related to the Manichaean polemic—an issue which may underwrite the project of the *Confessiones*. Thus not only Book XI but the *Confessiones* as a whole may be profitably examined in light of its Manichaean context. See *De Genesis contra Manichaeos* I,ii,3; also R. A. Markus, "Augustine's 'Confessions' and the Controversy with Julian of Eclanum: Manicheism Revisited," *Augustiniana* 41 (1991) 913–25; Edward Peters, "What Was God Doing Before He Created the Heavens and the Earth," *Augustiniana* 34 (1984) 53–74.

[10] *Confessiones* XI,xiii,15: *CC* XXVII,201–2.

[11] There are hints of this position even as early as Book X. After a rather extended analysis of the wonderful capacities of memory, Augustine indicates that, strictly speaking, God is not properly an object of memory. This would suggest that there is something unique to the existence of God which does not fit our ordinary categories of time and recollection. *Confessiones* X,xxvi,37: *CC* XXVII,174: *Neque enim iam eras in memoria mea, priusquam te discerem. Vbi ergo te inueni, ut discerem te, nisi in te supra me? Et nusquam locus, et recedimus et accedimus, et nusquam locus. Veritas, ubique praesides omnibus consultentibus te simulque respondes omnibus etiam diuersa consulentibus.*

[12] *Confessiones* XI,vi,8: *CC* XXVII,198.

[13] Callahan, p. 154.

[14] Ibid.

[15] What is it that prevents skepticism from carrying the day? "As always," Ricoeur remarks, "it is experience, articulated by language and enlightened by the intelligence" (Ricoeur, p. 9).

[16] *Confessiones* XI,xiv,17: *CC* XXVII,202–3: *Quid est tempus? Si nemo ex me quaerat, scio; si quaerenti explicare uelim, nescio: fidenter tamen dico scire me, quod, si nihil praeteriret, non esset praeteritum tempus, ... Si ergo praesens, ut tempus sit, ideo fit, quia in praeteritum transit, quomodo et hoc esse dicimus, cui causa, ut sit, illa est, quia non erit, ut scilicet non uere dicamus tempus esse, nisi quia tendit non esse?*

[17] In discussing the character of the three-fold present (Chapter 23) Augustine explicitly says that he is willing to tolerate ordinary language about time, but only to the extant that the inadequacy of such language is understood. Citing this same passage, Ricoeur steadfastly holds to his initial thesis about Augustine's penchant for ordinary language and awkwardly admits that "Everyday language is thus simply reformulated in a more rigorous manner" (Ricoeur, p. 11).

[18] *Confessiones* XII,xi,12: *CC* XXVII,222.

The Link between Faith and Time in St. Augustine

Roland J. Teske, S.J.

Twice in his writings Augustine cites Plato's *Timaeus* 29c: "As eternity ✓ stands to what has come to be, so truth stands to faith."[1] In the *De trinitate* he explains that the author used "what has come to be" for "temporal reality (*temporale*)"—the sort of thing human beings are in both body and soul by reason of their mutability. In the *De consensu euangelistarum* Augustine speaks of "what has come to be and faith" as "below (*deorsum*)" in contrast with "eternity and truth" which are "above (*sursum*)." Hence, one might paraphrase the citation: As the eternal is superior to the temporal, so truth is superior to faith. Augustine adds that we now believe "the things done in time on our behalf" so that we may later contemplate the truth in eternity.[2]

I. The Problem Posed by the Citation

The use of *Timaeus* 29c raises a number of problems, not the least important of which is that the text implies that faith has to do with temporal things and, it seems, *only* with temporal things. Later in *De trinitate* Augustine describes the things we believe as "those things in reality which are said to be now or to have been or to be still to come."[3] That is, the objects of faith are temporal events, even if the temporal events in question are the birth, life, suffering, death and resurrection of the Word. The temporal events which are the object of faith are not *merely* temporal events since one and the same Christ "who is the Truth in eternal things is for us faith in things that have come to be."[4] That is, the temporal reality of the humanity of the Word is "a great and ineffable sacrament (*magnum et inenarrabile sacramentum*)."[5] Nonetheless, though the objects of faith are not merely temporal events, since they are sacraments of the eternal Word, it seems that *only* temporal events are objects of faith. That is, it would seem that the eternal triune God would not, in Augustine's terms, be an object of faith, but an object of contemplation, even if he would be such only in the hereafter. My main question, then, is how Augustine could have held this position in view of the obvious structure of the creedal formulae which seem directed to the triune God, Father, Son and Holy Spirit.

Earlier, in *De uera religione*, Augustine stressed the importance for the Christian religion of the temporal economy of our salvation.

> The essential element in following this religion is the history
> and prophecy of the temporal dispensation of divine provi-
> dence for the salvation of the human race, in its reformation
> and restoration unto eternal life.[6]

Here "history" refers to an account of past events, as "prophecy" refers to the prediction of those yet to come. Among such objects of faith Augustine lists the assumption of the man, the virgin birth, the Son's death, resurrection and ascension, his sitting at the right hand of the Father, the destruction of sin, the day of judgment, and the resurrection of bodies.[7]

Later, in *De uera religione*, as well as in other texts, Augustine distinguished historical and temporal faith from spiritual and eternal faith, the former owed to history, the latter to understanding.[8] In *De agone christiano* Augustine also distinguished between a faith in temporal events and a faith in divine and eternal realities and points out that the eternal things cannot yet be known by those who are carnal.[9] Thus he implies that the eternal reality of God can be known by those who are no longer carnal, but have become spiritual.[10] In a number of his works, Augustine speaks of faith in eternal things as well as faith in temporal things.[11] Nonetheless, his speaking of faith in eternal things remains, I believe, a minor theme. In any case, the former objects of faith become objects of knowledge once one has become an adult or a spiritual person in the Church. Hence, only temporal things remain always and for everyone objects of faith.[12]

II. The Platonic Source and Background

In the passage quoted from the *De trinitate* Augustine attributes the quotation to one of the wise men among the Greeks, but in the slightly earlier *De consensu* he attributes it specifically to Plato in the *Timaeus*. Augustine most probably read before 400 the part of the *Timaeus* translated by Cicero.[13] Eugene TeSelle, however, suggests that Augustine got the text from Porphyry and claims that he shows no awareness of its meaning in its Platonic context, "namely, that one must tell a story in order to describe appropriately the origin and destiny of a temporal universe."[14]

Despite TeSelle's claim, Augustine does, I believe, agree with Plato that faith is a mode of cognition requisite for and appropriate to the order of temporal events and the destiny of temporal beings.[15] Indeed, as we shall see, Augustine views faith as necessary precisely for our knowledge of the destiny of humans at least, if not of the universe.

In the *Timaeus* passage Plato is dealing with the origin of the sensible world as a copy of the archetypal intelligible world. The ontological inferiority of the world of becoming to the world of being requires the epistemic inferiority of the account of the world of becoming to an account of the world of being, that is, of belief to knowledge. Here truth (*alêtheia*) in the sense of knowledge (*epistêmê*), having for its object the archetypal world of ideas, is certain and absolute, while belief (*pistis*), having for its object the world of becoming (*genesis*), is merely probable or conjectural.

Augustine was clearly aware of Plato's distinction between the intelligible world where truth resides and this sensible world that we can see and touch, as well as the distinction between knowledge (*scientia*) of the intelligible world and opinion (*opinio*) with regard to this world. In his earliest writing he says,

> Plato thought there were two worlds, one the intelligible world, in which truth itself resides, and the other this sensible world, which it is clear that we perceive by sight and touch. Thus that is the true world, and this is like the true one and made to its image. From that one the truth, so to speak, shines forth and becomes, as it were, clear in the soul that knows itself. Of this world, not knowledge, but opinion can be generated in the minds of the foolish....[16]

Furthermore, Augustine also claimed that by his own time

> there has...been filtered out one teaching that is the true philosophy. It is not the philosophy of this world, which our sacred mysteries rightly detest, but of the other intelligible world....[17]

This one true philosophy is not, of course, a natural human wisdom distinguished from theology, but rather the knowledge of eternal things that Augustine will later call wisdom (*sapientia*) as opposed to knowledge (*scientia*).[18] Augustine is also clear that

> subtle reasoning would never call souls blinded by all sorts of error and stained deeply with filth from the body back [to this intelligible world], had God not in his mercy toward the people bowed down and submitted the authority of the divine intellect to a human body. Stirred by his commands and deeds, souls can return into themselves and regain a taste for the fatherland even without the struggle of debates.[19]

That is, from his first writing at Cassiciacum Augustine held that the philosophy of Plato, which has recently shone forth so clearly in Plotinus that the latter seemed almost to be Plato returned to life, was correct in its teaching about the intelligible world.[20] And Christ himself taught that "there is this other world remote from these eyes, which the intellect of a few healthy men can see," when he said to Pilate, "My kingdom is not of this world" (Jn 18:36).[21]

Both Plato and Augustine are dealing with two modes of cognition, a superior mode dealing with immutable reality and an inferior mode dealing with temporal reality. As Camelot notes, Plato is comparing two modes of cognition possible in this present life: the one, *epistêmê*, having as its object *ousia*, is certain and absolute, while the other, *pistis*, having as its object *genesis*, is probable and conjectural. Augustine, Camelot adds, is comparing two *successive* modes of cognition: the first, faith belongs to this life and deals with the historical events worked by providence on our behalf, while the second, vision or contemplation, belongs to the next life and has for its object the eternal and immutable Truth that is God. As Camelot also notes, though for Augustine faith is temporary or provisional and inferior to vision, faith is not uncertain or conjectural.[22] This comparison is, I believe, correct except for two qualifications: One, the emphasis upon faith and vision as belonging respectively to this life and to the next overlooks the fact that for Augustine vision or contemplation of God always remained a possibility for some few in this life, whether these be the Platonists or Christian spirituals or mystics.[23] And, two, Augustine uses faith and truth not merely for modes of cognition, but also for the objects known by these modes of cognition. In this sense, Christ in his humanity is faith for the carnal, little ones and in his divinity is the truth.[24]

III. The Context of the Quotation in *De trinitate*

In *De trinitate* IV, Augustine is dealing with the incarnate Word as one true mediator of our salvation. In the preceding paragraphs he speaks of those "who think that they can be purified in order to contemplate God and to cling to him by their own power...."[25] He explains that the reason for such pride is that

> some of them were able to raise the highest point of their mind beyond every creature and to touch to some small degree the light of immutable truth, and they laugh at many Christians living from faith alone who cannot as yet do this.[26]

These proud men are the Platonists who "see from afar the fatherland across the sea," while they refuse in their pride the *lignum* that would carry them there—the wood of a boat that is at the same time the cross of Christ.[27] While these Platonists blame the Christians for their belief in the resurrection of the body, they want the Christians to listen to them "with regard to the changes of mutable things and the hidden order of the ages."[28] Augustine again concedes that "they were able to know that lofty and immutable substance through those things which were made."[29] He further concedes that they were able to show that "all temporal things occur in accord with the eternal reasons."[30] But he is adamant that they cannot, thereby, know in those reasons, that is, in the divine ideas, the number of individuals of various kinds, their origin, development, life span and demise, or their inclinations and aversions. All such things he insists they

> searched out through the history of places and times and they believed such things on the basis of the experience of others and their written records.[31]

Since they could not see these things in the divine wisdom, we should not be surprised that they could not search out the series of the ages and the limit to which the human race progressed in its downward flow and its turning back toward its goal.[32] Historians too could not write such things before they happened, and these philosophers did not contemplate them in the eternal ideas.[33] Augustine allows that prophets were able to foretell the future in various ways, but only to the extent God judged necessary.[34] From this Augustine concludes that

> with regard to the resurrection of the dead and the succession of the ages we ought not to consult even those philosophers who knew—to the extent they were able—the eternity of the creator....[35]

That is, in terms of knowledge of God's eternal being the Platonists were correct, but with regard to contingent historical matters they are not to be listened to. The reason for not heeding them with regard to temporal events is that they

> were unsuited to fix the highest point of their mind on the eternity of the spiritual and immutable nature so steadily that they could see in the wisdom of the creator and ruler of the universe the changes of the ages...and see there the conversions for the better not only of souls, but also of human bodies....[36]

Their unsuitability did not prevent them from fixing the highest part of their mind upon God's eternity, but from fixing it there so steadily that they could read off the course and goal of human history in God's wisdom. Moreover, they were not judged worthy to receive revelations concerning the course and goal of history as were the prophets of Israel.[37]

At this point Augustine moves from the unsuitability of the Platonists to that of all of us weighed down by sin and in need of purification. He sets forth a principle: "We could not be purified so as to be suited to eternal things except through the temporal things to which we were suited and by which we were held."[38] That is, we need a temporal medicine suited to our illness that can heal us and bring us, once healed, to eternal things. Thus

> just as, when the rational mind has been purified, it owes contemplation to eternal things, so when it is still in need of purification, it owes faith to temporal things.[39]

At this point Augustine cites Plato's words from the *Timaeus* with which this paper began.

In commenting on Augustine's emphasis on history and prophecy in *De uera religione* Eugene TeSelle observes that in the Cassiciacum dialogues "the authoritative character of revelation...meant, for all practical purposes, the Creed, which converged almost completely with the results of speculative philosophy...." I take TeSelle to mean by the Creed the doctrine of God as eternal and triune.[40] From this perspective Augustine could say of the Platonists of old,

> if those men could again live this life with us, they would see whose authority more readily has care for men and, by changing a few words and statements, they would become Christians, as several Platonists of the recent past and of our times have done.[41]

But by the time of *De uera religione* Augustine's new concern is with the contingent historical events that he now sees as constituting the essentials of the Christian religion.[42] TeSelle's suggestion also squares with the main thrust of the central section of *Confessiones* VII, where Augustine recounts his reading of the *libri Platonicorum* with the alternating *"ibi legi"* and *"ibi non legi."* What he read there concerned God's eternal reality; what he did not read there was the history and prophecy of those contingent historical events by which we have been and will be saved.[43] We have seen that in *De trinitate* IV Augustine grants to the Platonists a contemplative knowledge of God's eternal reality at least from afar; what they lacked was the humble faith in the temporal events by which they might draw near to and cling to God. Without faith in what has come about in time they could not return to the fatherland they saw. I suggest that Augustine's linking faith with temporal events in the way he does had to do with his conviction that the Neoplatonists certainly did not lack knowledge of the *aeternalia Dei*, though they did lack the humble faith in the Way who would lead them to the Truth, because he who in his humanity is the Way is also in his divinity the Truth.[44]

For Plato in the *Timaeus* faith was necessary as a mode of cognition appropriate to temporal things, their origin and their destiny. In Augustine faith is also needed—most of all and necessarily—for our grasp of the temporal being of Christ who is also our eternal destiny. Augustine says that we believe in Christ who has been born, has died, was raised up and taken into heaven.[45] In ourselves we recognize the first two, but the second two we believe have taken place in him. Because we believe that the second two have come to be in him, we hope that they will come to be in us.

> Because we believe that what had come to be in him has passed over to eternity, [what has come to be] of ours will pass over when faith has come to the truth....[46]

That is, our faith in the *transitus Domini* not merely grounds our hope of sharing in the Paschal mystery, but makes us part of it and brings us to the true immortality, true incorruptibility, true immutability that is eternity itself.[47] Despite the Platonists' vision of God's immutable substance, they did not have the faith in the history and prophecy of the temporal dispensation that grounds our hope and will make us sharers in the resurrection and ascension of the Lord. It is faith in the temporal events worked by providence for our salvation that discloses to us our human destiny and realizes it.

Notes

[1] *De trinitate* IV,xviii,24: *CC* L,191–93, and *De consensu euangelistarum* I,xxxv,53: *CSEL* XLIII,59: *Quantum ad id quod ortum est aeternitas ualet, tantum ad fidem ueritas.*

[2] *De trinitate* IV,xviii,24: *CC* L,191–92: *Nunc ergo adhibemus fidem rebus temporaliter gestis propter nos et per ipsam mundamur ut cum ad "speciem" uenerimus quemadmodum succedit fidei ueritas ita mortalitati succedat aeternitas.... quia rebus ortis adcommodamus fidem credulitatis sicut in aeternis speramus ueritatem contemplationis....* Augustine is here alluding to 2 Co 5:7: *Dum sumus in corpore, peregrinamur a Domino (per fidem enim ambulamus et non per speciem)....*

[3] *De trinitate* XIII,ii,5: *CC* L/A,386: *Illa quippe in rebus sunt quae vel esse vel fuisse vel futurae dicuntur....*

[4] *De consensu euangelistarum* I,xxxv,53: *CSEL* XLIII,60: *Ipse est nobis fides in rebus ortis qui est ueritas in aeternis.*

[5] Ibid.

[6] *De uera religione* VII,13: *CC* XXXII,196: *Huius religionis sectandae caput est historia et prophetia dispensationis temporalis diuinae prouidentiae pro salute generis humani in aeternam uitam reformandi et reparandi.*

[7] *De uera religione* VIII,14: *CC* XXXII,197: *Illa hominis sacrosancta susceptio et uirginis partus et mors filii dei pro nobis et resurrectio a mortuis et in caelum ascensio et consessus ad dextram patris et peccatorum abolitio et iudicii dies et corporum resuscitatio....*

[8] *De uera religione* L,99: *CC* XXXII,251: *Distinguamus ergo, quam fidem debeamus historiae, quam fidem debeamus intelligentiae, quid mandemus memoriae, uerum esse nescientes, sed credentes tamen, et ubi sit uerum, quod non uenit et transit, sed semper eodem modo manet...et quae sit stabilis fides siue historica et temporalis siue spiritualis et aeterna....*

[9] *De agone christiano* xiii,15: *CSEL* XLI,118: *Fides in ecclesia brevissime traditur, in qua commendantur aeterna, quae intelligi a carnalibus nondum possunt; et temporalia praeterita et futura, quae pro salute hominum gessit et gestura est aeternitas divinae providentiae.* Cf. also *De fide et symbolo* iv,6: *CSEL* XLI,10 and *De trinitate* XIV,i,3: *CC* L/A,423–24.

[10] On the distinction between spiritual and carnal persons in the Church, cf. T. J. van Bavel, "L'humanité du Christ comme *lac parvulorum* et comme *via* dans la spiritualité de saint Augustin," *Augustiniana* 7 (1957) 245–81, as well as my "Spirituals and Spiritual Interpretation in Augustine," *AS* 15 (1984) 65–81 and *"Homo spiritalis"* in St. Augustine's *De Genesi contra Manichaeos*," *Studia Patristica* 22 (1989) 351–55.

[11] Cf., for example, *De agone christiano* xvii,19: *CSEL* XL,120: *Credentes ergo incommutabilem trinitatem, credamus etiam dispensationem temporalem pro salute generis humani.*

[12] *De diuersis quaestionibus* LXXXIII,48: *CC* XLIV/A,75: *Alia sunt quae semper creduntur et numquam intelleguntur, sicut est omnis historia temporalia et humana gesta percurrens; alia quae mox ut creduntur intelleguntur, sicut sunt omnes rationes uel de numeris uel de quibusque disciplinis; tertium quae primo creduntur et postea intelleguntur, qualia sunt ea quae de diuinis rebus non possunt intellegi nisi ab his qui mundo sunt corde....*

[13] "En revanche, il a lu dès avant 400 la partie du *Timée* traduite par Cicéron: il cite dans le *De consensu Evangelistarum* et dans le *De Trinitate* la définition de l'éternité...." P. Courcelle, *Lettres grecques en occident: De Macrobe à Cassiodore* (Paris: De Bocard, 1948), pp. 156–57. Th. Camelot agrees with Courcelle and refers to *De civitate dei* XIII,xvi,1, where Augustine explicitly refers to Cicero's translation of the *Timaeus*. Cf. Th. Camelot, "A l'éternel par le temporel (*De trinitate*, IV, xviii, 24)," *REA* 2 (1956) 164, n. 3. Du Roy also claims that Courcelle "a montré qu'Augustin l'avait en tous cas lu dans cette trad. [Cicero's] avant 400." Cf. O. du Roy, *L'intelligence de la foi en la trinité selon saint Augustin: Genèse de sa théologie trinitaire jusqu'en 391* (Paris: Études Augustiniennes, 1966), p. 139, n. 5. Du Roy adds, "Voir les nombreuses références qu'il donne et qu'il faut compléter par celles du *De civ. Dei* (éd. *Corpus Christ.*) et par celles de l'édition Teubner (p. 172 B par exemple)." In any case, it would seem that Augustine got the quotation from Cicero's translation, since, though the Greek text has: "As being (*ousia*) stands to becoming (*genesis*), so truth (*alêtheia*) stands to belief (*pistis*)," Augustine follows Cicero's translation in which "eternity" replaces "being."

[14] "What makes it likely that Augustine acquired this passage at second hand is the fact that it is used as an isolated slogan, with no awareness of its meaning in the context of Plato's dialogue (namely, that one must tell a story in order to describe appropriately the origin and destiny of a temporal universe), for its purpose here is to support an anagogic theory of religious symbols" (Eugene TeSelle, *Augustine the Theologian* [New York: Herder and Herder, 1970], p. 240).

[15] Van Bavel writes, "Le seul point commun entre lui et Platon, c'est que la foi a trait aux choses commencées dans le temps" (p. 260). But he adds "Augustin n'exclut pas pour autant qu'ici-bas la foi a aussi les choses éternelles, invisibiles pour objet dont l'homme attend la révelation complète" (pp. 260–61), thus illustrating the tension in Augustine's use of *Timaeus* 29c.

[16] *Contra academicos* III,xvii,37: *CC* XXIX,57: *Platonem sensisse duos esse mundos, unum intelligibilem, in quo ipsa ueritas habitaret, istum autem sensibilem, quem manifestum est nos uisu tactuque sentire; itaque illum uerum, hunc ueri similem et ad illius imaginem factum, et ideo de illo in ea quae se cognosceret anima uelut expoliri et quasi serenari ueritatem, de hoc autem in stultorum animis non scientiam sed opinionem posse generari....* Augustine's early use of *"stulti"* as opposed to *"sapientes"* gives way to his speaking of *"parvuli"* as opposed to *"spirituales."* On this point, cf. van Bavel, pp. 256–57.

[17] *Contra academicos* III,xix,42: *CC* XXIX,60: *Sed tamen eliquata est, ut opinor, una uerissimae philosophiae disciplina. Non enim est ista huius mundi philosophia, quam sacra nostra meritissime detestantur, sed alterius intellegibilis....*

[18] *De trinitate* XIV,i,3; *CC* L/A,423–24. On Augustine's understanding of the role of *philosophia*, cf. G. Madec, "A propos d'une traduction de *De ordine* II, v, 6," *REA* 16 (1970) 179–85.

[19] *Contra academicos* III,xix,42: *CC* XXIX,60: *Cui animas multiformibus erroris tenebris caecatas et altissimis a corpore sordibus oblitas numquam ista ratio subtilissima reuocaret, nisi summus deus populari quadam clementia diuini intellectus auctoritatem usque ad ipsum corpus humanum declinaret atque submitteret, cuius non solum praeceptis sed etiam factis excitatae animae redire in semet ipsas et resipiscere patriam etiam sine disputationum concertatione potuissent.*

[20] Cf. *Contra academicos* III,xviii,41: *CC* XXIX,59–60.

[21] *De ordine* I,xi,32: *CC* XXIX,106: *Esse autem alium mundum ab istis oculis remotissimum, quem paucorum sanorum intellectus intuetur, satis ipse Christus significat, qui non dicit: "regnum meum non est de mundo," sed: "regnum meum non est de hoc mundo".*

[22] Camelot, p. 167.

[23] On this point, cf. C. Butler, *Western Mysticism: The Teaching of Augustine, Gregory and Bernard on Contemplation and the Contemplative Life*, 2nd ed., with Afterthoughts (New York: Harper and Row, 1966), pp. 20, 27. Cf. also my "St. Augustine and the Vision of God," in *Collectanea Augustiniana* II.

[24] *De consensu euangelistarum* I,xxxv,53: *CSEL* XLIII,60: *Ipse est nobis fides in rebus ortis qui est ueritas in aeternis.* "Dem Dualismus von credere-intelligere entspricht die Zweiheit der Naturen in Christus" (Magnus Löhrer, *Der Glaubensbegriff des hl. Augustinus in seinen ersten Schriften bis zu den Confessiones* [Einsiedeln: Benziger, 1955], p. 175. Cf. also pp. 133–37.

[25] *De trinitate* IV,xv,20: *CC* L,187: *Sunt autem quidam qui se putant ad contemplandum deum et inhaerendum deo uirtute propria posse purgari....*

²⁶ *De trinitate* IV,xv,20: *CC* L,187: *Nonnulli eorum potuerunt aciem mentis ultra omnem creaturam transmittere et lucem incommutabilis ueritatis quantulacumque ex parte contingere, quod christianos multos ex fide interim sola uiuentes nondum potuisse derident.*

²⁷ The Platonists were able *de longinquo prospicere patriam transmarinam* (*De trinitate* IV,xv,20: *CC* L,187). Augustine alludes to *Ennead* I,vi,8, where Plotinus speaks of the fatherland from which we have come and to which we are returning. Cf. also *Tractatus in Euangelium Ioannis* II,4: *CC* XXXVI,13, where Augustine explicitly links the images of wood, ship, cross, and sea: *Illud potuerunt uidere quod est, sed uiderunt de longe. Noluerunt tenere humilitatem Christi, in qua naui securi peruenerint ad id quod longe uidere potuerunt; et sorduit eis crux Christi. Mare transeundum est, et lignum contemnis?*

²⁸ *De trinitate* IV,xvi,21: *CC* L,188: *De conuersione rerum mutabilium aut de contexto saeculorum ordine consulendi sunt.*

²⁹ *De trinitate* IV,xvi,21: *CC* L,188: *Praecelsam incommutabilemque substantiam per illa quae facta sunt intelligere potuerunt.*

³⁰ *De trinitate* IV,xvi,21: *CC* L,188: *Verissime disputant et documentis certissimis persuadent aeternis rationibus omnia temporalia fieri.*

³¹ *De trinitate* IV,xvi,21: *CC* L,188: *Per locorum et temporum historiam quaesierunt et ab aliis experta atque conscripta crediderunt.*

³² *De trinitate* IV,xvi,21: *CC* L,188: *Quo minus mirandum est nullo modo eos potuisse prolixiorem saeculorum seriem uestigare et quandam metam huius excursus quo tamquam fluuio genus decurrit humanum atque inde conuersionem ad suum cuique debitum terminum.*

³³ Cf. *De trinitate* IV,xvi,21: *CC* L,188.

³⁴ Cf. *De trinitate* IV,xvii,22: *CC* L, 189.

³⁵ *De trinitate* IV,xvii,23: *CC* L,189–90: *Ergo de successionibus saeculorum et de resurrectione mortuorum philosophos nec illos consulere debemus qui creatoris aeternitatem "in quo uiuimus, mouemur et summus" quantum potuerunt intellexerunt....*

³⁶ *De trinitate* IV,xvii,23: *CC* L,190: *Et cum idonei non essent in aeternitatem spiritalis incommutabilisque naturae aciem mentis tam constanter infigere ut in ipsa sapientia creatoris atque rectoris uniuersitatis uiderunt uolumina saeculorum...atque ut ibi uiderunt conuersiones in melius non solum animorum sed etiam corporum humanorum....*

³⁷ *De trinitate* IV,xvii,23: *CC* L,190.

³⁸ *De trinitate* IV,xviii,24: *CC* L,191: *Purgari autem ut contemperaremur aeternis non nisi per temporalia possemus qualibus iam contemperati tenebamur.*

³⁹ *De trinitate* IV,xviii,24: *CC* L,191: *Mens autem rationalis sicut purgata contemplationem debet rebus aeternis, sic purganda temporalibus fidem.*

⁴⁰ TeSelle, p. 124.

⁴¹ *De uera religione* IV,7: *CC* XXXII,192: *Ita si hanc uitam illi uiri nobiscum rursus agere potuissent, uiderent profecto, cuius auctoritate facilius consuleretur hominibus, et paucis*

mutatis uerbis atque sententiis Christiani fierent, sicut plerique recentiorum nostrorumque temporum Platonici fecerunt.

[42] Cf. *De uera religione* VII,13: *CC* XXXII,196.

[43] Cf. *Confessiones* VII,ix,13–14: *BA* 13,608–12.

[44] Cf. *Tractatus in Euangelium Ioannis* XXXIV,9: *CC* XXXVI,315–16.

[45] Cf. *De trinitate* IV,xviii,24: *CC* L,192.

[46] *De trinitate* IV,xviii,24: *CC* L,193: *Duo autem reliqua, id est resuscitari et assumi iuste in nobis futura speramus quia in illo facta credidimus. Itaque in illo quia et id "quod ortum" erat transiit ad aeternitatem, transiturum est et nostrum cum fides peruenerit ad ueritatem. ... "Et ueritas," inquit, "liberabit uos." Unde nisi a morte, a corruptione, a mutabilitate.*

[47] Cf. *De trinitate* IV,xviii,24: *CC* L,193.

IV

Human Existence

Augustine

An illud negatis, sublimem quandam esse creaturam tam casto amore cohaerentem deo uero et uere aeterno, ut, quamuis ei coaeterna non sit, in nullam tamen temporum uarietatem et uicissitudinem ab illo se resoluat et defluat, sed in eius solius ueracissima contemplatione resquiescat? Quoniam tu, deus, diligenti te, quantum praecipis, ostendis ei te et sufficis ei, et ideo non declinat a te nec ad se? Haec est domus dei non terrena neque ulla caelesti mole corporea, sed spiritalis et particeps aeternitatis tuae, quia sine labe in aeternum.

Confessiones XII,xv,19

Augustinism: Locating the Center

Robert J. O'Connell, S.J.

Each of us can remember, no doubt, some brilliant phrase that seemed to sum up, to get to the very heart of some great character with whom we had grown gradually familiar. Such phrases work like the sudden fire-flash Plato describes as marking the moment of genuine insight. After years of closer and warmer acquaintance with someone, someone who may have begun as a remote figure from an alien clime and a distant age, a single master-stroke can enable us to behold and recognize, truly become the familiar of—a Cleopatra or a Joan of Arc, a Plato, say—or, an Aurelius Augustine! I can still recall, for instance, the moment when first I read Von Harnack's ringing summary: that Augustine saw his heart as his own "worst possession, and the living God his highest good."[1] In a soberer register, it seemed to me that Gilson hit the nail squarely when he wrote that the history of philosophy, for Augustine, was simply one extended meditation on how to achieve happiness, one long *De beata vita*.[2] And more recently, Robert Markus's observation seemed to ring equally true: that for Augustine "No area of human existence escapes the dire effects of Adam's sin" so that Augustine's notion of the Fall "left no aspect of human life and activity untouched."[3]

Sharpening the Focus

I have recalled only three well-known stabs at locating Augustine's "center," and surely each of you could add another, or two or three. But even were one to stay with these three, how differently they approach, and yet how unerringly each of them seems to penetrate to the very same heart of the very same man.

Despite that sameness of target, however, those differences of approach entail a certain fuzziness at the point of penetration: we seem to have located the center, fair enough, but the moment we try to fine-tune our focus on it, our instruments fail us: what promised to assume sharpness of line and firmness of shape turns, instead, to formless blur. We turn to Harnack, Gilson, Markus with a question in our eyes: how are we, exactly, to envisage what Augustine pictures as the life of happiness? And exactly how does God, and our own hearts, and the mystery of our fallenness figure in and relate to each other in that picture? Can we "locate that center" even more accurately and sharply than we have done up to now?

A Caution: My Personal Focus

But even for me to raise such a cluster of questions must put many of you on your guard. You know that if there is one thesis about Augustine— some would say one private heresy—I have been bugling over the years, it is the claim that he thought of us as fallen souls: quite literally, souls, who once, clothed in spiritual bodies, inhabited the "heaven of heaven" along with the angels. We sinned by turning away from our heart's bright happiness, which consisted in possessing our highest good, God's radiant splendor, in a vision which made us ineffably blissful. Our fall took the form of plunging downward into the sensible world of time, mortality, and restless bodily activity, and our hearts are restless till they rest in that vision, that paradise regained.

You are right to be on your guard, for this is the portrait of Saint Augustine I have come to be convinced is an accurate likeness. But, as one well-known critic put it, to expend one's energies as repeatedly as I have done, on verifying that particular feature of Augustine's teaching, may very well result in a skewed and distorted picture of the man's more comprehensive thought-world.

That is a danger, certainly. Or, rather, it would be a danger if the fall of the soul were merely one particular feature of Augustine's thought. Imagine the man's synthesis on the analogy of a geographical map, and think of his belief about the fall as though it were one particular island on that map: in that case, narrowing one's concentration to that particular island would entail ignoring not only a host of other islands, but entire continents along with vast expanses of ocean: surely that would amount to the distorted view of Augustine's thought-world our critic is concerned about.

But envisage our problem in another way: choose an organic metaphor, and think of Augustine's synthesis as a living reality, like a tree. In this case one could picture the fall of the soul much as Markus may be implying: as the root from which the entire tree, with all its particularities, emerges. The design of any tree's trunk, and the pattern of all its branchings, its every twig and leaf with their exquisitely balanced interrelationships, must not be considered primarily as *other* than, separate or even distinct from the root, but as united to, organically *one with* the root. The particularities of the root must be viewed as accounting for, and resonated by, the particularities of every leaf and twig on every branch of the tree. In this metaphor, meticulous study of the root-structure, precisely as root-structure, instead of distracting us, would actually direct our attention to the remainder of the tree in more crucial and illuminating ways than would otherwise be possible.

My Proposal Here: Center as "Root"

That is the kind of proposition I would like to offer for your consideration here: that the view of us humans as fallen souls is either the root, or so very close to the root of Augustine's entire intellectual synthesis, that virtually all the significant particularities of that synthesis slide into sharper focus, become more naturally intelligible, once we envisage them as emerging from that root vision. And the converse is also true: whether we start from root or branch, the features of the root will compel us to examine more closely and identify more accurately certain resonant features of the branches, and vice versa. Then, I submit, the blurring effect we spoke of earlier yields to a sharpness of line and form which tells us we have truly "located the center": our picture is in focus.

The "Fall" and Augustine's Aesthetic

My own conviction about how Augustine viewed our fallen condition emerged, as some of you doubtless know, from my earliest efforts to understand why Augustine attributed the somewhat anemic, the almost purely instrumental value he assigned to the creative arts. I had become convinced that heroes like Svoboda, Chapman, Finaert and others left too many gaps and imprecisions in attempting to answer that question. Yet nothing appealed to me less than the chilling prospect of getting mired down in that intellectual peonage known as source-research: up until then I had succeeded in escaping forced labor in those salt-mines. Yet Augustine's theory of art seemed clearly to root in a theory of man, and it was not at all clear to me—or, I suspected, to Svoboda, Chapman, Finaert and company—what that theory of man might be. When it finally became clear that I could no longer honorably shirk the task of digging in order to locate what sources Augustine had tapped in constructing his theory of the human, the answer to my question came to this: Augustine's view of the human condition amounted to a Christian adaptation (and I must stress that *Christian* adaptation) of Plotinus's theory of the soul's fall. I have often wondered whether that most genial of mentors, Henri-Irénée Marrou, had some later regrets about the Frankenstein monster he once so cheerfully spawned, but at that time he agreed that the resulting picture of Augustine's aesthetic was far more accurate and more sharply focused than previous scholars had succeeded in making it: identifying the root of that esthetic, in other words, had greatly bettered our understanding of the particularities of that individual branch of Augustine's synthesis, at least.

But can the same be said of the other branches of the Augustinian tree? I can only deal with a few of those branches here today, but perhaps you will find them typical enough to represent an honest promissory note for the remainder of his synthesis.

The "Fall" and Some Augustinian "Negatives"

Let me first begin with an Augustinian "negative." Scholars have repeatedly acknowledged that one of the most refractory difficulties in Augustine's thought is his theory of man. The complaint goes back to Etienne Gilson[4] and beyond him: Augustine conceived of the relation between soul and body in such slack, or better, such frankly oppositional terms, that it seems positively enigmatic that soul and body were conjoined in the first place. And explaining how they interact—think of that awkward construct, Augustine's "active" theory of sensation—only leads one into a nest of comparable enigmas.

Now Augustine probably had more than one reason for propounding that awkward relationship of soul to body, and one such reason was, admittedly, a measure of ignorance. Something closer to the Aristotelian notion of the soul as entelechy of the body would have provided Augustine with a far happier solution to the problem of thinking out the Christian mystery of bodily resurrection,[5] but his early work on *The Immortality of the Soul* indicates that Augustine simply confused that entelechy theory with a materialist view of the soul, and *The Literal Interpretation of Genesis* shows that he never abandoned that position.[6]

And yet, I would like to propose now that even if he had properly understood Aristotle's theory, Augustine might well have wound up preferring that looser, and even oppositional relationship of soul to body, which he had found in Plotinus's own treatise on the soul's immortality. Both early and late, we find him stressing the soul's capacity to detach its attention utterly from all bodily and sensible phenomena, as well as the soul's power of opposing the body's unruly drives and desires. That oppositional relationship boasts a long and respectable lineage: it goes back through Plotinus all the way to Plato's *Phaedo*. And yet, Augustine's preference for this sort of theory seems to have sprung much less from servile reverence toward Platonic authority, much more from its consonance with the view of human souls as fallen from another, loftier world into "this" sensible world of our present experience.

The Question of "Appeal": Anti-Traducianism

But why, you may well ask, why should such a conception of the human soul have exercised so powerful an appeal on Augustine?

For I am convinced that it was just such a powerful appeal, an appeal emotionally charged, that this conception of the soul exerted on him. We are dealing here with something much more electric than a reasoned preference, much more passion-laden than a purely intellectual conviction. Read once again that section of his *Literal Interpretation of Genesis* (X,xxiii–xxvi,39–45) where he apostrophizes the dead Tertullian and Tertullianists who may still be among the living: he pleads with them to abdicate the materialist notion of the soul he had elsewhere stigmatized as madness, simple madness: *dementia*.[7] Now he denounces the consequences of that view as no less than terrifying: *tremenda ista sunt*! he cries, and *Quid autem absurdius*? The note of passion is unmistakable.

But what fuels that passion? Think of the soul as material, Augustine reasons, and the materialism will invade your thinking about God. Tertullianists must be brought to see what the Platonist books had brought Augustine to see: that both God and soul are of another sort entirely, are spiritual.

That passion, moreover, is all the more remarkable given its context in his Genesis commentary. Augustine has been reviewing the four different accounts of the soul's origin proposed in his day; he is striving to determine which of those accounts will best square with the Apostle Paul's teaching—as he understands it—that every post-Adamic soul (save Christ's) is guilty with the guilt of Adam's sin. One by one, he has excluded three of the regnant theories: the only possibility which apparently remains is traducianism, the theory favored by Tertullian and his followers. But traducianists clung stubbornly to the notion, evidently inherited from the Stoics, that everything, including the soul and even God himself, was material. Otherwise, they thought (shades of Augustine himself when he was young) that neither the soul nor God could be truly and solidly real.

The momentum of his analysis has brought him to the point where traducianism alone seems acceptable to anyone who is resolved to cling to the *fundatissima fides*, that "bedrock belief" in original sin as preached by St. Paul. And plainly, Augustine is so resolved. Yet in spite of that resolve, and in spite of how inexorably his faith seems to impose the unwelcome traducianist conclusion, Augustine's reply is a tormented *cri de coeur*, an anguished "never, never, never, never." *"Admoneo sane, quantum valeam,"* he cries: he would strain every nerve to change their minds. It meant a great deal to him; in fact, one surmises, it would have broken his heart to admit that traducianism was true. But why?

The "Discovery of the Spiritual" in the *Confessiones*

Augustine hints broadly at the answer to that question at a number of points in his *Confessiones*, and notably in describing what has been called his "discovery of the spiritual" in Book Seven. All through the preceding books he has complained of his inability to think of God except in materialist terms; but then he tells us that, reflecting on the "books of the Platonists" which he first read at Milan in his thirty-second year, he learned how to think of God as *aliud, aliud valde*: "other, vastly other" than the realities of the sense world. His heart went soaring with the conviction that he had finally caught a glimpse of this radiant Beauty Who was so totally other, so stunningly beyond the loftiest beauty this bodily and sensible world could offer. What did he love when he loved his God? Augustine's first word in answer is a resounding "not." *Non speciem corporis nec decus temporis, non candorem lucis...non dulces melodias*: there is no beauty, no charm, no radiance or melody in the world of sense, which remotely resembles this entirely-other Beauty, ever ancient, ever new. The materialist, the sensist, would offer us happiness, and then depress the happiness they offer to the level of a sense world which, when compared to that other, spiritual world, is, alas, all too familiar to us, all too flat, stale, unexciting.

Now one of the intellectual convictions Augustine came to by virtue of his Platonic readings was this: that he would find happiness in nothing else, and nothing less, than in "clinging" to God in direct and immediate vision of the Divine Splendor. *Mihi autem inhaerere Deo meo bonum est*: "my good is to cling [literally to 'stick to'] my God." The point is of capital importance for our purposes; it brings us back to Gilson's reminder that, for Augustine, the central preoccupation of any and all philosophies was the quest for happiness. "Philosophy," he puts it pungently, "professes to teach humans how to become happy."[8] That is unquestionably true of Augustine's own philosophy: from the *De beata vita*, the first work he completed after his conversion, to *De ciuitate dei*—whose publication date seems to get pushed further back every time some scholar scouts the question—the quest for happiness lies at the very center of it.

Happiness and "Naked Vision"

But with that in mind, we can now focus in on that center even more sharply: Augustine is convinced that happiness will be found in the direct, immediate vision of God, and only there. The center of Augustine's thinking, accordingly, now comes down to discovering how one may attain this vision. This was the burden of that treatise from Plotinus's *Enneads*, "On Beauty" (I, vi), which was so influential on Augustine's early thought. Indeed, years later, when dictating *The City of God*, the memory of it comes flooding back upon him; "For that vision of God is a vision of so great a beauty, and is worthy of so great a love, that Plotinus does not hesitate to say that he who enjoys all other blessings in abundance, and has not this, is supremely miserable."[9]

Like all the children of Adam, Augustine had to begin his quest for vision by believing, and growing in belief. At Milan, however, in A.D. 386, he claims to have passed upward from simple belief to that half-way house between belief and immediate vision, the half-way house of *intellectus*. That term is normally translated as "understanding," but Augustine regularly envisages the meaning of the term in an image reflecting its etymology: it is a seeing, or "reading *through*": *inter-legere*. Any number of passages in his preached works encourage us to picture *intellectus* as the filtered kind of vision Augustine describes in the *Contra academicos*:[10] we catch sight of the divine Light as it shines through the clouds which half conceal, half reveal its radiance behind them; we see *per lucidas nubes*.[11] Compared to the filtered view of the Light attained by *intellectus*, faith resembles the trusting gaze of one who has been assured that the Sun is shining *there*, right *there*, though its Light remains totally obscured by the intervening clouds. This image illustrates why, as Magnus Löhrer has shown, belief, for Augustine, entails no insight into what is believed.[12] Still, the simple believer hears, "just keep your eyes directed toward that spot, and the light will eventually pierce through. Believe, and you will come to understand."

But that filtered vision of understanding, like the *dianoia* of Plato's Divided Line analogy, is only an intermediate stage: what Augustine longs for, and what he insists every human soul longs for, is that the clouds should part, should vanish entirely, and that our eyes become strong enough to gaze directly and immediately upon the Divine Sun.

This impatience with all intermediaries, this insistence that we leave everything bodily and sensible behind in pursuit of a vision that is absolutely direct and immediate, is what I found puzzling in Augustine's aesthetic theory. For no one proclaims more confidently than does the artist that unique power which aesthetic experience possesses, to weld the sensual and intellectual components of our humanity into a smoothly harmonious operation: nowhere is our capacity for wedding body and mind in unified performance more strikingly manifest. And nowhere, I was convinced, nowhere except in interpersonal relationships, do humans succeed in acting in a more distinctively human way.

Now this was precisely the unity of performance one found in Augustine's spontaneous activity as an artist. Analyze some of the most evocative and powerful passages of his *Confessiones*, and the fusion of word, image, passion and idea is seamless; yet glance at Augustine's analysis of artistic performance, and the components he so seamlessly fuses in practice, he insists on dislocating in theory. His theory, as Marrou once expressed it, does less to explain artistic performance than to explain it away.[13]

Again the Question of "Appeal"

Once again, though, one is compelled to ask "why?" Why should so accomplished a poet cling so stubbornly to a theory which would make poetry a second rate activity, meant to be transcended by a mind which—so the theory would have us believe—can and must cut all its moorings to the workings of sense and imagination, in a headlong quest for the kind of vision one would think more proper to utterly disembodied angelic spirits?

That mention of disembodied spirits is, I suggest, the key to answering our question. I want to suggest to you that the crucial reason why Augustine insisted on an oppositional relationship between body and mind-soul, the crucial reason why he adopted the view that we are fallen souls, was that these two positions were closely akin to each other, and both akin to his passionate conviction that our origin and our destiny, both, must be consonant with our nature as denizens—*de jure*—of another, higher world. I am suggesting, in other words, that the very center of Augustine's thinking lies in this passionately held conviction: just as God is *aliud, aliud valde*, "other, vastly other" from the realities of this visible world, so our beatitude must be no less "other, vastly other" from any imitation of bliss our sensible experience affords us. And in the thought-world of his time, the only way Augustine could find to express the radical otherness of our ultimate beatitude, was to shear off from it every trace of the sensible and material, every trace of this-worldliness, and in that way depict it as purely spiritual, radically other-worldly. Further, it made sense to Augustine to think of the soul's origin as proportioned to its destiny; but then, in the thought-world of his day, the only theory of the soul's origin which seemed coherent with this view of its destiny was the equally other-worldly and radically spiritual view: that we were originally created for a direct and immediate vision-union with God, in the "heaven of heaven," in that loftiest realm of the other world which was "home" to both the angelic spirits and ourselves.

Thus far I have tried to suggest that Augustine's theory that humans are creatures originally destined for, and fallen from another, higher world, was partner to his view of God as entirely "other," as well as with his view of human happiness as ecstatic contemplative union with that entirely Other. It was this "otherness" of our contemplative nature that entailed the oppositional relationship of soul and body we began with. But there are other features of Augustine's thought which come into clearer focus when examined through the lens of this same theory.

Some Additional Touchstones

One such feature is what Augustine tells us of that place he calls that "heaven of heaven." I have endeavored elsewhere to show that both Georg Nicholas Knauer and Jean Pépin, in two remarkable articles,[14] seemed simply unable to believe their eyes when the *Confessiones* assured them not only that our souls longed to return to this "our home" which was identical with God's own "eternity," but that our souls originally fell from there. T. S. Eliot was not the first to appreciate the symmetry of that conception: "in my end is my beginning." But consciously employ this notion of the soul's other-worldliness as a lens for understanding him, and you will find still other places in Augustine's works where it functions exactly as a "thought-center" should: it not only permits, but virtually compels us to read his text more accurately, and interpret it more faithfully, than we had previously done.

Consider the *De Trinitate* as such an instance: read it from Book Eight to the end with this theory as heuristic searchlight, and it becomes plain that Augustine's dominant intention was to show that God's original creative intention, in making "man" to his own image, was to make him not an embodied, nor a sense-using, nor even a believing soul using practical "knowledge" to guide him in making the ethical decisions for a temporal life: all these are "adventitious" features of our humanity, resulting from our fall. And that fall was from the status for which the God who created us "in his image" originally intended us: the status of soul, and precisely contemplative soul, united to him in the blissful union of immediate vision. God could never have intended a soul of that sort, Augustine was convinced, for the miserable kind of incarnate existence we now experience.

Indeed, it is partly the dim memory we still harbor of that blissful vision we once enjoyed that underlines the misery of incarnate existence, that sharpens the pangs of our restless "journey"—our distant *peregrinatio* through "this life"—*ista vita*—of time. Unless that haunting memory of our origin kept us on the stretch toward our other-worldly "home," we might easily become reconciled to the amenities of those pleasant inns and verdant oases that ease our journey through the menacing desert of "this" lower world: but, just as Odysseus never allowed the Circes and Calypsos of this world to make him forget he was "the Ithacan," we must always remember that we, too, are still far from our other-worldly home, the only home where our restless heart can find rest.

There are few themes of Augustine's preaching more tirelessly repeated or poignantly embroidered than that theme of *peregrinatio*. It has been suggested that he was being cautiously reticent, secretive, perhaps even deceptive about his view that we are fallen angels;[15] nothing will banish any such suspicions more decisively than reading Augustine's unambiguous affirmations that his hearers' journey of soul is a circular one: our "going" is a "going back," *redeamus*! Just as the Prodigal *returned* to the Father's house, as Odysseus *returned* to the Ithaca he had left, or as the lost sheep was borne *back* to the flock from which it had strayed away, so we must walk, run, fly *back*—to the heaven of heaven, the house of God, the celestial Jerusalem we once blissfully inhabited.[16] Here we have the underlying image which lends such impassioned urgency to Augustine's exhortations that we must never lapse into feeling "at home" in this lower world, that we positively foster that sense of being aliens and foreigners in this "dying life, living death." And it is that same impassioned nostalgia, I suggest, which keeps Augustine's *uti-frui* distinction so rigorously intransigent that he can never truly countenance our loving even our marriage partners and dearest friends with anything beyond the love of "use."[17]

Here, too, I suggest, we have identified the soil which brought forth those grim characterizations of our temporal life which have inspired so many meditations on the "pessimism" of Augustine. But what, when all is said, is wrong with human life as we experience it? Analyze Augustine's indictment, and in great part it comes down to this: our lives are not the kind of life Augustine imagines it could, and should have remained: a serene and peaceful bliss, like that of the angels, totally transparent to each other, and rapt in unchanging contemplation of God. Instead of an angelic, ours is a human life.

Here, too, I respectfully submit, we may have located the nerve of Augustine's teaching on sexuality. Peter Brown is correct, I suggest, in speaking of the "ascetical paradigm" which commanded Augustine's thinking in this area; my further suggestion to Brown's view still remains this: he might take much more account of the "mystical" component in that paradigm, the otherworldly nostalgia for the immediate vision of God which fuels and fires it.[18] It is more than a taste for the facile metaphor that inspires Augustine to describe that vision of God as a clinging, a cleaving, an embrace—*amplexus*—which has all the airs of sexual union about it.[19] Augustine's unembarrassed candor in blazoning the sexual flavor of his mysticism merits far more thoughtful recognition that it has received.

Sexuality, Mysticism, and the Young Augustine

That connection between Augustine's mysticism and his sexuality brings me to a final set of considerations. Thus far I have tried to show that taking the fall of the soul as Augustine's root insight both permits and compels us to sharpen our focus on a number of neuralgic elements of his thought-system: on the soul-body relationship underlying his aesthetic and epistemology, on his discovery of the spiritual and of God as "other, vastly other," on his passionate anti-materialism and anti-sensism, on our beatitude as consisting in the direct, immediate, angelistic vision of the Divine Beauty, on the graduated ascent from faith through understanding but ultimately to that same vision, on memory and our sense of alienation and restlessness during our *peregrinatio* of return to the heaven of heaven from which we originally wandered, on the uncompromising rigor of the *uti-frui* distinction, and finally, on the image of God as located in the contemplative mind-soul.

I should like to turn, now, from this macroscopic survey of Augustine's thought in order to show how the fallen-soul lens may also function as a microscope, or perhaps more modestly, as a Sherlockian magnifying glass. Let us narrow our focus for a few minutes, and fix our gaze on that moment in the *Confessions* when Augustine suddenly, and for the first time, becomes recognizably his unique, individual self. That moment, I suggest, coincides with his initial adolescent experiences of sexual passion.

For the Augustine of Book One of the *Confessions* is, on his own admission, a construct drawn from studying your typical infant, your typical little boy: so, too, is that highly theologized icon, the Adam-figure of Book Two who stole those pears. But when Augustine tells us of the tumult of puberty in his sixteenth year, and the stormy onslaughts of sexual passion after his arrival at Carthage, there is no question of icons or constructs, we detect instead the vividness of direct recall, the sharp poignancy which only memory can engender. And by the same stroke, we suddenly recognize that unique individual we know as Aurelius Augustine.

Augustine's Sexual Awakening

Listen to him, the accent is unmistakably his own.[20] He begins with the first of several word-plays on the term for love: he is confessing all of this out of love for God's love: *amore amoris tui*. He "burned," he tells us, *exarsi*, with love for this world's beauties (II,i,1), but on reflection he now sees that what delighted him was to "love and be loved": *amare et amari* (II,ii,2). There is something diffuse, undirected in all this, and a bit further on (III,i,1) Augustine himself calls attention to it: having arrived at Carthage, he realized that "I did not yet love" but "I loved loving" itself: *amare amabam*. And "Since I loved loving, I sought for something to love": *quaerebam quid amare*. So he battened in love on the sensible beauties in the world about him, and tasted only disappointment and frustration.

Nineteen years of age, away from home, and buffeted by the psychic storms of adolescence, it should be no surprise that Augustine did not always succeed in drawing the line between love and lust, or succeed in discerning how the bright reality of friendship might consort with the feverish tides of sexual passion. But these are scarcely grounds for depicting him as a randy monster of sexual indulgence. Give me an adolescent and he will know what I mean.

A Romantic Idealist

Indeed, anyone with a memory of his adolescence will resonate with the other side of the picture Augustine presents of himself. For those troubled years were also, for Augustine, a time for lofty ideals, for dreams of heroism, for those "thoughts of youth" which are "long long thoughts." And bear in mind that the same emotional fires may burn in both the sexual and heroic passions. "I was in love with love": to attribute its proper weight to that phrase, we must first evoke, but then transcend the echoes it prompts from Richard Rodgers, or am I thinking of Lorenz Hart? Though it must be admitted that Augustine was clearly a young romantic. But a romantic idealist as well. How strongly he was moved by the passions and partings of Dido and Aeneas, but of that Aeneas, remember, who was almost inhumanly dedicated to his ideal dream of Rome. That same idealistic streak kept him from joining or approving those gangs of "over-turners"—*eversores*—who ran wild in Carthage. And when he agreed to a common-law marriage, bear in mind that he was faithful to that un-named spouse for all the thirteen years or so of their union. For alongside the tumult of adolescent sexuality, not in opposition to it (I suggest) but as integral part of that ambiguous passage to manhood, Augustine fell in love, not simply with this girl or that, but *amare amabam*, he fell in love with love. What does he hope his readers will detect in that expression?

A Clue from the *De trinitate*: on "Loving Love"

Looking back on this period of his life, he tells us that he now realizes that his hunger for some satisfying love-object could be stilled only by that other-worldly reality, God himself. But those word-plays, *amare amabam, amore amoris*, suggest that the young Augustine already gleaned some measure of that self-knowledge from his youthful experience of love. But if we may be permitted an Augustinian interpretation of Augustine, the self-knowledge gained then was of the sort he later terms, in the *De trinitate, notitia*[21] that vague and implicit awareness even the sinful soul has that it is *imago Dei*, so that it needs but to love love itself—*diligere dilectionem*—in order to "embrace" by that love the very God Who is love.[22]

Confirmation from the *Hortensius* Episode

It may sound forced to claim that as early as his nineteenth year and even earlier, Augustine had already dimly felt a connection between sexual passion and the burning desire for an other-worldly vision of a "Beauty, ever ancient, ever new." But the next episode in his story—his reading of Cicero's *Hortensius*—makes that claim much more plausible. Examine this incident through the lens of the fallen-soul hypothesis, and that lens both permits and compels us to read the whole of Book Three more carefully, and I think insightfully, than ever before.

For one thing, it confirms what Olivier duRoy's laborious analysis[23] of Augustine's early works illustrates on virtually every page: to understand Augustine, we must learn how to capitalize a number of key terms in his writings —especially the terms which are his code-words for the Eternal Christ: words like Philosophy, Reason, Intellect, Order, Truth—and Wisdom. *Augustine's Quest of Wisdom* was an excellent title for Vernon Bourke to choose,[24] but I submit that in nine-tenths of its occurrences in the text, Wisdom—the object of the other-worldly vision Augustine is questing for—should have been capitalized.

Capitalize the term "Wisdom" as it occurs in the *Hortensius* account, and you will come as close as one can to Augustine's own version of where the center of his thought-world lay. Recall for a moment exactly how Augustine tells the story. In the ordinary course of study, he came upon the dialogue, *Hortensius*, which, he tells us, contains Cicero's "exhortation to philosophy." "This book changed my heart-set": he assures us of this, or of its equivalent, three distinct times in his *Confessiones*, and at least on three occasions in his early dialogues.[25] Note the moral and religious tone he injects into what we could mistakenly take to be a purely intellectual experience:

> It turned my prayers to you, Lord, and redirected my purposes and desires. All my vain hopes suddenly became worthless to me, and with incredible ardor of heart I yearned for the immortality of Wisdom. I began to rise up, in order to return to you....[26]

Let's pause for a moment and ponder those expressions. And first, remember that, in exhorting his readers to *philosophia*, Cicero was not recommending that they sign up for a few extension courses in logic or psychology at some neighboring university: he was urging them to abandon the life of worldly activity altogether, along with all the "vain hopes" and empty ambitions bound up with such activity. He was urging them to adopt the contemplative *life-style* of study and meditation: to become, in a word, a kind of secular monk. The dramatic effect this book had on him shows, accordingly, that as early as his nineteenth year Augustine was already sensitized by a lively inclination toward that kind of contemplative life. Was he a "born mystic"? Perhaps; but he was certainly a born contemplative.

An Other-Worldly Soul with Other-Worldly Longings

Most of this one could glean from Testard's treatment of this episode in his *Augustin et Cicéron*.[27] But focus on the text through the lens of fallen-soul theory and a number of further specifics surface:

> How I burned, O my God, [*ardebam*: the same word we saw a moment ago in a sexual connection], how I burned with

> desire to fly back to You from earthly things....for Wisdom
> is with You (*apud Te est enim Sapientia*)....[28]

Now notice once again the multiplication of fire- and flame- words, and
the lexicon of sexual passion more generally:

> What delighted me in [Cicero's] exhortation was only this: I
> was stirred up, and enkindled, and enflamed to love, to seek
> after, to attain and strongly embrace—not this or that sect,
> but Wisdom Itself, whatsoever Wisdom might be.[29]

But not only is Wisdom, *Sapientia,* a feminine noun in Latin, Augustine is here
envisaging Wisdom as an unmistakably feminine target of erotic desire: hence
the translation would more accurately say that he longed to embrace "Wisdom *her*self, *who*ever *she* might be."

> In so great a blaze, only one thing held me back: that the
> name Christ was not in it....Whatever lacked that name, no
> matter how well-written, polished, and truthful it might be,
> could not wholly bear me away: *non me totum rapiebat.*[30]

Here Augustine is probably telling us as much what he himself brought
to his reading of Cicero, as what Cicero actually wrote. In any case, he is telling us that he envisaged the contemplative life as a search, not for this or that
version of "human wisdom," not for the doctrine of this or that philosophical
sect, but for immortal "Wisdom herself"—Wisdom with a capital "W"—whoever she might be.

But Augustine soon qualifies that mysterious "whoever" with some telling specifics. And first, that search for Wisdom herself implied flying upwards
from all "earthly realities": Augustine is clearly thinking of that "Wisdom herself" along the lines of a Platonic hypostatic reality, or of a Biblical personifi-
cation, or as a fusion of both. Wisdom here means a fullness of Wisdom
somehow apart from, in another "world" from all human wisdoms.

But there is more: that other-worldly Wisdom is to be found "with
God": *apud Te.* That peculiar preposition, *apud,* alerts us to the fact that Augustine is thinking of this celestial Wisdom as identical with the Eternal
Christ, the Divine Word which, St. John's Prologue tells us, is "with God":
apud Deum. This identity was undoubtedly one of the reasons why Augustine

could be so disappointed that the *Hortensius* failed to mention the name "Christ."

The Prodigal and the "Loss of Wings"

The next two features to observe about this episode form a pair: first, Augustine describes himself as beginning to "rise up" in order to return to God: *surgere coeperam*, he tells us. Second, in another metaphor, he puts it that he burned to "fly back" to God from "earthly things": *revolare a terrenis ad te*. This latter, of course, is a stock expression from the platonist lexicon which described our souls as once, previous to this "earthly" life, winged, and dwelling in the heavenly realms; we have fallen from that realm, but even now, when suitably reminded, we yearn to sprout those wings again, and fly back— *revolare*—to our heavenly abode. The former of the two expressions, *surgere coeperam*, Augustine has taken from the fifteenth chapter of St. Luke's Gospel; there it applies to the Prodigal Son, whom Augustine invariably takes as a figure of fallen humanity.[31] The Prodigal journeyed far from the celestial mansion of God, his Father, collapsed out of hunger and exhaustion, but now "stands up" in order to "return" to his Father. But just as the soul now shorn of its wings once dwelt in heaven, so too the Prodigal once dwelt in the Father's house to which he is now resolved to return. The soul is other-worldly both in its origin and in its destiny.

Augustine is telling us, accordingly, that he found Cicero's *Hortensius* awakening a deep nostalgia for "returning" from the earthly realities he has loved until now, to the other-worldly God he had once abandoned. His subsequent returns to this episode make it unquestionably clear that it invariably provoked the same desire for a contemplative "return" to God. Augustine can, moreover, depict that "return" in the Platonic metaphor of the fallen soul, or in the gospel metaphor of the wandering Prodigal: to all appearances, he himself sees no conflict whatever between those metaphors; the Prodigal simply is, for him, the principal Christian metaphor for our condition as fallen souls.

Augustine's "erotic intellectualism"

Notice once again, though, how charged this episode is with an unambiguous erotic tonality. At its most intense, Augustine's intellectualism invariably assumes this erotic quality. Here, he would have us believe that Cicero's invitation electrified him in much the same way as, centuries later, his first glimpse of Beatrice electrified Dante. He "burned," Augustine tells us, burned with desire, with "incredible ardor of heart." He cannot find synonyms enough to dramatize his reaction: he was stirred up, enkindled, enflamed, to love, seek after, attain, and strongly embrace...(notice that word "embrace," again!). That unmistakably feminine *Sapientia* puts one in mind of the equally feminine *Continentia* from the Milanese garden-scene; one thinks also of the feminine figure of *Philosophia* in the *Contra academicos*, or (most striking of all) the bold evocation in the *Soliloquia* of Wisdom herself as a beautiful woman whom her ardent lovers are on fire to behold, stripped of "every intervening veil."[32]   Then one has to think of those poetic images of wisdom which Ecclesiasticus, the Proverbs, and the Book of Wisdom string together, all of them alluringly feminine....

And so the *Hortensius* lends definiteness to the answers which Augustine's earlier description of his sexual awakening left relatively hazy: we know much more explicitly now what that anonymous object of Augustine's searching was when he found himself in love with love itself; for God himself is as much sheer Wisdom as he is pure Love. We can understand more clearly, too, why no creaturely love-object could satisfy him, any more than this or that instance of human wisdom could still his hunger for Wisdom herself. He himself still has a great deal of growing to do before this relatively vague *notitia* becomes fully explicit *cogitatio sui*. But from this time forward, the architectonic lines of his thinking have taken form, and will never substantially alter. He has located the center from which, henceforth, all his thinking and aspiration spring. We are beings whose native air was once the loftier world where beauteous Wisdom dwelt with God; we have sinfully fallen into this lower realm of darkness, struggle, and misery; and we long to fly back to the bright home, to the rapturous embrace we spurned and left behind.

The Appeal of Manichaeism

This, then, was the human bundle of contradictions who got married, then tumbled on Cicero's *Hortensius*, and a short while later yielded to the attractions of Manichaeism. Augustine recounts these incidents serially, each set off from the incidents preceding and following it. But we must not let such narrative divisions deceive us. Surely there was as much underlying continuity between these successive episodes as there was distinction. Augustine's youthful idealism must have been interwoven as thoroughly through his personal and literary experiences of sexual passion and noble love, as through his reading of the *Hortensius*. And, I am now suggesting, the same predispositions must have been just as intensely at work in Augustine's conversion to Manichaeism.

Indeed, despite the episodic serialism of Augustine's narrative, Manichaeism was almost certainly exerting its appeal on Augustine at the same time as the events which led up to his common-law marriage, as well as during those days and weeks when he was wrestling with the challenge of the *Hortensius*. Granted, Augustine recounts his enrollment as a Manichee as actually occurring subsequently to those two events, but it must certainly have been the fruit of a growing acquaintance with that sect and its adherents, and that growing acquaintance must, in all likelihood, have run concurrently with his sexual difficulties, marriage, and reading of the *Hortensius*. But perhaps these working hypotheses will gain confirmation from the way they result in a mind-satisfying picture of all three events in their interrelationship.

Putting the Mosaic Together

It was then, I submit, a sexually troubled youth (by which I mean a pretty normal adolescent!) with a romantic and idealistic streak, who read the *Hortensius*; a youth who had settled into a common-law marriage which had its spats and reconciliations; a youth about whose ears were already buzzing both Manichee objections to the faith of the *Catholica*, and Manichee descriptions of the glorious Kingdom of Light.

By this time the quotidian domesticities of marriage must have de-romanticized the young man's sexual activity to some extent, drained it of the adventurous, even dangerous aura which can make it so bewitching to the roving young blade. Marriage invariably proves that the promise forbidden sex holds out to the callow adolescent is an extravagant promise which sex itself can never truly fulfill.

But Augustine must also have begun to suspect that what is true of sex is equally true of so many of "this" life's other extravagant promises: of security, of loving and being loved, of worldly achievement, success, even glory. And yet, those promises are there: is the world which holds them out to us no more than a giant deception? Or could it be that their promised fulfillment awaits in another world than the one we inhabit: could it be that security, love, achievement, glory, as well as the unabating ecstasy so fleetingly promised by sexual union, are hints, suggestions—what Plato would call "imitations"—of a perfect fulfillment which can occur only in a world we dream about, long for —or (is it possible?), a world which we "remember"?

But if all this be true, the ideal world of our hopes and dreams must be "other, vastly other" from "this" world of our experience. What could possibly have gone wrong to account for our finding ourselves in "this" frustrating world of misery and disappointment?

Here the Manichaean dualism must already have been making inroads on Augustine's consciousness at the time he was poring over Cicero's *Hortensius*. In any case, the Manichees offered a version of the happy life remarkably in accord with the one Augustine claims to have found in Cicero. The Manichees insisted that our souls are other-worldly beings, both in origin and destiny. They trumpeted an ascetic ideal of purity, and notably of sexual purity. Finally, their depreciation (at least in principle) of earthly achievement, may well have resonated with what Testard describes as Cicero's austere ethical counsels.

But in addition, Augustine tells us, the "name of [God] and of our Lord Jesus Christ," which he had missed so sorely in the *Hortensius*, that name was forever on the Manichees' lips;[33] indeed, Mani proclaimed himself the Apostle of Jesus Christ. Years later, moreover, Augustine is able to remind the Manichee bishop, Faustus,[34] of that tenet of theirs which must have made a deep impression on his youthful mind: their teaching on the Luminous Christ and his mythical analogue the *Splenditenens*: the One who held that world of spiritual splendor together.[35] That *Splenditenens* Augustine none too subtly recalled by the striking expression he coins in the *Confessions* for the all-upholding creative Word of God: *Omnitenens manu veritate*.[36]

And so we have circled back to that immortal Wisdom who is also Word "with God"—*apud Deum*—which Augustine glimpsed between the lines of Cicero's *Hortensius*. But this was only one feature of Manichee teaching which answered to what the young Augustine considered the truest of the religious and moral ideals he then held dear. And more specifically he could, and almost certainly did feel, that in adopting Manichaeism he was adopting a higher form of Christianity than he had found in the North African *Catholica* of his day.

Mani and the Regard for Intelligence

But another common characteristic of which the *Hortensius* and Manichaeism boasted, and which strongly appealed to the young Augustine, was the high regard for the workings of human intelligence they both displayed. Augustine is so insistent about this feature in the dialogues written shortly after his conversion, that one might almost be tempted to think it was the only reason for Manichaeism's appeal to him. He was *factus erectior*, he tells us, he was "made more erect,"[37] and he explains that phrase as meaning that he was no longer content to bow down and believe blindly in the intimidating pronouncements of the authoritarian teachers and preachers in the North African Catholic Church. It is significant that he applies the same interpretation to the phrase which describes what the Prodigal did in the gospel: he "rose up" to direct his gaze toward the higher world of truths which only the power of understanding can grasp.[38]

So the summons to philosophical meditation he had read in the *Hortensius* chimed in with the challenging promise that Manichees held out to him: they claimed that they would never require him to believe anything which they could not explain to him so cogently that he would see the truth of what they taught by the light of human reason.

But there is a significant distinction between the contributions Augustine describes as Cicero's, on the one hand, and the Manichaeans', on the other.[39] It is a distinction which must be kept in mind whenever we use that famous phrase, so often proffered in hopes of locating the "center" of Augustine's intellectual effort: "faith seeking understanding." Augustine repeatedly credits the Manichees with encouraging him to reject the authoritarianism of "infantile" blind faith, and "rise up" to stand on his own two feet as an adult rational being, capable of thinking things out for himself. Undoubtedly the Manichees had more in mind than this: the whole point of their religion was the soul's recovery of that peaceful union with the divine which had been disturbed. But for some reason, when he speaks of "faith seeking understanding" in a Manichee-related context, Augustine more often has in mind this imperative of moving from an infantile dependence on authority to the mature reliance on reason.

Now Augustine seems to credit Cicero with doing that, but more than that: Cicero's invitation to *philosophia* suggested to him that attaining the capacity to reason things out for himself was only a halfway-house: the reach of the human mind went beyond those operations of discursive reason; "understanding" in the full sense aimed well beyond the task of "reasoning things out" and so establishing this or that version of human wisdom against its competitors. No, Augustine found Cicero suggesting to him, the human mind hungered for a vision that would be ecstatic union with Wisdom itself, or more exactly now, Wisdom herself. Our souls' reach stretches into another world entirely, the world from which we literally other-worldly creatures must originally have come. In the image Augustine uses frequently to describe our situation, "understanding" is like the act of gazing steadily at the hazily luminous point where the sun's rays are filtering through a blanket of cloud. We are "seeing" that Sun, but *per lucidas nubes*: "through light-filled clouds." But our deepest yearning is for those clouds to disappear entirely, leaving us to behold that Sun directly, immediately: like that Lady Wisdom beheld with every intervening veil removed. "Love, love understanding," Augustine exclaims in that famous exhortation to Consentius;[40] but why? Ultimately because that way lies our hope of attaining, perhaps even in this mortal life, to the "very summit of contemplation," the "vision" which Paul describes as "face to face."[41]

For that, may I suggest for one last time in concluding, was the very center of the man we know as Augustine; and we recognize him as that unique individual from the moment when he steps forward at the dawning of sexuality and discovers he was fashioned to fall in love with love, to sense that the meaning of sex and passion of every sort pointed outward and upward to the other-worldly Beauty of a Wisdom who was somehow strangely familiar, somehow dimly remembered. From that moment forward "philosophy," for Augustine, became the single-minded pursuit of happiness, yes: but more precisely, of happiness as concentrated in the vision which we contemplative souls had once enjoyed, wrenched ourselves away from, but restlessly long to embrace again, this time forever. To this born poet, contemplative, and maybe even mystic, not only sex, but every delight, every pang, absolutely everything and everyone we encounter here below, was sign and shadow of that splendorous reality waiting for us at home. But compared to every such sign and shadow, that Reality was *aliud, aliud valde*: "other, vastly other." Which is why

Augustine tirelessly wrote, and preached, that we humans—or better, we fallen and wayfaring souls—must settle for nothing less!

Notes

[1] *History of Dogma* (New York: Dover Books, 1961) vol. 5, p. 64.

[2] *The Christian Philosophy of Saint Augustine*, tr. L. E. M. Lynch (New York: Random House, 1960), p. 115. (Henceforth: *Christian Philosophy*.)

[3] *Saeculum: History and Society in the Theology of Saint Augustine*, rev. ed. (Cambridge, England: Cambridge University Press, n.d. [1988]), p. xiii.

[4] *Christian Philosophy*, pp. 44–45.

[5] Compare the exceptional texts hypothesizing the soul's "natural" desire for a body, which Gilson exploits in *Christian Philosophy*, p. 280, n. 16.

[6] See my *Saint Augustine's Early Theory of Man, A.D. 386–391* (Cambridge, MA: The Belknap Press of Harvard University Press, 1968), pp. 135–45, and *The Origin of the Soul in St. Augustine's Later Works* (New York: Fordham University Press, 1987), pp. 238–41. (Henceforth *Early Theory* and *Origin*, respectively.)

[7] *Epistula CXC* IV,14–15: *CSEL* LVII,148–49.

[8] *De ciuitate dei* XVIII,xxxix: *CC* XLVIII,634: *Nam quod adtinet ad philosophiam, quae se docere profitetur aliquid, unde fiant homines beati ....*

[9] *De ciuitate dei* X,xvi: *CC* XLVII,289: *Illa namque uisio Dei tantae pulchritudinis uisio est et tanto amore dignissima, ut sine hac quibuslibet aliis bonis praeditum atque abundantem non dubitet Plotinus infelicissimum dicere.*

[10] *Contra academicos* I,i,3: *CC* XXIX,4–5.

[11] This "image" of the act of *intellectus* also occurs frequently in Augustine's preached works; see for example *Sermo CXXXV* VII,8: *PL* XXXVIII,749–50; *Sermo CCXLI* I,1: *PL* XXXVIII,1133–34; *Tractatus in Euangelium Ioannis* XIX,5: *CC* XXXVI,190.

[12] See his *Der Glaubensbegriff des hl. Augustinus* (Einseideln: Benziger, 1955), p. 111.

[13] H.-I. Marrou, *Augustin et la fin de la culture antique* (Paris: Boccard, 1938), p. 184, n. 1.

[14] See Knauer's *"Peregrinatio Animae"*: zur Frage der Einheit der *Konfessionen*," *Hermes* 85 (1957) 216–48, and Pépin's "Recherches sur le sens et les origines de l'expression 'caelum caeli' dans les *Confessions* de saint Augustin," *Archivum Latinitatis Medii Aevi* 23 (1953) 185–274. For my analysis, see "The Fall of the Soul in the Confessions," *Atti* II of the *Congresso Internazionale su S. Agostino* (Rome: Augustinianum, 1986), pp. 45–58.

[15] See the review of my *Origin* by John Rist, in *International Philosophical Quarterly* 29 (1989) 221–27, esp. 223.

[16] See, for example, *Sermo CLXXXIX* I,1: *MA* I,209–210; *Enarratio in Psalmum CXXI* 2, 5: *CC* XL,1801–1802, 1805–1806; *Enarratio in Psalmum CXLVIII* 4: *CC* XL,2168–69; *Enarratio in Psalmum XC, Sermo II* 1: *CC* XXXIX,1265–67. A fuller treatment of Augustine's imagery is forthcoming from Fordham University Press.

[17] See the most recent contribution to this troubled question, *The Problem of Self-Love in St. Augustine*, by O. O'Donovan (New Haven: Yale University Press, 1980), pp. 112–36.

[18] This was the tenor of my contribution to *Colloquy* 46 of the Center for Hermeneutical Studies, of the University of California at Berkeley, on "Augustine and Sexuality," 1983. The drift of Professor Peter Brown's thinking on that suggestion (he was main speaker and respondent on the occasion) may be fairly judged from his recent book, *The Body and Society* (New York: Columbia University Press, 1988), where (on page 405 particularly) he firmly rejects the "fallen soul" assumption on which my suggestion rested. His understanding of that hypothesis, however, leaves something to be desired in the way of precision.

[19] *Confessiones* X,vi,8: *BA* 14,152–54.

[20] What immediately follows is a conflation of the opening paragraphs of Books Two and Three of the *Confessiones*: both sections are cognate in treating of Augustine's difficulties with adolescent sexuality. Cf. *Confessiones* II,i,1–ii,2: *BA* 13,332–34; III,i,1: *BA* 13,362–64.

[21] *De trinitate* XIV,iv,7–viii,11: *CC* L/A,429–38.

[22] *De trinitate* VIII,viii,12: *CC* L,286–87.

[23] See his *L'intelligence de la foi en la Trinité selon Saint Augustin* (Paris: Études Augustiniennes, 1966).

[24] Milwaukee: Bruce, 1945.

[25] In addition to this section, *Confessiones* III,iv,7–8: *BA* 13,372–76, see: VI,ix,18: *BA* 13, 556–58; VIII,vii,17: *BA* 14,42–44; *De beata vita* I,4: *CC* XXIX,66–67; *Contra academicos* I,i,4: *CC* XXIX,5; *Soliloquia* I,x,17: *CSEL* LXXXIX,26.

[26] *Confessiones* III,iv,7: *BA* 13,374: *ille uero liber mutauit affectum meum et ad te, domine, mutauit preces meas et uota ac desideria mea fecit alia. uiluit mihi repente omnis uana spes et inmortalitatem sapientiae concupiscebam aestu cordis incredibili et surgere coeperam, ut ad te redirem.*

[27] Paris: Études Augustiniennes, 1958, pp. 19–49.

[28] *Confessiones* III,iv,8: *BA* 13,374: *Quomodo ardebam, deus meus, quomodo ardebam reuolare a terrenis ad te,...apud te est enim sapientia.*

[29] *Confessiones* III,iv,8: *BA* 13,376: *...hoc tamen solo delectabar in illa exhortatione,*

quod non illam aut illam sectam, sed ipsam quaecumque esset sapientiam ut diligerem et quaererem et adsequerer et tenerem atque amplexarer fortiter, excitabar sermone illo et accendebar et ardebam....

[30] *Confessiones* III,iv,8: *BA* 13,376: *...et hoc solum me in tanta flagrantia refrangebat, quod nomen Christi non erat ibi...quidquid sine hoc nomine fuisset quamuis litteratum et expolitum et ueridicum, non me totum rapiebat.*

[31] Augustine presents what appears to have been his quasi-normative personal interpretation of this parable in his *Libri duo quaestionum evangeliorum* II,xxxiii: *PL* XXXV, 1344-49, written around the year 400. He does not hesitate, however, to make slight adaptations to his views to fit different preaching occasions.

[32] For *Continentia*, see *Confessiones* VIII,xi,27: *BA* 14,62; for *Philosophia*, *Contra academicos* II,iii,7: *CC* XXIX,21–22; for *Sapientia*, *Soliloquia* I,xiii,22: *CSEL* LXXXIX,34.

[33] *Confessiones* III,vi,10: *BA* 13,378: *...nominis tui et domini Iesu Christi.... haec nomina non recedebant de ore eorum....*

[34] *Contra Faustum* XV,5–6: *CSEL* XXV.VI.1,424-28.

[35] Samuel N. C. Lieu, *Manichaeism* (Manchester, England: Manchester University Press, 1985), pp. 134–35.

[36] *Confessiones* VII,xv,21: *BA* 13,624.

[37] I have dealt with this image more at length in "On Augustine's 'First Conversion': *Factus Erectior* (*De Beata Vita* 4)," *Augustinian Studies* 17 (1986) 15–29.

[38] See note above.

[39] The distinction is not air-tight, chiefly, I suspect, because Augustine himself does not seem reflectively to have drawn it. In *Contra academicos* I,iii,8: *CC* XXIX,7–8 and I,ix, 24: *CC* XXIX,16–17, for example, Cicero is cited in connection with the need to pass from reliance on authority to the mature use of reason.

[40] *Epistula CXX* III,13: *CSEL* XXXIV,715–16.

[41] *Epistula CXX* I,4: *CSEL* XXXIV,707–8; II,8: *CSEL* XXXIV,711.

Sin and Punishment: The Early Augustine on Evil

William S. Babcock

Augustine's *De libero arbitrio* opens with a passage that has not, I think, received the attention it deserves.[1] If I am right about the passage's import, it holds an important clue to the development of Augustine's early thinking about evil and, at the same time, to the way in which Latin Christianity took shape at the point of transition from late antiquity to the early medieval era. But let me start by attempting a sketch of the argument that appears in the passage itself.

The *De libero arbitrio* was written, of course, in the form of a dialogue; and it begins with the interlocutor's request to be shown whether God is not the author of evil. In response, Augustine distinguishes two senses in which we are accustomed to use the word *evil*: "one when we say that someone has acted evilly, the other when we say that someone has suffered something evil."[2] This distinction provides the instrument that Augustine will use to sort out the question that he faces and to set the lines that he will follow in attempting an answer to it. His first step is to appeal to the acknowledged goodness and justice of God. If God is good—and it is not licit to think otherwise (*neque enim aliter fas est*)—then God does not act evilly. If God is just—and it is sacrilege to deny the point (*nam et hoc negare sacrilegum est*)—then, just as God distributes rewards to the good, so God distributes punishments to the wicked. And these punishments are certainly evils to those who suffer them. Now, given the further premise that no one undergoes punishments unjustly—which we must believe since we hold that this universe is governed by divine providence—we can reach the double conclusion that God is not the author of evil in the first sense (as good, God does not act evilly), but is the author of evil in the second sense (as just, God punishes the wicked).[3]

In this first stage of his argument, then, Augustine has subtly, but decisively, altered the shape of the problem. More or less by fiat, he has exempted God from the authorship of evil in the first sense: since God is good, God does not act evilly. But he has not exempted God from the authorship of evil in the second sense (the evils that persons suffer). Rather he has renamed these evils, labeling them punishments, and thus made them not only compatible with divine authorship but also the very expression of divine justice and of God's providential rule of the universe. The question of theodicy does not arise; at least, it does not arise if the relabeling of these evils as just punishments can be sustained. Thus Augustine's reshaping of the problem has the effect of putting all the pressure on the question of whether or not we can legitimately think of the evils people suffer as punishments that they rightly undergo. The next step in the argument will address this point.

God is not the author of evil in the sense of acting evilly. But we have still to ask whether there is some other author of evil in this sense, and it is just this question that the interlocutor now poses. Augustine replies that most certainly there is, for we could not have evil in this sense if it were not authored by someone. There is, however, no one author. Rather each evil person is the author of his (or her) evil actions. In support of this point, Augustine appeals to his previous assertion that evil actions are punished by God's justice and then draws the crucial conclusion: evil actions are not punished *justly* unless they are performed willingly (*voluntate*).[4] The point seems clear enough: evil actions will not count as evil in the relevant sense—i.e., the sense that makes them liable to punishment—unless they can rightly be said to be authored by those who perform them, and to be the author of one's actions one must enact them willingly. Thus Augustine, in refining and completing the argument of this opening passage of the *De libero arbitrio*, has again shifted the point at which the pressure falls. The claim that the evils people suffer can be construed as punishments rightly applied will be sustained if, and only if, the evils people do can be construed as moral evils, as evils willingly performed—in short, as sins. It is this point that Augustine will argue in the remainder of the *De libero arbitrio*.

In a few deft strokes, then, Augustine has recast the question of evil at the very outset of his treatise, transforming it into the question of sin and punishment.[5] What is the significance of the change? In effect, Augustine has translated the question from one realm to another. In its new form, it is no longer a question about the presence of evil in the cosmos, but is rather a question about the interactions of moral agents—the person who sins, on the one hand, and the God who is just, on the other. And, of course, the dimension in which the interactions between moral agents play themselves out is the dimension of time and of history, not the dimension of space or of cosmos. By taking the distinction between the evil persons do and the evil persons suffer as an exhaustive reckoning of evil, and by labeling the first *sin* and the second *punishment*, Augustine has recast the question of evil as a question of divine-human interaction in time, as a question of divine providence and human sin, as a question of history. It has been suggested that the *De libero arbitrio*—or, at least, its first two books—might more properly have been called *De malo*.[6] But the suggestion rests on a failure to take due account of the work's opening passage. The whole point of that passage is to redefine the question *de malo* as the question *de libero arbitrio*, the question of moral agency exercised in time and under God's rule.

The *De libero arbitrio* was not, of course, the first of Augustine's works to take up the question of evil. In the *De ordine*, written at Cassiciacum, he had already made a sustained, if somewhat murky, attempt to come to grips with the issue. Like the *De libero arbitrio*, the *De ordine* is also a dialogue, and its principal participants are Augustine himself and his two young pupils, Licentius and Trygetius. Their discussions, however, do not lead to any true conclusion with respect to the problem initially posed. Instead they turn to a delineation of the training required for those who wish to pursue such philosophical inquiries, and the question itself is left hanging in the air.

Despite the elusiveness of the *De ordine*, however, it is possible to sketch at least the main lines of the argument it develops and to catch at least intimations of the position it adopts with regard to the question of evil. Particularly important—because it sets the issue that stands at the center of the work—is the nighttime discussion that dominates the first book of the treatise and in which Licentius, fired by a fresh enthusiasm for philosophy, takes the lead.[7] The central theme, already announced in the address to Zenobius with which the work begins, has to do with discerning and expounding the universal order by which this world is controlled and governed,[8] and the first night's conversation culminates in Licentius' avid declaration that nothing happens outside or apart from order (*praeter ordinem*).[9] But this assertion immediately evokes some probing counter-questions from Trygetius: if evils are contained in order and if order both stems from and is loved by God, must we say that evils come from God or that God loves evils?[10]

Licentius responds that, in fact, it belongs to order that God should not love evils (i.e., order includes both God's loving goods and God's not loving evils), and he suggests that this very order itself makes evils necessary. The contrast between good and evil, like antithesis in human discourse, contributes to the harmony (*congruentia*) and enhances the beauty (*pulchritudo*) of the whole, the unity in which all things cohere (the *universitas*).[11] As a by no means irrelevant afterthought, Licentius adds that divine justice consists in rendering to each its due. Consequently, if there were no distinction between good and evil, there could be no such rendering, and there would be no distinction if all were good. Thus God's justice means precisely that God renders their due both to the good *and to the evil* so that all is included in order.[12] Licentius seems, then, to have elaborated a position that (a) brings evil within the realm of order (since evil does not remain an unordered or disordered element outside the universal scheme of things as divinely governed), (b) suggests that evil, in fact, enhances the beauty of the ordered whole (since it constitutes a contribution to rather than a fault in or a diminution of order's scheme), and (c) reconciles the existence of evil with divine justice (since, if there were no evil, divine justice would lack its sphere of application).

But there are problems. When Augustine returns to the question of evil and divine justice in the second book of *De ordine*, it is in order to expose and to query the implication that, if God is always just, evil must always have existed. Trygetius is the one who discovers an escape. He suggests that, just as Cicero had the virtues of prudence, temperance, justice, and fortitude before he put them to use in dealing with Catiline's conspiracy, so we can say that God was just before God put justice into practice, i.e., before the distinction between good and evil arose. Thus divine justice does not entail that evil always existed.[13] Augustine is quick to point out, however, that Trygetius' gambit leads directly to a new and greater difficulty. If evil had a beginning, we can hardly say that it took its beginning by the ordering activity of God—i.e., we can hardly say that God is the one who brings about the origin of evil.[14] Thus it seems that something does occur *praeter ordinem* after all, namely, evil's start.

Licentius, caught off guard by this challenge to his position, leaps to the suggestion that order itself began when evil began. But Augustine observes that this view also leaves the beginning of evil *praeter ordinem*, and Licentius, defeated on this front, turns to Trygetius' strategy. *Ordo*, he asserts, was always with God but was not put to use until evil arose. The difficulty, however, remains: on this account, too, evil arises outside of and apart from order. Thus Licentius faces a critical dilemma: either he must concede that something happens *praeter ordinem* or he must embrace the consequence of asserting that everything happens according to order, the consequence that evil itself must have arisen according to order and thus by divine design.[15]

At this stage, it would seem, the critical issue has at last been defined, and the argument is at last ready to move toward a resolution. In fact, however, it is just here that Augustine breaks off the discussion of the question of order and evil and turns the *De ordine* in a quite different direction. He now makes it explicitly what it has been implicitly all along: a pedagogical exercise in the training and forming of those who wish to pursue philosophical inquiry into such delicate and difficult regions as the problem of evil in a cosmos governed by divine design. Those who love order, he insists, will follow the order that such an enterprise requires, i.e., the *ordo docendi* or the *ordo studiorum sapientiae*,[16] which he then expounds under the two headings of authority and reason through the remainder of the work.

Nevertheless Augustine does not leave us utterly without hints as to how his mind stood on the matter at hand. In this regard, two points are particularly important. The first is that, in the *De ordine*, Augustine regards the question of evil as first of all a matter of failed vision. In a well known passage that occurs early in the work, he suggests that people who take offense at the evil in the world are like people examining a mosaic from so close a range that they can see only a single tile. They object that the artist knew nothing of arrangement (*ordinatio*) and composition (*compositio*) when, in fact, the problem arises entirely from their own lack of perspective. If they would only step back, they would see how the pieces to which they object come together to make a figure of unified beauty (*in unius pulchritudinis faciem*).[17] It might seem, then, that Augustine has shifted the question of evil from the viewed to the viewer, dissolving the apparent evil in the bright harmony of the wider whole seen in proper perspective. This impression, however, is quite wrong. Looking at the mosaic from a distance does not eliminate the evil; rather it shows how the evil fits into and enhances the beauty of the whole. It shows, we might say, that there is no such thing as unordered or disordered evil, that there is no such thing as evil that has not already been brought under the governance of the divine design. It does not show that there is no evil at all.

The second point, then, is that it is not failed, but precisely corrected vision that makes the dilemma facing Licentius an urgent and weighty matter. If we are to secure the claim that there is no such thing as unordered evil, and never has been, then we must somehow come to grips with the question of evil's beginning. But to admit that evil had a beginning appears to entail one or the other of two wholly unacceptable corollaries: either evil arose *praeter ordinem* (and thus there is, after all, an unordered, uncontrolled form of evil) or evil arose *ordine Dei* (and God is, after all, the one responsible for the presence of evil—and not merely for its harmonization—in the ordered whole). The only escape, it would seem, is to grant that evil always existed.

In a tantalizing and elusive passage near the end of the *De ordine*, Augustine lists the "obscure and yet divine" matters that are to be approached only through the *ordo eruditionis*, only through the appropriate training of the philosopher for philosophic inquiry.[18] At the head of the list stand these questions: "how it is that God both makes no evil and is omnipotent, and yet such terrible evils occur; for what benefit God made the world when God had need of nothing; and whether evil always existed or began to be in time...." Taking the assumption that evil always existed, Augustine continues by asking,

> whether, if evil always existed, it was always under God's control; and, if so, whether this world also always existed, in which evil is governed by divine design; or, if this world began at some point in time, how evil was held in check by God's power before this world existed and what need there was to construct this world in order to direct evil to the punishment of souls (*ad poenas animarum includeretur*) when God's power was already reining evil in; or, if there was a time when evil was not under God's dominion, what suddenly happened that had not happened through all the preceding eternity of time....[19]

But we do not need to follow Augustine's list of questions any further. He uses the remaining portions of this passage to rule out the Manichaean possibility of an evil that once was not controlled by God and to exclude, as well, the notion that this present world was not created.

Although a succession of questions can hardly be construed as a set of conclusions, this passage does give us significant intimations of Augustine's view of evil while he was still at Cassiciacum. It is noteworthy, in the first place, that he does not take up or explore the possibility that evil did not always exist. That alternative, once mentioned, simply drops from sight, and we can conclude, with Olivier du Roy, that Augustine, at the time he wrote the *De ordine*, considered evil always to have existed.[20] Furthermore, since he also rules out both the possibility that evil once stood beyond the reach of divine control and the possibility that this world existed eternally, we can see exactly where he located the problem of evil in relation to divine order and precisely what he took the dimensions of the problem to be. Evil always existed and was always under divine control; this world, which is the present instrument through which evil is governed by divine design, did not always exist. Thus two questions follow: how was evil held in check—i.e., by what order and in what design was it held in check—before this world came into existence? and, given that some such design or order was already in effect, what need was there to create this world in order to direct evil toward the punishment of souls (for that is the role, Augustine asserts, that evil plays in this world)? Paraphrasing a little more loosely, we might say that, for all its annoying elusiveness, the *De ordine* ends by casting the question of evil in this unexpected form: why the creation of this world when God had already and always controlled evil within a divine order? why this apparent shift in the divine design? For Augustine, we can only presume, the question was a dead end. By the time he started the *De libero arbitrio*, two years later, all that survived was the notion that, in this world, evil serves for the punishment of souls.

The line of thought that Augustine intimated in the *De ordine* ended, then, in a muddle. The muddle presumably arose because Augustine, intent on warding off the haunting specter of the Manichees, could conceive of no irruption of evil into the divinely ordered scheme of things that did not represent in some sense a defeat for God, an unwanted happening that occurred *praeter ordinem*. Consequently the only acceptable answer seemed to be that evil had always been contained and controlled within the divine design—and therefore that evil had always existed. But this conclusion jostled uneasily against the claim that the present world, the created order in which evil functions for the punishment of souls, did have a beginning. To give up this claim would, in Augustine's eyes, have been an impiety and a sacrilege.[21] But holding to it suggested a shift in the divine design, a change from one way of holding evil in check to another. And why, if evil was already successfully constrained, was there any need for such a change?

The Platonic notion of evil as privation, although certainly at work in both the *De ordine* and the *De libero arbitrio*,[22] held no resources for the reduction or the solution of this puzzle. It served well as a weapon against the Manichaean claim that evil has an independent ontic status of its own, a base camp, as it were, from which it might sally forth to attack the good. The Platonic notion served the purpose of reducing evil to a parasite upon the good which, as a parasite, requires the good if it is to exist at all. But it does not account for the origin of evil; and, above all, it does not capture the active force of evil as a power exerting itself in opposition to—even if wholly constrained by—the divine design. Augustine needed something more if he was to escape from the muddle into which the *De ordine* had led him. He found that "something more" in the categorization of evil under the two headings of the evil we do and the evil we suffer and, far more important, in the labeling of these two forms of evil as respectively sin and punishment. I want to conclude with some observations about the outcome of this reconceptualization of the question of evil.

The first and most obvious thing to say is that, by construing the question of evil as a matter of sin and punishment, Augustine locates it squarely in the moral realm, the realm in which we have to do with the actions and interactions of moral agents—and therefore, we can reiterate, he locates it squarely in the dimension of time, for time is the dimension in which such actions and interactions transpire. The image of the mosaic which holds such a prominent place in the *De ordine* is, of course, a spatial image. It has to do with the arrangement of *tesserae* in relation to each other within a spatial matrix. But already in the *De ordine* itself Augustine had suggested an alternate imagery. The way in which evil might be said to enhance the beauty of a wider scheme can be pictured not only as the contribution of a single tile to a mosaic whole, but also as the contribution of antithesis to the elegance of human speech.[23] And speech, unlike the visual image, achieves its effects through time. This verbal image lends itself to a historical rendering, and that is exactly how Augustine does use it in the *City of God*: in creating human beings, God foreknew their future evil, and God would not have created them at all without also knowing how to turn them to account in the interests of the good and so to enrich the order of the ages (*ordo saeculorum*) "by the kind of antithesis which gives beauty to a poem," thus producing "a kind of eloquence in events, instead of in words."[24] The mosaic tiles are, so to speak, reconstrued as episodes in the course of time.

In order to sustain this relocation of the question of evil in the moral and the historical realm, of course, Augustine had to secure the claim that the evil we do genuinely counts as sin, i.e., that in acting evilly we act willingly or, to say the same thing another way, that we act as moral agents. As I have already suggested, this argument is perhaps the central point of the *De libero arbitrio*. But more is required. Around and with this central argument, Augustine—if he was to move beyond the muddle of *De ordine*—had also to show that evil can have its origin in the willing action of moral agents (a) without implicating God as the ultimate author of the evils done by the moral agents God created, (b) without implying an irruption of evil that constitutes a defeat for God, and (c) without falling outside the order of the divine design. The first of these Augustine attempted to show by arguing that the will is a good which, just because it is a good, was rightly given to human beings by

God.[25] The giver of a good gift is not implicated in the misuse of the gift by its recipients. The second Augustine tried to accomplish by arguing that there is no cause of evil willing. The movement of aversion from a higher to a lower good is a defective movement; and defect, Augustine urges in good Platonic fashion, comes from nothing.[26] It does not have its source in God or in any other outside force. Thus the origin of evil is not to be construed as an irruption from without, but as a defection from within. And it constitutes no defeat for God because this defection most certainly does not escape the ordering of the divine design. Rather sin so entails its own penalty that to sin is already—in the consequent disorder of the self—to enter a penal state, a state in which one is penally afflicted with ignorance and moral difficulty in all one's subsequent dispositions and actions (so much so, in fact, that only the first instance of sinning counts as sin in the proper sense while subsequent sinning counts rather as the penalty of sin and thus as sinning only in a secondary sense).[27] Thus sin, the evil that persons do, so far from blemishing the order of the whole, is compelled by penalty into congruity with its beauty. The penalty of sin corrects the ugliness of sin, and whatever the soul chooses, the universe, created and administered by God, remains beautiful and ordered in the full seemliness of its parts.[28] Thus Augustine, in the *De libero arbitrio*, was able not only to sustain the notion that we sin willingly but also, and on this basis, to elaborate a treatment of evil that resolves the puzzles that the *De ordine* left unresolved. Despite the number of years over which it was composed, the *De libero arbitrio*, I suspect, has more unity of purpose and program than we are sometimes ready to suppose.

Finally, I want to suggest that we do not catch the full import and impact of Augustine's new treatment of the question of evil if we view it only as a solution to a set of intellectual puzzles. Consider, in this regard, one of Paulinus of Nola's annual poems in honor of Felix, his patron saint. In Poem 23, Paulinus tells the story of Theridius, one of his friends at Nola. One evening, in the dark, Theridius was moving through a darkened corridor where, as it happened, one of the lamps had been lowered to be refilled with oil and, by inadvertence, had not been raised again. At the base of the lamp, hanging just at eye-level, there were three metal rods sticking out horizontally like hooks. Unable to see in the dark and not expecting any danger, Theridius ran into the lamp, and one of the metal pieces pierced his eye.

In despair, Theridius prayed to St. Felix for help, and his prayer began in this way:

> How great, alas, must be the sins compelling these pains of
> mine, since I, poor wretch, have deserved to sustain so griev-
> ous a wound, in spite of my having Felix as my patron and my
> neighbor, and on this his very birthday! Huge must be my
> guilt and great my crime, for punishment strikes me on the
> day it usually withdraws. Dear saint, I beg you, help your
> son.[29]

I suspect that most modern readers, even those who have studied Peter
Brown's *The Cult of the Saints* with some care, would find at least this portion
of Theridius' prayer both alien (or, perhaps, all too familiar) and distasteful.[30]
He has made the mistake, it would seem, of taking an accident for a punishment and has compounded the error by manufacturing some imagined, personal crime to fit the punishment. The incident of the lamp, we might guess,
has brought Theridius' over-ready and obsessive sense of guilt into play, and
to support the guilt, he has ascribed to himself a great sin that even he cannot
discern.

But we psychologize too much; or, at least, we psychologize in the wrong
way. If Theridius has manufactured a great sin for himself, it is not an expression of an over-active sense of guilt but rather a way of supplying what is needed to sustain the schematization of evil in terms of sin and punishment[31]
—and, in this way, to bring the accidental within a pattern of meaning. The
accidental is the quintessentially senseless. It just happens, without rhyme or
reason, and for just this reason, when the accidental is evil, it represents evil
unordered and uncontrolled, evil as a purely random factor, untamed and
striking where it will without design or cause or purpose. And it leaves those
whom it strikes utterly helpless; for what help can there be against the random, the senseless, the purposeless, the uninterpretable? Against the backdrop of this question, we can see the point of Theridius' prayer. It serves the
purpose of drawing the accidental into the realm of meaning and thus of can-
celling its random character. It locates the evil in the realm of the action and
the interaction of moral agents, and in this realm Theridius is not helpless: he
knows what to do, and what he does makes sense. The appeal to Felix is an
appeal for help in negotiating the arena in which moral agents interact, and it
makes sense so long as the world can be construed as such an arena. That is
the bearing of the Augustinian scheme of sin and punishment on the way
Christians of the Latin West in late antiquity conceived their world and nego-
tiated its dangers.

It remains only to report that, with Felix's aid, Theridius was able to remove the metal rod without damaging his eye.

Notes

[1] I make no attempt here to review the literature on Augustine's treatment of evil. Most general works on Augustine include some discussion of the matter. For an older, but still useful study, see R. Jolivet, *Le Problème du mal d'après Saint Augustin* (Paris: Beauchesne, 1936). G. R. Evans' more recent *Augustine on Evil* (Cambridge: Cambridge Univ. Press, 1982) must be used with reservations (see my review in *The Second Century* 5 [1986] 52–54). There is a good summary in J. P. Burns, "Augustine on the Origin and Progress of Evil," *Journal of Religious Ethics* 16 (1988) 9–27. Evans (p. 114) briefly recapitulates the opening passage of the *De libero arbitrio*, but without capturing its full significance. For a brief, philosophical assessment of the passage's argument, one can turn to C. Kirwan, *Augustine* (London and New York: Routledge, 1989), pp. 69–71 and 77–78. None of these works gives attention, however, to Augustine's recasting of the question of evil in terms of sin and punishment either in its relation to his previous thought on evil or in its import for his subsequent approach to the question.

[2] *De libero arbitrio* I,i,1: *CC* XXIX,211:...*uno, cum male quemque fecisse dicimus, alio, cum mali aliquid esse perpessum.*

[3] *De libero arbitrio* I,i,1: *CC* XXIX,211. The full argument runs as follows: *At si Deum bonum esse nosti uel credis—neque enim aliter fas est—, male non facit. Rursus, si Deum iustum fatemur—nam et hoc negare sacrilegum est—, ut bonis praemia, ita supplicia malis tribuit; quae utique supplicia patientibus mala sunt. Quamobrem si nemo iniuste poenas luit, quod necesse est credamus, quandoquidem diuina prouidentia hoc uniuersum regi credimus, illius primi generis malorum nullo modo, huius autem secundi auctor est Deus.*

[4] *De libero arbitrio* I,i,1: *CC* XXIX,211. The full text of Augustine's reply is: *Est certe; non enim nullo auctore fieri posset. Si autem quaeris, quisnam iste sit, dici non potest; non enim unus aliquis est, sed quisque malus sui malefacti auctor est. Vnde si dubitas, illud attende quod supra dictum est, maleficia iustitia Dei uindicari. Non enim iuste uindicarentur, nisi fierent uoluntate.*

[5] The distinction between the evil we do and the evil we suffer goes back at least as far as Plato's *Gorgias*. The labeling of these two as respectively sin and punishment may, however, be new with Augustine (although the *Gorgias* also deals with punishment as one form of the evil people suffer)—as may the assumption that the two represent an exhaustive classification of evil. The resulting scheme is not without its problems. It seems, for instance, to rule out the case of innocent suffering (see Kirwan, p. 71), although Augustine does, in fact, discuss the suffering of innocent babies in *De libero arbitrio* III,xxiii,66–68: *CC* XXIX,314–15. Nor does it establish the correlation between level and degree of punishment and level and degree of evil in a person's actions that such a view would seem to require. On this point, however, it should be noted that Augustine appears to have chiefly in

mind an internal rather than an external relation between sin and punishment. To act evilly is already to incur—and, in fact, to exemplify—that ignorance of the supreme good and that subjection of the soul to the disruptive passions which are themselves the primary forms that divine punishment takes (see, e.g., *De libero arbitrio* I,xi,22–23; III,xviii,52: *CC* XXIX,215; 283). Augustine obviously construes punishment (and therefore the evils people suffer?) primarily in psychic rather than physical terms; and in these terms the question of appropriate correlation between sin and punishment apparently answers itself. G. Bonner misses the psychic emphasis in Augustine's view of punishment when he remarks that, for Augustine, sin "draws upon itself a condign penalty, which is physical evil" (*St Augustine of Hippo: Life and Controversies* [London: SCM Press, 1963], p. 207).

    [6] The suggestion was made by G. Bardy. It is discussed by Madec in *BA* 6,162–63, but without reference to Augustine's transformation of the question of evil into the question of sin and punishment.

    [7] *De ordine* I,iii,6–viii,21: *CC* XXIX,91–99.

    [8] *De ordine* I,i,1: *CC* XXIX,89: *Ordinem rerum, Zenobi, cum sequi ac tenere cuique proprium tum uero uniuersitatis, quo cohercetur hic mundus ac regitur, uel uidere uel pandere difficillimum hominibus atque rarissimum est.*

    [9] *De ordine* I,iii,8: *CC* XXIX,92:...*nam praeter ordinem nihil mihi fieri uidetur*; I,iii,9: *CC* XXIX,93:...*nihilque praeter ordinem fieri posse asseram*; I,v,14: *CC* XXIX,96: *Quis neget, deus magne, inquit, te cuncta ordine administrare?*; I,vii,19: *CC* XXIX,98:...*totum igitur ordine includitur.*

    [10] *De ordine* I,vii,17: *CC* XXIX,97: *Certe enim et mala dixisti ordine contineri et ipsum ordinem manare a summo deo et ab eo diligi. Ex quo sequitur, ut et mala sint a summo Deo et mala Deus diligat.*

    [11] *De ordine* I,vii,18: *CC* XXIX,97–98.

    [12] *De ordine* I,vii,19: *CC* XXIX,98.

    [13] *De ordine* II,vii,22: *CC* XXIX,118–19.

    [14] *De ordine* II,vii,23: *CC* XXIX,119–20.

    [15] *De ordine* II,vii,23: *CC* XXIX,120: *Nam siue apud deum fuit ordo siue ex illo tempore esse coepit, ex quo etiam malum, tamen malum illud praeter ordinem natum est. Quod si concedis, fateris aliquid praeter ordinem posse fieri...si autem non concedis, incipit dei ordine natum malum uideri et malorum auctorem deum fateberis, quo sacrilegio mihi detestabilius nihil occurrit.*

    [16] *De ordine* II,vii,24: *CC* XXIX,120; Augustine uses the phrase *ordo studiorum sapientiae* in II,xviii,47: *CC* XXIX, 133.

    [17] *De ordine* I,i,2: *CC* XXIX,89–90; see also II,iv,11: *CC* XXIX,113.

    [18] *De ordine* II,xvii,46: *CC* XXIX,132:...*ergo de his atque huius modi rebus aut ordine illo eruditionis aut nullo modo quicquam requirendum est.*

[19] *De ordine* II,xvii,46: *CC* XXIX,132:...*quomodo deus et nihil mali faciat et sit omnipotens et tanta mala fiant et cui bono mundum fecerit, qui non erat indiguus, et utrum semper fuerit malum an tempore coeperit et, si semper fuit, utrum sub conditione Dei fuerit et, si fuit, utrum etiam iste mundus semper fuerit, in quo illud malum divino ordine domaretur—si autem hic mundus aliquando esse coepit, quomodo, antequam esset, potestate dei malum tenebatur et quid opus erat mundum fabricari, quo malum quod iam dei potestas frenabat, ad poenas animarum includeretur? Si autem fuit tempus, quo sub dei dominio malum non erat, quid subito accidit, quod per aeterna retro tempora non acciderat?* For a careful analysis and sound estimate of this passage, see O. du Roy, *L'intelligence de la foi en la trinité selon Saint Augustin* (Paris: Études Augustiniennes, 1966), p. 183, n.4.

[20] Du Roy, p. 184, n.4.

[21] *De ordine* II,xvii,46: *CC* XXIX,132: *Si autem istum mundum non factum dicamus, impium est atque ingratum credere, ne illud sequatur, quod Deus eum non fabricarit*....

[22] See *De ordine* II,iii,10: *CC* XXIX,112–13 (folly as lack of wisdom); II,vii,23: *CC* XXIX,119 (a reference to the *nihil quod dicitur malum*); *De libero arbitrio* II,xx,54: *CC* XXIX,272–73; III,xiii,36: *CC* XXIX,297; III,xiii,41: *CC* XXIX,299–300.

[23] *De ordine* I,vii,18: *CC* XXIX,97–98; see also II,v,13: *CC* XXIX,95.

[24] *De civitate Dei* XI,xviii: *CC* XLVIII,337:...*atque ita ordinem saeculorum tamquam pulcherrimum carmen etiam ex quibusdam quasi antithetis honestaret*....*ita quadam non uerborum, sed rerum eloquentia*...The translation is from *Augustine: City of God*, tr. H. Bettenson (Harmondsworth: Penguin Books, 1972), p. 449. The rendering of *rerum* by "events" seems justified in this temporal context.

[25] *De libero arbitrio* II,xviii,47–xx,54: *CC* XXIX, 268–73.

[26] *De libero arbitrio* II,xx,54: *CC* XXIX,272–73; also III,xvii,48–49: *CC* XXIX,269–70. Augustine later used a more sophisticated and more highly elaborated version of the same argument in *De civitate Dei* XII,vi–xi: *CC* XLVIII,359–66. For an assessment, see my "Augustine on Sin and Moral Agency," *Journal of Religious Ethics* 16 (1988) 44–49.

[27] *De libero arbitrio* I,xi,22; II,xix,53; III,xv,44; III,xviii,51–xix,54: *CC* XXIX,226; 272; 301–2; 305–7.

[28] *De libero arbitrio* III,ix,26: *CC* XXIX,291: *Sed uoluntaria quae in peccato fit turpis adfectio est. Cui propterea poenalis adhibetur ut ordinet eam ubi talem esse non turpe sit, et decori uniuersitatis congruere cogat, ut peccati dedecus emendat poena peccati*; III,ix,27: *CC* XXIX,291:...*ut quodlibet elegerit [anima] semper sit pulchra uniuersitas decentissimis partibus ordinata, cuius est conditor et administrator deus*; III,xv,44: *CC* XXIX,301: *Nullo autem interuallo temporis ista [sin and punishment] diuiduntur*...*ne uel puncto temporis uniuersalis pulchritudo turpetur, ut sit in ea peccati dedecus sine decore uindictae.*

[29] *Carmen* XXIII,201–6: *CSEL* XXX,201: *ei mihi! quanta meos urgent peccata labores / qui tantam merui plagam Felice patrono / vicinoque simul Felicis et insuper ipso / natali miser excipere? heu! magno reus ingens / crimine, quem tunc poena ferit, cum soluere suevit / sancte, precor, succurre tuo*...The translation is from *The Poems of St. Paulinus of Nola*, tr. P. G. Walsh, Ancient Christian Writers 40 (New York: Newman Press, 1975), p. 216.

Human Existence

[30] Brown discusses the saint as friend and patron, with special reference to Paulinus' relationship to Felix, in *The Cult of the Saints* (Chicago: Univ. of Chicago Press, 1981), pp. 50–68.

[31] It should be noted, however, that Paulinus—unlike Augustine (see n. 5 above)—clearly presumes an external rather than an internal relation between sin and punishment in his account of Theridius.

Friendship and the State

Donald X. Burt, O.S.A.

I. Introduction

In his life and in his thought Augustine was driven by two thirsts: the thirst for happiness and the thirst for "getting it all together"—a thirst for union.

For Augustine the central tragedy of being human just now is alienation —a state of being fractured in which we are separated from ourselves, each other, and the infinite God. At the same time it is a glorious thing to be human because we have the power of understanding our condition and remedying it. Love is the binding glue by which our internal and external divisions can be corrected, and we express this love most perfectly in the love of friendship.

In another place I have examined the nature of friendship and argued that Augustine believed that it should be the foundation of the family and the religious community. In this paper I will argue that he held that friendship is also the foundation and perfection of the state. I shall support this claim by examining three areas of his thought: (1) his definition of the state, (2) his description of the ideal ruler and (3) his views on the best form of government in the ideal state.

II. The Essential Characteristics of the State

In his definition of the state Augustine wished to establish the minimal requirements for having a true political society. Thus in a letter to his friend Marcellinus, Augustine asks: "What is the state if it is not a group of human beings bound together by some bond of agreement?"[1]

In *The City of God* Augustine lays out his reasons for defining the State in this way. In the twenty-first chapter of book two, he examines and rejects Scipio's position (reported and seconded by Cicero) that a state cannot exist unless it contains the perfection of justice. Augustine argues that, if this were a necessary condition for statehood, none of the classical political societies could be called states. Since the perfection of justice means giving everyone their due, this includes recognition of the supreme rule of the one true God. Obviously none of the pagan empires of history met this criterion, but it would be unreasonable to claim that they were not true political societies. In varying degrees all of them, especially Rome in its days of glory, were concerned about the public good: the *res publica*.[2]

A more modest definition of the state seems to be in order, one which demands some justice but not perfect justice. This Augustine provides in the twenty-fourth chapter of book nineteen where he writes that a political society is nothing else than "…a multitude of reasonable beings voluntarily associated in the pursuit of common interests."[3]

This broad description of the state allows Augustine to place under that umbrella such disparate entities as the truly Christian state (which he believed never existed), Israel, Rome, and many other secular civil societies. Though they may vary greatly in their observance of justice, each one exists under the direction of divine providence and therefore serves a purpose in God's grand plan for creation.[4]

In Augustine's view the primary purpose of the state is to promote temporal peace, one of the "good gifts of God suited to human existence on earth." This peace will include such things as health, security and human fellowship. This purpose will also include those things necessary or useful for preserving the peace and for regaining it once it is lost. If there is a "oneness of heart" about these common goals, this is enough for a political society to exist. It is also at very least a step in the direction of that "oneness of heart" that is the essence of friendship.[5]

What a people includes among those things essential for its peace and *how* it goes about attaining those things determines what *sort* of people it is. But *having* such common interests is sufficient to *constitute* it as a people. It is sufficient and also necessary. Without some common purpose no state, indeed, no society can exist. As Augustine says: "If there is unity, a *populus* exists; if there is no unity, it becomes a mob. For what else is a mob except a chaotic multitude?"[6]

Even in the worst state there is some justice, at least that justice implied in unity of purpose and a rule of law directing all to the common good. If citizens are united in the social good that they love, there is some ground for respecting each other. Their concern for distributive and legal justice (each one receiving and giving their fair share to the society) can lead to the beginnings of commutative justice whereby they respect the rights of each other. Justice is the preserver of the necessary order in society whereby the members

love more that which is more important and love less that which is less important.[7] Such modest ordering of love can be the seed of that perfect justice
which Augustine would wish for every individual and every society: the justice
which is love serving God and therefore ruling well all things subject to humans.[8] The driving force in the state, as in friendship, is therefore mutual love
even though admittedly in the more perverse states the only manifestation of
this love will be found in some agreement about a common goal and agreement to sometimes subordinate private interests in order to achieve this goal.
In this agreement and subordination of private interests there is at least the
seed of the recognition of equality and concern for the other that is the root of
friendship.

III. The Good Ruler

This recognition of equality and concern for the other is also reflected
in what Augustine will say about the duties of the ruler and the ruled. In the
twenty-fourth chapter of the fifth book of *The City of God*, Augustine gives his
own version of the classical "Mirror of Princes," the description of the ideal
ruler. In his view the best rulers should first of all be humble, never forgetting
that they remain human beings despite all their princely powers. Rather than
indulging their greater freedom to satisfy personal desires, they should recognize that their greater opportunity for vice gives greater reason for virtue.
They should remember their past weakness and rejoice more in controlling
their passions than in controlling the world. They should rule with justice
tempered by mercy. They should make harsh decrees when these are required
and should not be reticent about punishing those who disobey. They should
take such action not out of revenge or personal animosity but out of love for
the common good. They should be generous with their mercy when they see
that this will lead to reform and not cause others to take the law lightly. The
best rulers will see their vocation as a divine calling, a ministry of divine providence, and will exercise their function not for the sake of glory but as a means
of personal salvation through service to God and fellow citizens.[9]
It is clear that Augustine believed that part of being a good human being was to be a good member of the state either as a ruler or as citizen. Thus,
when he advises his young students at Cassiciacum on how they should plan
their lives, he does not tell them to flee from political life but rather to accept
their position in the state gracefully and exercise their political duties virtu-

ously. If they do happen to find themselves in charge of others, they should
not forget that they are fellow human beings. They should rule so consider-
ately that it becomes a pleasure to obey them. If it is their lot in life to be
subject to the authority of others, they should be so respectful that it becomes
somewhat embarrassing to give them a command. Whether as ruler or ruled,
the guideline for dealing with others should be: "Don't do to others what you
would not want them to do to you." They should not wish to take a position
in the state until they are ready for it, but they should not hesitate to get prepared for such service. Finally, in all their human relationships "in every circumstance of life, in every place, at all times...they should have friends or
earnestly seek to make friends."[10]

From Augustine's instruction to rulers actually in place and from his
advice to young people considering such positions of authority, it is clear that
he saw no contradiction between the exercise of civil authority and the "oneness of heart" that is characteristic of friendship. Indeed, his advice to have
friends or make friends in every circumstance of life would certainly not preclude such "oneness of heart" existing between ruler and ruled in civil society.

Augustine certainly did not believe that "being in charge" of others
stood in the way of being their friends...having the equality, agreement on
goals, mutual caring, trust, and honesty that are the marks of friendship. The
fact that some command and others obey does not weaken that peace nor
stand in the way of a union of hearts as long as the relationship is based on
love. Augustine agrees with Cicero that some subordination of one to another
is natural. It is just and proper that the soul rule the body, that God rule
humans, and that the ruler have sovereignty over a community when such
authority serves the good of the community.[11]

When subordination of ruled to ruler is based on friendship, its harsh-
ness is softened. In its exercise it respects the equality and dignity and goodness of the other. Although true authority is present, an authority that assumes some sort of superior-inferior relationship, there is no denigration of
the subject. As Augustine writes:

> Where charity is not present, the command of the authority is
> bitter. But where charity exists, the one who commands does
> so with sweetness, and the charity makes the very work to be

almost no work at all for the one who is commanded, even though in truth he is bound to some task.[12]

If rule is based on love there will not be a desire to have mastery over the other person.[13] Rather there will be a desire to make all humans equal to you, "each one dependent on him to whom nothing need be given."[14] The good ruler should so act as to make oppressive subordination unnecessary because the society is composed of true friends. In such an environment the commanding and obeying is done out of mutual love, not out of fear. Augustine observes that when love is absent, the demands of authority are a bitter burden but when love is present the demands are welcome. Even though the one commanded must undertake a difficult task, love makes this work light and almost negligible.[15]

Some of the things that Augustine said about the rule of the superior in the religious life have application to other societies as well. Van Bavel is quite right when he remarks:

> "It should be one's object more to be loved by others than to be feared." This is a thought that recurs repeatedly in Augustine. In his time this principle also constituted the ideal line of conduct for politicians.[16]

Such love will involve mutual respect and to that extent will involve a type of fear, but it is not the fear of a slave. Rather it is the fear of a lover who fears to lose a loved one or fears doing him some injury. The obedience of the ruled will be prompted by a love of the ruler and a caring concern about the burdens and temptations that rulers take upon themselves in accepting lofty positions of authority.[17] As Van Bavel remarks, "Augustine had a strong tendency to deal with questions of authority and obedience always in a context of mutual love."[18] Such a context is nothing other than a context of friendship.

Of course unnatural subordination of ruled to ruler in the state is antithetical to friendship, but this is so not because it is *subordination* but because it is *perverse*. In such subordination the goal is the "*ruler's* peace, the *ruler's* good" rather than the common good. Such rulers reject the equality of all humans under God and try to *be* God, acting as though every other human being were essentially inferior.[19] But such subordination is not a necessary characteristic of authority or of subordination. Nothing can be more subordinate in the order of being than the human body to the human spirit and yet Augustine will insist that these radically diverse entities are meant to be and some day *will be* friends. If none of the characteristics of friendship exist between king and subject, this is so not because one happens to be ruler and the other is ruled, but rather because they are both "cracked" human beings.

IV. The Best Form of Government

As has been said above, Augustine believed that authority should exist in a context of friendship. If in the ideal state the ruler serves the good of the community, it seems reasonable that the community should also have some say in the choice of their rulers. Augustine firmly believed that order demanded that rule should be by the "best," and the best ruler will be the one who is "best" in promoting and protecting the public good.[20] Since all humans are equal as humans there is nothing in the nature of humanity that will make any "one person" intrinsically superior to another in political society. There is no "natural subordination" as there is for example in the case of a minor child and a parent. How then is a leader to be selected? Who will decide which member (or members) of human society are "best" for the common good?

Augustine believed that in an ideal situation the people should decide. Such an ideal is realized when (1) the state is well ordered and serious, (2) it is a most watchful guardian of the common interest, and (3) it contains citizens who place public good above private interests. In such a state Augustine writes, "A law is rightly established which gives to the people the power to select their own officials to see to the public welfare."[21]

Of course all authority ultimately comes from God, but the issue here is not about the *source* of authority but rather about the appropriate *way* for it to come to specific human beings. If there is a natural superiority of one over another (as there is in the case of parent/child), then authority is given in virtue of what one is. But if all are equal, then authority can only come through choice. Thus, if in a particular state every citizen is dedicated equally and "whole-heartedly" to the common good, such dedication should give them some right to have their views counted in determining the policies of the society and in selecting the officials who are to administer these policies. The ruled are thus ruled "voluntarily," a sensible way of deciding "who shall be in charge" in a society of dedicated friends.

In point of fact no state (nor any human family and certainly no religious community) has ever enjoyed completely dedicated subjects or perfectly wise leaders. Augustine somberly observes that in ordinary political life the wise and the pious are not usually found in seats of power and fear rather than love is the corrective force for most citizens.[22]

But this sad fact of life is not caused by a defect in the nature of civil society. A state can be no better than the people who are its seeds, and every one of these has been "tested in the fire and has come out somewhat cracked."[23] It may be that every human is a "vessel of God," but the vessel is cracked. Despite our pretensions to the contrary, every society, every family, and certainly every state is made up of "cracked pots." As a consequence it has always been necessary to protect order by judging and punishing miscreants. Since Adam and Eve first raised Cain, pious exhortations to civility have never been enough in human society. The state has always faced the unfortunate necessity of dealing with actions against the public good which "it must punish in order to keep peace among ignorant men."[24]

Augustine recognizes that, although democracy may be the best form of government ideally, in the real world it will not work if the citizens are depraved. If the people universally favor their private desires over the public good, if there is a general buying and selling of votes, if the society is so corrupted by those who love power that government is handed over to the evil and criminal elements, then (Augustine asks): "...isn't it right that at such a time a good man who is outstanding and has the greatest ability, should take the power of conferring offices from this people and reduce the government to a few noblemen or even to one?"[25]

What he is saying is that when the people are the "worst," there is no room for the "best" and the constitutional law which sets up the state as democracy is rightly overridden "by the eternal law under which it is always just for a serious people to confer offices and for a fickle people to be unable to do so."[26] The rationale for such radical change is rooted in the fact that no state can exist without some orderly movement towards a common good. What makes a state "good" is not its form of government but its attempt to fulfill its duty to love God and neighbor. As Augustine says:

> ...the best city is erected and safeguarded on no other foundation than the bond of faith and unbreakable concord. This

happens when the common good is loved, when God is the
highest and truest good, and when humans love each other
most sincerely because they love themselves for the sake of
him from whom they cannot hide the true sentiment of their
hearts.[27]

He would be the first to agree that such a "perfect" city united by the
love of friends will not exist until the next life, but he will also insist that it
should be the goal of every city existing now.

V. Objection: "Shepherds, Not Kings"

An objection to the claim that Augustine wanted the state to be a society of friends is sometimes raised by pointing to texts where he seems to be
saying that political authority of human over human is not a natural state.
Such rule is either the result of sin or is an unfortunate necessity caused by the
turmoil in human relationships caused by sin. It is not an aspect of the natural
good of friendship; it is rather a contradiction.

A troublesome text is found in the fifteenth chapter of the nineteenth
book of *The City Of God*. There Augustine states:

God did not want rational beings, made in his own image, to
dominate any being except the non-rational. He did not
want a human to dominate another human; humans were
meant to dominate only beasts.[28]

At first blush it would seem that Augustine is saying here that the relationship
of king to subject is a relationship that comes only as a result of sin. If so, it
obviously cannot be claimed that it rests on the admittedly "natural" relationship of friendship. However the context suggests that Augustine is not speaking about the normal or ideal relationship between ruler and citizen. He is
speaking about a dominion that comes from war where the losers are sometimes made, not citizens, but slaves of the conqueror. Obviously such a situation can only be a result of sin. Without sin there would be no war and thus
no conqueror. Without sin there would be no condition whereby a human
treats another human as a lower order of being. The natural condition of

human to human is absolute equality and any perversion of that is obviously wrong.

However the chapter before this makes it clear that every relationship of ruler to ruled does not involve such sinful domination of another. The fundamental command upon the human race is that we must love three beings: God, ourselves, and our neighbor. This means that we must harm no one, help whomever we can, and allow ourselves to be helped by others when we need help. If a man is a husband and father, he must help his wife, children, servants, and all others whom he can influence. The fact that a person has authority over the household (an authority which Augustine clearly believes is rooted in nature) does not interfere with the goal of having ordered "oneness of heart." In the family, authority does not interfere with the oneness of heart that is friendship because

> those who command serve those whom they seem to order about. They do not give orders out of desire to dominate but because of their duty to look out for the interests of others. They command not from pride of being in charge but from the compassion of one who cares about others.[29]

The language Augustine uses to describe the caring rule and respectful obedience in the ideal family is the same sort of language that he uses to describe the ideal relationship between the ruler and the citizen in the state. If the relationship of authority does not stand in the way of friendship in the family, neither does it in the state. Indeed, in both societies friendship is the foundation for such exercise of authority.

It is obvious that in the text from *The City of God* XIX,xv, Augustine is not speaking about the relationship of ruler and citizen in the ideal state. He is speaking about a master-slave relationship which unfortunately sometimes results from the spoils of war. Slavery is indeed antithetical to friendship, but slavery is not the Augustinian model for civil society.

VI. Concluding Remarks

Augustine writes:

> Peace among humans is ordered "oneness of heart." The
> peace of the family is ordered "oneness of heart" among
> those who live together, with some commanding and others
> obeying. The peace of the state is ordered "oneness of
> heart" among citizens with some commanding and others
> obeying. The peace of the heavenly city is found in that soci-
> ety which rejoices in the enjoyment of God and in the enjoy-
> ment of each other in God...that society which is most well-
> ordered and most perfectly "one in heart."[30]

The individual, the family, the state, and the heavenly city are related as concentric circles. The individual is at the center, body and soul, passion and reason, impulse and freedom...a division in himself/herself that makes the life of
each person a battle. This is the source of the problem in all human societies.
Without peace in the individual, it is difficult to have peace in the family.
Without virtuous individuals and peace-filled families, it is difficult to have a
peaceful state. We must be friends with ourselves and with our families before we can have any hope of being friends with fellow-citizens.[31]

When there is peace at the center (in the individual human), this creates
ripples of love that flow out in ever widening circles embracing more and
more in the bond of friendship. To use Augustine's felicitous phrase, we love
others because they are friends or in order that they may become our
friends.[32] On earth this expansion is necessarily imperfect and limited, but it
hints at that perfect and infinite friendship of the heavenly city once its membership is fixed beyond time.

Examination of friendship in the eternal city of God must wait for another time. It is enough now to note that its traces can be found even here.
The friendship we experience in all human societies is but a prelude and a
promise of what is to come.[33]

Notes

[1]*Epistula CXXXVIII* 10: *CSEL* XLIV,135:...*quid est autem ciuitas nisi hominum
multitudo in quoddam uinculum redacta concordiae? De ciuitate dei* XV,vii: *CC* XLVIII,

464: *Ciuitas, quae nihil aliud est quam hominum multitudo aliquo societatis uinculo colligata. Epistula CLV* iii,9: *CSEL* XLIV,440: *cum aliud ciuitas non sit quam concors hominum multitudo.* Cf. also *De ciuitate dei* XIX,xiv: *CC* XLVIII,681.

[2] Cf. *De ciuitate dei* II,xxi: *CC* XLVII,54-55.

[3] *De ciuitate dei* XIX,xxiv: *CC* XLVIII,695: *Populus est coetus multitudinis rationalis rerum quas diligit concordi communione sociatus.*

[4] *De ciuitate dei* V,xxvi,1: *CC* XLVII,161-63. Cf. D. J. MacQueen, "The Origin and Dynamics of Society and the State," *AS* 4 (1973) 86-89.

[5] *De ciuitate dei* XIX,xiii: *CC* XLVIII,680: *Deus...dedit hominibus quaedam bona huic uitae congrua, id est pacem temporalem pro modulo mortalis uitae in ipsa salute et incolumitate ac societate sui generis, et quaeque huic paci uel tuendae uel recuperandae necessaria sunt....*

[6] *Sermo CIII* III,4: *PL* XXXVIII,614: *Da unum, et populus est: tolle unum, et turba est. Quid est enim turba, nisi multitudo turbata?* Cf. *In Ioannis Epistulam ad Parthos tractatus* VI,10: *PL* XXXV,2025.

[7] *De uera religione* XLVIII,93: *CC* XXXII,248: *Et haec est perfecta iustitia, qua potius potiora, et minus minora diligimus.*

[8] *De moribus ecclesiae Catholicae et de moribus Manichaeorum* I,xv,25: *PL* XXXII, 1322: *...iustitiam, amorem deo tantum seruientem, et ob hoc bene imperantem caeteris quae homini subiecta sunt.*

[9] *De ciuitate dei* V,xxiv: *CC* XLVII,160.

[10] *De ordine* II,viii,25: *CC* XXIX,121: *nemini faciant, quod pati nolunt....In omni autem uita loco tempore amicos aut habeant aut habere instent.*

[11] *De ciuitate dei* XIX,xxi: *CC* XLVIII,688.

[12] *In Ioannis Epistulam ad Parthos tractatus* IX,1: *PL* XXXV,2085: *ubi charitas non est, amarus exactor est: ubi autem charitas est, et qui exigit dulcis est; et a quo exigitur, etsi aliquem laborem suscipit, facit eumdem laborem prope nullum et levem ipsa charitas.*

[13] *In Ioannis Epistulam ad Parthos tractatus* VIII,8 and 14: *PL* XXXV,2040 and 2044. Cf. *De doctrina christiana* I,xxiii,23: *CC* XXXII,18; *De ciuitate dei* XIX,xv: *CC* XLVIII,682.

[14] *In Ioannis Epistulam ad Parthos tractatus* VIII,5: *PL* XXXV,2038: *ut ambo sub uno sitis cui nihil praestari potest.*

[15] *In Ioannis Epistulam ad Parthos tractatus* IX,1-3: *PL* 35,2045-47.

[16] T. J. Van Bavel, O.S.A., *The Rule of St. Augustine with Introduction and Commentary*, trans. R. Canning, O.S.A. (London: Darton, Longman and Todd, 1984), p. 109.

[17] *Enarratio in Psalmum CVI* 7: *CC* XL,1573-74. Cf. Van Bavel, p. 110.

[18] Van Bavel, pp. 113-14.

[19] *De ciuitate dei* XIX,xii,2: *CC* XLVIII,677.

[20] D. J. MacQueen, pp. 84-85.

[21] *De libero arbitrio* I,vi,14: *CC* XXIX,219: *Ergo si populus sit bene moderatus et grauis, communisque utilitatis diligentissimus custos, in quo unusquisque minoris rem priuatam quam publicam pendat, nonne recte lex fertur, qua huic ipsi populo liceat creare sibi magistratus, per quos sua res, id est publica, administretur?*

[22] Cf. *De trinitate* III,iv,9: *CC* L,135-36: *hoc quidem uerum est; sed sicut meliores sunt, quos dirigit amor, ita plures sunt, quos corrigit timor.* *Epistula CLXXXV* VI,21: *CSEL* LVII, 19.

[23] *Enarratio in Psalmum XCIX* 11: *CC* XXXIX,1399:...*missi sunt in fornacem, et crepuerunt.* Cf. *Enarratio in Psalmum IX* 8: *CC* XXXVIII,62.

[24] *De libero arbitrio* I,v,13: *CC* XXIX,218: *Videtur ergo mihi et legem istam, quae populo regendo scribitur, recte ista permittere et diuinam prouidentiam uindicare. Ea enim uindicanda sibi haec adsumit, quae satis sint conciliandae paci hominibus imperitis....*

[25] *De libero arbitrio* I,vi,14: *CC* XXIX,219:...*nonne item recte, si quis tunc extiterit uir bonus, qui plurimum possit, adimat huic populo potestatem dandi honores et in paucorum bonorum uel etiam unius redigat arbitrium.*

[26] *De libero arbitrio* I,vi,15: *CC* XXIX,220: *Nam si populus ille quodam tempore iuste honores dedit, quodam rursus iuste non dedit, haec uicissitudo temporalis ut esset iusta ex illa aeternitate tracta est, quo semper iustum est grauem populum honores dare, leuem non dare....*

[27] *Epistula CXXXVII* V,17: *CSEL* XLIV,122:...*hic etiam laudabilis rei publicae salus, neque enim conditur et custoditur optima ciuitas nisi fundamento et uinculo fidei firmaeque concordiae, cum bonum commune diligitur, quod summum ac uerissimum deus est, atque in illo inuicem sincerissime se homines diligunt, cum propter illum se diligunt, cui, quo animo diligant, occultare non possunt*; trans. by Wilfrid Parsons, *St. Augustine: Letters*; FC 20,34.

[28] *De ciuitate dei* XIX,xv: *CC* XLVIII,682: *Rationalem factum ad imaginem suam noluit nisi inrationabilibus dominari; non hominem homini, sed hominem pecori.*

[29] *De ciuitate dei* XIX,xiv: *CC* XLVII,681-82: *Sed in domo iusti uiuentis ex fide.... etiam qui imperant, seruiunt eis quibus uidentur imperare. Neque enim dominandi cupiditate imperant, sed officio consulendi, nec principandi superbia, sed prouidendi misericordia.*

[30] *De ciuitate dei* XIX,xiii: *CC* XLVIII,679:...*pax hominum ordinata concordia, pax domus ordinata imperandi atque oboediendi concordia cohabitantium, pax ciuitatis ordinata imperandi atque oboediendi concordia ciuium, pax caelestis ciuitatis ordinatissima et concordissima societas fruendi Deo et inuicem in Deo, pax omnium rerum tranquillitas ordinis.* Cf. *Contra academicos* III,vi,13: *CC* XXIX,42, and *Epistula CCLVIII* 1: *CSEL* LVII,605.

[31] *De ciuitate dei* XIX,xvi: *CC* XLVIII,683:...*pacem ciuicam pax domestica referatur, id est, ut ordinata imperandi oboediendique concordia cohabitantium referatur ad ordinatam imperandi oboediendique concordiam ciuium.*

[32] *In Ioannis Epistulam ad Parthos tractatus* X,7: *PL* XXXV,35,2059: *Ubicumque fratrem diligitis, amicum diligitis. ...tu dilige, et fraterno amore dilige: nondum est frater, sed ideo diligis ut sit frater.* Cf. *De diuersis quaestionibus LXXXIII* LXXI,6: *CC* XLIV/A,205.

[33] Cf. *De bono conjugali* XVIII,21: *CSEL* XXXI,214–15. Cf. Peter Brown, *The Body and Society* (New York: Columbia University Press, 1988), p. 404.

The Significance of *Ordo* in St. Augustine's Moral Theory

N. Joseph Torchia

An examination of nearly any aspect of Augustinism reveals the importance of a specific understanding of order in that particular philosophical outlook. Such an understanding of order is especially evident in Augustine's interpretation of iniquity, the perverse use of the will, which for him constitutes the basis of moral evil. This paper will investigate the significance of the notion of order, that is, *ordo*, in St. Augustine's philosophy, with a special focus upon its role in his deliberations regarding the origins of iniquity.

In and of itself, the term *iniquitas* connotes an imbalance, injustice, or unreasonableness. In the context of Augustine's ethics, the term assumes a special meaning as a principle of moral disorder. But the very idea of "disorder" is meaningless without some prior sense of order. Indeed, Augustine's widespread deliberations—throughout his early writings—on the roots and expressions of *iniquitas* presuppose a well-articulated vision of *ordo*, the framework within which humans make their choices. In this respect, it would appear that an adequate grasp of the implications of Augustine's interpretation of *iniquitas* requires a clarification of the more fundamental notion of *ordo* and the extent to which it defines the parameters of his moral theory.

In what follows, I will examine the metaphysical and moral dimensions of *ordo* in certain select discussions. The very pervasiveness of references to *ordo* in Augustine's writings necessitates a narrowing of textual materials. Accordingly, I will concentrate primarily upon three early works: the *De moribus ecclesiae catholicae et de moribus Manichaeorum* (written toward the end of 387 and beginning of 388), the *De Genesi contra Manichaeos* (written in 389), and the *De libero arbitrio* (Book I written in 388, Books II and III written from 391 to 395).[1]

These works are useful for the present purposes because they provide some central Augustinian statements on *iniquitas* and its place within the hierarchy of creation. But more importantly, they represent key components of the early Augustine's ongoing anti-Manichaean polemic. In that series of writings, where he wrestled with such issues as the nature of God and the problem of evil (among others), the proper depiction of *ordo* was of paramount importance. For Augustine's response to such questions proceeded from a world-view that stood in direct opposition to that of his Manichaean opponents. Let us begin with a consideration of his interpretation of the *ordo* of reality as a whole.

The *Ordo* of Reality

In the opening chapters of the second book of the *De moribus ecclesiae* (II,i–ix), Augustine provides a concise but rich explication of the metaphysical implications of *ordo*. The discussion unfolds against the background of his theory of participation, the means whereby he delineates the relationship between God and creatures.[2] Implicit in that theory are two key teachings: first, the absolute perfection of God; secondly, the complete contingency and derivative perfection of creatures, including that of goodness. As Augustine contends, "...to be made means to receive goodness from another."[3] In this respect, God is viewed as good by his very nature, and creatures only by a participation or sharing in the supreme goodness.[4]

Augustine thus recognizes a hierarchy of goodness with God at its summit. But this hierarchy of goodness corresponds to an ontological hierarchy in which God provides the fullness of being upon which all creaturely existence is dependent. In Augustinian terms, only God represents "being" in its truest sense, that is, a nature "which subsists in itself and is altogether changeless."[5] Such a primary Being can be neither corrupted nor affected in any way. Accordingly, God cannot be subjected to that which is contrary to his nature, that is, to non-being.[6] This point underscores one of Augustine's chief goals in this polemical context, namely, the refutation of the Manichaean cosmogony and its dualistic doctrine of competing realms of light and darkness, absolute good and absolute evil, respectively.[7]

On the basis of these metaphysical insights, Augustine addresses the question concerning the ontological status of evil. In his reply to the Manichaeans, who viewed evil as a substance, Augustine applied the term exclusively to the privation of reality. From an Augustinian standpoint, evil can exist only in relation to some created substance and not in its own right.[8] But if this is so, how does evil manifest itself and how are creatures subjected to its negative effects? For Augustine, evil involves a corruption or, more precisely, a perversion (*perversio*) of created being.[9] While order is correlative with the good, perversion is correlative with evil.

Augustine highlights the meaning of *perversio* in this context by juxtaposing it with *conversio* (i.e., conversion), a term which assumes such a profound import in the *Confessiones*, the account of his own spiritual journey. Here, *conversio* signifies the means whereby creatures undergo positive change, turning from fleeting images to God, the paradigm of being, goodness, and order. In contrast, *perversio* entails an undermining of being or "loss of essence," the consequence of a movement away from God and enduring reality.[10]

Yet, such a destructive movement never renders something completely devoid of the good. Rather, it deprives it of an order which things should rightfully possess.[11] In metaphysical terms, that which is so disordered is reduced from a state of being (and by implication, a condition of stability and permanence) to one of instability and impermanence.[12]

In Augustinism, that which truly is exists as one, that is, as a unified whole.[13] In this respect, a thing exists or has being in proportion to the unity which it possesses. As a simple nature and pure unity, God most fully exists. Composite realities, however, exist only insofar as they imitate this higher unity. By virtue of order, their parts are conjoined and harmonized for the good of the whole. In this way, creatures attain that measure of being appropriate to composite, mutable things. Order, then, characterizes everything which exists and is conducive to being.[14] Disorder, on the other hand, is an earmark of non-being, the deficiency of the real and the antithesis of unity.

But the recognition that created being undergoes corruption prompts consideration of an aspect of the problem of evil that receives more thoroughgoing treatment in the *De libero arbitrio*. This issue concerns the reconciliation of the human capacity for evil with the absolute goodness of a God who is held creatively responsible for our status as free moral agents. At this point, however, Augustine's major concern lies in challenging the Manichaean contention that creatures can fall into a state of complete corruption.

His response to this claim rests upon the conviction that Divine Providence allocates a suitable place to each thing according to its just merits. Only such providential ordering saves those souls which fall from God from the utter annihilation of non-being.[15] In this respect, the "loss of essence" which accompanies sin is not caused by God. Instead, God orders those things that tend toward nothingness so that their defection can never completely deprive them of some participation in the good. Thus, even evil things are subject to *ordo*, and through an ordered movement, they have the capacity to return to their source.[16] In a hierarchical arrangement wherein all things (whether good or evil) are related to a larger whole, the human soul occupies a unique place.

I will now consider Augustine's interpretation of the soul's status in the *ordo* of creation.

Ordo and the Soul

Augustine views the soul as a spiritual, incorporeal reality. Like God, the human soul and other spiritual creatures are immutable. But their immutability is a limited one: in contrast to the supremely perfect and absolutely changeless Divine nature, the soul is immutable only in spatial terms. As an imperfect creature, it is subject to the effects of temporal process and capable of growth and error, both intellectually and morally.[17]

While the soul possesses a rational faculty enabling it to grasp eternal truths, it also has freedom of will, whereby it can direct itself to God and subsistent being or toward lower, mutable ends.[18] For, in addition to spiritual realities, being also encompasses corporeal natures. Unlike the soul, these are mutable in every way, and because of this susceptibility to change and corruption, they are counted as least real among created beings.[19]

Augustine, then, posits three levels of reality, ranked according to the degree of being which each possesses: God occupies the highest position, souls assume a mid-rank position, and bodies occupy the lowest position.[20] One of Augustine's clearest statements regarding the soul's mid-rank position is found in the *De Genesi contra Manichaeos* (II,ix), his elaborate attempt to refute Manichaean teachings through an exegesis of Scripture. In that work, his view of the soul as situated between God and lesser realities grows out of a commentary upon two trees planted in the "middle of paradise." The biblical reference to "the tree of life" is interpreted as the soul's intelligence, whereby it understands its ordered position among existent things, that is, its subordination to God and its superiority over all corporeal nature. In Augustine's language, such a properly ordered soul neither "claims for herself what is not" (that is, the non-being of lesser things), nor "contemns what is through negligence" (that is, God, the fullness of being).[21]

Augustine next explicates the significance of "the tree of knowledge of good and evil." This tree is interpreted as the soul's mid-rank itself, that is, its *medietas*. The soul which accepts its mid-rank likewise conforms itself to *ordo*, submitting to the higher authority of God and renouncing the entanglements of lower earthly desires. Here, Augustine relies upon St. Paul's distinction in Ph 3:13–14 between what should be "before" and what should be "behind" the soul in its esteem.[22] By means of this Pauline imagery, he defines the correct attitude of the properly ordered soul: it must extend itself to God Who is ontologically prior or "before" it and shun those corporeal passions that are inferior or "behind" it. The soul's failure to maintain this attitude is the source of its iniquity.

It should be noted that in the *De Genesi contra Manichaeos*, Augustine refined his interpretation of iniquity in terms of the operation of pride (*superbia*), curiosity (*curiositas*), and carnal concupiscence (*concupiscentia carnis*).[23] His subsequent discussions on the origins of moral evil relied heavily upon this triadic interpretation. For him, each expression of iniquity represents a source of disruption for the soul, upsetting its balance between submission to what is "above" and regulation of what is "below." In the case of pride, the soul claims for itself what is most appropriate for God; in the case of curiosity and carnal concupiscence, it surrenders its God-given integrity to lesser things.[24] Such a disordering impairs its special relationship with God.

According to Augustine's exegesis, the soul's identity as "image of God" is reflected in the upright posture of humans, a stature signifying the soul's bond with eternity, its true dwelling place.[25] In this respect, the soul's true fulfillment consists in a transcendence of the world. But Augustine distinguishes its condition before and after sin. Prior to sin, he maintains, the soul enjoyed a privileged status, existing as an invisible, spiritual creature. He further depicts the soul in this perfect state as sustained by an "inner fountain" which communicated Truth directly to reason.[26] After sin, the soul is subjected to the limitations of human mortality, assuming all of the weaknesses associated with a corruptible body.[27] As Scriptural support for this theory of the soul's penalization, Augustine could refer to God's various "curses" on Adam and the serpent which are enumerated in Genesis.

But to what extent does iniquity detract from the goodness of creation? In a manner consistent with his Christian optimism, Augustine holds that the condition of human mortality damages the beauty of creation only in part, while the excellence of the whole remains intact. For, he contends, a beautiful object formed of many diverse parts is more praiseworthy in the whole than in the part.[28] This is a variation of arguments which are more fully developed in both the *De ordine* and the *De musica*. In effect, Augustine attempts to resolve the apparent disorder in our world by reference to an all-embracing *ordo* which harmonizes and governs the totality of being.[29] From his intellectualist perspective, an appreciation of the goodness and coherence inherent in creation necessitates an expansion of our cognitive vision beyond the immediate data of sense experience. Any imperfection disclosed by the senses must be judged in terms of that *ordo* wherein nothing (including iniquity and the moral disorder it precipitates) is "unarranged, unclassed, or unassigned."[30] The stage is now set for a more in-depth consideration of Augustine's classic statement on the source of moral evil as presented in the *De libero arbitrio*.

Ordo and Iniquity

In the first book of the *De libero arbitrio*, Augustine confronts the problem that by his own admission, perplexed him from an early age and drove him into "the company of heretics."[31] He frames the issue in these terms:

> ... if sins come from souls created by God, while these souls
> in turn come from God, how is it that sins are not at once
> chargeable to God?[32]

Augustine's response to this question was based upon his theory of volition and its emphasis upon individual responsibility for moral wrongdoing. In this respect, moral evil has its source neither in God nor in some cosmic conflict of the Manichaean variety, but rather, in the human will.

But Augustine's ongoing analysis of the cause of evil in terms of free will is closely bound up with an ideal of the properly ordered individual. For him, our life is ordered when reason, mind, or spirit regulates the body and its accompanying desires.[33] As we have seen, *ordo* dictates that what is less perfect must be subordinate to what is more perfect. The soul's sovereignty over the body and its passions is an implication of this principle and, according to Augustine, consistent with eternal law.[34] This model of the properly ordered individual, which affirms the primacy of spiritual over corporeal reality, provides something of a general standard for judging the will's affective movements.

For Augustine, will manifests itself as love or, in broader terms, as desire: like a "weight," love or desire draws the soul toward those things in which it finds delight.[35] In this sense, Augustine's valuative distinction between the good and evil wills refers to different expressions of the soul's natural eudaemonistic orientation. The goods toward which the soul tends and, more importantly, the manner in which it loves them, determine the moral quality of the will.

As defined by Augustine, the good will is consistent with the virtuous life, prompting the soul toward immutable goods and subsistent reality.[36] The evil will, the cause of sin, is initially defined in terms of either *cupiditas* or *libido* (lust and passion, respectively, but for Augustine, almost synonymous in meaning), those irrational movements which point the soul toward lower mutable reality.[37] But this statement must be qualified: since Augustine views creation as fundamentally good, moral error proceeds from an inordinate preoccupation with bodily life rather than from the desire for material things alone.[38]

In anticipation of a key distinction that emerges in his mature writings, Augustine defines this blameworthy desire in terms of the "use" that we make of goods.[39] The evil will (and the lust or passion which motivates it) entails a "bad use" of things: one who uses them in this manner is enslaved to the rule of passion, "held fast," in Augustine's words, "by their love," and making them "members of his own soul."[40] In effect, the soul's attachment to such things constitutes a subjection to that which should rightfully be subjected to its governance and care. In this context, the bad use of things amounts to a misplaced or disordered love, that is, a love which fails to conform to *ordo* and the prescriptions of a Divine Law which assigns a proper place to each good, both in reality and in the scope of our affections.[41]

From this standpoint, conformance to *ordo* demands a degree of indifference to the world and temporal pursuits. For Augustine, one who attempts to ground his or her happiness solely upon mutable realities can never attain true happiness: the very fragility and uncertainty of such things does not allow for that sense of peace and freedom from care which are necessary conditions of the good and happy life.[42] These sentiments are reflected in the comprehensive definition of iniquity which appears at the end of the first book of the *De libero arbitrio*:

> ...the pursuit of temporal things...as if they were great...
> which are perceived by the lowest part of man...his body...
> and the neglect of those things which the mind enjoys and
> perceives of itself, and which cannot be lost....[43]

This definition is further refined in Book II, where Augustine links his understanding of iniquity as the will's aversion from "what is Divine and abiding" with the "whole"/"part" analysis that we encounter throughout his moral deliberations. At this point, sin is viewed as a rejection of the universal Good in favor of limited, partial goods proper to oneself alone.[44] In this context, moral error constitutes an unwillingness to align private concerns with the requirements of Divine Law and the interests of the common Good. Accordingly, moral living demands an elevation of will to an immutable, all-encompassing Good and an attunement of intellect to the contemplation of eternal, all-embracing truth. The order of our loves, then, must parallel the order of the whole: that which is highest in being should hold the highest place in our scale of loves; creatures, in turn, should be loved in proportion to their varying degrees of dignity and worth.[45]

Conclusion

Augustine's conception of *ordo* enlightens us about his overall understanding of reality. In Augustinian terms, the universe is a *"cosmos"* in the classical sense of that term—that is, an ordered scheme whose parts share in and derive their intelligibility from a greater whole. As we have seen, this world-view (supported by a belief in a good and providential God) has important implications for Augustine's ethical theory. In moral terms, Augustine presupposes a Divine Law which provides the ultimate standard of right conduct. Accordingly, iniquity entails a violation of Law, and in effect, a subversion of *ordo*.

In the texts under scrutiny in this paper, iniquity constitutes a "disordering" in three senses. In the *De moribus*, it is treated as a defective movement from God, the fullness of being, to the corruptibility of non-being. In the *De Genesi contra Manichaeos*, Augustine develops a more refined interpretation of this defective movement in the context of his theory of the soul's mid-rank between God and corporeal natures. By virtue of this position, the soul finds its proper order, that is, a condition of loving submission to the authority of God and the stewardship of lower creation. In the *De libero arbitrio*, in the context of his fully developed theory of volition, Augustine defines iniquity in terms of a disordered love, a misuse of things in a manner which fails to respect their relationship to the whole and an elevation of personal desires over the common Good.

But while the negative effects of iniquity are far-reaching, Augustine stresses that such disorder only affects the parts and never the whole of things. This conviction reveals the vast differences between his vision of reality and that of the Manichaeans. If, in fact, a notion of order can be attributed to such a pessimistic scheme, it is one characterized by conflict and upheaval rather than harmony and stability. In Manichaeism, as in all forms of Gnosticism, cosmos assumed a pejorative connotation.[46] For the Gnostics, as Hans Jonas has observed, *cosmos* becomes "an emphatically negative concept," coinciding with an experience of an "absolute rift" between humans and the world in which they find themselves.[47] Accordingly, such outlooks tended to rely upon metaphysical dualisms which drew a sharp division between a transcendent Godhead and humanity on the one hand, and between humanity and the world at large on the other.

Augustine, as we have seen, likewise resorts to something of a dualism in his distinctions between the immutable and mutable, the eternal and the temporal. For him, such distinctions underscore the vast disparities between spiritual and corporeal reality, as well as the deficiencies inherent in that which is subject to process and change. In Augustine, however, the relationship between these ontological levels is essentially one of order and harmony rather than conflict and tension. From his Christian perspective, reality is fundamentally good because everything is subjected to *ordo*.

According to its famous formulation in the *De civitate dei*, *ordo* is "the arrangement of things equal and unequal in a pattern which assigns to each its proper position."[48] In the earlier *De musica*, Augustine spoke in terms of a "poem of the universe" (*carmen universitatis*), a beautiful scheme of interrelated components, wherein "terrestrial things are subjected to celestial, and their time circuits join together in harmonious succession."[49] Such statements reflect Augustine's intellectual commitment to the rationalism of the Greek philosophical tradition, as articulated by Plato, by the Neoplatonists, and by the Stoics. A basic presupposition of this tradition was the goodness and rationality of the whole, and by implication, its components.

This affirmation of a harmony and kinship between whole and parts was a prominent feature of classical theories of human nature. From this teleological perspective, humans were viewed as microcosms of the whole, reflecting and imitating its perfection by virtue of rational thought and purposeful action. Augustine upheld this cosmic ideal, adapting it to suit his own Christian outlook. In keeping with Scriptural teaching, he views humans as created in God's "image and likeness." For Augustine, we are free, morally responsible beings rather than passive spectators caught in some dualistic struggle between opposing natures. But as free agents, humans can either adhere to the dictates of *ordo* by directing their choices to the Good or they can challenge it through iniquity. Paradoxically, the will which Augustine numbers among the chief goods given to us by God is capable of sin. For us, as for Augustine, the reason for this defective movement toward nothingness eludes our understanding. We are left, then, with an unresolved problem, namely, that human souls, which can freely fall from God, are likewise necessary for the perfection of the universe.[50]

Notes

[1] There is some debate as to the precise chronology of Augustine's writings. I have relied upon Gustave Bardy's chronology, as found in *BA* 12,563–71.

[2] For a concise statement on the main lines of Augustine's participation metaphysics, see Vernon J. Bourke's *Augustine's View of Reality*; The Saint Augustine Lecture, 1963 (Villanova: Villanova University Press, 1964), pp. 24–25 and 117–23.

[3] *De moribus ecclesiae catholicae et de moribus Manichaeorum* II,iv,6: *PL* XXXII, 1347: *Neque naturaliter bona res est, quae cum facta dicitur, utique ut bona esset, accepit. Ita et Deus summum bonum est, et ea quae fecit, bona sunt omnia, quamvis non sint tam bona, quam est ille ipse qui fecit; FC* 56,69.

[4] *De moribus ecclesiae catholicae et de moribus Manichaeorum* II,iv,6: *PL* XXXII, 1347: *quae aliud dicit bonum quod summe ac per se bonum est, et non participatione alicujus boni, sed propria natura et essentia; aliud quod participando bonum et habendo; habet autem de illo summo bono ut bonum sit, in se tamen manente illo, nihilque amittente.*

[5] *De moribus ecclesiae catholicae et de moribus Manichaeorum* II,iv,6: *PL* XXXII, 1345: *Hoc enim maxime esse dicendum est, quod semper eodem modo sese habet, quod omnimodo sui simile est, quod nulla ex parte corrumpi ac mutari potest, quod non subjacet tempori, quod aliter nunc se habere quam habebat antea, non potest. Id enim est quod esse verissime dicitur. Subest enim huic verbo manentis in se atque incommutabiliter sese habentis naturae significatio.*

[6] *De moribus ecclesiae catholicae et de moribus Manichaeorum* II,iv,6: *PL* XXXII, 1345: *Hanc nihil aliud quam Deum possumus dicere, cui si contrarium recte quaeras, nihil omnino est. Esse enim contrarium non habet, nisi non esse. Nulla est ergo Deo natura contraria.*

[7] *De moribus ecclesiae catholicae et de moribus Manichaeorum* II,iii,5: *PL* XXXII, 1346–47.

[8] *De moribus ecclesiae catholicae et de moribus Manichaeorum* II,iv,6: *PL* XXXII, 1347: *Ita et malum ostenditur quomodo dicatur; non enim secundum essentiam, sed secundum privationem verissime dicitur: et natura cui noceri possit apparet.*

[9] *De moribus ecclesiae catholicae et de moribus Manichaeorum* II,v,7: *PL* XXXII, 1348: *Item quod corrumpitur, profecto pervertitur; quod autem pervertitur, ordine privatur: ordo autem bonum est. Non igitur quod corrumpitur, bono caret: eo namque ipso quo non caret, viduari dum corrumpitur potest.*

[10] *De moribus ecclesiae catholicae et de moribus Manichaeorum* II,vi,8: *PL* XXXII, 1348: *Nam quod mutatur in melius, non quia manebat mutatur, sed quia pervertebatur in pejus, id est, ab essentia deficiebat: cujus defectionis auctor non est qui est auctor essentiae. Mutantur ergo quaedam in meliora, et propterea tendunt esse: nec dicuntur ista mutatione perverti, sed reverti atque converti. Perversio enim contraria est ordinationi. Haec vero quae tendunt esse, ad ordinem tendunt: quem cum fuerint consecuta, ipsum esse consequuntur, quantum id creatura consequi potest. Ordo enim ad convenientiam quamdam quod ordinat redigit.*

[11] *De moribus ecclesiae catholicae et de moribus Manichaeorum* II,vi,8: *PL* XXXII, 1348: *Quare ordinatio esse cogit, inordinatio vero non esse; quae perversio etiam nominatur atque corruptio. Quidquid igitur corrumpitur, eo tendit ut non sit.*

[12] *De moribus ecclesiae catholicae et de moribus Manichaeorum* II,vi,8: *PL* XXXII, 1348: *Deficiunt autem omnia per corruptionem ab eo quod erant, et non permanere coguntur, non esse coguntur. Esse enim ad manendum refertur. Itaque quod summe et maxime esse dicitur, permanendo, in se dicitur.*

[13] *De moribus ecclesiae catholicae et de moribus Manichaeorum* II,vi,8: *PL* XXXII, 1348: *Nihil est autem esse, quam unum esse. Itaque in quantum quidque unitatem adipiscitur, in tantum est.*

[14] *De moribus ecclesiae catholicae et de moribus Manichaeorum* II,vi,8: *PL* XXXII, 1348: *Unitatis est enim operatio, convenientia et concordia, qua sunt in quantum sunt, ea quae composita sunt: nam simplicia per se sunt, quia una sunt; quae autem non sunt simplicia, concordia partium imitantur unitatem, et in tantum sunt in quantum assequuntur.* In the *De moribus ecclesiae catholicae et de moribus Manichaeorum* II,vi,8, "order" is designated as an earmark of being, along with "measure" and "harmony." But Augustine's writings posit different combinations of such general characteristics of the really real. For a convenient survey of relevant Augustinian texts (and translations), see Vernon J. Bourke's *Augustine's View of Reality*, pp. 46–53; 66–75; 84–87; 92–95; 108–9. Among the texts cited by Bourke are the *De Genesi contra Manichaeos* I,xvi,26 and the *De libero arbitrio* II,xx,54 (for the combination of "measure," "number," and "order"); the *De uera religione* VII,13 and the *De trinitate* VI,x,12 (for the combination of "one," "species," and "order"); the *De musica* VI,xvii,56–57 (for the combination of "unity," "number," and "order"); the *De natura boni* III and the *De ciuitate dei* XI,15 (for the combination of "mode," "species," and "order"); the *De Genesi ad litteram* IV,iii,7–iv,9 and the *De trinitate* XI,xi,18 (for the combination of "measure," "number," and "weight").

[15] *De moribus ecclesiae catholicae et de moribus Manichaeorum* II,vii,9: *PL* XXXII, 1349: *Sed Dei bonitas eo rem perduci non sinit, et omnia deficientia sic ordinat, ut ibi sint ubi congruentissime possint esse, donec ordinatis motibus ad id recurrant unde defecerunt. Itaque etiam animas rationes, in quibus est potentissimum liberum arbitrium, deficientes a se, in inferioribus creaturae gradibus ordinat, ubi tales esse decet. Fiunt ergo miserae divino judicio, dum convenienter pro meritis ordinantur.*

[16] *De moribus ecclesiae catholicae et de moribus Manichaeorum* II,vii,9: *PL* XXXII, 1349: *Facere enim est, quod omnino non erat; condere autem, ordinare quod utcumque jam*

erat, ut melius magisque sit. Ea namque condit Deus, id est ordinat, cum dicit, Condo mala, quae deficiunt, id est, non esse tendunt; non ea quae ad id quo tendunt, pervenerunt. Dictum est enim: Nihil per divinam providentiam, ad id ut non sit pervenire permittitur. Augustine bases this distinction between the role of God as maker of all things and orderer of evil things upon Is 45:7.

[17] *De uera religione* X,18: *CC* XXXII,199.

[18] Cf. *De moribus ecclesiae catholicae et de moribus Manichaeorum* II,vii,9: *PL* XXXII,1349.

[19] *De uera religione* X,18: *CC* XXXII,199.

[20] *De diversis quaestionibus LXXXIII* XLV: *CC* XLIV/A,67: *Mens enim humana de uisibilibus iudicans, potest agnoscere omnibus uisibilibus se ipsam esse meliorem. Quae tamen, cum etiam se propter defectum profectumque in sapientia fatetur esse mutabilem, inuenit supra se esse incommutabilem ueritatem;* cf. *De doctrina christiana* II,xxxviii,57: *CC* XXXII,72:...*constituta tamen inter incommutabilem supra se ueritatem et mutabilia infra se cetera....*

[21] *De Genesi contra Manichaeos* II,ix,12: *PL* XXXIV,203: *Lignum autem vitae plantatum, in medio paradisi, sapientiam illam significat, qua oportet ut intelligat anima, in meditullio quodam rerum se esse ordinatum, ut quamvis subjectam sibi habeat omnem naturam corpoream, supra se tamen esse intelligat naturam Dei: et neque in dexteram declinet, sibi arrogando quod non est; neque ad sinistram, per negligentiam contemnando quod est: et hoc est lignum vitae plantatum in medio paradisi.*

[22] *De Genesi contra Manichaeos* II,ix,12: *PL* XXXIV,203: *Ligno autem scientiae boni et mali, ipsa item medietas animae et ordinata integritas significatur: nam et ipsum lignum in medio paradisi plantatum est; et ideo lignum dignoscentiae boni et mali dicitur, quia si anima quae debet in ea quae anteriora sunt se extendere, id est in Deum, et ea quae posteriora sunt oblivisci....*

[23] For a more detailed discussion of the evolution of Augustine's understanding of iniquity, see my contribution, "St. Augustine's Triadic Interpretation of Iniquity in the *Confessiones*" in *Collectanea Augustiniana* I (New York: Peter Lang Publishing, Inc., 1989), pp. 159–73.

[24] *De Genesi contra Manichaeos* I,xxiii,40; II,v,6; II,ix,12; II,xv,22; II,xvi,24; II,xviii,27; II,xxvi,40: *PL* XXXIV,192; 199; 203; 207–8; 208–9; 210; 217–18.

[25] *De Genesi contra Manichaeos* I,xvii,28: *PL* XXXIV,187: *Quo significatur, etiam animum nostrum in superna sua, id est in aeterna spiritualia, erectum esse debere.*

[26] *De Genesi contra Manichaeos* II,iv,5: *PL* XXXIV,198–99: *Ante peccatum vero, cum viride agri et pabulum fecisset Deus, quo nomine invisibilem creaturam significari diximus, irrigabat eam fonte interiore, loquens in intellectum ejus: ut non extrinsecus verba exciperet....*

[27] *De Genesi contra Manichaeos* I,xviii,29: *PL* XXXIV,187:...*cum in hujus vitae mortalitatem damnatus est, et amisit perfectionem illam qua factus est ad imaginem Dei;* cf. *De Genesi contra Manichaeos* II,xx,30; II,v,6.

[28] *De Genesi contra Manichaeos* I,xxi,32: *PL* XXXIV,188–89: *Omnis enim pulchritudo quae partibus constat, multo est laudabilior in toto quam in parte...et quod eos propter conditionem nostrae mortalitatis in parte offendit....*

[29] Cf. *De ordine* II,iv,11: *PL* XXXII,1000; *De musica* VI,xi,29: *PL* XXXII,1179.

[30] *De ordine* II,iv,11: *PL* XXXII,1000: *Si autem mentis oculos erigens atque diffundens, simul universa collustret, nihil non ordinatum, suisque semper veluti sedibus distinctum dispositumque reperiet.*

[31] *De libero arbitrio* I,ii,4: *CC* XXIX,213: *Eam quaestionem moues, quae me admodum adulescentem uehementer exercuit et fatigatum in haereticos impulit atque deiecit*; *FC* 59, 75.

[32] *De libero arbitrio* I,ii,4: *CC* XXIX,213: *Mouet autem animum, si peccata ex his animabus sunt quas deus creauit, illae autem animae ex deo, quomodo non paruo interuallo peccata referantur in deum.*

[33] *De libero arbitrio* I,viii,18: *CC* XXIX,222–23.

[34] *De libero arbitrio* I,viii,18; I,x,20; II,xviii,48: *CC* XXIX,222–23; 224–25; 269–70.

[35] Augustine frequently uses "weight" imagery in the context of discussions regarding the soul's love. In the *De Musica* VI,xi,29: *PL* XXXII,1179, he explicitly defines that in which the soul takes "delight" as its ordering principle. Cf. *Confessiones* XIII,ix,10: *CC* XXVII,246–47.

[36] *De libero arbitrio* I,xii,25: *CC* XXIX,227–28.

[37] *De libero arbitrio* I,iii,8: *CC* XXIX,215. The characterization of passion as the decisive factor in wrongdoing demands further clarification. While Augustine speaks of such inordinate desire as "blameworthy," he still attributes a primacy to free will in the dynamics of moral decision-making. For him, the soul's submission to the influence of *cupiditas* or *libido* ultimately depends upon will (*De libero arbitrio* I,xi,21; I,xvi,34: *CC* XXIX,225–26; 234–35). By virtue of free will, the soul chooses either to control or to be controlled by its appetites. Strictly speaking, then, sin does not proceed from passion alone, but from volition.

[38] *De libero arbitrio* I,xiii,28; I,xvi,34: *CC* XXIX,230; 234–35.

[39] I refer here to the later distinction between use (*uti*) and enjoyment (*frui*) which, for Augustine, provides another means of contrasting the proper and improper disposition on our part toward goods. Cf. *De doctrina christiana* I,iv,4: *CC* XXXII,8; *De trinitate* X,x,13; X,xi,17–18: *CC* L,326–27; *De diversis quaestionibus LXXXIII* XXX: *CC* XLIV/A,38–40.

[40] *De libero arbitrio* I,xv,33: *CC* XXIX,1239: *Cum igitur eisdem rebus alius male alius bene utatur, et is quidem qui male, amore his inhaereat atque implicetur—scilicet subditus eis rebus quas ei subditas esse oportebat, et ea bona sibi constituens quibus ordinandis beneque tractandis ipse esse utique deberet bonum—, ille autem qui recte his utitur, ostendat quidem bona esse, sed non sibi—non enim eum bonum melioremue faciunt, sed ab eo potius fiunt—, et ideo non eis amore agglutinetur neque uelut membra sui animi faciat, quod fit amando, ne*

cum resecari coeperint, eum cruciatu ac tabe foedent, sed eis totus superferatur, et habere illa atque regere, cum opus est, paratus et amittere ac non habere paratior....

⁴¹ *De libero arbitrio* I,xvi,34: *CC* XXIX,234–35. Conversely, Augustine defines the virtuous life in terms of an ordered love: *De ciuitate dei* XV,xxii: *CC* XLVIII, 488: *Creator autem si ueraciter ametur, hoc est si ipse, non aliud pro illo quod non est ipse, ametur, male amari non potest. Nam et amor ipse ordinate amandus est, quo bene amatur quod amandum est, ut sit in nobis uirtus qua uiuitur bene. Unde mihi uidetur, quod definitio breuis et uera uirtutis ordo est amoris....*

⁴² *De libero arbitrio* I,xvi,34: *CC* XXIX,234–35. This insight, frequently expressed in the *De libero arbitrio*, reflects Augustine's reliance upon the Stoic dictum that no one finds happiness in those things which can be lost against one's will. For a more detailed discussion of the Stoic element in the early Augustine, see Robert J. O'Connell's "De Libero Arbitrio I: Stoicism Revisited," *AS* I (1970) 49–68.

⁴³ *De libero arbitrio* I,xvi,34: *CC* XXIX,234–35: *Quocira licet nunc animaduertere et considerare utrum sit aliud male facere quam neglectis rebus aeternis, quibus per se ipsam mens fruitur et per se ipsam percipit et quas amans amittere non potest, temporalia et quaeque per corpus, partem hominis uilissimam, sentiuntur et nunquam esse certa possunt quasi magna et miranda sectari. Nam hoc uno genere omnia malefacta, id est peccata, mihi uidentur includi. Tibi autem quid uideatur exspecto cognoscere.*

⁴⁴ This understanding of iniquity, which is developed in terms of the distinction between the *commune* and the *proprium*, emerges in the *De libero arbitrio* II,vii,15–xiii,37: *CC* XXIX,247–63. Cf. *De musica* VI,xiii,39–40; VI,xiv,48; VI,xvi,53: *PL* XXXII,1184–85; 1188; 1190.

⁴⁵ Augustine discusses the differences between the eternal and the temporal laws, and the gradation of loves which each prescribes, in the *De libero arbitrio* I,xv,31–32: *CC* XXIX,232–33.

⁴⁶ I am interpreting Manichaeism as a brand of Gnosticism, that religious tendency which was extremely widespread in the Hellenistic world. The Gnostics shared in common some salient features—e.g., a sense of alienation on the part of individuals from the world and God; metaphysical dualisms; a spirit of pessimism about human existence; a belief in an "elect" who were assured of salvation by virtue of their possession of a privileged "gnosis."

⁴⁷ Hans Jonas, *The Gnostic Religion*, 2nd edition (Boston: Beacon Press, 1963), pp. 250–51.

⁴⁸ *De ciuitate dei* XIX,xiii: *CC* XLVIII,679: *Ordo est parium dispariumque rerum sua cuique loca tribuens dispositio*; tr. Henry Bettenson *Concerning the City of God against the Pagans* (Harmondsworth: Penguin Books, 1972).

⁴⁹ *De musica* VI,xi,29: *PL* XXXII,1179; *FC* 2,355: *Ita coelestibus terrena subjecta, orbes temporum suorum numerosa successione quasi carmeni universitatis associant.*

⁵⁰ *De libero arbitrio* II,xx,54; III,ix,24–28: *CC* XXIX,272–73; 289–92.

V

Belief and Understanding

Augustine

*Quoniam igitur diuina prouidentia non solum singulis ho-
minibus quasi privatim, sed universo generi humano tamquam
publice consulit, quid cum singulis agatur, deus qui agit atque
ipsi cum quibus agitur sciunt, quid autem agatur cum genere
humano, per historiam commendari uoluit et per prophetiam.
Temporalium autem rerum fides siue praeteritarum siue futura-
rum magis credendo quam intellegendo ualet, sed nostrum est
considerare, quibus uel hominibus uel libris credendum sit ad
colendum recte deum, quae una salus est.*

De uera religione XXV,46

Augustine on Faith and Reason

Eduardo J. Echeverria

I

Michael Polanyi has written that "In the fourth century A.D., St. Augustine brought the history of Greek philosophy to a close by inaugurating for the first time a post-critical philosophy."[1] Augustine, argues Polanyi, restored the balance of our cognitive powers by rescuing belief from its inferior status as opinion in Greek philosophy. "He taught that all knowledge was a gift of grace, for which we must strive under the guidance of antecedent belief: *nisi credideritis, non intelligetis. Credo ut intelligam,* as Anselm formulated Augustine's doctrine six centuries after his death, ruled the minds of Christian scholars for a millennium, says Polanyi. The decisive shift in sensibility occurred, however, when Augustinian doctrine waned and rationalism[2] gained superiority. Polanyi does not say what contributed to this shift, but he does suggest that by the end of the seventeenth century John Locke had "thoroughly discredited" belief and "reduced [it] to the status of subjectivity." Moreover, the modern Western intellectual takes Locke's view of faith and knowledge for granted. Says Polanyi, "belief is...no longer a higher power that reveals to us knowledge lying beyond the range of observation and reason, but a mere personal acceptance which falls short of empirical and rational demonstrability." Polanyi's response to Locke and his successors urges us to go back to Augustine in order to restore, once again, the balance of our cognitive powers of faith and reason. We need, he says, for the second time in the history of Western philosophy to establish a "post-critical philosophy."

The shift in sensibility from Augustine to Locke, which Polanyi describes here, is not entirely clear, nor persuasive. Augustine certainly focuses upon faith in revealed truth as the first and obligatory step toward knowledge, but does reason, on his view, work only within the context of faith? Is reason merely a handmaid in the exploration of the content of divine revelation? To be sure, there is a clear sense in which faith precedes reason, but is there not an equally clear sense, on Augustine's view, in which reason precedes faith? Indeed, is not the claim that faith precedes reason itself a reasonable principle? Yes, it is precisely this point that Augustine articulates in the following passage: "It is, then, a reasonable requirement that faith precede reason, for, if this requirement is not reasonable, then it is contrary to reason, which God forbid. But, if it is reasonable that faith precede a certain great reason which cannot yet be grasped, there is no doubt that, however slight the reason which proves this, it does precede faith."[3] Thus we see that for Augustine the primacy of faith over reason is itself a principle of rationality. If so, then it may seem fairly plausible to say that, though reason does not have priority over faith on the lower level of "first-order" beliefs, it does have priority on the higher level, because the belief that faith precedes reason is itself a reasonable principle.

Etienne Gilson, in his book *Reason and Revelation in the Middle Ages*, sets forth an interpretation of Augustine similar to Polanyi's. There is a crucial difference between their views, however, which has a bearing on the issue before us. The way to knowledge starts with faith in revealed truth, but "even the faith of an Augustinian," says Gilson, "presupposes a certain exercise of natural reason. We cannot believe something, be it the word of God Himself, unless we find some sense in the formula we believe. And it can hardly be expected that we will believe in God's revelation, unless we be given good reasons to think that such a Revelation has indeed taken place."[4] Gilson's point suggests that reason itself, without revelation, is capable of determining, indeed, must determine, whether the proposition that P has been revealed by God. Once again, we see this priority of reason to faith in Augustine's *Of True Religion* where he speaks of reason's two functions—one following after authority, the other in relation to authority itself: "There are two different methods, authority and reason. Authority demands belief and prepares man for reason. Reason leads to understanding and knowledge. But reason is not entirely absent from authority, for we have got to consider whom we have to believe."[5] At first glance, then, Polanyi's reading of Augustine does not recommend itself.

If we turn now to Polanyi's interpretation of Locke, we find it to be questionable as well. Significantly, although Locke holds that reason precedes faith's knowledge of God, he still wants to hold on to revelation as an independent ground of authority.[6] Locke distinguishes between faith and knowledge. As he says, there "are two ways whereby truth comes into the mind, wholly distinct, so that one is not the other. What I see, I know to be so by the evidence of the thing itself; what I believe, I take to be so upon the testimony of another." Locke immediately adds this condition, however: "but this testimony I must know to be given, or else what ground have I of believing? I must see that it is God that reveals this to me, or else I see nothing." In raising this point, Locke does not doubt whether any revelation from God is true. We can be certain, says Locke, that whatever God reveals is true, because any theist who believes, as Locke does, that God is a perfectly truthful being will assent to the proposition that any revelation from God is true. But saying this, even if true, does not settle the epistemological question of how anyone knows whether or not a particular proposition is revealed by God. Here, then, Locke's claim is that a person believes a putative revelation because it has been proved that it was revealed. Locke makes clear that reason needs evidence to support the claim that P has been revealed by God; we do not need evidence to support P itself (the content of the putative revelation) to be justified in accepting it.

The distinction between the proposition that P has been revealed by God and P itself is important in order to grasp Locke's attempt to retain the status of revelation as an independent ground of assent. The proposition that P has been revealed—call it Q—is itself a proposition distinct from P, and a true one at that, should the fact of its being revealed be proved. In this way Locke hopes to retain the possibility that God might reveal to us for our belief things that are beyond reason's power to reach. Nonetheless, because the fact of their being revealed can be proved, he claims, faith is not in conflict with reason but is a rational state of mind. Moreover, since Locke holds the principle that God is a perfectly truthful being, and hence that whatever God reveals is true, this principle, along with the judgment that P has been revealed by God, entails that the purportedly revealed proposition P is true. Consequently, having this argument that P is true, the mind is permitted access to truths which we could not justifiably believe by the unaided use of our intellect.[7] Thus, pace Polanyi, since revelation retains its status, on Locke's view, as an independent ground of assent, faith does have access to truths lying beyond the range of observation and reason.

It will be clear from this brief and somewhat simplified sketch of Augustine and Locke that their positions on the relation of faith and reason is not as simple as Polanyi makes it. In particular, we have already encountered Augustine's thesis that there is a place for reason both before and after accepting revelation. To give a place to reason prior to faith means that one must have independent reasons for accepting the proposition that God revealed something. The rationale behind this thesis, at least in the modern period, is to build a bridge from rational knowledge to faith. Is that what Augustine intends as well with his thesis that there is a place for reason before faith? If so, then Augustine would seem to be much closer to what Polanyi calls the "critical mind-set" of modern Western intellectuals like Locke. Let us call this critical mind-set evidentialism, which I will define as any view affirming that people can be counted fully rational only if they can supply reasons for everything they believe. The question before us now is whether Augustine is an evidentialist. Does he adopt the epistemic policy of believing only what he himself is able independently to justify? Alternatively: does he attach evidentialist preconditions to the act of faith? In order to answer this question, I turn now to consider more closely Augustine's doctrine of faith and reason.

II

It is Augustine's central thesis that faith and reason should never be conceived as antagonists, contradictories, but always as coadjutants, cooperating to a common end in our noetic enterprise, which is the search for truth. There are two ways whereby truth comes into the mind: by faith or by reason. "No one doubts," Augustine tells us, "that we are incited to learn by the double weight of authority and of reason."[8] The difference here in modes of mental acts or states by which truth may be laid hold of, between "believing that P" and "knowing that P," is simply as follows. In the case of things we believe, we accept the truth of P on someone's say-so, on testimony; it is to take something on the word of another, on his authority. In the case of things we know, we see the truth of P for ourselves, defined by Augustine as the direct knowledge human beings have when they 'see' self-evident truths or when inference adds to knowledge by strict logical demonstration.[9]

When I believe that P, I accept P as true on someone's say-so; belief takes the place of a direct knowledge which is lacking. Surely in doing this, says Augustine, I am doing what humans do generally: rely upon the testimony of others for the overwhelming majority of their beliefs. Facing head on the charge of the Manichees, who claim that one may not believe anything one has not seen for oneself, and recalling how God set his thoughts in order, Augustine writes in the *Confessions*:

> I began to realize that I believed countless things which I had
> never seen or which had taken place when I was not there to
> see—so many events in the history of the world, so many
> facts about places and towns which I had never seen, and so
> much that I believed on the word of friends or doctors or

various other people. Unless we took these things on trust, we should accomplish absolutely nothing in this life.[10]

"Since in all these things we have believed the testimony of others,"[11] as Augustine writes in *On The Trinity*, belief can be adequately warranted by authority alone. Of course, in cases where I take another's word that something is the truth, I can in principle establish the truth of P for myself and thus dispense with the appeal to someone's testimony or say-so. Nonetheless, to be warranted in believing that P, I do not require the independent evidence of reason, not only because such reasons are often impossible to obtain, but also because it is beyond the capacity of any individual, however intelligent and well informed, to suspend his acceptance of beliefs, which is founded on the testimony of others, until he has independently worked it all out for himself.

So, for Augustine, testimony is an independent source of warrant for an enormously large proportion of our beliefs. It is in this sense that there is nothing unreasonable in what one might call, following Thomas Reid, our disposition to trust testimony. As Reid sees it, testimony has "a native and intrinsic authority," because "the Wise Author of Nature hath implanted in the human mind a propensity to rely upon human testimony before we give a reason for doing so."[12] Augustine would agree with Reid. This means that, in Augustine's view, it would be wrong, therefore, to adopt an epistemic policy, as the evidentialist suggests, of believing only what we ourselves are able independently to justify. Thus, Augustine's complaint against the evidentialist is not only that he gives an unrealistic account of how we acquire and maintain our beliefs; it is the evidentialist's epistemology that he wishes to find fault with. Faith and authority can never be dispensed with in favor of rational evidence alone. This is the case for ordinary, common sense beliefs, but it is no less so for religious beliefs. Faith and authority lie at the very basis of both.

Authority is not only an absolutely fundamental and indispensable part of our noetic enterprise, but also the necessary pedagogue to knowledge. Acceptance of P as true on the grounds of authority, on the testimony of others, need not be a final act but only a stage on the way to knowledge. Every learner must first be a believer, in order that he may come to knowledge. Thus the dynamic of the noetic enterprise is one in which believing strives to replace itself with knowing. Says Augustine, "We are of necessity led in a twofold manner: by authority and by reason. In point of time, authority is first; in the order of reality, reason is prior. What takes precedence in operation is one thing; what is more highly prized as an object of desire is something else."[13]

This dynamic also explains why faith, now in the specifically religious sense, seeks understanding. Faith in revelation, in divine testimony, is the first in time, but rational insight, understanding, is indeed first in dignity. Faith must precede the knowledge which appropriates and comprehends it intellectually. So faith is not so much a substitute for knowledge as a preparation for knowledge. And the effort of the knowledge-seeker should be to transmute his faith into knowledge, gradually to replace faith by sight, that is to say, some rational insight into the contents of revelation.

Here we come to an important point. Our question is: why ought we, in the case of religious belief, to begin with authority, and not with reason. "For, although we grant that it is one thing to believe, another to be credulous, it does not follow, that it is no fault to believe in matters of religion.... [Therefore] make plain, how in the case of religion it be not base to believe before one knows."[14] Augustine's initial reply to this question is as follows. Suppose then that our knowledge of God could be ascertained through proofs or arguments, yielding knowledge of the truth, here and now, instead of mere belief. "[B]ut, it being so great a matter, that you are by reason to come to the knowledge of God, do you think that all are qualified to understand the reasons, by which the human soul is led to know God, or many, or few?"[15] Only a few people can arrive at a knowledge of God in this way, of course, for the arguments are relatively complex. What, then, Augustine asks, would be the condition of humanity, if all our knowledge of God depended only on human reason? Would it not be unfair of God to deny this knowledge to the many who cannot construct proofs or arguments?[16] "For you cannot think," says Augustine, "that any one whatever in a case where he desires so great a thing, ought by any means to be abandoned or rejected." Because of this, there is yet another mode, which is no less certain, even though it is the indirect and slower path, of attaining knowledge of God. That additional mode is faith. "What way can there be more healthful, than for a man to become fitted to receive the truth by believing those things, which have been appointed by God to serve for the previous culture and treatment of the mind?"[17] This way, says Augustine, consists in accepting, by faith, something on testimony, which is proposed by God for our belief. Faith, taking us by the hand, so to speak, puts us on the right road towards rational understanding.[18]

But why is it necessary to have faith in the divine revelation anyway? The answer to this is simply that, human beings are, in their present condition, sinful; thus, the noetic effect of sin is such that it weakens the human intellect. To overcome this *debilitas rationis* man has, therefore, need of divine revelation; and this is what faith offers him. God's revelation, divine testimony, meets the sin-bred inability of human beings to attain right knowledge of God. Significantly, this is only an extension, on Augustine's view, of the provision he discerns, in human testimony, for meeting the immaturity of man's cognitive powers. The need for revelation and the provision of revelation for sinful man is analogous to the need and provision of testimony in its role as the necessary pedagogue to knowledge. God meets the needs of sin-blinded human beings, by offering to them, on the authority of divine testimony, the truth which they are as sinners incapable of ascertaining for themselves. Augustine is admirably explicit on this point: "For I not only judge it most healthful to believe before reason, when you are not qualified to receive reason, and by the very act of faith thoroughly to cultivate the mind to receive the seeds of truth, but altogether a thing of such a sort as that without it health cannot return to sick souls."[19]

It may well be pointed out that, if faith is a necessary and effective condition for attaining knowledge of God, how, then, can reason precede faith, as Augustine suggests, in the evaluation and acceptance of authority. How can Augustine, in short, allow for the evaluation of authority by independent rational criteria? This is a major question, and the difficulty is that Augustine does not elaborate. Let me now try to state precisely what Augustine is and is not claiming.

III

Augustine does not claim that all truth must be discovered by reason; but neither does he claim that the content of revelation must be proved by reason. This is not to deny that some revelatory truths can also be objects of knowledge, truths about God, viz., the existence, infinity, and immutability of God, which men can know, and not just believe, on their natural powers alone.[20] What he does deny is the ability of unaided reason to bring us to a saving knowledge of God through its own resources alone. Still less does Augustine claim that one should proportion one's degree of assent to what is warranted by the amount or weight of the evidence in support of one's beliefs. Augustine holds, we remember, that it is wrong to adopt an epistemic policy of believing only what we ourselves are able independently to justify.

Looking back to Locke, it is important to remark, moreover, that Augustine does not share his epistemological strategy in justifying revelational

claims. Yet, precisely this affinity with Locke is suggested by Protestant evi-
dentialists. Benjamin Warfield, for example, in his interpretation of Augustine suggests the following interpretation which bears striking resemblance to
Locke's views adumbrated above.[21] For Augustine, says Warfield, the proper
acceptance of any revealed truth, P, depends on a judgment that P has been
revealed by God. But once we have that judgment authority, not reason, is
then the ground for accepting the particular teachings which reason can eluci-
date. For Augustine has the principle that God is a perfectly truthful being,
and that therefore whatever is revealed by God is true. Thus, this principle,
and the judgment that P has been revealed by God, implies that P is true. If
so, we can go on to believe things that we could not justifiably believe by the
unaided use of our minds. So Augustine's strategy, on Warfield's view, is as
follows: (1) "the validation of a revelation as such on its appropriate grounds,"
(2) "the acceptance by faith of the contents of revelation on the sole ground of
its authority," and (3) "the comprehension by the intellect of the contents of
the revelation and the justification of them severally to reason so far as that
may prove to be possible to us." This is an argument of considerable force for
the existence of a God who might reveal himself by communicating with men.
For if one is warranted in believing the proposition that God has revealed P,
then one cannot fail to believe P itself.

   The problem with this argument is that it is difficult to see how the revelation, once accepted, is intrinsically authoritative, as far as its revelational
content is concerned, for, as Warfield claims, its warranty is valid only if it is
indeed a genuine revelation, and whether this is so must first be judged by
reason. To be sure, Warfield says that we "neither need nor are entitled to
wait until each of these [revealed] truths is separately validated to us on the
grounds of reason before we give our assent it." Still, what he does say is that
"the rational ground on which we accept each truth is the proof that the authority by which it is commended to us is adequate." If so, it follows that we
can never properly be more certain of the truth of a revealed proposition than
is warranted by the amount or weight of the evidence in support of thinking
that it is revealed. And this conclusion, I suggest, is inconsistent with Augustine's rejection of evidentialist epistemology.[22]

   We still need to answer the question of how Augustine can allow for the
evaluation of testimony by independent rational criteria. If I am right about
rejecting Warfield's Lockian reading of Augustine, then how should Augustine be interpreted? I shall now argue that Thomas Reid can help us to answer this question.[23]

Reid says that our disposition to trust testimony is an innate "original principle of our constitution" implanted in us by God. Reid calls this principle the credulity principle.[24] This disposition, he adds, is "unlimited in children, until they meet with instances of deceit and falsehood." Our response to encountering such instances does not lead to eliminating the credulity principle, but instead to its refinement: we learn to discriminate between reliable and unreliable kinds of testimony. As Reid sees it, of particular significance in this refining process is the interaction of reason with our credulity disposition. Reid writes:

> When brought to maturity by proper culture...Reason learns to suspect testimony in some cases, and to disbelieve it in others. But still, to the end of life, she finds a necessity of borrowing light from testimony....And as, in many cases, reason even in her maturity, borrows aid from testimony, so in others she mutually gives aid to it, and strengthens its authority. For, as we find good reason to reject testimony in some cases, so in others we find good reason to rely upon it with perfect security....The character, the number, and the disinterestedness of the witnesses, the impossibility of collusion, may give an irresistible strength to testimony, compared to which its native and intrinsic authority is very inconsiderable.

This brings us back to Augustine. In his *Confessions*, Augustine tells us that he came to the conviction that some authority is indispensable to life. This conviction led him to consider the possibility of there being a divine authority. But the question remained where to find that authority. There were so many conflicting claims to such authority. How was he to decide? "It remained to inquire what that authority might be, since among so many dissentient voices each one professed to be able to hand it [authority] on to me. An inextricable thicket confronted me, most tiresome to be involved in; and here without any rest my mind was agitated by the desire to find the truth."[25]

So Augustine faces the problem of conflicting authorities. This problem blocks the flow of his disposition to trust testimony. What, then, is the role of what Reid calls "good reasons" in resolving such a problem? Suppose he realizes on reflection that there is rationally persuasive evidence for the resurrection of Jesus. I suggest that in finding some such "good reasons" for taking one testimony over the other, Augustine can come to believe the testimony of the New Testament, but he need not be relying on this evidence instead of his native credulity disposition to do so. Instead, the problem of conflicting authorities may be resolved by virtue of the evidence functioning as a discriminating feature, cutting a channel for his basic credulity disposition, which itself then forcefully carries his belief toward trusting the Bible.

Earlier in this essay, I noted Polanyi's claim that the change in the epistemic status of belief is clearly evident at the end of the seventeenth century with Locke's evidentialism. Polanyi fails, however, to say what contributed to the rise of evidentialism at least as it bears on the matter of religious epistemology. Some scholars argue that evidentialism is already anticipated at the beginning of the seventeenth century in Descartes' *Meditations*. Others claim that evidentialism is anticipated much earlier in medieval philosophers and theologians with their project of natural theology. Thomas Aquinas is generally singled out here as the key figure who set the evidentialist tradition of religious epistemology in motion by giving primacy to reason, allegedly arguing that an act of faith is unreasonable without the benefit of rational arguments. Since Augustine himself engaged in this project, in offering his argument for the existence of God from the existence of truth, and in arguing that there is some evidence that the Bible is God's revelation, they draw the conclusion that he, too, must be an evidentialist—although in Augustine's case, this conclusion is hesitantly drawn, given the affirmation he repeats most assiduously that "faith is the starting-point of knowledge."

If this is a mistaken reading both of Augustine and Aquinas,[26] and I am convinced that it is, what then is Augustine's view, in particular, of the role of evidences and arguments in the believer's assent to the knowledge of God and to the revelational character of that knowledge? Simply this: there is no denying that there are enough evidences and arguments to lead most people to the truth of the faith, which is not to say that there is enough to compel acceptance; but it is denied that the believer's assent to revealed truths is grounded on these.[27] To be sure, arguments and evidences may serve to recommend faith to an individual. Such evidence and argument, although sufficient to show that belief is not foolish and although capable of increasing the believer's confidence, is not sufficient to compel assent by all rational persons, however. They are, as the Catholic tradition puts it, motives of credibility. So ultimately, even taken together, they are not able to effect in a person's heart the faith that motivates him to believe that God has spoken, and that what God has said is true. Indeed, the act of responding in faith involves, not only the presence to the mind of evidence (a content that must be considered and weighed in the act of believing), but also the divine power of the *testimonium Spiritus Sancti* who moves the will to respond in faith. That is because the act of faith is not simply rational. Of course, far from inviting us to do away with reason, the Word of God itself promises to all those who seek truth in God's divine testimony the reward of understanding. "Faith is to believe that which you do not yet see," says Augustine, "the reward of that faith is to see that which you believe."[28]

To summarize: for Augustine, the sufficient cause of faith must lie beyond the evidences and arguments for three reasons. First, the certainty of faith does not and cannot be accounted for in terms of the arguments and evidences, because it does not depend on fallible human insight; it involves the unshakable certitude that God has spoken, and that what God has said is true, even though the object of faith, that which is believed, is "unseen." Second, there is a large group of persons possessing these same evidences who do not come to have faith. It is important to remark here that in such circumstances Augustine would say that the noetic influence of sin makes its presence felt by producing what one might call epistemic blindness. What prevents an individual from responding in faith is the resistance to the available arguments and the accessible evidences, not so much the lack of these.[29] And thirdly, the revelation given to us in divine testimony is for everyone, for the learned as well as for the unsophisticated individual; its truth may not hinge on arguments and evidences which are accessible only to the wise and learned.

Notes

[1] M. Polanyi, *Personal Knowledge: Towards a Post-Critical Philosophy* (1958; repr. New York: Harper and Row, 1964), p. 266, for this and the following quotations.

[2] In its restricted and technical sense, rationalism is invariably contrasted with empiricism. I do not mean to use the word rationalism in this sense, but rather in the broader sense proposed by John Cottingham (*Rationalism* [London: Paladin Books, 1984], p. 2), who writes that the rationalist is "one who places special emphasis on man's rational capacities and has a special belief in the value and importance of reason and rational argument."

[3] Augustine, *Epistula CXX* 3: *CSEL* XXXIV,706–7: *Proinde ut fides praecedat rationem, rationabiliter iussum est. nam si hoc praeceptum rationabile non est, ergo irrationabile est; absit. si igitur rationabile est, ut magnam quandam, quae capi nondum potest, fides antecedat rationem, procul dubio quantulacumque ratio, qua hoc persuadet, etiam ipsa antecedit fidem*; tr. in *Introduction to the Philosophy of Saint Augustine: Selected Readings and Com-*

mentaries, ed. by John A. Mourant (University Park, Pennsylvania: Pennsylvania State University Press, 1964), p. 47.

[4] E. Gilson, *Reason and Revelation in the Middle Ages* (New York: Charles Scribner's Sons, 1938), pp. 17–18. Gilson's formulation is misleading if it is meant to suggest that, in Augustine's view, belief is a two-step process, with reason coming first and faith following —or so, at least, that is what I shall argue in this essay.

[5] Augustine, *De uera religione* XXIV,45: *CC* XXXII,215: *Tribuitur enim in auctoritatem atque rationem. Auctoritas fidem flagitat, et rationi praeparat hominem. Ratio ad intellectum cognitionemque perducit, quamquam neque auctoritatem ratio penitus deserit, cum consideratur cui credendum sit*; tr. J. H. S. Burleigh in *Augustine: Earlier Writings* (Philadelphia: Westminster, 1953), p. 247.

[6] John Locke, *An Essay Concerning Human Understanding* (London: William Tegg, 1689), Book IV, Chapters xviii–xix. The phrases quoted are found in IV,xix,10.

[7] I have profited from George Mavrodes's discussion of Locke's doctrine of revelation. See his *Revelation in Religious Belief* (Philadelphia: Temple University Press, 1988), especially Chapter 1. See also his essay, "Revelation and the Bible," *Faith and Philosophy* 6 (1989) 398–411.

[8] Augustine, *Contra academicos* III,xx,43: *BA* 4,200: *Nulli autem dubium est gemino pondere nos impelli ad discendum, auctoritatis atque rationis*; tr. M. P. Garvey, *Against The Academicians* (Milwaukee: Marquette University Press, 1957), p. 82.

[9] One might ask Augustine whether faith is a form of knowledge. Is the Bible not full of references to the "knowledge" of God? For example, Paul says that "if we died with Christ, we believe that we will also live with him. For we know that since Christ was raised from the dead, he cannot die again" (Rm 6:8–9 NIV). And again, "we also believe and therefore speak, because we know that the one who raised the Lord Jesus from the dead will also raise us with Jesus and will bring us with you in his presence" (2 Co 4:13–14 NIV). Among other passages, see Jn 6:69, 17:8, and 1 Jn 4:16. Augustine has a two-fold reply to this question. First, he agrees that the Bible uses the words for knowledge and belief interchangeably, but its usage reflects an understanding of knowledge in a popular and common sense of knowledge, not a more technical or theoretical sense of knowledge. Augustine makes this point in *Retractationes* I,xiv,3: *BA* 12,358: *Proprie quippe cum loquimur, id solum scire dicimus quod mentis firma ratione comprehendimus. Cum vero loquimur verbis consuetudini aptioribus, sicut loquitur etiam divina Scriptura, non dubitemus dicere scire nos et quod percipimus nostri corporis sensibus et quod fide dignis credimus testibus, dum tamen inter haec et illud quid distet intelligamus.* "When we speak strictly we are said to know that only which by the mind's own firm reason we comprehend. But when we speak in words more suited to common use, as also Divine Scripture speaketh, we should not hesitate to say we know both what we have perceived with our bodily senses, and what we believe of trustworthy witnesses, whilst however between one and the other we are aware what difference exists."

Second, he also thinks that the Bible in some places distinguishes between knowledge and belief. In *De libero arbitrio* II,ii,6: *BA* 6,218: Augustine writes: *Ipse quoque Dominus noster et dictis et factis ad credendum primo hortatus est, quos ad salutem vocavit. Sed postea cum de ipso dono loqueretur, quod erat daturus credentibus, non ait, Haec est autem vita aeterna ut credant; sed, Haec est, inquit, vita aeterna, ut cognoscant te solum Deum verum, et quem misisti Jesum Christum* [Jn 17:3]. *Deinde jam credentibus dicit, Quaerite et invenietis* [Mt 7:7]: *nam neque inventum dici potest, quod incognitum creditur; neque quisquam inveniendo Deo fit idoneus, nisi antea crediderit quod est postea cogniturus*; tr. Anna S. Benjamin and L. A. Hackstaff, *On Free Choice of the Will* II,ii,18–19 (Indianapolis: Bobbs-Merrill, 1964), p. 39: "Our Lord Himself, by His words and deeds, first urged those whom He called to salvation to believe. Afterwards, when He spoke about the gift He was to give to those who believed, He did not say, 'This is life eternal so that they may believe.' Instead He said, 'This is life eternal that they may know Thee, the one true God and Him whom Thou didst send, Jesus Christ.' Then, to those who believed, He said, 'Seek and you shall find.' For what is believed without being known cannot be said to have been found, and no one can become fit for finding God unless he believes first what he shall know afterwards."

[10] Augustine, *Confessiones* VI,v,7: *BA* 13,530: *deinde paulatim tu, domine, manu mitissima et misericordissima pertractans et conponens cor meum, consideranti, quam innumerabilia crederem, quae non uiderem neque cum gererentur adfuissem, sicut tam multa in historia gentium, tam multa de locis atque urbibus, quae non uideram, tam multa amicis, tam multa medicis, tam multa hominibus aliis atque aliis, quae nisi crederentur, omnino in hac uita nihil ageremus*; tr. R. S. Pine-Coffin, *Confessions* (London: Penguin Books, 1961), pp. 116–17.

[11] Augustine, *De trinitate* XV,xii,21: *BA* 16,482: *quia haec omnia testimoniis credidimus aliorum*; tr. A. W. Haddan, *On The Trinity*, NPNF I:III,212.

[12] Thomas Reid, *Inquiry into the Human Mind* (Edinburgh: Maclachlan, Stewart, and Co., 1846), VI,24.

[13] Augustine, *De ordine* II,ix,26: *BA* 4,408: *Ad discendum item necessario dupliciter ducimur, auctoritate atque ratione. Tempore auctoritas, re autem ratio prior est. Aliud est enim quod in agendo anteponitur, aliud quod pluris in appetendo aestimatur; Divine Providence and the Problem of Evil*, tr. R. P. Russell, FC 5,303.

[14] Augustine, *De utilitate credendi* X,23: *BA* 8,260: *Neque enim si concedimus aliud esse credere, aliud credulum esse, sequitur ut nulla culpa sit in religionibus credere.…nunc expedi quomodo in religione turpe non sit credere, antequam scire*; tr. C. L. Cornish in NPNF I:III,357.

[15] *De utilitate credendi* X,24: *BA* 8,262: *sed cum res tanta sit, ut Deus tibi ratione cognoscendus sit, omnesne putas idoneos esse percipiendis rationibus, quibus ad divinam intelligentiam mens ducitur humana, an plures, an paucos?* tr. in NPNF I:III,358.

[16] Aquinas makes a similar point in the *Summa contra gentiles* I,4,22b–26; ed. by C. Pera et al. (Turin and Rome: Marietti, 1961), p. 6: *Sequerentur autem tria inconvenientia si huiusmodi veritas solummodo rationi inquirenda relinqueretur. Unum est quod paucis hominibus Dei cognitio inesset.…Secundum inconveniens est quod illi qui ad praedictae veritatis inventionem pervenirent, vix post longum tempus pertingerent.…Tertium inconveniens est quod investigationi rationis humanae plerumque falsitas admiscetur, propter debilitatem intellectus*

nostri in iudicando.... Et ideo oportuit per viam fidei fixam certitudinem et puram veritatem de rebus divinis hominibus exhiberi. Salubriter ergo divina providit clementia ut ea etiam quae ratio investigare potest, fide tenenda praeciperet: ut sic omnes de facili possent divinae cognitionis participes esse, et absque dubitatione et errore; tr. Anton C. Pegis *Summa Contra Gentiles* (Garden City, New York: Doubleday and Company, 1955), pp. 66–68: "If this [divine] truth were left solely as a matter of inquiry for the human reason, three awkward consequences would follow. The first is that few men would possess the knowledge of God.... The second awkward effect is that those who would come to discover the abovementioned truth would barely reach it after a great deal of time.... The third awkward effect is this. The investigation of the human reason for the most part has falsity present within it, and this is due...to the weakness of our intellect in judgment.... That is why it was necessary that the unshakable certitude and pure truth concerning divine things should be presented to men by way of faith. Beneficially, therefore, did the divine Mercy provide that it should instruct us to hold by faith even those truths that the human reason is able to investigate. In this way, all men would easily be able to have a share in the knowledge of God, and this without certainty and error." The same points are made again by Aquinas in his *Commentary on the De Trinitate of Boethius* III,1. See also *Summa theologiae* IIaIIae,2,4.

[17] *De utilitate credendi* X,24: *BA* 8,262.264: *Neque enim tibi quivis homo in rei tantae cupiditate ullo modo deserendus aut respuendus videri potest. ...Postremo quae potest esse via salubrior, quam idoneum primo fieri percipiendae veritatis, adhibendo iis fidem, quae ad praecolendum et ad praecurandum animum sunt divinitus constituta?* tr. in NPNF I:III,358.

[18] In addition, it is important to remark that Augustine does not regard faith as a species of opinion. Rather, it is midway between understanding and opinion. *De utilitate credendi* XI,25: *BA* 8,266.268.270: *Quod intelligimus igitur, debemus rationi: quod credimus, auctoritati: quod opinamur, errori.... Quae si per se ipsa considerentur, primum semper sine vitio est; secundum, aliquando cum vitio; tertium, nunquam sine vitio.... Haec dicta sunt, ut intelligeremus nos retenta fide, illarum etiam rerum quas nondum comprehendimus, a temeritate opinantium vindicari.... profecto erroris et inhumanitatis atque superbiae crimen vitabit*; tr. in NPNF I:III,359: "What then we understand, we owe to reason; what we believe, to authority; what we have an opinion on, to error." Of these three mental states, "the first is always without fault, the second sometimes with fault, the third never without fault." Understanding is faultless because it knows the truth and hence cannot be mistaken. Holding an opinion, however, is an altogether faulty credulity, because it is a pretense to knowledge —those who think that they know what they do not know. Believing, on the other hand, lies midway between understanding and opinion; for it can "escape the charge of error," or be "set free from the rashness of such as have an opinion," as when it follows the proper authority; and it can be faulty, when it collapses into mere credulity.

[19] *De utilitate credendi* XIV,31: *BA* 8,280: *Nam ergo credere ante rationem, cum percipiendae rationi non sis idoneus, et ipsa fide animum excolere excipiendis seminibus veritatis, non solum saluberrimum judico, sed tale omnino, sine quo aegris animis salus redire non possit*; tr. in NPNF I:III,362.

[20] On this, see Augustine, *De ciuitate dei* VIII,3–12: *CC* XLVII,218–29.

[21] B. B. Warfield, *Studies in Tertullian and Augustine* (New York: Oxford University Press, 1930), p. 174 for this and the following quotations. For a Catholic interpretation of Augustine similar to Warfield's, see G. van Noort, *Dogmatic Theology*, Volume II: *The Sources of Revelation, Divine Faith* (Westminster, Maryland: The Newman Press, 1961).

[22] Locke does, of course, in the end leave it to human judgment to determine whether communications which purport to be revelatory are so or not. On Locke's view, justifying revelational claims on valid grounds requires the support of reasons which are independent of the putative revelation. In this requirement we discern something of the evidentialist challenge that Locke issued to the conviction that a revelation, a communication-type revelation, has occurred. According to Locke, if one is to believe responsibly that God has revealed P, one must believe it rationally. Correspondingly, if one is to believe rationally that God has revealed P, one must believe it on the basis of good evidence. So Locke assumes that the religious believer may believe only on the basis of good arguments, and hence that unless one has good reasons for one's religious beliefs, one ought to give them up.

[23] My discussion of Reid is generously indebted to S. J. Wykstra, "Toward a Sensible Evidentialism: On the Notion of 'Needing Evidence'," in *Philosophy of Religion: Selected Readings*, ed. by W. Rowe and W. J. Wainwright (New York: Harcourt, Brace, Jovanovich, Pub., 1989). See also N. Wolterstorff, "Evidence, Entitled Belief, and the Gospels," *Faith and Philosophy* 6 (1989) 429–59.

[24] Thomas Reid, *Inquiry into the Human Mind* (Edinburgh: MacLachlan, Stewart, and Co., 1846) VI,XXIV.

[25] Augustine, *De utilitate credendi* VIII,20: *BA* 8,252: *Restabat quaerere quaenam illa esset auctoritate, cum in tantis dissensionibus se quisque illam traditurum policeretur. Occurrebat igitur inexplicabilis silva, cui demum inseri multum pigebat: atque inter haec sine ulla requie, cupiditate reperiendi veri animus agitabatur;* tr. J. H. S. Burleigh in *Augustine: Earlier Writings* (Philadelphia: Westminster, 1953), p. 307.

[26] On the Protestant side, this mistaken interpretation has been corrected by A. Vos, *Aquinas, Calvin, and Contemporary Protestant Thought: A Critique of Protestant Views on the Thought of Thomas Aquinas* (Grand Rapids, Michigan: Eerdmans, 1985); see also N. Wolterstorff, "The Migration of the Theistic Arguments: From Natural Theology to Evidentialist Apologetics," in *Rationality, Religious Belief, and Moral Commitment*, ed. by R. Audi and W. J. Wainwright (Ithaca: Cornell University Press, 1986), pp. 38–81. On the Catholic side, see R. McInerny, *St. Thomas Aquinas* (Notre Dame: University of Notre Dame Press, 1977).

[27] Augustine says as much in his *De praedestinatione sanctorum* II,5: *BA* 24,472–74: *Nullus quippe credit aliquid, nisi prius cogitaverit esse credendum…. Non enim omnis qui cogitat, credit, cum ideo cogitent plerique, ne credant; sed cogitat omnis qui credit, et credendo cogitat, et cogitanto credit. Quod ergo pertinet ad religionem atque pietatem (de qua loquebatur Apostolus), si non samus idonei cogitare aliquid quasi ex nobismetipsis, sed sufficientia nostra ex Deo est; profecto non sumus idonei credere aliquid quasi ex nobismetipsis, quod sine cogitatione non possumus, sed sufficientia nostra qua credere incipiamus, ex Deo est;* tr. in

Mourant, *Saint Augustine: Selected Readings*, p. 44: "No one believes anything unless he has first thought that it is to be believed.... [I]t is not everyone who thinks that believes, since many think in order that they may not believe; but everybody who believes, thinks—both thinks in believing and believes in thinking. Therefore in what pertains to religion and piety if we are not capable of thinking anything as of ourselves, but our sufficiency is of God, we are certainly not capable of believing anything of ourselves, since we cannot do this without thinking; but our sufficiency, by which we begin to believe, is of God."

[28] Augustine, *Sermo XLIII* 1: *PL* XXXII,254: *Est autem fides, credere quod nondum vides: cujus fidei merces est, videre quod credis*; tr. in Mourant, *Saint Augustine: Selected Readings*, p. 39.

[29] Augustine puts it this way in *De utilitate credendi* XVI,34: *BA* 8,290–92: *Sed id nunc agitur, ut sapientes esse possimus, id est, inhaerere veritati: quod profecto sordidus animus non potest. Sunt autem sordes animi, ut brevi explicem, amor quarumlibet rerum, praeter animum et Deum: a quibus sordibus quanto est quis purgatior, tanto verum facilius intuetur. Verum igitur videre velle, ut animum purges, cum ideo purgetur ut videas, perversum certe atque praeposterum est. Homini ergo non valenti verum intueri, ut ad id fiat idoneus, purgarique se sinat, auctoritas praesto est*; tr. in NPNF I:III,364: "This is now the business in hand, that we may be able to be wise, that is, to cleave to the truth; which the filthy soul is utterly unable to do; but the filth of the soul, to say shortly what I mean, is the love of any things whatsoever save God and the soul: from which filth the more any one is cleansed, the more easily he sees the truth. Therefore to wish to see the truth, in order to purge your soul, when it is purged for the very purpose that you may see, is surely perverse and preposterous. Therefore to man unable to see the truth, authority is at hand, in order that he may be fitted for it, and may allow himself to be cleansed."

Faith Seeks Understanding:
Augustine's Alternative to Natural Theology*

Dewey J. Hoitenga, Jr.

Can we know God in this life? That is, can we know that he exists and something of what he is, given the conditions and limitations of our finite and morally corrupted existence? Augustine's answer to these questions is, Yes; but he develops this answer along two quite different lines. One line, found in *On Free Will*, is that of inference and proof. The other line, found in the *Soliloquies, Confessions*, and elsewhere, is that of vision. I take "vision" to be Augustine's characteristic term for knowledge by acquaintance or experience, although John Burnaby is certainly correct when he observes that "for this profoundly personal apprehension of God, the term 'vision' is indeed inadequate."[1] In this paper I argue that the way of vision, thus understood, not the way of proof, offers the more authentic interpretation of the formula associated with Augustine's name, faith seeks to understand.

Advocates of natural theology, in contrast, have typically taken the formula to warrant an inferential approach to God. Recently, for example, Norman Kretzmann takes the formula as the charter for Christian philosophy, which he defines as not only clarifying Christian beliefs by analysis but also supporting them by argument.[2] For paradigms of Christian philosophy so defined he recommends Aquinas's two *Summae* and Augustine's *On Free Will*. In the latter he singles out from Book II Augustine's proof for the existence of God from the existence of truth.[3]

As I have shown elsewhere, major objections can be brought against taking Augustine's proof as a plausible paradigm of faith seeking understanding.[4] First, the faith that God exists, which is essential to the formula, is not essential for the soundness of a proof; what is essential is acceptance of its premises. If faith were essential for the proof, moreover, it would imply, mistakenly, that only Christians, because they alone have faith, are capable of proving the existence of God. Second, the duty of faith to seek understanding that Augustine sees entailed by the formula, if applied to the way of proof, would imply the false conclusion that every Christian is obliged by his faith to be a natural theologian. Third, the condition of moral purity which Augustine builds into the formula implies the wrong prerequisite for constructing or following a proof. Fourth, the continuity Augustine suggests between the understanding that faith finds in this life and the beatific vision in the next suggests the dubious consequence that non-Christian natural theologians, too, can by their natural theology enjoy a taste of the vision promised only to those who are pure in heart. To these objections may be added the disappointment that Augustine himself expresses after reaching the conclusion of his proof. He discovers that he has attained only a "tenuous form of knowledge," which is not the wisdom faith seeks when it seeks understanding.[5]

Augustine's doctrines of divine illumination and of the divine teacher suggest his more characteristic concept of the knowledge of God. These doctrines lead us away from proof towards vision as identifying the kind of understanding which faith seeks. Augustine best exhibits this interpretation of the formula in the comparatively early *Soliloquies* (386–87) and in his great religious autobiography, the *Confessions* (397–400). In the former, Augustine speaks with himself; in the latter, with God. In the former he anticipates descriptively what he personally embodies in the latter, for in the *Confessions* he shows by his own example what he thinks it is to know God. To know God is to acknowledge him with praise, confession, and contemplation and to recognize his presence in one's mind and his providence in one's life. I shall focus here mainly on the *Soliloquies*, however, since it has been overlooked as a key to Augustine's view of the knowledge of God.

The *Soliloquies* contains Augustine's first extended discussion of faith and reason following his conversion. In his *Retractations*, he describes his motive in writing this dialogue. It was "zeal and love for searching out, by reason, the truth concerning those matters which I especially desired to know,...questioning myself and answering myself as if we were two—reason and I—although I was alone."[6] And what are "those matters" which Augustine especially wants to know? Two, as he says in his famous answer, early in the *Soliloquies*: "I desire to know God and the soul."[7] Notice that Augustine says he wants to search out these matters by reason. He does not say "by faith." He was, of course, already a believer. Why, then, does he not say he will search out these matters by faith? Because he wants to see, to know, to understand, and these are not the function of faith. The functions of faith, for Augustine, are to believe and to trust, that is, to believe the testimony of an authority that it trusts. By contrast, it is the function of reason to see, to know, to understand. If there is something to see in the incorporeal world, it is for reason to see it—not the senses, not faith—even though, of course, these, too, depend in their own way upon reason to formulate the propositions that represent what is seen by the senses or what is believed by faith.

Incidentally, the project of sorting out these various functions of faith, the senses, and reason's involvement in them is for reason itself to undertake, not for the senses or faith. What knowing and believing are, what are their objects, and what are the faculties with which we do these things is an inquiry of reason. Augustine's name for this inquiry is "dialectics," which includes much of modern logic and epistemology. In *Divine Providence and the Problem of Evil*, he defines it as follows: "This science teaches both how to teach and how to learn. In it, reason itself exhibits itself, and reveals its own nature, its desires, its powers. It knows what knowledge is; by itself, it not only wishes to make men learned, but also can make them so."[8] Reason alone can discover the truth about such matters, because they, like numbers and justice, are not corporeal but incorporeal things. The *Soliloquies*, then, nicely exhibits what Augustine elsewhere in *Divine Providence* calls the priority of reason "in the order of reality," in virtue of which it "is more highly prized as an object of desire."[9] Nowhere does Augustine engage in a similar dialogue with faith!

What does it mean to know God? This question is center stage throughout Book I of the *Soliloquies*. Augustine must begin, says Reason, by searching for God. Augustine already is a believer, of course; he begins his dialogue with an extended prayer to God, at the behest of Reason. Actually, then, his faith, insofar as it manifests itself in prayer, is still his starting point. If reason is prior in the order of reality, faith is still first in the order of time.[10] Still, in order to know God, he must search, and that involves the use of reason. His faith seeks understanding, which reason alone can give. About ten years later, Augustine begins his *Confessions* in the same way, by praying to God, asking whether he should call on God in order to know him, or know him in order to call upon him. Scripture answers: he must call on God in order to know him; but to call on God, he must first believe.[11] Faith (i.e., trust in what Scripture says) is thus the first step, understanding the reward.

Thus far, the *Soliloquies* and the *Confessions* parallel *On Free Will* exactly; the great difference is that Reason says nothing in the *Soliloquies*, nor does Augustine writing in his own voice in the *Confessions*, about reaching that understanding by inference or proof. It is important to be clear on this, for at one point in the *Soliloquies* Reason asks, "But first explain how, if God is demonstrated to you, you will be able to say that it is enough."[12] The term "demonstrate" (*demonstrare*) might suggest that Reason will try to prove to Augustine that God exists. It is the same term he uses to describe his proof in

On Free Will (II,ii,6). In the *Soliloquies*, however, Reason is not offering to prove the existence of God (no proof is given), but to show God to Augustine in a way which assumes that Augustine already knows that he exists. As John Burnaby says, "The aim is not to demonstrate theological propositions, but to show God, to bring Him into the heart so that he may be felt."[13] The existence of God is not the issue at all, but knowing God definitely is. What, then, is the difference? How can Reason not need to prove the existence of God, and yet desire to know him?

The answer to the first part of this twofold question is: Reason does not need to prove that God exists because it already knows that God exists, which it does by having directly seen him with its "interior eye." That is why reason "pledges to make God known to your mind just as the sun is shown to the eyes."[14] In this analogy,

> the senses of the soul are, as it were, the mind's own eyes.... I—Reason—am in minds as the act of looking is in the eyes. To have eyes is not the same as to look, and to look is not the same as to see. Therefore the soul needs three distinct things: that it have eyes which it can properly use, that it look, and that it see.[15]

Thus knowing God is not the result of reasoning—the discursive activity associated with inference, demonstration, and proof. Rather it is a matter of directly seeing him with the mind—reason in its intuitive sense. The import of the analogy between God and the sun can be elaborated in three points: first, that knowing God is to see him, just as knowing the sun is to see it; second, that having seen God is to have no need to prove his existence, just as having seen the sun is to have no need to prove its existence; and third, that just as no one first comes to know the sun by proof, so no one first comes to know God by proof. This third point is the most important one. The ability to see is the original and sufficient way to know not only that there is a world of physical objects but also that there is a world of incorporeal objects, the highest one of which is God.

The answer to the second part of the question removes a paradox. How can Reason still desire to know what it already knows because it sees it? To explain this, Reason draws a second analogy, one from the knowledge we have of our friends. Would it satisfy Augustine, Reason asks, if he could "know God just as you know Alypius"?[16] Augustine replies that he would be grateful for such knowledge, but that it would not be enough. It would not be enough, "Because I do not even know God as I do Alypius, and yet I do not know Alypius enough."[17] This analogy holds the key to the deepest sense of what it means to desire the knowledge of God. Again, as with the sun, it is not a knowledge which proves existence. For once we have come to know our friends, their existence is not even in question (nor was it, really, when we first came to know them). What we still want to know, when we already know our friends, is to know them better.

Here, then, is a kind of knowing which we can seek even though we already have it. This is not so paradoxical as it may sound. The point is that this kind of knowing, unlike knowing that something exists, is one that comes in degrees. Unless we already know our friend, however slightly, we cannot even desire to know him better. Indeed, we only want to know him better because, as Augustine brings out, we love him. And we love him because we have found him, and his friendship, to be something good. But, as Augustine discusses at length in *On the Trinity*: "no one can love at all a thing of which he is wholly ignorant."[18] We are not wholly ignorant of our friend, not because we proved his existence after having believed he exists on the testimony of others, but because we have seen him and made his acquaintance. Having thus known him and found his friendship good, we are also made happy. Our happiness consists not only in knowing him but also in coming to know him better. And we are able to know him better because of the depth in the reality of a human being; there is always more to our friend than we already know. There is infinitely more to God, of course, than we already know.

The combined implications of these two analogies for what it means to know God are evident. First, the knowledge of God is by an intellectual vision, which is analogous to the corporeal vision by which we know that there is a sun. We also know by corporeal vision a little of what the sun is, for example, that it is the brightest object in the sky. So, we can know by an intellectual vision not only that God exists, but a little of what he is, for example, that he is the brightest object in the world of incorporeal things. Second, the intellectual vision of God is also like that vision by which we know our friends. Just as the more we know them, the more we want to know them because we love them, so the more we know God, the more we want to know him because knowing him is good and gives us joy.

It is true, of course, that the knowledge we have of God in this life is only a partial knowledge of him, just as the knowledge we have of the sun or of our friends is never exhaustive or complete. And, of course, we cannot

know or see very much of the goodness of God without also believing what he
has revealed himself to be and to have done for us in the incarnation of his
son, Jesus Christ. Thus the believer's total knowledge of God will be a fusion
of what his Reason sees by the natural divine light and what he believes (and
begins to understand) on the divine testimony in his revelation. Faith and
reason, for Augustine, form an organic epistemic whole.

Here is the deepest meaning of the Augustinian formula, faith seeking
to understand. Faith, by which Christians trust God and therefore believe
many things about him which he reveals to them, seeks to know him better in
those things which reason already sees for itself and to know him for the first
time in those other things which reason does not yet see for itself. Thus, too,
it becomes evident what Augustine means when he says that Christian believers can never, for all their beginning to know God in this life, leave their faith
behind. They must always trust the God they have come to see and know, for
much of what he says about himself they can only believe, since they do not as
yet see and know it, or at least do not as yet see and know it very clearly, even
though they are acquainted with him. Augustine puts the point nicely in *On
the Trinity* as he struggles to know God as three persons in one being: "Let us
therefore so seek as if we should find, and so find as if we were about to
seek."[19]

Reason is limited in two important ways, by its finitude and by the effects of sin. Reason can have only a dim, partial knowledge of God in this life
because of God's overwhelming radiance. "For the light is God himself,
whereas the soul is a creature; yet, since it is rational and intellectual, it is
made in his image. And when it tries to behold the Light, it trembles in its
weakness and finds itself unable to do so."[20] Augustine's language is reminiscent of Plato, who shrinks from defining the Good (*Republic* 505–6), and of
Plotinus, who hesitates to name the One (*Ennead* VI,9,1). The Platonic response to transcendence is not alien to Augustine's Christian sensibility, for
Scripture, too, declares that God "alone has immortality and dwells in unap-
proachable light, whom no man has ever seen or can see" (1 Tm 6:16 RSV;
see also Ps 36:9; 43:3; Jn 1:4). No wonder Augustine exclaims at the outset of
his *Confessions*: "What does any man say when he speaks of you? Yet woe to
those who keep silent concerning you, since even those who speak much are as
the dumb."[21]

But reason is weak also because it has been vitiated by sin. What reason
most needs for its knowledge of God is the purging of a rebellious will which
has turned it away from loving God to loving the lower goods of his creation.

And it is just at this point that faith is necessary for the healing which reason needs. Augustine distinguishes that faith from all other faith. The faith that heals is, of course, the Christian faith. Like all faith, it requires trust; but the object of its trust is the God who reveals himself in the Bible and in Jesus Christ. The faith which so trusts and so believes purifies reason for its seeing God: "The mind is like healthy eyes when it is cleansed of every taint of the body, that is, detached and purged of the desires of earthly things—which cleansing it obtains, at first, only by Faith."[22] In short, Christian faith is divine faith, dramatically different from everyday human faith. It is a virtue, with God as its special object of trust and the moral purification of the soul by God as its special consequence. When such faith seeks understanding, we see Augustine's formula at work in its most important sense—faith seeking true wisdom, the pious knowledge of God. No wonder, then, that Augustine at one point classifies the belief that has "divine matters" as its object in a division by itself.[23]

Augustine's emphasis upon reason suggests his deep concern with the intellectual (propositional) aspect of faith—what it is we are to believe. We see now, however, that when faith is divine faith, its intellectual aspect is embedded in a moral framework that includes trust in God himself. Trust, in turn, involves the will. Accordingly, Reason's final admonition, at the close of Book I of the *Soliloquies*, sounds like a Scriptural command from God himself, requiring this element of trust:

> Believe steadfastly in God and, as far as you can, entrust
> yourself wholly to Him. Do not choose to be, so to speak,
> your own master and under your own dominion, but proclaim
> yourself the servant of him who is our kindest and most help-
> ful Lord. For, if you do this, he will not cease to lift you up
> to himself, and He will allow nothing to happen to you which
> is not for your good, even though you do not know it.[24]

Augustine's response to the admonition reflects the full complexity of Biblical faith. Such faith includes not only belief and trust but also obedience: "I hear, I believe, and, as far as I am able, I obey; I pray very much to God Himself in order that I may accomplish much."[25]

Augustine writes here as a new convert, at the threshold of a Christian life of faith seeking understanding. There is no suggestion yet that such understanding consists in finding a proof for the existence of a God in whom

Augustine believes on the testimony of others. Instead, Augustine has set himself to see God—whom he already sees—more clearly and deeply in a continuing life of faith, confession, love, obedience, and prayer. Of course, he has heard about God in the testimony of the Church and of Scripture, but now he has also begun to see God, that is, to know and experience God for himself. His faith not only seeks, it also has begun to find what it seeks, in a vision of heart and mind.

Notes

*This paper is reprinted (with editorial modifications) from D. Hoitenga, Jr., *Faith and Reason from Plato to Plantinga: An Introduction to Reformed Epistemology* (Albany: State University of New York Press, 1991), pp. 85, 98–105, 120, by permission of the publisher.

[1] J. Burnaby, *Amor Dei* (London: Hodder and Stoughton, 1968), p. 156.

[2] N. Kretzmann, "Faith Seeks, Understanding Finds: Augustine's Charter for Christian Philosophy," in *Christian Philosophy*, ed. T. Flint (Notre Dame: University of Notre Dame Press, 1990), p. 1.

[3] N. Kretzmann, pp. 1, 8–18.

[4] D. Hoitenga, Jr., *Faith and Reason from Plato to Plantinga: An Introduction to Reformed Epistemology* (Albany: State University of New York Press, 1991), ch. 4.

[5] *De libero arbitrio* II,xv,39–40: *CC* XXIX,264: *A. Quod jam non solum indubitatum, quantum arbitror, fide retinemus, sed etiam certa, quamuis adhuc tenuissima, forma cognitionis attingimus....*
    A. Sed, quaeso te, numquid iam sapientes et beati sumus? an adhuc eo tendimus, ut id nobis esse proueniat? E. Ego nos potius tendere existimo; tr. J. H. S. Burleigh, *Augustine: Earlier Writings* (Philadelphia: Westminster Press, 1953).

[6] *Retractationes* I,iv,1: *BA* 12,288: *Inter haec scripsi etiam duo volumina secundum studium meum et amorem, ratione indagandae veritatis de his rebus, quas maxime scire cupiebam, me interrogans mihique respondens, tanquam duo essemus, ratio et ego, cum solus essem*; tr. M. I. Bogan, *Retractations, FC* 60.

[7] *Soliloquia* I,ii,7: *CSEL* LXXXIX,11: *A. Deum et animam scire cupio*; tr. T. F. Gilligan, *Soliloquies, FC* 1.

[8] *De ordine* II,xiii,38: *CC* XXIX,128: *Haec docet docere, haec docet discere; in hac se ipsa ratio demonstrat atque aperit, quae sit, quid uelit, quid ualeat. Scit scire, sola scientes facere non solum uult, sed etiam potest*; tr. R. P. Russell, *Divine Providence and the Problem of Evil, FC* 1.

[9] *De ordine* II,ix,26: *CC* XXIX,122: *Tempore auctoritas, re autem ratio prior est. Aliud est enim, quod in agendo anteponitur, aliud, quod pluris in appetendo aestimatur.*

[10] Ibid.

[11] *Confessiones* I,i,1: *CC* XXVII,1: *Da mihi, Domine, scire et intelligere utrum, …scire te prius sit an inuocare te…. Quaeram te, domine, inuocans te et inuocem te credens in te: praedicatus enim es nobis.*

[12] *Soliloquia* I,ii,7: *CSEL* LXXXIX,11: *R. Sed prius explica, quomodo, tibi si demonstretur deus, possis dicere: 'Sat est.'*

[13] J. Burnaby, p. 65.

[14] *Soliloquia* I,vi,12: *CSEL* LXXXIX,19: *R. Promittit enim Ratio, quae tecum loquitur, ita se demonstraturam deum tuae menti, ut oculis sol demonstratur.*

[15] *Soliloquia* I,vi,12: *CSEL* LXXXIX,19–20: *R. Nam mentes quasi sui sunt sensus animae…. Ego autem Ratio ita sum in mentibus, ut in oculis est aspectus. Non enim hoc est habere oculos quod aspicere aut item hoc est aspicere quod videre. Ergo animae tribus quibusdam rebus opus est: ut oculos habaeat, quibus iam bene uti possit, ut aspiciat, ut videat.*

[16] *Soliloquia* I,iii,8: *CSEL* LXXXIX,13: *R. Sed tamen si quis tibi diceret: 'faciam te sic deum nosse, quomodo nosti Alypium,' nonne ageres gratias et diceres: 'Satis est'?*

[17] *Soliloquia* I,iii,8: *CSEL* LXXXIX,13: *A. Quia deum ne sic quidem novi quomodo Alypium, et tamen Alypium non satis novi.*

[18] *De trinitate* X,i,1: *CC* L,311: *Rem prorsus ignotam amare omnino nullus potest*; tr. A. W. Haddan, rev. W. G. T. Shedd, in *NPNF* I:III.

[19] *De trinitate* IX,i,1: *CC* L,293: *Sic ergo quaeramus tanquam inuenturi, et sic inueniamus tamquam quaesituri.*

[20] *De Genesi ad litteram* XII,xxxi,59: *BA* 49,436: *Nam illud [ipsum lumen] iam ipse Deus est, haec [anima] autem creatura, quamuis rationalis et intellectualis ad eius imaginem facta, quae cum conatur lumen illud intueri palpitat infirmitate, et minus ualet*; tr. J. H. Taylor, in *The Essential Augustine*, ed. V. Bourke (Indianapolis: Hackett, 1974).

[21] *Confessiones* I,iv,4: *CC* XXVII,3: *Quid dicit aliquis, cum de te dicit? et vae tacentibus de te, quoniam loquaces muti sunt*; tr. J. K. Ryan, *The Confessions of St. Augustine* (Garden City: Doubleday, 1960).

[22] *Soliloquia* I,vi,12: *CSEL* LXXXIX,20: *Oculi sani mens est ab omni labe corporis pura, id est a cupiditatibus rerum mortalium iam remota atque purgata. Quod ei nihil aliud praestat quam fides primo.*

[23] *De diuersis quaestionibus LXXXIII* XLVIII: *CC* XLIV/A,75: *Credibilium tria sunt genera…tertium quae primo creduntur et postea intelliguntur, qualia sunt ea quae de diuinis rebus non possunt intelligi nisi ab his qui mundo sunt corde, quod fit praeceptis seruatis, quae de bene uiuendo accipiuntur.*

[24] *Soliloquia* I,xv,30: *CSEL* LXXXIX,44: *R. Constanter deo crede eique te totum committe quantum potes. Noli esse velle quasi proprius et in tua potestate, sed eius clementissimi et utilissimi domini te servum esse profitere. Ita enim te ad se sublevare non desinet nihilque tibi evenire permittet, nisi quod tibi prosit, etiam si nescias.*

[25] *Soliloquia* I,xv,30: *CSEL* LXXXIX,44: *A. Audio, credo et quantum possum obtempero plurimumque ipsum deprecor, ut plurimum possim . . . .*

Augustine on Language and the Nature of Belief

Kevin M. Staley

In this paper, I will examine the relationship between faith and reason from the standpoint of Augustine's philosophy of language. I would like to show how Augustine's account of language and, more specifically, his explanation of the meaningfulness of language dramatically influenced his understanding of the necessity and nature of faith in his earlier writings and led to a fundamental ambiguity in his middle-to-late work, *De trinitate*. I suspect that this ambiguity remains with Augustine for the rest of his career and that a study of his latest works will confirm this suspicion. A detailed investigation of his latest works, however, lies beyond this study.

Augustine's account of the meaningfulness of language can be found scattered throughout his writings, but is present in its most concentrated form in the *De magistro*, written about 389. To summarize briefly Augustine's position, there are three things necessary for meaningful language: verbal tokens or signs, things, and cognitions of the things to which the signs refer. The meaningfulness of verbal tokens is dependent upon and is a function of the cognition of the thing to which the sign refers. The term "cat," for example, is meaningful because it calls to mind from memory one's cognition of what it is to be a cat. Without this prior, non-verbal cognition of things, words are no more than noise.

From this principle, Augustine draws the rather paradoxical conclusion that a teacher can teach us nothing with words. For if his words are meaningful, then we must already know the things to which they refer. So the teacher is useless. If, on the other hand, we have no cognition of the things to which his discourse refers, then his words will be meaningless and in vain. This is not to say that teaching is impossible; it says only that teaching is not to be found in verbal interchange, rather: "He alone teaches me anything who sets before my eyes, or one of my other bodily senses, or my mind the things [themselves] which I desire to know."[1]

In the *De magistro*, Augustine uses this account of meaning, and its implications for the nature of teaching, to argue for the doctrine of illumination. We can easily account for the meanings of terms which refer to sensible things, for we perceive them with our senses. Terms such as "justice," "eternity," and "goodness," on the other hand, do not refer to something known through sense or imagination. The cognition of the things to which they refer must therefore be referred to the teacher of the inner man, Christ, the light which illumines all human persons.

In 392, three years later, we can see Augustine using the conclusions of the *De magistro* in the *De utilitate credendi* in order to refute an error of the Manichees on the matter of the relationship between faith and reason. The Manichees promised that "they would put aside all overarching authority [faith], and by pure and simple reason would bring to God those who were willing to listen to them."[2] Augustine intends to demonstrate that faith, belief in things that are not seen, is an inescapable fact of human life by pointing out the sorts of things which must be believed, since they can never be understood. Our "knowledge" of history, for example, necessarily requires belief. Augustine remarks, "I believe that the most wicked conspirators once put to death the virtuous Cicero. Not only do I not know that, but I am quite certain that I cannot possibly know it."[3] Moreover, the love which children ought to show their parents depends on belief, for one can never know who one's parents really are: "who the father is is believed on the authority of the mother, and as to the mother, midwives, nurses, and slaves have to be believed...."[4] Finally, even the Manichees deign to teach only those whom they deem to be sincere of heart. But should you desire their instruction, "you will say that your conscience is clear, that you are void of deceit. You will assert this with all the words you are master of, which are, however, only words. For you cannot lay bear the lurking places of your mind, that you may be intimately known as man to man."[5]

The examples which Augustine uses have two things in common: they point to things or events which are inaccessible either to the senses or to the illumined intelligence. And, because they cannot be presented to the senses or intelligence, they cannot strictly speaking be known or understood. They must be believed on the authority of those who see or have seen them. These examples of belief are not, of course, examples of faith or religious belief; but Augustine uses them in order to isolate the characteristic marks of religious belief. First, the object of religious belief is inaccessible to one's intellect or sense. Secondly, it is embraced solely on the authority of one to whom it was or is accessible. Given these characteristics of belief, faith comes to be associated principally with matters historical—at least in Augustine's earlier writings.

In the *De uera religione*, for example, written between the *De magistro* and the *De utilitate credendi* (391), Augustine repeatedly defines religious faith in terms of the historical: "In following religion, our chief concern is with the prophetic history of the dispensation of divine providence in time."[6] And again, "...God, in his ineffable mercy, by a temporal dispensation has used the mutable creation.... to remind the soul of its original and perfect nature, and so has come to the aid of individual men and indeed of the whole human race. That is the Christian religion of our times."[7] Miracles become the paradigmatic objects of religious belief. Miracles are certain historical events demonstrating the power or mercy of God. As historical events they are in principle inaccessible to later generations of Christians. As witnessed by the authors of Scripture, they are presented for belief solely on the authority of those authors.

Augustine finds it especially fitting that faith should be proposed first to those disposed to search for God, and this for two reasons. First, belief in matters temporal is especially fitted to our sinful state. We are sinful because we have too great a love for matters temporal. Thus, Augustine notes, "because we dwell among temporal things, and love of them is an obstacle to our reaching eternal things, a kind of temporal medicine, calling not to those who know, but those who believe back to health, has priority by the order, not of nature or its inherent excellence, but of time."[8] Secondly, to submit to the rightful authority of another is in itself an act of obedience and constitutes principally a moral rather than an intellectual perfection. But man's sinful condition requires just such a moral conversion before it can be illumined so as to see matters both eternal and divine. Faith, precisely because it demands humble obedience, purifies the soul. And this is to say, the principal function of faith for the early Augustine seems to be more purgative than informative.

In the *De utilitate credendi*, for example, Augustine notes that the authority of faith "has two ways of appealing to us, partly by miracles and partly by the multitude who accept it. Neither of these is necessary for the wise man. No one denies that...[but].... For the man who is not able to behold the truth, in order that he may become able and allow himself to be purified, authority is available."[9] In his treatise of 393, *Faith and the Creed*, Augustine again emphasizes the themes of obedience, submission, and purification when treating of the matter of faith: "This is the faith which is handed over to young Christians, expressed in a few words, which they are to hold faithfully. These few words are made known to believers, that, believing, they may subject themselves to God, being so subject they may live righteous lives, living righteously they may cleanse their hearts, and with a pure heart may know what they believe."[10]

Authority is not necessary for the wise, for wisdom regards things eternal, things which are immediately accessible in the light of divine illumination. But the problem which faith addresses is how one is to become wise. To the extent that the mind is clouded by sin, purification is required so that we might see what is in itself otherwise accessible to the intellect. Faith functions as this purgative medicine. There is little hint, at least at this stage in Augustine's thought, that faith might also be required to inform us of matters concerning what is eternal and divine, that what is eternal and divine might so transcend our intellects that we require not only purification but information about so exalted an object.

The ultimate error of the philosophers, as Augustine sees it, is not that they strove to attain too exalted an object for the human intellect—nor even that they strove after this object with reason alone. As the divine is eternal and immutable, reason or intellect is the only faculty with which it can be perceived. The error of the philosophers lies in the fact that they "promise themselves cleansing by their own righteousness for this reason, because some of them have been able to penetrate with the eye of the mind beyond the whole creature, and to touch, though it be in ever so small a part, the light of the unchangeable truth."[11] Their error is one of pride; they deem themselves capable of raising themselves to the divine in spite of their fallen condition, and so fall from what little wisdom they manage to attain: "Since, knowing God through those things which are made, they have not glorified Him as God, neither were thankful; but professing themselves to be wise, they became fools."[12]

So far, then, we might characterize faith as a submission of one's will to due authority in regards to the truth of statements, the referents of which are historical in nature. Faith is required for the sake of purification; and purification is required so that the soul might be further enlightened concerning matters divine and eternal. So formulated, however, Augustine's definition of faith is problematic, and it is so from the very same perspective which leads him to this formulation—namely, his philosophy of language. For if the meaningfulness of any statement depends upon the cognition of the things to which its terms refer, and statements of faith refer to historical events which cannot be known by the present generations of Christians, then does it not follow that statements of faith are ultimately meaningless?

This problem occupies Augustine's attention most explicitly in the eighth book of the *De trinitate* (399/419). His solution is fairly straightforward: "It must needs be, that, when by reading or hearing of them, we believe in any corporeal things which we have not seen, the mind frames for itself something under bodily features or forms, just as it may occur to our thoughts."[13] Thus, when we read that God was made man, for example, we frame some image of a man gathered from experience and utilize "a notion of human nature implanted in us, as it were by a rule."[14] There are many things which we do not know about the things which we believe: the countenance of the Virgin, the body of Lazarus, the town of Bethany, the very stone Christ commanded to be rolled from the tomb, Christ's own tomb, or the Mount of Olives. Nevertheless, "we believe those things most steadfastly, because we imagine them according to a special and general notion, of which we are certain."[15] For example, "we believe that Christ was born of a virgin who was called Mary." Now we certainly know what a virgin is, what it is to be born, and what a proper name is. As to Mary's countenance, "we neither know at all, nor believe."[16] That is, we can say that Mary was perhaps of dark hair without violating the faith; but we could not say that Christ perhaps was born of a virgin.

Faith thus appears to be constituted by the following: 1) notions or rules, either gathered from experience or implanted by nature or illumination, which give meaning to the terms used in the propositions which express matters of faith; 2) incidental conceptions or images which accompany our consideration of things of the faith, but are not matters of faith (Mary's dark hair); 3) a core historical event, essential to the faith which is not accessible in the notions or rules, nor which is incidental (Christ's actually having been born of a virgin). Let us call these elements the notional, the incidental, and the factual elements of a belief.

Essential to the faith are the notional and factual elements. The incidental element accompanies our understanding of faith, but is not of the faith. But of the two essential elements, it is the factual which is most proper to the faith, for the notional elements are available to the enlightened or experienced mind. It is belief in the factual which sets the Christian apart. It is belief in the factual which takes the form of a proposition which is either true or false. The notional element is required only so that the proposition asserting the reality of the factual element might be a meaningful one.

Thus, in the case of Christ's raising Lazarus from the dead, the incidental elements would include what Lazarus looked like, the shape of the rock Christ had rolled from the tomb, etc. The notional elements include what power is, what death is, what life is, what returning from death to life is, what omnipotence is, etc. The factual core is that Lazarus was really dead, that Christ really raised him from the dead, and that Lazarus really lived after having been dead.

Note that on this account, faith itself requires some prior understanding of matters both sensible and temporal (what a tomb is, what death is) and intelligible and eternal (what omnipotence is, what mercy is). For this reason, Augustine argues that faith constitutes a kind of knowledge, but he denies that it is a wisdom. Wisdom, for Augustine, regards only matters eternal. Knowledge represents the application of eternal truths to the judgment of sensible, temporal things. Because matters of faith are temporal, historical events to which we only apply concepts known through illumination, faith cannot be a wisdom. Thus, Augustine remarks: "And all these things which the Word made flesh did and bore for us in time and place, belong, according to the distinction which we have undertaken to demonstrate, to knowledge, not to wisdom. And as the Word is without time and place, it is co-eternal with the Father, and in its wholeness everywhere; and if anyone can, and as much as he can, speak truly concerning this Word, then his discourse will pertain to Wisdom."[17]

Augustine can give a fairly convincing account, then, of just how it is that statements of the faith can be meaningful, but not without introducing a serious ambiguity in the heart of his account of the nature of faith. For one might ask Augustine whether statements about the Trinity, for example, are matters of faith and knowledge or matters belonging to wisdom. Statements about the Trinity, it seems, cannot be matters of faith and knowledge, for they do not have as their referent any temporal/historical fact. As the Trinity is both eternal and immutable, statements of the Trinity belong, if anywhere, to wisdom. Moreover, even if it remains the case that we believe that God is triune and cannot see that God is triune, how can such statements about the Trinity be meaningful if we do not see or know the thing to which they refer? It seems, then, that statements about the Trinity are either not matters of faith, or, if they are, they must be meaningless.

In solving this dilemma, Augustine turns our attention to the nature of love: "No other thing, then, is chiefly to be regarded in this inquiry, which we make concerning the Trinity, and concerning knowing God, except what is true love."[18]

He asks his reader first to consider the love which we bear for St. Paul. As we have seen above, "no one loves what he believes and does not see, except by some rule of a general or special notion."[19] Augustine denies that the general notion operative in this case is that of what it is to be a man, for we love Paul even now, though we consider him to have passed away as a man. What we love of Paul is his righteous mind. There are operative in our love two general notions under the aspects of which we love Paul, namely the notions of mind and righteousness. What it is to be a mind we gather from within ourselves. What is most remarkable, however, is that we have also a notion of righteousness, though we ourselves fail to be righteous. Our knowledge of righteousness is the work of illumination. Since whenever we love something rightly we love it because of righteousness, Augustine concludes that before all else we love the form of righteousness itself. Unlike the love of Paul, which is mediated, our love of righteousness is unmediated: "For we do not find any other such thing besides itself, so that by believing we might love it [righteousness] when it is unknown.... For whatsoever of such a kind one may have seen, is itself; and there is not any other such thing, since itself alone is such as itself is."[20]

According to Augustine, he who loves his brother "knows the love with which he loves, more than the brother whom he loves." He concludes, "so now he can know God more than he knows his brother: clearly known more, because more present; known more because more certain." Thus, Augustine ends with this exhortation: "Embrace the love of God, and by love embrace God."[21]

Augustine's strategy is fairly apparent here. By utilizing the example of the love of Paul's righteous mind, whom we presently love because we hold him presently to exist, Augustine eliminates just that historical element proper to belief in such matters as the resurrection of Christ. We are here wholly within the interior and notional realm. Of course, even presently loving the Apostle Paul involves some element of belief; for that we should love some present mind precisely as St. Paul's requires that we believe what we read of the historical Paul in Scripture. But Augustine's point in the above is that our love of righteousness lacks even this reference to the historical past. The love of Paul is mediated; our love of righteousness is unmediated and directly present to the mind. It is here, in our love of righteousness, that we are to look for that cognition which will render our speech about the Trinity meaningful.

Augustine's confidence in this regard is nowhere greater than at the end of the eighth book of the *De trinitate*. He states: "Well, but you will say, I see love, and as far as I am able, I gaze upon it with my mind, and I believe the Scripture saying that 'God is love; and he that dwelleth in love dwelleth in

God;' but when I see love, I do not see in it the Trinity." Augustine's response is critical: "Nay, thou dost see the Trinity if thou seest love. But if I can, I will put you in mind, that thou mayest see that thou seest it."[22]

If, indeed, we can see the Trinity, and faith pertains to those things which cannot be seen, then this passage bears out our original judgment: given Augustine's account of faith thus far, the doctrine of the Trinity seems to belong to the domain of wisdom rather than to that of faith and knowledge. Moreover, because this wisdom presupposes true love of righteousness, one can understand why such wisdom requires the purgative effects of faith as a condition for its possibility, without requiring faith to provide additional information about that which is seen and which could not be known otherwise.

In the succeeding books of the *De trinitate*, Augustine sets for himself the task of elucidating and elaborating this embryonic vision of the Trinity. In the final book of the *De trinitate*, however, Augustine's earlier confidence that he would be able to lead his reader to see that he really sees the Trinity is replaced with resignation that all of his endeavors have shown but an image of the Trinity, and a poor one at that. He points out that the Apostle says that we see God "through a glass" and "in an enigma." The glass is the human mind, which is a mirror in which we might glimpse at a reflection of the Trinity. This image is called an enigma because the image is "obscure and difficult to see through."[23] Most of the fifteenth book is dedicated to showing just how far all of the images fall short of expressing the Unity and Trinity proper to God, and how these images cannot resolve the questions Augustine had hoped to resolve with their aid. In fact, Augustine points out that one can master all that is to be known of the human mind, and never see the Trinity: "They, then, who see their own mind, in whatever way this is possible, and in it that Trinity of which I have treated.... and yet do not believe it or understand it to be an image of God, see indeed a glass, but do not see through the glass Him [God].... And if they despise the faith that purifies the heart, what do they accomplish by understanding the most subtle disputes concerning the nature of the human mind, unless that they be condemned also by the witness of their own understanding."[24] In order to see this glass precisely as an image, in order to see through the glass, one requires faith. One must believe that God is triune in order to see one's own memory, understanding and will as its image. One must believe that God is triune, that is, without seeing it.

Augustine thus ends the *De trinitate* with a prayer: "O Lord, Our God, we believe in Thee, the Father, Son, and Holy Spirit."[25] But surely, the term "believe" cannot here mean what Augustine has defined as faith in his earlier writings. There remains an element of authority; we believe that God is triune on the authority of Scripture; but the Trinity is unique in that it is neither a matter of historical fact nor, it would seem, accessible through the illumination we enjoy in our present state. Here faith would seem to be genuinely informative of the nature of God, and not merely purgative. Moreover, if the Trinity itself is not accessible, a serious question remains about the meaningfulness of discourse about the Trinity—even in Scripture. We may use the term meaningfully only if we have grasped the thing to which it refers, yet this is precisely what we lack. It is not surprising then that Augustine should include in his prayer, which begins with faith, an imprecation to be freed from his very speech: "Set me free, O God, from that multitude of speech which I suffer inwardly in my soul, wretched as I am in Thy sight."[26]

But if the *De trinitate* ends in silence, it is for good reason. Augustine's early account of the necessity and nature of faith, which he seems to have held as late as the writing of the eighth and thirteenth books of *De trinitate*, has failed him in the fifteenth. Some new account of the nature of faith, and some new explanation of the meaningfulness of statements of the faith would seem to be called for—a notion of faith which is genuinely informative of the divine and rightfully called wisdom; and some explanation of meaning not so heavily reliant on illumination.

How Augustine might solve this difficulty on his own grounds remains a topic for further study. Let it suffice to have shown that an ambiguity lies deep within Augustine's account of the nature and necessity of religious belief —an ambiguity which arises from his doctrines of the nature of language and illumination. If it could be shown that terms referring to the Trinity could be meaningful by way of analogy on the basis of our knowledge of things belonging to the temporal and created order, then this ambiguity could be resolved. Augustine certainly anticipates such a resolution in suggesting that language expressing beliefs about the Trinity relies on our knowledge of ourselves as enigmas, as obscure likenesses of the divine. However, should this suggestion be developed to its fullest, then would not Augustine begin to look more like a Thomas Aquinas than an Augustinian? Or is it that Thomas himself was not so much the Thomist as he was simply a mature Augustine?

Notes

[1] *De magistro* XI,36: *CC* XXIX,194: *Is me autem aliquid docet, qui uel oculis uel ulli corporis sensui uel ipsi etiam menti praebet ea, quae cognoscere uolo.* English citations from the *De magistro, De uera religione, De fide et symbolo,* and the *De utilitate credendi* are taken from or based upon J. H. S. Burleigh's *Augustine: Earlier Writings* (Philadelphia: The Westminster Press, 1953). English citations from the *De trinitate* are based upon *St. Augustine: On the Holy Trinity*; *NPNF* I:III.

[2] *De utilitate credendi* I,2: *PL* XLII,66:…*se dicebant, terribili auctoritate separata, mera et simplici ratione eos qui se audire vellent introducturos ad deum*….

[3] *De utilitate credendi* XI,25: *PL* XLII,83: *Credo enim sceleratissimos conjuratos virtute Ciceronis quondam interfectos: atqui id non solum nescio, sed etiam nullo pacto me scire posse, certo scio.*

[4] *De utilitate credendi* XII,26: *PL* XLII,84:…*sed interposita matris auctoritate de patre creditur, de ipsa vero matre plerumque nec matri, sed obstetricibus, nutricibus, famulis.*

[5] *De utilitate credendi* X,23: *PL* XLII,81: *Dices, bona tua conscientia nihil te fingere, quantis poteris idipsum asserens verbis, sed tamen verbis. Non enim animi tui latebras, ita ut intime sciaris, homo homini aperire possis.*

[6] *De uera religione* VII,13: *CC* XXXII,196: *Huius religionis sectandae caput est historia et prophetia dispensationis temporalis diuinae prouidentiae pro salute generis humani in aeternam uitam reformandi atque reparandi.*

[7] *De uera religione* X,19: *CC* XXXII,199–200:…*ineffabili misericordia dei temporali dispensatione per creaturam mutabilem…ad commemorationem primae suae perfectaeque naturae partim singulis hominibus partim uero ipsi hominum generi subuenitur. Ea est nostris temporibus Christiana religio, quam cognoscere ac sequi securissima ac certissima salus est.*

[8] *De uera religione* XXIV,45: *CC* XXXII,215: *Sed quia in temporalia deuenimus et eorum amore ab aeternis impedimur, quaedam temporalis medicina, quae non scientes, sed credentes ad salutem uocat, non naturae excellentia, sed ipsius temporis ordine prior est.*

[9] *De utilitate credendi* XVI,34: *PL* XLII,89–90:…*[auctoritas] dupliciter nos movet; partim miraculis, partim sequentium multitudine. Nihil horum est necessarium sapienti; quis negat?…Homini ergo non valenti verum intueri, ut ad id fiat idoneus, purgarique se sinat, auctoritas praesto est*….

[10] *De fide et symbolo* X,25: *PL* XL,196: *Haec est fides quae paucis verbis tenenda in Symbolo novellis christianis datur. Quae pauca verba fidelibus nota sunt, ut credendo subjugentur Deo, subjugati recte vivant, recte vivendo cor mundent, corde mundato quod credunt intelligant.*

[11] *De trinitate* IV,xv,20: *CC* L,187: *Hinc enim sibi purgationem isti virtute propria pollicentur quia nonnulli eorum potuerunt aciem mentis ultra omnem creaturam transmittere et lucem incommutabilis ueritatis quantulacumque ex parte contingere, quod christianos multos "ex fide" interim sola uiuentes nondum potuisse derident.*

[12] *De trinitate* IV,xvii,23: *CC* L,190:...*quia per ea quae facta sunt cognoscentes deum non sicut deum glorificauerunt aut gratias egerunt, sed dicentes se esse sapientes stulti facti sunt* —that is, Augustine quotes Rm 1:21.

[13] *De trinitate* VIII,iv,7: *CC* L,275: *Necesse est autem cum aliqua corporalia lecta uel audita quae non uidimus credimus, fingat sibi animus aliquid in lineamentis formisque corporum sicut occurrerit cogitanti....*

[14] *De trinitate* VIII,iv,7: *CC* L,276:...*habemus enim quasi regulariter infixam naturae humanae notitiam secundum quam quidquid tale aspicimus statim hominem esse cognoscimus uel hominis formam.*

[15] *De trinitate* VIII,v,7: *CC* L,277:...*et tamen ea firmissime credimus quia secundum specialem generalemque notitiam quae certa nobis est cogitamus.*

[16] *De trinitate* VIII,v,7: *CC* L,277: *Vtrum autem illa facies Mariae fuerit quae occurrerit animo cum ista loquimur aut recordamur nec nouimus omnino nec credimus.*

[17] *De trinitate* XIII,xix,24: *CC* L,415: *Haec autem omnia quae pro nobis "uerbum caro factum" [Jn 1:14] temporaliter et localiter fecit et pertulit secundum distinctionem quam demonstrare suscepimus ad scientiam pertinent non ad sapientiam. Quod autem uerbum est sine tempore et "sine loco" est patri coaeternum et "ubique totum," de quo si quisquam potest quantum potest ueracem proferre sermonem, "sermo" erit ille sapientiae.*

[18] *De trinitate* VIII,vii,10: *CC* L,284: *Quapropter non est praecipue uidendum in hac quaestione quae de trinitate nobis est et de cognoscendo deo nisi quid sit uera dilectio....*

[19] *De trinitate* VIII,vi,9: *CC* L,280:...*superius demonstrauimus neminem diligere quod credit et non videt nisi ex aliqua regula notitiae generalis siue specialis.*

[20] *De trinitate* VIII,vi,9: *CC* L,283: *Neque enim inuenimus aliquid tale praeter ipsam ut eam cum incognita est credendo diligamus ex eo quod iam tale aliquid nouimus. Quidquid enim tale aspexeris ipsa est, et non est quidquam tale quoniam sola ipsa talis est qualis ipsa est.*

[21] *De trinitate* VIII,viii,12: *CC* L,286: *Diligat fratrem et diligat eandem dilectionem; magis enim nouit dilectionem qua fratrem quem diligit. Ecce iam potest notiorem deum habere quam fratrem, plane notiorem quia praesentiorem, notiorem quia interiorem, notiorem quia certiorem. Amplectere dilectionem deum et dilectione amplectere deum.*

[22] *De trinitate* VIII,viii,12: *CC* L,287: *"At enim caritatem uideo, et quantum possum eam mente conspicio, et credo scripturae dicenti: 'Quoniam deus caritas est, et qui manet in caritate in deo manet' [1 Jn 4:8]. Sed cum eam [caritatem] uideo non in ea uideo trinitatem." Immo uero uides trinitatem si caritatem uides. Sed commonebo si potero ut uidere te uideas....*

[23] *De trinitate* XV,ix,16: *CC* L/A,482: *Proinde quantum mihi uidetur sicut nomine speculi imaginem uoluit intelligi, ita nomine aenigmatis quamuis similitudinem tamen obscuram et ad perspiciendum difficilem.*

[24] *De trinitate* XV,xxiv,44: *CC* L/A,522-23: *Qui ergo uident suam mentem quomodo uideri potest et in ea trinitatem istam de qua multis modis ut potui disputaui, nec tamen eam*

316 Belief and Understanding

credunt uel intelligunt esse imaginem dei. Speculum quidem uident, sed usque adeo non ui-dent per speculum…. Qua fide cordium mundatrice contempta quid agunt intelligendo quae de natura mentis humanae subtilissime disputantur nisi ut ipsa quoque intelligentia sua teste damnentur?

[25] *De trinitate* XV,xxviii,51: *CC* L/A,533: *Domine deus noster, credimus in te patrem et filium et spiritum sanctum.*

[26] *De trinitate* XV,xxviii,52: *CC* L/A,534–35: *Libera me, deus meus, a multiloquio quod patior intus in anima mea misera in conspectu tuo….*

VI

The Interpretation of Scripture

Augustine

Demonstrandus est igitur prius modus inueniendae locuti-onis, propriane an figurata sit. Et iste omnino modus est, ut quidquid in sermone diuino neque ad morum honestatem neque ad fidei ueritatem proprie referri potest, figuratum esse cognos-cas. Morum honestas ad diligendum deum et proximum, fidei ueritas ad cognoscendum deum et proximum pertinet.

De doctrina christiana III,x,14

Figure and History:
A Contemporary Reassessment of Augustine's Hermeneutic

Curtis W. Freeman

Introduction

Since the mid-nineteenth century, the historical-critical method has regulated scholarly exegesis of Scripture. We do well to remember that this hermeneutical hegemony is a relatively recent development in the history of interpretation. Although patristic and medieval exegetes acknowledged the normative role of the *sensus litteralis*, they also recognized its limitations. Thus, pre-critical hermeneutics accounted for multiple levels of meaning in Scripture—the *sensus plenior*.[1]

The modern critical paradigm, however, is exhibiting signs of insurgency as biblical critics confront the insuperable barrier of recovering the historical meaning of a text and the additional unwelcome fact that the objective perspective supposedly required by the critical method may conflict with the spiritual character of the Bible.[2] Moreover, post-modern literary theory has vigorously challenged the formalist notion that a text has a single meaning which the interpreter must discern.[3] The purpose of this paper will be to explore the pre-critical paradigm of biblical interpretation. Specifically, it will attempt to display Augustine's figural hermeneutic both in theory and application with a view toward its contemporary relevance.

Letter and Spirit

In the early second century, Marcion began to teach a Christian faith that rejected the God of the Hebrew Bible and proclaimed that Christ had revealed a deity previously unknown. Although the Church Fathers dismissed Marcion's gnostic theological and christological assertions, they nevertheless agreed with him in one important respect: the literal-historical meaning of the Old Testament held little value for Christians.[4] Early Christian exegetes, thus, became experts in allegory and typology as they transformed the Hebrew Bible into Christian Scripture.[5] Through spiritual exegesis, the Fathers came to see that the New Testament is concealed in the Old, and the Old Testament is revealed in the New. In his justly famous essay on figural interpretation, E. Auerbach defined the use of *figura* by the Church Fathers:

> Figural interpretation establishes a connection between two events or persons, the first of which signifies not only itself but also the second, while the second encompasses or fulfills the first. The two poles of the figure are separate in time, but both, being real events or figures are within time, within the stream of historical life.[6]

Although John Cassian would become a more popular exegete, Augustine played a formative role in the conventionalization of figural interpretation.

Augustine took as his point of departure the words of the apostle Paul: "The letter kills, but the spirit gives life" (2 Co 3:6).[7] He first learned from Ambrose to understand this Pauline text as a hermeneutical axiom which juxtaposes the literal meaning of Scripture ("the letter") and the symbolic meaning ("the spirit").[8] Augustine, however, was clearly troubled by the allegorical extremism of writers like Origen and Clement of Alexandria who justified their interpretations on the basis of this same principle. Drawing from the *Liber regularum* of Tyconius, in *De doctrina christiana* Augustine proposed a set of guidelines to regulate the practice of figural exegesis.

First, it is necessary *to safeguard against the error of taking figural expressions as if they were literal*.[9] This hermeneutical mistake leads to the kind of spiritual bondage that enslaved Augustine during his Manichaean years. In the *Confessions*, he explains:

> [My liberation occurred] when I heard, rather often, one after another of the obscure passages from the Old Testament being explained, passages wherein I was slain (*occidebar*) when I took them literally (*cum ad litteram acciperem*).[10]

Second, it is equally essential *to prevent the opposite error of taking literal expressions as if they were figural*.[11] Although the spirit is to be given superiority over the letter, Augustine was concerned that this not be regarded as license to dismiss the literal meaning of Scripture as unimportant. In order to execute figural exegesis successfully, one must determine whether a biblical text should be taken as literal or figural.

A *prima facie* rule for an exegete is that a text should be understood figurally if, when taken literally, it cannot be referred to purity of life (*morum honestatem*), soundness of doctrine (*fidei veritatem*), and hope in one's conscience (*Spes autem sua cuique est in conscientia propria*).[12] Specifically, Scripture is given to nurture the theological virtues of faith (*fides*), hope (*spes*), and love (*caritas*).[13] Texts which in the plain literal sense teach Christian virtue are morally edifying and thus need not be given a figural interpretation. Not all the parts of the Bible, however, are morally edifying as they stand. What spiritual significance can possibly be found, for example, in the Psalmist's imprecation to crush the heads of Babylonian children (Ps 137:9)? Such passages which have an unedifying literal sense should be given a figural interpretation.

Augustine, however, does not mean that the interpreter is given free rein to pursue the avenues of unchecked imagination or autonomous reason. There are at least three normative criteria which serve as guides in the process. First, because "Scripture asserts nothing but the catholic faith (*Non autem adserit nisi catholicam fidem*)," true exegesis must be guided by the Church as an interpretive community.[14] Second, a valid interpretation "tends to establish the reign of love (*ad regnum caritatis interpretatio perducatur*)," thus, it produces truthful character.[15] Third, obscure biblical texts (*in locis…obscuris*) should be read in light of clear ones (*Vbi autem apertius ponuntur*), which makes spiritual meanings dependent on *manifest testimonies*.[16] By employing the norms of Church, virtue, and Scripture, Augustine limits the range of interpretation and in so doing attempts *to avoid the extreme of biblical spiritualism*, which understands the Bible as a hermetic book. Conversely, because he does not limit Scripture to a single meaning but leaves it open to a variety of interpretations, Augustine also endeavors *to evade the trap of biblical literalism*, which mistakes story for history.

Figure and History

For Augustine, the two Testaments are not so much allegorically related as they are typologically united. This typological unity presupposes—indeed it depends upon—the literal (*littera*) and historical (*historia*) meaning of the biblical narrative because he believes there is historical continuity as well as theological homogeneity between the Old and the New.[17] Furthermore, *figura* is the hermeneutical middle term between *littera* and *veritas*. He warns against venturesome exegetes who maintain that in Scripture "everything is bound up in allegorical meanings" and who "carve out some spiritual interpretation" without taking "good care first and foremost to adhere to the historical fact (*historiae veritate*)."[18] Similarly, he advises that an allegorical interpretation of the Genesis narrative of the Garden of Eden is permissible only "so long as we believe in the historical truth (*historiae ueritas*) manifest in the faithful narrative of these events."[19] Augustine, however, ironically concedes that Origen's allegorizations of the Genesis narrative are legitimate.[20] It then remains unclear why the literal meaning is essential to the spiritual meaning if there is no substantive difference from allegorical interpretations that do not grant the historicity of the biblical narrative. That is, this seems to be *a difference that does not make a difference*.

Moreover, Augustine's hermeneutic, which maintains an insistence on the facticity of *littera* and *historia* in all the Bible as a necessary precondition for *figura* and *veritas*, leads him to make some rather bizarre and absurd assertions in light of modern science and history. He is compelled to account for the origin of freakish races of people in Adam, e.g., Hermaphrodites (humans with both male and female sexual organs that impregnate themselves and give birth to their own offspring), Sciopodes (people with a single leg that has two feet), and Cynocephalae (a species with dog-like heads and barking voices).[21] Additionally, Augustine accepts the historicity of antediluvian giants, and he defends this view on the basis of his claim to have seen a human tooth that was one hundred times the size of a modern tooth.[22] He emphatically insists that the earth is less than six thousand years old.[23] Furthermore, because he insists that Scripture is "divinely inspired history (*divinae...historiae*),"[24] he defends the chronological veracity of the biblical account of antediluvian lifespans, e.g., that Methuselah was 969 solar years old.[25]

The implicit force of Augustine's interpretation is that one cannot accept the truth of the figural sense (viz. the redemptive sacrifice of Christ or the sacramental presence of the Church) without also recognizing the facticity of the literal sense (viz. the chronological accuracy of Genesis). Both meanings must be accepted for either one to be valid. Augustine should not be faulted for endorsing primitive "science" and "history" which he had little reason to question. However, the patent absurdity of these literal meanings—in view of sixteen centuries—seems to overwhelm the organic linkage between history and figure.

What is at stake for Augustine in these passages, however, is not history qua history, but rather the biblical narrative as the mimesis of history. Consequently, he does not see Scripture as having merely symbolic meaning. The verisimilitude of Scripture begins with the literal, which cannot be disregarded. Once the literal sense is accepted, biblical realism then extends to the figurative. The figural understanding is true, but it becomes truth for Augustine only when the fulfillment is seen as cloaked within the literal meaning. Therefore, the literal and the figural, although distinct, are interrelated. More precisely for Augustine, while the literal may exist without the figural, the figural is never independent of the literal. Augustine believes that interpreters who dispense with the literal dimension inevitably undermine the full truth of both Scripture and history. In order to understand more fully the meaning of Augustine's use of figural exegesis, it will be helpful to display his application of this hermeneutical theory.

Figures of the Church

How is one to read the Old Testament? During the time that Augustine embraced Manichaeism, he found that, if taken literally, the Old Testament was unedifying at best and patently immoral at worst. As he embraced Catholic Christianity, however, Augustine began to discover that the Old Testament speaks in shadows of things to come. Through figural exegesis, he learned to read the Old Testament, not as Hebrew Bible, but as Christian Scripture which adumbrated Christ and the Church. One of the clearest examples of ecclesial typology is the ark.

The ark, Augustine writes, is "a symbol (*figura*) of the city of God on its pilgrimage in history, a figure of the Church."[26] Just as Noah and his family are strangers in the world, so the pilgrims of the city of God are strangers in the earthly city. Thus, the ark is an *eschatological figure of the Church*. Moreover, as the residents of the ark are saved by its wood, so the pilgrim city of God receives salvation by virtue of the wood of the cross, on which Christ as the Mediator gives his life. Thus, the ark is *a soteriological figure of the Church*. And as every species of animal enters the ark, even so is the Church filled with multitudes from every nation—Jews and Gentiles. Thus, the ark is *a tropological figure of the Church*.[27]

Augustine confesses that every detail symbolizes some feature of the Church. The measurements of the ark foreshadow Christ's body, and the door of the ark symbolizes the wound in his side, that is, the sacraments which are the door of the Church. Even the squared timbers are symbolic of the holy life.[28] Augustine ends his discussion of the ark with three conclusions:

    (1) That the events really took place (*et gesta esse*);

    (2) That what took place had a symbolic meaning (*et significare aliquid*);

    (3) That the meaning is a foreshadowing of the Church (*et ipsum aliquid ad praefigurandam ecclesiam pertinere*).[29]

The story of the ark, which Augustine emphatically accepts as literal and which he goes to great lengths to defend as historical, thus, is a foreshadowing image of the Church.[30]

Figures of Christ

Augustine finds in Abel, Seth, and Enosh a triform figure of Christ. Abel is a luminous figure of Christ crucified and "a marvelous symbol (*mirabili sacramento*) of the persecuted City of God."[31] The name Abel, taken to mean "sorrow" (*iuctus*), thus signifies the first aspect of Christ's fulfillment of salvation—death.[32] Seth means "resurrection" (*resurrectio*); and thus, as the replacement of Abel, he is a figure of the second aspect of Christ's fulfillment of salvation—resurrection.[33] The name Enosh, the son of Seth, means "man" (*homo*). Specifically, "Enos[h] was a 'son' of 'resurrection' (*filius resurrectionis*)."[34] But this trifold figuration is itself multivalent as it operates at two levels. Augustine explains:

> The "son of resurrection" is a man who lives in hope (*in spe*). The City of God, which is the child of faith (*quae gignitur ex fide*) in the Resurrection of Christ, lives in hope (*in spe vivit*) so long as its pilgrimage on earth endures.... It is from faith in the Resurrection that the City of God is born—the City in the sense of mankind hoping to "call upon the name of the Lord." "For in hope," says the Apostle, "were we saved. But hope that is seen is not hope. For how can a man hope for what he sees? But if we hope for what we do not see, we wait for it with patience (*per patientiam expectamus*)."[35]

Abel, a figure of Christ crucified, also models the earthly travail of the pilgrim city. Seth, a type of Christ resurrected, likewise exemplifies the ultimate triumph of the pilgrim city. Enosh, the son of resurrection, envisions the hope of salvation accomplished in Christ and embodies the waiting in patience epitomized by Christ. As one who hopes to call upon the name of the Lord, Enosh prefigures those who by grace become part of the city of God. As one who longs to see the salvation of God, Enosh typifies those who wait with patience and thus endure the pilgrim journey.

Augustine concludes his interpretation with a summary statement about Abel, Seth, and Enosh as Christological figures:

> The invocation of God is the whole and the highest preoccupation of the City of God during its pilgrimage in this world and it is symbolized (*commendandum*) in the one 'man' (Enos[h]) born of the 'resurrection' (Seth) of the man who was slain (Abel). That one man, in fact, is a symbol of the unity of the whole heavenly City, which is not yet in the fullness (*nondum quidem conpleta*) which it is destined to reach, and which is adumbrated in this prophetic figure (*prophetica praefiguratione conplenda*).[36]

In Augustine's trio of figures, Enosh is the linchpin. He is the conjunction between Abel and Seth. But more importantly, Enosh is the link between Christ, the one who is exemplary of the pilgrim, and Christians, the people who imitate Christ's example through the virtues of faith, hope, and patience. Therefore, Augustine's Christological figuration is not merely *typological*; it is also *tropological* and *anagogical*.

Conclusions

What has Augustine's hermeneutical method to say about exegetical theory and practice after sixteen centuries?

1. *Augustine reminds us to attend to the recovery of the spiritual meanings of Scripture.* The modern commitment to the literal sense of the Bible and the historical-critical method as the key to unlocking its meaning are results of the Protestant revolution against esoteric interpretations. Although historical criticism has produced many benefits, it has not proven sufficient as the sole hermeneutical criterion. Augustine and the Fathers recognized that because Scripture has multiple levels many interpretations are necessary. One of the

evidences that Scripture is a truly classic text may not be that it possesses an inexhaustible meaning, but rather that it inspires an indefatigable interest. The sacredness of Scripture, thus, becomes evident as we find in it light which illumines our lives with new possibilities.

2. *Augustine cautions us about the necessity of a communal interpretation of Scripture.* For Augustine, the authority of Scripture is dependent upon the Church; therefore, interpretation must be guided by the Church. Scripture was and is eucharistically formed. Augustine asserted against the Manichees, "I should not believe the gospel except as moved by the authority of the Catholic Church."[37] Because it abstracts Scripture from the ecclesial context, the historical-critical method is a distortion of Christian tradition. It proceeds under the assumption that individual interpreters can discern the meaning of the biblical text without taking account of the good ends of the community for which this text is Scripture. It is simply a mistake to assume that the text of the Bible makes sense apart from a community that makes it make sense. Augustine helps us to see that we will understand the significance of the Bible when we become concerned about finding an interpretative community under whose tutelage we might learn what it means to read the Bible as Scripture.

3. *Augustine challenges us to reflect on continuity in a literal reading of Scripture.* Although Augustine illustrates some of the problems of making an ostensible link between a realistic narrative and historical events, he nevertheless maintained the valuable insight that the biblical narrative depicts the real world. Unfortunately, much of "the real world" as represented in the literal sense of the Old Testament was found to be unedifying. Thus, pre-critical exegesis turned to allegory and typology in order to find theological significance in the Old Testament. If the Church today is to make credible the claim of the unity of God's revelation against neo-marcionism and neo-manichaeism, biblical exegesis and theology must continue to search for ways of finding continuity between the Old and the New at the literal level as well as at the spiritual.

Notes

[1] R. E. Brown and S. M. Schneiders, "Hermeneutics," in *The New Jerome Biblical Commentary*, ed. R. E. Brown (Englewood Cliffs: Prentice Hall, 1990), pp. 1153–58; J. S. Preus, *From Shadow to Promise: Old Testament Interpretation from Augustine to the Young Luther* (Cambridge: Harvard Univ. Press, 1969), pp. 1–149; and D. Steinmetz, "The Superiority of Pre-Critical Exegesis," chap. in *Memory and Mission: Theological Reflections on the Christian Past* (Nashville: Abingdon, 1988), pp. 143–63.

[2] Thus, W. Wink asserts that "historical biblical criticism is bankrupt," in *The Bible in Human Transformation: Toward a New Paradigm for Biblical Study* (Philadelphia: Fortress Press, 1973), p. 1.

[3] For a brief summary of the literary-critical debate see S. Fish, "How I Stopped Worrying and Learned To Love Interpretation," chap. in *Is There a Text in This Class?* (Cambridge: Harvard University Press, 1980), pp. 1–17.

[4] Preus, *From Shadow to Promise*, p. 10.

[5] R. A. Greer, *Early Biblical Interpretation* (Philadelphia: Westminster Press, 1986), pp. 126–54. J. W. Trigg incisively comments that attempts have been made "to distinguish 'typology' in which historical events in the Bible foreshadow later historical events...from 'allegory' in which earthly realities symbolize heavenly realities." Such a distinction, however, does not conform to the practice of exegesis by Augustine or other early Christian writers. See Trigg, *Biblical Interpretation*, Message of the Fathers of the Church, vol. 9 (Wilmington: Michael Glazier, 1988), p. 18.

[6] E. Auerbach, "Figura," in *Scenes From the Drama of European Literature* (Minneapolis: University of Minnesota Press, 1984), p. 53.

[7] *De doctrina christiana* III,v,9: *CC* XXXII,82: *NPNF* I:II,559: *Littera occidit, spiritus autem uiuificat.*

[8] *Confessiones* VI,iv,6: *CC* XXVII,77: *FC* 21,136.

[9] *De doctrina christiana* III,v,9: *CC* XXXII,82: *NPNF* I:II,559.

[10] *Confessiones* V,xiv,24: *CC* XXVII,71: *FC* 21,126. *[M]axime audito uno atque altero et saepius aenigmate soluto de scriptis veteribus, ubi, cum ad litteram acciperem, occidebar. Spiritaliter itaque plerisque illorum librorum locis expositis iam reprehendebam desperationem meam illam dumtaxat.*

[11] *De doctrina christiana* III,x,14: *CC* XXXII,86: *NPNF* I:II,560–61.

[12] *Ibid.*.

[13] *De doctrina christiana* I,xxxix,43: *CC* XXXII,31: *NPNF* I:II,534. It is important to note that in this passage Augustine argues that, except for catechetical purposes, Scripture is not necessary for the Christian who possesses the cardinal virtues. *Homo itaque fide et spe et caritate subnixus eaque inconcusse retinens non indiget scripturis nisi ad alios instruendos.*

[14] *De doctrina christiana* III,x,15: *CC* XXXII,87: *NPNF* I:II,561. For Augustine, the authority of Scripture is dependent upon the Church. In one of his earliest assertions (396) of this insight, Augustine wrote: "I should not believe the gospel except as moved by the authority of the Catholic Church": *ego uero euangelio non crederem, nisi me catholicae ecclesiae conmoueret auctoritas: Contra epistulam quam vocant Fundamenti* 5: *CSEL* XXV,197: *NPNF* I:IV,131. As Eugene TeSelle has reminded me, this passage is often misconstrued by careless readers. Augustine's consent to Catholic authority should not be taken as an irrational form of ecclesial fideism. Indeed, his intent in the text was to refute the Mani-

chaean claim to "truth." When Augustine speaks of the Catholic Church in *Contra epistu-lam*, the referent of "Church" includes the empirical Catholic community as well as the sacramental ecclesial communion. However, the broader sense of a historical Church (as in *De ciuitate dei*) which includes Old Testament saints is not developed in *Contra epistu-lam*. Moreover, as W. S. Babcock perceptively notes, Augustine's hermeneutic in *De doctri-na christiana* was informed by the *Liber regularum* of Tyconius, in which the ecclesial con-text of exegesis is made explicit. That is, Tyconius' "exegetical guides are, at the same time, rules for discerning and understanding the character of the church." Babcock, "Augustine and Tyconius: A Study in the Latin Appropriation of Paul," *Studia Patristica* 17 (1982) 1212.

¹⁵ *De doctrina christiana* III,xv,23: *CC* XXXII,91: *NPNF* I:II,563.

¹⁶ *De doctrina christiana* III,xxvi,37: *CC* XXXII,99: *NPNF* I:II,566.

¹⁷ *De ciuitate dei* XV,xxvii: *CC* XLVIII,495–97: *FC* 14,480–84.

¹⁸ *De ciuitate dei* XVII,iii: *CC* XLVIII,554: *FC* 24,22–23: *Mihi autem...multum ui-dentur...audere, qui prorsus ibi omnia significationibus allegoricis inuoluta esse contendunt. ... Hoc enim existimo, non tamen culpans eos, qui potuerint illic de quacumque re gesta sensum intelligentiae spiritalis exsculpere, seruata dumtaxat primitus historiae ueritate.*

¹⁹ *De ciuitate dei* XIII,xxi: *CC* XLVIII,404: *FC* 14,332: *dum tamen et illius historiae ueritas fidelissima rerum gestarum narratione commendata credatur.*

²⁰ *De ciuitate dei* XIII,xxi: *CC* XLVIII,404: *FC* 14,331–32.

²¹ *De ciuitate dei* XVI,viii: *CC* XLVIII,508–10: *FC* 14,501–4.

²² *De ciuitate dei* XV,ix: *CC* XLVIII,465–66: *FC* 14,432–34.

²³ *De ciuitate dei* XII,xi: *CC* XLVIII,365–66: *FC* 14,263–65.

²⁴ *De ciuitate dei* XVIII,xl: *CC* XLVIII,635: *FC* 24,148.

²⁵ *De ciuitate dei* XV,xi–xiv: *CC* XLVIII,467–74: *FC* 14,436–47. Augustine's excur-sus on chronology (the *littera*) is important because it is contained in XV,x–xvi which forms a parenthesis in his exegesis of the Abel-Seth-Enosh typology (the *figura*) in XV,i–ix and XV, xvii–xxi.

²⁶ *De ciuitate dei* XV,xxvi: *CC* XLVIII,493: *FC* 14,477: *figura est peregrinantis in hoc saeculo ciuitatis Dei, hoc est ecclesiae..*

²⁷ *De ciuitate dei* XV,xxvi: *CC* XLVIII,493–94: *FC* 14,477–79. See also *De ciuitate dei* XV,xxvii and XVI,vii: *CC* XLVIII,495–97 and XLVIII,507–8: *FC* 14,480–84 and 14, 500–501.

²⁸ *De ciuitate dei* XV,xxvi: *CC* XLVIII,493–94: *FC* 14,478.

²⁹ *De ciuitate dei* XV,xxvii: *CC* XLVIII,497: *FC* 14,484.

³⁰ Although Augustine's theology distinguishes between the empirical Church and the pilgrim city, his figural identification of the ark and the Church illustrates that he often

uses these overlapping concepts interchangeably. F. E. Cranz has settled the matter of the identification of the Church and the city of God in *"De Civitate Dei*, XV,2 and Augustine's Idea of the Christian Society," in *Augustine: A Collection of Critical Essays*, ed. R. A. Markus (Garden City, N.Y.: Anchor Books, 1972), p. 419, note 21.

[31] *De ciuitate dei* XV,xvii: *CC* XLVIII,479: *FC* 14,454.

[32] *De ciuitate dei* XV,xviii: *CC* XLVIII,480: *FC* 14,457.

[33] *De ciuitate dei* XV,xvii: *CC* XLVIII,480: *FC* 14,456.

[34] *De ciuitate dei* XV,xviii: *CC* XLVII,480: *FC* 14,455.

[35] *De ciuitate dei* XV,xviii: *CC* XLVIII,480: *FC* 14,457: *In spe igitur uiuit homo filius resurrectionis; in spe uiuit, quamdiu peregrinatur hic, ciuitas Dei, quae gignitur ex fide resurrectionis Christi. …Ex qua fide gignitur hic ciuitas Dei, id est homo, qui sperauit inuocare nomen Domini Dei. "Spe enim salui facti sumus," ait apostolus. "Spes autem quae uidetur, non est spes. Quod enim uidet quis, quid sperat? Si autem quod non uidemus speramus, per patientiam expectamus."*

[36] *De ciuitate dei* XV,xxi: *CC* XLVIII,486: *FC* 14,466: *Hoc est quippe in hoc mundo peregrinantis ciuitatis Dei totum atque summum in hac mortalitate negotium, quod per unum hominem, quem sane occisi resurrectio genuit, commendandum fuit. Homo quippe ille unus totius supernae ciuitatis est unitas, nondum quidem completa, sed praemissa ista prophetica praefiguratione conplenda.*

[37] *Contra epistulam quam vocant Fundamenti* 5: *CSEL* XXV,197: *NPNF* I:IV,131: *Ego uero euangelio non crederem, nisi me catholicae ecclesiae conmoueret auctoritas:* Bonner perceptively notes that the ecclesial quality is the most important feature of Augustine's hermeneutic. He writes, for Augustine "the Bible must be read and understood within the framework of the life and doctrine of the Christian community and not interpreted by mere private judgment, however learned." G. Bonner, "Augustine as Biblical Scholar," in *The Cambridge History of the Bible* (Cambridge: Cambridge Univ. Press, 1970), 1:561.

Local Setting and Motivation of *De doctrina christiana*

Charles Kannengiesser

Identified as a *pastoral* work, *De doctrina christiana* may well betray its real setting and motivation in the local context of the African Church. In the sequence of Augustine's literary productions, the thirtieth of his numerous essays, it remains linked with earlier products of the same sort, responding to similar needs and developing approximately the same topics. But being the newly nominated bishop's first properly literary work, it is also the first by which he applied his life-long familiarity with rhetoric to the problem of how to interpret Scripture.

What was it more specifically that motivated Augustine's involvement in such a programmatic task? To reach an answer to that question we must read simultaneously the introduction of *De doctrina christiana* and the last part of Book III added in 426.

The newly appointed bishop sounds amazingly defensive in this introduction. In the first sentence of it, he announces "precepts for treating the Scriptures"[1] which may be of profit to students who read anyway "the work of expositors."[2] In his second sentence he emphasizes the fact that these rules are precisely his own: "if God our Lord will not deny me, in writing, those things which he usually suggests to me in thought."[3] And then he goes immediately over, in his own terms, "to answer those who will condemn these precepts."[4] He distinguishes three types of opponents: the first one being those who would not understand, because they are too ignorant, or illiterate; the second type being people who would read the precepts, but not understand how to apply them by themselves; and the third type being actually the only one against which he would become vocal until the end of the introduction, from par. 2 through par. 9. He calls them "detractors who either treat the Sacred Scripture well, or think they do."[5] What he dislikes in them particularly is that "they are already equipped to expound the sacred books without having read any of the observations which I have set out to make, so that they will declare that these regulations are necessary to no one, but that everything which may laudably be revealed about the obscurities of those books can be revealed with divine assistance" (par. 2).[6]

In other words *De doctrina christiana* is introduced as a response to a kind of biblical hermeneutic based on principles of which Augustine disapproves. He opposes well-established interpreters of the Bible who feel no need to share his own rhetorical approach to it. In his own words, they don't care about "the observations which I have set out to make." Let me note here that it would certainly be misleading to identify those virtual opponents as "anti-paideia"-oriented African Christians,[7] Augustine insisting on their good reasons for thinking that they "treat the Sacred Scripture well."[8] Nor should one reduce them to being irrational charismatics, misled by their fantasies, rather than guided by sound reason.

For Augustine does not deny that they have their own hermeneutical logic with its proper rules. He only regrets in advance that they would not accept *his* precepts. Their system of interpretation leads them to be people "who exult in divine assistance and who glory in being able to understand and to treat the sacred books without precepts of the kind which I have undertaken to supply herewith, so that they think these precepts superfluous" (par. 4).[9] We are obviously dealing here with a conflictual context, in which Augustine seems hardly able, or at least not inclined, to give names or more explicit data. He keeps a prudent reserve in denouncing a general attitude rather than specific interpreters in the field of biblical exegesis. And what he insists on the most is, surprisingly enough, the *religious* character of the form of exegesis which he opposes. In that exegesis, remarks Augustine, "whoever, instructed by no precepts, glories in his understanding of whatever is obscure in the Scriptures through a divine gift, believes correctly in thinking that his ability does not come from himself but is divinely given, so that he seeks the glory of God and not his own" (par. 8).[10] But he adds immediately a stern warning against spiritual pride, in reminding the opponents of the humble and down-to-earth babbling of their first childhood.

A particular insistence on certain obscurities of Scripture and a candid claim to become able to eliminate them thanks to the assistance of the Holy Spirit seem to have impressed Augustine more than anything else in the local form of exegesis which he opposes at the start of *De doctrina christiana*.

But did he really address a *local* hermeneutic by the polemical overtones of this introduction? In fact, one hears nothing more about such opponents in the rest of *De doctrina christiana* that was written in 396. We are, however, immediately faced with them as soon as the writing starts again thirty years later. But the tension has gone. The adversaries are no longer denounced from afar, as an indifferent audience which would in any case refuse to receive Augustine's teaching. Now, in 426, their characteristic taste for the obscurities of Scripture adds a new flavor to Augustine's own exegetical understanding. After having taken over the figure of "leaven," with a good sense in one place and a bad sense in another, a figure with which the writing had ended in 396, Augustine adds a few more examples of that sort, and goes over quickly to a very different case of enigma, namely, the case with a figure remaining in itself enigmatic in all places where it is used, for instance, "the wrath of God," pointing to "the ultimate penalty" or to "the grace of the Scriptures passing from the Jews to the Gentiles" (par. 36).[11] Such a central theological category had never occurred before in *De doctrina christiana*, nor had the Johannine Apocalypse been referred to as here in order to signify "the Holy Spirit" through the image of "water."[12] Augustine focuses now directly on how to interpret things "in obscure places" (par. 37).[13] He adds an explicit statement on the Holy Spirit as the primordial author of Scripture, who providentially disposed it in view of the present readership. Again, such theological insights about the hermeneutical nature of Scripture were totally missing so far in *De doctrina christiana*. I quote:

> He who examines the divine eloquence, desiring to discover the intention of the author through whom the Holy Spirit created the Scripture, whether he attains this end or finds another meaning in the words not contrary to right faith, is free from blame if he has evidence from some other place in the divine books. And certainly the Spirit of God, who worked through that author, undoubtedly foresaw that this meaning would occur to the reader or listener. Rather, he provided that it might occur to him, since that meaning is dependent upon truth. For what could God have more generously and abundantly provided in the divine writings than that the same words might be understood in various ways which other no less divine witnesses approve? (par. 38).[14]

One may admit that Augustine had matured and was deeply enriched as an interpreter of Scripture after 30 years of leadership in the field, so there should be no surprise if his discourse sounds more substantial in its theological hermeneutics from *De doctrina christiana* III,x,15 on. But the tone of what he has now to say about scriptural obscurities, the examples and references produced, even his occasional wordings betray too much of a distinctive source for it to be attributed only to Augustine's general experience and old age—for instance, when he focuses again in par. 39 on "passages obscured by figurative words," about which he certifies that "we shall walk much more safely with the aid of the Scriptures themselves."[15] After the transition bound to his writing of 396, as secured in par. 36 through 39, Augustine seems to come in par. 40 to the real complementary section which he wanted to add to Book III. It is about *tropes*.[16] He describes and enumerates them as *allegoria, aenigma, parabola*, or as "metaphor," "catachresis," or again as "irony" and "antiphrasis."[17] He stresses the need to be aware of them in order to find "a solution of the ambiguities of Scripture," and he concludes confidently that "in this way many hidden things are discovered" (par. 41).[18]

Since par. 36 the bishop actually had in mind Tyconius, whom he starts quoting in par. 42 and who will occupy the whole scene until the end of Book III in par. 56. Augustine had paraphrased Tyconius in an allusive way from the moment when he decided to complete *De doctrina christiana* in 426. More correctly he was eager to integrate into that complementary part of his work the essential wisdom which he had appropriated during the past three decades through his assiduous reading of Tyconius. By the way, he also evidenced at once how he had finally understood Tyconius's teaching. In 396, introducing *De doctrina christiana*, he still felt more than reserved about a hermeneutic involving special assistance of the Holy Spirit, focusing on the Apocalypse and on decisive obscurities of Scripture, or claiming to possess rules proper to give an "understanding of whatever is obscure in the Scriptures" (par. 8).[19] Now he feels free to quote the outspoken leader of such a school of thought. Par. 42 starts: "A certain Tyconius who wrote most triumphantly against the Donatists, although he himself was a Donatist..., wrote a book which he called *Of Rules*...."[20]

It is worth recalling to our attention at this point that Tyconius was the only African exegete with whom Augustine was seriously concerned at the time when he conceived his essay, *De doctrina christiana*, in 395–96. As an assistant bishop in Hippo, he had just struggled with Tyconius's interpretation of Paul in some of the *83 Diverse Questions* sent to Simplicianus as a gift for his election to the see of Milan after the death of Ambrose in April, 397. He did this precisely in Questions 69 and 81, as A. Pincherle had noted 50 years ago.[21] There is also a striking affinity with Tyconius noted in the Commentary on Psalm 54, written near Easter, 395. In addition to it, we are lucky enough to possess a letter written by Augustine to Aurelius, bishop of Carthage, in 396 (*Epistula XLI*), in which he mentions that it was Aurelius who had urged the priest and then bishop Augustine to read Tyconius. Moreover, in that letter, Augustine insists on the fact that he was at a loss with Tyconius's work and that, after multiple requests to hear what Aurelius himself thought about the work of the Donatist, he was begging again for some clues. I must quote Augustine's own words, because dating from 396, they evidence dramatically that, at the very time of the conception of *De doctrina christiana*, Tyconius was already on Augustine's mind exactly as he would be in his explicit writing of the last part of *De doctrina christiana* III thirty years later: *Nam et ego quod iussisti non negligo et de Tyconii septem regulis vel clavibus sicut saepe iam scripsi, cognoscere quid tibi videatur exspecto:*[22] "For I myself do not neglect what you have prescribed, and as I wrote to you many times, I still want to know what you think about the seven rules or keys of Tyconius."

Now, in 426, Augustine introduces his spectacular quotation of the Donatist's hermeneutic with the statement: "A certain Tyconius...wrote a book which he called *Of Rules*, since in it he explained seven rules with which, as if with keys, the obscurities of the Divine Scriptures might be opened" (par. 42).[23] He enumerates the "rules," and denounces at once Tyconius's pride or candid illusion, as he claims that all obscurities in Scripture would be cleared up by them. What counts foremost is Augustine's equation between "rules" and "keys" repeated identically in 396 (*septem regulis vel clavibus*) and in 426 ("seven rules with which as with keys").[24] Here we may perceive the reason why Augustine could not enter into Tyconius's logic in 396, but also why he succeeded in learning essential lessons from the same Tyconius after further studies, to the point of quoting and recommending him now in 426, as never any heretic or schismatic leader has anywhere been celebrated in a Patristic writing. Should I add that Augustine's specific equation between Tyconius's "rules" and "keys," which one might see as perfectly fitting with Augustine's own hermeneutic, but which misses completely Tyconius's point, could as well signal why Aurelius hesitated in 396 to express his own opinion to Augustine about Tyconius's *Book of Rules*. Aurelius was more informed at that time about Donatist matters than Augustine was. The latter did not yet have any clear idea about the Donatist doctrine of baptism, only a couple of years earlier, according to his pamphlet *Contra epistolam Donati*. He was still a newcomer on the scene of the African Church as such, but a newcomer powerfully gifted with a creative hermeneutic of his own. Aurelius could not help letting him work out his original response to Tyconian principles of interpretation at the cost of failing entirely to understand those principles in their own right, but in using them finally for a deeper and more theological account of his own hermeneutical precepts. In any case, we benefit from that enrichment in the final part of *De doctrina christiana* III, added in 426.

After having carefully introduced the Tyconian "rules" as "keys," with which "the obscurities of the Divine Scriptures might be opened," Augustine goes over, in par. 43, to quote at length the prologue of Tyconius's treatise: "I thought it necessary before all the other matters which occurred to me to write a book of Rules, and to fabricate, as it were, keys and windows for the secrets of the Law."[25] In this first proposition Augustine understood two juxtaposed sentences repeating the same thing: "to write a book of Rules" equalled, then, by a simple apposition, "to fabricate keys and windows." And such was the understanding of the medieval copyists who diligently modified the wordings of the next sentences, as well as the understanding of modern translators, who wrote for instance: "For there are certain mystic rules which reveal what is hidden in the whole Law and make visible the treasures of truth which are invisible to some."[26] This is truly consistent with Augustine's mind, but it is also in perfect contradiction with what Tyconius had written: *Sunt enim quaedam regulae mysticae, quae uniuersae legis recessus obtinent et ueritatis thesauros aliquibus inuisibiles faciunt.*[27] A study of Tyconius's *Book of Rules* shows without any doubt that the category of "mystic rules" was central for him.[28] Those "rules" were called by him "mystic" because they were the rules applied by the Holy Spirit in creating Scripture. They were, in other words, objective structures operating in the Holy Book with a revelatory power of their own. They were "obtaining," or "holding back,"[29] the "hidden places"[30] of the whole Scripture; and by the way they kept *invisible* for some people the real treasures of biblical truth. The role of the interpreter, in Tyconius's mind, was only to "fabricate keys"[31] which would give access to such structures. It was by no means to fabricate the "rules" themselves, which were "mystic,"[32] out of reach, and properly owned by the Holy Spirit in Scripture.

Augustine never entered into that African and very consistently theological hermeneutic witnessed by Tyconius and proper to the Donatist tradition, as shown by Parmenian through quotations of Optatus of Miletus, and by other sources.

At least we may have identified a local setting and motivation for *De doctrina christiana* worth a further consideration.[33]

Notes

[1] *De doctrina christiana* Prooemium,1: *CC* XXXII,1: *praecepta...tractandarum scripturarum*; tr. D. W. Robertson, Jr., *On Christian Doctrine* (Indianapolis: The Liberal Arts Press, 1983), p. 3.

[2] *De doctrina christiana* Prooemium,1: *CC* XXXII,1: *legendo alios, qui diuinarum litterarum operta aperuerunt.*

[3] *De doctrina christiana* Prooemium,1: *CC* XXXII,1: *si dominus ac deus noster ea, quae de hac re cogitanti solet suggerere, etiam scribenti mihi non deneget.*

[4] *De doctrina christiana* Prooemium,1: *CC* XXXII,1: *respondendum esse his, qui haec reprehensuri sunt aut reprehensuri essent.*

[5] *De doctrina christiana* Prooemium,2: *CC* XXXII,1: *qui diuinas scripturas uel re uera bene tractant uel bene tractare sibi uidentur.*

[6] *De doctrina christiana* Prooemium,2: *CC* XXXII,1-2: *qui quoniam nullis huiusmodi obseruationibus lectis quales nunc tradere institui, facultatem exponendorum sanctorum librorum se assecutos uel uident uel putant, nemini esse ista praecepta necessaria, sed potius totum quod de illarum litterarum obscuritatibus laudabiliter aperitur, diuino munere fieri posse clamitabunt*; tr. D. W. Robertson, Jr., p. 3.

[7] As suggested by E. Kevane, "Paideia and Anti-Paideia: The *Prooemium* of St. Augustine's *De doctrina christiana*," *AS* 1 (1970) 153–80.

[8] *De doctrina christiana* Prooemium,2: *CC* XXXII,1: *re uera bene tractant.*

[9] *De doctrina christiana* Prooemium,4: *CC* XXXII,2: *Iam uero eorum qui diuino munere exultant et sine talibus praeceptis, qualia nunc tradere institui, se sanctos libros intellegere atque tractare gloriantur et propterea me superflua uoluisse scribere existimant*; tr. D. W. Robertson, Jr., p. 4.

[10] *De doctrina christiana* Prooemium,8: *CC* XXXII,5: *Postremo quisquis se nullis praeceptis instructum diuino munere, quaecumque in scripturis obscura sunt intellegere gloriatur, bene quidem credit, et uerum est, non esse illam facultatem quasi a se ipso existentem, sed diuinitus traditam; ita enim dei gloriam quaerit et non suam*; tr. D. W. Robertson, Jr., 6.

[11] *De doctrina christiana* III,xxv,36: *CC* XXXII,98: *Incertum est enim, utrum iram dei significet non usque ad nouissimam poenam,…an potius gratiam scripturarum a Iudaeis ad gentes transeuntem*; tr. D. W. Robertson, Jr., p. 100.

[12] *De doctrina christiana* III,xxv,36: *CC* XXXII,99: *quod aqua…significat, sicut in Apocalypsi legimus, et spiritum sanctum.*

[13] *De doctrina christiana* III,xxvi,37: *CC* XXXII,99: *in locis…obscuris*; tr. D. W. Robertson, Jr., p. 101.

[14] *De doctrina christiana* III,xxvii,38: *CC* XXXII,100: *eo conante, qui diuina scrutatur eloquia, ut ad uoluntatem perueniatur auctoris, per quem scripturam illam sanctus operatus est spiritus; siue hoc assequatur, siue aliam sententiam de illis uerbis quae fidei rectae non refragatur, exsculpat, testimonium habens a quocumque alio loco diuinorum eloquiorum. Ille quippe auctor in eisdem uerbis, quae intellegere uolumus, et ipsam sententiam forsitan uidit et certe dei spiritus, qui per eum haec operatus est, etiam ipsam occursuram lectori uel auditori sine dubitatione praeuidit, immo ut occurreret, quia et ipsa est ueritate subnixa, prouidit. Nam quid in diuinis eloquiis largius et uberius potuit diuinitus prouideri, quam ut eadem uerba pluribus in-*

tellegantur modis, quos alia non minus diuina contestantia faciant approbari? tr. D. W. Robertson, Jr., p. 102.

¹⁵ *De doctrina christiana* III,xxviii,39: *CC* XXXII,100: *per scripturas enim diuinas multo tutius ambulatur; quas uerbis translatis opacatas cum scrutari uolumus.*

¹⁶ *De doctrina christiana* III,xxix,40: *CC* XXXII,100: *quos grammatici graeco nomine tropos uocant*; tr. D. W. Robertson, Jr., p. 102.

¹⁷ *De doctrina christiana* III,xxix,40–41: *CC* XXXII,101: *allegoria, aenigma, parabola —metafora—catachresis—ironia uel antifrasis*; tr. D. W. Robertson, Jr., pp. 102–3.

¹⁸ *De doctrina christiana* III,xxix,41: *CC* XXXII,102: *cognitio...scripturarum ambiguitatibus dissoluendis est necessaria...et sic pleraque inuenta sunt, quae latebant*; tr. D. W. Robertson, Jr., p. 104.

¹⁹ *De doctrina christiana* Prooemium,8: *CC* XXXII,5: *quaecumque in scripturis obscura sunt*; tr. D. W. Robertson, Jr., p. 6.

²⁰ *De doctrina christiana* III,xxx,42: *CC* XXXII,102: *Ticonius quidam, qui contra Donatistas inuictissime scripsit, cum fuerit donatista,...fecit librum, quem 'Regularum' uocauit*; tr. D. W. Robertson, Jr., p. 104.

²¹ A. Pincherle, *La formazione teologica de S. Agostino* (Rome, 1947: a collection of articles published in *Ricerche Religiose* in the years 1930–34), pp. 185–86, 203, n. 43.

²² *Epistula XLI* 2: *CSEL* XXXIII,83, translation mine.

²³ *De doctrina christiana* III,xxx,42: *CC* XXXII,102: *Ticonius quidam...fecit librum quem 'Regularum' vocavit, quia in eo quasdam septem regulas exsecutus est, quibus quasi clauibus diuinarum scripturarum aperirentur occulta*; tr. D. W. Robertson, Jr., p. 104. P. Bright, *The Book of Rules of Tyconius. Its Purpose and Inner Logic.* Christianity and Judaism in Antiquity. Vol. 2 (Notre Dame, Indiana: University of Notre Dame Press, 1988), offers up to the present day the only introduction available to Tyconius' work in an essay format. See also William Babcock's introduction in *Tyconius: The Book of Rules.* Translated with an Introduction and Notes by W. S. Babcock; SBL: Text and Translations 31, Early Christian Literature Series 7 (Atlanta: Scholars Press, 1989).

²⁴ See supra, notes 22 and 23.

²⁵ *De doctrina christiana* III,xxx,43: *CC* XXXII,103: *Necessarium duxi ante omnia, quae mihi uidentur, libellum regularum scribere et secretorum legis ueluti claues et luminaria fabricare.* Cf. F. C. Burkitt, ed., *The Book of Rules of Tyconius* (Cambridge: Cambridge University Press, 1894, repr. 1967), p. 1.

²⁶ D. W. Robertson, Jr., p. 105.

²⁷ *De doctrina christiana* III,xxx,43: *CC* XXXII,103.

²⁸ For some preliminary remarks on Tyconius' "mystic rules": C. Kannengiesser, *A Conflict of Christian Hermeneutics in Roman Africa: Tyconius and Augustine* (Colloquy 58) (Berkeley, CA: Center for Hermeneutical Studies in Hellenistic and Modern Culture.

Graduate Theological Union and U.C.-Berkeley, 1989): III "Mystic Rules: The Key-Notion of Tyconian Hermeneutic," pp. 6–8.

[29] Professor William S. Anderson (U.C.-Berkeley) suggested "hold back," or "blockaded": Minutes of Colloquy 58 mentioned in the preceding note, p. 71.

[30] *De doctrina christiana* III,xxx,43: *CC* XXXII,103: *secretorum legis*; cf. supra, n. 25.

[31] *De doctrina christiana* III,xxx,43: *CC* XXXII,103: *claves...fabricare*; cf. supra, n. 25.

[32] *De doctrina christiana* III,xxx,43: *CC* XXXII,103: *regulae mysticae*.

[33] More comments on this issue in my paper on "The Interrupted *De doctrina christiana*" in *Augustine's De doctrina christiana: A Classic of Western Culture*. A Colloquy held at the University of Notre Dame, 4–7 April 1991. To be published by the University of Notre Dame Press in 1992.

Serpent, Eve, and Adam:
Augustine and the Exegetical Tradition

Eugene TeSelle

When Augustine develops a theory of willing systematically—and he does it very early, from 390 on[1] —he isolates three factors. First, he says, comes the *suggestion*, which occurs to us either through the senses or through our own free association of ideas. This in turn arouses *delight* in what is presented to us. In Latin as well as English it could be said both that something "delights us" and that we "delight in" it. But delight is only an inclination; it does not issue in action, either inward or outward, until there is *consent* which is freely given in the center of the self. In consent we "cede to," give in to, ratify some inclination that has already been aroused. Or perhaps we "resist" the inclination and do not cede to it. But there is no action until there is consent.

In the very first statements of the triad "suggestion-delight-consent," Augustine says that the serpent of the Eden narrative represents the "suggestions" which come to us, inwardly or outwardly; Eve represents the affections aroused, the inclinations toward what is offered, the delight taken in the object; and Adam represents the consent that is given in the center of the self.[2]

Augustine was not alone in interpreting the Eden narrative in this way. There are parallels (but not exact parallels) which we shall examine. This line of interpretation, we would say today, is sexist in that it puts the male at the center of decision and identifies the woman with impulse. That is not surprising. It was developed by and from the standpoint of males, for whom women were "the other"—but an other which invited appropriation and could be delight itself. The culture, furthermore, gave males the dominant role, reinforcing and justifying a perspectival limitation rather than questioning it in the name of mutuality.

Even under such circumstances, however, this interpretation was not inevitable. Some Gnostic texts take the alternative position that Eve represents the higher principle of "spirit," Adam the lower principle of "soul."[3] And yet this fact is not quite as impressive as it seems. On this alternative interpretation, Adam still represents the center of decision or consent; the difference is that Eve represents a higher rather than a lower inducement, one that is redeeming rather than imprisoning. In these Gnostic texts, furthermore, the female principle, while higher than "Adam," is still derived from a supreme "masculine" deity and represents that portion of the spiritual realm which, being fallible, comes to be confined within the creaturely.[4]

There is in fact a similar complexity in Augustine, who in the end does better than the Gnostics. Although it could be said that he made the female principle of delight "lower" in dignity, it would be more accurate to say that he made it *penultimate* in the process of willing, preparatory to the final act of consent. And in so doing he also appropriated, internalized, and affirmed the "female" principle of delight as an indispensable factor in the working of the psyche. He did this, we should add, not only in the negative sense that delight often constitutes temptation, but (especially in his later writings) in the positive sense that delight in the good, given immediately by the Spirit of God, is what makes it possible to persist in virtue. And this Spirit is God's own self-delight.[5]

This allegorization, with all its complexities, was important to the ancient world. Whatever our modern reactions to it may be, let us ask about the origin and the meaning of this interpretation of the Eden narrative.

In Search of Augustine's Sources

Some key features of the allegory clearly resemble the interpretation of Ambrose, the bishop of Milan who had a major influence in Augustine's conversion.[6] One of Ambrose's first works was "On Paradise," written about 377; his interpretation would have been available to Augustine, either in writing or orally, at the time of his conversion nine or ten years later. As in Augustine's interpretation, the garden is the human self, and the three figures illustrate factors or processes within it. But the details are different. For Ambrose, as for Philo several centuries earlier, Eve is sense, Adam is mind, and the serpent is pleasure, which is to be fled like a serpent, for it leads away from the spiritual delights of Paradise and is the beginning of the passions.[7]

The allegorization is in the Platonist tradition, emphasizing the difference between "higher" and "lower" capacities and the objects of their attention. It could have been the beginning of Augustine's reflections. But it does not have the sequence "suggestion-delight-consent," and the symbolism of Eve and the serpent is the reverse of Augustine's. The difference is that Philo, followed by Ambrose, moves *outward*, from the center of the self to that which is not only more contingent but is, at least in principle, avoidable; Augustine, by contrast, moves *inward*, from the circumstances to which human willing is intrinsically receptive to the definitive act of consent to those preconditions.

From reading Ambrose one would not guess that his interpretation comes from Philo of Alexandria, the Jewish writer of the first century; indeed, Philo is mentioned by name only once, and then critically, with a slur at his Jewish inability to grasp spiritual things. Had Ambrose read Philo? He was able to use Greek, and Jerome, a contemporary, criticized Ambrose for plagiarizing from Greek works without mentioning his dependence on them. There is some evidence that Philo's writings were preserved in Italy, in a manuscript tradition different from that of Origen at Caesarea. In addition, some of Philo's works were translated into Latin, probably around 380, and thus were available for use by both Ambrose and Augustine. But it could also be that Ambrose took the material, not directly from Philo, but from Origen, and specifically from his lost commentaries on Genesis, which would have reported and evaluated Philo's own extensive commentaries on the same work.[8]

Origen seems to be indicated by *another* figurative interpretation of Scripture, which first appears in Augustine's writings at the same time as the Eden allegory. In the gospels Christ is said to have raised three persons from the dead: the daughter of the ruler of the synagogue (Mk 5:35–43), who had just died; the only son of the widow of Nain (Lk 7:11–17), who was being carried out of the city for burial; and Lazarus (Jn 11:17–44), who had been in the tomb for four days and was putrefying. These seem, then, to represent three degrees of spiritual death: within the heart (i.e., within the house), by consenting to desire; issuing in external action (i.e., going out the gates of the city); and pressing upon the soul with the weight of custom (that is, decomposing within the tomb). Each of these degrees of death is overcome through faith, as one responds to Christ saying, "Talitha cumi" (Mk 5:41), or "I say to you, rise" (Lk 7:14), or "Lazarus, come forth" (Jn 11:35).[9]

The Philosophical Debate

The question of Augustine's sources becomes even more complex when we look at the triple formula "suggestion-delight-consent." In its essentials it comes from the Stoics. The most evident source is Aulus Gellius, whose *Attic Nights* is quoted several times by Augustine. He tells how a Stoic philosopher was on a ship tossed in a storm. When the philosopher grew pale with terror, the other passengers twitted him for not achieving Stoic imperturbability. But he answered that it only confirmed Stoic theory: we cannot control what impressions will be made on us from outside ourselves, seeking our acknowledgment; they even cause involuntary "movement" through the force of their appeal; but approval or assent or acknowledgment is within our own power. In other words, there are no "passions" except when we give way to this appeal and consent to it.[10] The point is made even clearer in another passage,[11] when Augustine deals with the statement (Gn 15:12) that "at the setting of the sun, dread rushed upon Abraham, and behold, a great fear befell him." The question involved here is whether those who are wise—which Abraham certainly was—can experience such "perturbations." Gellius is recalled in order to make the point that there is a difference between *affects*, which are not within our power but to which we do not necessarily yield, and *passions*, which arise once we consent to these affects. (The outcome is not always favorable, of course. In the *Confessions* Augustine tells how his friend Alypius, on going to Rome, was taken against his will to the gladiatorial games by his fellow students, vowing that he would neither look nor enjoy; but when heard the shouts of the crowd he opened his eyes, was delighted with the cruelty of combat, and became an enthusiast, dragging others with him.)[12]

In all of this we catch a glimpse of the ongoing disputes among the differing philosophical schools. In part it was a matter of definition—what is and is not a "passion"?—and Augustine quoted with favor the assertion of Cicero that the Stoics and the Aristotelians were disputing about words.[13] But of course there remained important issues of describing human experience accurately and conceptualizing it correctly.

The Stoics, like modern behaviorists or philosophers of action, did not like the way Plato talked about the "parts" of the soul, or Aristotle about its "powers." They preferred to see human beings as unified organisms. Whenever we act, they insisted, it is we ourselves who do it. For them the basic differentiation is between the experiences that "occur" to us and our response or "assent" to them. The former are not within our power; the latter, by the nature of the case, is always within our power. The former come to us as "propositions" seeking our assent; but it is we ourselves who give consent, sometimes in the cognitive mode by saying, "That's true," sometimes in the practical mode by saying, "I'll do it."[14] (For the Stoics cognitive and practical assent were essentially the same kind of response. Even Augustine uses "assent" and "consent" more or less equivalently. But he begins to anticipate the medieval and modern differentiation between them, so that assent is more cognitive, acknowledging the truth of a proposition concerning some state of affairs, while consent is more affective, a yielding to and agreeing with some purpose or some project.) The point is that the Stoics tended to emphasize a yes or no to what is proposed to us in experience; they did not think in terms of the Aristotelians' deliberation about alternatives or the Platonists' contemplation of ideals.

But the Platonists and Aristotelians could bring to bear certain experiences which seemed to confirm their language about "parts" or "powers" of the soul. We do have inner conflicts, and these suggest that we feel various impulses from the "irrational" parts of the soul before, and even after, we consent to a particular course of action. The Aristotelians, furthermore, drew attention to the practical value of emotions such as anger and desire, at least when they are kept within proper measure. Finally, there are experiences which suggest that the "rational soul" is able to rise above the immediate data of the situation, deliberating on alternative possibilities for action (this was the Aristotelian emphasis) or even considering abstract ideals which completely transcend the sensory realm (and this was the Platonist emphasis).[15]

In the encounter every party conceded something. Here we find one of the many instances of genuine inquiry and innovation, not the mere repetition of dogmatic positions, in the philosophy of the Hellenistic and Roman periods. The Platonists came to acknowledge, perhaps more strongly than before, that much of our life is indeed enmeshed in the sensory world and that irrational impulses must be taken seriously. The Stoics, for their part, came to acknowledge a greater complexity in our inner life. Although they did not speak in terms of Aristotelian deliberation or Platonist awareness of ideals, they did add a new factor prior to assent—what they called προπάθειαι or "pre-passions," involuntary affective reactions which come prior to consent and thus are different from the true passions, which are based upon consent.[16] In this way they were able to retain their older doctrine that the only impulses which lead to action are those which *follow* consent.

Augustine learned about this Stoic doctrine—in its later form, acknowledging involuntary inclinations prior to consent—from Aulus Gellius, as we have seen, and from Cicero, and perhaps from Seneca as well.[17] And yet no Stoics summarized their doctrine in the triple formula "suggestion-delight-consent," probably because they admitted the middle stage somewhat reluctantly or even defensively, as a concession to their opponents. It is quite possible, then, that Augustine developed the triple formula on his own, following the suggestions he had encountered in Gellius.

On the other hand, Augustine's use of the triple formula is linked from the first with the allegorical interpretation of the temptation story in Genesis. This suggests a link with an earlier tradition of Biblical interpretation, and Origen is the one who springs most readily to mind.[18]

It would not be foolish to look even farther back. There was a tradition of discussion using the tripartite formula "sense-impulse-assent."[19] It seems to summarize a question debated among the rival schools. In what appears to be a *reductio ad absurdum* of Stoic "necessity," Carneades of the "New Academy" and Colotes the Epicurean pointed out that sense and impulse cannot be eliminated from human experience; if assent were denied an independent role, then these others factors would become determinative, and assent itself would be caused by them. The Stoics, answering the accusation of necessity, drew an important distinction. Assent, which is within our power, is the *principal cause* of our action; outward impressions and inward impulses are only *disposing causes*.[20] In contrast to physical objects which are moved "from without," or animals which are moved "from within" by impulse, human action always presupposes judgment and assent.[21]

But this tripartite discussion of human action is chiefly the outline of a controversy among the schools. It does not represent, by itself, anything like a "doctrine," though alternative doctrines could be developed from it (the Stoics would emphasize rational judgment and assent, while Aristotelians would acknowledge the role, and even the positive role, of inclination).

We must hold open the possibility, then, that something like the tripartite formula "suggestion-delight-consent" was used prior to Augustine, and also the possibility that someone prior to Augustine linked it with the serpent, Eve, and Adam. But it is just as likely that he formulated it on his own in a synthetic insight, linking (1) an exegetical tradition which already allegorized the Eden narrative, but assigned different values to Adam, Eve, and the serpent; (2) a philosophical discussion of the problem of "sense-impulse-assent," which the opposing schools treated in very different ways, none of them expressing their own doctrines with a tripartite formula, and none of them stating the triad "suggestion-delight-consent"; and (3) a new way of formulating the synthesis, suggested by Plotinus.[22] For the crucial concept is that of delight as orienting the soul "downward" or "upward," and this acquires a major role in the sixth book of *De musica*, completed in 389 or 390:

Delight is, so to speak, the weight of the soul. "For where your treasure is, there will also be your heart" (Mt 6:21): where delight is, there is treasure; but where the heart is, there is happiness or misery.[23]

Augustine had begun to quote the Canticles (Sg 2:4):

"Give order to love within me."[24]

He had long since known a verse from Vergil's *Eclogues*, which the pagan Maximus of Madaura, writing to Augustine in 389, quoted apropos of a different and more trivial point:

Each is drawn by one's own pleasure.[25]

And of course he also knew of the passage about the Stoic in Aulus Gellius' *Attic Nights*, which comes close to enunciating a triadic theory of willing. What Plotinus added to all of this was the imagery of gravitating downward or upward in ways which affect one's entire being, indeed, which determine whether the soul is "with God" or "in the body." A few years later Augustine states the point systematically. He not only notes that delight in sensible beauty can be a temptation to sin, and makes the more general point that we will pursue what delights us most, but also speaks of the "fruits of the Spirit" (Ga 5:22–23) as those delights through which higher good is able to rule human responses.[26]

The search for direct "influences," then, while it must always be undertaken, may be of limited value. Even when we find such influences, an idea can be transformed by a creative thinker, especially in a new situation; indeed, when a number of different influences come together they *must* be combined in an individual way.

More important, then, than the *answers* given by successive thinkers is the *question* with which they were dealing, the sense of uncertainty which they shared, the problem that made them uneasy and drove them to seek some resolution, the inquiry in which they were engaged without being sure that it would arrive at a satisfactory answer. In the present case we have a convergence of *two* traditions of discussion—one of them a philosophical inquiry into willing and its preconditions, which has just been discussed, the other an exegetical consideration of the Eden narrative, to which we shall now turn, for it is not only interesting as a problem of interpretation but may be especially revealing, precisely because it is symbolic, of the thinker's connections with his own affective life.

What Happened in the Garden?

Augustine shares the same *problem* with many others before him, going back at least to the generation of Philo—and of Paul—early in the first century. It is a major problem, the origin of human sin. And the narrative in Genesis, in the process of dealing with this problem, creates other problems as well. For it is the narrative itself that introduces the serpent, the woman, and the man—in that order, and at least three times: in tracing the origin of sin (Gn 3:1–7), in narrating the explanations given by the guilty ones (Gn 3:12–13), and in reporting God's punishment of all three (Gn 3:14–19). According to the narrative, furthermore, the prohibition against eating of the tree of knowledge was addressed only to Adam, prior to Eve's creation, while Eve alone had contact with the serpent and thus was the mediator of temptation. It was not inaccurate, then, when a New Testament writing, often quoted by Augustine in summarizing the problem, said: "Adam was not deceived, but the woman was deceived ['seduced' is the Latin, but it simply means 'deceived' and 'led astray,' with or without sexual connotations] into transgression" (1 Tm 2:14). And it was not merely male self-justification when rabbinic interpretations tended to minimize the responsibility of Adam and emphasize the roles of Eve and the serpent; the text itself—perhaps out of misogyny or male self-justification—had already suggested their importance in initiating the process that led to sin.[27]

All of this exacerbated the problem of the origin of sin by increasing the number of factors involved—and placing them, furthermore, in an earthly setting. Celsus, the second-century opponent of Christianity, made fun of the Eden narrative with its forming of the man by God's hands, and the drawing of the woman from his side, and the weakness of a deity whose persuasive power was less than the serpent's. He knew that Jews and Christians, being ashamed of these things, had already tried to allegorize them. Origen could only hurl a *tu quoque* in reply: the Greeks allegorize Homer and Hesiod all the time, therefore the "barbarians" should be able to do likewise with their own sacred literature.[28]

But how is one to allegorize? The double creation narrative in Genesis 1 and 2 mentioned both the humanity, "male and female," which is created in—or to—the *image of God* (Gn 1:27), and the humanity which is formed from the *earth* (Gn 2:7, 21–22), of which only males—Adam and Seth—are said to be in God's image (Gn 5:1–3). It was possible to say, then, that males alone are the image and glory of God, as Paul indeed suggests (1 Co 3:18 and 4:4–6). But it was also possible to do what Philo and many others did, namely to assert that the true humanity is that which is after the image of God, in which males and females are identical, and that the differentiation into male and female, if it is not the *result* of sin (a fall from heaven to earth), is at least the *occasion* of sin (through the addition of a lower mind which could be drawn to lesser things, or through sexual differentiation with its new opportunities for sexual pleasure).

From its beginnings the Christian church had several possibilities for thinking about males and females and what they signified.

First, there were without doubt attempts to nurture a community without sexual dualisms and without patriarchy, a community in which there is a vision of "inclusive wholeness," in which marriage is equal partnership, in which no one is called father or rabbi (Mt 23:8–10), and in which women are assumed, as in the gospel narratives, to have a significant role.[29]

Second, as an alternative to earthly equality between males and females —which could be upsetting, socially and culturally and even politically—there were attempts, along the lines manifested in Philo and in Gnosticism, to go behind the differentiation of male and female to the primal humanity, created after God's image, of Genesis 1:27. The "spiritual" party at Corinth probably had this character, and a number of recent studies have tried to identify, from Paul's attacks on them, the teachings of his opponents—and not only teachings, for in addition to their theories about the origin of the human situation, or their contemplative attempts to return to the primal state, they also had their own interpretation of rituals like baptism or the eucharist, perhaps even ritual actions of their own. One of the most obscure questions, but one directly pertinent to our inquiry, concerns Paul's discussion of head coverings (veils? long hair?) for women (1 Co 11:2–16).[30] If it was a matter of hair length, it meant that they were challenging the culturally established differences between the sexes and trying to reintroduce the primal unity of the human race. If it was a matter of removing their veils, perhaps only in the setting of ecstatic worship, it may have symbolized a spiritual or ritual return to the primal humanity, once again by denying the importance of sexual differentiation.

Paul himself took a third and more complex approach. He asserted that there is no difference between men and women—at least "in Christ" (1 Co 11:11–12 and especially Ga 3:27–28). But at the same time he did not deny sexual differentiation. In effect he reversed Philo's sequence: first there is the earthly humanity, and only then the heavenly (1 Co 15:45–50). His direction is not "protological" but "eschatological."[31] This had ambiguous benefits from the standpoint of women. It rejected any requirements of their disembodiment or becoming like men—but at the price of their being acknowledged precisely as women, and therefore of being valued, at least during the present age, primarily for their reproductive role, and in a subordinate status.[32]

Here we have a trajectory reaching at least from Paul to Augustine, a trajectory unified not by agreed answers, even when attention was focused upon texts regarded as authoritative, but by a set of hermeneutical problems. Thus it is not surprising to see Augustine wrestling with centuries-old themes, and to see both similarities (which suggest lines of influence) and differences (which suggest either unknown sources or originality of insight). He himself had once been contemptuous of the Genesis narrative; he himself had joined in the Manichaeans' mockery of it; he himself had then welcomed Ambrose's allegorizing, which made it intelligible and acceptable for the first time. Later he began to wonder whether allegorization was too spiritualizing, too fearful of the literal meaning, too devaluing of the body.[33]

The Augustinian Interpretation

The characteristics of Augustine's answers, as he develops them over a period of years and in various contexts, are, first, the affirmation of a *plurality* of factors and, second, a tendency to *internalize* them, so that the outward differentiation between male and female and serpent becomes a parable for the plurality of factors within the psyche.

From an early time Augustine found saving value in the complexity of the human fall. At one extreme, the angels who never fell away from God have no need of a mediator; and at the other extreme, the angels who fell by their own choice, without persuasion by another, cannot be reconciled to God by a mediator. By contrast humanity, having fallen through persuasion to pride by the proud mediator of sin, can be restored through persuasion to humility by the humble mediator of reconciliation.[34] The *mediated* character of human life turns out, then, to be an extenuating circumstance; indeed, it is the condition of possibility for salvation.

Furthermore Augustine, when he asked why Adam yielded to temptation, gave a "social" explanation: Adam did not want to disappoint Eve, believing that she would waste away and die without his presence, and thus he ate out of friendly benevolence;[35] or, even less magnanimously, he ate out of fear of losing his only companion.[36] This "companionate" side of marriage came to be emphasized after 401, when Augustine tried to soften Jerome's attacks on marriage in the twin works *On the Good of Marriage* and *On Holy Virginity* (we should also add the contemporaneous writing *On the Work of Monks*).[37] Here, and in *The City of God*, marriage is made the first and most natural sign of the social character of human life.[38] It helps to understand why Adam followed Eve in eating the forbidden fruit.

But to *understand* Adam is not to *excuse* him. The social motive of his sin "accuses more than excuses," Augustine says. Against all those, ancient and modern, who blame Eve for the origin of human sin, he firmly points out that there is no one—not even one's sole companion—to whom consent ought to be yielded ahead of God.[39] In this respect the situation of Adam is by no means unique. Augustine notes that the devil also tempted Job through a woman, when his wife urged him to curse God. But Job was not another Adam. While Adam was vanquished in the midst of delights, Job conquered in the midst of pain; while Adam consented to positive inducements, Job did not yield even to negative torments.[40]

By now it has become clear that Augustine assumes the primacy of the male partner. He is the one who makes decisions, who consents or refuses to yield, while the female is the one who urges him in the wrong direction.

One reason is symbolic: the male represents the mind, the center of the self where decisions are made, while the female represents the inclinations which may or may not be ratified by the mind. The New Testament assertion that it was not Adam but Eve who was deceived (1 Tm 2:13–14) can suggest this kind of allegorization. And even if it is *not* allegorized it still suggests that the woman is the "weaker" partner.

The other reason is altogether literal: Augustine assumes that the subjection of female to male is the one kind of subjection that belongs to the "order of nature" and is not the result of sin.[41] Paul's assertion that the male is "the image and glory of God" (1 Co 11:7) seems to confirm this. And yet Augustine knows very well that male and female are both said to be created in the image of God (Gn 1:26–27) and that in Christ, that is, in the renewed humanity, there is neither male nor female (Ga 3:27–28). How is this exegetical puzzle to be resolved?

Augustine distinguishes between different aspects of human life. Creation in the image of God and renewal in Christ have to do with the mind, the "inward person," which males and females have in common. But sexual difference in the body becomes an appropriate symbol for a difference within each person—that between mind and affection, between that which should rule and that which should be subjected. The apostle was speaking in terms of this "sacrament" when he said that only women should be veiled because men are the image and glory of God.[42] Thus Augustine sets for himself the complex task of speaking both about what is *inwardly shared* by males and females and about what *inwardly and outwardly differentiates* them. The former is suggested by the creation account in Genesis 1, the latter by that in Genesis 2. In Augustine's age the former tended to reinforce beliefs in the preexistence of the soul, since it emphasized those aspects of human life which can be thought of "apart from" or even "before" embodiment, while the latter required a consideration of precisely the aspects of embodiment, difference, reproduction, and physical descent—though even these, as we have seen, could also be interpreted symbolically.

The full complexity of Augustine's thinking along these lines is reflected in Book XII of *On the Trinity*.[43] Once again he affirms that the image of God, which is the mind, is complete in both the male and the female. But when the woman is referred to separately, in terms which apply to her alone, she is *not* called the image of God. In such contexts she signifies the "lower reason" which concerns itself with temporal affairs. And the serpent here represents sense experience.

In mind, then, man and woman have a common nature. But their bodily difference becomes a figure for a complex and hierarchically structured "distribution" of that one mind. In any single person we find *sense*, which human beings have in common with animals; *lower reason*, whose appetites are close to the senses; and *higher reason*, which because of its independence is in a position to give final consent. Human life, therefore, is in every way "in the middle," related to God, to sensible things—and to itself. It can turn away from God to itself, and then, through its own "middleness," to lower things. And yet this complexity of human life is not only the occasion of temptation and sin; it also constitutes the potentiality for redemption, as we have seen, since it exhibits the extenuating circumstances under which sin occurs and makes possible a lifelong struggle between good and evil.

An Appraisal

Augustine's allegorization of the serpent, Eve, and Adam has often been criticized; his theory that the allegorization is appropriately expressed in the biological difference between males and females has been attacked even more severely. Let us ask, not only what defects have been found in his interpretation of male and female, but how it reflects its own cultural setting and where it is better or worse than other expressions of that setting.

First, it does accept the social conventions of male superiority, which were promoted, of course, not only in the culture of late antiquity but in the language of the Bible itself. More precisely, it assumes that the difference between male and female must signify higher and lower, not a diversity that can be lived out in equality and mutuality. The other possibility of viewing sexual difference as an invitation to friendship or companionship was recognized by many ancients, including Augustine; but this alternative insight was unable to dislodge the conviction that male and female are unequal by nature.

This culturally-based attitude reinforced, and was reinforced by, the ascetic movement, which turned away from interpersonal relationships (since it did not see a central human value in them but viewed them as distracting or misleading) and sought the "singleness," the simplicity and unrelatedness, of mind, usually conceived as male even with reference to female ascetics.[44]

And when there was allegorizing—when there was recognition that the Eden narrative cannot simply be left in the past, that it has some meaning for the present, that human life is receptive to influences from outside itself and even within itself, that mind can be affected in many ways, that it is not totally independent and autonomous—the point of view was that of male exegetes, who, not surprisingly, identify their own subjectivity with Adam and assume that Eve represents a penultimate factor which is experienced by and is judged by mind but does not have the same rights to judge the male self.

Given the male point of view, the linking of Eve with the affections has positive as well as negative implications, for the aspects of "affection" and "receptivity" associated by the culture with women can be internalized by males as part of their own personality. A less male-centered theory, however, might have considered in this connection the other classic impulse of *anger*, defensiveness, assertiveness, which is culturally linked with masculinity, so that the responsive inclinations of the soul would be *both* feminine and masculine, and the center of the self, which gives consent, would be thought of as ungendered or, more appropriately, androgynous.[45] Augustine's own thought has potentialities for such a move. But even though he appreciated the role of fear—not only in driving human life toward evildoing but in "deterring" it through fear of punishment—he recognized that we are more often drawn toward that which attracts us. That is to say, the "feminine" principle of desire and delight is psychologically stronger than the "masculine" principle of anger and fear and confrontation.

When the affections are symbolized by a female figure, they are not merely negative in their connotations, as a principle of temptation and movement "downward." Some Gnostic texts, as we have noted, identified Eve with the higher, though fallible, principle of spirit or wisdom.[46] And Augustine himself, late in his career, developed the theme of *delectatio uictrix*, a victorious delight in the good or in justice.[47] Its interpretation has been controversial ever since the theme was highlighted by the Jansenists, making it seem to impose a kind of inevitability upon human willing. The typical response in Catholic theology is to deny inevitability (which would make this victorious delight a "concupiscence in reverse") and instead to emphasize a sort of "positive reinforcement loop" between delight and consent, such that only those who consent to the good can take delight in it, and delight in turn stimulates the next act of consent.[48]

What the ancient trajectory of interpretation seems to have overlooked was a genuinely interpersonal understanding of human life, one which could see it not only as open and vulnerable to the other (this was recognized in the literature on friendship) but as involving the affections, perhaps even sexual affections, perhaps even a willing self-abandon. There were those who loved spouses or partners and wrote eloquently about it. But this belonged chiefly to poetry, not to philosophy. Interpersonal and especially sexual love was sublimated by the philosophical tradition, often nobly. The classic statement was Plato's *Symposium*.[49] The corresponding "last word," at least for our purposes, was uttered by the Augustine of the Cassiciacum dialogues, who, having just abandoned woman's embrace, wrote passionately about a spiritual embrace with divine Wisdom or Truth[50] and initiated his lifelong intoxication with the *caritas* which comes from God and returns to God.

Perhaps it was necessary for classical and Christian thought to discover and strengthen the self before it could discover and give itself to the human other. Perhaps the betrayals endemic to human friendship and the disappointments inevitably resulting from human mortality made human affection seem too risky, so that emotional security was to be sought within and above the self. But it also seems likely that the social customs and kinship systems of the ancient world collected their tribute from the interpreters of Scripture, pointing them toward the male, not to the "male and female" of Genesis 1:27, when they looked for the image of God.

Notes

[1] *De Genesi aduersus Manichaeos* II,xiv,20–21; xviii,28: *PL* XXXIV,206–7, 210; *De sermone Domini in monte* I,xii,34: *CC* XXXV,36–38.

[2] Besides the texts cited above, see *De catechizandis rudibus* xviii,30: *CC* XLVI,154–55; *Enarratio in Psalmum LXXXIII* 7: *CC* XXXIX,1151–52; *De trinitate* XII,xii,17: *CC* L, 371–72; *De ciuitate dei* XIV,xi: *CC* XLVIII,431–33, and *Contra Julianum* VI,xxii,68: *PL* XLIV,864–65. A partial parallel is Augustine's interpretation of the statement (Gn 3:15) that the woman will watch (*obseruabit*) the serpent's head: the serpent's head is the initial "suggestion" of evil, which one should repel before delight and consent follow (*Enarratio in Psalmum XLVIII, Sermo I* 6: *CC* XXXVIII,555–57; cf. *Enarratio in Psalmum CIII, Sermo IV* 6: *CC* XL,1525–26; both from 412). For the texts and their context see K. E. Børresen, *Subordination and Equivalence: The Nature and Role of Women in Augustine and Thomas Aquinas* (Washington: University Press of America, 1981), pp. 51–56; the "Notes complémentaires" by P. Agaësse et A. Solignac in *BA* 49,516–30, 541–45, 555–59 (including responses to Børresen, originally published in 1968); R. J. McGowan, "Augustine's Spiritual Equality: The Allegory of Man and Woman with Regard to Imago Dei," *REA* 33 (1987) 255–64; and R. J. O'Connell, S.J., *The Origin of the Soul in St. Augustine's Later Works* (New York: Fordham University Press, 1987), pp. 260–64 and 312–19.

[3] E. Pagels, "Adam and Eve and the Serpent in Genesis 1–3," *Images of the Feminine in Gnosticism*, ed. K. L. King (Philadelphia: Fortress Press, 1988), p. 414; *Adam, Eve, and the Serpent* (New York: Random House, 1988), pp. 66–68.

[4] K. L. King, "Sophia and Christ in the Apocryphon of John," *Images of the Feminine in Gnosticism* (Philadelphia: Fortress Press, 1988), pp. 173–74.

[5] *De trinitate* VI,x,11–12: *CC* L,241–43. At the same time Augustine refuses to make the Holy Spirit a "feminine" principle in God, or the "mother" of the Son (*De trinitate* XII, v,5: *CC* L,359–60), as Marius Victorinus had done (*Aduersus Arium* I,57–58).

[6] For citation and interpretation of the passages, see F. H. Dudden, *The Life and Times of St. Ambrose* (Oxford: Clarendon Press, 1935), p. 615; R. J. O'Connell, S.J., *St. Augustine's Early Theory of Man, A.D. 386–391* (Cambridge: Harvard University Press, 1968), p. 157; E. Clark, "Heresy, Asceticism, Adam, and Eve: Interpretations of Genesis 1–3 in the Later Latin Fathers," *Ascetic Piety and Women's Faith: Essays on Late Ancient Christianity*, Studies in Women and Religion 20 (Lewiston/Queenston: Edwin Mellen Press, 1986), also printed in *Genesis 1–3 in the History of Exegesis: Intrigue in the Garden,*

ed. G. A. Robbins, Studies in Women and Religion 27 (Lewiston/Queenston: Edwin Mellen Press, 1988), pp. 99–134.

[7] R. A. Baer, Jr., *Philo's Use of the Categories of Male and Female*, Arbeiten zur Literatur und Geschichte des hellenistischen Judentums 3 (Leiden: E.J. Brill, 1970), pp. 40–44, and T. H. Tobin, S.J., *The Creation of Man: Philo and the History of Interpretation*, Catholic Biblical Quarterly Monograph Series 11 (Washington: Catholic Biblical Association of America, 1983), pp. 33–35, 146–49, trace the complexity of the problem of the double creation in Gn 1 and 2, which Philo (perhaps following earlier interpreters) discusses along several different lines; both of them also emphasize that his purpose is to make the creation narrative an "allegory of the soul," referring not only to the past but to the present. D. Sly, *Philo's Perception of Women*, Brown Judaic Studies 209 (Atlanta: Scholars Press, 1990) looks more connectedly at Philo's evaluations of women (both literally and allegorically), and finds a consistent pattern of hierarchical control, whether in the household or in the soul; thus lack of control within the psyche compromises its unity and makes the mind vulnerable to desire (pp. 91–110 on Eve), while proper control makes the mind of a man or a woman "virginal" or "male" and ready to receive guidance from the "feminine" principle of wisdom or virtue (pp. 145–60 on Sarah and Rebecca).

[8] These issues are discussed at length in E. Lucchesi, *L'Usage de Philon dans l'oeuvre exégétique de saint Ambroise. Une 'Quellenforschung' relative aux commentaires d'Ambroise sur la Genèse*, Arbeiten zur Literatur und Geschichte des hellenistischen Judentums 9 (Leiden: E.J. Brill, 1977), esp. pp. 71–77, 86–88, and A. Solignac, "Philon d'Alexandrie, II. Influence sur les Pères de l'Église," *Dictionnaire de spiritualité*, XII.1 (Paris: Beauchesne, 1983), pp. 1368–74.

[9] This is first developed in *De sermone Domini in monte* I,xii,35: *CC* XXXV,38–39. It reappears later in three sermons preached between 415 and 418: *Tractatus in Euangelium Ioannis* XLIX,3: *CC* XXXVI,420–21; *Sermo XCVIII* 5–6: *PL* XXXVIII,593–94; and *Sermo CXXVIII* 14: *PL* XXXVIII,720. The source is likely to be Origen, who not only mentions these three raisings from the dead—in the same order—but emphasizes the symbolic interpretation of all Christ's miracles (*Contra Celsum* II,48).

[10] *De ciuitate dei* IX,iv: *CC* XLVII,251–53, paraphrasing *Noctes Atticae* XIX,1. This was written about 417. For all the relevant texts see H. Hagendahl, *Augustine and the Latin Classics*, Studia Graeca et Latina Gothoburgensia 20.1 (Stockholm: Almqvist and Wiksell, 1967), pp. 179–84 and 674. Three similar narratives, from modern novels or biographies, are quoted in B. Inwood, *Ethics and Human Action in Early Stoicism* (Oxford: Clarendon Press, 1985), p. 181.

[11] *Quaestiones et locutiones in Heptateuchum* I,30: *CC* XXXIII,12–13, written in 419. Here it is clear that Augustine is recalling the passage from memory; there is even a note (to himself or the scribe), "Consider how A. Gellius said this and carefully insert it"—a note which was ignored (Hagendahl, p. 674).

[12] *Confessiones* VI,viii,13: *CC* XXVII,82–83. The rhetoric of the passage is analyzed with much insight in E. Auerbach, *Mimesis: The Representation of Reality in Western Literature*, tr. W. R. Trask (Princeton: Princeton University Press, 1953), pp. 66–76.

[13] *De ciuitate dei* IX,iv–v: *CC* XLVII,251–55.

[14] Note the similarity with the interpretation of experience that we find in the modern philosopher A. N. Whitehead, *Process and Reality: An Essay in Cosmology* (New York: Macmillan, 1929), pp. 280–316, for whom experience is filled with "propositions" or "lures for feeling" which might be appropriated as one's own through action or self-definition. The difference is that Whitehead emphasizes a freedom for decision among various propositions, while the Stoics were determinists, holding that every proposition, even when it concerns the future, is either true or false, so that its realization does not depend upon free choice among alternatives but will take place without fail, either with or without our consent. Augustine, like the Stoics, asserted that propositions about the future are either true or false. He differentiated himself from them by affirming both human choice and divine foreknowledge, which, though "definite" or "determinate," do not impose "necessity" (*De ciuitate dei* V,ix–x: *CC* XLVII,136–41). Elsewhere he added to this his belief in predestination, according to which God works with human freedom by offering precisely those suggestions, and infusing those inclinations, which will infallibly lead to consent.

[15] Inwood, pp. 72–86. On the Roman appropriation of Stoicism, see M. L. Colish, *The Stoic Tradition from Antiquity to the Early Middle Ages*, 2 volumes, Studies in the History of Christian Thought 34–35 (Leiden: E.J. Brill, 1985).

[16] Inwood (pp. 175–81) suggests that they were invented at some point between Chrysippus, who made the classic statement of the Stoic position, and the "middle Stoicism" of Posidonius in the first century B.C.E., who clearly acknowledged that affects are not merely the result of wrong consent. For citations see P. Merlan, "Greek Philosophy from Plato to Plotinus," *The Cambridge History of Later Greek and Early Medieval Philosophy*, ed. A. H. Armstrong (Cambridge: University Press, 1970), p. 126. It should be noted that part of the debate focused upon Euripedes' *Medea*, and specifically the conflict expressed (lines 1078–79) between passion and thought—an issue that may have influenced Paul's reflections in Romans 7. Chrysippus saw Medea's flaw as one of judgment, turning away from what reason itself dictated. Galen, in criticism of his excessive rationalism, saw it as a conflict of different impulses in the parts of the soul. This issue was identified by A. Dihle, *Euripedes' Medea*, Sitzungsberichte der Heidelberger Akademie der Wissenschaften. Philosophisch-historische Klasse 1977.5 (Heidelberg: Carl Winter, 1977), p. 25, and has been discussed at greater length by G. Theissen, *Psychological Aspects of Pauline Theology*, tr. J. P. Galvin (Philadelphia: Fortress Press, 1987), pp. 211–21.

[17] Seneca clearly states that between the impression made by experience and the assent freely given there is inclination, a tentative "first movement" which foreshadows the movement of affection which is really one's own (*De ira* I,xvi,7; II,iii,1; iv,1). But Augustine mentions Seneca only a few times, and never in connection with the themes involved here (Hagendahl, pp. 676–80).

[18] I have already noted the possibility that this topic was discussed in Origen's long commentary on Genesis. The other channel, perhaps even more likely, would be his homilies on Genesis, translated by Rufinus. Of these only 16 survive, and their subjects leap from creation (Homily 1) to Noah's Ark (Homily 2). If the later manuscript tradition (whose source is southern Italy) is a truncated one, a homily on Eden and the serpent might

well have been included. Augustine did make use of Rufinus's translation of these homilies, as early as *De Genesi aduersus Manichaeos*, according to B. Altaner, "Augustinus und Origenes," *Historisches Jahrbuch* 70 (1951) 15–41, reprinted in *Kleine patristische Schriften*, hrsg. von G. Glockmann, Texte und Untersuchungen 83 (Berlin: Akademie-Verlag, 1967), pp. 234–35, 246–47. For a complete survey of Origen's multifaceted interpretations of the Eden narrative, see C. P. Bammel, "Adam in Origen," *The Making of Orthodoxy: Essays in Honour of Henry Chadwick*, ed. R. Williams (Cambridge: Cambridge University Press, 1989), pp. 62–93. No evident correlations come to light.

[19] W. Theiler, "Tacitus und die antike Schicksalslehre," *Phyllobolia für Peter von der Müll* (Basel: B. Schwabe, 1946), pp. 61–62, reprinted in *Forschungen zum Neuplatonismus*, Quellen und Studien zur Geschichte der Philosophie 10 (Berlin: Walter de Gruyter, 1966), pp. 73–74. In Plutarch's *Aduersus Colotem* 1122B–D, the terms are *aisthesis/phantasia-horme-synkatathesis*; in Cicero's *De fato* 40–41, they are *visum-appetitus-assensio*.

[20] Cicero, *De fato* 18, quoting Chrysippus. It is to be noted that Augustine, in defending the infallible foreknowledge of God in *De ciuitate dei* X,ix–x: *CC* XLVII,281–84, favors many of the Stoics' formulations as against Cicero, who adopted a position of indeterminism in order to defend free choice. The importance of Cicero's *De fato* for Augustine is highlighted by M. Djuth, "Stoicism and Augustine's Doctrine of Human Freedom after 396," *Collectanea Augustiniana*, ed. J. C. Schnaubelt and F. Van Fleteren (New York: Peter Lang, 1990).

[21] Origen, *De principiis* III,i,2–3; cf. *De oratione* VI,1–2. It has been argued that the passage is derived from Chrysippus himself. See B.D. Jackson, "Sources of Origen's Doctrine of Freedom," *Church History* 35 (1966) 13–26. In any event, the distinctions persisted in ancient philosophy, as noted by H. Koch, *Pronoia und Paideusis. Studien über Origenes und sein Verhältnis zum Platonismus* (Berlin: Walter de Gruyter, 1932), pp. 284–85.

[22] R. J. O'Connell, *St. Augustine's Early Theory of Man*, pp. 156–82, traces parallels between Plotinus and the passages in which Augustine discusses the imagery of serpent, woman, and man. While they indicate how Augustine utilized Plotinian concepts in interpreting the Eden narrative, they cannot be the sole source of his interpretation. Motifs that sound Plotinian—especially the "middle" position of the soul between the spiritual and material worlds, which Augustine reads out of the statement that the tree of knowledge was in the middle of the garden—are by no means unique to him; on the contrary, the same imagery was crucial to Philo and to almost every Christian theologian after the second century.

[23] *De musica* VI,xi,29: *PL* XXXII,1179–80: *Delectatio quippe quasi pondus est animae.* Cf. *Confessiones* XIII,ix,10: *CC* XXVII,246–47: *Pondus meum amor meus; eo feror, quocumque feror.* O'Connell shows (pp. 170–72) how the image of weight is derived from *Ennead* IV,iii,13, Plotinus' discussion of the movement of the soul downward and upward.

[24] *De moribus ecclesiae catholicae et de moribus Manichaeorum* I,xxv,46: *PL* XXXII, 1330–31: *Ordinate in me caritatem.* The work was begun in Rome in 387 and finished in Tagaste by 389.

[25] *Eclogae* II,65: *Trahit sua quemque uoluptas.* Augustine, quite naturally, recognized the quotation and replied with further displays of learning (*Epistula XVI* 3; *Epistula XVII* 3: *CSEL* XXXIV,38–39, 42–43). This would be only a "subliminal" or, at most, an "unacknowledged" influence, for Augustine does not use the passage from Vergil until one of the sermons on the Gospel according to John (*Tractatus in Euangelium Ioannis* XXVI,5: *CC* XXXVI,262), which comes from 418 or later (A.-M. La Bonnardière, *Recherches de chronologie augustinienne* [Paris: Études Augustiniennes, 1965], p. 87). Augustine knew the verse from Vergil, but probably did not deem it appropriate for citation in the exposition of Christian texts (as opposed to a polemical writing); indeed, the surprise is that he uses it at all in a sermonic setting.

[26] *Expositio epistulae ad Galatas* 49: *CSEL* LXXXIV,126.

[27] For a brief summary of these see N. Aschkenasy, *Eve's Journey: Feminine Images in Hebraic Literary Tradition* (Philadelphia: University of Pennsylvania Press, 1986), pp. 39–50. The full complexity of rabbinic interpretations is highlighted by M. Poorthuis, "Sexisme als zondeval: Rabbijnse interpretaties van het paradijsverhaal belicht vanuit de verhouding tussen man en vrouw," *Tijdschrift voor theologie* 30 (1990) 234–58, who points out that the "weakness" of the woman was sometimes viewed as the self-justifying and erroneous opinion of the man, whose sin would thus be the result of sexism from the very first.

[28] *Contra Celsum* IV,36–39.

[29] E. Schüssler Fiorenza, *In Memory of Her: A Feminist Theological Reconstruction of Christian Origins* (New York: Crossroad, 1985), pp. 118ff., 144–47.

[30] See D. R. MacDonald, *There Is No Male and Female: The Fate of a Dominical Saying in Paul and Gnosticism,* Harvard Dissertations in Religion 20 (Philadelphia: Fortress Press, 1987), which summarizes the history of scholarship on this passage (pp. 72–91) and then develops a thesis (pp. 92–111).

[31] Perhaps the classic argument for this is J. Jervell, *Imago Dei. Gen. 1,26f. im Spätjudentum, in der Gnosis und in den paulinischen Briefen,* Forschungen zur Religion und Literatur des Alten und Neuen Testaments, N.F. 58 (Göttingen: Vandenhoeck und Ruprecht, 1960), pp. 55, 59–60, 64–66. It is the thesis developed by MacDonald.

[32] MacDonald, pp. 99–100.

[33] This point is made well in Clark, "Heresy, Asceticism, Adam, and Eve." The relevant passages in Augustine's writings—especially the mature ones—are translated in *Women in the Early Church,* Message of the Fathers of the Church 13 (Wilmington: Michael Glazier, Inc., 1983), pp. 27–28, 39–41, 44–47, 55–69.

[34] *Expositio epistulae ad Galatas* 24: *CSEL* LXXXIV,86–87.

[35] *De Genesi ad litteram* XI,xlii,59: *BA* 49,324–26.

[36] *De ciuitate dei* XIV,xi: *CC* XLVIII,431–33. A different perspective on the social origins of sin is found in a number of Jewish traditions noted by Poorthuis (pp. 247, 250, 254). According to them, Eve wished Adam to join her in eating from the tree, either out of jealous fear that God might create another woman to take her place, or out of a more

360		*The Interpretation of Scripture*

positive desire that Adam share her destiny with her—a theme that also appears in Milton's *Paradise Lost* IX,827–33.

[37] See E. Clark, "'Adam's Only Companion': Augustine and the Early Christian Debate on Marriage," *Recherches Augustiniennes* 21 (1986) 139–62, and also *La Genèse, BA* 49, pp. 525–26.

[38] The unity of the human race as a family, all coming "from one," plays a major role in *De ciuitate dei,* esp. XII,xxi–xxvii, XIV,xxvii–xxviii, XV,vii–viii: *CC* XLVIII,376–84, 450–52, 459–65.

[39] *De ciuitate dei* XIV,xiv: *CC* XLVIII,436.

[40] *De patientia* 9: *PL* XL,616.

[41] R. A. Markus, *Saeculum: History and Society in the Theology of St. Augustine* (Cambridge: Cambridge University Press, 1970), pp. 201–3, citing *De Genesi ad litteram* VIII,xxiii,44 and XI,xxxvii,50: *BA* 49,74–76, 312–14. Augustine's reason for this judgment of natural superiority appears to be the physiological receptivity of the female in the process of procreation (*De mendacio* VII,10: *PL* XL,495–96).

[42] *De opere monachorum* XXXII,40 (written in 401): *CSEL* LX,591–94. This passage is highlighted by A. Solignac, "La condition de l'homme pécheur d'après saint Augustin," *Nouvelle revue théologique* 88 (1956) 369, n. 31; cf. *La Genèse, BA* 48,558. But much earlier, about 394, Augustine had already allegorized Paul's statement in 1 Co 11:3 and the narrative of the Samaritan woman in Jn 4:5–53 in the following way: the woman had had five husbands, who represent the five bodily senses, but she is told to call her true husband, her own mind, which alone is capable of being related to the divine Word as its true Head (*De diuersis quaestionibus octoginta tribus* q. LXIV,6–7: *CC* XLIV/A,142–45). This passage is emphasized in C. Wolfskeel, "Some Remarks with Regard to Augustine's Conception of Man as the Image of God," *Vigiliae Christianae* 30 (1976) 63–71.

[43] The pertinent section is *De trinitate* XII,vii,9–xiii,21: *CC* L/A,363–64, written about 413. Concerning the issues for Augustine's thought which were raised in writing this book —begun about 413, completed about 417 or 418, see O'Connell, *The Origin of the Soul,* chapter 9, esp. pp. 260–65.

[44] Following a different line of reflection, Cardinal J. Ratzinger, in "Concerning the Notion of Person in Theology," *Communio* 17 (1990) 453–54, deplores the individualistic turn in Augustine's doctrine of the Trinity, arguing that the trinitarian "we" promotes and offers space for the human "we."

[45] That this line of interpretation was a possibility in the ancient world is shown by Clement of Alexandria, who states it in his *Stromateis* III,xiii,93.

[46] See note 4 above.

[47] The expression is used in *De peccatorum meritis et remissione* II,xix,32: *CSEL* LX, 103, and the doctrine is often stated, especially in *Enchiridion* LXXXI,22: *PL* XL,271.

[48] See Gustave Combès, *La charité d'après saint Augustin* (Paris: Desclée de Brouwer, 1934), p. 8 and Appendix II; Etienne Gilson, *The Christian Philosophy of St. Augustine* (New York: Random House, 1960), Part II, chapter 3; and Henri de Lubac, *Augustinianism and Modern Theology*, tr. Lancelot Sheppard (New York: Herder and Herder, 1965), pp. 75–85.

[49] The multivalence of this dialogue is explored in David M. Halperin, "Why is Diotima a Woman? Platonic Eros and the Figuration of Gender," in *Before Sexuality: The Construction of Erotic Experience in the Ancient Greek World*, ed. David M. Halperin, John J. Winkler, and Froma I. Zeitlin (Princeton: Princeton University Press, 1990), pp. 254–308.

[50] See especially *De beata uita* IV,33: *CC* XXIX,83–84; *De ordine* I,viii,24: *CC* XXIX, 100–101; *Contra academicos* II,ix,22: *CC* XXIX,29–30; and *Soliloquia* I,xiii,22: *CSEL* LXXXIX,34. The imagery of spiritual embrace is influenced by Plotinus' *Ennead* VI,v,10, as Robert J. O'Connell shows in "*Ennead* VI, 4 and 5 in the Works of Saint Augustine," *REA* 9 (1963) 21–24.

The Meaning and Purpose of Animals
According to Augustine's Genesis Commentaries

Wanda Cizewski

During the years 388 to 389, having turned homeward from Milan through Rome and Carthage, Augustine busied himself with a commentary on Genesis against the Manichees. A few years later, after his sudden ordination to the priesthood at Hippo, he returned to the topic and started a commentary *De Genesi ad litteram* (392–93). The project went unfinished, but again in the year 401, after completing his *Confessiones*, he took up the text of Genesis and, in the course of just over a decade, gradually completed the *Libri duodecim de Genesi ad litteram*.[1] What seems surprising about all this is not so much that Augustine should have kept going back over the same material again and again, but that he should have felt bound to enter territory that had already been staked out by no less authorities than Basil of Caesarea among the Greeks, and Ambrose of Milan, with a version of Basil in Latin (prob. 387).[2]

The focus of this paper is a very narrow segment of Augustine's work on Genesis, namely his interpretations of hexaemeral days five and six. Nevertheless, I hope I may show how his distinctive principles of interpretation shaped a very different reading from that of his distinguished predecessors, and how those principles of interpretation were applied to the special problem of animals and their relation to human beings. How did Augustine himself define his principles of interpretation? In the search for a concise and relevant statement of method, I hit upon the famous passage in book two, chapter ten of his handbook, *De doctrina christiana* (ca. 395 to 426). Augustine states:

> There are two reasons why things written are not understood: they are obscured either by unknown or by ambiguous signs. For signs are either literal [*propria*] or figurative [*translata*]. The are called literal when they are used to designate those things on account of which they were instituted; thus, we say *bos* [ox] when we mean an animal of a herd, because all who use the Latin language call it by that name, just as we do. Figurative signs occur when that thing which we designate by

a literal sign is used to signify something else; thus, we say
'ox' and by that syllable understand the animal which is ordinarily designated by that word, but again by that animal we
understand an evangelist, as is signified in the scripture, according to the interpretation of the apostle, when it says,
'Thou shalt not muzzle the ox that treads out the corn' (Dt
25:4).[3]

The passage seems especially apt for my purposes, since it not only gives
us a general statement of exegetical principles, but also relies for illustration
on the example of an animal—*bos, bovis*, or the ox. Three distinct objects of
thought occur when that word is uttered. First, there occurs the name, as such
—*bos* in Latin, or in English "ox." That single syllable is an audible sign by
which speakers of a language refer to the animal in question. Meanwhile, singular instances of the animal so named occur in nature even now. Finally, a
figurative sense may occur to the exegete, in the allegorical significance of the
animal named. In Augustine's example, the allegorical significance of the
hardworking ox is the hardworking evangelist, since both exert themselves for
the benefit of human beings, and both may claim a little reward and compassion.

The risk in the figurative sense is that it may have the effect of promoting an allegorical interpretation at the expense of the literal or historical
meaning of a text. Thus, for example, in the Pauline passage to which Augustine refers, the law requiring humane treatment of domestic animals is erased
by the needs of the apostle. "Do you suppose God's concern is with oxen,"
asks Paul, "or is the reference clearly to ourselves?" (1 Co 9:9; cf. 1 Tm 5:18)
The task of the exegete, who seeks "to understand things written," consequently demands that where a word or sign is ambiguous, the exegete should
determine whether it is to be taken in the literal or in the figurative sense.
While interpreting the hexaemeron, therefore, the exegete must decide
whether the signs contained therein are to be regarded as ambiguous, and
then choose between a literal and a figurative reading of the text.

It would not have been unthinkable for Augustine to read hexaemeral
days five and six in the figurative sense, so as to interpret the animals by
means of allegory. Some two hundred years before, Origen had set the exegetical tone by listing the "beginning of Genesis" with the Song of Songs and
parts of the book of Ezechiel as the most difficult texts in Hebrew scripture.[4]
All three required mature exegetical judgement, and, by implication, a much

deeper than literal interpretation. Had he adopted the allegorical mode, moreover, Augustine would have followed the examples of his mentor Ambrose, and Ambrose's model Basil. Their readings of days five and six rely heavily on allegory, recounting anecdote after anecdote from the animal lore of classical literature and the *Physiologus*, and for each one supplying a suitable moral.

To illustrate, let me cite one example from several included in reference to the *reptilia* created on day five (Gn 1:20). Both Basil and Ambrose describe an apocryphal courtship of the viper and the eel, and both interpret it in the figurative sense to point out a series of moral lessons for married life. In Ambrose's *Exameron*, it runs as follows:

> When the viper, the deadliest animal and the most cunning of the whole species of serpents, evinces a desire for copulation, he searches for a moray eel already known to him, or he seeks a new mate. Proceeding towards the shore, he makes his presence known by a hissing sound, whereby he invites the conjugal embrace. The moray eel does not repulse the appeal, and yields to the poisonous serpent the desired enjoyment of their conjugal bond.[5]

Ambrose then proceeds into a series of four allegorical interpretations, in which the viper is understood to signify: 1) an abusive or repulsive husband, whose embraces must be endured by a properly obedient wife; 2) a spiteful and embittered wife who rejects or brings suit against her husband; 3) the same abusive husband, admonished to mend his evil ways; and finally, 4) an adulterous lover of another man's wife. Realizing that his multiple morals are mutually contradictory, Ambrose hastens to add:

> Do not form the opinion that we have based our argument on contradictions, in that we have made use of the example of a viper to point out both a good and a bad moral. It serves the purposes of instruction to bring forward a twofold consideration.[6]

Be that as it may, the tortuous coils of his allegory seem even more complicated than the fictitious reptilian romance on which they are built, and, incidentally, explain neither the language of the text, nor the nature of the animals named in it.

There are no allegorical eels or vipers in Augustine's Genesis commentaries. Unlike his predecessors, he chooses to interpret the potentially ambiguous text of the hexaemeron according to the literal sense, by which the names of the animals are signs of those creatures "on whose account they were instituted." His intention in so doing is explicitly stated in the title and preface of the first of the series: *De Genesi contra Manichaeos*. The purpose of his work is to make sense of a text dismissed by the Manichees as nonsense, and to account for the material creation described therein so as to refute the Manichee doctrine that the material world is evil.[7] Accordingly, his starting-point in the text is always some word or phrase which seems ambiguous or obscure or suggests some absurd conclusion. He will then proceed to pose questions and offer possible answers to resolve the difficulty. Sometimes he illustrates with a literary tag, an item from contemporary philosophical sources, or an anecdote based on personal experience. For each hexaemeral day, moreover, he seems to find a unifying philosophical theme or focus, and this problem orientation endures as if "between the lines" from one commentary to the next.

The philosophical problem lurking under the surface of hexaemeral day five is the question of the elements as they constitute bodies. It emerges in connection with the text of Gn 1:20, where the waters are commanded to bring forth both reptiles and birds. Augustine notes that some would ask, "Why are birds as well as fish said to have been formed from water, when only fish live in water?"[8] His response in the commentary *De Genesi contra Manichaeos* cites the opinion of "most learned persons" (*doctissimi homines*) and a tag from Lucan's *Pharsalia* to show that there are differences in the layers of atmosphere which surround the earth. The "water," therefore, from which birds are said to be created can reasonably be identified as the moist and foggy lower air.[9] In the incomplete commentary *ad litteram*, Augustine adverts again to the problem, and points out that it is the vaporous and humid lower air to which the phrase, *sub firmamento caeli* (Gn 1:20) refers. The *firmamentum*, by contrast, seems identified as "the most pure air,"[10] far above earth's surface, in regions where no birds can fly.

Neither of his two earlier interpretations seem to have satisfied Augustine, and in his later work *De Genesi ad litteram*, we find him searching again for an adequate interpretation of the phrase, *sub firmamento caeli*. He notes initially that the word *caelum* can have a variety of meanings, and in scripture may refer, sometimes in the plural and sometimes in the singular, to different parts of the cosmos.[11] The sense of the word *firmamentum*, too, is made the more difficult to grasp by a statement in 2 P 3:5–7, to the effect that it perished in the flood. Augustine attempts to harmonize that text with Gn 1:20 by suggesting a sort of vast condensation, by which the vaporous lower air became liquid in the flood and rose to cover the mountain peaks (Gn 7:20).[12]

Moving back from the words of the text as if to offer a broader perspective, Augustine proceeds to report a series of contemporary opinions on the elements. First, he notes, some hold that the elements are mutable and may be changed from one into another. Second, he reports the contrary opinion, that the elements are immutable, so that the qualities of one cannot be turned into the qualities of another. Third, he relates a theory of correlation between the senses and the elements: according to some authorities, vision is associated with fire, hearing with air, and scent and taste with water as vapor and liquid, respectively. Touch, meanwhile, is associated with earth. These authorities also note that fire and earth intermingle in the activity of all bodies, and that the finer elements of fire or air may readily interpenetrate the grosser elements of water and earth. All sensation is governed by the soul, however, and as spirit it interpenetrates the body but remains independent of it.[13]

Having surveyed a variety of secular opinions on the natural order and the interaction of the elements, Augustine is in a position to explain and vindicate the language and teachings of his text. Scripture must not be supposed to omit the element of air when only sky (*caelum*), water, and earth are mentioned. Air is included in the general phrase, *caelum et terra*, both in its higher form, with *caelum*, and in its lower, moist, and turbulent state, with *terra*. Indeed, the word *terra* is often used in Scripture to indicate all of the lower region of the cosmos, including the moist and cloudy lower air, water, and dry land. It follows that creation of the birds from water as vapor, and reptiles from water in its liquid state, perfectly respects the known natural order.[14] Later, the text will as reasonably be seen to describe the creation of other animals from earth.

It may be that for moderns, Augustine's Ptolemaic cosmology and rival elemental theories seem as fantastic as the seaside affair of the viper and eel in Ambrose's *Exameron*. The philosophical problem underlying Augustine's investigation of day six, however, remains unfortunately perennial. It is the problem of physical evil. Augustine first states the issue in his commentary *De Genesi contra Manichaeos*, by citing a Manichee gibe against the creation:

> They say: Why did God create so many animals, whether in
> the waters or on earth, which would not be necessary to hu-
> man beings? Many are even dangerous and fearsome.[15]

Augustine's response argues from the beauty of a well-ordered totality, to the
beauty and so also the value of each of its parts. He retorts:

> When they say such things, they do not understand how ev-
> erything is beautiful for its founder and shaper, who makes
> use of everything to govern the universe that he controls by
> his supreme law.[16]

Every creature, Augustine continues, is part of a totality that can be compared
to the workshop where a master craftsman plies his trade. If some ignorant
visitor cannot guess the purpose of an odd-looking tool, but handles it care-
lessly so as to injure himself, the craftsman is not to blame, for he knows the
use and value of each instrument.

Should the reader inquire more closely, Augustine admits that he, too,
is an ignorant spectator in the divine workshop, but not so foolish as to criti-
cize what he does not understand. Concluding, he offers, with a touch of irony, to summarize his limited grasp of the divine work: there are three types of
animal. Some are useful, some are harmful, some are superfluous.[17] Who can
object to the existence of useful creatures, and what concern of ours is the
existence of the superfluous? As for the harmful, these punish, exercise, or
terrify us so that we may the more earnestly cherish the hope of heaven and
set minimal store by fleeting temporal goods.

Apparently satisfied with his response to Manichee criticisms of the animal creation, Augustine does not return to the question in his brief, incomplete commentary *ad litteram*. In his third reading of the text, however, he
looks again at the problem of physical evil. The ironical, confident style of *De
Genesi contra Manichaeos* is dropped, as is the rather simplistic image of creatures as implements in the hands of a craftsman-Creator. Instead, Augustine
develops a rather complex and difficult interpretation of the problem, unfold-
ed in a series of interlocking questions about the variety of animal species and
behavior.

Following his usual method, Augustine first quotes the Latin text of Gn
1:24–25, and then selects words and phrases from it for close interpretation.[18]
Initially, he seeks to account for the various names used to designate the vari-

ous kinds of animals created on day six, and here he relies on solutions already sketched in the *liber imperfectus*.[19] The next problem is posed by the phrase, *secundum genus*. Is there some reason for its repetition after the name of each animal? Does the phrase refer to the "higher" or spiritual reasons according to which these animals were created? But in that case, why does the phrase not occur after the name of every created thing? Augustine points out that the phrase is first introduced at day three, describing the varieties of herbs and trees, and then reappears in the account of day five, at the mention of all the variety of creatures produced from water (Gn 1:21). The answer, Augustine then suggests, is that the phrase *secundum genus* signals the propagation of offspring, since these creatures reproduce according to their *genus*. Granting that this must, indeed, be the solution, Augustine then asks one last set of questions: why is the phrase not used in the text describing the creation of human beings? And what does the blessing of the primal couple signify, instead (Gn 1:28)?[20] Reserving details for later, Augustine simply points out that there is only one kind, or *genus*, of human being. Hence, the phrase *secundum genus* is unnecessary in reference to humankind, although it serves to distinguish among all the various kinds of plant and animal species.

Having mentioned the benediction of Gn 1:28, Augustine recalls the prior blessing uttered in Gn 1:22: "Increase, and multiply, and fill the waters of the sea, and let the birds multiply on the earth." What purpose does that blessing serve? Augustine answers: a blessing was uttered over the first of those creatures which were made to feel an instinct for procreation, and is subsequently understood to apply to the creatures of day six as well. However, he adds:

> It was necessary to repeat the blessing for the human being, so that no one might say that there was any sin in the function of begetting children, as there is in lustful acts whether of fornication or of the improper use of marriage.[21]

It must be recalled, at this point, that Augustine's polemical target is the Manichee condemnation of the material creation in general, and human procreation in particular. Apart from that debate, Augustine's shift, in what follows, from speculation about the use of the phrase, *secundum genus*, to the problem of vermin and predator species, may seem irrational. Instead, let me suggest that having vindicated the reproduction of both animal and human bodies, Augustine then proceeds to confront a series of related problems:

1) Does the vindication of animal reproduction include the apparently un-natural reproduction of certain kinds of tiny vermin from corrupt or decaying organic matter—or is the pullulation of life from rotting bodies an after-effect of sin? 2) Does the Creator's benediction extend to the dangerous predator species as well as to their animal and human prey—or is the predator-prey relation an after-effect of sin? 3) Did the Creator include among his good works of the hexaemeral week those thorns and thistles explicitly named in the curse of Gn 3:18—or was there an evil second creation after the fall? To each of these questions, Augustine unfolds an answer urging the unqualified goodness and integrity of the material creation.[22] Each particular thing was created good, *secundum genus*, and even in the predator-prey relation, a terrible beauty is discerned. Augustine states:

> ...one animal is the nourishment of another. To wish that it were otherwise, would not be reasonable. For all creatures, as long as they exist, have their own measure, number, and order. Rightly considered, they are all praiseworthy and all the changes that occur in them, even when one passes into another, are governed by a hidden plan that rules the beauty of the world and regulates each according to its kind.[23]

As in the first commentary *contra Manichaeos*, Augustine refuses to condemn the dangerous and fearsome beasts. They are parts of the good creation, and may serve to test, punish, or admonish human beings. However, his tone has changed from that of a philosopher's ironical detachment, to the mature compassion of the priest. He describes the salvation of the prophet Daniel and the Apostle Paul from deadly animal attack, and suggests a moral:

> For by means of [such deadly animals], examples of patience must be revealed for the benefit of others, and thus, too, in-dividuals acquire a deeper self-knowledge in temptation and, quite appropriately, the eternal salvation that was shamefully lost by self indulgence is bravely regained by endurance of pain.[24]

The moral falters, however, as Augustine confronts the suffering of animals and so also of all who cannot understand but must endure their pain. Again, it seems that Augustine's earlier detachment has been replaced with compassion, as he describes the busy struggle of animals for daily survival. Such instinctual fortitude, he suggests, should admonish human beings in our quest for spiritual and eternal survival. And yet, that is not his last word. Augustine's investigation of the animal creation has disclosed the insoluble problem of physical pain, and cannot stop at facile moralizing. Instead, he closes with a description of the urge to survive which animates even the smallest creatures:

> Physical pain in any animal acts in a strange and powerful manner upon the soul. For the soul by its mysterious vital powers mingles with the whole organism and holds it together, and it strives to maintain the unity that belongs to its nature when it feels, not with indifference but with a kind of indignation, that unity wasting away and disintegrating.[25]

No allegory or moral can be extracted from the body's humble resistance to its death, and none is sought. Augustine's reading of the text *ad litteram* has instead plumbed its depths so as to reach, but not explain away, the paradoxical coexistence of goodness and suffering in the living works of God.

Notes

[1] For chronology, see P. Brown, *Augustine of Hippo: A Biography* (Berkeley: University of California Press, 1969), pp. 74 and 184.

[2] See F. E. Robbins, *The Hexaemeral Literature* (Chicago: University of Chicago Press, 1912), p. 58.

[3] *De doctrina christiana* II,x,15: *CC* XXXII,41: *Duabus autem causis non intelliguntur, quae scripta sunt, si aut ignotis aut ambiguis signis obteguntur. Sunt autem signa uel propria uel translata. Propria dicuntur, cum his rebus significandis adhibentur, propter quas sunt instituta, sicut dicimus bouem, cum intelligimus pecus, quod omnes nobiscum latinae linguae homines hoc nomine uocant. Translata sunt, cum et ipsae res, quas propriis uerbis significamus, ad aliquid aliud significandum usurpantur, sicut dicimus bouem et per has duas syllabas intellegimus pecus, quod isto nomine appellari solet, sed rursus per illud pecus intelligimus euangelistam, quem significauit scriptura interpretante apostolo dicens: bouem triturantem non infrenabis*; tr. D. W. Robertson, Jr., *Augustine on Christian Doctrine* (New York: Bobbs-Merrill, 1958), p. 43. For *propria* and *translata*, see Cicero, *De oratore* III,xxxvi,149, ed. and tr. H. Rackham, *Cicero de oratore* II (London: Heinemann, 1948), pp. 118–19.

[4] Origen, *In canticum canticorum*, praef., ed. D. A. B. Caillau and D. Guillon in *Origenis opera* IV (Paris, 1892), pp. 356–57.

[5] Ambrose, *Exameron* V,vii,18: ed. C. Schenkl in *Sancti Ambrosii episcopi mediolanensis opera* I (Milan: Bibliotheca Ambrosiana, 1979), pp. 259–60: *Vipera, nequissimum genus bestiae et super omnia quae serpentini sunt generis astutior, ubi coeundi cupiditatem adsumpserit, muraenae maritimae notam sibi requirit copulam uel nouam praeparat progressaque ad litus sibilo testificata praesentiam sui ad coniugalem amplexum illam euocat, muraenae autem inuitata non deest et uenenatae serpenti expetitos usus suae coniunctionis impertit*; tr. John J. Savage, *FC* 42,173.

[6] Ambrose, *Exameron* V,vii,20: Schenkl, 264; *Nec quisquam uelut contraria posuisse nos credat, ut et ad bonum et ad malum uiperae huius exemplo uteremur, cum ad institutionem utrumque proficiat…*; tr. John J. Savage, *FC* 42,175–76.

[7] *De Genesi contra Manichaeos* I,i–ii: *PL* XXXIV,173.

[8] *De Genesi contra Manichaeos* I,xv,24: *PL* XXXIV,184: *Haec solent reprehendere, quaerentes vel potius calumniantes, quare animalia non solum ea quae in aquis vivunt, sed etiam ea quae in aere volitant et omnia pennata de aquis nata scriptum sit.*

[9] Lucan, *Pharsalia* 2,271; compare Augustine, *Quaestiones in Heptateuchum* I,ix: *CSEL* XXVIII,2, and *De ciuitate dei* XV,xxvii: *CC* XLVIII,495.

[10] *De Genesi ad litteram liber imperfectus* XV: *CSEL* XXVIII,495; compare *De ciuitate dei* XV,xxvii: *CC* XLVIII,495; see also *De ciuitate dei* XI,xxxiv: *CSEL* XLIII,354–55.

[11] *De Genesi ad litteram* III,1: *CSEL* XXVIII,62.

[12] *De Genesi ad litteram* III,2: *CSEL* XXVIII,64.

[13] *De Genesi ad litteram* III,3: *CSEL* XXVIII,65–66; see Plato, *Timaeus* 65B–68D, Aristotle, *De anima* 416B–424B, and Cicero, *De natura deorum* II,ix,23: ed. and tr. H. Rackham (London: Heinemann, 1933), pp. 144–49.

[14] *De Genesi ad litteram* III,6: *CSEL* XXVIII,68.

[15] *De Genesi contra Manichaeos* I,xvi,25: *PL* XXXIV,185: *Quid opus erat ut tam multa animalia Deus faceret, sive in aquis, sive in terra, quae hominibus non sunt necessaria? Multa etiam perniciosa sunt et timenda.*

[16] *De Genesi contra Manichaeos* I,xvi,25: *PL* XXXIV,185: *Sed cum ista dicunt, non intellegunt quemadmodum omnia pulchra sint conditori et artifici suo, qui omnibus utitur ad gubernationem universitatis cui summa lege dominatur.*

[17] *De Genesi contra Manichaeos* I,xvi,26: *PL* XXXIV,185.

[18] *De Genesi ad litteram* III,11: *CSEL* XXVIII,75.

[19] *De Genesi ad litteram liber imperfectus* XV,53–XVI,54: *CSEL* LX,496–97.

[20] *De Genesi ad litteram* III,13: *CSEL* XXVIII,79.

[21] *De Genesi ad litteram* III,13: *CSEL* XXVIII,79: *Necessarium autem fuit hoc in homine repetere, ne quisquam diceret in officio gignendi filios ullum esse peccatum, sicut est in libidine siue fornicandi siue ipso coniugio immoderatius abutendi*; tr. J. H. Taylor, *St. Augustine and the Literal Meaning of Genesis* I, *ACW* 41,89.

[22] *De Genesi ad litteram* III,14–18: *CSEL* XXVIII,80–84.

[23] *De Genesi ad litteram* III,16: *CSEL* XXVIII,82: *[A]liae cibi sunt aliarum. Nec recte possumus dicere, non essent aliae, quibus aliae uescerentur. Habent enim omnia, quamdiu sunt, mensuras, numeros, ordines suos; quae cuncta merito considerata laudantur nec sine occulta pro suo genere moderatione pulchritudinis temporalis, etiam ex alio in aliud transeundo mutantur.*

[24] *De Genesi ad litteram* III,15: *CSEL* XXVIII,81: *[Q]uia et exempla sunt demonstranda patientiae ad profectum ceterorum, et ipsi sibi homo in temtationibus certius innotescit, et iuste salus illa perpetua, quae turpiter amissa est per uoluptatem, fortiter recipitur per dolorem*; tr. Taylor, p. 91. I prefer the alternate reading at 1.22 to that in the body of the text, *voluntatem.*

[25] *De Genesi ad litteram* III,16: *CSEL* XXVIII,82: *Nam et ipse corporis dolor in quolibet animante magna et mirabilis animae uis est, quae illam compagem ineffabili permixtione uitaliter continet et in quamdam sui moduli redigit unitatem, cum eam non indifferenter, sed, ut ita dicam, indignanter patitur corrumpi atque dissolui*; tr. Taylor, p. 92. Augustine follows Cicero in referring to the life principle of animals as the soul (*anima*), see, e.g., Cicero, *De natura deorum* II,ix,23: Rackham, pp. 146–47.

"The Glue Itself Is Charity": Ps 62:9 in Augustine's Thought

Joseph T. Lienhard, S.J.

I. Introduction

In Augustine's writings, an intriguing concept recurs in two important passages on friendship.

One is the famous definition of friendship in the fourth book of the *Confessiones*, where Augustine writes: "Friendship cannot be true unless you glue it together [*eam tu agglutinas*] among those who cleave to one another by the charity 'poured forth in our hearts by the Holy Spirit, who is given to us.'"[1]

The other is the place in the *De trinitate* where Augustine writes that the Holy Spirit is the consubstantial and coeternal communion of the Father and the Son, and adds the startling comment, "If this can rightly be called 'friendship,' let it be called this."[2] The context of this statement about friendship in God is a reflection on unity. Augustine writes: "We are blessed because, by His gift, we are one among ourselves. But with Him we are 'one spirit' (1 Co 6:17), because our soul is glued to him [*quia agglutinatur anima nostra post eum*]."[3]

In both passages, Augustine uses the interesting word *agglutinare*—here deliberately translated "glue," hamfistedly, perhaps, and certainly with malice aforethought. God glues two friends together, and glues our souls to Himself. What led Augustine to use this seemingly graceless image? What is its source? Does he use it elsewhere? Does it have any theological significance?

One point can be clarified immediately, namely the source of the words *quia agglutinatur anima nostra post eum* in the passage just quoted from the *De trinitate*. Mountain, in his critical edition of this work, does not identify the phrase. But Augustine is here adapting Ps 62:9, which he sometimes read as: *Agglutinata est anima mea post te*. The search, however, does not end here.

The word *agglutinare* is hardly a common philosophical or theological term. Concretely, it means "to cause to adhere," "to glue," "to paste on," "to solder," "to bring into contact with." Pliny the Elder writes of warming shards of glass and sticking (*agglutinare*) them together. Metaphorically, the word could mean "to attach one person to another," but the effect was comic.[4]

The word is rare in the Vulgate. There are only four instances, all in the Old Testament.[5] Ezekiel (29:4), condemning Pharaoh to be a fish, says that God will attach (*agglutinabo*) the fish of the Nile to Pharaoh's scales. In Baruch (3:4), evils are bonded (*agglutinata sunt*) to Israel. Jeremiah (13:11) uses *agglutinare* of God's bonding Israel to Himself. And Sirach (25:16) writes of the *initium fidei* that makes a man adhere (*agglutinandum est*) to God.[6]

The version of Ps 62:9 that Augustine quotes in the *De trinitate* is not the common reading. At Ps 62:9 neither the Old Latin nor the Vulgate reads *agglutinata est*, but rather *adhesit anima mea post te; me suscepit dextra tua*.[7] And Augustine himself quotes two different versions of Ps 62:9. The one he learned first was *adhaesit anima mea post te*. The second, which he introduces later, is *agglutinata est anima mea post te*. It is worth noting that *adhesit* is active, and implies that the soul causes the adherence, whereas *agglutinata est* is passive, and leaves room for a divine agent. Augustine's new translation corresponds to his growing understanding of the gratuity of grace.

I would like to proceed by looking first at how Augustine understood Ps 62:9 in the translation with *adhesit*; then considering his use of the image of "glue"—the noun *gluten* and the verb *agglutinare*—as a metaphor for love and as the love that the Holy Spirit causes; and, finally, examining his understanding of Ps 62:9 in the new translation, with *agglutinata est*.

II. Ps 62:9: *Adhaesit*

Augustine cites Ps 62:9 with *adhaesit* four times. Three instances are early, and the word that catches Augustine's attention is *post*. *Post* suggests to him the right order of things, and the psalm verse is a warning against pride and an exhortation to humility. Commenting on Ps 3:9 he says that we should beware of pride and say instead: *adhesit anima mea post te*.[8] He urges his readers to cling to God, and not to be proudly independent, *inordinati*. In chapter 45 of *De diuersis quaestionibus octoginta tribus*, entitled *Aduersus mathematicos*, Augustine is trying to place the human mind in the right order of things. The mind judges visible things and realizes that it is superior to them. But it also realizes, on account of defect and progress in wisdom, that it is mutable, and finds immutable truth above itself. "And thus, clinging to that truth (*post eam*), as Scripture has said: *Adhesit anima mea post te*, it is made blessed, finding within the very creator and Lord of all things visible."⁹ Finally, in chapter 66 of the same work, Augustine is treating Romans 7 and 8. Ps 62:9 again suggests humility. The desire to sin is useful, he says, because the soul realizes that it cannot extricate itself from servitude to sin. Its swelling diminishes, all pride is extinguished, and the sinner says sincerely, *Adhaesit anima mea post te*. He is no longer under the law of sin, but under the law of justice; the sinner discovers the right *ordo*.¹⁰

III. *Gluten Amoris, Caritatis, Dilectionis*

My first conclusion has to be negative. Augustine's use of Ps 62:9, in the earlier version with *adhaesit*, leads nowhere, and he all but drops the translation after 396.

Another approach is more fruitful. From 388 on, Augustine began to use *gluten* as a metaphor for the bond of love. At first he used it without reference to the Scriptures; then he found a passage in Job which confirmed his usage. Charity as glue becomes a minor, but not insignificant, theme in Augustine's works.

Augustine used the phrase *amore agglutinari* soon after his baptism, in *De libero arbitrio* I, written in Rome in 388. In this instance, and only in this one, the image indicates a disordered love: "[The man who uses things aright] is not glued [*adglutinetur*] to them by love, making them parts of his soul, as is done by loving them."¹¹

A little later, but not after 400, Augustine discovered the word *agglutinare* in Job 38:38. The Latin text he followed was wholly different from the Vulgate, and read: "But ashes have been spread abroad like earth, and they cause him to adhere [*adglutinauit*] like food to stone."¹² The verse makes so little sense that Augustine was sure to find a profound meaning in it. According to Augustine's interpretation, the "adhering like food" applies to the Incarnation and the Eucharist. Christ adheres as a man to men, the mediator between God and men (1 Tm 2:5), giving himself to them as food through the mystery of his body and blood.¹³ What makes Christ adhere to men is the *gluten caritatis*, Augustine writes, where *caritatis* is an exepegetical genitive: that is, "the glue that is charity."

Augustine never cited the text from Job again, but the comparison of charity with glue apparently intrigued him.

In his *Contra Faustum Manichaeum*, written between 397 and 400, at about the same time as the *Adnotationes in Iob*, Augustine interpreted the *bitumen*, the pitch that Noah applied to the ark, as *gluten*, and *gluten* in turn as *dilectio*. Faustus is arguing that the Hebrew prophets said nothing about Christ. Augustine disagrees, and begins to give examples, including some difficult ones like Henoch and Noah. The ark was covered with pitch (*bitumen*) inside and out. The bond of unity (*compages unitatis*) signifies the tolerance of charity (*tolerantia caritatis*). The two layers of pitch protect the Church from scandal, from within and from without. Augustine then interprets the word "pitch": "For bitumen is a very fervid and violent glue, signifying the ardor of love by the great force of its strength in holding together a spiritual society that can endure everything."[14]

Gluten is *caritas*: this becomes a fixed equation in Augustine's mind, and he uses it several more times, without reference to Ps 62:9—in a sermon preached around 412, and twice in the *De trinitate*.[15]

IV. *Agglutinante Spiritu Sancto*

Around 396 or 397, Augustine added another dimension to his use of the image of *gluten*: he makes the subject of the verb *agglutinare* the Holy Spirit. The Holy Spirit is the agent within the Trinity who binds or glues us to the Godhead.

Augustine first uses this image in the *De doctrina christiana*, without reference to the Scriptures. He writes: "For when we come to [Christ], we also come to the Father, because the Father, to whom the Son is equal, is known through His equal. And the Holy Spirit binds and, as it were, glues us. By the Holy Spirit we can abide in the highest and the immutable Good."[16]

At about the same time, 397 or so, Augustine wrote the famous definition of friendship in the *Confessiones*, quoted once already: "Friendship cannot be true unless you glue it together among those who cleave to one another by the charity 'poured forth in our hearts by the Holy Spirit, who is given to us.'"[17] There is a new element here: Augustine quotes Rm 5:5. God, he says, bonds the friendship "by the charity 'poured forth in our hearts by the Holy Spirit, who is given to us.'" The crucial role of Rm 5:5 in Augustine's thought is well known. In his work *On the Trinity*, the verse from Paul allowed Augustine to call the Holy Spirit charity. And Rm 5:5 was his most convincing scriptural refutation of Pelagianism.[18]

V. Ps 62:9: *Agglutinata Est*

From 388 on, Augustine uses *gluten* as an image for love—*amor, caritas,* or *dilectio*. He found one scriptural echo in Job 38:38, but did not exploit it. Beginning around 396, he says that the agent of the action *agglutinare* is the Holy Spirit; and in the fourth book of the *Confessiones* he appeals to the important verse Rm 5:5 to confirm this point. His next step takes place some time around the year 405, when he adopted a new translation of Ps 62:9, using *agglutinata est* instead of *adhaesit*. Neither the Old Latin nor the Vulgate uses *agglutinata est* here, nor does any other Father, before or after Augustine, quote this form. Did Augustine change the translation of Scripture on his own authority, perhaps to accommodate it to his thought?

The new translation is found in the *Epistula ad catholicos de secta Donatistarum (De unitate ecclesiae)*. The authenticity of this work has been questioned, but recent opinion inclines toward accepting it as genuine. It dates from around the year 405. On the supposition that the *Epistula* is authentic, it is the first time that Augustine uses *agglutinata est* in Ps 62:9.

Here again, Augustine is comparing Noah's ark with the Church. This time he is playing, like a supremely confident cat with a frightened mouse, not with Faustus the Manichee, but with a Donatist bishop. The Donatist bishop interprets the double layer of pitch on Noah's ark as demonstrating the exclusive validity of the Donatists' baptism: their water cannot get out, and profane water cannot get in. "He seems to say something," Augustine begins. But really, one layer of pitch, either inside or outside, would suffice, for if water cannot leak out, then it cannot leak in, either. Hence: the passage must have some other significance. Augustine continues: Why can't I make something else of it? The pitch rather signifies charity, he writes, and quotes Ps 62:9 to prove it. *Bitumen* is *gluten*, and *gluten* is *caritas*.[19]

But Augustine's principal interpretation of Ps 62:9 with *agglutinata est* is found in his sermon on that psalm, preached in Hippo, during Lent in 412.[20]

Augustine applies the psalm verse *adglutinata est anima mea post te* to the Christian who longs for God, thirsts for God. Such a Christian adheres to God. Augustine wants this *affectus* to be born in us and, using a tree as his metaphor, to be rained upon and grow, if it is sprouting, until it becomes so strong that we say: *Adglutinatur anima mea post te.*

And where, he asks, is the glue itself? "The glue itself is charity." Charity is that glue by which your soul is glued to God—not *cum Deo*, but *post Deum*. God must precede, the believer must follow, just as the Lord said to Peter, *Redi post me*; that is the proper order of things.

Who is the speaker of the verse, *Adglutinata est anima mea post te*? First of all, Augustine says, the speaker is Christ in us, the *totus Christus*. But the Church, too, says these words—she says them in Christ, her head.

Augustine ends with a homely image. "The devil and his angels are like vultures. We are like chicks, under the wings of that hen, and the vulture cannot touch us. For the hen that protects us is brave. The hen is weak for our sakes, but brave in herself—our Lord Jesus Christ, the very wisdom of God. Hence the Church, too, says: *Adglutinata est anima mea post te.*"

VI. *Adglutinari Spiritu Sancto* with Ps 62:9

The last text to be considered is one of the first mentioned, from the sixth book of the *De trinitate*. Here most of the themes we have been considering come together. Here Augustine cites Ps 62:9 with *agglutinatur*. Here he writes of the Holy Spirit, although not as the agent of love, but as the agent of unity: *ipsius munere inter nos unum*. But far from neglecting love, Augustine makes the Spirit substantial love, or rather, substantial friendship. Advancing in his understanding of Rm 5:5, he writes here that the Holy Spirit is not *amor* or *dilectio* or *caritas*, but *amicitia*. The Holy Spirit is the consubstantial and coeternal communion of the Father and the Son. Augustine then adds a statement that is unique in his writings: "If this can rightly be called 'friendship,' let it be called this."[21] In other words, Augustine calls the Holy Spirit the substantial friendship of the Father and the Son. The passage is remarkable because Augustine, in most of the rest of the *De trinitate*, resists any suggestion that would lead to a social trinity, and forcefully rejects the notion that Father, Son, and Holy Spirit are three friends.

VII. Conclusion

What has been accomplished? At worst, one footnote has been added to the *De trinitate* at VI,v,7: the phrase *agglutinatur anima nostra post eum* is a paraphrase of Ps 62:9.

If more is permitted, then I have traced Augustine's use of one, admittedly minor image. In the *De libero arbitrio, gluten* is negative; the man whose life is rightly ordered does not glue temporal things to his soul. Commenting on Job, Augustine applies *gluten* to the Incarnation and the Eucharist, and to Christ's bond of love with the human race. In the *Contra Faustum, gluten* binds together the spiritual society of the Church. From his first year as bishop, Augustine begins to make the Holy Spirit the subject of the verb *agglutinare*. The Spirit binds us to the Good, and the Holy Spirit is the bond that joins true friends. (Augustine here radically revises the classical idea of friendship found in Aristotle, Cicero, and others, according to which friendship is ultimately self-serving. Augustine realizes that two friends are bound not by personal advantage, but by their common love of the God who also unites them in friendship.) Around 405, Augustine revises his translation of Ps 62:9, perhaps to accommodate the verse to his theology of grace, and to the image of *gluten* he has been developing. Adhering to God is the goal of progress in the spiritual life, spoken by the *totus Christus* and by the Church. Finally, in the sixth book of the *De trinitate*, the Spirit is the agent first of unity among Christians and then—precisely because He is the agent of unity—the agent of love. The Spirit is the consubstantial and coeternal communion of Father and Son, a communion that may be called *amicitia,* and He thereby makes Christians, united into one, adhere to God the Trinity.

I would like to add one final point. In my own limited reading of the Fathers, I have been consistently surprised at how often an apparent obscurity in their writings is clarified by realizing that they were using, explaining, or accounting for a single word in the Scriptures. The ancients' first unit of understanding was not the pericope, or the sentence, but the single word. The word as the starting point for understanding was an assumption of ancient education in poetics and rhetoric; Augustine's *De magistro* illustrates this point superbly. Much remains to be learned about the Fathers and their writings from a closer study of ancient education. If I am correct, I have traced the path of Augustine's interest in one word.

Notes

[1] *Confessiones* IV,iv,7: *CC* XXVII,43: *Est uera amicitia, quia non est uera, nisi cum eam tu agglutinas inter haerentes tibi caritate diffusa in cordibus nostris per spiritum sanctum, qui datus est nobis.* The translation is by J. K. Ryan (Garden City: Doubleday, 1960), p. 97, altered, quoting Rm 5:5.

[2] *De trinitate* VI,v,7: *CC* L,235: *Quae si amicitia conuenienter dici potest, dicatur.*

[3] *De trinitate* VI,v,7: *CC* L,235: *Nos autem...beati quia ipsius munere inter nos unum; cum illo autem "unus spiritus" quia agglutinatur anima nostra post eum.*

[4] The *Oxford Latin Dictionary* gives three quotations for this meaning, all from Plautus (*Cistellaria* 648, *Menaechmi* 342, and *Aulularia* 801; but the last does not refer to persons).

[5] Further: *glutinum* occurs only at Is 41:7; *gluten* is never found.

[6] The Vulgate has *fidei autem initium adglutinandum est ei.* The Jerusalem Bible translates the Vulgate version as: "It is by faith that a man begins to cling to him."

[7] This is the version in the *Psalmi iuxta LXX* and the *Psalmi iuxta Hebraeos*. It is also the form used by Hilary (*Tractatus in psalmum LXII* 10: *CSEL* XXII,222), Ambrose (*De Isaac uel anima* 3,7: *CSEL* XXXII,i,646, and *Expositio psalmi CXVIII* XI,4: *CSEL* LXII, 235), Gaudentius of Brescia (*Tractatus paschales* I,23: *CSEL* LXVIII,23), and Cassiodorus (*Expositio in psalterium*, Ps. LXII,9: *PL* LXX,436D).

[8] *Enarratio in Psalmum III* 10: *CC* XXXVIII,13: *Cauenda superbia est et dicendum: "Adhaesit anima mea post te. Et super populum tuum benedictio tua,"* hoc est super unumquemque nostrum. The second phrase is from Ps 3:9.

[9] *De diuersis quaestionibus LXXXIII* XLV,1: *CC* XLIV/A,67: *Atque ita adhaerens post ipsam, sicut dictum est: "Adhaesit anima mea post te," beata efficitur, intrinsecus inueniens etiam omnium uisibilium creatorem atque dominum.* Augustine even adopts the awkward Latin phrase *post te*, and says, of clinging to the truth, *post eam*.

[10] *De diuersis quaestionibus LXXXIII* LXVI,1: *CC* XLIV/A,151–52: *Quod quidem ad hoc utile est, ut sentiat anima se ipsam non sufficere ad extrahendum se de seruitute peccati, atque hoc modo detumescente atque extincta omni superbia subdatur liberatori suo, sinceriterque homo dicat: "Adhaesit anima mea post te," quod est iam non esse sub lege peccati, sed in lege iustitiae.* The last quotation of Ps 62:9 with *adhaesit* is in *Enarratio in Psalmum XLIII* 25: *CC* XXXVIII,492, a sermon on Ps 43 preached during the Lent of 412. Augustine may have reverted to *adhaesit* to match Ps 62:9 with Ps 72:28, *Mihi adhaerere Deo bonum est*, which he quotes immediately after Ps 62:9. In *Enarrationes in psalmos* LXII,28: *CC* XXXIX,806, he paraphrases Ps 62:9 with *adhaesit*, because *gluten* is nearby.

[11] *De libero arbitrio* I,xv,33,113: *CC* XXIX,234: *...Et ideo non eis amore adglutinetur neque uelut membra sui animi faciat, quod fit amando.* The translation is by J. H. S. Burleigh, *Augustine: Earlier Writings* (Philadelphia: Westminster, 1953), p. 132, altered.

[12] *Adnotationum in Iob* 38: *CSEL* XXVIII,ii,614: *Diffusus est autem sicut terra cinis, et adglutinauit eum sicut lapidibus cibum.* The notations are Augustine's; around 400 an unknown scribe attached them to a running text. The Vulgate has: *Quando fundebatur pulvis in terram et glebae conpingebatur.*

[13] *Adnotationum in Iob* 38: *CSEL* XXVIII,ii,614: *Cohaereret eis tamquam glutine caritatis, homo hominibus, ut mediator esset dei et hominum, se ipsum illis dans cibum per sacramentum corporis et sanguinis sui.*

[14] *Contra Faustum Manichaeum* XII,14: *CSEL* XXV,345: *Est enim bitumen feruentissimum et uiolentissimum gluten significans dilectionis ardorem ui magna fortitudinis ad tenendam societatem spiritalem omnia tolerantem.*

[15] In Sermon 349 Augustine also calls *gluten* the glue of charity. He speaks of licit human charity: toward spouses, children, friends, fellow-citizens. *Sermo CCCXLIX* II,2: *PL* XXXIX,1530: *Liceat vobis humana charitate diligere conjuges, diligere filios, diligere amicos vestros, diligere cives vestros. Omnia enim ista nomina habent necessitudinis vinculum, et gluten quodam modo charitatis. Sed videtis istam charitatem esse posse et impiorum, id est, Paganorum, Judaeorum, haereticorum.* The title of the sermon is *De charitate, et de caeco illuminato 1.* In the tenth book of the *De trinitate*, Augustine wrote: *Tanta uis est amoris ut ea quae cum amore diu cogitauerit eisque curae glutino inhaeserit attrahat secum etiam cum ad se cogitandam quodam modo redit* (*De trinitate* X,v,7: *CC* L,321); and *Cohaeserunt enim mirabiliter glutino amoris* (*De trinitate* X,viii,11: *CC* L,324).

[16] *De doctrina christiana* I,xxxiv,38: *CC* XXXII,28: *Cum enim ad ipsum peruenitur, etiam ad patrem peruenitur; quia per aequalem ille, cui est aequalis, agnoscitur vinciente et tamquam agglutinante nos sancto spiritu, quo in summo atque incommutabili bono permanere possimus.*

[17] See note 1.

[18] See, for example, *De spiritu et littera* iii,5: *CSEL* LX,157.

[19] *Epistula ad catholicos de secta Donatistarum* (*De unitate ecclesiae*) V,9: *CSEL* LII, 241: *Bitumen, quia uiolentum gluten et res feruentissima est, significatam esse caritatem. unde enim dicitur in psalmo: "agglutinata est anima mea post te," nisi flagrantissima caritate?* This sentence is so close to the sentence quoted in note 13 from the *Contra Faustum Manichaeum* that some direct dependence must be postulated: either Augustine's disciple copied his thought, or Augustine repeated the same phrases he had used earlier.

[20] *Enarratio in Psalmum LXII* 17–18: *CC* XXXIX,805–6: *"Adglutinata est anima mea post te." Videte desiderantem, uidete sitientem, uidete quomodo haeret Deo. Nascatur in uobis iste affectus. Si iam germinat, compluatur, et crescat; perueniat ad tale robur ut et uos dicatis ex toto corde: "Adglutinata est anima mea post te." Vbi est ipsum gluten? Ipsum gluten caritas est. Caritatem habe, quo glutine adglutinetur anima tua post Deum. Non cum Deo, sed post Deum; ut ille praecedat, tu sequaris....Dixit hoc Christus in nobis; id est, in homine quem gestabat pro nobis, quem offerebat pro nobis, dixit hoc. Dicit hoc et ecclesia in Christo, dicit in capite suo; quia et ipsa passa est hic persecutiones magnas, et singillatim etiam modo patitur....Sic sunt diabolus et angeli eius, quasi milui; sub illius gallinae alis sumus, et non nos*

potest contingere: gallina enim quae nos protegit, fortis est.   Infirma est propter nos; sed fortis est in se Dominus noster Iesus Christus, ipse sapientia Dei.   Ergo dicit hoc et ecclesia: "Adglu-tinata est anima mea post te; me suscepit dextera tua."

[21] See notes 2 and 3.

The Theological Structure of Augustine's Exegesis in the
Tractatus in Euangelium Ioannis

John M. Norris

Augustine interprets Scripture in the *Tractatus in Euangelium Ioannis* according to his understanding of God's revelation to humanity through the incarnation of the Word. Many of the disparate elements of Augustine's exegesis, his allegorical interpretation, his rhetorical style, the way in which he interprets Scripture by Scripture, can all be better understood in the light of this theological principle. In this paper we shall focus on his figurative interpretation of the Gospel of John, especially his notion of the signifying power of Christ's life in all of its aspects. In the Incarnation, the Word accommodates himself to humanity's capacity for knowledge, dwelling beneath the cover of flesh so that humanity can progress from a knowledge of Christ in the flesh to a knowledge of the Word in the beginning. For Augustine, the descent of the Word into flesh is a model for his theory of signs, for his doctrine of the inspiration of Scripture, for his understanding of the sacramental function of Scripture, and for the role of the preacher. Augustine bases his understanding of God's revelation in the Scriptures upon the mystery of God's revelation in Christ. God speaks to humanity in signs and figures, and the greatest of these sacraments is the Incarnation.

When we begin to study Augustine's exegetical method, we do so with a practical look at Augustine's preaching. Although sociological and cultural studies are now in the ascendancy in the scholarly world, there is an even better reason for this down-to-earth look at Augustine. Augustine is not a systematician or a contemplative monk. First and foremost, Augustine is a bishop and pastor. His theological concerns are pastoral ones. When scaling the heights of Augustine's theological output, it is always wise to keep one's feet planted solidly on the historical situation to which Augustine was responding. As E. Gilson writes: "Speculation abounds in Augustine but its aims are always practical and its term of reference is always man."[1] Therefore, when we attempt to find the theological basis of Augustine's exegesis in the practical relationship between Augustine and his congregation, we are not doing anything that Augustine himself would not find most appropriate. As Augustine's theories of grace and predestination stem from his own understanding of the nature of sin and the search for grace, so his theory of exegesis and revelation in Scripture comes from his practical experience as a pastor trying to convey the Word of God to his congregation.

When looking at Augustine's exegesis in his *Tractates on the Gospel of John* we can never forget the circumstances in which this work was produced.[2] The *Tractates* are not a commentary on the Gospel written for a learned audience, nor a critical theological work, but a pastoral work preached by a bishop to his congregation in Hippo. These sermons function on several different theological and rhetorical levels. As homilies, they reflect the oratorical style and customs of North Africa in the early years of the fifth century. They also reflect the serious theological concerns of Augustine's great battle with the Donatists and the beginnings of his struggle against Pelagius and his followers, for Augustine conducted his campaign against these heresies mainly from the preacher's chair. These theological concerns are a dimension of Augustine's concern for his flock, a part of his responsibility for the Church he shepherded. Augustine also offered his congregation practical moral advice for a Christian life; he encouraged them in their faith, and most importantly he labored along with them in a never-ending attempt to follow Christ, to live in Christ, and to know more of Christ. Augustine's exegesis in these *Tractates* must be seen as his attempt to explain the Word of the Lord to his congregation.

In order to understand these *Tractates*, we must recognize that Augustine preached to his congregation according to their ability to understand him. Augustine's efforts as a preacher were defined by this effort to make the gospel understood in as complete a fashion as possible to the various levels of his congregation. The preacher himself had a certain role, if not many roles, as Augustine learned in his many years as bishop of Hippo. A preacher, as Augustine wrote in the *De doctrina christiana*, "should conciliate those who are opposed, arouse those who are remiss, and teach those who are ignorant."[3] The end of preaching was to make Christ better known, to continue the work of the Incarnation.[4] Augustine's exegesis of Scripture in his preaching must be seen in light of this desire to make Christ better known. When studying Augustine's exegesis, one should not confuse the exegesis of the preacher, which speaks to the faithful, with that of the commentator, which is written for readers. The preacher is not a reasoner who proceeds from arguments, but is in the service of the Word of God as he is in the service of the sacraments. He is the mediator between the text and the faithful, and he knows his authority comes from the Word of God upon which he comments and which he himself listens to in prayer and reflection.[5] The preacher searches the Scriptures to apprehend the voice of God speaking to his people rather than apprehending the human voice of the inspired author.[6] The preacher also searches his own soul, seeking the Spirit within himself and giving this knowledge to the congregation.[7] Augustine gladly offered the deepest theological insights of his studies of the Word of God to his congregation in his preaching, giving to others what the Spirit had given him. Augustine's exegesis of Scripture is not a simple historical understanding of what the text literally says. Augustine also takes into account the intention of the Lord toward his congregation and the inspiration of the Spirit in his own heart.

One metaphor which Augustine uses in the *Tractates* to understand the role of the preacher is that of ascent and descent. Like the adult bird who ascends to gather food for its infants, and then offers it back to them in readily digestible portions, Augustine searches the heights of the Scriptures and returns to his congregation and offers them in his sermons nourishment fit for their present stage of spiritual development. Augustine offers this metaphor for the office of preaching in his commentary on the passage in Gn 23:10–22, where Jacob, dreaming, sees angels descending and ascending on a ladder reaching to heaven. In his allegorical interpretation of this text, Augustine compares the angels to Christian preachers. In their ascending and descending the ladder, they preach Christ, ascending and descending upon the Son of Man. St. Paul gives him an explanation of this interpretation, and probably is also the origin of this idea. Using Paul as a model for all preachers of the truth, Augustine writes:

> Look, he who had ascended descended. Seek where he had ascended: 'Up to the third heaven' (2 Co 12:2–4). Seek where he had descended: To giving milk to little ones (1 Co 3:1–2). Hear that he descended: 'I became a little one,' he says, 'in your midst, as if a nurse were fondling her own children' (1 Th 2:7).[8]

Paul had ascended and descended, just as the angels of God. The ascent is the preacher's own internal and spiritual contemplation of God in Christ, whereas the preaching itself is the actual descent, where one attempts to communicate through the deficiencies of language the inner words of the heart and mind.

Augustine enlarges upon this metaphor by an example from daily life. Mothers and nurses descend to little ones and, as Augustine writes: "somehow switch their speech so that they may be able to compose childish cajoleries from eloquent language; for if they should speak correctly, the infant does not hear with understanding but neither does he benefit."[9] Augustine attributes this pattern of ascent and descent not only to imitation of Paul, but also to imitation of Christ. Augustine writes: "If the Lord himself ascended and descended, it is clear that his preachers also ascend by imitation and descend by preaching."[10] Preaching in this image is tied together with the imitation of the work of the Incarnation. Descending, the preacher clothes the great truths of the Word who was in the beginning with God, through whom all things were made, in language and images that can be understood by the faithful. The preacher must couch his message in a language that his people can understand, in imitation of God who makes himself known to his people through Christ in the flesh, so that those who can only understand carnally may come to know spiritually. Augustine's rhetorical and exegetical style is an imitation of what he sees as God's humble accommodation to humanity as it is revealed in the Incarnation and in the Scriptures.

Augustine's understanding of the Incarnation is not only a metaphorical basis for his own actions as a preacher. Augustine's conception of the revelatory power of the Word made flesh influences his interpretation of the Scriptures, especially how the narrative of Scripture acts as a sign. Augustine inherits this figurative understanding of the Scriptures from St. Paul, as well as from Christian tradition and his classical training. Augustine in fact borrows Paul's figures. He writes of the figure of Christ and the Church found in Adam and Eve:

> For no man will say that I misunderstand the meaning when I produce, not my own, but the apostle's. How great a mystery, then, does that one statement contain about Christ, which the Apostle recalls when he says, 'And they shall be two in one flesh. This is a great mystery' (Ep 5:31–32).[11]

Augustine finds Biblical support for his figurative interpretation of the Old Testament in these passages from Paul. Beyond this notion of the figurative interpretation of the Old Testament, Augustine has the firm conviction that all the words and deeds of Christ's life on earth offer a spiritual meaning.[12]

Augustine finds support for his understanding of the allegorical significance of Christ's deeds in Paul's notion of the unity of the Body of Christ with Christ, its head. Augustine shows how a passage from Acts illustrates this unity of signification, whereby a spiritual meaning can be applied to Christ's action that refers to us, his Body:

> For Christ is not simply in the head and not in the body, but Christ whole is in the head and body. What, therefore, His members are, that He is; but what He is, it does not necessarily follow that his members are. For if His members were not Himself, He would not have said, 'Saul, why do you persecute me?' (Ac 9:4). For Saul was not persecuting Himself on earth, but His members, namely, His believers.[13]

In the case above, it is clear that the person of Christ is to be interpreted in terms of his followers. If the words were taken literally, then Saul would somehow be persecuting Christ physically, so a figurative interpretation is required to give proper meaning to the passage.

We see Augustine employ this type of interpretation when Christ's feet are anointed with nard by Mary. Augustine interprets her actions according to the moral responsibilities of his flock:

> Anoint the feet of Jesus: follow by a good life the Lord's footsteps. Wipe them with your hair: what you have of superfluity, give to the poor, and you have wiped the feet of the Lord; for the hair seems to be the superfluous part of the body. You have something to spare of your abundance: it is superfluous to you, but necessary for the feet of the Lord. Perhaps on this earth the Lord's feet are still in need. For of whom but of his members is he yet to say in the end, 'Inasmuch as you did it to one of the least of mine, you did it unto me' (Mt 25:40)?[14]

In this interpretation of Christ according to his members, Augustine follows the first of Tyconius' seven exegetical rules which he presents in the *De doctrina christiana*. The first rule Augustine describes is: "'Of the Lord and His Body,' according to which it is understood that sometimes the head and the body, that is, Christ and the Church, are indicated to us as one person."[15] Yet the examples which Augustine uses to illustrate this rule stem not from the New Testament but from the Old Testament. When Augustine interprets all of the actions and words of Christ as signs, he goes beyond Tyconius' original intentions.

Augustine goes a step further when he makes it a rule that whatever the deeds or words of Christ, they may be taken to have a spiritual meaning that can apply to his disciples, to the Church, to the Body of Christ, to Augustine's own congregation. Augustine writes:

> For surely the Lord's deeds are not merely deeds, but signs. And if they are signs, besides their wonderful character, they have some real significance: and to find out this in regard to such deeds is a somewhat harder task than to read or hear of them.[16]

In this method of interpretation, the literal meaning, the historical meaning, is not discarded because it is absurd or contradictory. The figurative interpretation is added on to the literal meaning. Christ's actions and words are edifying both on a historical and a spiritual level. Augustine, speaking about Christ's healing of the blind man, says:

> I proceed, therefore, to set forth briefly the mystery of this blind man's enlightenment. All, certainly, that was done by our Lord Jesus Christ, both works and words, are worthy of our astonishment and admiration: his works, because they are fact; his words, because they are signs. If we reflect, then, on what is signified by the deed here done, that blind man is the human race....[17]

Here in this figure, Augustine is not interpreting Christ in terms of his members. Instead, the human race is being represented by the blind man who is cured by Christ. Throughout Augustine's preaching on the Gospel of John, he consistently treats the narrative portions of John's writing as an opportunity for allegorical interpretation, where each detail and each action becomes a sign for his congregation, bearing a message intended by Christ himself.

In these *Tractates*, Augustine concentrates his attention on the revelatory function of Christ's humanity as a sign of the presence of the Word of God. Following the soteriology of John, Augustine speaks more often of Christ's saving power as the way to God than of the saving power of the cross and res-urrection. In this sense, Christ's deeds are physical signs of deeper truths. Human hearts are darkened by sin and do not know God; the eyes of the heart cannot see God, but the eyes of the flesh can see Christ. Christ acts in ways that the soul can see so that it might recognize the God hidden within. Through the story of Christ's life, we are shown signs whereby we might un-derstand his divine nature and the purpose of his Incarnation. Augustine, in describing the cure of the sick man at the Sheep pool, writes: "For what he became for men is more valuable for our salvation than what he did among men; and that he healed the vices of souls is more valuable than that he healed the maladies of bodies which were going to die."[18] Augustine is con-cerned with the Word made flesh as a sign pointing to the Word in the begin-ning. The flesh of Christ is an instrument by which we may come to know God in himself. Therefore, the deeds of Christ's life are of interest to Augus-tine not for themselves as much as for their significance, what they tell of Christ's nature.

Like the preacher who must nourish his flock with milk before giving them solid food, Christ nourishes us with his physical actions that we might come to know his divine nature. Augustine writes: "We are nourished by out-ward signs that we might be able to come to the enduring realities them-selves.... Accordingly the Lord feeds us too, while we toil with these signs of the Scriptures."[19] For example, in this cure of the sick man, Augustine pre-sents a figure of Christ's healing of the world from sin. He chooses one man to signify the unity of the human race. The pool represents the Jewish people, for bodies of water often represent people. The five porticoes are the books of Moses which shut in the people, for the Law brings forth sinners but con-victs them and cannot acquit them. The hidden angel who disturbs the water is Christ, who was hidden from his people. To go down into the water is to believe in Christ's death. Only one is healed to represent unity, that those who are outside unity cannot be healed. The man's thirty-eight years of sick-ness represent the equation forty less two: the perfection of the law in good works less the two precepts of love, of God and the neighbor, signifying the man's weakness. Christ supplies these two precepts in his two commands to take up his bed and walk.[20] Thus every detail of Christ's healing is given a figurative significance beyond its literal meaning.[21] In his preaching, Augus-tine attempts to find the inner signification of these outward signs, always seeking the enduring realities, always looking beyond the historical occurrence to find its permanent and lasting significance, so that his congregation may come to know Christ more intimately.

In conclusion, a pastoral and Christological understanding of Augustine's interpretation of Scripture can help to shed light on one of the most discussed aspects of Augustine's exegesis, his use of allegorical interpretation. For Augustine, allegorical interpretation is not just a concession to his audience, or an unconscious cultural fault that can be excused from a later historical vantage. Allegorical interpretation is intimately connected to his understanding of how a preacher should lead his congregation from a simple level of understanding to the depths of wisdom, from carnal to spiritual understanding, from the literal sense to the spiritual sense of Scripture. Augustine thinks in this way because he sees that God speaks to humanity in figures, not only in the figures of the Old Testament, but in the sacraments of the Church and most importantly through the Incarnation of the Word. Augustine interprets Scripture allegorically because God speaks to humanity most profoundly when he speaks in figures.

Notes

[1] *The Christian Philosophy of St. Augustine*, tr. L. M. Lynch (1960; repr. New York: Octagon Books, 1983), p. 3.

[2] H. Rondet, "La théologie de saint Augustin prédicateur," *Bulletin de littérature ecclésiastique* 72 (1971) 246.

[3] *De doctrina christiana* IV,iv,6: *CC* XXXII,119:...*conciliare auersos, remissos erigere, nescientibus, quod agitur, quid exspectare debeant intimare*; tr. D. W. Robertson, Jr., *On Christian Doctrine* (Indianapolis: Bobbs-Merrill Publishing Company, 1958), pp. 120–21.

[4] M. F. Berrouard makes this analysis in the introduction to *Homélies sur l'évangile de saint Jean 1–16, BA* 71,23.

[5] M. F. Berrouard writes: ". . . on ne peut pas confondre l'exégèse du prédicateur qui parle à des fidèles et celle du commentateur qui écrit pour des lecteurs....Le prédicateur n'est pas 'un raissoneur' qui procède à coups d'argumentations, mais il est au service de la Parole comme il est au service des sacrements; se tenant en médiateur entre le texte qu'il vient de faire lire et les fidèles qui l'ont entendu, il sait que sa parole ne tire son autorité que de la Parole de Dieu qu'il commente et qu'il commencé par écouter lui-même dans la prière et la refléxion," "L'exégèse de saint Augustin prédicateur du quatrième évangile. Le sens de l'unité des écritures," *Freiburger Zeitschrift für Philosophie und Theologie* 34 (1987) 314.

[6] G. Bonner takes this view of Augustine in "Augustine as Biblical Scholar," *Cambridge History of the Bible I: From the Beginnings to Jerome* (Cambridge: Cambridge University Press, 1970), p. 547.

[7] C. Mohrmann mentions this self-search in "Saint Augustin prédicateur," *La Maison Dieu* 39 (1954) 84.

[8] *Tractatus in Euangelium Ioannis* VII,23; *CC* XXXVI,80: *Ecce descendit qui adscenderat. Quaere quo adscenderat. Vsque in tertium caelum. Quaere quo descenderit. Vsque ad lac paruulis dandum. Audi quia descendit: Factus sum paruulus, inquit, in medio uestrum, tamquam si nutrix foueat filios suos*; tr. J. W. Rettig, *Tractates on the Gospel of John 1-10*, FC 78,177.

[9] *Tractatus in Euangelium Ioannis* VII,23: *CC* XXXVI,81:...*et quassant quoddammodo linguam suam, ut possint de lingua diserta fieri blandimenta puerilia; quia si sic dicant, non audit infans, sed nec proficit infans*; FC 78,177.

[10] *Tractatus in Euangelium Ioannis* VII,23: *CC* XXXVI,81: *Si ipse Dominus ascendit et descendit, manifestum est quia et praedicatores ipsius adscendunt imitatione, descendunt praedicatione*; FC 78,177.

[11] *Tractatus in Euangelium Ioannis* IX,10: *CC* XXXVI,96: *Nemo enim me dicet praue intellexisse, quando intellectum non meum, sed apostoli profero. Illud ergo unum quantum mysterium de Christo continet, quod commemorat apostolus, dicens: et erunt duo in carne una; sacramentum hoc magnum est*; FC 78,204.

[12] M. Comeau, *Saint Augustin, exégète du quatrième évangile* (Paris: Gabriel Beauchesne, 1930), p. 142. Comeau is clearly wrong when she states that Augustine uses the allegorical method only for the Old Testament and not for the New Testament. Augustine attempts to allegorize almost all the narrative sections of the gospel of John.

[13] *Tractatus in Euangelium Ioannis* XXVIII,1: *CC* XXXVI,277: *Non enim Christus in capite et non in corpore, sed Christus totus in capite et in corpore. Quod ergo membra eius, ipse; quod autem ipse, non continuo membra eius. Nam si non ipse essent membra eius, non diceret: Saule, quid me persequeris? Non enim Saulus ipsum, sed membra eius, id est fideles eius, in terra persequebatur*; *Homilies on the Gospel of John*, tr. J. Gibb and J. Innes, *NPNF* I:VII,178-79.

[14] *Tractatus in Euangelium Ioannis* L,6: *CC* XXXVI,435: *Vnge pedes Iesu: bene uidendo dominica sectare uestigia. Capillis terge: si habes superflua, da pauperibus, et Domini pedes tersisti; capilli enim superflua corporis uidentur. Habes quod agas de superfluis tuis; tibi superflua sunt, sed Domini pedibus necessaria. Forte in terra Domini pedes indigent. De quibus enim nisi de membris suis in fine dicturus est: Cum uni ex minimis fecistis, mihi fecistis?* tr. Gibb and Innes, *NPNF* I:VII,280.

[15] *De doctrina christiana* III,xxxi,44: *CC* XXXII,104: *Prima de domino et eius corpore est; in qua scientes aliquando capitis et corporis, id est Christi et ecclesiae, unam personam nobis intimari*; tr. Robertson, p. 106.

[16] *Tractatus in Euangelium Ioannis* XLIX,1: *CC* XXVI,420: *Domini quippe facta non sunt tantummodo facta, sed signa. Si ergo signa sunt, praeter id quod mira sunt, aliquid profecto significant; quorum factorum significationem inuenire, aliquanto est operosius, quam ea legere uel audire*; tr. Gibb and Innes, *NPNF* I:VII,270.

[17] *Tractatus in Euangelium Ioannis* XLIV,1: *CC* XXXVI,381: *Breuiter ergo caeci huius illuminati commendo mysterium. Ea quippe quae fecit Dominus noster Iesus Christus stupenda atque miranda, et opera et uerba sunt: opera, quia facta sunt; uerba, quia signa sunt. Si ergo quid significet hoc quod factum est cogitemus, genus humanum est iste caecus...*; tr. Gibb and Innes, *NPNF* I:VII,245.

[18] *Tractatus in Euangelium Ioannis* XVII,1: *CC* XXXVI,169–70: *Plus est enim ad salutem nostram quod factus est propter homines, quam quod fecit inter homines; et plus est quod uitia sanauit animarum, quam quod sanauit languores corporum moriturorum*; tr. J. W. Rettig, *FC* 79,108.

[19] *Tractatus in Euangelium Ioannis* XVII,5: *CC* XXXVI,172: *Significationibus pascimur, ut ad res ipsas perdurantes peruenire possimus. ...Proinde et nos Dominus in istis scripturarum significationibus laborantes pascit*; tr. Rettig, *FC* 79,113.

[20] *Tractatus in Euangelium Ioannis* XVII,1–9: *CC* XXXVI,169–75; tr. Rettig, *FC* 79, 108–16.

[21] The miracles in the Gospel of John are well suited for this type of interpretation, for more than any other Gospel, the miracles in John are meant to be understood as signs of Christ's nature rather than of his miraculous power.

The Immateriality and Eternity of the Word in St. Augustine's Sermons on the Prologue of John's Gospel

Michael Heintz

One of the more interesting aspects of St. Augustine's thought is his Christology. However, as one theologian has observed, Augustinian Christology has gone "relatively unnoticed by modern scholarship."[1] One relatively unmined resource[2] for our knowledge of Augustinian Christology is the ten extant sermons in which Augustine treats all or part of the prologue (1:1–18) of John's Gospel,[3] about which there are more Augustinian sermons than any other passage in the Scriptures.[4] It has been noted that Augustine's Christology is rather simple in expression,[5] and this is certainly true in his sermons, in which his goal is to teach with clarity.[6] Thus, methodologically, the sermons of Augustine on John's prologue provide an example of Christological reflection whose guiding principle is catechetical effectiveness. At the same time, these sermons give contemporary scholarship a glance at Augustinian Christology in the simple, clear language of the preacher, who constantly provides his listeners with images, metaphors, and analogies, by which to grasp the central mystery of the faith, the Word Incarnate.

Two of the recurring themes in these sermons[7] are the immateriality and eternity of the Word as God. Augustine expresses both a pastoral and a theological concern that the Word not be conceived of in material terms: the Word is bounded by neither space nor time. The Word should not be thought of as a "body."[8] Augustine continually urges his hearers to transcend corporeal conceptions of God, and he often places this movement within the rhetorical antithesis (drawn from Paul) *animalis* or *carnalis* versus *spiritualis*.[9] The carnal man is bound by his usual manner of perceiving things, which is limited to the senses, and seeks to understand spiritual realities in terms of carnal realities.[10] The flesh, which passes away, cannot understand the Word, which abides.[11] But this antithesis *carnalis* versus *spiritualis* is not crypto-dualistic for Augustine, since he expresses the paradox of the Incarnation: while flesh has blinded us, the flesh which the Word assumes heals us.[12]

At the root of Augustine's concern that the Word not be conceived materially or temporally is the problem of divine incomprehensibility; as Augustine frequently reminds his listeners, we are incapable of fully understanding

God; if we think we have fully understood God, then what we have understood is certainly not God, but something else.[13] Employing such phrases as *Extendite corda vestra*,[14] *Erigite corda vestra*,[15] and *Erige cor, genus humanum*,[16] he encourages his listeners to enlarge their limited conceptions of divinity, but also assures them that the divine Word is ultimately an ineffable mystery.[17] And it is far safer to confess one's ignorance of so great a mystery than to presume to comprehend it.[18] In fact, silence is a perfectly reverent response.[19]

The Word is not bounded by space, nor is it limited by place. Obviously, Augustine does not deny the real, physical existence of Jesus Christ. Rather, he insists that the Incarnation did not change, limit, or diminish the divinity of the Word; conversely, it added to the humanity: "But He added what He was to our nature; for He came to what He was not, but did not lose what He was."[20] In one particularly interesting passage,[21] Augustine compares the Word-made-flesh to solid food, which, having been ingested by a mother, is transformed into mother's milk, with which she may nourish her child. Yet Augustine notes one significant difference:

> when a mother makes food, which has become part of her
> flesh, into milk, the food is changed into milk; but the abid-
> ing Word unchangeably assumed flesh, that there might
> somehow be an interweaving of the two.[22]

The Incarnation did not "cramp" the Word; He is the all-powerful Word of God, who both abides with the Father and comes to us, without parting from the Father.[23] He was in the world in an altogether remarkable and inexpressible way.[24]

The Word cannot be thought of as existing in part or parts; He exists wholly in Himself.[25] Augustine repeatedly uses the concept of the *Verbum totum* or *integrum*, which is in no manner lessened, diminished, or diffused, but abides eternally without time and without space.[26] He contrasts the spiritual vision of the Word with the human vision of corporeal things. Even physical realities cannot be comprehended as a whole, but only one part at a time; through memory, we form a mental construct of the various parts to imagine the whole. But how much more impossible for us to comprehend the *Verbum totum*—we can only hope, with purified vision, to touch it spiritually; yet this touch is sufficient for our beatitude.[27] Elsewhere, using the paradigm of human speech, he tells his hearers that the divine Word, like human words, goes out to each and to all, but is not diminished or diffused; no matter how many hear it, it comes to each as a whole.[28] There seem to be two dimensions involved here, one epistemological, the other ontological. Epistemologically, God cannot be comprehended or fully grasped in knowledge. Yet, ontologically, He is nonetheless wholly present to each individual. Thus, the limitations of our relation to the divine are ours, not God's.

The Word is eternal; it is not bound by time. Augustine warns of the dangers of drawing comparisons between temporal realities and eternal realities.[29] He makes a key distinction, one which he notes that the Arians had failed to make. The Arians conceive of the Son begotten in time,[30] but in so doing have misapplied categories. One cannot properly determine the relation of God the Father and the Son by an analogy drawn from the relation of temporal father and son.[31] So Augustine distinguishes between coeternal realities and coeval realities. The former exist together without time, while the latter exist together in time. One can legitimately compare two coeval, though temporal, realities, to two coeternal realities, because in each case, one member of the pair does not precede the other in existence.[32] He gives two examples of coeval things which are analogous to the relation of Father and Son. A candle, when lighted, has a flame which produces brightness. The flame and the brightness which it emits are coeval, for the flame does not precede the brightness in time.[33] Another, more developed example is the shrub which sprouts near a pool of water. From the moment it sprouts, its image, reflected in the pool, exists coevally with the shrub.[34] Augustine suggests that this is a helpful way to seek to understand the eternal relation of Father and Son, mindful, of course, of the substantive disparity in the analogy.[35] Another tack by which Augustine expresses the eternity of the Word is through the use of the paradigm of human speech. While the example of human speech is useful in affirming the immaterial nature of the Word,[36] the comparison clearly limps: human words sound forth and are gone, but the Word of the Father, spoken eternally, abides forever.[37] There is no time for the Word, who abides from eternity to eternity,[38] and it is through Him that time itself was made.[39]

God, though present in the world, is not confined to or contained by the world, but, inversely, maintains the world by His indwelling presence.[40] In fact, God, while unseen, is certainly more present to us than anyone or anything else.[41] The Incarnation is explained by Augustine, not in terms of God becoming present to humanity (for He is that), but as an act which, through divine humility, makes God, who is eternally present, recognizable to us.[42]

The immateriality and eternity of the Word are just two of the many recurring themes in Augustine's sermons on the prologue of John's Gospel. It is my hope that this brief presentation may spur and encourage further research into the Christology of these sermons; to examine, for example, the paradigms used by Augustine to explain the Incarnation, or the developed manner in which Augustine treats the relationship of Christ and John the Baptist as a means of showing the unique place of Christ in relation to humanity.

Notes

[1] B. Daley, "A Humble Mediator: The Distinctive Elements in Saint Augustine's Christology," *Word and Spirit* 9 (1987) 101, n. 5.

[2] Even T. van Bavel, in his classic study, *Recherches sur la christologie de saint Augustin*, Paradosis X (Fribourg: Editions Universitaires 1954), draws from them only five times: p. 60, n. 157: *Tractatus in Euangelium Ioannis* II,8; p. 77, n. 5: *Sermo CXXI* 5; p. 126, n. 6: *Sermo CXIX* 7; p. 146, n. 3: *Sermo Caillau I* 57,3; p. 168, n. 47: *Sermo CXVII* 4.

[3] *Sermones CXVII–CXXI*: *PL* XXXVIII,661–80, cf. *NPNF* I:VI,458–70; *Sermo CCCXLII*: *PL* XXXIX,1501–4; *Tractatus in Euangelium Ioannis* I–III: *CC* XXXVI,1–31, cf. *FC* 78,41–92, and the fragmentary *Sermo Caillau I* 57: *MA* I,245–47; this count does not include *Sermo I*: *CC* XLI,2–6, in which Augustine compares the first verse of Genesis and the first verse of John's Gospel.

[4] There are 32 sermons on Psalm 118 in the *Enarratio in Psalmum CXVIII*: *CC* XL, 1664–1776. However these represent a rather systematic attempt to deal with the lengthy and profound psalm in an orderly manner and in effect comprise one unit; see Augustine's remarks prefacing his treatment of this psalm: *CC* XL,1664–65.

[5] Van Bavel, p. 5: "les premières formules de saint Augustin pour exprimer le mystère de l'union du divin et de l'humain dans le Christ sont des plus simples"; cf. pp. 40–41; Daley, p. 101.

[6] *De doctrina christiana* IV,viii–xi: *CC* XXXII,131–35; cf. C. Mohrmann, "Augustine and the Eloquentia," *Études sur le latin des chrétiens* (Rome: Edizioni di storia e letteratura 1958–77) I,351–70.

[7] It is not within the scope of this paper to treat these sermons with regard to their chronology; for questions of chronology, see the summary of contemporary scholarship in P. Verbraken, *Études critiques sur les sermons authentiques de saint Augustin*, Patristica XII (Steenbrugis: In abbatia S. Petri, 1976).

[8] E.g., *Sermo CXVII* III,4: *PL* XXXVIII,663: *Pars corporis humani, verbi gratia, brachium: utique minus est brachium quam totum corpus. Et si minus est brachium, breviorem locum occupat. Item caput, quia pars est corporis in minore loco est, et minus est quam totum corpus, cui caput est. Sic omnia quae sunt in loco, minora sunt in parte quam in toto. Nihil tale de illo Verbo sentiamus, nihil tale cogitemus*; *Sermo CXX* 2: *PL* XXXVIII,676–77: *Videte aliam differentiam, quam longe sit a Creatore creatura, maxime corporalis. Quando in oriente*

est sol, in occidente non est. Lux quidem ejus de illo grandi corpore effusa, pertendit usque in occidentem; sed ipse non est…. Numquid Verbum Dei sic est? Numquid quando est in oriente, non est in occidente; aut quando est in occidente, non est in oriente? This concern is certainly not limited to his sermons, cf. *Confessiones* VII,i: *CC* XXVII,92–93; *De trinitate* I,i: *CC* L,27–31.

⁹ *Sermo CXVII* V,7; X,16: *PL* XXXVIII,665; 670; *Sermo CXIX* III,3: *PL* XXXVIII, 674; *Tractatus in Euangelium Ioannis* I,1, 4: *CC* XXXVI,1, 2; III,19: *CC* XXXVI,28.

¹⁰ *Sermo CXVII* V,7: *PL* XXXVIII,665: *Et quid facimus, fratres, quando carnalibus spiritualia insinuamus: si tamen et nos ipsi non carnales sumus, quando carnalibus ista spiritualia intimamus, homini assuefacto nativitate terrena, et videnti istius creaturae ordinem, ubi successus et decessus, gignentes et genitos aetate distinguit? Post patrem enim nascitur filius, patri utique morituro successurus. Hoc in hominibus, hoc in aliis animantibus invenimus, parentes priores tempore, filios tempore posteriores. Hac consuetudine videndi carnalia transferre illi ad spiritualia cupiunt, et intentione carnalium facilius seducuntur.* The context is a polemic against the Arians, who seek to understand the Son's being begotten of the Father in the same manner as a human father begets a son; as Augustine later points out, the Son was not begotten in time, cf. *Sermo CXVII* VI,10: *PL* XXXVIII,666; also, *Sermo CXVII* III,4: *PL* XXXVIII,663: *non de suggestione carnis spiritualia imaginemur.*

¹¹ *Sermo CXIX* III,3: *PL* XXXVIII,674: *Quis comprehendat Verbum manens? Omnia verba nostra sonant et transeunt. Quis comprehendat Verbum manens, nisi qui in ipso manet? Vis comprehendere Verbum manens? Noli sequi flumen carnis. Caro quippe ista fluvius est: non enim manet. Tanquam de fonte quodam secreto naturae nascuntur homines, vivunt homines, moriuntur homines: nec unde veniant novimus, nec quo eant novimus.*

¹² *Tractatus in Euangelium Ioannis* II,16: *CC* XXXVI,19: *Omnia enim collyria et medicamenta nihil sunt nisi de terra. De puluere caecatus es, de puluere sanaris; ergo caro te caecauerat, caro te sanat. Carnalis enim anima facta erat consentiendo affectibus carnalibus, inde fuerat oculus cordis caecatus. "Verbum caro factum est:" medicus iste tibi fecit collyrium. Et quoniam sic uenit ut de carne uitia carnis exstingueret, et de morte occideret mortem;* cf. *Sermo CXIX* IV,4: *PL* XXXVIII,674.

¹³ *Sermo CXVII* III,5: *PL* XXXVIII,663: *Sed non potes tale aliquid cogitare. Magis pia est talis ignorantia, quam praesumpta scientia. Loquimur enim de Deo. Dictum est, "Et Deus erat Verbum." De Deo loquimur, quid mirum si non comprehendis? Si enim comprehendis, non est Deus. Sit pia confessio ignorantiae magis, quam temeraria professio scientiae.*

¹⁴ *Sermo CXIX* III,3: *PL* XXXVIII,674.

¹⁵ *Sermo CXX* 2: *PL* XXXVIII,676.

¹⁶ *Sermo CCCXLII* 5: *PL* XXXIX,1504.

¹⁷ Cf. *Sermo CXVII* II,3: *PL* XXXVIII,662–63: *Non modo, fratres, tractamus, quomodo possit intelligi quod dictum est. "In principio erat Verbum, et Verbum erat apud Deum, et Deus erat Verbum." Ineffabiliter potest intelligi: non verbis hominis fit ut intelligatur. Verbum Dei tractamus, et dicimus quare non intelligatur…. Dicimus quam incomprehensibile sit quod*

lectum est: tamen lectum est, non ut comprehenderetur ab homine, sed ut doleret homo quia non comprehendit, et inveniret unde impeditur a comprehensione, et removeret ea, et inhiaret perceptioni incommutabilis Verbi, ipse ex deteriore in melius commutatus.

[18] See note 12.

[19] Cf. *Sermo CXVII* V,7: *PL* XXXVIII,665: *Et quid facimus nos? Silebimus? Utinam liceret. Forsitan enim silendo aliquid dignum de re ineffabili cogitaretur…. Itaque, fratres, melius erat si possemus tacere, et dicere: hoc habet fides, sic credimus.*

[20] *Sermo CXXI* 5: *PL* XXXVIII,680: *Sed addidit quod erat naturae nostrae. Accedit enim ad id quod non erat, non amisit quod erat.*

[21] *Sermo CXVII* X,16: *PL* XXXVIII,670; Augustine puns repeatedly in the word *incarnatum*: *Verbum incarnatum [Dei] …cibum incarnatum [matris]*.

[22] *Sermo CXVII* X,16: *PL* XXXVIII,670: *Quia quando cibum mater incarnatum lac facit, cibus in lac convertitur; incommutabiliter autem manens Verbum carnem assumpsit, ut esset quodammodo contextum.*

[23] Cf. *Sermo CXIX* VI,6: *PL* XXXVIII,675: *Sed quomodo, inquit, fieri potuit ut Verbum Dei, quo gubernatur mundus, per quod et creata sunt et creantur universa, coarctaret se in virginis carnem; dimitteret mundum, et desereret Angelos, in utero unius feminae includeretur? Nec nosti divina cogitare. Verbum Dei (tibi loquor, o homo, de omnipotentia Dei Verbi tibi loquor) prorsus totum potuit, quia et Verbum Dei omnipotens est, et manere apud Patrem, et venire ad nos; et in carne procedere ad nos, et apud ipsum latere*; cf. also *Sermo CXX* 3: *PL* XXXVIII,677.

[24] *Sermo CCCXLII* 3: *PL* XXXIX,1502: *ergo miro et ineffabili modo in hoc mundo erat.*

[25] *Sermo CXX* 3: *PL* XXXVIII,677: *Verbum episcopus facit. Verbum facio de Verbo. Sed quale verbum, de quali Verbo? Mortale verbum, de immortali Verbo; mutabile verbum, de immutabili Verbo; transitorium verbum, de aeterno Verbo. Tamen attendite verbum meum. Dixeram enim vobis, Verbum Dei ubique totum est. Ecce facio vobis verbum: ad omnes pervenit quod dico.…Ecce loquor, et omnes habetis. Parum est quia omnes habetis: et omnes totum habetis. Pervenit ad omnes totum, ad singulos totum.* Cf. *Sermo CXVII* III,4–5: *PL* XXXVIII,663–64.

[26] *Sermo CXVII* II,3: *PL* XXXVIII,663: *Non enim Verbum proficit aut crescit accedente cognitore; sed integrum si permanseris, integrum si recesseris, integrum cum redieris; manens in se, et innovans omnia. Ergo est forma omnium rerum, forma infabricata, sine tempore, ut diximus, sine spatiis locorum.*

[27] *Sermo CXVII* III,5: *PL* XXXVIII,663–64: *Attingere aliquantum mente Deum, magna beatitudo est; comprehendere autem, omnino impossibile…. Quid ergo de illo Verbo, fratres, dici potest?…Quis ergo oculus cordis comprehendit Deum? Sufficit ut attingat, si purus est oculus. Si autem attingit, tactu quodam attingit incorporeo et spirituali, non tamen comprehendit; et hoc, si purus est. Et homo fit beatus contingendo corde illud quod semper beatum manet.*

[28] *Sermo CXX* 3: *PL* XXXVIII,677: *Pervenit ad omnes totum, ad singulos totum.*

[29] *Sermo CXVII* VIII,11: *PL* XXXVIII,667: *Arbitror sanctitatem vestram jam intellexisse quod dico, non posse comparari temporalia aeternis; sed posse ex aliqua tenui et parva similitudine coaeva coaeternis. Inveniamus itaque coaeva, et de scripturis admoneamur ad has similitudines.*

[30] *Sermo CXVII* IV,6: *PL* XXXVIII,664: *Itaque Verbum Dei, fratres charissimi, incorporaliter, inviolabiliter, incommutabiliter, sine temporali nativitate, natum tamen intelligamus a Deo. Putamusne possumus aliquo modo persuadere quibusdam infidelibus non abhorrere a vero, quod dicitur a nobis fide catholica, quae contraria est Arianis, a quibus Ecclesia Dei saepe tentata est, cum carnales homines id facilius accipiunt quod videre consueverunt? Ausi sunt enim quidam dicere, Major est Pater Filio, et precedit eum tempore: id est, major est Filio Pater, et minor est Patre Filius, et a Patre in tempore preceditur.*

[31] *Sermo CXVII* VI,10: *PL* XXXVIII,666: *Et revera, fratres, non sum inventurus temporales similitudines, quas aeternitati possim comparare. Sed et tu quas invenisti, quid sunt? Quid enim invenisti? Quia pater major est tempore quam filius: et ideo vis ut Filius Dei tempore minor sit quam Pater aeternus, quia invenisti minorem filium patre temporali. Da mihi aeternum patrem hic, et invenisti similitudinem.*

[32] *Sermo CXVII* VI,10: *PL* XXXVIII,666: *Aliud est enim coaeternum, aliud coaevum. Coaevos quotidie dicimus eos qui eamdem habent mensuram temporum: non alter ab altero preceditur tempore, ambos tamen esse coepisse, quos dicimus coaevos.*

[33] *Sermo CXVII* VIII,11: *PL* XXXVIII,667; he uses the same analogy in *Sermo CXVIII* 2: *PL* XXXVIII,672–73.

[34] *Sermo CXVII* IX,12: *PL* XXXVIII,668: *Nascitur ergo cum imagine sua, et simul esse incipiunt virgultum et imago ejus. Numquid non fateris imaginem esse de illo virgulto, non virgultum de imagine genitum? Ergo de illo virgulto confiteris imaginem. Itaque et generans, et quod genitum est, simul esse coeperunt. Ergo coaeva sunt.*

[35] *Sermo CXVII* IX,12: *PL* XXXVIII,668: *Non potuisti invenire coaeterna genita aeternis genitoribus, et invenisti coaeva nata temporalibus gignentibus. Intelligo coaeternum Filium natum aeterno gignenti. Quod enim est temporali coaevum, hoc est aeterno coaeternum.*

[36] Cf. *Sermo CXIX* VII,7: *PL* XXXVIII,675: *Ecce ego verbum quod vobis loquor, in corde meo prius habui; processit ad te, nec recessit a me: coepit esse in te, quod non erat in te; mansit apud me, cum exiret ad te. Sicut ergo verbum meum prolatum est sensui tuo, nec recessit a corde meo: sic illud Verbum prolatum est sensui nostro, nec recessit a Patre suo. Verbum meum erat apud me, et processit in vocem: Verbum Dei erat apud Patrem, et processit in carnem. Sed numquid ego possum id facere de voce mea, quod potuit ille de carne sua?*

[37] *Sermo CXIX* III,3: *PL* XXXVIII,674: *Quis comprehendat Verbum manens? Omnia verba nostra sonant et transeunt. Quis comprehendat Verbum manens, nisi qui in ipso manet?* Cf. *Sermo CXX* 3: *PL* XXXVIII,677 and *Tractatus in Euangelium Ioannis* I,8: *CC* XXXVI, 4–5.

[38] *Sermo Caillau I* 57,2: *MA* I,246: *Ab aeternitate in aeternitatem manens, aequalis numquam non fuit; nec dicendum Fuit, Est, et Erit, sed Est: quod ergo dicitur, Fuit, iam non est; quod autem dicitur, Erit, nondum est.*

[39] *Sermo CXVIII* 1: *PL* XXXVIII,672: *Noli ergo quaerere tempus ei, per quem facta sunt tempora. "Erat Verbum." Sed tu dicis, Aliquando non erat Verbum. Mentiris, nusquam legis. Ego autem lego tibi, "In principio erat Verbum." Quid quaeris ante principium? Si autem aliquid invenire potueris ante principium, ipsum erit principium. Insanit qui aliquid quaerit ante principium. Quid ergo dicit quia fuit ante principium?* Cf. *Sermo CXIX* VI,6: *PL* XXXVIII,675; *Sermo CXXI* 1: *PL* XXXVIII,678; *Sermo Caillau I* 57,2: *MA* I,247.

[40] *Sermo CCCXLII* 3: *PL* XXXIX,1502: *Deus enim habitando continet, non continetur; Tractatus in Euangelium Ioannis* II,10: *CC* XXXVI,16: *Deus autem mundo infusus fabricat, ubique positus fabricat*; cf. *Confessiones* VII,15: *CC* XXVII,106.

[41] *Tractatus in Euangelium Ioannis* I,7: *CC* XXXVI,4: *Sed forte dicetis, quia ego uobis sum praesentior quam Deus. Absit. Multo est ille praesentior.*

[42] *Tractatus in Euangelium Ioannis* II,4: *CC* XXXVI,14: *Propter te crucifixus est, ut humilitatem doceret; et quia si sic ueniret ut Deus, non agnosceretur. Si enim sic ueniret ut Deus, non ueniret eis qui uidere Deum non poterant. Non enim secundum id quod Deus est aut uenit aut discedit, cum sit ubique praesens, et nullo loco contineatur. Sed secundum quid uenit? Quod apparuit homo.*

VII

The Church and Christian Life

Augustine

*Diffusa ecclesia per gentes loquitur omnibus linguis; eccle-
sia est corpus Christi, in hoc corpore membrum es; cum ergo
membrum sis eius corporis quod loquitur omnibus linguis, crede
te loqui omnibus linguis. Vnitas enim membrorum caritate con-
cordat; et ipsa unitas loquitur quomodo tunc unus homo loquebatur. Accipimus ergo et nos Spiritum sanctum, si amamus
ecclesiam, si caritate compaginamur, si catholico nomine et fide
gaudemus. Credamus, fratres, quantum quisque amat ecclesiam
Christi, tantum habet Spiritum sanctum.*

Tractatus in Euangelium Ioannis XXXII,7-8

A Ministry Characterized by and Exercised in Humility: The Theology of Ordained Ministry in the Letters of Augustine of Hippo

All but 20 of Augustine's almost 300 letters were written during his 39 years as a cleric of the Catholic Church. Since his letters have rarely been the subject of a study of his theology of the ordained ministry, I hope that this communication will increase our understanding of Augustine's views on this important aspect of Church life.

My thesis is that in his letters Augustine presents the ordained ministry as one characterized by and exercised in humility. The ordained minister exercises this humility both ontologically and epistemologically. The theological basis of Augustine's stress on humility is found primarily in his Christology. The social roots of his stress on humility stem from the economic, social, and legal privileges granted to clergy in the Christian Church during the fourth and fifth centuries.[1]

A Ministry Characterized by Humility

For Augustine, the ordained minister demonstrated humility ontologically by remembering that he, too, was a member of the people of God, a fellow-disciple along with all other Christian faithful under the one Master, Jesus Christ. In acknowledging that he was a fellow disciple along with all the other Christian faithful, in remembering that his ministry was but an instrument of the Lord's power and grace, and in treating others with gentleness and patience, the cleric demonstrated humility.

Augustine characterized himself as the servant of Christ and of the servants of Christ;[2] the bishop of Hippo referred to his brother bishop, Severus, as "one of our fellow disciples";[3] and he called Paulinus and Therasia "fellow disciples under our Master, the Lord Jesus Christ."[4]

This co-discipleship is seen in Augustine's famous understanding of being at the head of the local church community in a position of authority only by being at the side of the community as a fellow disciple.[5] The bishop could not be at the head of the community as leader unless he was first and also at the side of the community, sitting together with them at the feet of the one Master, the Lord Jesus Christ.[6]

Augustine's language indicates his awareness that he was a fellow disciple along with all other Christians, even though as bishop he had authority over them.[7] He never referred to the congregation at Hippo as "my people." Rather, he would speak of them as "the people of the heavenly Jerusalem,"[8] "members of Christ,"[9] "the sheep of the Lord."[10] He tells Darius that "we [bishops] are your guardians, you are the flock of God,"[11] not using the possessive pronoun.

Augustine also demonstrated this ontological humility by describing the ordained ministry as an instrument of divine grace. God is the source and goal of all ministry in the Church, and the ordained minister is but an instrument through which the Lord works.[12] As a presbyter, Augustine told Bishop Valerius that he commended himself to God, begging the Lord to work through his powers.[13] He also reminded Valerius that it was not the clergy who were to be feared because of their power, but rather God because of their words.[14] Augustine wrote Paulinus of Nola that any glory associated with the latter's ministry was not his, but belonged to the Lord.[15] Augustine and Alypius informed the lady Juliana that she received the Word of God through their ministry.[16] Augustine exhorted the Donatists to return to the unity of the Catholic Church by listening to the word that is God's, not his.[17] He urged Count Boniface, who was contemplating resigning his military charge and entering monastic life, to hear not so much him, but the Lord, who was speaking through the bishop, his feeble minister.[18] He described the people of Hippo as God's trees, which the Lord watered continuously through his ministry.[19]

This ontological humility is also demonstrated in the ordained minister's treatment of the people entrusted to his care. As a presbyter, Augustine recommended that abuses in pastoral life be done away with not by harsh or severe measures, not by commands or threats, but by teaching and persuasion.[20] Thus he hoped that the Donatists could be won over by insistent but gentle warning rather than by force.[21] In comparing governance of Church and state, Augustine told the proconsul Apringius that ruling a province is best done by instilling fear, but ruling a church is to be made lovable by the use of mildness.[22]

Such humility would even lead a bishop to ask forgiveness of one he had wronged. Augustine's frank criticism of Jerome's exegesis occasioned an apology from the bishop to the presbyter in Bethlehem. Augustine acknowledged that his sin of offending Jerome could not be disavowed and he asked his forgiveness.[23]

A Ministry Exercised in Humility

Augustine's letters also indicate that the ordained minister was to exercise humility by relying on Scripture, the teaching and decisions of Church councils, and the leadership of the see of Rome for guidance in pastoring the flock of God entrusted to him and regulating Church life. This epistemological humility flows from the ontological humility described above, since the ordained minister was a fellow disciple with all the other Christian faithful.

For Augustine, the Bible was primarily the Bible of a pastor;[24] as pastor he ceaselessly used the Bible in his daily ministry as shepherd of the flock of Christ.

In his first letter as a presbyter to Bishop Valerius he stated how the ordained minister would find instruction for pastoral guidance in the Scriptures.[25] A later letter from Augustine the presbyter related how he appealed to the Scriptures in a successful campaign to eliminate the boisterous drinking bouts at the tombs of martyrs on feast days.[26]

Augustine's refutations of heretics and schismatics relied heavily on the Scriptures, since he believed that these errors came about through misinterpretation of the Scriptures. Augustine often reminded the Donatists of the parables of the wheat and the weeds (Mt 13:24–30) and of the threshing floor mentioned in Mt 3:12.[27] Many times the Pelagians heard Augustine refer to passages from the Psalms[28] and especially from Romans[29] in his letters opposing their views on sin and grace. The Arian Pascentius found in Augustine one who had carefully searched the Scriptures, and therefore one over whom a victory in truth could not easily be won.[30]

The Bible continued to be the guide for Augustine the pastor. While he reminded Bishop Possidius that Scripture does not provide an answer to every particular problem a person might encounter, Augustine did find some relevant remarks in 1 Corinthians about female dress and behavior to help Possidius deal with some women in Camala who were wearing amulets and painting their faces.[31] When faced with Bishop Hesychius' claim that one could determine the date of the end of the world from clues given in Scripture, Augustine not only used Scripture to refute all of Hesychius' proofs, but then reminded the bishop of the futility of such a venture by recalling the Lord's words in Ac 1:7 that even the Apostles were not to know such a date.[32]

After the absolute primacy of the Scriptures for pastoral guidance, Augustine held Church councils in the highest regard for providing norms for the exercise of the pastoral ministry. Although Scripture alone could demonstrate that eliminating the boisterous drinking parties at the martyrs' tombs was a necessity, Augustine believed that the abuse had become so widespread that only conciliar authority could eliminate it.[33] Augustine also referred to conciliar decisions for liturgical matters, replying to the notary Januarius that some liturgical seasons and practices came from plenary councils which had great authority in the Church.[34] Conciliar decisions also promulgated policies forbidding the transference of presbyters and bishops from one see to another,[35] as well as that of monks from one monastery to another.[36] Augustine would often remind a correspondent of how actions which are contrary to conciliar decrees and decisions must not be undertaken, so as not to make a mockery of the councils or provide cause for scandal.[37]

A cleric also turned to the see of Rome for guidance and assistance in resolving pastoral situations, especially in cases of heresy. The Council of Carthage sought the help of Innocent, the bishop of Rome, in fighting Pelagianism.[38] The Council of Milevis sent its minutes to that same bishop, hoping that the Pelagian heretics would submit to the authority of the bishop of Rome, which is derived from the authority of the Scriptures.[39] Augustine was willing to refer the case of Count Classicianus, whose whole family had been excommunicated by the brash young Bishop Auxilius, not only to a bishops' council but also to the Apostolic See if necessary for resolution.[40] Arguments in the case of the corrupt and unworthy Bishop Antoninus of Fussala were sent to Rome for arbitration by both the wily Antonius and Augustine and the African bishops.[41] Augustine also suggested sending other particularly delicate and difficult ecclesiastical matters to the Roman see for arbitration and decision.[42]

As bishop, Augustine admitted frequently his ignorance about many things and his need and desire to learn from those who knew more than he. Ordination and the clerical office gave no guarantee of superior wisdom. In his correspondence with Jerome, Augustine insisted that the presbyter in Bethlehem help the bishop of Hippo correct his errors and learn from the biblical scholar.[43] Even though a bishop ranks higher than a presbyter, Augustine ranked lower than Jerome in many things, and correction from an inferior is not to be refused or disdained.[44] The author of *De magistro* always considered himself first and foremost as a learner. He told Florentina, a young lady whom he tutored, that he acted not so much as a finished master, but as one who needed perfecting along with his pupils.[45] Augustine informed the zealous Bishop Hesychius that he would rather confess a cautious ignorance than profess a false knowledge.[46]

Christology as the Theological Basis
for Augustine's Stress on Humility
in His Theology of the Ordained Ministry

We will now argue that this stress on humility comes primarily from Augustine's Christology, in which Christ is presented as the model, teacher, and pattern of humility. We shall also argue this thesis from the fact that Augustine sees the ordained ministry as one primarily devoted to ministering Christ's Word and Sacraments to the people of God.

Since for Augustine, all sin was pride,[47] the work of the Redeemer and Savior was to teach humility to the sinful human race. Thus humility becomes a central aspect of Augustine's Christology.[48] Augustine saw Christ as the Doctor of Humility, the Divine Physician who healed the human race of its sinful pride through the medicine of humility. Christ is both doctor and medicine, being the model and teacher of humility, instructing the sinful human race to subject itself to the Creator through humility and restoring the proper balance between Creator and creature.[49] Thus Augustine saw humility as the key to understanding Christ and the Christian way of life.[50]

Augustine saw humility demonstrated in every stage of Christ's life and ministry. From both John 1 and Ph 2:5-8, the bishop of Hippo saw Christ demonstrate humility in the Incarnation.[51] The Savior whom the whole world could not contain slept in the straw of a manger.[52] Christ the Master was baptized by John the servant.[53] Christ, who was equal to the Father, solemnly declared that he sought not his own glory, but that of his Father.[54] When he washed his disciples' feet at the Last Supper, the Savior taught us that we, too, must be so humble as to be willing to wash each other's feet.[55] Even the institution of the Eucharist is an act of humility on Christ's part, since only through humility could Christ become food and drink for our eternal life.[56]

In Christ's passion and death Augustine saw the greatest demonstration of humility. Christ was crucified for us in order to teach us humility.[57] The Christological hymn in Philippians 2 gave Augustine more Scriptural evidence for seeing humility in the passion and death of Christ. The Christ preached throughout the world is the crucified Christ, the Christ whose divine humility conquered the pride of earth.[58]

It is precisely in Augustine's own description of the ordained ministry that we see the connection between his theology of ordained ministry and his Christology. Augustine often described the ministry of the cleric as one devoted to ministering Christ's Word and sacrament to the people of God.[59] The Word and sacrament of which the cleric is the minister are not his, but Christ's. Since Christ is the model and pattern of true humility, the cleric who ministers Christ's Word and sacraments to the people of God must himself be a man of great humility. He who ministers the word and sacraments of the Doctor of humility must be an example of that humility by which the Divine Physician healed the human race of its sinful pride.

We can see a most evident link between Augustine's Christology and his theology of the ordained ministry in the letter sent by the Catholic bishops of Africa to Marcellinus before the Conference of Carthage held in 411. After the Conference, the Catholic bishops are willing to let any converted Donatist bishops join them as "co-bishops" in ministering to the people of God. If the people find such an arrangement spiritually distressing, the Catholic bishops suggest that both Catholic and converted Donatist bishops resign and that a single new bishop then be chosen for each diocese.

The rationale for this surprising suggestion is Christological in nature. Since Christ came down from the heavens in an act of humility to dwell among his human members, should the bishops fear to come down from their episcopal thrones to save the Church from further divisions and scandal? The office of bishop would bring them greater reward if in an act of humility they laid it aside so as to gather the flock of Christ together rather than hold on to the episcopal office and keep the flock of Christ scattered and in distress.[60] The Catholic bishops provide a Christological basis for their offer of resigning their offices in an act of humility for the spiritual good of the people of God.

The Social Roots of Augustine's Stress on Humility in the Practice of the Ordained Ministry

I would also argue that we can detect social roots for Augustine's stress on humility in the practice of the ordained ministry. Specifically, I would argue that the clerical privileges in Late Antiquity provide a social basis for Augustine's stress on humility.

Expositions of these privileges have been ably documented and detailed elsewhere,[61] and will only be summarized here briefly. The Catholic clergy of Late Antiquity were recipients of exemptions from property, inheritance, and business taxes, as well as curial duties and other civic obligations for the Roman Empire. Bishops were paid higher salaries than some professionals and government officials of the day. The clergy's clothing gave them the appearance of imperial senators and consuls. Clergy were granted immunity from certain types of punishments and penalties from which ordinary citizens were not. Clergy exerted social prestige in law courts through personal interventions; eventually there had to be laws which prevented clerical intercession in some kinds of trials. Clergy were also among the elite group of citizens who elected a city's *defensor civitatis*. Although titles of honor given to bishops carried no legal or juridical weight, these titles are evidence of the high respect in which the Empire held bishops. As is well known, bishops served as judges and later arbiters in civil cases.

All these economic, legal, and social privileges made the clerical state a respected and enviable state of life. We can see how well-known and desirable the clerical state in Late Antiquity was by noting that Constantine had to legislate against rich pagans who were impersonating Catholic clergy in order to claim the privileges and exemptions granted to the Church's ministers.[62]

Such a privileged state of life could easily distract a cleric from his primary responsibility as minister of word and sacrament in the Church. Augustine's letters contain references to clerics who have abandoned the spiritual dimensions of their ministry in order to pursue economic gains and social prestige by means of the clerical state. Bishop Paul of Cataquas is severely scolded for his dealings in illegal tax exemptions and property deals;[63] Antoninus of Fussala was able to tyrannize and bully the people there because of the social prestige and ecclesiastical authority that was his as bishop.[64]

This privileged clerical state would require the humility Augustine called for if the cleric was to remain faithful to his ministry of word and sacrament among the people of God. Remembering that he must give an account on Judgment Day of the spiritual well-being of the flock entrusted to his care would keep the ordained minister steadfast and faithful in the exercise of his spiritual ministry.[65] The possibility of worldly honors tempting the cleric to neglect or even abandon his spiritual duties could be avoided if he practiced the ontological and epistemological humility called for in Augustine's letters.

These worldly honors and the temptations they presented to clerics give Augustine's stress on humility in the ordained ministry social roots as well as the Christological basis we have presented earlier in this paper.

In conclusion, I believe we must insist that the Christological basis we have outlined was the primary basis for Augustine's stress on humility, since in Augustine's letters the cleric first and foremost was minister of the word and sacraments of him who was the teacher, pattern, and doctor of all humility. But we should also not overlook the economic, legal, and social privileges granted to clergy in Augustine's day as another factor in understanding the bishop of Hippo's stress on humility in the practice of the ordained ministry.

Notes

[1] The episcopal ministry is the one most frequently mentioned in Augustine's letters. Since the presbyter and the deacon work with the bishop and share in his ministry, what Augustine says of the bishop can usually be applied to the presbyter and the deacon as well.

[2] Salutations in *Epistula CXXX: CSEL* XLIV,40; *Epistula CCXVII: CSEL* LVII,403; *Epistula CCXXXI: CSEL* LVII,504.

[3] *Epistula XXXI* 9: *CSEL* XXXIV,ii,8: *(b)eatissimus frater Seuerus de condiscipulatu nostro.*

[4] Salutation in *Epistula XCV: CSEL* XXXIV,ii,506: *sub magistro Domino Iesu condiscipuli.*

[5] *Epistula CXXXIV* 1: *CSEL* XLIV,85: *non tam praeesse quam prodesse desidero.* This famous pairing of *praeesse* and *prodesse* seems to be Augustine's creation. It represents, in the view of Y. Congar, not only a sacramental view of Augustine's ontology (*ut enim sit quisque sit verus sacerdos, oportet ut non solo sacramento, sed iustitia quoque induatur*; see *Contra litteras Petiliani* II,xxx,69: *BA* 30,310), but was also very influential in the bishop of Hippo's theologico-ethical synthesis which unites the ideas of justice, humility, obedience, peace, and liberty. See Y. Congar, "Quelques expressions traditionnelles du service chrétien," in *L'épiscopat et l'église universelle*, eds. Y. Congar and B.-D. DePuys (Paris: Les éditions du Cerf, 1962), pp. 101–2.

[6] A. Mandouze, *Saint Augustin: l'aventure de la raison et de la grâce* (Paris: Études Augustiniennes, 1968), pp. 159–62.

[7] É. Lamirande, "The Priesthood at the Service of the People of God according to Saint Augustine," *The Furrow* 15 (1964) 507, highlights well Augustine's emphasis on the bishop's being a co-disciple along with all other Christian faithful.

[8] *Epistula XCV* 5: *CSEL* XXXIV,ii,510: *populi...Hierosolymitani caelestis.*

[9] *Epistula CXXII* 1: *CSEL* XXXIV,ii,742: *membra Christi.*

[10] *Epistula CXXV* 2: *CSEL* XLIV,4: *oues dominicae*. Mandouze (p. 160) reminds us, "il [Augustine] parle toujours du 'peuple de Dieu' ou du 'peuple chrétien', étant entendu que l'évêque en est lui-même membre avec les autre fidèles." See also M. Jourjon, "L'évêque et le peuple de Dieu," in *Saint Augustin parmi nous*, ed. H. Rondet (Paris: Le Puy, 1954), p. 151; A. Mandouze, "L'évêque et le corps presbyteral au service du peuple fidèle selon saint Augustin," in *L'évêque dans l'église du Christ*, ed. H. Bouësse (Paris: Desclée de Brouwer, 1963), pp. 138–39.

[11] *Epistula CCXXXI* 6: *CSEL* LVII,509: *praepositi uestris sumus, grex dei estis*.

[12] É. Lamirande, "'Non sibi arroget minister plus quam quod ut minister,' (*Sermo* 266, 3): notes sur la théologie augustinienne du ministère" in *Études sur l'ecclésiologie de saint Augustin* (Ottawa: University of Ottawa Press, 1969), p. 129, reminds us that the use of *dispensator* and *minister* by Augustine underscores the mediating role of the ordained minister in the economy of salvation. See also E. Sauser, "Gedanken zum priesterlichen Dienst in der Theologie des heiligen Augustinus," *Trierer theologische Zeitschrift* 77 (1968) 93.

[13] *Epistula XXII* I,1: *CSEL* XXXIV,i,54.

[14] *Epistula XXII* I,5: *CSEL* XXXIV,i,58.

[15] *Epistula XXXI* 6: *CSEL* XXXIV,ii,6.

[16] *Epistula CLXXXVIII* I,1: *CSEL* LVII,119–20.

[17] *Epistula CLXIII* 1: *CSEL* XLIV,640.

[18] *Epistula CCXX* 3: *CSEL* LVII,432.

[19] *Epistula CCLXVIII* 3: *CSEL* LVII,654.

[20] *Epistula XXII* I,5: *CSEL* XXXIV,i,58.

[21] *Epistula XXIII* 7: *CSEL* XXXIV,i,71–72.

[22] *Epistula CXXXIV* 3: *CSEL* XLIV,86.

[23] *Epistula LXXIII* II,3: *CSEL* XXXIV,ii,265–66.

[24] A. M. la Bonnadière, "Augustin, ministre de la parole de Dieu," in *Saint Augustin et la Bible* (Paris: Beauchesne, 1986), p. 51.

[25] *Epistula XXI* 3–4: *CSEL* XXXIV,i,51–52.

[26] *Epistula XXII* I,3–II,8: *CSEL* XXXIV,i,56–61.

[27] *Epistula XLIII* VIII,21: *CSEL* XXXIV,ii,103; *Epistula LIII* III,6: *CSEL* XXXIV, ii,156; *Epistula LXXVI* 2: *CSEL* XXXIV,ii,326; *Epistula LXXXVII* 8: *CSEL* XXXIV,ii,404; *Epistula XCIII* IV,15: *CSEL* XXXIV,ii,459; *Epistula CV* V,16: *CSEL* XXXIV,ii,609; *Epistula CVIII* VI,17: *CSEL* XXXIV,ii,631; *Epistula CXLII* 3: *CSEL* XLIV,249; *Epistula CLXXXV* IV,16: *CSEL* LVII,15.

414 The Church and Christian Life

[28] *Epistula CLVII* III,16: *CSEL* XLIV,464; *Epistula CLXXVII* 5: *CSEL* XLIV,673; *Epistula CLXXXVII* passim: *CSEL* LVII,45–80.

[29] *Epistula CLVII* passim: *CSEL* XLIV,449–88; *Epistula CLXXIX* passim: *CSEL* XLIV,691–97; *Epistula CLXXXVI* passim: *CSEL* LVII,45–80; *Epistula CXCIV* passim: *CSEL* LVII,176–214; *Epistula CCXVII* passim: *CSEL* LVII,403–25.

[30] *Epistula CCXXXVIII* II,14;IV,27: *CSEL* LVII,543, 554.

[31] *Epistula CCXLV*: *CSEL* LVII,581–83.

[32] *Epistula CXCIX* IV,13: *CSEL* LVII,254.

[33] *Epistula XXII* I,4: *CSEL* XXXIV,i,57–58.

[34] *Epistula LIV* I,1: *CSEL* XXXIV,ii,161–62.

[35] *Epistula LXIV* 3: *CSEL* XXXIV,ii,230–31; *Epistula XXII** 5: *BA* 46B,352.

[36] *Epistula LXIV* 3: *CSEL* XXXIV,ii,230–31.

[37] *Epistula XX** 8: *BA* 46B,304; *Epistula XXVI** 2: *BA* 46B,392.

[38] *Epistula CLXXV* 2: *CSEL* XLIV,655.

[39] *Epistula CLXXVI* 5: *CSEL* XLIV,667–68.

[40] *Epistula I** 5: *BA* 46B,50.

[41] *Epistula CCIX* 1, 6: *CSEL* LVII,347, 350; *Epistula XX** 12, 25, 26: *BA* 46B,312, 330, 332.

[42] *Epistula XXII*A* 4–5: *BA* 46B,378, 380.

[43] *Epistula LXVII* I,2: *CSEL* XXXIV,ii,238–39; *Epistula LXXIII* 1: *CSEL* XXXIV,ii, 264–65.

[44] *Epistula LXXXII* IV,33: *CSEL* XXXIV,ii,385.

[45] *Epistula CCLXVI* 2: *CSEL* LVII,648.

[46] *Epistula CXCVII* 5: *CSEL* LVII,234–35.

[47] *De ciuitate dei* XIV,xiii: *CC* XLVIII,434.

[48] Ibid. A. von Harnack, *Lehrbuch der Dogmengeschichte*, 5th ed., vol. 3 (Tübingen, J. C. B. Mohr, 1932), p. 132, saw humility as the very center of Augustine's Christology. "Damit ist das wahre Wesen Jesu Christi wirklich erkannt: 'robur in infirmitate perficitur.' Dass Niedrigkeit, Leiden, Schmach, Elend und Tod Mittel der Heiligung sind, ja dass die selbstlose und daher stets leidende Liebe das einzige Mittel der Heiligung ist ('ich heilige mich für sie'), dass die Demuth allein ein Auge hat, das Göttliche zu sehen, dass jede Stimmung im Guten das Gefühl, begnädigt zu sein, zum Begleiter hat—das ist die Christologie Augustin's in ihrem letzten Kern." See also A. Zumkeller, *Augustine's Ideal of the Religious Life* (New York: Fordham University Press, 1968), pp. 233–35.

[49] See R. Arbesmann, "The Concept of Christus Medicus in St. Augustine," *Traditio* 10 (1954) 1–28.

[50] *Epistula CXVIII* III,22: *CSEL* XXXIV,ii,685–86. For a lengthier discussion of this Christological basis for Augustine's theology of humility, see P. Adnès, "L'humilité vertu spécifiquement chrétienne d'après saint Augustin," *Revue d'ascétique et de mystique* 28 (1952) 208–33; idem, "L'humilité à l'école de saint Augustin," *Revue d'ascétique et de mystique* 31 (1955) 28–46.

[51] *Sermo Mai XXII* 1: *MA* I,314–15; *Confessiones* VII,ix,14: *CC* XXVII,101–2.

[52] *Sermo Frangipane IV* 4: *MA* I,211.

[53] *Sermo LII* 1: *PL* XXXVIII,354–55.

[54] *Tractatus in Euangelium Ioannis* XXIX,8: *CC* XXXVI,288.

[55] *Tractatus in Euangelium Ioannis* LVIII,4: *CC* XXXVI,474.

[56] *Enarratio in Psalmum XXXIII, Sermo I* 6: *CC* XXXVIII,277.

[57] *Tractatus in Euangelium Ioannis* II,4: *CC* XXXVI,13–14; *Enarratio in Psalmum XXXI, Sermo II* 18: *CC* XXXVIII,239.

[58] *Epistula CCXXXII* 6: *CSEL* LVII,516.

[59] *Epistula CCXXVIII* 2: *CSEL* LVII,485; *Epistula CCLIX* 2: *CSEL* LVII,612.

[60] *Epistula CXXVIII* 3: *CSEL* XLIV,32.

[61] For example, K. Baus et al., *The Imperial Church from Constantine to the Early Middle Ages*, History of the Church 2 (New York: Seabury Press, 1980), pp. 284–87; A. H. M. Jones, *The Later Roman Empire: A Social, Economic and Administrative Survey* (Norman: University of Oklahoma Press, 1964), 2:904–29; J. Gaudemet, *L'église dans l'empire romain* (Paris: Sirey, 1958), pp. 172–368.

[62] *Codex Theodosianus* XVI,ii,3,6: *Theodosiani libri XVI cum constitutionibus sirmondianis et leges novellae ad Theodosianum pertinentes*, ed. Th. Mommsen and P. M. Myer (Berlin, 1905) 2:1481–83.

[63] *Epistula LXXXV* 2: *CSEL* XXXIV,ii,395; *Epistula XCVI* 2: *CSEL* XXXIV,ii,515.

[64] *Epistula CCIX* 9: *CSEL* LVII,351–52; *Epistula XX** 4–7: *BA* 46B,298, 300, 302, 304.

[65] *Epistula XXIII* 6: *CSEL* XXXIV,i,70; *Epistula XXIV* 7: *CSEL* XXXIV,i,118.

Conversion in the Church
As Found in the Letters of St. Augustine

Mary Jane Kreidler

Introduction

Augustine's conversion led him on a journey from intellectual pride and self-sufficient knowledge to true wisdom and humility in solidarity with the crucified Christ.[1] As he came to believe, Augustine discovered in Jesus Christ a savior who:

> raised up there to himself those who had been brought low. Amid the lower parts he has built for himself out of our clay a lowly dwelling, in which he would protect from themselves those ready to become submissive to him, and bring them to himself. He heals their swellings, and nourishes their love, so that they may not go on further in self-confidence, but rather become weak. For at their feet they see the Godhead, weak because of its participation in our "coats of skin," and in their weariness they cast themselves on it, while it arises and lifts them up.[2]

The purpose of this paper is to discuss Augustine's ecclesiology as a relationship of solidarity between the savior, who participates "in our 'coats of skin,'" and weak, sinful humanity, which is lifted up[3] —a solidarity in sin and grace. Such an ecclesiology presumes the dynamism of an organic body—a savior and a people, exclusive of none, on a journey through this world toward fulfillment in the next.

Augustine's letters are invaluable resources for such a study. They trace the development of his thought throughout the years of his active ministry, contain some of his most persuasive rhetoric, and are addressed to a wide and varied audience. For the purpose of this paper, selected letters addressed principally, but not exclusively, to the Donatists will provide the texts for the discussion.

The dynamic quality of Augustine's ecclesiology provides a contrast to perfectionist groups such as the Donatists. Augustine saw the Church as the source of relationship between Christ and the Christian where Christians were also united to one another in Christ. Solidarity in sin and grace is the foundation of this body, which finds its identity in the Spirit-filled community of the Acts of the Apostles rather than in the closed community of Donatists, run aground in a sealed Ark, celebrating and preserving what was, with little attention to what was to come.[4]

Christ

Christ is central to Augustine's ecclesiology precisely because that ecclesiology presumes sinners in need for a redeemer. If Christ's role in the order of salvation is denied, he quickly becomes the exemplar of the Pelagian or one priest among many for the Donatist, locked into the ritual purity of a former day. For its part, the Church becomes an elitist sanctuary for the perfect, and its sectarian membership celebrates its own perfection while sitting in judgment on the presumed sinfulness of others. There is no room for the sinner in such a church.

In the conversion scene in the *Confessions*, Augustine read Rm 13:13–14, which invited him to put on the Lord Jesus Christ.[5] In fact, such a union of God and Augustine was possible because humanity and divinity were already united irrevocably and forever in the God-Man Jesus Christ who through his incarnation, death and resurrection

> "emptied himself," not losing the form of God, but "taking the form of a servant. He humbled himself, becoming obedient unto death, even to the death of the cross" (Ph 2:7–8).[6]

Jesus Christ, the suffering servant of Isaiah (Is 53:4),[7] endured that humanity might be healed.[8] He served by taking as His own the weaknesses and infirmity of the human condition.[9] According to Augustine's reading of Rm 5:12, Adam bore responsibility for humanity's sin and the subsequent need for redemption.[10] Human beings stand in solidarity with sinful Adam, for "By one man, sin entered into the world and by sin death, and so, death passed upon all men in whom all have sinned" (Rm 5:12).

But human beings stand in solidarity with the grace of Jesus Christ as well. If Adam is the source of death, Christ the new Adam is the source of life (1 Co 15:22) through justification.[11] He "is both the just one and the justifier, but we are 'justified freely by his grace'" (Rm 3:24).[12] If Adam is the source of carnal birth which is now subject to sin and damnation, Christ through spiritual rebirth in his grace destroys the first sin and in the case of an adult, personal sin as well.[13] No matter what harm Adam has accomplished as the "figure in reverse of Him that is to come, the good done by Christ to the regenerated is greater than the harm done by Adam to his descendants."[14]

Christ is the light who illumines the soul,[15] who gives humanity the power to become the sons of God (Jn 1:10). This, says Augustine, is adoption.[16]

> From this begetting by grace we distinguish that son who, although He was the Son of God, came that He might become the son of man, and might give us, who were sons of man, the power to become the sons of God.[17]

The centrality of Christ to the mystery of the Church is precisely what distinguishes Augustine's ecclesiology from that of other religious groups of his day. Augustine's ecclesiology focused on faith in Incarnate Love expressed in Christ's death and resurrection. Death and resurrection became the salvific hope for the Church in this world, a promise based on relationship, to be fully realized only in the world to come.

> "Rising from the dead he dieth no more, death hath no more dominion over him" (Rm 6:9); but after such Resurrection had taken place in the Lord's Body, so that the head of the Church might foreshadow what the body of the Church hopes for at the end....[18]
>
> Therefore, the universal Church, which is now in the pilgrimage of mortal life, awaits at the end of time what was first shown in the body of our Lord Jesus Christ, who is "the first born from the dead" (Col 1:18), because the Church is His Body, of which He is the Head.[19]

Augustine's understanding of conversion in the Church presupposed a belief in the reality of sin and the need for redemption. To deny sin and the need for redemption is an attempt to negate the human condition and alter the meaning of, or even eliminate the need for the cross and resurrection.

Donatism

While the Donatists were not so naive as to posit the sinlessness of their entire community, they did believe that one type of sinfulness, especially among the clergy, was worse than any other—that of *traditor*. Peter Brown states that Donatist purity depended on a "church that had preserved the *'total'* Christian law"[20] and who understood "Catholic" in that sense. By not sacrificing to idols or giving over sacred writings or objects, the Donatists identified themselves as the Chosen People who had preserved ritual purity without compromise.[21] They isolated themselves from the church they judged unclean and formed, as Brown says, an Ark that could save and protect its inhabitants from the sinful world around it.[22]

Loyal as they were to their interpretation of ritual purity and priestly law inherited from Cyprian, the Donatists denied the validity of baptism outside their community, believing that sacramental validity depended on the holiness of the minister which they understood as union with the Church.[23] In spite of this, they allowed for baptism within their communion performed by ministers who by their own definition were less than worthy.[24] In Letter 105, addressed specifically to the Donatists, Augustine chided them for this inconsistency, stated the source of grace, and rather sarcastically suggested that an evil minister would at least assure God's sanctification.

> See now how wrong and wicked is that customary saying of yours that if a man is good he sanctifies the one whom he baptizes; if he is bad and the one baptized does not know it, then God sanctifies him. If this is true, men ought to pray to be baptized by bad men whose wickedness is unknown to them rather than by good men, known to be such, so as to be sanctified by God rather than by men. God forbid that we should accept such foolish beliefs. Why not speak truly and recognize that the grace is always God's and the sacrament is God's, but the ministry is man's?[25]

Letters to Donatist bishops and laity illustrate how diligently Augustine worked to establish the legitimacy of Christ as the heir of the promises of the Old Testament as Paul had done in Rm 11:5 and Ga 3:16. Like Cyprian, Augustine uses Ps 2:7–8 to show the presence of Christ in the Old Testament.[26] Similarly, no fewer than eight letters use psalm 2 to show that Christ is the Son who has received the nations for his inheritance.[27] Another seven use Gn 22:18 and Ga 3:16 to illustrate that the descendants of all the nations of the earth shall find their blessing in the descendant who is Christ.[28]

As Letter 105 to the Donatists continues, Augustine reminds his readers that Scripture teaches both Christ and the Church.[29] Christ is *the seed* to whom the promise was given (Ga 3:16) and the Church is the reality of the nations to be blessed (Gn 22:18). The letter proceeds with a series of references to Christ from the Old Testament including titles such as "son" (Ps 2:7), "God of gods" (Ps 49:1), "bridegroom" (Ps 18:6), "king's son" (Ps 71:2), and "stone cut from the mountain" (Dn 2:34–35). Similarly, the Church is described as "nations" (Gn 22:18), "the Gentiles" (Ps 2:8), "the earth" (Ps 49:2), "the earth and the world set in the sun" (Ps 18:6), "the kingdom" (Ps 21:28–29), and "the glory over all the earth" (Ps 53:7). Christ is the mute lamb led to slaughter (Is 53:7), and the Church is the barren one that sings forth praise (Is 54:1–4).[30]

Augustine finds both Christ and the Church present in the Old Testament—important for understanding Augustine's ecclesiology. It marks a major point of divergence between Augustine and the Donatists—namely, the fact that Augustine understood that the Church received her identity in Christ. The perfection of the Church derived from Christ, not from its leadership. If the members of the Donatist church claim perfection by virtue of association with their hierarchy, their understanding of the Church is far from Augustine's. He wonders why the Lord's Prayer is said if "forgive us our debts" has no meaning.[31]

The Donatist church, as Augustine understood it, lacked both the dynamism of a living body and a purifying journey of return. The Donatists had no significant sinfulness to bring to their union with Christ. The perfection present within their communities belonged to the leadership and not to Christ. The Donatists show little need for Christ the Savior as they sail through life on a protective Ark removed from the reality of their own sinfulness. They have appropriated the Law of the Old Testament but deny the Redeemer of the New.

If, as Luc Verheijen maintains in his work *St. Augustine's Monasticism in the Light of Acts 4:32–35*, Augustine's understanding of Church is that of an organic body,[32] then the members are held together by the love of Christ as unifying principle.[33] In this world, members are sinners, while Christ their Head is perfect. Yet the Church is a unity because the Head and Body are united irrevocably in the God-Man Jesus Christ. Thus, as Adolar Zumkeller notes in his work *Augustine's Ideal of the Religious Life*, the Church as body is the "already and not yet" of Paul—the "already" of Christ and the "not yet" of the Christian on a journey joined together in love by the Spirit.[34]

What is predicated of the individual on a journey of conversion Augustine predicates of the body called Church as well. In bringing sin and weakness to the Church, humanity is invited to put on the Lord Jesus Christ (Rm 13:12–13). As a living body, it is called to life and growth in Christ its head. "Put you on the Lord Jesus Christ" is, then, a dynamic process—not a once-and-for-all experience, not the experience of the individual, but the experience of a corporate entity whose members are not only related to Christ but in him to each other. Verheijen seems to agree with Zumkeller when he says that Augustine believed the Church to be dynamic—that is, called to be "one heart and one mind *into God*" (Ac 4:32).[35]

Christ the seed, Son, Lord, Bridegroom, enlivens and fulfills the nation or the Kingdom that includes the whole world, not merely North Africa. In Letter 23 to the Donatist bishop Maximinus, Augustine affirms this when he says:

> I know, indeed, what the Catholic Church is. The nations are
> the inheritance of Christ, and the ends of the earth are His
> possession.[36]

A Church that includes the whole world must include both the good and the bad. In Letter 93 to Vincent the Rogatist bishop, Augustine explains that the good will not be harmed by the inclusion of the bad.[37] However, failure to include the bad is to judge prematurely, since it is not yet the end time. The parables of the wheat and the tares (Mt 13:24–30 with 3:12) and the fish and the net (Mt 13:47–48) indicate that not all those present in the Church are holy but that final judgment belongs to God and then only in the end time.

> So the Church, which increases among all nations, has been
> preserved with the Lord's grain (Mt 13:24–30, 38–39) and

will be preserved to the end, until it includes all nations, even the barbarian ones. The Church is symbolized by the good seed, which the Son of Man sowed, and of which He foretold that it would grow, intermingled with cockle, until the harvest time. The field indeed is the world, and the harvest the end of the world.[38]

Again in Letter 105, Augustine quotes 1 Co 1:10,12,13, written by Paul to combat the sectarianism of the Corinthians. Augustine denounces schisms and concludes that it was Christ, not Paul or Donatus, who was crucified, redeemed humanity, and in whose name the Christian is baptized.[39]

Christ has fulfilled Old Testament prophecies and redeemed the human race while introducing a new era of salvation. Augustine's term is the "grace of the New Testament,"[40] which he contrasts in the anti-Pelagian Letter 140 with the age that was. What God created was good;[41] those who "made known the Old Testament in accord with the time,…belonged to the New Testament."[42] Grace, which had been concealed in the Old Testament, is now revealed in Christ.[43] Human beings are "changed for the better,"[44] for "they are reborn through spiritual grace"[45] that is not their own. Further, they are subject to a new law, the command to love God and neighbor.

In Letter 185, chapter 36, written to the civil official Boniface in 417 regarding the treatment of the Donatists and the confiscation of their property, Augustine affirms that the basis of Christian unity in God is Christ. He sees the merger of Donatist and Catholic property as symbolic of his hope for a deeper union when he says:

> Let them enter into unity as partners with us, so that we may together administer not only what they call theirs, but also what is ours. For, it is written: "All things are yours, but you are Christ's and Christ is God's" (1 Co 3:22–23). Let us be one under that Head, in His one Body (cf. Ga 3:28; Ep 1:22–23; 3:15; 5:23; Col 1:18), and let us deal with such things as these in the manner described in the Acts of the Apostles: "They had one heart and one soul, neither did anyone say that aught was his own, but all things were common onto them" (Ac 4:32).[46]

Augustine's use of Ac 4:32 in this letter is indeed unusual and somewhat startling. It is a rare (and perhaps the only) citation of Ac 4:32 in the letters apart from Letter 211 to the nuns of Hippo. Viewed in that light, this passage, ostensibly written about the confiscation of Donatist property, becomes tremendously important. The duplication of churches and other goods was symptomatic of a deeper lack of unity that Donatism represented and that was the antithesis of Augustine's understanding of Church.

This short passage summarizes Augustine's ecclesiology. The English translation "partners" conceals the word *societas*—a people related to one another. Augustine is still calling the Donatists "into unity as partners" who can be one in Christ and live according to the example of Ac 4:32.

In the greeting to the nuns in Letter 211, Augustine calls them first to dwell "together in a house in unity (Ps 132:1), that [they] may have one soul and one heart (Ac 4:32) toward God."[47] That is, the nuns should be united in love. What is spoken to the nuns of the monastery of Hippo in Letter 211 is addressed to the whole Church and specifically the Donatists in Letter 185. Augustine continues:

> Let us love what we sing: "Behold how good and how pleas-
> ant it is for brethren to dwell together in unity" (Ps 132:1),
> that they may experience and may know how truthfully their
> Catholic mother calls out to them in the words written by the
> blessed Apostle to the Corinthians: "I seek not the things
> that are yours, but you" (2 Co 12:14).[48]

Yet, as Zumkeller notes, Augustine's *Exposition on Psalm 132* gives his views on the significance of monasticism.[49] Nevertheless, Augustine uses the passage here to describe for the Donatists why their "Catholic Mother" calls them and reinforces his statement with 2 Co 12:14: "I seek not the things that are yours but you."[50]

Zumkeller discusses the honored position afforded monasticism within the Mystical Body by Augustine.[51] But that honored position was always to be in dialogue with and at the service of the larger community. It is precisely in this discussion that the significance of the use of both Ac 4:32 and Ps 132 in Letters 185 and 211 is important.

For Augustine, the *monos* was not the rugged individualist who labored alone for perfection and salvation in some kind of accidental or convenient communal situation.[52] Rather, "monk" was a term that could be used of communities "who through their harmonious living together have become, as it were, a *monos*, that is, a single being, and possess only one heart and one soul toward God."[53] "Toward God" precisely describes Augustine's dynamic notion of Church and implies a journey that is not yet complete. Such was a major difference between the monk and the Donatist. Such was Augustine's invitation to the Donatists in Letter 185—to journey as one toward God.

Conclusion

Augustine's understanding of conversion in the Church went far beyond any individual idea of salvation. Rather the unity of humanity into Christ expressed itself as a society related to one another and to Christ the Redeemer.

Augustine's Church was not a closed community. It was open to all. If it had been closed it could have limited its membership to the monks and nuns of Letter 211 and formed a new kind of Donatism. The very fact that Augustine calls the Donatists of Letter 185 to be partners (*societas*)—to be in relationship—is important. Ac 4:32 is the model for the relationship for both the Donatists of Letter 185 and the nuns of Letter 211. For the Donatists it is a call to conversion. For the monks and nuns, Ac 4:32 was a reminder that their status and responsibility as honored members of the Body[54] was not to end in the unhealthy isolation of the perfect but in the service of the community.

For all the Church, Ac 4:32 modeled the Spirit-filled community moving forward in hope exclusive of none. The hope is the hope of a people on a journey of return. The hope is the hope of a people redeemed. Christ the Redeemer is precisely why Augustine's Church is open to all.

Notes

[1] R. Arbesmann, "The Concept of 'Christus Medicus' in St. Augustine," *Traditio* 10 (1954) 3–28. In his article Arbesmann describes conversion in Augustine as a redefinition of wisdom.

[2] Augustine, *Confessiones* VII,xviii,24: *CC* XXVII,108: *subditos erigit ad se ipsam, in inferioribus autem aedificauit sibi humilem domum de limo nostro, per quam subdendos deprimeret a se ipsis et ad se traiceret, sanans tumorem et nutriens amorem, ne fiducia sui progrederentur longius, sed potius infirmarentur uidentes ante pedes suos infirmam diuinitatem ex participatione tunicae pelliciae nostrae et lassi prosternerentur in eam, illa autem surgens leuaret eos.* Tr. by J. K. Ryan, *Augustine of Hippo: Confessions* (Garden City: Image Books, 1960), p. 176.

³ Ibid.

⁴ P. Brown, *Augustine of Hippo: A Biography* (Berkeley: Univ. of California Press, 1969), pp. 224–25.

⁵ Augustine, *Confessiones* VIII,xii,29.

⁶ Augustine, *Epistula CXL* IV,12: *FC* 20,66: *CSEL* XLIV,164: *"semet ipsum" tamen "exinaniuit" non formam dei amittens sed "formam serui suscipiens; humiliauit semet ipsum factus oboediens usque ad mortem, mortem autem crucis"* (Ph 2:7–8).

⁷ Augustine, *Epistula CXL* V,14–vi,15: *FC* 20,68–69.

⁸ See R. Duffy, *A Roman Catholic Theology of Pastoral Care*, Theology and Pastoral Care Series (Philadelphia: Fortress Press, 1983), p. 42. Duffy considers the *medicus* image of Christ.

⁹ Centuries later Martin Luther will develop this theme in his treatise "The Freedom of a Christian," in which he describes faith in Christ by using marital imagery:

> Let us compare these and we shall see inestimable benefits. Christ is full of grace, life, and salvation. The soul is full of sins, death, and damnation. Now let faith come between them and sins, death, and damnation will be Christ's, while grace, life, and salvation will be the soul's; for if Christ is a bridegroom, he must take upon himself the things which are his bride's and bestow upon her the things that are his. If he gives her his body and very self, how shall he not give her all that is his? And if he takes the body of the bride, how shall he not take all that is hers?

M. Luther, "The Freedom of a Christian," tr. by W. A. Lambert in *Three Treatises* (Philadelphia: Fortress Press, 1978), pp. 262–316.

¹⁰ Augustine, *Epistula CLVII* III,11: *FC* 20,327.

¹¹ Augustine, *Epistula CLVII* III,14: *FC* 20,330.

¹² Augustine, *Epistula CLXXXV* IX,40: *FC* 30,179: *CSEL* LVII,35: *dominus itaque Christus et iustus est et iustificans, nos autem "iustificati gratis per gratiam ipsius"* (Rm 3:24).

¹³ Augustine, *Epistula CLVII* III,11–14: *FC* 20,328–30.

¹⁴ Augustine, *Epistula CLVII* III,20: *FC* 20,337: *CSEL* XLIV,469: *quamuis ergo, inquit, Adam futuri forma sit a contrario, plus tamen praestat Christus regeneratis, quam eis nocuerat ille generatis.*

¹⁵ Augustine, *Epistula CXL* III,7–8: *FC* 20,63.

¹⁶ Augustine, *Epistula CXL* III,10: *FC* 20,64.

¹⁷ Augustine, *Epistula CXL* IV,10: *FC* 20,64: *CSEL* XLIV,161–62: *et ab hac generatione gratiae discernitur ille filius, qui, cum esset filius dei, uenit, ut fieret filius hominis donaretque nobis, qui eramus filii hominis, filios dei fieri.*

[18] Augustine, *Epistula LV* XIII,23: *FC* 12,279: *CSEL* XXXIV,2,194–95: *qui "resurgens a mortuis non moreretur et mors ei ultra non dominaretur"* (Rm 6:9), *ut, postquam facta est talis resurrectio in corpore domini, ut praeiret in capite ecclesiae, quod corpus ecclesiae speraret in finem* ....

[19] Augustine, *Epistula LV* II,3: *FC* 12,263: *CSEL* XXXIV,2,173: *hoc igitur uniuersa ecclesia, quae in peregrinatione mortalitatis inuenta est, expectat in fine saeculi, quod in domini nostri Iesu Christi corpore praemonstratum est, qui est "primogenitus a mortuis"* (Col 1:18), *quia et corpus eius, cui caput est ipse, non nisi ecclesia est.*

[20] P. Brown, *Augustine of Hippo*, pp. 218ff.

[21] P. Brown, *Augustine of Hippo*, p. 219.

[22] P. Brown, *Augustine of Hippo*, p. 224. See also Cyprian, *On the Unity of the Catholic Church* 6: *ACW* 25,48–49.

[23] See Yves M.-J. Congar, "Introduction Générale," *Traités anti-donatistes* I, *BA* 28, 7–133.

[24] See Cyprian, *De ecclesiae catholicae unitate* 11: *Quando aliud baptisma praeter unum esse non possit, baptizare posse se opinantur; uitae fonte deserto, uitalis et salutaris aquae gratiam pollicentur. Non abluuntur illic homines sed potius sordidantur, nec purgantur delicta sed immo cumulantur; non Deo nativitas illa sed diabolo filios generat: per mendacium nati veritatis promissa non capiunt, de perfidia procreati fidei gratiam perdunt.* Cyprian, *De Lapsis and De Ecclesiae Catholicae Unitate*, ed. and tr. by Maurice Bévenot (Oxford: Clarendon, 1971), p. 16. In this work Cyprian denies the validity of heretical Baptism. This view was condemned by Pope St. Stephen. See also the dissertation of Mary Jane Kreidler, *The Pastoral Theology of Augustine of Hippo as Found in His Letters* (Ann Arbor, Michigan: UMI, 1987), p. 63.

[25] Augustine, *Epistula CV* III,12: *FC* 18,205: *CSEL* XXXIV,2,604: *uidete enim, quam peruerse et impie dicatur, quod dicere soletis, quia, si bonus sit homo, ipse sanctificat eum, quem baptizat, si autem malus sit et nesciat ille, qui baptizatur, tunc deus sanctificat. hoc si uerum est, optare ergo debent homines, ut a malis ignoratis baptizentur potius quam a notis bonis, ut magis a deo quam ab homine possint sanctificari. sed absit a nobis ista dementia. quare ergo non uerum dicimus et recte sapimus, quia semper dei est illa gratia et dei sacramentum hominis autem solum ministerium, qui si bonus est, adhaeret deo et operatur cum deo, si autem malus est, operatur per illum deus uisibilem sacramenti formam, ipse autem donat inuisibilem gratiam?*

[26] Cyprian, *The Unity of the Catholic Church* 6–9.

[27] Letters include 23, 43, 49, 53, 76, 87, 105, 185. See Kreidler, *Pastoral Theology*, p. 68.

[28] Letters 53, 88, 89, 93, 105, 185, 199. Letters indicating Christ as descendant are 53, 76, 105, 196. See Kreidler, *Pastoral Theology*, pp. 68–69.

[29] Augustine, *Epistula CV* IV,14: *FC* 18,206.

[30] Augustine, *Epistula CV* IV,13: *FC* 18,207–8.

[31] Augustine, *Epistula CLXXXV* IX,39: *FC* 30,178–79.

[32] L. Verheijen, *Saint Augustine's Monasticism in the Light of Acts 4:32*–35, Saint Augustine Lecture Series, 1975 (Philadelphia: Villanova University Press, 1979), p. 10.

[33] Verheijen, *Monasticism*, pp. 11–16. In Letter 30 Paulinus had added *in domino* to Ac 4:32. Augustine added *in deum*, which is in harmony with *De moribus ecclesiae catholicae et de moribus Manichaeorum* I,xii,21.

[34] A. Zumkeller, *Augustine's Ideal of the Religious Life*, tr. by E. Colledge (New York: Fordham University Press, 1986), p. 109.

[35] Ibid.

[36] Augustine, *Epistula XXIII* 2: *FC* 12,59–60: *CSEL* XXXIV,1,65: *noui etenim, quae sit ecclesia catholica. gentes sunt hereditas Christi et possessio Christi termini terrae.*

[37] Augustine, *Epistula XCIII* X,39: *FC* 18,96. See also Kreidler, *Pastoral Theology*, pp. 71–72.

[38] Augustine, *Epistula XCIII* IX,31: *FC* 18,88: *CSEL* XXXIV,2,477: *ac sic ecclesia, quae per omnes gentes crescit, in frumentis dominicis conseruata est et usque in finem, donec omnino gentes omnes etiam barbaras teneat, conseruabitur. ipsa est enim ecclesia in bono semine, quod seminauit filius hominis et usque ad messem crescere inter zizania praenuntiauit. ager autem mundus est, messis finis saeculi.*

[39] Augustine, *Epistula CV* III,11; see also CVIII,i,3.

[40] Augustine, *Epistula CXL* III,9: *CSEL* XLIV,161: *haec est gratia novi testamenti.*

[41] Augustine, *Epistula CXL* II,5.

[42] Augustine, *Epistula CXL* II,5: *FC* 20,61: *CSEL* XLIV,158: *dispensabant ergo illi sancti pro congruentia temporis testamentum uetus, pertinebant uero ad testamentum nouum.*

[43] Augustine, *Epistula CXL* III,6.

[44] Augustine, *Epistula CXL* IV,12: *FC* 20,66: *CSEL* XLIV,163: *mutabiles in melius.*

[45] Augustine, *Epistula CXL* IV,11: *FC* 20,65: *CSEL* XLIV,163: *per gratiam renascuntur spiritalem.*

[46] Augustine, *Epistula CLXXXV* IX,36: *FC* 30,176: *CSEL* LVII,32: *sed intrent in unitatis societatem, ut pariter gubernemus non illa tantum, quae dicunt sua, uerum etiam, quae dicuntur et nostra. scriptum est enim: "Omnia uestra, uos autem Christi, Christus autem dei"* (1 Co 3:22–23). *sub illo capite in uno eius corpore unum simus et de istis talibus rebus faciamus, quod scriptum est in actibus apostolorum: "Erat illis anima una et cor unum et nemo dicebat aliquid proprium, sed erant illis omnia communia"* (Ac 4:32).

[47] Augustine, *Epistula CCXI* 2: *FC* 32,39: *CSEL* LVII,357: *uerum etiam in domo societatem eligeretis habitandi unanimes, ut sit uobis anima una et cor unum in deum.*

[48] Augustine, *Epistula CLXXXV* IX,36: *FC* 30,176: *CSEL* LVII,32–33: *amemus, quod cantamus: "Ecce quam bonum et quam iucundum habitare fratres in unum"* (Ps 132:1), *ut sic experiantur et sciant, quam ueraciter ad eos clamet mater catholica, quod scribit beatus apostolus ad Corinthios: "Non quaero, quae sunt uestra, sed uos"* (2 Co 12:14).

[49] Zumkeller, *Augustine's Ideal*, p. 110.

[50] Augustine, *Epistula CLXXXV* IX,36.

[51] Zumkeller, *Augustine's Ideal*, pp. 110–11.

[52] Ibid. Here Zumkeller is quoting A. Wucherer-Huldenfeld, "Mönchtum und kirchlicher Dienst bei Augustinus nach dem Bild des Neubekehrten und des Bischofs," *Zeitschrift für katholische Theologie* 82 (1960) 199f.

[53] Zumkeller, *Augustine's Ideal*, pp. 131–32; see *Enarratio in Psalmum CXXXII*, 6.

[54] Zumkeller, *Augustine's Ideal*, p. 110.

St. Augustine's Theology of Prayer: Gracious Conformation

Timothy Maschke

Prayer was a central and vital component in all of Augustine's life and work, especially as he served in his capacity as a Christian bishop of Hippo. From Augustine's writings, two contrasting emphases on prayer have emerged over the centuries: contemplative meditation and discursive communication. While these two views often represent opposite poles of spirituality, there is a higher unity in Augustine's theology of prayer which can be discovered as a thread in all of his writings on prayer. The nexus of Augustine's theology of prayer lies in what I have labelled a "gracious conformation," the humble re-structuring or reforming of the Christian's life to the divine will as empowered by the assurance of God's grace.

Although he never wrote an extended theological treatise setting forth a theology of prayer, Augustine came closest to such a work in his letter to the wealthy widow, Proba, which has been described as a "wonderful treatise on Prayer."[1] The letter to Proba served as a starting point for this study and is a thematic backbone for this paper.[2]

Material for this study was also taken from a wide selection of Augustine's other writings, especially from his expositions on the Psalms, the Sermon on the Mount, and the Gospel of St. John, and from several sermons on the Lord's Prayer.[3] Drawing from these works, this paper presents Augustine's view of prayer—its essence, expression, and effectiveness—in light of the concept of "gracious conformation." Specific prayers, times and kinds of prayers, and Augustine's interpretation of the Our Father were not the focus of this study, except as they related to the general concept of prayer.[4]

The Essence of Prayer

Already in Augustine's early philosophical works one finds him offering up prayers to God in a profoundly personal and conversational style.[5] Such conversation becomes a central mark of his later works, as Mary T. Clark points out: "We see Augustine in dialogue with Father, Son, and Spirit throughout the *Confessions*."[6] There, in his *Confessions*, Augustine portrays his early childhood as a time when he learned to speak with God and take his childhood concerns to him in prayer:

> Indeed, we discovered, Lord, that certain men prayed to You and we learned from them, and imagined You, as far as we could, as some sort of Mighty One who, even though not appearing before our senses, could hear us and come to our assistance. For while still a boy I began to pray to You, my Help and my Refuge, and in praying to You I broke the bonds of my tongue.[7]

For Augustine, prayer is clearly conversation with God, a communication with a personal source of power and help beyond himself.

Later in his preaching ministry as Bishop of Hippo, Augustine expanded the concept of prayer as conversation to include the idea of dialogue and two-way communication between heaven and earth, God and humanity. In a sermon for an Easter Vigil, Augustine describes how God speaks through his Word and people respond through prayer: "May God speak to us in His lessons; may we speak to God in our praying. If we listen to His words obediently, He whom we ask dwells among us."[8] In content and style, Augustine's prayers are conspicuously conversational. And he consistently encouraged his parishioners to engage in prayerful conversations with God. For him, God is One with whom he could and did talk in prayer as a dear friend with a gracious Friend.[9]

The Expression of Prayer

More basic than conversation, however, is Augustine's understanding that prayer is the expression of human desire. It is this desire which becomes a central factor for the idea of gracious conformation. "For it is your desire that is your prayer," he wrote in his exposition on Psalm 38, "and if your desire continues, your prayer continues."[10] Similarly, he proclaimed in a homily: "Desire prays always, though the tongue is silent. If you are always desiring, you are always praying."[11] Prayer is, therefore, the simplest expression to God of what the petitioner wants or desires.

Human desires which express spiritual concerns, says Augustine in a Lenten sermon, are of a much more preferable quality:

Prayer is certainly a spiritual thing, and therefore, it is more acceptable as it accomplishes the effects of its nature. However, it is uttered from a greater spiritual source as the soul, which utters it, is raised above carnal desires.[12]

Even when people express negative or inadequate feelings regarding their prayer life, says Augustine, they are praying:

Is not our prayer sometimes tepid or rather frigid and even ceases altogether, so that we do not even notice this condition in us with sorrow. For if we are sorrowful regarding this, already we are praying.[13]

The bishop of Hippo understood prayer simply as a sincere desire, regardless of how ill-expressed that desire might be.

What Prayer is Not

Although prayer is an expression of human desire, Augustine never viewed prayer as a means by which human beings could manipulate God or even inform him of their desires. In *The Teacher*, Augustine's son, Adeodatus, says: "…now we use words when we pray; but it is not proper to believe that God is taught anything by us or reminded of anything."[14] Augustine repeated this idea in his letter to Proba: "…We are not to believe that the Lord needs these [prayers], either to be informed or to be influenced."[15]

He explains this more fully to Proba, when he discusses the words of Paul in Ph 4:6, "Let your petitions be made known to God."

That saying of the Apostle…is not to be taken in the sense that [our desires] are actually made known to God, who certainly knew them before they were uttered, but that they are made known to us before God through patience.[16]

Augustine did not find words necessary to inform God, for he notes in an exposition on Psalm 38 that even sighs are heard by God.[17]

Frequently, when speaking of prayer, Augustine exhorts his listeners or readers to avoid long and wordy prayers. Wordiness is not to be equated with being heard, he tells Proba.[18] It is undoubtedly this abhorrence of long prayers that caused Augustine to mention the Egyptian ascetics who regularly recited brief prayers "rapidly like arrows."[19] Thus, it is not the words which matter, as much as the heart which experiences and expresses the desire.

Words do have a beneficial value in Augustine's theological view of prayer. They are particularly helpful in determining an individual's spiritual development and growth toward Christian maturity, according to Augustine. F. van der Meer's biography on the Bishop of Hippo notes Augustine's reason why actual words are to be used:

> From time to time we should also pray in actual words, so that by clear definition we may call to mind what we are praying about, and grow conscious of the extent to which our longing has grown....[20]

This idea is reiterated in Augustine's letter to Proba, where he writes about the benefits of praying specific prayers at fixed times and seasons:

> That is why at certain fixed hours and times we pray to God in words, so that we may urge ourselves on, as with these signs, how much progress we have made in this desire, and take note in ourselves and may excite ourselves more earnestly to increase it.[21]

Fixed prayers both enable individuals to mark their progress in their spiritual journey and also encourage them toward greater Christian maturity. Words serve as benchmarks for the Christians' progress toward maturity as members of the Body of Christ. In addition, words make Christians more aware of what it is that they actually desire. The use of words in prayer, then, has the purpose of developing those who pray spiritually and leads them forward toward gracious conformation.[22]

The Effect of Prayer

Henry Chadwick draws us into the heart of Augustine's theology of prayer as he notes, "Many sermons of Augustine warned that prayer is neither informing God nor cajoling him into a change of mind, but is the way to conform our wills to his."[23] This conformation seems to be a major purpose for Christian prayer in Augustine's theology of prayer.

Thomas Hand summarizes Augustine's view of prayer's conforming purpose in the following way:

> Let it be said at once, therefore, that the words we use in prayer are not intended for the instruction of God, but for the construction of our own desires. That is what God wishes to accomplish by means of the formulas of prayer. Not that he has any need of them for himself; but in the sense that he makes use of them to build up our desires for heavenly things.[24]

In many works by Augustine, this idea of reconstructing one's desires or conforming one's will to God's will through the activity of prayer is evident.

To Proba, Augustine clearly suggests that "we ought to ask, without doubting, what God considers and not what we ourselves will."[25] In his comments on The Sermon on the Mount, Augustine boldly underscores the confidence which stems from conformity:

> Therefore, in prayer, the heart is turned toward Him who is always prepared to give, provided that we are capable of accepting whatever He may give; and in that turning there is a cleansing of the inner eye through the exclusion of that longing for temporal things, in order that the gaze of the simple heart is able to bear the simple light divinely shining without any setting or change.[26]

Prayer is a way of orienting the heart toward God and conforming to his will.

A number of Augustine's sermons on prayer illustrate and expand upon this idea of conformation. In a Lenten sermon, the bishop of Hippo urges his hearers to pray prayers which conform to higher, eternal, and spiritual concerns rather than merely pray for mundane things: "For what do we ask?...

We ask for that which we may possess forever: that of which, once we have been filled with it, we shall never again want."[27] The petition of the Our Father, "Thy will be done," may even include the unspoken and unrecognized request for the conversion of one's enemies; this is something, Augustine says, which the petitioner might not consciously wish, but it is certainly something which would be in conformity to God's will.[28] This is undoubtedly why Augustine saw the Lord's Prayer as a model prayer for Christian conformation.

The Lord's Prayer becomes the ultimate model for such Christian prayer life.[29] Praying the Our Father leads to a conforming of the human will and desire to God's will:

> From the words and meaning of this prayer let us not fall away in our petitions, and whatever we ask, it shall be done for us. For only then may His words be said to remain in us, when we do what He has commanded us, and love what He has promised.[30]

The words of the Our Father serve as a guide and guard for conforming prayer.

The Lord's Prayer is more than a model prayer for Augustine. It is *the* prayer of conformation; by it the Christian believer is able to express the ultimate act of conformation, "to pray only in a spiritual manner."[31] Such conforming prayer accomplishes its purpose of bringing the human will into conformity with the divine will in the Christian's life.[32]

Prayers of conformation also provide the believer with a sense of certainty, says Augustine: "Whoever asks that one thing of the Lord, and keeps asking for it, asks with certainty and security, fearing nothing...."[33] Conforming one's life through the exercise of prayer explains the fact that believers' prayers seem to be more regularly answered, according to Augustine.[34]

This draws us into Augustine's understanding of faith in relation to prayer. Faith expresses itself in prayer, he tells Proba, because God wants "our desire to be exercised in prayer so that we may be able to receive what He is preparing to give."[35] As an individual's faith conforms to God's will, so also will that person's prayer life. Conforming prayer is an exercise of faith. The quality of a petitioner's faith becomes more clearly evident through the life of prayer. The stronger one's faith, the more one will pray. The prerequisite of all prayer, therefore, is faith, as Augustine explains in a sermon on Luke:

> If faith fails, prayer perishes....faith is the fountain of
> prayer....Faith, I say, pours out prayer, the pouring out of
> prayer secures strengthening even for faith itself.[36]

Prayer, for Augustine, is an exercise of true faith which desires to conform to
God's will.

What Prayer Needs

According to Augustine, conformation of the human will to the divine
will is beyond the capabilities of the natural human being who is born sinful.
He here manifests his strong theological emphasis as *Doctor Gratiae*. To Proba, he writes, "How, then, could you thus strive to pray to the Lord if you did
not hope in Him?"[37] Conforming prayer, and all prayer for that matter, according to Augustine, must be attributed only to the grace of God which the
one praying has received.[38]

The Lord's Prayer again is the clearest testimony of the need for God's
grace, Augustine says specifically in regards to the Sixth Petition.[39] If it were
possible for people not to be tempted based upon their own abilities or spiritual powers, continues Augustine in this line of argument, then that petition
would be silly and pointless.

Even the fact that prayer is an expression of desire and a conforming of
the will to God's will, says Augustine in a sermon on the Lord's Prayer, is a
result of God's gracious work.[40] This necessity of grace for prayer is emphasized again when Augustine speaks about prayer in his *Tractates on the Gospel
of John*. In discussing the relationship between the Father and the Son, Augustine stops to exhort his hearers to understand (or at least to ask God for
help in comprehending) the profound mysteries of this relationship: "...let
him turn to Him that opens the heart, that He may pour in what He gives...
and supplicate the divine goodness."[41] Similarly, in his *Expositions of the
Psalms*, Augustine points to the grace of God in the Christian's prayer life.
He notes that Christ is actually within the praying believer, as long as the believer prays in conformity to God's good and gracious will.[42]

In Book 13 of his *Confessions*, Augustine illustrates clearly that the longing of his soul is a result of God's gracious activity of breathing life into the
soul: "I call You into my soul, which You prepare to accept You, by the de-

sires that You breathe into it."[43] The very ability of the soul to desire is recognized as a grace-induced gift of God. More than any theologian before him, Augustine emphasized the grace of God operating in this vital area of Christian spirituality. The next section of this paper will illustrate this more fully.

The Effectiveness of Prayer

The effectiveness of a prayer does not lie in the one praying. Rather, a prayer's effectiveness lies in the gracious power and presence of God, and especially in the person of Jesus Christ, the one Mediator, who himself lifts us to himself.[44] Gracious conformation becomes a praying to, with, and in Christ, says Augustine:

> [It is] our Lord Jesus Christ, the Son of God, who not only prays for us, but prays in us, and is prayed to by us. He prays for us, as our Priest; He prays in us, as our Head; He is prayed to by us, as our God. Let us therefore recognize in Him our words, and His words in us.[45]

Christ makes prayers effective, because of his presence in and his praying for his people. The grace of God is seen in the person and work of Christ.

Augustine warns that this is not to be understood in some Manichaean materialistic way, as if Christ physically stood before the Father and offered petitions on behalf of Christians.[46] On the other hand, while the Father and the Son are distinct persons, they work in union with each other to aid and answer Christian prayer. Therefore, one should not think that Christ and the Father are separated when certain kinds of prayers are being prayed.[47] Similarly, Augustine asserts that the Holy Spirit is also active in the prayer life of a conforming Christian.[48] Augustine attributes prayer's effectiveness only to the mysterious economy of the Trinity, who graciously work together for the aid and effectiveness of the Christians' prayers.[49]

Prayer's effectiveness is clearly evident and most certainly unmistakable when Christians pray and believe in the saving work of Christ. The effectiveness of prayer is the result of conforming one's will to God's gracious order of salvation in Christ.

Whoever truly has such ideas of Him [Christ] as ought to be
experienced, asks in His name; and he receives what he asks,
if he asks nothing that is contrary to his own everlasting salvation.[50]

Such conformation is what Augustine means by praying "in Jesus' name."[51]
Prayer in Christ's name is nothing less than the conforming of the human will
to God's saving will. This is the goal for a true Christian prayer life and embodies the fullness of gracious conformation.

Conclusions

According to Augustine, prayer is, first and foremost, conversation with
God. Yet, prayer also expresses basic and natural human desires. Prayer is
never a means to communicate human needs or desires to God, nor to change
God's will. Audible words are even unnecessary in prayer although the Bishop of Hippo admits that they aid Christian consciousness of spiritual development by providing clearly discernible levels of maturity.

Human weakness and sin are at the heart of the requirement for the aid
of God's grace by which Christians are enabled to conform their prayers more
perfectly to the divine will. Conforming prayer is modelled and manifested
most clearly in the contents of the Lord's Prayer. The effectiveness of prayer
ultimately rests upon the Father's grace, in Christ's name, and the Spirit's
power.

The concept of gracious conformation permeates Augustine's writings.
Although Christianity would develop certain distinguishing and often contrasting aspects of Augustine's ideas on prayer, gracious conformation provides a clear and unifying connection for all later developments of prayer in
the Augustinian tradition.

Notes

[1] H. Pope, *Saint Augustine of Hippo* (London: Sands and Co., 1937), p. 197.

[2] *Epistula CXXX*: *CSEL* XLIV,40–77. Letter 130 is available in English translation
in *St. Augustine: Letters*, trans. W. Parsons; *FC* 18.

[3] T. Hand, *Saint Augustine on Prayer* (Westminster: Newman Press, 1963), pp. ix–
131, has collected more than five hundred quotations from Augustine's writings in which

Augustine speaks of prayer. Although the book is not developed into a theology of prayer, it is a very helpful resource for Augustine's ideas on prayer. Hand classifies his work as a devotional resource rather than a scholarly study.

⁴Excellent specialized studies have been done in some areas of Augustine's theology of prayer, including the following: A. Besnard, *Priez Dieu les Psaumes* (Paris: Les Editions du Cerf, 1982); B. Fischer, "The Common Prayer of Congregation and Family in the Ancient Church," *Studia Liturgica* 10 (1974) 106–24; M. Flores, *Prayer in Saint Augustine's Letter to Proba* (Diss. The Augustinian Institute, Valletta, Malta, 1985); G. Montaño, "Doctrina agustiniana de la oración," *Augustinus* 18 (1973) 279–302; G. Raeithel, "Das Gebet in den Soliloquien Augustins," *Zeitschrift für Religions- und Geistesgeschichte* 20:2 (1968) 139–53; L. Verheijen, "La prière dans la Règle de saint Augustin" in *Saint Augustin et la Bible*, ed. A.-M. La Bonnardière (Paris, Beauchesne, 1986); M. Vincent, "Actualité de la doctrine de saint Augustin sur la prière," *Revista augustiniana* 29 (1988) 593–609; but little has been done in English.

⁵P. Brown notes in *Augustine of Hippo* (Berkeley: Univ. of California Press, 1967), pp. 166f., that "prayer...was a recognized vehicle for speculative enquiry....The fact that they were couched in the form of a prayer, far from relegating them to a work of piety, would have increased their value as a philosophical exercise....Yet such prayers were usually regarded as part of a preliminary stage in the lifting of the philosopher's mind to God."

⁶M. T. Clark, *Augustine of Hippo: Selected Writings*; The Classics of Western Spirituality (Ramsey: Paulist Press, 1984), p. 9.

⁷*Confessiones* I,ix,14: *CC* XXVII,8: *Inuenimus autem, domine, homines, rogantes te et didicimus ab eis, sentientes te, ut poteramus, esse magnum aliquem, qui posses etiam non apparens sensibus nostris exaudire nos et subuenire nobis. Nam puer coepi rogare te, auxilium et refugium meum, et in tuam inuocationem rumpebam nodos linguae meae....*

⁸*Sermo CCIX*: *PL* XXXVIII,1088: *Deus nobis loquatur in lectionibus suis; Deo loquamur in precibus nostris. Si eloquia ejus obedienter audiamus, in nobis habitat quem rogamus.*

In his letter to Proba, Augustine encourages continual prayer and Bible-reading (*Epistula CXXX* II,5: *CSEL* XLIV,45). The idea of a mutual conversation is also expressed in his exposition of Psalm 85, where Augustine writes: "...We speak with Him, and He speaks with us; we speak in Him, He speaks in us the prayer of this Psalm...." *Enarratio in Psalmum LXXXV* 1: *CC* XXXIX,1177:*...dicimus cum illo, et dicit nobiscum; dicimus in illo, dicit in nobis psalmi huius orationem....*

In a Lenten sermon, which he specifically addresses to married couples, Augustine again equates conversation with God as prayer: The time which was formerly taken up with conjugal duties, spend in supplications. The body which was engaged in physical affections, prostrate in earnest prayer. The hands which were intwined in embraces, extend in prayer. *Sermo CCV*: *PL* XXXVIII,1040: *Tempus quod reddendo conjugali debito occupabatur, supplicationibus impendatur. Corpus quod carnalibus affectibus solvebatur, puris precibus prosternatur. Manus quae amplexibus implicabantur, orationibus extendantur.*

⁹Clark, *Augustine of Hippo*, p. 42.

[10] *Enarratio in Psalmum XXXVII* 14: *CC* XXXVIII,392: *Ipsum enim desiderium tuum, oratio tua est; et si continuum desiderium, continua oratio.*

[11] *Sermo LXXX* 7: *PL* XXXVIII,498: *Desiderium semper orat, etsi lingua taceat. Si semper desideras, semper oras.*
Writing to Proba, Augustine expands on this idea: "Truly, prayer is to be free of much speaking, but not of much entreaty....For to speak much in prayer is to do a necessary thing with superfluous verbiage; however, to entreat much of Him whom we entreat is to pulse with a long-continued and devout excitation of the heart. For this work is done more by sighs than by speech, more by weeping than by words." *Epistula CXXX* X,20: *CSEL* XLIV,62–63: *absit enim ab oratione multa locutio, sed non desit multa precatio. ...nam multum loqui est in orando rem necessariam superfluis agere uerbis; multum autem precari est ad eum, quem precamur, diuturna et pia cordis excitatione pulsare. nam plerumque hoc negotium plus gemitibus quam sermonibus agitur, plus fletu quam affatu.*
He modelled that simple desire in a short prayer in his *Soliloquies:* "Reason: Pray, then, as briefly and as perfectly as you can. Augustine: O God, always the same, let me know myself and let me know You. That is my prayer." *Soliloquia* II,i,1: *CSEL* LXXXIX, 45: *R. Itaque ora brevissime ac perfectissime, quantum potes. A. Deus semper idem, noverim me, noverim te. Oratum est.*

[12] *Sermo CCX* VI,9: *PL* XXXVIII,1052: *Oratio quippe spiritualis res est, et ideo tanto est acceptior, quanto magis suae naturae implet effectum. Tanto magis autem spirituali opere funditur, quanto magis animus qui eam fundit, a carnali voluptate suspenditur.*

[13] *De diuersis quaestionibus ad Simplicianum* I,ii,21: *CC* XLIV, 54: *Nonne aliquando ipsa oratio nostra sic tepida est uel potius frigida et pene nulla, immo omnino interdum ita nulla, ut neque hoc in nobis cum dolore aduertamus? Quia si uel hoc dolemus, iam oramus.*

[14] *De magistro* I,2: *CC* XXIX,158:*...dum oramus utique loquimur, nec tamen deum aut doceri aliquid a nobis aut commemorari fas est credere.*

[15] *Epistula CXXX* XI,21: *CSEL* XLIV,63:*...non quibus dominum seu docendum seu flectendum esse credamus.*

[16] *Epistula CXXX* IX,18: *CSEL* XLIV,61:*...quod idem apostolus ait...non sic accipiendum, est, tamquam deo innotescant, qui eas, et antequam essent, utique nouerat, sed nobis innotescant apud deum per tolerantiam....*

[17] *Enarratio in Psalmum XXXVII* 14: *CC* XXXVIII,392.

[18] *Epistula CXXX* VIII,15: *CSEL* XLIV,57. Likewise, in a sermon on the Lord's Prayer, he said: "Therefore, our Lord excluded loquaciousness, so that you might not address many words to God, as though you would teach God by a great many words. Therefore, when you pray, it is a work of piety, not verbosity." *Sermo LVI* III,4: *PL* XXXVIII, 378–79: *Dominus ergo noster primo amputavit multiloquium, ne multa verba afferas ad Deum, quasi velis multis verbis docere Deum. Quando ergo rogas, pietate opus est, non verbositate.*

[19] *Epistula CXXX* X,20: *CSEL* XLIV,62:*...raptim quodam modo iaculatus....*

[20] F. van der Meer, *Augustine the Bishop*, trans. B. Battershaw and G. R. Lamb (New York: Sheed and Ward, 1961), p. 166.

[21] *Epistula CXXX* IX,18: *CSEL* XLIV,60: *sed ideo per certa interualla horarum et temporum etiam uerbis rogamus deum, ut illis rerum signis nos ipsos admoneamus, quantumque in hoc desiderio profecerimus, nobis ipsis innotescamus et ad hoc augendum nos ipsos acrius excitemus.*

Augustine continues: "But because, by reason of our cares and preoccupation with other things, that desire grows somewhat lukewarm, we call our mind back to the duty of praying at fixed hours, and we urge ourselves in the words of our prayer to press forward to what we desire; otherwise, after our desire has begun to grow lukewarm, it then becomes entirely cold and is completely extinguished unless it is frequently inflamed." *sed ideo ab aliis curis atque negotiis, quibus ipsum desiderium quodam modo tepescit, certis horis ad negotium orandi mentem reuocamus uerbis orationis nos admonentes in id, quod desideramus, intendere, ne, quod tepescere coeperat, omnino frigescat et penitus extinguatur, nisi crebrius inflammetur.*

A little later he explained: "Therefore, words are necessary for us so that we may be reminded and may examine what we are asking for, but we are not to believe that the Lord needs these [prayers], either to be informed or to be influenced." *Epistula CXXX* XI,21: *CSEL* XLIV,63: *Nobis ergo uerba necessaria sunt, quibus commoneamur et inspiciamus, quid petamus, non quibus dominum seu docendum seu flectendum esse credamus.* Even in the Lord's Prayer, he sees the words as a model and guide for believers to stir their desires, rather than doing anything for God. See *Epistula CXXX* X,20 and XI,21: *CSEL* XLIV,62 and 63.

[22] Words are also to be used in prayer to build up those who may only be listening to them. F. van der Meer, *Augustine the Bishop*, p. 168, reports that some children listened to the audible prayers of adults in church and then mockingly repeated the contents in the streets. Thus, Augustine in *The Teacher* says: "In praying to God, whom we must not think needs to be taught or reminded, we use words in order either to remind ourselves or to admonish and teach others through them." *De magistro* VII,19: *CC* XXIX,177:...*et in orando deo, quem doceri aut commemorari existimare non possumus, id uerba ualeant, ut uel nos ipsos commonefaciamus uel alii commemorentur doceanturque per nos.* And in a *Lecture on the Gospel of John*, Augustine says that Jesus' High Priestly Prayer, although for himself, was also "a means of edification for His disciples." *Tractatus in Euangelium Ioannis* CIX,2: *CC* XXXVI,602:...*sed etiam pro ipsis ad Patrem oratio, discipularum est aedificatio.*

[23] Henry Chadwick, *Augustine* (New York: Oxford University Press, 1986), p. 72.

[24] Hand, *Saint Augustine on Prayer*, p. 10.

[25] *Epistula CXXX* XIV,26: *CSEL* XLIV,71: *quod dei non quod nostra uoluntas habuit, minime dubitare debemus.* He follows this with the example of Jesus himself praying in the Garden of Gethsemane.

[26] *De sermone domini* II,iii,14: *CC* XXXV,104: *Fit ergo in oratione conuersio cordis ad eum qui semper dare paratus est, si nos capiamus quod dederit, et in ipsa conuersione purgatio interioris oculi, cum excluduntur ea quae temporaliter cupiebantur, ut acies simplicis cordis ferre possit simplicem lucem diuinitus sine ullo occasu aut immutatione fulgentem....*

[27] *Sermo LXI* VI,7: *PL* XXXVIII,411:...*Quid petimus?...Hoc ergo petimus quod in aeternum habeamus: quo cum saturati fuerimus, ulterius non egeamus.*

[28] He says, "May our enemies believe, as we also believe in You. May they be friends, may enmities cease." *Sermo LVI* V,8: *PL* XXXVIII,380: *Credant inimici nostri, quomodo et nos in te credimus: fiant amici, finiant inimicitias.* Augustine repeats this particular aspect of conformation in his exposition on Psalm 38: "Sometimes we pray for what we do not want....Therefore, let them not pray for this, that their enemies may die; but pray for this, that they may be corrected; and their enemies will be dead; for from the time they are corrected, they no longer will be enemies." *Enarratio in Psalmum XXXVII* 14: *CC* XXXVIII,392: *Nam aliquando oramus quod non debemus....Non ergo hoc orent, ut moriantur inimici, sed hoc orent, ut corrigantur; et mortui erunt inimici; iam enim correcti, non erunt inimici.*

[29] K. Schnurr, *Hören und Handeln: Lateinische Auslegungen des Vaterunsers in der Alten Kirche bis zum 5. Jahrhundert* (Freiburg: Herder, 1985), p. 107, says, "Das Gebet des Herrn dient Augustinus an dieser Stelle seines Briefes beim Beten dazu, der Adressatin Proba zu zeigen, was man beten soll.... Das Vaterunser is demnach auch hier die zusammenfassende Beschreibung der Haltung, die sich für einen Christen gebührt."

[30] *Tractatus in Euangelium Ioannis LXXXI,4: CC* XXXVI,531: *Ab huius orationis uerbis et sensibus non recedamus petitionibus nostris, et quidquid petierimus, fiet nobis. Tunc enim dicenda sunt uerba eius in nobis manere, quando facimus quae praecepit, et diligimus quae promisit....*

[31] *Epistula CXXX* XII,22: *CSEL* XLIV,65: *non nisi spiritaliter deceat orare....* Later in Letter 130 Augustine says: "And if you were to run over all the words of holy prayers, you would find nothing, as far as I can judge, which is not contained and included in the Lord's Prayer. Hence, it is allowable to say the same things differently and in fact in different words, when praying, but it ought not to be allowable to say different things." *Epistula CXXX* XII,22: *CSEL* XLIV,66: *et si per omnia precationum sanctarum uerba discurras, quantum existimo, nihil inuenies, quod non ista dominica contineat et concludat oratio. unde liberum est aliis atque aliis uerbis eadem tamen in orando dicere, sed non esse debet liberum alia dicere.*

[32] Conformation of the human will to God through prayer is illustrated by Augustine himself in the following prayer from his *Confessiones*: "Behold, therefore, Lord, my King and my God; may whatever useful thing I learned as a boy serve You, may whatever I speak and I write and I read and I calculate, serve You." *Confessiones* I,xv,24: *CC* XXVII, 13: *Ecce enim tu, domine, rex meus et deus meus, tibi seruiat quidquid utile puer didici, tibi seruiat quod loquor et scribo et lego et numero....*

[33] *Epistula CXXX* XIV,27: *CSEL* XLIV,71: *Quisquis autem unam illam petit a domino et hanc requirit, certus ac securus petit nec timet....*

[34] Augustine notes in his *Sixth Homily on First John* that "[the prayers of] the saints are heard for the welfare of all things, always heard for the eternal welfare: And that is what they desire; to the end that they are always heard." *In Ioannis Epistulam ad Parthos tractatus VI,6: PL* XXXV,2023: *Sancti ad salutem per omnia exaudiuntur, semper exaudiuntur ad salutem aeternam: ipsam desiderant; quia secundum hanc semper exaudiuntur.*

[35] *Epistula CXXX* VIII,17: *CSEL* XLIV,59:....*exerceri in orationibus desiderium nostrum, quo possimus capere, quod praeparat dare.*

[36] *Sermo CXV* I,1: *PL* XXXVIII,655: *Si fides deficit, oratio perit.... fides fons orationis. ...Fides, inquam, fundit orationem, fusa oratio etiam ipsi fidei impetrat firmitatem.*

In the *Confessiones*, Augustine similarly quotes Scripture regarding his prayer life, "I believe, and therefore also I speak." *Confessiones* I,v,6: *CC* XXVII,3: *Credo, propter quod et loquor.* Augustine explained this close connection of faith and prayer to some of his catechumens in a sermon on Romans 10: "...He said, 'how shall they call upon Him in whom they have not believed?' Notice that you have not first received the Lord's Prayer, and after that the Creed; but first the Creed, where you might know what to believe, and afterwards the Prayer, where you might know whom to call upon...because it is he who believes, that is heard when he calls." *Sermo LVI* I,1: *PL* XXXVIII,377: *Quia ergo dixit, Quomodo invocabunt, in quem non crediderunt: ideo non accepistis prius Orationem, et postea symbolum; sed prius symbolum ubi sciretis quid crederetis, et postea Orationem, ubi nossetis quem invocaretis. ...Quia qui credit, ipse exauditur invocans.*

[37] *Epistula CXXX* I,1: *CSEL* XLIV,42: *quo modo enim tu sic studeres orare dominum, nisi sperares in eo?*

[38] Augustine wrote, "...For why does He say to us: 'Watch and pray,'...if this is not to be fulfilled by the help of divine grace...?" *Epistula CXLV* 8: *CSEL* XLIV, 273: *nam ut quid nobis dicitur: Vigilate et orate...si hoc non impletur ex adiutorio gratiae diuinae...?*

[39] *Epistula CLXXVII* 4: *CSEL* XLIV,673: *ipsa igitur oratio clarissima est gratiae testificatio....*

[40] Augustine says, "He Himself has implanted this desire. Therefore, the words which our Lord Jesus Christ has taught in his Prayer are the pattern of [our] desires." *Sermo LVI* III,4: *PL* XXXVIII,379:...*ipsum desiderium ipse insinuavit. Verbo ergo quae Dominus noster Jesus Christus in Oratione docuit, forma est desideriorum.*

[41] *Tractatus in Euangelium Ioannis* XX,3: *CC* XXXVI,204....*conuertat se ad illum qui cor aperit, ut infundat quod donat.... et supplicet diuinae bonitati.*

[42] *Enarratio in Psalmum LXXXVI* 1: *CC* XXXIX,1198. Pope Innocent heard this emphasis upon grace in response to the Pelagian controversy. Augustine had written to him regarding Pelagius, saying, "...Therefore, just as we acknowledge the will when these commands are given, so also let him acknowledge grace when these petitions are said." *Epistula CLXXVII* 5: *CSEL* XLIV,674–75: *sicut ergo agnoscimus uoluntatem, cum haec praecipiuntur, sic et ipse agnoscat gratiam, cum petuntur.*

[43] *Confessiones* XIII,i,1: *CC* XXVII,242: *Inuoco te in animam meam, quam praeparas ad capiendum te ex desiderio, quod inspiras ei....*

In a letter to Pope Sixtus, Augustine expresses the view, in contradistinction to some later theological developments, that God works through his means to create faith and that the ability to pray is the result of that faith: "Truly, however, we should not think that even the merit of prayer precedes grace, in which case it would not be a free gift—but then it would not be grace because it would be the reward which was due—besides prayer itself is counted among the gifts of grace." *Epistula CXCIV IV,16: CSEL LVII,188: uerum tamen ne saltem orationis putentur praecedere merita, quibus non gratuita daretur gratia—sed iam nec gratia esset, quia debita redderetur—, etiam ipsa oratio inter gratiae munera reperitur.*

[44] "There is one that hears prayer, do not hesitate to pray; but He that hears remains forever within....He that hears you is not beyond you. You do not have to travel long, nor lift yourself up, so as to reach Him as it were with your hands. Rather, if you lift yourself up, you will fall; if you humble yourself, He will draw near to you. Our Lord God is here, the Word of God, the Word made flesh, the Son of the Father, the Son of God, the Son of man; the Exalted One who makes us, the Humble One who makes us new...." *Tractatus in Euangelium Ioannis X,1: CC XXXVI,100: Est qui exaudiat, ne dubitetis orare; qui autem exaudit, intus manet. ...Qui te exaudit, non est praeter te. Non longe uadas, nec te extollas, ut quasi adtingas illum manibus. Magis si te extuleris, cades; si te humiliaueris, ipse adpropinquabit. Hic Dominus Deus noster Verbum Dei, Verbum caro factum, Filius Patris, Filius Dei, Filius hominis, excelsus ut nos faceret, humilis ut nos reficeret....*

[45] *Enarratio in Psalmum LXXXV 1: CC XXXIX,1176:...Dominus noster Iesus Christus Filius Dei, qui et oret pro nobis, et oret in nobis, et oretur a nobis. Orat pro nobis, ut sacerdos noster; orat in nobis, ut caput nostrum, oratur a nobis, ut Deus noster. Agnoscamus ergo et in illo uoces nostras, et uoces eius in nobis.*

[46] In a lecture on the Gospel of John, Augustine explains his Christology in these words: "Those who ask, ask in His name; for in the sound of that name they understand nothing else than the reality itself which is called by that name, and do not, in the vanity or infirmity of the mind, pretend as if the Father is in one place, the Son in another, standing before the Father and praying for us, with the material substances of both occupying each its own place, and the Word pleading verbally for us with Him whose Word He is, while a definite space interposes between the mouth of the speaker and the ears of the hearer; and other such ideas which those who are natural, and at the same time carnal, fabricate in their hearts." *Tractatus in Euangelium Ioannis CII,4: CC XXXVI,596: Tunc in eius nomine petunt qui petunt, quia in sono eius nominis non aliud quam res ipsa est quae hoc nomine uocatur, intellegunt, nec animi uanitate uel infirmitate confingunt tamquam in alio loco Patrem, in alio Filium ante Patrem stantem, et pro nobis rogantem, spatia sua quaeque amborum occupantibus molibus, et Verbum ad eum cuius est Verbum facere uerba pro nobis, interuallo interposito inter os loquentis et auriculas audientis, et alia talia quae sibi animales, iidemque carnales in cordibus fabricantur.*

[47] "...When we speak intercessions to God, we do not separate the Son from Him; and when the Body of the Son prays, it does not separate its Head from itself; for there is one Savior of His Body, our Lord Jesus Christ, the Son of God...." *Enarratio in Psalmum LXXXV 1: CC XXXIX,1176:...quando loquimur ad Deum deprecantes, non inde Filium separemus, et quando precatur corpus Filii, non a se separet caput suum, sitque ipse unus saluator corporis sui Dominus noster Iesus Christus Filius Dei....*

[48] G. Montaño, "Doctrina Agustiniana de la oración," *Augustinus* 18 (1973) 301, states that Augustine taught that "he who does not possess the Holy Spirit dwelling in him ...cannot say that he possesses the spirit of prayer; he cannot then pray properly. He who

possesses Him, on the other hand, really prays with genuine efficacy, which is translated into eternal salvation." "Quien no posee el Espíritu Santo habitando en sí...no se puede decir que posea el espíritu de oración; no puede pues orar saludablemente. Quien lo posee, en cambio, ora realmente con genuina eficacia, la cual se traduce en salvación eterna."

⁴⁹ *Tractatus in Euangelium Ioannis* CII,4: *CC* XXXVI,597. This idea is repeated in Augustine's sermon on Christ's High Priestly Prayer, when he states: "Christ prays and gives that for which He prays. The Lord Christ, who listens to us with the Father, deigned to pray for us to the Father. What is more definite of our happiness than that He prays for us who gives that for which He prays? For Christ is Man and God; He prays as Man; He gives that for which He prays as God." *Sermo CCXVII* 1: *PL* XXXVIII,1083: *Christus orat, et dat quod orat. Dominus Christus, qui nos exaudit cum Patre, orare pro nobis dignatus est Patrem. Quid felicitate nostra certius, quanto ille pro nobis orat, qui dat quod orat? Est enim Christus homo et Deus: orat ut homo; dat quod orat, ut Deus.*

⁵⁰ *Tractatus in Euangelium Ioannis* CII,1: *CC* XXXVI,594: *Qui uero quod est de illo sentiendum sentit, ipse in eius nomine petit; et accipit quod petit, si non contra suam salutem sempiternam petit.*

⁵¹ In another lecture on the Gospel of John, Augustine expands upon this idea: "...Therefore, whatever we ask that is adverse to the usefulness of salvation, we do not ask in the name of the Savior. And yet He is the Savior, not only when He does what we ask, but truly more so when He does not do so; since when He sees something asked as contrary to our salvation, by not providing it, He manifests Himself more fully as our Savior....Let us not, then, ask anything that is contrary to our own salvation; for if He does that, He does it not as Savior, which is His name to His faithful ones....If, however, one who believes in Him asks something through ignorance that is contrary to his salvation, he does not ask it in the name of the Savior; because his Savior He would not be if He did anything to impede his salvation." *Tractatus in Euangelium Ioannis* LXXIII,3: *CC* XXXVI,511:...*ac per hoc quodcumque petimus aduersus utilitatem salutis, non petimus in nomine Saluatoris. Et tamen ipse Saluator est, non solum quando facit quod petimus, uerum etiam quando non facit; quoniam quod uidet peti contra salutem, non faciendo potius se exhibet Saluatorem. ...Non ergo contra nostram salutem petamus; quod si fecerit, non ut Saluator facit, quod est nomen eius fidelibus eius. ...Si autem qui in eum credit, aliquid per ignorantiam contra suam salutem petit, non in nomine Saluatoris petit; quia Saluator eius non erit, si quod eius salutem impedit, fecerit.*

Augustine and the Thousand Year Reign of Saints

Pamela Bright

The Augustinian "Revolution":
The Spiritual Interpretation of the Millennium

In *De ciuitate dei*, Augustine turns his attention to the scriptural admonitions of the coming of "the date which is called peculiarly the day of judgment and sometimes the day of the Lord."[1] It is in the context of the final Judgment that Augustine discusses the interpretation of the "first resurrection," the thousand year reign of the saints in Jerusalem.

> And I saw the souls of those who had been beheaded because of the witness to Jesus and because of the word of God, and who did not worship the beast or his images, and did not accept his mark upon their foreheads or upon their hands. And they came to life and reigned with Christ a thousand years. The rest of the dead did not come to life until the thousand years were finished (Rv 20:4–6).

Augustine argues strenuously against a "future and bodily" interpretation of this passage from the Book of Revelation. It is not that he would deny, in principle, a kind of Sabbath celebration to the saints. In fact, the elderly bishop admits to having accepted, at an earlier stage of his ministry, the idea of an earthly Sabbath of the saints. In Sermon 259, preached during the Octave of Easter, Augustine had distinguished between the eighth day signifying "the new life at the end of the world" and the seventh day, "the future rest of the saints on earth."

In *De ciuitate dei* XX,vii Augustine remarks:

> And this opinion would not be objectionable if it were believed that the joys of the saints in the Sabbath shall be spiritual, and consequent on the presence of God; for I myself, too, once held this opinion. But, as they assert that those who then rise again shall enjoy the leisure of immoderate carnal banquets, furnished with an amount of meat and drink

such as not only to shock the feeling of the temperate, but
even to surpass the measure of credulity itself, such assertions can be believed only by the carnal.[2]

Obviously, the bishop who had long opposed the "immoderate carnal
banquets" at the tombs of the martyrs in his native Africa was consistent in his
disapproval of a scriptural validation for tippling martyrs![3] However, there is
a much more serious object in view. Augustine uses the opportunity to mount
a sustained attack on the millenarian interpretations so prevalent in the African Church. From chapters 5 to 10 of Book XX, Augustine argues against a
"carnal" interpretation of the Book of Revelation. As a result, he has often
been credited with "revolutionizing" the interpretation of the "thousand year
reign" of the saints of Revelation 20. A footnote of the Nicene and Post-
Nicene Fathers series asserts,

> Augustine, who had formerly himself entertained chiliastic
> hopes, revolutionized the prevailing Ante-Nicene view of the
> apocalyptic millennium by understanding it as the present
> reign of Christ in the Church.[4]

More recent studies of the millenarian debate in the fourth century have corrected this view, and have rightly demonstrated Augustine's dependence on
his older African compatriot, Tyconius, the author of the most influential
commentary on the Book of Revelation in the western tradition. According
to Gennadius, the fifth-century author of *De viris inlustribus*, it was Tyconius
who interpreted the Book of Revelation "spiritually." It was Tyconius who
argued that the "first resurrection" of the saints occurs not in some future
Sabbath, but that "the thousand year reign of the saints" has begun already in
baptism, "now" in the Church.[5]

In chapter 6 of Book XX of *De ciuitate dei*, Augustine cites Jn 5:22–24:

> "The hour is coming, and is now, when the dead shall hear
> the voice of the Son of God; and they that hear shall live.
> For the Father has life in Himself; so has he given to the Son
> to have life in Himself." As yet he does not speak of the sec-
> ond resurrection, that is the resurrection of the body, which
> shall be in the end, but the first, which is now. It is for the
> sake of making this distinction that He says, "The Hour is

coming, and now is." Now this resurrection regards not the body, but the soul.[6]

This is precisely the point that Tyconius makes in his *Book of Rules*. It is the same scriptural citation and the same argument that the "first resurrection" is present "now" in the church.[7]

It is not my intention to concentrate on the source of the Augustinian interpretation of the "thousand year reign of the saints." The Tyconian origin is abundantly clear.[8] Nor is it my intention to weigh up the effects of Augustine's espousing the "spiritual" millennium in the interpretative history of the western tradition. This question has been explored by other scholars, notably R. Landes in his excellent essay on the defusing of the millennium in the patterns of western chronography between 100–800 C.E.[9]

The focus of the present study is upon the ecclesiology that underlies Augustine's interpretation of the "reign of the saints." I would argue that there is a radical difference in the time frames of eschatology between Augustine and his Tyconian source in the interpretation of the "now" of the Church of the "first resurrection." It is precisely in this difference in eschatology that Augustine does "revolutionize" the western tradition.

The Church—Mixed or Bipartite

Around the same time that he was writing Book XX of *De ciuitate dei*, Augustine turned to an incomplete work from the early years of his episcopate, the *De doctrina christiana*. In completing Book III of *De doctrina christiana*, he summarized and commented on Tyconius' *Book of Rules*. Augustine agrees with Tyconius that the Church is the field that must wait until the Judgment for the separation of its wheat and its tares. This highly unorthodox Donatist theologian insisted that the mystery of evil is always insidiously at work within the Church, which he describes as "bipartite." Both Augustine and Tyconius use dualistic terms in speaking of the nature of the church. They use the image of two cities, even two societies which are mysteriously interwoven until the end of time, when their true natures will be revealed at the coming of the Son of Man.

While recommending the Donatist theologian's work as "useful and elaborate,"[10] Augustine took issue with Tyconius' insistence that the Church was "bipartite." In Rule 2, Tyconius claims that the church has a right and left side. Augustine has strong objections to this terminology.

> The second (rule) is "Of the Bipartite Body of the Lord" which should not be designated in that way since that is not actually the body of the Lord which will be with Him in eternity. Rather it should be called "Of the True or Mixed Body of the Lord" or "The True and Simulated," or something else, because hypocrites should not be said to be with Him either in eternity or even now, although they seem to be in His Church. Whence this rule might have been named in such a way that it designated the "mixed Church."[11]

Augustine's objection is no quibble over details. It is an objection rooted in a fundamental difference in perception of the church in relation to the eschaton; I would suggest that the Tyconian description of the church as "bipartite" is derived from his view of the Christian community as the martyr community of the last times of tribulation, while the Augustinian description of a "mixed" church is related to the image of the pilgrim state of the church far from the "fixed stability" of the heavenly city.[12]

The "bipartite" church of Tyconius, and the "mixed" church of Augustine are imagined in very different time frames. It is not that the pilgrim church of Augustine lacks an eschatological perspective. The whole point of the image of a pilgrim church is that the gaze of the church is fixed on the heavenly Jerusalem, rather than upon the landscape through which it is passing. But the journey is long. Augustine has sharp words for the inveterate finger-counters who are constantly scanning the horizon for the signs of the end-times. Augustine's image of the pilgrim church toiling through the ambiguities of time is not the same as the "bipartite church" of Tyconius, perched on the precipice of a collapsing world.

The Martyr Church and the Pilgrim Church

The "bipartite church" of Tyconius is set in the symbolic world of eschatological judgment. Against this background, Tyconius has argued not only for a symbolic interpretation of the thousand years of the Book of Revelation, but also for a symbolic—or rather a "spiritual" interpretation—of the signs of the end-times. The "bipartite church" is experiencing both the "thousand year reign of the saints" in baptism, "now," but it is just as really experiencing the horrors of the end-times, "now," in the reign of Antichrist in the midst of the church through rampant sin and hypocrisy. The "times" of tribulation have already begun "spiritually." But in these last hours, there is yet time for repentance. The gaze of the Christian should be on the manifestations of the sign of charity, the ultimate saving gift of the Spirit, rather than on the physical signs of the final tribulation, which will be manifest to all the world.[13]

Tyconius' contribution to eschatology is his careful distinction between the "now" of the time of repentance and the "then" of the saved community of saints, snatched "from the midst" of the destruction of the evil city of Babylon. But his vision of the church is filled with the traditional symbol-sets of the community of the imminent end-times, the times of the final tribulation. The grim shadow of Antichrist, enthroned secretly "in the midst" of the church, looms over every section of his *Book of Rules*. This vision of the last days is not only typical of Donatist sermons but is also the persistent theme of African literature. It is a constant in the writings of Cyprian, and in the lesser-known works of Commodianus and Quodvultdeus. In other words, from the third to the mid-fifth century the dominant ecclesial theme in Africa is that of the martyr church struggling to maintain its integrity and its holiness in the tribulations of the last days.

Although Tyconius incurred the wrath of Parmenian, his Donatist bishop, by insisting that evil had infiltrated the holy community of the church, he had not changed the symbolic time frame in which the struggle of the church was perceived. The final verses of the *Book of Rules*, as it has come down to us, focused not on the heavenly city but, typically in the African tradition, on the victory over Antichrist and his followers.[14]

Augustine and the "Now" of the "Reign of the Saints"

Augustine is no less aware of the "mystery of the iniquity" in the church than his fellow Africans. He quotes with approval Tyconius' concept of the secret presence of evil, already at work in the Church, and especially at work secretly within every heart. For both theologians, the thousand-year reign of saints has already begun. Augustine argues that the church even in her pilgrim state already hears the strains of the chorus of praise of the angels, fellow citizens of the heavenly Jerusalem.[15] But for Augustine, the "now" of the participation in such an angelic and everlasting liturgy raises the question—who in the "mixed" church already participates in such a heavenly chorus?

Under the searching gaze of Augustine the ecclesiological perspective shifts; the time frames shift. More significantly, the scriptural frame of reference begins to shift. The "now" of the "reign of the saints" in Augustine's meditation is set against a background of texts from the psalms, especially the pilgrim psalms, and a conflation of images of the heavenly city from the Book of Revelation and the Epistle to the Hebrews, a work rarely evidenced in the African tradition before Augustine. For Augustine, the "reign of the saints" is expressed in participating in angel choruses (Heb 12:22) rather than in "immoderate banquets" suggested to some by Rv 20:4–6.

Conclusion

The earlier commentator had suggested that Augustine had "revolutionized" the exegesis of Revelation by situating the "reign of the saints" in the "now" of the church. Rather, there was a shift in direction within a revolution already under way. Tyconius and Augustine shared the pastoral concern of urging the continuing need for vigilance and repentance on the part of the Christian in the "now" of the church, while at the same time offering the encouragement of the victorious "reign" that had already begun in baptism, which they both called the "first resurrection."

Augustine shifted the pastoral perspective within the Tyconian exegesis of the "now" of the "reign of the saints." This shift in perspective was achieved by superimposing a different landscape over the threatening contours of the earlier African "symbol-scape." Augustine's symbolic landscape is that of the winding pilgrim track, where the sojourners endure the fatigue and uncertainties of the journey, with hope-filled gaze fixed on the journey's end.

Pilgrims are constantly aware of their weakness and vulnerability, even while they rejoice in the distant strains of the angel voices in the heavenly city. It is this double image of pilgrim and citizen, within the "now" of the church, that Augustine introduces as he explores the pastoral implications of the "first resurrection of the saints" in the Book of Revelation.

Notes

[1] *De ciuitate dei* XX,ii: *CC* XLVIII,701: *cuius tempus iam proprie dies iudicii et aliquando dies Domini.*

[2] *De ciuitate dei* XX,vii: *CC* XLVIII,709: *Quae opinio esset utcumque tolerabilis, si aliquae deliciae spiritales in illo sabbato adfuturae sanctis per Domini praesentiam crederentur. Nam etiam nos hoc opinati fuimus aliquando. Sed cum eos, qui tunc resurrexerint, dicant inmoderatissimis carnalibus epulis uacaturos, in quibus cibus sit tantus ac potus, ut non solum nullam modestiam teneant, sed modum quoque ipsius credulitatis excedant: nullo modo ista possunt nisi a carnalibus credi.*

[3] See Epistle 10 in *St. Augustine: Select Letters*, ed. J. H. Baxter, Loeb Classical Library (London: Harvard Univ. Press, 1980), pp. 69–91.

[4] M. Dods, *NPNF* I:II,426.

[5] Gennadius, *De viris inlustribus* 18; ed. Richardson, Texte und Untersuchungen 14; *NPNF* II:III,285.

[6] *De ciuitate dei* XX,vi: *CC* XLVIII,706: *quia uenit hora et nunc est, quando mortui audient uocem filii Dei, et qui audierint uiuent. Sicut enim Pater habet uitam in semet ipso, sic dedit et Filio habere uitam in semet ipso. Nondum de secunda resurrectione, id est corporum, loquitur, quae in fine futura est, sed de prima, quae nunc est. Hanc quippe ut distingueret, ait: Venit hora, et nunc est. Non autem ista corporum, sed animarum est.*

[7] *Liber Regularum* 36:29–37:10; ed. F. C. Burkitt, *The Book of Rules of Tyconius* (Cambridge: Cambridge Univ. Press, 1894, repr. 1967).

[8] P. Bright, *The Book of Rules of Tyconius: Its Purpose and Inner Logic* (Notre Dame: Notre Dame Univ. Press, 1988), p. 25.

[9] R. Landes, "Last Millennium Be Fulfilled: Apocalyptic Expectations and the Pattern of Western Chronography 100–800 CE," *The Use and Abuse of Eschatology in the Middle Ages*, ed. W. Verbeke and A. Welkenhuysen (Louvain: Leuven Univ. Press, 1988), pp. 137–211.

[10] *De doctrina christiana* III,xxx,43: *CC* XXXII,103: *tam elaborato atque utili operi.*

[11] *De ciuitate dei* III,xxxii,45: *CC* XXXII,104: *Secunda est de domini corpore bipertito, quod quidem non ita debuit appellare; non enim re uera domini corpus est, quod cum illo non erit in aeternum, sed dicendum fuit: de domini corpore uero atque permixto aut uero atque simulato uel quid aliud, quia non solum in aeternum, uerum etiam nunc hypocritae non cum illo esse dicendi sunt, quamuis in eius esse uideantur ecclesia.*

[12] *De ciuitate dei* I,Praefatio: *CC* XLVII,1: *Gloriosissimam ciuitatem Dei siue in hoc temporum cursu, cum inter impios peregrinatur ex fide uiuens, siue in illa stabilitate sedis aeternae.*

[13] Rule 5 of Tyconius, *De temporibus*, and rule 6, *De recapitulatione*. For a further discussion of these rules, see *The Book of Rules of Tyconius*, pp. 46–48, 76–84.

[14] See Tyconius' exegesis of the destruction of the prince of Tyre, Ezk 28:2–19, Rule 7. W. Babcock, *Tyconius: The Book of Rules* (Atlanta: Scholars Press, 1989), pp. 129–45.

[15] *Expositions On the Book of Psalms by Augustine*, Psalm XLII, 8, ed. A. C. Coxe, *NPNF* I:VIII,134.

The Cynic Monks of Carthage:
Some Observations on *De opere monachorum*

Kenneth B. Steinhauser

Augustine's *On the Work of Monks* is considered by many the only piece of literature from Christian antiquity dedicated entirely to the topic of human labor.[1] Nevertheless, in spite of its title a careful reading of the treatise reveals that human work is actually a secondary concern. Augustine presents no theoretical definition of work. He does not deal with the origin of work. He does not develop a theology of work. In fact, if one desires a more complete picture of Augustine's views on work, one must look elsewhere. In *De Genesi ad litteram* Augustine observes that work existed before the fall.[2] Therefore, work in itself is not evil; nor may human work be considered the result of original sin. Before the fall, agricultural labor—the ideal work in antiquity—was a tremendous pleasure to the laborer. In the work of husbandry, the laborer could see the activity of God in his creation. Augustine does concede that work would not be such a burden today if the bliss which prevailed in the garden had endured. Only after the fall does work become difficult and painful. In evaluating work as a positive good Augustine would not have been at odds with the contemporary secular tradition. One need only peruse Cato's *De agricultura* and Varro's *De re rustica* to discover two outstanding examples of the Roman agricultural manuals dedicated to the mastery of the contemporary economy.

Certainly Augustine is much more concerned with the dissident monks themselves than with their work. Aurelius, bishop of Carthage, had written to Augustine requesting that he instruct a vocal faction of beatnik monks on the matter of work. Citing Mt 6:26, the rebellious monks had decided not to work: "Look at the birds in the sky. They do not sow or reap, they gather nothing into barns; yet your heavenly Father feeds them. Are not you more important than they?"[3] Augustine countered with 2 Th 3:10: "Anyone who would not work should not eat." The first thirty chapters of Augustine's treatise are dedicated to explaining these two biblical quotations and some related passages. Then, in the last three chapters Augustine turns his attention to the physical appearance of these rebellious monks, who also refuse to cut their hair. Once again Augustine shows his fondness for Paul: "It is dishonorable for a man to wear his hair long" (1 Co 11:14). And once again the beatnik monks respond with Matthew: "Those who have castrated themselves for the sake of the kingdom of heaven are no longer men."[4] Augustine, in turn, attacks them for debasing themselves.

Augustine's subsequent description of the treatise in the *Retractationes* also emphasizes these same two characteristics of the dissident monks: their refusal to work and their long hair.[5] Augustine describes the Carthaginian situation as a quarrel between two factions, one which relied on Paul's Letters and the other which appealed to Matthew's Gospel.

In addition to exposing some aspects of Augustine's understanding of work and his clever intervention in a delicate situation, *De opere monachorum* also divulges characteristics of the dissident monks themselves. Who were they? What was their reason for not working? What were they attempting to demonstrate by their refusal to work? What was the purpose of the faction?

G. Folliet has attempted to demonstrate the presence of heretical monks in Africa prior to Augustine's establishment of monasteries in the region.[6] Essentially Folliet's hypothesis is based upon two references in Augustine's writings. In *De haeresibus* Augustine describes Messalians or Euchites as monks who refuse to work. Their Syrian name and its Greek translation come from their desire to obey the Lord's command to pray without ceasing. Therefore, they do not work in order to dedicate themselves entirely to prayer.[7]

Folliet then explains that the Euchites mentioned in *De haeresibus*, written in the year 428, were known to Augustine in 400 when he wrote *De opere monachorum*, which is first and foremost a reproach against a faction of monks who refuse to work in order to dedicate themselves to prayer and contemplation. Having connected these two references, Folliet comes to the conclusion that the Euchites had their own monasteries, which had been established before Augustine's. Of course, this conclusion destroys the traditional hypothesis that Augustine was the father of monasticism in Latin-speaking Roman Africa.

Not long after the publication of his article, Folliet's hypothesis was attacked by Lope Cilleruelo[8] and subsequently by Juan-Manuel del Estal.[9] Both Cilleruelo and del Estal take exception to Folliet's conclusion that Euchite monasteries existed in Africa prior to Augustine's foundations. Del Estal disagrees with Folliet's assertion that entire monasteries, where all the monks do not work, had been founded in the heretical Euchite tradition. Augustine is rather addressing a disciplinary problem involving a faction of monks within a monastery or within some monasteries at Carthage. Furthermore, del Estal objects to identifying the Euchites in *De haeresibus* with the non-working monks in *De opere monachorum*, which was written some twenty-eight years earlier, because there is no concrete evidence that the two references are related to one another. Adolar Zumkeller has taken a middle road in the debate maintaining that Augustine was the father of monasticism in Roman Africa but conceding an Euchite influence on the non-working monks of Carthage.[10]

In reopening this debate, I wish to avoid the question whether or not Augustine was the father of monasticism in Roman Africa. Nevertheless, my sympathies do lie with Cilleruelo, del Estal and Zumkeller because Folliet has clearly drawn an unwarrantable conclusion. In other words, his conclusion that heretical Euchite monasteries had been established in Roman Africa prior to the Augustinian foundations goes far beyond the evidence which he has brought to support that conclusion. Here I prefer rather to turn my attention to these monks and perhaps more closely describe them and their beliefs and practices. From Augustine's treatment of the problem in *De opere monachorum* and from subsequent comments on that work in his *Retractationes*, one is able to develop a descriptive profile of these monks and identify some of their significant characteristics. Then, on the basis of that profile constructed from the available evidence, one may advance a reasonable hypothesis concerning what motivated these monks and how the faction began. Six fundamental characteristics emerge.

First, as a matter of principle these monks refused to work.[11] The bulk of the treatise deals with this issue, which was obviously foremost in the mind of Augustine, whose argument is primarily exegetical. Identifying the saying of the Lord concerning the lilies of the field as a parable, Augustine calls for a spiritual interpretation of the Matthean passage.

Second, the renegade monks earned their living begging.[12] This was especially problematic for Augustine because he certainly did not want idle and lazy riffraff invading the monasteries. Nor did he want the lazy monks to give scandal to the laity who were already donating substantial resources for the maintenance of African monasteries.

Third, the monks wore their hair long.[13] Augustine spends a full three chapters dealing with this issue, which is unfortunately frequently overlooked by scholars. Both sides cite biblical authorities to justify their positions. This aspect of long hair is important for two reasons: these monks are readily identifiable in public as belonging to the faction, and they are also engaging in a practice which Augustine considered self-degrading.

Fourth, some wandered about the countryside propagating their views.[14] Augustine states that "they boasted."[15] He also states that they teach perversely.[16] The interests of these dissident monks were neither academic nor literary but popular and practical. Allowing themselves to be easily identifiable in public, they appealed directly to the masses.

Fifth, the monks showed a marked preference for the Gospel of Matthew while Augustine relied on the Letters of Paul. Of course, Augustine's predilection for Paul is no secret. Every quotation or paraphrase from Matthew's Gospel by Augustine is of a saying of Jesus. This would indicate that the dissident monks were using the sayings of Jesus to support their actions.

Sixth, in his argument against the non-working monks, Augustine lays a great emphasis on social responsibility. "There is one commonwealth of all Christians,"[17] he writes. The Ciceronian concept of the *respublica*, translated here as "commonwealth" and treated later in the *City of God*, is the harmonious cooperation of citizens from various levels of society.[18] These monks had removed themselves from the *respublica*. They were counter-cultural to the point of being asocial.

What kind of people or what group in antiquity possessed all of the above characteristics? The dominant similarity which the Syrian Messalians and the Carthaginian dissidents share is their refusal to work. However, the Messalians or Euchites do not match the entire profile. There is no evidence that they wandered about the countryside or wore long hair. The beatnik monks of Carthage are remarkably similar to the ancient Cynic philosophers. Cynics did not work. They wore long hair and a distinctive garb. They acquired their livelihood begging. They engaged in various self-debasing practices. They wandered about the countryside. They propagated their views in public. They were social critics. They formed a clique. They collected the sayings of their hero.

Three illustrations from antiquity should be sufficient to demonstrate similarities between the Cynic philosophers and the dissident Carthaginian monks: Diogenes, Maximus, and Julian the Emperor.

Diogenes was the founder of Cynicism and Cynic *par excellence*. Despite the famous Cynic "diatribe," Cynicism was not an academic but a popular philosophy, so that few literary witnesses remain. For the most part we must rely on fragments and anecdotes. Diogenes was called a "cynic" or a "dog." Although the label was pejorative, he accepted the name as an indication of his self-sufficiency. He was proud to be called a dog because he, like a dog, depended on no one. He was free and totally independent.[19] Self-sufficiency and independence was also the goal of the Carthaginian Cynic monks.

Maximus provides the example and, thus, the theoretical possibility of a Christian Cynic. A native of Alexandria, Maximus supported Athanasius in the Arian dispute. His involvement cost him a beating and exile in 374. The last historical reference to him was the council of Constantinople declaring his ordination invalid in 381. In this context, Gregory Nazianzen praised Maximus as one who is a Cynic through his simplicity of life. He also admired Maximus for his neglect of speculative philosophy, his philanthropy and his cosmopolitanism.[20] The actual existence of a Christian Cynic serves to demonstrate that Cynicism and Christianity could be compatible in a concrete historical situation.

The emperor Julian, who died in 363, had delivered two speeches against the Cynics, whom he criticized for their ostentatious asceticism. Julian explicitly called monks the Cynics of the present age.[21] Rigorous asceticism, bordering on self-abasement, and antisocial behavior are essential and recurring Cynic themes.[22] That Cynicism with its counter-cultural value system could appeal to some monks is not an unreasonable conclusion especially when contemporaries had already noted similarities between Cynicism and monasticism.

Who were these beatnik monks of Carthage? In spite of distinct similarities with Cynicism, an historical connection between the dissident monks and Cynic philosophers cannot be proved just as an historical connection with the heretical Euchite monks cannot be proved. Nevertheless, a plausible chain of events may be constructed. As an individual, each monk had entered the monastery. Each monk on his own had earned a fairly decent reputation. Only after having entered the monastery did the individual monks form themselves into a faction. In attempting to cajole them to his point of view Augustine makes the flattering statement that in all other respects these were good monks.[23] This would indicate a prior good standing within the monastic community. It would also eliminate any possibility of an heretical or Euchite association.

Their long hair seems to have been derived from a non-Christian or extra-ecclesiastical practice. There is no basis in the Gospel for wearing long hair. In his criticism Augustine does refer to the Nazarite vow and the prophets. However, the main justification for long hair advanced by the dissident monks appears to have been the indirect and defensive argument from the Gospels against Paul who states that women, not men, wear long hair. The monks retorted that because of their vow of celibacy they were eunuchs for the kingdom and not men anyway. The lack of a clear and coherent biblical foundation for their position indicates that they had first acquired the practice of wearing long hair elsewhere and then developed a rather feeble theoretical defense of their practice. We know that some Cynics wore a distinctive garb and long hair.

Cynicism as a movement or a philosophy extended from the fourth century before Christ to the sixth century after in both the east and the west. According to the emperor Julian Cynicism had been practiced in all ages. Although Cynicism was not a driving intellectual force in Augustine's Africa, some contact with this popular philosophy was certainly possible. Carthage was a port city and significant urban center of cultural diversity. The region was home to descendants of the Romans, Phoenicians and Berbers. There was even an ethnic Greek minority. Amidst Manichaeans, Donatists and Platonists, one should not be surprised to find other philosophies or life-styles in varying degrees. In another context, defending the Cynics against accusations of indecency, Augustine himself documents their presence in Africa: "Even now we see that there are still Cynic philosophers among us."[24]

After having entered the monastery, these dissident monks had come into contact with popular Cynic philosophy. They adopted some of the practices of Cynicism and began propagating a christianized version of Cynicism or perhaps a "cynicized" version of Christianity. They were social critics emphasizing autonomy or independence through simple living. The Carthaginian movement was ultimately short lived. Augustine does not deal with the problem again and his *Retractationes* indicates that the issue was closed. Neither Christianity nor monasticism were as a matter of principle impervious to external philosophical influences. The reason why the beatnik monks failed may very well lie in the nature of the monastic community itself. Although monasticism could easily assimilate Stoic indifference (ἀπάθεια), there appears to have been no place for Cynic individualism (αὐτάρκεια).

Notes

[1] See H. Holzapfel, *Die sittliche Wertung der körperlichen Arbeit im christlichen Altertum* (Würzburg: Rita Verlag, 1941), pp. 122–36, and A. T. Geoghegan, *The Attitude towards Labor in Early Christianity and Ancient Culture*, Studies in Christian Antiquity 6 (Washington: The Catholic University of America Press, 1945), pp. 201–12.

[2] *De Genesi ad litteram* VIII,viii,16: *BA* 49,36.

[3] Biblical quotations are from the New American Bible.

[4] *De opere monachorum* XXXII,40: *CSEL* XLI,591–94; tr. M. S. Muldowney, *FC* 16, 390; cf. Mt 19:12.

[5] *Retractationes* II,xxi: *CC* LVII,106–7.

[6] G. Folliet, "Des moines euchites à Carthage en 400–401," *Studia Patristica* 2, Texte und Untersuchungen 64 (Berlin: Akademie Verlag, 1957), pp. 386–99.

[7] On the Euchites or Messalians see also B. Lohse, *Askese und Mönchtum in der Antike und in der alten Kirche*, Religion und Kultur der alten Mittelmeerwelt in Parallelforschungen 1 (Munich: R. Oldenbourg, 1969), pp. 211–13, and I. Gobry, *Les Moines en Occident*, vol. 1 (Paris: Fayard, 1985), pp. 423–24.

[8] L. Cilleruelo, "Nota sobre el agustinismo de los monjes de Cartago," *La Ciudad de Dios* 172 (1959) 365–69.

[9] J. M. del Estal, "Descertada opinión moderna sobre los monjes de Cartago," *La Ciudad de Dios* 172 (1959) 596–616.

[10] A. Zumkeller, *Augustine's Ideal of the Religious Life* (New York: Fordham University Press, 1986), p. 77; see also I. I. Gavigan, *De vita monastica in Africa Septentrionali inde a temporibus S. Augustini usque ad invasiones Arabum* (Rome: Marietti, 1962), pp. 241–44.

[11] *De opere monachorum* I,2: *CSEL* XLI,531–32.

[12] *De opere monachorum* III,4: *CSEL* XLI,535–37.

[13] *De opere monachorum* XXXI,39: *CSEL* XLI,590–91.

[14] *De opere monachorum* XXIX,37: *CSEL* XLI,586–89, and *Retractationes* II,xxi: *CC* LVII,106–7.

[15] *Retractationes* II,xxi: *CC* LVII,107: *se…iactarent*.

[16] *De opere monachorum* XXXIII,41: *CSEL* XLI,594–95.

[17] *De opere monachorum* XXV,33: *CSEL* XLI,580: *omnium enim Christianorum una respublica est*; tr. *FC* 16,378.

[18] See A. Wachtel, *Beiträge zur Geschichtstheologie des Aurelius Augustinus*, Bonner Historische Forschungen 17 (Bonn: Ludwig Röhrscheid Verlag, 1960), p. 137.

[19] See M. I. Finley, *Aspects of Antiquity: Discoveries and Controversies* (New York: Penguin Books, 1977), pp. 88–98.

[20] See D. R. Dudley, *A History of Cynicism: From Diogenes to the 6th Century A.D.* (Cambridge, 1937; rpt. Chicago: Ares Publishers, 1980), pp. 204–7.

[21] C. N. Cochrane, *Christianity and Classical Culture: A Study of Thought and Action from Augustus to Augustine* (New York: Oxford University Press, 1957), pp. 269–71.

[22] R. Höistad, *Cynic Hero and Cynic King: Studies in the Cynic Conception of Man* (Uppsala: n.p., 1948), p. 198.

[23] *De opere monachorum* XXXI,39: *CSEL* XLI,590–91.

[24] *De ciuitate dei* XIV,xx: *CC* XLVIII,442: *et nunc uidemus adhuc esse philosophos Cynicos*; tr. P. Levine, Loeb 414,368–71. Cf. Höistad, p. 18.

VIII

Relations and Comparisons

Augustine

Arbitror iam manifestum esse omnibus posse auctoritatem beati Cypriani ad retinendum uinculum pacis nulloque modo uiolandam unitatis ecclesiae saluberrimam caritatem magis pro nobis quam pro Donatistis esse proponendam. si enim Cypriani exemplo uti uoluerint ad rebaptizandos catholicos, quia ille censuit in catholica baptizandos haereticos, nos potius exemplo eius utimur, quo apertissime statuit a catholica communione id est a christianis toto terrarum orbe diffusis etiam malis et sacrilegis admissis nullo modo per separationem communionis esse recedendum, quandoquidem nec eos qui, ut eidem uidebatur, non baptizatos sacrilegos in communionem recipiebant, a iure communionis uoluit amouere dicens: 'neminem iudicantes aut a iure communionis aliquem si diuersum senserit amouentes'.

De baptismo III,i,1

Augustine and Aristotle on Causality

Montague Brown

At first sight, the idea of comparing Augustine with Aristotle on the nature of causality might seem like an effort in futility. After all, Augustine is a Platonist, and Aristotle differs from Plato in many fundamental ways. Where Plato says we are souls trapped in bodies, Aristotle claims that these bodies, as informed by rational souls, are what we are. Where Plato says we learn by turning away from the material world and recollecting what we innately know, Aristotle insists that learning is a process of abstracting meaning from material things themselves. While Plato thinks of the material world as a mere shadow of a true Reality which lies in a separated world of Forms, Aristotle holds that this material world is really real, that the actuality and intelligibility of things lies in themselves. In short, the views of reality of Augustine the Platonist and Aristotle would appear to be as far apart as those of Plato and Aristotle. But there is more. Not only does Augustine differ from Aristotle in his Platonic leanings, he is also a Christian and primarily a theologian. As a Christian, he holds that God is the free creator of the universe, a notion absolutely foreign to Greek metaphysics. For a Christian Platonist, the principles of explanation of the things of this world might appear to be even more distanced from that world since they exist in the mind of the creator, who is utterly different from his creatures. As a theologian, Augustine's method is most often a meditation on Scripture. He takes what he knows by faith, and then relates this to the world. Aristotle's thinking always moves in the other direction, from things to the cause of things. Such basic and plentiful problems in trying to compare Augustine and Aristotle have prompted the eminent Augustinian scholar Vernon Bourke to declare: "It is vain...to attempt to relate the Augustinian treatment of causality to the Aristotelian theory of the four causes (agent, final, formal and material). St. Augustine does not think as Aristotle does."[1]

Despite Bourke's warning, I shall, in this paper, compare the notions of causality of Augustine and Aristotle. Such a comparison will have two main foci: on the one hand, it will raise the question whether or not Augustine has a strong doctrine of secondary causality; on the other hand, it will ask whether or not one can find in the thought of Augustine a parallel to Aristotle's four causes. Thus, in the first part of the paper, I shall consider the issue of secondary causality in Augustine, and in part two, I shall look at Augustine's ideas about kinds of causality. In the concluding section I shall offer some suggestions as to why Augustine the Platonist should end up rather close to Aristotle in his understanding of causality.

I

There is a theory called "occasionalism" which developed among philosophers who held that God is creator. Occasionalism holds that every apparent action between created things is really only the action of God. For example, the presence of cold hands before a fire on a winter's day is merely the "occasion" for God to make the hands feel warm. If such a view is true, then clearly there is no such thing as secondary causality. There was a tradition among Muslim philosophers which held this view.[2] In the Christian West, Nicholas Malbranche, a seventeenth-century Oratorian priest, was the major exponent of the occasionalist philosophy. Malbranche considered himself the disciple of Descartes and, before Descartes, of Augustine.[3] Thus, the denial of secondary causality is a possible interpretation of Augustine's thought. Let us see whether such an interpretation is justified.

As I said above, St. Augustine is first and foremost a theologian, and philosophically a Platonist: either of these points might lead one to believe that Augustine has little concern for secondary causality. For Augustine the paradigm of causality is the creative act. God is cause in the fullest sense. As creator, the most obvious kind of causality God displays is efficient causality. God makes the world out of nothing. The question arises as to whether God's efficient causality is the only causality at work in creation. Vernon Bourke writes: "Causality meant efficient production to Augustine; in a very real sense, all efficacy in the inanimate universe is directly and immediately supplied by God."[4] But if all efficacy is directly supplied by God, then the apparent secondary causality of creatures is just that—apparent, not real.

I would like to divide my treatment of secondary causality in Augustine into two parts. First, I shall consider texts in which Augustine speaks to the issue of creaturely causality directly and in general. Then, I shall examine in some detail Augustine's view of matter. This, it seems to me, is of critical importance, for if matter is just "stuff" created by God to be made into various things, then the notion of God alone acting in the world seems rather plausible. However, if Augustine's notion of matter turns out to be more like Aristotle's prime matter, then, since the latter only exists as a component of a material thing in continuity with other material things, and since God as creator is not the things he has made, there must be a world of real things with specific natures, whose interrelations would constitute real secondary causality.

Augustine's general treatment of secondary causality may be understood by considering two problems: 1) are there any creatures at all which exercise proper causality? and 2) are there any creatures without free will which exercise proper causality? Addressing the first question, the answer would most certainly have to be yes. Angels and human beings exercise real secondary causality in terms of acts of will. If this were not so, God would be the direct cause of sin, which is inadmissible, since God as creator is perfect being. Thus, creatures with rational wills, at least, are real secondary causes. As Augustine says, "whatever power they have, is most certainly power."[5]

It is not so clear that creatures without freedom exercise real secondary causality. In point of fact, Augustine says that "there are no efficient causes except voluntary causes...therefore, bodies are subjected to wills."[6] This would seem to be diametrically opposed to Aristotle's notion of the coming to be of creatures on the earth through the influence of the heavenly bodies. But is it? Aristotle did, indeed, hold that the heavenly bodies were the efficient causes of things coming to be. However, it is clear that they are not independent causes: they are moved by spiritual beings, the separate substances, which are the ultimate causes for things coming to be. But as Aristotle's separate substances are final causes, not efficient causes, there is not for him the same difficulty in reconciling simultaneous primary and secondary causality as there is for a philosopher of creation who holds that God, in addition to being final cause, is also efficient cause of all things.

While it might seem that a creating God usurps causality from the world more than Aristotle's Unmoved Mover, just the opposite, I think, proves to be true. For God as creator makes it true to say that his existence and causality are not the only existence and causality. God's presence to created things is not a usurpation of their natural powers; rather it is their guarantee. "From within, however, it [the corporeal universe] is helped incorporeally, God acting upon it so that it is entirely natural, since all things are from him, through him, and in him."[7] Clearly there is nothing unnatural about being from God, through God, and in God. God's presence to things neither adds to their natures nor subtracts from them. God's presence to things makes them to be precisely what they are. As Augustine says, things are created "in order that they might be natures,"[8] not so that their natural powers might be usurped by Divine power.

> Thus he [God] so administers all the things which he has created that each is allowed to show forth and exercise its own power. For although without him nothing could exist, created things are not the same as what he is himself.[9]

Thus, occasionalism is certainly not implied by Augustine's thought, either for creatures with rational wills or for inanimate things. If God had wanted everything to be his power alone, he would never have created. This is not to say that anything escapes the divine power, for nothing would exist unless created by God, nor act except moved by the source of all activity; but it is to say that the created world is really real, and the causality which is the concomitant of having a universe of different kinds of things on different levels of perfection is also real. The universe is an ordered whole with interdependent creatures, not some charade in which what appears to be order is just an illusion. It is a wise creation, created so that it might be.[10] Even the way Augustine speaks of God as the one "from whom are all powers"[11] indicates that Augustine certainly thought that there were causes other than God.

If we turn to the task of discovering what Augustine meant by matter, we may find more reason to affirm the presence of secondary causality in his view of reality. For if Augustine has a notion of material cause similar to Aristotle's, that is, matter as potency to all material forms, then there is a continuity among creatures in terms of causality: one thing really does change into another through the agency of some higher cause. Professor Bourke expressly rejects this notion: "There is no theory of potency and act in Augustine's thought; so matter simply means the original stuff that God created out of nothing."[12] Let us consider some texts to see just how true Professor Bourke's position is.

There is no question that Augustine often does speak of matter in the way Bourke says he does. In his *Confessions* Augustine writes: "For you, Lord, made the world from formless matter, which you made out of nothing. By this matter which was nearly nothing you made great things at which the sons of men wonder."[13] Augustine is commenting here on the creation story in Genesis where it is said that "the earth was without form and void" (Gn 1:2 RSV). The literal meaning of the passage seems to be that God first created this formless matter and then created things out of it. Such a reading would explain the interpretation that Augustine meant by matter "stuff" out of which God makes other things. This interpretation provides the framework for the notion of "seminal reasons," those "invisible seeds" in the elementary matter which allow the active power of God to draw forth different things.[14] However, it is clear that this notion of seminal reasons cannot be Augustine's notion of formless matter itself since these reasons, like seeds, have formal properties which direct their growth into what they will become. Then what does Augustine mean by "formless matter"?

In trying to answer this question, Augustine draws closer and closer to an Aristotelian notion of prime matter. He realizes that this unformed matter could never have existed on its own, as "stuff" which was later given form. For anything material is changing (a fundamental precept of Platonic and Aristotelian philosophy) and hence measurable by time. But this invisible and unorganized earth is said to be without form.

> Neither is the creation of that formless, uncomposed matter of the invisible, unformed earth numbered among the days of creation. For where there is no species and no order, nothing comes to be nor wears away; and where there is not this process of succession, there are no days nor any change of spatial or temporal things.[15]

Since time is the measure of motion, and motion is a characteristic of material things, only material things (things with distinct natures through their forms) can be said to exist in time. Since formless matter is without form, it cannot exist in time: it cannot exist prior to being informed. Thus, formless matter is not a barely formed "stuff" which is created first in time and later made into things; rather, matter is a principle of things.

Once we understand that this "formless matter" is a principle of things and not a kind of thing itself, its similarity to Aristotle's prime matter as potency becomes clearer. "But by Hyle I mean a certain material entirely formless and without quality, whence those qualities that we sense are formed, as the ancients said."[16] Matter has no form of its own, not even the form of "stuff"; rather, it is actual through form. What exists as created material nature is a world of things—matter structured by form.

There is another passage in which Augustine speaks of matter in language even more explicitly like Aristotle's. Meditating on what "formless matter" could be, Augustine confesses: "I was thinking of it together with numerous and varied forms; and so I was not thinking about it."[17] Imagination must always picture "formless matter" as having some form, even if only the confused form of "stuff." But Augustine insists that this "picture thinking" is not really thinking. Realizing that trying to think of matter in itself always leads to false imaginings, Augustine turns to a functional formulation of matter. Matter is the principle of mutability in things: it explains why things change. Matter represents the potentiality of one thing to change into another.

> Directing my attention to bodies themselves, I looked more
> deeply into their mutability, by which they cease to be what
> they were and begin to be what they were not. I suspected
> that this transition from form to form was by means of some
> unformed thing, not by means of complete nothingness.[18]

Defining prime matter satisfactorily is an impossible task, for definition always shows forth form, and prime matter lacks all form. To understand what Aristotle, and I would claim Augustine, meant by matter, one must consider the fact that there are beings in the world which share in common the ability to become other things. It is this "ability" that is pointed out by the principle of prime matter. "For the mutability of mutable things is itself capable of all the forms into which mutable things are changed."[19]

When one understands that for Augustine matter is not "stuff" but a principle of potency only real when informed, one becomes aware of the existence of things other than God—things in continuity with other things, each with its own distinct nature capable of natural action. If one were to miss this presence of real secondary causality in Augustine's thought by focusing on God as ultimate efficient cause and matter as "stuff," then one would be likely to read Augustine as an occasionalist or as a precursor to modern science with its emphasis on ultimate forces of nature (replacing God as efficient cause) moving matter into various accidental quantitative patterns which are the various "things" of our experience. From the point of view of occasionalism or modern physical science, the universe is not so much populated by real things, which act in accord with their own natures so as to perfect those natures and the order of the whole universe, as by accidental structures, which happen to be gathered together from some basic "stuff" by the arbitrary will of God (occasionalism) or the four forces of physics (modern science). Such is a view of the created universe shorn of formal and final causality, that is, of meaning and purpose. But this notion of the arbitrariness of God's activity and the reduction of things to chance patterns of atoms is certainly rejected by Augustine, who states that God is omnipotent, "not by thoughtless power, but by virtue of wisdom."[20]

II

If there is a principle of potency in material things, there must be a corresponding principle of act. Granted that Augustine thinks that there are real secondary causes operating in the universe, how does he see their activity? Does he see them acting in ways analogous to Aristotle's efficient, formal, and final causes? The answer to this question I think is most certainly yes, and the focus of his thinking on this point is a text from the book of Wisdom: "You ordered all things by measure, number and weight" (Ws 11:21 Jerusalem Bible). Augustine sees this text as indicating three kinds of cause which correspond to three questions one can ask about any existing thing.

> For everything that exists, that whereby it is established, that whereby it is distinguished, and that whereby it is in agreement are different. Therefore, the created universe, if it exists in some way and is far from being utterly nothing and yet is in agreement with itself and its parts, there must be a threefold cause, by which it is, by which it is this, by which it is in agreement with itself.[21]

We may ask three questions about any particular thing. Translated into Aristotelian terminology they are: what is its efficient cause? what is its formal cause? and what is its the final cause? Pursuing these questions about things, one comes to know God as the efficient cause of all things, their exemplary cause, and their final cause.

But, as we have said, God is not the only thing that is: he has created a universe of creatures, each of which has its own three-fold causality. "I would like to say beforehand that it must be kept in mind that these three, measure, number, and weight, are also found in all other things."[22] Let us look at these three causes one at a time, considering what Augustine says about them, and whether or not this is along the same lines as Aristotle's three principles of act. Augustine applies such principles of act on three levels: to God, to human beings, and to inanimate creatures.

First let us consider "measure." Augustine reads measure as being the principle of origin of anything—that thing's participation in existence itself. Speaking of God, Augustine remarks that "the measure without measure is that to which all other measures are compared, but which is itself from no other."[23] As for the human being, in the position of "measure" in the three-fold schematization, Augustine places "the beginning of the act of being."[24] And lest one think that Augustine attributes this principle of measure only to creatures with wills, he says in the same passage that from the light of God comes "to all bodies the measure by which they subsist."[25] In Augustine's own words: "Measure is also some kind of principle of action."[26]

In Augustine's trio of causes, "number" is a quite straightforward analogate for formal causality. Aristotle himself uses the notion of number in his definition of formal causality.[27] In speaking of God, Augustine writes: "number without number is that by which all things are formed, but is not itself formed."[28] When discussing human beings, Augustine replaces "number" in his account with "the reason of the act of knowing."[29] This makes for an easy comparison to Aristotle for whom the rational soul is the form of the body. As for inanimate things, they, too, are all said to possess this intrinsic formal principle. Augustine often substitutes "species" (which can be translated as form) for "number" in his analysis of the causal structure of all things.[30]

Finally, "weight" is an analogate for final causality in the thought of Augustine. God is said to be "the weight that draws everything to rest and stability."[31] For human beings, our "weight" is "the law of loving."[32] "Weight applies to will and love."[33] Aristotle speaks of the final causality by which the Unmoved Mover causes motion in the world as being love.[34] Everything, says Augustine, whether animate or inanimate, "either seeks or holds fast to a certain order."[35] This is its weight. A thing's weight indicates its own internal order to perfection and its place in the order of the universe. In many places, in fact, the word "order" is substituted for "weight" in the trio of causes.[36]

However Augustine may formulate his three principles, whether as the original "measure, number and weight," or as "one, species and order,"[37] or as "mode, species and order,"[38] as "measure of being, species and a certain kind of peace,"[39] or in other variations on the theme, it is clear that Augustine distinguishes three ways in which the causality of God and creatures operates. Like Aristotle, Augustine understands that there are three fundamental questions one raises when confronted with any real thing: how did it come to be? what is it? what is it for? Aristotle names these three efficient, formal, and final causality. If Augustine does not use these terms, it is not because he does not have an understanding of what they mean.

Conclusion

We have seen how Augustine's notion of causality turns out to be very close to that of Aristotle. Like Aristotle, Augustine clearly holds that there is real secondary causality, and the component features of that causality turn out to be parallels to Aristotle's four causes—material, formal, efficient (or moving), and final. Why is it that a confirmed Platonist such as Augustine should end up agreeing with Aristotle on these fundamentals of causality?

As a first step toward answering this question, one can point out the well-known fact that there were some Aristotelian influences on Augustine. As he points out in his *Confessiones*, Augustine read and understood Aristotle's *Categories*.[40] Thus, he would have been directly acquainted with Aristotle's distinction between substance and accidents. In addition, it is clear that Augustine read the works of Plotinus.[41] The philosophical system of Plotinus, and of Neoplatonism in general, was a conscious attempt to synthesize the thought of Plato and Aristotle.[42] However, the elements drawn from Aristotle were primarily from his discussions on logic and the soul. When it comes to causality, Neoplatonism follows Plato. The reality and causality of this material world is not integral to it, but is to be found in the realm of Ideas and ultimately in the One. Thus, neither his direct contact with Aristotle nor his Neoplatonism can explain sufficiently why Augustine's notion of causality is close to that of Aristotle.

There is a second, and I think more important, factor which helps to explain the kinship of Augustine and Aristotle in terms of causality. While we mentioned in the introduction that the Christian doctrine of creation might seem to further divide Augustine from Aristotle, I think, in fact, that the opposite proves to be true. While Augustine's Platonism keeps turning him away from the world of material things, his understanding of God as creator requires him to grant to those things the status of real being. If God creates, he makes something else to exist besides himself. A proper understanding of creation, such as Augustine's, must recognize that God's presence to things is not a violation of their natures: rather, he is precisely the giver of those natures. Thus, the refusal to grant reality to this material world, whether in Platonism, Neoplatonism, or occasionalism, is a misunderstanding of God's absolute power as creator. When once we recognize that there are real things other than God, we know that there must be secondary causality. Things will act according to their natures; and, since God has created various natures, he has created causal relationships among them. There is real order and structure, not just in each thing, but among the things of the created universe.

In fact, Augustine, far from holding that God usurps from creatures their intrinsic causality as occasionalism would have it, claims that a study of the causal structure of things actually reveals the creator in three ways, according to Aristotle's three-fold character of active causality. "Therefore, it must be that, since we see by our intellect the creator through those things that have been made, a fitting trace of him is apparent in creatures. For in that trinity is the highest origin, the most perfect beauty, and the most blessed delight of all things."[43] Thus, while Augustine the theologian begins with God where he finds a trinity of causality operating: "From him (efficient causality) and through him (formal causality) and to him (final causality) are all things" (Rm 11:36, RSV); Augustine the philosopher recognizes real secondary causality among the things of this world, and this activity reveals to him the presence of God.

Notes

[1] V. J. Bourke, *Augustine's View of Reality* (Villanova: Villanova University Press, 1964), p. 131.

[2] The Ash'arites, followers of Al Ash'ari (d. 936), held this "occasionalist" view of the relationship between God and his creation. See E. Gilson, *History of Christian Philosophy in the Middle Ages* (New York: Random House, 1955), pp. 184–85.

[3] "Cartesianism and the philosophy of Augustine were the dominant influences of his philosophy" (W. Doney, "Nicholas Malbranche," in *The Encyclopedia of Philosophy*, ed. P. Edwards [New York: Macmillan Publishing Co., 1967] vol. 5, p. 140).

[4] V. J. Bourke, *The Essential Augustine* (Indianapolis: Hackett Publishing Co., 1978), p. 44.

[5] *De ciuitate dei* V,ix,4: *CC* XLVII,140:....*quidquid ualent, certissime ualent.* Unless otherwise noted, all translations are my own.

[6] *De ciuitate dei* V,ix,4: *CC* XLVII,139:....*non esse causas efficientes omnium quae fiunt nisi uoluntarias...corpora igitur magis subiacent uoluntatibus.*

[7] *De Genesi ad litteram* VIII,xxv,46: *BA* 49,78: *Intrinsecus autem adiuuatur incorporaliter, Deo id agente, ut omnino natura sit, quoniam ex ipso et per ipsum et in ipso sunt omnia.*

[8] *De Genesi ad litteram* VIII,xxv,46: *BA* 49,78:…*ut naturae sint.*

[9] *De ciuitate dei* VII,xxx: *CC* XLVII,212: *Sic itaque administrat omnia, quae creauit, ut etiam ipsa proprios exserere et agere motus sinat. Quamuis enim nihil esse possint sine ipso, non sunt quod ipse.*

[10] "For not by thoughtless power, but by virtue of wisdom is he [God] omnipotent." *De Genesi ad litteram* IX,xvii,32: *BA* 49,138: *Neque enim potentia temeraria, sed sapientiae uirtute omnipotens est….*

[11] *De ciuitate dei* V,viii: *CC* XLVII,135:…*a quo sunt omnes potestates.*

[12] Bourke, *The Essential Augustine*, p. 98.

[13] *Confessiones* XII,viii,8: *CC* XXVII, 220: *Tu enim, Domine, fecisti mundum de materia informi, quam fecisti de nulla re paene nullam rem, unde faceres magna, quae miramur filii hominum.*

[14] See *De Genesi ad litteram* IX,xvii,32: *BA* 49,138–40, and *De trinitate* III,viii,13: *CC* L,139–41.

[15] *Confessiones* XII,ix,9: *CC* XXVII,221: *Ista uero informitas, terrae inuisibilis et incomposita, nec ipsa in diebus numerata est. Vbi enim nulla species, nullus ordo; nec uenit quidquam nec praeterit, et ubi hoc non fit, non sunt utique dies, nec uicissitudo spatiorum temporalium.*

[16] *De natura boni contra Manichaeos* XVIII: *PL* XLII,556: *Sed hylen dico quamdam penitus informem et sine qualitate materiem, unde istae quas sentimus qualitates formantur, ut antiqui dixerunt.*

[17] *Confessiones* XII,vi,6: *CC* XXVII,218:…*eam cum speciebus innumeris et uariis cogitabam et ideo non eam cogitabam.*

[18] *Confessiones* XII,vi,6: *CC* XXVII,219:…*intendi in ipsa corpora, eorumque mutabilitatem altius inspexi, qua desinunt esse quod fuerant et incipiunt esse quod non erant, eumdemque transitum de forma in formam per informe quiddam fieri suspicatus sum, non per omnino nihil.*

[19] *Confessiones* XII,vi,6: *CC* XXVII,219: *Mutabilitas enim rerum mutabilium ipsa capax est formarum omnium, in quas mutantur res mutabiles.*

[20] *De Genesi ad litteram* IX,xvii,32: *BA* 49,138: *Neque enim potentia temeraria, sed sapientiae uirtute….*

[21] *De diuersis quaestionibus LXXXIII* XVIII: *CC* XLIV,23: *Omne quod est aliud est quo constat, aliud quo discernitur, aliud quo congruit. Vniuersa igitur creatura si et est quoquo modo, et ab eo quod omnino nihil est plurimum distat, et suis partibus sibimet congruit, causam quoque eius trinam esse oportet: qua sit, qua hoc sit, qua sibi amica sit.*

[22] *De trinitate* XI,xi,18; *CC* L,355: *Quapropter haec tria, mensuram, numerum, pondus, etiam in ceteris omnibus rebus animaduertenda praelibauerim.*

[23] *De Genesi ad litteram* IV,iv,8: *BA* 48,290: *Mensura autem sine mensura est, cui aequatur quod de illa est, nec aliunde ipsa est….*

[24] *Contra Faustum Manichaeum* XX,7: *PL* XLII 42,372:...*initium existendi.*

[25] *Contra Faustum Manichaeum* XX,7: *PL* XLII 42,372:...*omnibus corporibus mensura ut subsitant.*

[26] *De Genesi ad litteram* IV,iv,8: *BA* 48,290: *Est autem mensura aliquid agendi....*

[27] "In general, a number and the parts in the formula," *Physics* II,3 194b29; tr. H. Apostle in *Aristotle's Physics* (Grinell, Iowa: Peripatetic Press, 1980), p. 29.

[28] *De Genesi ad litteram* IV,iv,8: *BA* 48,290:...*numerus sine numero est, quo formantur omnia, nec formatur ipse....*

[29] *Contra Faustum Manichaeum* XX,7: *PL* XLII,372:...*ratio cognoscendi.*

[30] For *species*, cf. *De Genesi ad litteram* IV,iii,7: *BA* 48,290; *De uera religione* VII,13: *CC* XXXII,196–97; *De natura boni contra Manichaeos* III: *PL* XLII,554; *De trinitate* VI,x,12: *CC* L,242.

[31] *De Genesi ad litteram* IV,iii,7: *BA* 48,290:...*pondus omnem rem ad quietem ac stabilitatem trahit....*

[32] *Contra Faustum Manichaeum* XX,7: *CSEL* XXV,542:...*lex amandi.*

[33] *De Genesi ad litteram* IV,iii,8: *BA* 48,290:...*est pondus uoluntatis et amoris....*

[34] *Metaphysics* XII,7 1072b.

[35] *De trinitate* VI,x,12: *CC* L,242:...*ordinem aliquem petit aut tenet.*

[36] For *ordo*, cf. *De Genesi contra Manichaeos* I,xvi,26: *PL* XXXIV,185–86; *De libero arbitrio* II,xx,54: *CC* XXIX,273; *De uera religione* VII,13: *CC* XXXII,196–97.

[37] For *unum, species, ordo*, cf. *De trinitate* VI,x,12: *CC* L,242.

[38] For *modus, species, ordo*, cf. *De ciuitate dei* XI,xv: *CC* XLVIII,336.

[39] *De ciuitate dei* XII,v: *CC* XLVIII,359:...*modum suum, speciem suam, et quamdam secum pacem suam.*

[40] *Confessiones* IV,xvi,28: *CC* XXVII,54.

[41] See, for example, *Soliloquia* I,iv,9: *CSEL* LXXXIX,15, where Augustine mentions Plotinus by name.

[42] The Aristotelian elements are quite easy to pick out in reading the *Enneads*, especially those which discuss the Intelligence or the Soul, such as IV,iii,27; V,i,10; or V,ix,5. E. O'Brien in *The Essential Plotinus* (repr., Indianapolis: Hackett, 1975) points out some of these elements in his notes on sources.

[43] *De trinitate* VI,x,12: *CC* L,242: *Oportet igitur ut creatorem per ea quae facta sunt intellecta conspicientes cuius in creatura quomodo dignum est apparet uestigium. In illa enim trinitate summa origo est rerum omnium et perfectissima pulchritudo et beatissima delectatio.*

The Giant's Twin Substances:
Ambrose and the Christology of Augustine's
Contra sermonem Arianorum

Brian E. Daley, S.J.

St. Augustine's Christology has not been the object of a great deal of study. Three or four serious books,[1] it is true, and several weighty articles[2] have appeared over the last three and a half decades, discussing Augustine's understanding of the person and work of Christ and adding substantially to the handful of earlier works on the subject.[3] Yet in comparison with the abundance of scholarly works on other aspects of the Bishop of Hippo's thought, the attention paid to his Christology by modern scholarship has been strikingly small.

The reason, undoubtedly, lies to a large extent in the subject itself. Although Augustine's theology and spirituality, taken as a whole, can justly be characterized as Christocentric, technical questions about the identity and achievement of Christ were not subjects of controversy or prolonged investigation for him, in the way that sin and grace, or the reality of the Church, or "the Trinity, which is God" surely were. So aside from several fine Christmas sermons,[4] a short, early refutation of Apollinarian Christology in the *Eighty-Three Various Questions*,[5] and the eloquent apologetic for the notion of an incarnate God that he sent to the senator Volusianus in 412,[6] Augustine generally deals with Christological issues warmly and movingly, but in passing. And while the centrality of Christ's role as mediator between God and the human race, as the "way" of humility leading us to "the humble God,"[7] remains clear from his earliest works, most of what Augustine has to say about the person of Christ is couched in fairly untechnical terms, and seems not to offer a ready analytical hand-hold for the modern interpreter.

The one set of works that offer an exception to this general observation —curiously neglected by scholars, yet an important part of Augustine's later theological development—are his works against the Arians. Not usually regarded as one of his major disputes, Augustine's public controversy with Arian Christians may have begun as early as 406, in a discussion held by the bishop and his friend Alypius with Count Pascentius, an imperial fiscal official[8] who was also an enthusiastic but somewhat confused Arian. After a single meeting, the dialogue was interrupted, and sputtered out in a series of increasingly petulant letters from both sides.[9] Towards the end of his life, Augustine took part in a more professional public disputation with the bishop Maximinus, the accomplished Arian preacher and apologist who seems to have come to Africa, perhaps from Illyria, with the imperial army commanded by the Gothic general Sigisvult in 427.[10] The transcript of their debate, together with the two books Augustine later wrote to refute Maximinus' position, provide us with his most complete treatment of the issues and Scriptural *loci* at stake in the later Arian controversy in the West. But Augustine mounted substantial arguments against the Arian position in a number of other places, too: a letter, of unknown date, to a certain Elpidius, who had sent him an Arian treatise;[11] several of the later *Tractates on John*;[12] Books V–VII of *De trinitate*; and a number of explicitly anti-Arian sermons, none of them, as far as we can tell, delivered earlier than 416.[13] The key work for interpreting and dating all of these efforts, however, is a modest treatise that has not often been studied—an occasional piece, which bears signs of having been hastily written, yet a work that seems to mark both a turning point in his Christological thought and a new assimilation of the anti-Arian polemic of his old mentor, Ambrose of Milan: his little essay *Contra sermonem Arianorum*.[14]

In the second book of his *Retractationes*,[15] Augustine explains the context of this treatise: he has been sent a copy of an anonymous tract setting forth the principles of Arian theology, and has been urgently asked to reply. One of the letters of Augustine recently discovered by Johannes Divjak— *Epistle* 23*A—allows us to specify these circumstances, with cautious certainty, even more closely. Writing to an unnamed correspondent—perhaps his biographer, Possidius of Calama—in December of 419, Augustine there lists the works he has dictated since their return together from Carthage the previous September: an output of some 6000 lines, he says, including "something against the Arians, in reply to what our friend Dionysius sent me from Vicus Juliani."[16] Among Augustine's extant anti-Arian works, only the *Contra sermonem Arianorum* is a direct reply to a document sent to him by a correspondent, so it seems plausible to identify it with the work mentioned in this letter. Although this means dating the *Contra sermonem Arianorum* about a year later than is usually supposed,[17] such a chronology fits smoothly into the general sequence of works given in the *Retractationes*, and sets this treatise, along with *Epistles* 190 and 202A, the first book of *De natura et origine animae*, and some of the *Tractates on John,* in the busy period between September 11 and December 1, 419.[18]

The Arian treatise Dionysius sent Augustine is apparently not so much a discourse or an organically developed tract as a set of propositions or theses, arranged in the general order of the ancient baptismal creeds and explaining in patient detail the anti-homoousian understanding of the relationship of the Son and the Spirit to each other and to the eternal Father. The Arian theology it presents is not the radical, dialectically grounded "anomoean" variety, against which the Cappadocians had aimed their efforts, but the older, more moderate "homoean" strain current among the Goths and represented in Latin, in the late fourth century, by the writings of Palladius of Ratiaria and Maximinus: a theology that recognized both Son and Spirit as truly divine, truly *like* the Father in deserving our worship, but that saw in their missions and their hierarchically ordered relationships, to each other and to the Father, proof that each is different (*alius*) from the others "in nature and rank, position and condition, dignity and power, ability and action."[19]

Augustine's point-by-point, thesis-by-thesis reply to the document's conception of God is brief, but consistent with the position he expounded at such length in the *De trinitate,* the last parts of which he seems to have written shortly after *Contra sermonem Arianorum.*[20] God is radically, indivisibly one, he argues, in nature and operation, even though Father, Son and Spirit may never be confused with one another.[21] "The whole [Trinity], whatever it is, is the ultimate, true, unchangeable God."[22] The distinction of the persons, then, rests not in their works—which they perform as one[23] —but in their relationships of origin;[24] even taking flesh, which is proper to the Son alone, is not a sign of a lesser nature, and is done with the active cooperation of the Father and the Spirit.[25] So Augustine's argument in the treatise moves quickly and inevitably from a consideration of the Arian understanding of God's trinity and unity to the issue of the unity and distinction within the person of Christ. Recognizing that the Arian position, probably since Arius himself, had been largely based on the assumption that a God capable of direct contact with the world—capable of creation and providence, of incarnation and suffering— must be God in a lesser sense than the God of transcendent mystery, Augustine articulates here a portrait of Christ that distinguishes, with a technical precision and a concentration of phrasing infrequent in his earlier works, between a complete human reality and the complete reality of God, both within the unity of a single, acting person.

Augustine begins the section of his treatise that deals directly with the person of Christ—chapters V through XIV—with the observation that what the Arian document in his hands says about the Son assumes "that Christ took up human flesh without a human soul."[26] This is, he says, "the particular heresy of the Apollinarians," but it has always been characteristic of Arian theology as well.[27] In his *De haeresibus*, written in 428, Augustine repeats this point, and says he found it to be true in his own reading and discussions, though he has not found it said against the Arians by any other Catholic writers except Epiphanius.[28] The point is well taken; a strong *logos-sarx* model of the person of Jesus had, in fact, been characteristic of Arian theology since the beginning, and had formed an essential element in their portrait of the Lord as a mediating figure between the transcendent God and the world of fallen creatures.[29] What is curious here is Augustine's apparent surprise at his discovery, since Ambrose had made the same point fairly clearly in his *De incarnationis dominicae sacramento*.[30] And this fact becomes even stranger when one realizes, in reading on in Augustine's treatise, how similar his own terminology and line of argument are to those used by Ambrose himself in his anti-Arian treatises. In the six chapters that follow, Augustine proceeds to refute the propositions in his Arian tract that deal specifically with the human experiences and behavior of Jesus, and does so by insisting over and over that the Biblical evidence shows us not a soulless hybrid, superior to humans in his godlike internal constitution but always subordinate in being to the ultimate God, as the Arian Christ is, but rather that Christ "has joined to the only-begotten Word not only flesh, but also a human soul,"[31] and "that there is one person in both natures—that is, the nature of God and of a human person."[32] The emphasis on the soul of Christ is, of course, not new for Augustine; in *Confessions* VII, for instance, he recalls that while his friend Alypius, in their pre-conversion days, thought all Catholics had an effectively Apollinarian notion of Christ, the two of them already saw clearly that the New Testament presented him as a complete human being.[33] Augustine continued to stress the importance of Christ's human soul throughout his works, especially as the point of contact between the Word and his humanity.[34] What is new here is his explicit, metaphysically precise reflection on the continuing, functional completeness of Christ's human nature, within the unity of a single subject, as a way of showing the continuity between the New Testament evidence and the faith of Nicaea. In doing this, Augustine seems unmistakably to echo, in ways he has not done since his very earliest Catholic writings, the categories and arguments of Ambrose, especially of several passages in his *De fide* and *De incarnationis dominicae sacramento*.

The most obvious clue to a link with Ambrose here is Augustine's reference to Christ as a "twin-substanced giant," *geminae gigas substantiae*,[35] a striking phrase from Ambrose's Christmas hymn, *Veni, redemptor gentium*, which Augustine and later Latin writers delighted in quoting.[36] Giants, to the classical mind, were "sons of the earth," often referred to in Latin poetry, with other mythic monsters, as "composite" (*gemini*) or even "two-bodied," (*bicorpores*) because they combined various characteristics of humans and beasts.[37] Philo saw in the giants of Gn 6:4 a figurative allusion to souls who had left their "better situation" to dwell in an inferior place, by abandoning the path of reason and transforming themselves "into the lifeless and inert nature of flesh," thus becoming "sons of the earth" in a negative sense.[38] So when Ps 18:6, in the old Latin version, referred to the sun's course with the phrase,

> He has come forth like a bridegroom leaving his chamber,
> He has rejoiced, like a giant, to run his way,[39]

the application to Christ, the "sun of justice" who became flesh for us, lay close at hand, particularly since this psalm appears to have been used in the liturgy for the key Christological feasts of Christmas and the Ascension since the late fourth century.[40]

In the mind of Ambrose (who knew both his Latin literature and his Philo), and later of Augustine, it was the Incarnation, the conjunction of the two realities of God and a human being in the intimacy of a single womb and the strenuous course of a single life, that made Christ both "bridegroom" and joyful "giant," Son of God and "son of the earth." Ambrose writes:

> The holy prophet David described him as a giant, because he is one in a double, composite nature, and shares both in divinity and in humanity; "coming forth like a bridegroom from his chamber, he has rejoiced like a giant to run his way": the bridegroom of the soul, according to the phrase, and a giant of the earth, who, passing through all the duties of our way of life, even though he was always the eternal God, took on himself the mysteries of the Incarnation—not divided, but

one, because each element is one person and one person is in
both elements, namely divinity and the body.[41]

The one who had "joined himself to our human nature" like a spouse in his
bridal chamber, Augustine later remarked, then "rejoiced to run the way": "he
was born, he grew, he taught, he suffered, he rose, he ascended—he *ran* the
way, he did not *cling* to the way!"[42] The psalm-verse clearly spoke to both authors of the mystery of the Incarnation, of the earthy vitality of the Lord; yet
for Augustine in the *Contra sermonem Arianorum*, it is not merely the psalm-
verse that comes to mind, apparently, but Ambrose's use of it: not only does
he quote Ambrose's poetic phrase in full, but twice more, in this same section
of the work, he refers to Christ as *gemina substantia...sed una persona*, language otherwise rare in Augustine's Christological terminology.[43]

This Christological part of his treatise has other similarities, too, to arguments of Ambrose in the *De incarnationis dominicae sacramento*: each of
them fairly insignificant in itself, but all significant in their convergence. In
chapter VII, for instance, just before his first reference to the *gemina substantia* in the one person of Christ, Augustine argues: "He revealed that there is
indeed one person in both natures—that is, the natures of God and the human being—lest, if he should make two [persons], there should begin to be a
quaternity, not a trinity."[44] Ambrose, too, in his argument against the Apollinarian Christology of both Arians and Nicenes, had made the same point neg-
atively:

> Nor am I afraid of seeming to introduce a tetrad [i.e., instead
> of a triad or trinity]. For we, who make this profession [of a
> human soul in Christ], worship only a trinity. I do not divide
> Christ, when I distinguish the substance of his flesh from his
> divinity, but I preach one Christ with the Father and the Spir-
> it of God....For he is not one person (*unus*), because he
> shares the same substance, but one thing (*unum*).[45]

Ambrose turns his point in a slightly different direction from Augustine's,
arguing that it is the Apollinarians who, by making the flesh of Christ "one
substance" with God, alongside the Word, seem to be introducing a *quartum
increatum* into the divine Mystery.[46] But it is nonetheless striking that Augustine's echo of his "twin-substance" language should also echo concern to show

that such a conception of Christ does not endanger the Church's Trinitarian confession.

A few paragraphs later, Augustine quotes from the Arian document a curious passage depicting Christ entering the glory of the Father "with his very body, like a shepherd with his sheep and a priest with his offering and a king with his purple garment."[47] He asks, ironically, what kind of sheep this might be: "If it is flesh without a soul that [Christ] brought back [to the Father], what is that sheep but senseless earth, which cannot give thanks? What can flesh do without a soul?"[48] Ambrose, in the same seventh chapter of *De incarnationis dominicae sacramento* that I have just cited, asks a similar question of those who propose a Christ made up of Word and flesh:

> What use would it be to take up flesh without a soul, since after all senseless flesh and an irrational soul are neither susceptible of sin nor worthy of reward? He took up, then, for my sake, what was more seriously endangered in us. What good is it to me, after all, if he did not redeem all of me?[49]

Although Augustine, characteristically, focuses on the ability to give thanks to God as the fulfillment of salvation, the soteriological uselessness of a Christ with human flesh but no human soul is the point of his question as it had been of Ambrose's.

A few paragraphs later, Augustine is replying to the Arian contention that God's command to his Son, "Sit at my right hand," implies—in the very glorification of Christ—obedient subordination. Augustine points out that words such as this, spoken within the Trinity, are always to be taken as metaphors for eternal relationships:

> How, after all, does the Son hear the Father? How are many words said by the Father to the one and only Word? How does he speak in a passing way to the one whom he speaks everlastingly? How does he say something in a temporal way to the one, coeternal with himself, in whom all things were already present which he says at their proper times?[50]

Ambrose, too, in an earlier passage in the *De incarnationis dominicae sacramento,* insists that the Word of God is not to be understood as too closely analogous to temporal, human speech:

> The Son is not such a Word, because the Father of the Word
> is not such a Father. We must be careful, then, not to seem
> to raise in his case a question taken from corporeal speaking:
> God is incorporeal; he does not, then, as incorporeal, have
> corporeal speech. If there is no corporeal speech in the Fa-
> ther, the Son is not a corporeal word. If there is no body in
> the Father, there is no time in the Father; if there is no time
> in the Father, surely there is none in the Son.[51]

This theme of the difference between temporal speech and the wholly internal, bodiless and timeless utterance of the Word of God is, of course, a familiar one in Augustine's works, and need not, of itself, show that he is thinking of Ambrose here.[52] Still, it is worth noting that this argument appears in both treatises in the context of arguments for the equality of Son to Father, and for the necessity of distinguishing between his humanity and his divinity as two complete substances.

Besides these Ambrosian resonances in the specifically Christological part of Augustine's treatise, there are also echoes in the same section, less verbal than structural, but at least as striking, of another anti-Arian work of Ambrose: the second book of his *De fide,* addressed to the emperor Gratian. The Arian treatise Augustine is refuting has begun its own Christological section by asserting that the Incarnation of "the Lord Jesus" is proof of the honor in which God holds his human creatures, whom he has made "a little less than the angels."[53] So God sent the Son to carry out his will and redeem humanity by his death; but the very obedience of Jesus, according to the treatise, also shows his subordination, as divine Son, to the Father. Further, the treatise interprets his death as a separation of his body from the mediating divine Word that took the place, in him, of a human soul. Augustine responds, as we have already said, by a long and complicated argument for the equality of Son and Father based on the distinction of two complete and functioning substances— the divine and the human—within the single subject, Jesus. But the point of his argument, and the scriptural passages on which he bases it, also resemble closely the argument of Ambrose for the completeness and mutual harmony of two wills in Christ, and for the paradoxical unity of the divine and the hu-

Ambrose, *De fide* 41-73

Augustine, *Contra serm. Arian.* V-IX

V. Real texts at issue in Arian debate on Christ:
Heb 2:7 (with Ps 8:5f.);
Jn 14:28;
allusion to Ph 2:7.

41. Mt 26:39: does Gethsemane prayer show Son is not omnipotent?
42-45. He speaks here *quasi homo*.
46. The real problem text is Jn 6:38 (I have come down not to do own will but will of Father). Is Son not free?
47-49. Jn 3:8 shows Spirit is free; Ps 39.9 (I want to do your will) and the miracles of Jesus show Son is free.
50-51. Jn 5:21 shows Father and Son both will to give life.
52-53. Mt 26:39: *alia voluntas hominis, alia dei.* Agony of Jesus reveals his human will and suffering.
54-57. Jesus struggles and suffers in human soul.
58. The paradoxical unity of Christ, revealed in:
    1 Co 2:8 (crucified Lord of glory), and
    Jn 3:13 (Son of Man who descended from heaven).
59-64. - He is less as man:
    Jn 14:28 (Father is greater);
    Ps 21:7; Is. 53:7 (passion)
    Ph 2:5-8 (self-emptying and exaltation);
    Ps 8:5f. and Heb 2:7-9;
65-73. - He is equal as God:
    Jn 5:18f. (made self equal to God);
    Heb 6:13f. (Abraham and Melchisedech);
    Jn 10:30 (I and Father are one).

VI. Arian texts on subordination of Son:
    Ga 4:4 (born of woman);
    Jn 6:38;
    Lk 4:43 (mission of Christ);
    Jn 12:49 (mandate of Father);
    Mt 26:39 (Gethsemane).

VII. Augustine discusses Jesus' contrasting wills:
    Jn 6:38, drawing on
    - Rm 5:12-19 (sinful will of Adam as *propria voluntas contra voluntatem Dei*);
    - 1 Tm 2:5 (as mediator, Jesus has one will with God);
    so the two wills in Christ are those of fallen humanity and God.

VIII. Paradoxical unity of two natures in one person, shown by:
    Jn 3:13;
    1 Co 2:8;
    Ph 2:5-8.
    Contrasted texts, used of one person:
    Jn 14:28;
    Jn 10:30;
    Jn 6:38;
    Jn 5:21.

IX. Gethsemane and Calvary show both human soul and human will in Christ:
    Mt 26:39;
    - texts referring to soul of Christ (Jn 10:18; Jn 15:13; Ps 15:10, cited in Acts);
    - texts using "flesh" to mean "person" (Ps 64:3; Rm 3:20; Ga 3:11);
    Summation: 1 Tm 2:5;
    Jn 14:28;
    Jn 10:30.

Figure 1

man in Christ's single person, which Ambrose developed in *De fide* II,v,41–
ix,73. This similarity is best seen schematically (cf. Figure 1 on the preceding
page).

Although Augustine here is replying to a specific Arian document, with
its own Scriptural proof texts and its own particular assumptions used in interpreting them, it seems striking that he himself relies, to a large extent, on texts
of his own, and that the texts on which he rests most of his argument are in
most cases texts Ambrose used in this section his *De fide*. Similarly, the main
Christological points developed here by Augustine are the points Ambrose
labors to establish in the passage I have cited: the implications of the two complete natures of Christ for the internal struggles of his will, as revealed in
Scripture, and the paradoxical liberty a two-nature Christology gives us to
predicate divine attributes of the man Jesus and human experiences of God
the Son—the structural character of the person of Jesus known by later Christological writers as the "communication of idioms."

One may well ask just what these similarities prove. The Scriptural texts
Augustine draws into the argument here were doubtless familiar from a century of controversy over the relation of Jesus to God, and some—like Jn 10:30
and Jn 14:28—had been classic *testimonia*, evidence that had to be either welcomed or explained away, since the days of Tertullian and Hippolytus. Some
of the likeness between Ambrose's thought and Augustine's on the issues at
hand is also inevitably due to the likeness of their opposition: the Arians Augustine criticized in Africa, in 419 and afterwards, were the successors of the
same Latin-speaking *homoeans* Ambrose had opposed at Sirmium and Aquileia and Rome in the years between 375 and 382, and against whom he directed his earlier polemical tracts; Palladius was their ablest spokesman, and
Maximinus, who later debated with Augustine, Palladius' leading defender.
Inevitably, then, the anti-Arian arguments of Ambrose and Augustine could
be expected to show similarities.

Nevertheless, risky though it always is to speculate on the influence of
one ancient theologian upon another, I want to suggest that Augustine probably had at least these two works of Ambrose—the *De incarnationis dominicae
sacramento* and the first two books of the *De fide*—in mind, and perhaps even
in hand, as he dictated his critique of the Arian manifesto sent to him in the
autumn of 419. In subtle but important ways, the Christology of this brief
treatise marks a change of emphasis from the Christology of his earlier mature works. Augustine had emphasized, certainly, since the early 390s, the
completeness both of the humanity of Jesus—internally and externally, soul

and body—and of his divinity as Word; he saw these two realities as functional, active, yet united in the eternal *persona* of the Wisdom of God.[54] Yet in his works written between the mid-390's and about 412, Augustine usually stresses the transformation and elevation of the human nature of Christ in its assumption by the Word,[55] and sees the human acts of Christ essentially as accomplishing instrumentally, and revealing sacramentally, the divine acts of the Word,[56] much as the body, in Neoplatonic anthropology, acts fundamentally as revealer and instrument of the human being's personal center, the soul.[57]

Concern with the Arian question, however, began to be a real issue for Augustine around 413, if not before,[58] and this seems to have brought with it a clearer understanding that the human experiences and human reality of Christ had to be distinguished more unambiguously, more metaphysically, from his divine nature, as somehow coordinate and mutually complementary within the subjective unity of his person, if one were not to be drawn into the Arian error of conceiving the Word as limited by the created bounds of the human being he assumed, as made less than God by his very identity with a human soul and body. So it is in the *Enarratio* on Psalm 93, delivered at Thagaste in the summer of 414, that Augustine—without referring to the Arians—elaborates seriously for the first time on the two complete wills in Christ, revealed in his struggle at Gethsemane;[59] and it is in these same years that he comes to speak more reflectively on the paradox of the reciprocal predication of divine and human attributes for the two natures in Christ—what has come to be known as the *communicatio idiomatum*—a procedure that presupposes a structural symmetry in the constitution of the Incarnate Word.[60]

With the *Contra sermonem Arianorum*, we find the first full-scale articulation, in precise language, of this new Christological perspective. Not only does Augustine use here—three times—Ambrose's picturesque phrase *gemina substantia* for the two realities in Christ: a formula echoing the older Latin tradition of Tertullian's *Adversus Praxean* but not found, to my knowledge, in Augustine's earlier works.[61] He also insists here, more clearly than before, on the reality of Christ's two wills and the propriety of *communicatio idiomatum* language as concrete, existential implications of these two natures or substances.[62] The "one person," who is Christ, is now presented unabashedly as "Word and human being; but that human being is soul and flesh, and for this reason Christ is Word, soul and flesh."[63] True, this same way of expressing the mystery of Christ's person appears in one of Augustine's earliest sermons: *Sermon* 214, *In traditione symboli*, delivered at Easter 391, shortly after his ordination as a presbyter. There, too, the principle of the *communicatio idiomatum* is both enunciated and applied.[64] But the earliest works of Augustine, in their presentation of the doctrines of the Trinity and the person of Christ, show similarities to the thought of Ambrose that would not emerge again with such clarity until Arianism became for him, as it had been for Ambrose, a matter of direct concern.[65]

The balance and metaphysical clarity of Augustine's picture of Christ in the *Contra sermonem Arianorum*, a balance that continues in his later *Sermons* and *Tractates on John*, seems perhaps less "Augustinian" than the strongly integrated, explicitly Word-centered Christ of his works from the mid-390s on; yet this model of Christ anticipates more clearly than those earlier writings do the Christological symmetry of Leo and Chalcedon, a point that may explain Leo's direct use of the work in his *Tome to Flavian*.[66] And while Augustine makes no explicit mention of Ambrose in this treatise—he seldom does acknowledge his theological debts publicly, after all—still the clearest inspiration for such a symmetrical portrait of Christ, a portrait that stressed the parallel completeness of his substances or natures rather than the central dominance of the Word, was to be found in the early writings of the great bishop of Milan, developed and perhaps even invented by him as a weapon against the Arians.[67] As Augustine struggled to meet the challenge posed by the specious attractiveness of an Arian Christ, it seems more than likely that he turned again to a Christological model he had used in the early years of his ministry, and reached for the treatises, as well as the familiar hymn, of the anti-Arian bishop of Milan, whose faith had reshaped his own at the time of his conversion. It was Ambrose's giant now, not simply the self-emptying Word and the humble mediator of Augustine's earlier mature writings, who was to "run the way" of fifth-century Western Christology.

Notes

[1] The most thorough and important study of Augustine's Christology remains that of T. J. Van Bavel, *Recherches sur la christologie de saint Augustin* (Paradosis 10; Fribourg: Editions universitaires, 1954). Also important are W. Geerlings, *Christus Exemplum. Studien zur Christologie und Christusverkündigung Augustins* (Mainz: Grünewald, 1978); G. Remy, *Le Christ médiateur dans l'oeuvre de S. Augustin*, 2 vols. (Paris: Champion, 1979); H. Dröbner, *Personexegese und Christologie bei Augustinus* (Leiden: Brill, 1986).

[2] Among recent articles on Augustine's Christology, see especially J. T. Newton, "The Importance of Augustine's Use of the Neoplatonic Doctrine of Hypostatic Union for the Development of Christology," *AS* 2 (1971) 1–16; B. Studer, "Le Christ, notre justice,

selon S. Augustin," *Recherches Augustiniennes* 15 (1980) 99–143, and "'Una Persona in Christo.' Ein augustinisches Thema bei Leo dem Grossen," *Augustinianum* 25 (1985) 453–87; G. Bonner, "Christ, God and Man in the Thought of St. Augustine," *Angelicum* 61 (1984) 268–94. See also my survey, "A Humble Mediator: The Distinctive Elements in St. Augustine's Christology," *Word and Spirit* 9 (1987) 100–117.

³ Aside from brief treatments in standard works on the history of dogma, the main earlier study is the controversial book of Otto Scheel, *Die Anschauung Augustins über Christi Person und Werk* (Tübingen: J. C. B. Mohr, 1901).

⁴ *Sermones CLXXXIV–CXCVI*: *PL* XXXIII,995–1021. Sermons 190 and 196 seem to date from the 390s; the rest were probably delivered between 410 and 416. In citing works of Augustine, I will give the date, when known, in square brackets immediately after the chapter numbers.

⁵ *De diuersis quaestionibus LXXXIII*, q. 80 [c. 395]: *CC* XLIV/A,232–38. Several other of these questions deal with the relation of Jesus to the Father, in terms that suggest Augustine is thinking of the Arian controversy, although he nowhere mentions the Arians by name: see Qq. 16, 23, 37, 50, 60 and 69: *CC* XLIV/A,21,27f.,59,77,184–96 (esp. 185,53f.; 193,204–11; 194f,230–41).

⁶ *Epistula CXXXVII* [412]: *CSEL* XLIV,96–125.

⁷ See, for example, *Confessiones* VII,xviii,24 [397–401]: *CC* XXVII,108; *De catechizandis rudibus* IV,8 [399]: *CC* XLVI,129; *Sermo CCLXI* 7 [Ascension, 410]: *PL* XXXVIII, 1206; *De ciuitate dei* XI,ii [417]: *CC* XLVIII,322.

⁸ Possidius, *Vita Augustini* 17, tells us that Pascentius was *comes domus regiae* and a *fisci vehementissimus exactor* (*PL* XXXII,47,14ff.). For a discussion of what actual office Pascentius may have held, see J. R. Martindale, *The Prosopography of the Later Roman Empire* II (Cambridge: Cambridge University Press, 1980), pp. 834f.

⁹ *Epistulae CCXXXVIII–CCXLI*: *CSEL* LVII, 533–62.

¹⁰ For Maximinus' career, see M. Meslin, *Les ariens d'occident* (Paris: Editions du Seuil, 1967), pp. 92–96; M. Hanssens, "Massimino il Visigoto," *La Scuola Cattolica* 102 (1974) 474–514. For a general discussion of Augustine's controversies with Arians, see M. Simonetti, "Agostino e gli Ariani," *REA* (1967) 55–84; W. A. Sumruld, *Augustine's Theological Opposition to the Gothic Arians, AD 418–430* (unpublished dissertation, Southwestern Baptist Theological Seminary, 1985).

¹¹ *Epistula CCXLII*: *CSEL* LVII, 563–67.

¹² The most important anti-Arian passages in the *Tractates on John* are Tractates 18; 20 (both on Jn 5:19); 26,5–10 (on Jn 6:41–59); and 71 (on Jn 14:10–14). The first three of these are usually dated in 413, the last 418: see S. Zarb, "Chronologia operum Sancti Augustini," *Angelicum* 10 (1933) 50–110; 359–96; 478–512; 11 (1934) 78–91. Because of similarities of argument in some passages to the *Contra sermonem Arianorum*, Anne-Marie La Bonnardière dates all the *Tractates* from 24 on after 418: *Recherches de chronologie Augustinienne* (Paris: Études Augustiniennes, 1965), pp. 72–118. However, if the newly discovered

Epistle 23*A is, as seems likely, referring to the *Contra sermonem Arianorum* as one of the works Augustine wrote in the autumn of 419 (see below), La Bonnardière's *terminus a quo* will have to be moved back a further year.

[13] *Sermo CXVII* 6–17 [418]; *Sermo CXXXV* 2–5 [417]; *Sermo CXXXIX* [416–18]; *Sermo CXL* against Maximinus [Christmas 427 or 428]; *Sermo CLXXXIII* [after 416]; *Sermo CCXXVI* [416–17]; *Sermo CCCXLI* [December 12, 418]; *Sermo CCCLXXX* 3–6 [June 24, 417]; *Sermo Guelferbytanus XVII* [421–23]. See La Bonnardière 96f., 111.

[14] *PL* XLII,683–708.

[15] *Retractationes* II,lii [426/27]: *CSEL* XXXVI,188f.

[16] *Epistula XXIII*A* (ed., Divjak): *CSEL* LXXXVIII,122,12f:...*dictaui contra Arrianos ad illud quod mihi Dionysius noster de Vico Iuliani miserat.* Dionysius is otherwise unknown; Vicus Iuliani is about 25 miles from Hippo.

[17] See, for example, Meslin, *Les ariens d'occident*, pp. 132ff.; La Bonnardière, *Recherches*, pp. 96ff.

[18] For this chronology, as well as the identification of references in the letter, see the notes of Robert B. Eno in *Saint Augustine, Letters VI (1*–29*)* FC 81,165–67. I am grateful to Fr. George Lawless, OSA, for directing me to this passage in Epistle 23*A.

[19] *Sermo Arianorum* 31: *PL* XLII,681f: *Alium esse [Spiritum] a Filio, et natura et ordine, gradu et affectu, dignitate et potestate, virtute et operatione, sicut et Filius natura et ordine, gradu et affectu, divina dignitate et potestate, unigenitus Deus alius est ab ingenito Deo.* On the theology of the Western Arians in the late fourth and early fifth century, see the works of Meslin and Simonetti, and R. P. C. Hanson, "The Arian Doctrine of the Incarnation," in R. C. Gregg (ed.), *Arianism: Historical and Theological Reassessments* (Patristic Monograph Series 11; Cambridge, MA: Philadelphia Patristic Foundation, 1985), pp. 181–211. For a careful portrait of Homoean Arianism, Western and Eastern, see R. P. C. Hanson, *The Search for the Christian Doctrine of God* (Edinburgh: T. and T. Clark, 1988), pp. 557–97.

[20] See La Bonnardière, 75, 111, 166f., where she argues that at least *De trinitate* II,iii,5 and XV,xx,38 reflect arguments already set forth in *Contra sermonem Arianorum*.

[21] *Contra sermonem Arianorum* XV,9: *PL* XLII,694,53–695,2.

[22] *Contra sermonem Arianorum* XXVII,23: *PL* XLII,702,33f: *Totum quidquid illud est, summum, verum, immutabilem Deum.*

[23] *Contra sermonem Arianorum* XV–XVI, 9: *PL* XLII,694,4–696,3.

[24] See, for instance, *Contra sermonem Arianorum* XIV,9; XV,9; XXIII,19: *PL* XLII, 693,19–25; 694,4–695,2; 700,9–21.

[25] *Contra sermonem Arianorum* XV,9: *PL* XLII,695,4–24.

[26] *Contra sermonem Arianorum* V,5: *PL* XLII,686,54ff:...*hoc volunt intellegi, quod humanam carnem sine humana anima Christus assumpserit.*

[27] *Contra sermonem Arianorum* V,5: *PL* XLII,686,56–687,1:...*quae propria haeresis Apollinaristarum est: sed etiam istos, id est, Arianos, in eorum disputationibus, non solum Trinitatis diversas esse naturas, sed etiam hoc sentire deprehendimus, quod animam non habeat Christus humanam.*

[28] *De haeresibus* 49: *CC* XLVI,321,6–11; for Epiphanius' treatment of the same point, see *Ancoratus* 35: *GCS* 1,44; *Panarion* 69,60,1f.: *GCS* 3,208f.

[29] For a thorough discussion of the role of this Christological model in the development of Arian theology in East and West, see especially Hanson, "The Arian Doctrine of the Incarnation" (above, note 19).

[30] *De incarnationis dominicae sacramento* VI,49: *CSEL* LXXIX,249.

[31] *Contra sermonem Arianorum* IX,7: *PL* XLII,690,16ff.:...*fateanturque Christum non tantum carnem, sed animam quoque humanam Verbo unigenito coaptasse.*

[32] *Contra sermonem Arianorum* VII,6: *PL* XLII,688,16ff.: *Unam quippe ostendit esse personam in utraque natura, hoc est, Dei et hominis....*

[33] *Confessiones* VII,xix,25: *CC* XXVII,108,7–109,30.

[34] For references, see Van Bavel, pp. 51–54; Daley, "A Humble Mediator," 102ff.

[35] *Contra sermonem Arianorum* VIII,6: *PL* XLII,689,27.

[36] The fifth strophe of the hymn is as follows:

> *Procedat e thalamo suo,*
> *pudoris aula regia,*
> *geminae gigans substantiae;*
> *alacris occurrat viam.*

For the text of the hymn and a full discussion of the literary questions surrounding it, see A. S. Walpole, *Early Latin Hymns* (Cambridge: Cambridge University Press, 1922), pp. 50–57; M. Simonetti, *Studi sull' innologia popolare cristiana dei primi secoli* (Atti dell'accademia nazionale dei Lincei VIII,4,6: Rome, 1952), pp. 382–87. Both Simonetti and Walpole regard this hymn as certainly by Ambrose; Simonetti dates it around 385–87, because of its anti-Arian content (see Paulinus, *Vita Ambrosii* 13; Augustine, *Confessiones* IX,vii,15 on the origin of Ambrose's composition of hymns). For the later use of the phrase *geminae gigas substantiae*, see J. De Ghellinck, "Note sur l'expression 'Geminae Gigas Substantiae'," *Recherches de science religieuse* 5 (1914) 416–21.

[37] See, for instance, the reference to Runcus and Purpureus, "sons of the earth," as *bicorpores gigantes* in Naevius, *De Bello Punico* I, Frag. 19 (20): ed. W. Morel, *Fragmenta Poetarum Latinorum Epicorum et Lyricorum* (Stuttgart: Teubner, 1963), p. 20. For references to centaurs, Triton the merman, and the Minotaur (half bull, half man) as *gemini*, see, e.g., Ovid, *Metamorphoses* XII,449; Manilius, *Astronomica* II,552; IV,785; Seneca, *Medea* 641; Statius, *Thebaid* V,707; *Silvae* I,iv,98.

[38] Philo, *De gigantibus* XV,65; cf. XIII,60.

[39] *Et ipse tamquam sponsus procedens de thalamo suo;*
      exultavit sicut gigas (gigans) ad currendam viam....

[40] For the use of Ps 18:6 in the liturgy of both feasts, see Augustine, *Sermones CCCLXXII* 2 (Christmas) and *CCCLXXVII* (Ascension): *PL* XXXIX,1662 and 1672. Both sermons are listed among the *sermones dubii* of Augustine, but are probably from the early fifth century; *Sermo CCCLXXII* 3 alludes to the fact that the congregation has just sung the Ambrosian hymn containing this expression (*PL* XXXIX,1663,25–31). In the pre-Vatican II Latin liturgy, Ps 18:6 appeared in both the Gradual and the Communion antiphon for the Ember Saturday in Advent, in antiphons for both Matins and Second Vespers of Christmas Day, in a responsory for the feast of the Visitation, and in an antiphon for matins on the feast of the Ascension: see C. Marbach, *Carmina Scripturarum* (Strassburg, 1907), *ad loc.*

[41] *De incarnationis dominicae sacramento* V,35: *CSEL* LXXIX,240f.,10–19: *Quem quasi gigantem sanctus David propheta describit, eo quod biformis geminaeque naturae unus sit, consors divinitatis et corporis, qui "tamquam sponsus procedens de thalamo suo exultavit tamquam gigans ad currendam viam," sponsus animae secundum verbum, gigans terrae, quia usus nostri officia percurrens, cum deus semper esset aeternus, incarnationis sacramenta suscepit, non divisus, sed unus, quia utrumque unus et unus in utroque, hoc est vel divinitate vel corpore.* For Augustine's similar interpretation of the verse, see *Enarratio in Psalmum XVIII, Sermo I* 6 [392]: *CC* XXXVIII,103,9–12; *Enarratio in Psalmum XVIII, Sermo II* 6 [411/412]: *CC* XXXVIII, 109,27–110,34; *Enarratio in Psalmum XLIV* 3 [403]: *CC* XXXVIII,495,14–17; *Enarratio in Psalmum LXXXVII* 10 [414/416]: *CC* XXXIX,1215,36–40; *Confessiones* IV,xii, 19 [397–401] *CC* XXVII,50,22–25; *De consensu evangelistarum* I,xxx,46 [400]: *CSEL* XLIII, 47,7–11; *In Ioannis Epistulam ad Parthos tractatus* I,2 [407?]: *PL* XXXV,1979,28–40. Following the Psalm, Augustine usually emphasizes the strength implied in the image of the giant, rather than his earthiness.

[42] *Enarratio in Psalmum XVIII, Sermo II* 6 [411–12]: *CC* XXXVIII,110,31–34: *Hoc est enim "gigas exultauit ad currendam uiam": natus est, creuit, docuit, passus est, resurrexit, ascendit; cucurrit uiam, non haesit in uia.* Compare his interpretation in the "dubious" Christmas sermon mentioned above: *Sermo CCCLXXII* 2: *PL* XXXIX,1662: *"Processus ut sponsus," "exultavit ut gigas." Pulcher et fortis: pulcher ut sponsus, fortis ut gigas. Pulcher, ut ametur; fortis, ut timeatur; pulcher ut placeret, fortis ut vinceret....*

[43] *Contra sermonem Arianorum* VII,6: *PL* XLII,688,19f: *Quoniam itaque gemina quidem substantia, sed una persona est...*; ibid. IX,7: *PL* XLII,690,16–22: *fateanturque Christum non tantum carnem sed animam quoque humanam Verbo unigenito coaptasse, ut esset una persona; quod Christus est Verbum et homo, sed ipse homo anima et caro, ac per hoc Christus Verbum, anima et caro. Et ideo sic intelligendus geminae substantiae, divinae scilicet et humanae....* On Augustine's use of *substantia* for speaking of the underlying divine and human realities in Christ, a term going back to Tertullian, see Van Bavel, p. 45; V. Bourke, *Augustine's View of Reality* (Villanova, PA: Villanova University Press, 1964); for the background and implications of this and related terms, see A. De Halleux, "'Hypostase' et 'Personne' dans la formation du dogme Trinitaire (ca. 375–81)," *Revue d'histoire ecclésiastique* 79 (1984) 313–69, 625–70.

[44] *Contra sermonem Arianorum* VII,6: *PL* XLII,688,16–19: *Unam quippe ostendit esse personam in utraque natura, hoc est, Dei et hominis, ne si duas faciat, quaternitas incipiat esse, non trinitas.* For a similar argument, also in the context of "two-substance" language about Christ, see Augustine, *Sermo CXXX* 3: *PL* XXVIII,727,10–12 (see below, n. 60).

45 *De incarnationis dominicae sacramento* VII,77: *CSEL* LXXIX,263,140–48: *Nec timeo, ne "tetrada" videar inducere. Nos enim vere solam, qui hoc adserimus, colimus trinitatem. Non enim Christum divido, cum carnis eius divinitatisque distinguo substantiam, sed unum Christum cum patre et spiritu dei praedico.... Non enim, quod eiusdem substantiae est, unus, sed unum est.*

46 Ibid. 77f.

47 *Contra sermonem Arianorum* X,8: *PL* XLII,690,50ff.: ...*cum ipso corpore, ut pastor cum ove, et sacerdos cum oblatione, et rex cum purpura.*

48 *Contra sermonem Arianorum* X,8: *PL* XLII,690,52–57: *Quaerendum est ab eis qui ista dicunt, qualem ovem pastor reportaverit Patri. Si enim caro sine anima est quam reportavit, quid est ovis ista nisi terra sine sensu, quae nec agere gratias potest? Quia sine anima caro quid potest?*

49 *De incarnationis dominicae sacramento* VII,68: *CSEL* LXXIX,259,63–67: *Quid autem opus fuit carnem suscipere sine anima, cum utique insensibilis caro et inrationabilis anima nec peccato sit obnoxia nec digna praemio? Illud ergo pro nobis suscepit, quod in nobis amplius periclitabatur. Quid autem mihi prode est, si totum me non redemit?*

50 *Contra sermonem Arianorum* XII,9: *PL* XLII,692,20–26: *Quomodo autem Filius audit Patrem? quomodo dicuntur a Patre multa verba unico Verbo? quomodo transeunter loquitur ei quem stabiliter loquitur? quomodo aliquid temporaliter ei dicit in quo sibi coaeterno jam erant omnia quae congruis quibusque temporibus dicit?*

51 *De incarnationis dominicae sacramento* III,19f.: *CSEL* LXXIX,233,63–69: ...*non tale verbum filius, quia non talis est pater verbi. Cavendum ergo, ne et illi quaestionem vocis corporalis videamur inferre: incorporeus est deus; vocem utique incorporeus corporalem non habet. Si vox corporalis non est in patre, nec filius verbum est corporale. Si corpus in patre non est, nec tempus in patre est; si tempus in patre non est,utique nec in verbo est....*

52 See, e.g., *Sermo CXIX* 7: *PL* XXXVIII,675f. [date uncertain].

53 *Contra sermonem Arianorum* V,5: *PL* XLII,686,43–54.

54 See, for instance, *Expositio epistulae ad Galatas* 27 [394/95]: *PL* XXXV,2125,3–9; *De agone christiano* XX,22 [396]: *CSEL* XLI,122f.; *De consensu evangelistarum* I,xxxv,53 [c. 400]: *CSEL* XLIII,59. On Augustine's use of the terms "nature" and "person" to express the union of the divine and the human in Christ, see Van Bavel, pp. 13–23, 47–57.

55 For references, see Van Bavel, p. 53; referring to this elevation and perfection of the human nature assumed by the Word, Van Bavel asserts: "Plus que n'importe quel Père avant lui, saint Augustin insiste sur ce point" (ibid.).

56 See, e.g., *De diuersis quaestionibus LXXXIII*, q. 73,2: *CC* XLIV/A,211,45–212,67; for further references, see Van Bavel, p. 64f.

57 For his instrumental conception of the body in his earlier writings, see, e.g., *De moribus ecclesiae catholicae et de moribus Manichaeorum* I,xxvii,52 [387/89]: *PL* XXXII, 1332,46f.; *De quantitate animae* XIII,22 [387/88]: *CSEL* LXXIX,158,6ff. Augustine con-

tinued, throughout his life, to conceive of the union of Word and human being in the Incarnation on the analogy of the union of soul with body: see, e.g., *Epistula CXXXVII* [411/12]: *CSEL* XLIV, 96–125. The purpose of the Incarnation is to help our human weakness "see" the divine Word (*Sermo CCCXLI* 3, *contra Arianos* [418/19]: *PL* XXXIX,1495,7–10); Jesus' humanity is the "ass" on which the Word, like the Good Samaritan, lays the wounded body of humanity (e.g., *Sermo CXIX* 7: *PL* XXXVIII,676,1–3; *Sermo CCCXLI* 3 [418/19]: *PL* XXXIX,1495,12–15). See also Geerlings, pp. 110–14.

[58] See Tractates 18 and 20 on the Gospel of John, usually dated about 413, which deal directly with the Arian interpretation of the relation of the Son to the Father, in connection with Jn 5:19.

[59] *Enarratio in Psalmum XCIII* 19: *CC* XXXIX,1319–21.

[60] See, for instance, *De peccatorum meritis et remissione* I,xxxi,60 [411]: *CSEL* LX,61, 1–8; *Epistula CLXXXVII* 3,9 [417]: *CSEL* LVII,88; *Tractatus in Euangelium Ioannis* XXVII, 4; CXI,2 [after 418?]: *CC* XXXVI,271,11–30; 629,11–14; *Contra Maximinum* II,xx,3: *PL* XLII,789f. See Van Bavel, p. 57.

[61] *Sermo CXXX* 3: *PL* XXXVIII,727,8–10, speaks of *duae substantiae, sed una persona* in Christ, but the date of this sermon is uncertain. Augustine uses the phrase *gemina substantia* in *Tractatus in Euangelium Ioannis* LIX,3 (an anti-Arian passage, using Ambrose's phrase directly), and *Tractatus* LXXVIII,3, both passages presumably from after 418, and in the late anti-Arian work, *Contra Maximinum* II,x,2: *PL* XLII,765. For his reservations about the use of *substantia*-language for the persons in God, because of its suggestion of the possibility of accidents and its identification both with universal reality (= Greek *ousia*) and with concrete individuals (= Greek *hypostasis*), see *De trinitate* V,ii,3–iii,4; V, viii–ix,10; VII,iv,7–vi,11: *CC* L,207ff., 216f., 255–65; La Bonnardière suggests these books also, which deal directly with Arian arguments, may have been composed as late as 418.

[62] See *Contra sermonem Arianorum* VII,6–VIII,6: *PL* XLII,687,38–689,35. For a formulation of the principle of the "communication of idioms," note the following: *Hanc unitatem personae Christi Jesu Domini nostri, sic ex natura utraque constantem, divina scilicet atque humana, ut quaelibet earum vocabulum etiam alteri impertiat, et divina humanae, et humana divinae, beatus ostendit Apostolus…. Ergo et illa divinitas hujus humanitatis nomen accepit…. et ista humanitas illius divinitatis nomen accepit. Apparet tamen idem ipse Christus, geminae gigas substantiae, secundum quid obediens, secundum quid aequalis Deo; secundum quid Filius hominis, secundum quid Filius Dei….* Ambrose's phrase seems to be, for Augustine here, the picturesque summary of the principle of reciprocal predication.

[63] *Contra sermonem Arianorum* IX,7: *PL* XLII,690,16–21 (repunctuated): *Fateanturque [sc. Ariani] Christum non tantum carnem, sed animam quoque humanam Verbo unigenito coaptasse, ut esset una persona; quod Christus est Verbum et homo, sed ipse homo anima et caro, ac per hoc Christus Verbum anima et caro.* For further argument that Augustine's conception of the *una persona* in Christ takes on a new, more metaphysically precise connotation in his anti-Arian works after 418, see Basil Studer, "Una Persona in Christo. Ein augustinisches Thema bei Leo dem Grossen," *Augustinianum* 25 (1985) 453–87.

[64] *Cum enim sit totus Filius Dei unicus Dominus noster Iesus Christus Verbum et homo, atque ut expressius dicam, Verbum, anima, et caro; ad totum refertur quod in sola anima tristis fuit usque ad mortem* (Mt 26:38); *quia Filius Dei unicus Iesus Christus tristis fuit, ad totum refertur quod in solo homine crucifixus est...: PL* XXXVIII,1068. This same formula, that the person of Christ is *Verbum, anima et caro,* appears later in the *Tractates on the Gospel of John,* which seem to have been written after the *Contra sermonem Arianorum:* see, e.g., *Tractatus in Euangelium Ioannis* XXVII,4; XLVII,10–11: *CC* XXXVI,271, 410.

[65] For a discussion of the similarity to Ambrose's Christology in the earliest works of Augustine, up to *De fide et symbolo* [393], see C. Basevi, "Alle fonti della dottrina agostiniana dell'incarnazione: l'influenza della cristologia di Sant'Ambrogio," *Scripta Theologica* 7 (1975) 499–529.

[66] Without mentioning his source, Leo cites *Contra sermonem Arianorum* VIII,6: *PL* XLII,688,37–51 in the *Tome,* Ep. 28,5 (*PL* LIV,771 A9–B5). There are also echoes of *Contra sermonem Arianorum* VII,6: *PL* XLII,688.6–25 in chapter 3 of the *Tome* (*PL* LIV,763 A12–B8).

[67] For the suggestion that Ambrose is the first writer to use a clear two-nature/one-person conception of Christ specifically as a polemical weapon against the Arians, see L. Herrmann, "Ambrosius von Mailand als Trinitätstheologe," *Zeitschrift für Kirchengeschichte* 69 (1958) 212.

Augustine and Gregory of Nyssa:
Is the Triune God Infinite in Being?

Leo Sweeney, S.J.

It seems one may appropriately study Augustine (354–430) and Gregory of Nyssa (ca. 331–95) in a single paper in the light of Bernard C. Barmann's remarks: Nyssa deserves "to be ranked among the truly leading Christian philosophers and...as one of the greatest minds produced by the Christian East .... The Christian philosophy of Nyssa in the East marks an achievement as significant as that of Augustine in the West."[1]

Let us begin with the Greek author, who antedates the Latin Father by a couple of decades and whose answer as to whether God's very being is infinite is clearly "yes"—a clarity arising because of the manner in which the Arians had formulated the question. Both Arius and Eunomius discussed the Trinity in terms of "being": the divine Being consists (so they say) in Unbegottenness, and thus, only the Father is God. In replying, Gregory had to speak in terms of "being" too—God, although triune in really distinct persons, is also one Being, with which the three persons are identical: they are *homoousioi*. Within the parameters of debate drawn by the Arians, then, a Neoplatonic God who is nonbeing because beyond being obviously would not do.[2] Nor would anything less than an infinity consonant with God as supreme Being suffice: in His very entity He is infinitely perfect.

The Arian formulation of the problem in terms of "being" or "essence" (*ousia*) and Gregory's reply in similar terms will set the stage for investigating Augustine, who might be expected to reply in a similar fashion in his *De trinitate*.

First let us consider one of the many texts in which Gregory sets forth his understanding of how the triune God of Father, Son and Holy Spirit is infinite in being, as well as in goodness, wisdom, power, love, and truth. Such a text is *Contra Eunomium* Book I, ch. 19, where we shall first outline its context, to be followed by its translation or paraphrase, which in turn issues into a commentary.

Contra Eunomium, Book I, ch. 19[3]

The context for this capital text will be twofold: remote (historical facts on the Trinitarian heresies Gregory faced and on relevant documents) and proximate (the movement of thought in Gregory's response to Eunomius).

Remote context. (a) Arianism, which takes its name from Arius of Alexandria (c. 250–336), has as its fundamental tenet "that the Son of God is a creature" and receives the title "God" only in a moral sense and by participation; the Son was not begotten out of the substance or entity (*ousia*) of the Father but was made out of nothing. The Holy Spirit is subordinate to the Son.[4]

(b) Eunomius, who was bishop of Cyzicus for a short time (c. 360) and died in 394, held a theory describable as Neo-Arianism: the very essence or being (*ousia*) of God is unbegottenness (*agennesia*) and thus only the Father is God; His operation (*energeia*) begot the Son (*ergon*), who is less than the Father; the Son's operation or *energeia* produced the Holy Spirit (*ergon*), who is less than the Son and, of course, the Father. Neither Son nor Spirit is identical in *ousia* with God the Father.[5]

(c) The stages of debate between Eunomius and the Cappadocians and the relevant documents are as follows.

(1) Eunomius, *Apologia*, written c. 360, to explain and defend his position;[6]

(2) Basil of Caesarea, *Adversus Eunomium* (Books I–III), c. 363;

(3) Eunomius, *Apologia apologiae* (Books I and II), c. 378;

(4) Gregory of Nyssa, *Contra Eunomium* (Books I and II), c. 380–81;

(5) Eunomius, *Apologia apologiae* (Book III), c. 382;

(6) Gregory, *Contra Eunomium* (Book III), c. 383.

(d) The text of Gregory about to be investigated is taken from *Contra Eunomium* named above in (c) (4) and edited by Werner Jaeger.[7]

Proximate context. (e) Gregory's ch. 19 depends upon ch. 13, where he quotes Eunomius: "The whole account of our doctrines is summed up thus. There is the supreme and absolute being (*ousia*), and another being (*ousia*) existing by reason of the first but after it, though prior to all others; and a third being (*ousia*) not ranking with either of these but inferior to the one [the Father] as to its cause, and to the other [the Son] as to the operation which produced it."[8]

(f) He begins ch. 19 by again turning to Eunomius: "Each of those beings (*ousiai*) [Father, Son, Holy Spirit] is absolutely simple and totally one when considered according to its own proper worth [and nature]; and since operations are circumscribed by their products, which in turn are commensurate with the operations, one must conclude that the operations which are consequent upon each being are greater and lesser—the former pertain to beings of first rank, the latter to those of second rank."[9]

(g) What Eunomius proposes, Gregory adds, is to establish that the Father has no connection (*synapheia*) with the Son or the Son with the Spirit; rather they are *ousiai* which are separate from one another and possess natures foreign and unfamiliar to each other. Besides this they differ also in the magnitude and unequal ranking of [the perfections which constitute] their worth and in other such ways.[10]

(h) Accordingly (Gregory warns), let us not be taken in: by his words Eunomius makes the underlying being (*ousia*) of each [person] be different from that of the others so that he is speaking of several entities (*ousiai*), each with its own unique differences which alienate them from one another.[11]

Key Text[12]

[1] But let us again examine Eunomius' words, "Each of those entities or beings (*ousiai*) is simple and totally one." Of course they are: the divine and blessed nature is simple—how can anyone conceive of that which is formless, entirely structureless and separate from quantified mass to be multiform and composite? *Contra Eunomium* I,231:

... τὴν γὰρ ἀειδῆ τε καὶ ἀσχημάτιστον πηλικότητός τε πάσης καὶ τῆς ἐν τῷ μεγέθει ποσότητος κεχωρισμένην πῶς ἄν τις πολυειδῆ καὶ σύνθετον ὑπολάβοι;[13]

[2] In fact, this description of the supreme Being as "simple" is inconsistent with the rest of his system. Who does not realize that simplicity with reference to the Holy Trinity does not admit of more or less? There one does not think of a mixture or confluence of qualities but rather we intellectually grasp their power which is without parts and is incomposite—how can one be aware there of any differentiation of more and less? [3] For to mark differences somewhere one must be aware of qualities in a subject underlying them —e.g., differences of largeness and smallness re quantity or differences

through abundance and lessening of goodness, power, wisdom or other such factors worthy of application to God.

[4] But in neither case [i.e., of quantitative or qualitative differences] can one escape the notion of composition, for nothing which possesses wisdom or power or any other good by reason of what it is by nature and not as a gift from outside can allow a lessening in such perfections. [5] The result is that if anyone says he detects smaller and greater beings in the divine nature, he is surreptitiously making what is divine be composed of dissimilar parts in such a way that he conceives of the subject as one constituent, what is participated as another—by participating in this latter that which was not good before becomes so now.

[6] If he had been thinking of Being which is really simple and entirely one and of Being which is good as it is itself and not by becoming so through acquisition, he would not be computing it in terms of more or less.

[7] As we said above,[14] the good can be lessened only by the presence of evil and where there is a nature which is incapable of deteriorating, there is no conceivable limit to its goodness, [8] for the unlimited (*to aoriston*) is not such because of a relationship to anything else but, considered precisely in itself, it escapes limit. How can anyone reflect accurately and think one infinity to be greater or less than another infinity? [9] Consequently, if he acknowledges that the supreme Being is simple and self-consistent, then let him also grant that it combines and associates simplicity and infinity. [10] But if he divides and estranges the Beings from each other so that the Only Begotten is an *ousia* other than the Father's and that of the Spirit is other than the Only Begotten's inasmuch as he attributes a more and less to them, then let his hidden snares not deceive us: he verbally attributes simplicity, but in reality he fraudulently inserts composition into God.[15] The Greek for [5]–[6] and [8]–[9] of the key text, *Contra Eunomium* I,234–35, 236–37:

> ...ὥστε ὁ λέγων ἐλάττους τε καὶ μείζους ἐν τῇ θείᾳ φύσει
> καταλαμβάνειν τὰς οὐσίας λέληθεν ἑαυτὸν σύνθετον ἐξ ἀνο-
> μοίων κατασκευάζων τὸ θεῖον, ὡς ἄλλο μέν τι νοεῖν εἶναι τὸ
> ὑποκείμενον, ἕτερον δὲ πάλιν τὸ μετεχόμενον, οὐ κατὰ μετ-
> ουσίαν ἐν τῷ ἀγαθῷ γίνεσθαι τὸ μὴ τοιοῦτον ὄν. εἰ δὲ ἀληθῶς
> ἁπλῆν καὶ πάντη μίαν ἐνενόει τὴν οὐσίαν, αὐτὸ ὅπερ ἐστὶν
> ἀγαθὸν οὖσαν, οὐ γινομένην ἐξ ἐπικτήσεως, οὐκ ἂν τὸ μεῖζον
> καὶ τὸ ἔλαττον περὶ αὐτὴν ἐλογίζετο....

...τὸ δὲ ἀόριστον οὐ τῇ πρὸς ἕτερον σχέσει τοιοῦτόν ἐστιν, ἀλλ' αὐτὸ καθ' ἑαυτὸ νοούμενον ἐκφεύγει τὸν ὅρον. ἄπειρον δὲ ἀπείρου πλέον καὶ ἔλαττον λέγειν οὐκ οἶδα πῶς ὁ λελογισμένος συνθήσεται. ὥστε εἰ ἁπλῆν ὁμολογεῖ τὴν ὑπερκειμένην οὐσίαν καὶ οἰκείως ἔχειν αὐτὴν πρὸς ἑαυτήν, συντιθέσθω τῇ κατὰ τὸ ἁπλοῦν καὶ ἄπειρον κοινωνίᾳ συναπτομένην....[16]

Commentary

Having established through his quotations from Eunomius [(e)–(f)] that the Arian was intent on disconnecting the Father from the Son and the Son from the Spirit because they are all separate beings differing in perfections and rank [(g)–(h)], Gregory begins his refutation in the key text.

As Eunomius himself proclaims, each of those three *ousiai* is simple and absolutely one. Why? Because each is without form, structure and extension ([1]). But their simplicity excludes their being compared as more and less (whether in goodness, power, wisdom or any other divine attribute ([2]–[3]). Why? Because each divine person is good, wise and powerful by and in what it is by nature and not by receiving such perfections from some outside source ([4]–[6]). Otherwise one has introduced into each a composition of recipient and perfection received, of participant and perfection participated in [and a process] whereby what was not good before [= the participant] is made good [by the perfection received; [5]] and [whereby the perfection itself is limited by and to the participant]. But the divine Being is goodness and completely transcends evil [7] and, thus, He is unlimited in and of Himself and, as infinite, rises above any comparison of more or less [8]. If, then, Eunomius grants that the supreme Being is simple, then let him also concede He is infinite in unlimited perfection [9]. Otherwise, we have unmasked him as injecting composition into God by denying that the Father, Son and Holy Spirit are identical in being because the Father is greater than the Son, who is greater than the Spirit [10].

Such is the refutation, from which we shall extricate Gregory's position on divine infinity. For the Cappadocian, the Father, Son and Holy Spirit are one and the same God, who is being, goodness, wisdom, power and, thus, is subsistently so. He also is infinitely so because those perfections are not participated or received in a participant, which would thereby determine them.

They are identical with the divine Being (itself identical with the three divine persons). Therefore, the divine Being is itself infinite as without the determination which would arise were participation to occur.[17]

In Gregory, then, we come upon the twofold determination needed if an author is to propose God as infinite in His very being: that which goodness, wisdom and other perfections exercise upon their recipients or participants and, secondly, that which the recipients or participants exercise upon the perfections themselves.

Such a theory of determination fits neatly within the theology which resulted when Gregory was confronted with Arius' [see above, (a) and (b)] and Eunomius' [(c)–(h)] discussion of the Trinity in terms of being: the divine Being consists (so they say) in Unbegottenness and thus only the Father is God. In replying Gregory had to speak in terms of being too—God, although triune in really distinct persons, is also one Being, with which the three persons are identical: they are *homoousioi*. Within the parameters of debate drawn by the heretics, then, a Neoplatonic God who is nonbeing because beyond being obviously would not do. Nor would anything less than an infinity consonant with God as supreme Being suffice: in His very entity He is infinitely perfect. Such apparently is the Cappadocian's message in the key text just studied.

Augustine of Hippo

Do we find a similar message in Augustine's *De trinitate*, "composed over a long period of years from 400 to 416"?[18] Although this work in Oates' view "was not written against any antagonist, nor indeed was it precipitated, as were so many of his works, by the heat of controversy,"[19] still Augustine explicitly mentions Arius himself in Book VI,[20] distinguishes between his earlier and later followers[21] and in the final book of the treatise explains and refutes Eunomius' view that the Son of God is Son not by nature (that is, not born of the substance of the Father) but by His will.[22]

Another similarity Augustine has with Gregory is that he, following the Nicene and other *symbola*,[23] can be interpreted as speaking of the Trinity in terms of "being" inasmuch as he applies "substance" and "essence" to God. For example, the Father, the Son and the Holy Spirit are rightly said, believed and understood to be "of one and the same substance or essence".[24] In fact, all previous Catholic expounders of the divine Scriptures have taught that "the Father, Son and Holy Spirit entail a divine unity of one and the same substance in an indivisible equality."[25] Two chapters later, Augustine relies upon the Prologue to John's Gospel to stress that the incarnate Word not only is God but also is of the same substance with the Father and thus is not a creature.[26]

Finally, in his lengthy discussion of how the Greek Catholic authors speak of the Trinity as involving *una essentia, tres substantiae* in contrast to the Latins, whose language is *una essentia uel substantia, tres personae*,[27] he pauses midway to consider whether and how *subsistere* may be predicated of God. A body subsists and thus is a "substance," whereas its color and shape are not substances but are in a substance. Hence, only mutable and composite things are properly called "substances." From this perspective "substance" is only improperly said of God,[28] who truly and rightly is "essence." Why? He is immutable, and hence only He is truly. Thus "essence" is the name God revealed to Moses (Ex 3:14): "I am who am" and "Say to them: He who is has sent me to you."[29] But (Augustine continues) whether "essence" is properly and "substance" improperly said of God, what matters is that each expresses God as such and not the persons. Accordingly, for God to be is for Him to subsist and, thus, if the Trinity is one essence, it is also one substance. Hence, the Latin manner of describing the Trinity as *tres personae* is perhaps better than *tres substantiae*.[30]

Rather obviously, Augustine has tentatively sided with the Latins rather than the Greeks in expressing the Trinity. Would this preference coincide with a distance between his and Nyssa's conceptions of the triune God as infinite being?

Let us reflect on the two instances so far found of his applying *infinitum* to the Trinity. Each is found in the final paragraph of the last chapter of Book VI, which discusses what Hilary of Poitiers intended by stating, *Aeternitas in patre, species in imagine, usus in munere*.[31] In this complicated and rather contrived discussion Augustine speaks of *aeternitas, species* and *usus* with reference first to the Trinity, then to creatures and finally to the Trinity again. In this last section he classifies the three persons both as determined and as infinite. Let us follow him in that threefold movement of thought.

[a] "Eternity" signifies that the Father does not himself have a father, whereas the Son is from the Father and thus is co-eternal: as perfect image the Son is co-equal to the Father (lines 8–12).

[b] The Son is named *species*[32] to designate the beauty issuing from His primal equality, likeness and identity with the Father in being, life and intellection. This is to be expected in Him who is the perfect Word and exemplar

(filled with all immutable, living and unified *rationes*) of the omnipotent and wise God,[33] who thereby knows everything He has made (lines 12–26).

[c] The Holy Spirit is named *usus* to indicate the love, joy and happiness which exist between the Father and the Son and which allow all creatures to achieve their order and proper rank (lines 30–36).

[d] All these created existents manifest an inner unity, beauty (*speciem*) and order: unity in the natures of their bodies and in the abilities of their souls; beauty in their physical shapes and qualities and in their knowledges and skills; order in their physical juxtapositions and in their loves and delights (lines 37–44).

[e] Consequently, from creatures so disposed to be signposts (*uestigia*) we should know the Trinity, which is the supreme origin of all things, most perfect beauty and most blessed delight (lines 45–49).

[f] [Now come the key lines:] Thus those three [origin, beauty, delight or, by reduction, Father, Son and Holy Spirit] are seen to be mutually determinate [as persons] but to be infinite in themselves [as God] (lines 47–50).[34]

[g] But in corporeal things one is not as much as three, and two is more than one. In the Trinity, though, one is as much as three, and two is not more than one, and the three [persons] are mutually infinite [because they are the same God] (lines 52–54).[35]

[h] Thus, any one person is individually in each of the other two, and all three are in any one, and each is in all and all in all and each is all (lines 54–56).[36]

[i] May whoever glimpses this truth either partially or darkly as in a mirror rejoice in that he knows God, whom he should honor and thank. But anyone without such a glimpse should strive to attain it since God is one and yet triune (lines 56–60).

Thus far has Augustine's *De trinitate* VI,x been translated or paraphrased. Manifestly he speaks of the three persons as somehow *infinita* (see [f] and [g]) but the term is not applied to God as such or to the divine essence and substance. Accordingly, one might infer that Augustine differs from Nyssa in this application.

Etienne Gilson

Such an inference, however, must contend with the interpretation of none other than the eminent historian of philosophy, Etienne Gilson, who has located *De trinitate* VI,x among passages in which Augustine is developing a doctrine of divine infinity where the "future speculations of theologians are contained in germ" and which makes a definitive contribution to the Christian theologians of the Middle Ages and, specifically, to Thomas Aquinas.[37] What is that doctrine? Basically, this: Because He is immaterial and, thus, is not contained in place and has no direct connection with anything corporeal or quantitative, God is Himself infinite and without limitation.[38] Such is Augustine's message, Gilson maintains, in the lines from *De trinitate*: although the divine persons are three, still number here does not imply limitation since the persons are infinite in their absolute immateriality.

> Sa position favorite est celle que nous avons vue, et il y revient spontanément lorsque l'occasion l'invite à s'expliquer sur ce point. Par example, les personnes divines sont trois, mais elles n'en sont pas moins infinies pour cela, parce qu'elles sont incorporelles. Il s'agit de refuser que le nombre entraîne en Dieu aucune limite; donc l'infinité entre en jeu.[39]

What should one's reaction be to Gilson's exegesis? Whether or not God's freedom from matter and place is ground for inferring Him to be infinite being and reality must be postponed until later, but rereading ch. 10 of *De trinitate* VI discloses no direct mention of matter or place. Rather, that chapter conveys a meaning of infinity very different from that proposed by Gilson, as is evident from consulting three thirteenth-century commentaries on Peter Lombard's twelfth-century *Sentences*, Book One, Distinctions 19 and 31, who quotes the key text from Augustine's *De trinitate*.[40]

Three Medieval Commentators

The first of these commentators is Stephen Langton (d. 1228). Coming upon Augustine's statement, *Itaque illa tria et a se invicem determinari videntur et in se infinita sunt,* he restricted his explanation to one word. "'Infinite'" he asserted, "means 'indistinct according to essence'."[41]

Some years later Hugh of S. Cher, teaching at the University of Paris
between 1230 and 1235, was more generous. "The word 'three' in the phrase,
Itaque illa tria," he began, "stands for Father, Image and Gift" (the last two
terms refer, as we have seen, in Hilary's and in Augustine's texts to the Son
and the Holy Spirit). "The word *determinari*," he added, "means, are distinguished by eternity, beauty, and joy," which also Hilary and, after him, Augustine set up as properties of the Father, Son and Holy Spirit. "The word *infinita*, in the phrase, *In se infinita sunt*, can be understood in a two-fold manner. If
applied to the divine persons qua persons, it is synonymous with 'incomprehensible.' If applied to them [qua divine—inasmuch as they have identically
one and the same divine nature] it means 'not-finite, that is, not-different in
their nature.'"

> "*Itaque quia illa tria*," id est, tres: *Pater, Imago, Munus.*
> "*Determinari*," id est, distingui per haec alia tria, scilicet eterni-
>   tatem, speciem, usum.
> "*In se infinita sunt*," id est, respectiva vel incomprehensibilia vel
>   non finita, i.e., in natura sua indifferentia.[42]

Approximately a decade later Richard Fishacre wrote comments which
are in many respects similar to those of Hugh. "The word 'three,' in the
phrase *illa tria*," he began, "stands for Father, Image and Gift," an explanation
which exactly reproduces what Hugh had said. "*Determinari*," he continues,
"signifies 'are distinguished'." Finally, "The word, *infinita*, in the phrase, *et in
se infinita sunt*, indicates one of two things. Either the three persons are not-
different in nature [which is one and the same for all three]. Or each of the
three persons, who are distinct from one another qua persons, is incomprehensible or, even, is infinite in power and magnitude."

> "*Illa tria*," id est, tres: *Pater, Imago, Munus.*
> "*Determinari*," id est, distingui.
> "*Et in se infinita sunt*," id est, incomprehensibilia vel [in] natura
>   indifferentia. Quod dicit: illi tres sic distinguuntur, et
>   tamen in se incomprehensibilis est unusquisque eorum.
> "*Vel infinita*" secundum potentiam et magnitudinem.[43]

What interpretation, then, of the key sentence in *De trinitate* VI,x, can
be gathered from those three medieval commentators? First of all, Augustine

intends to speak of the three divine persons, to whom *tria* in the phrase, *Itaque illa tria*, refers. In the next words, *et ad se invicem determinari videntur*, he says that qua persons they are distinct from one another. In the final portion, *et in se infinita sunt*, however, he reminds us that they are nonetheless indistinct with reference to the divine essence—they are one and the same God and have identically one and the same divine nature.[44] Putting the phrases together, then, we learn that according to Augustine the three divine persons are distinct qua persons but are indistinct in the divine nature, with which each is identical. They are three qua persons but are one qua divine or, to say the same thing, God is one and yet triune.

Notice how neatly the sentence, when so understood, fits into the immediate context. Beginning with chapter six, Augustine aims at establishing God's absolute simplicity.[45] Truly, God is great, good, wise, happy, true and the like. Nevertheless, His magnitude of power is the same as His wisdom, His goodness the same as His wisdom and magnitude, His truth the same as all three.[46] In fact, even divine trinity, the bishop continues in chapter seven, is no obstacle to divine simplicity. God is triune, not tripartite, since the Father or Son or Holy Spirit alone is as much as the Father, Son and Holy Spirit together.[47] The Son is equal to the Father, we read in chapter eight, and the Holy Spirit is equal to both. Perfect is the Father, perfect is the Son, perfect is the Spirit, and a perfect God is the Father, Son and Holy Spirit. Accordingly, there is a trinity, not a triplicity.[48] "Having, then, demonstrated that the three persons are equal and are one and the same substance," Augustine concludes in chapter nine, "nothing should prevent us from acknowledging the supreme equality of the Father, Son and Holy Spirit."[49]

Chapter ten immediately follows. Let us with St. Hilary apply Eternity, Augustine begins, to the Father as the sourceless source even of the Son. Let us characterize the Word as Beauty, the Holy Spirit as subsistent Joy. Let us even recognize the Trinity in creatures, all of whom bear its imprint to some degree, for in that Trinity one discovers the ultimate source of all things, as well as most perfect beauty and maximal joy. And its three divine persons are distinct as persons and yet are not distinct from one another in respect to the divine essence, with which each is identical (*illa tria et ad se invicem determinari videntur et in se infinita sunt*). In material things one is not as much as three such items taken together, and two are more than one. But in the august Trinity one person is as much as all three together, nor are two any more than one, for qua divine they are not distinct from one another but are one and the same God (*et in se infinita sunt*). For this reason, each person is in each other and all in each and each in all and all in all, and one is all. Whoever even partially understands this doctrine should rejoice in his knowledge and should give thanks. But should someone not understand it, let him be brought through piety to understand and not through blindness to calumniate, for truly God is one and yet is triune.[50]

Conclusions

If we follow the lead of such medieval commentators as Stephen Langton, Hugh of S. Cher and Richard Fishacre, and if we then re-read the key sentences from Augustine's *De trinitate* VI,x, in the light of their immediate context, what else can we conclude but that "infinity" there is a technical trinitarian term? It is synonymous with "absence of distinction" or, expressed positively, "complete identity" in nature. As "infinite" the divine persons are not distinct from the divine nature which they all have in common or, in that sense, from one another. They are, in short, one and the same God.

In this passage Augustine is not dealing with whether or not the divine being is itself infinite and, thus, is not comparable here with Gregory's refutation of the Arians which stressed that the Son and Spirit, as well as the Father, are the same divine and infinite being and thus are equal and are equally God.

What does Augustine say elsewhere? He expresses his mind in at least three other series of passages, in one of which infinity is merely synonymous with incomprehensibility[51] and in a second, infinity is applied to divine power.[52]

The third consists of lines in *Epistula CXVIII* iv,24[53] immediately following that application where Augustine discusses Cicero's opposition (in his *De natura deorum* I,x,28 sq.) to Anaxagoras' theory of mind (*nous*). For Cicero nothing can be added, Augustine states, to the infinite if this latter is a body because bodies necessarily have limits (line 20, line 1). Yet the intellect or mind cannot be infinite (as Anaxagoras would want) because it also must sentiently know (and thus be a soul) if it is to be the *ordinatrix et moderatrix rerum omnium* (line 7). Why? Because the soul, wherever it senses, does so throughout its whole nature (line 9: *totam sentire animam*) since any body perceived does not escape the soul's entire attention (lines 9–10: *totam...non latet*). But if the whole nature of the soul is engaged in the sensation (line 11: *totam naturam sentire*), it cannot be infinite since any sense of the body it animates starts at a particular spot and then terminates as its own proper organ

—characteristics excluded from what is infinite. Then come the key lines, 16–19:

> That which is incorporeal is in another fashion called a whole because it is conceived without limitations from places: it is whole because of its completeness, it is infinite because it is not surrounded by spatial limits.

> *Aliter dicitur totum quod incorporeum est, quia sine finibus locorum intellegitur, ut et totum et infinitum dici possit: totum propter integritatem, infinitum quia locorum finibus non ambitur.*

If Augustine identifies this incorporeal whole (line 16: *totum quod incorporeum est*) with God, He is infinite because free of spatial limitations, which if they were present would determine Him and thus make Him be determinate and finite. But they are absent from God, who thus can Himself be termed "infinite." Notice, though, Augustine does not explicitly say "The divine being is infinite."

But this explicitation is found in the fourth and last text, where infinity is linked with the divine substance:

> *Quid est ergo illud in corde tuo, quando cogitas quamdam substantiam, uiuam, perpetuam, omnipotentem, infinitam, ubique praesentem, ubique totam, nusquam inclusam? Quando ista cogitas, hoc est uerbum de Deo in corde tuo.*[54]

But despite that link with substance Augustine does not explain what such divine infinity consists in—is it because God is incomprehensible or/and omnipotent or/and nonspatial (as one finds in the previous three passages)? Or is it because He is free from all determination of matter and potency, as one might expect if Augustine had been Aristotelian in his metaphysics?[55] As yet no answer is clear.

Obviously, much research and reflection remain to be done on Augustine's theory of infinity.[56] At least this is manifest: in *De trinitate* VI,x, the Latin author is directly predicating infinity of God not as being but as triune.

Notes

[1] *The Cappadocian Triumph Over Arianism*, Revised Doctoral Dissertation; Stanford University, 1966 (Ann Arbor: University Microfilms), pp. 323 and 441.

[2] On the important but complicated question of Gregory's relationship to Plotinus and, more generally, to Neoplatonism, Jean Daniélou's remarks appear accurate: "Grégoire ne se rattache donc à aucune école néo-platonicienne définie. Il utilise Plotin pour sa mystique, Porphyre pour la logique et l'ontologie, Jamblique pour la cosmologie. Il est d'ailleurs très indépendant dans cette utilisation. *Il n'est pas un néo-platonicien.* Mais il connaît bien les courants du néo-platonisme" ("Orientations actuelles de la recherche sur Grégoire de Nysse" in *Ecriture et culture philosophique dans la pensée de Grégoire de Nysse*, ed. M. Harl [Leiden: E. J. Brill, 1971], p. 6 [italics added to the quotation]). For a helpful summary of the contrast between Daniélou's and H. Cherniss' assessments of Gregory and Platonism, see W. Jaeger, *Two Re-discovered Works of Ancient Christian Literature: Gregory of Nyssa and Macarius* (Leiden: E. J. Brill, 1954), p. 71, n. 1: "Cherniss [*The Platonism of Gregory of Nyssa*] finds in Gregory much that is Platonic but thinks that Gregory has not improved Platonism by applying and adjusting its ideas to Christian problems. Daniélou [*Platonisme et théologie mystique*], on the other hand, believes that Gregory's 'Platonism' is no longer Platonic and that it must be judged on the basis of its Christian motifs rather than its original philosophical intention—in other words, there has been a complete metamorphosis of its traditional meaning." J. Quasten, *Patrology* III (Utrecht/Antwerp: Spectrum Publishers, 1966), pp. 284–86, sides with Daniélou over Cherniss. Also see David L. Balás, *Metousia Theou: Man's Participation in God's Perfections According to Saint Gregory of Nyssa* (Rome: Herder, 1966), pp. 163–64; E. Mühlenberg, "Die philosophische Bildung Gregors von Nyssa in den Büchern Contra Eunomium" in *Ecriture et culture*, pp. 230–52; all the articles in *Gregor von Nyssa und die Philosophie*, ed. Heinrich Dörrie et al. (Leiden: E. J. Brill, 1976), with special attention given to Jean Daniélou, "Grégoire de Nysse et la philosophie," pp. 3–18 (esp. p. 17: "L'élément le plus remarquable est que Grégoire, s'il dépend pour une part du néoplatonisme, est aussi l'expression d'une réaction antiplatonicienne et d'un renouveau du moyen stoicisme") and to T. Paul Verghese, "*Diastema* and *Diastasis* in Gregory of Nyssa," pp. 243–60) esp. p. 257; "Gregory's view of the relation of God and the world is fundamentally different from that of Plotinus or others of the so-called Neoplatonic School, [so] that it is not correct to class Gregory among Neoplatonists or Christian Platonists. There is no theory of emanation in Gregory, no ontological continuity between the One and the Many."

[3] *Contra Eunomium libri. Pars prior: Libri I et II*, Gregorii Nysseni Opera (hereafter, *GNO*), I (Leiden: E. J. Brill, 1960), pp. 94–96.

[4] See R. Williams, *Arius: Heresy and Tradition* (London: Darton Longman and Todd, 1987), pp. 82–91, 95–116, and 230–32 (helpful references throughout to Abramowski, Opitz, Kannengiesser, Gregg, Groh, Meijering, Simonetti). R. J. Deferrari (tr.), *Saint Basil: The Letters* I; Loeb Classical Library (London: William Heinemann, 1926), pp. xxv–xxxii, is still helpful on the complex history of the Arian controversy, which had both religious and political dimensions. Also see G. L. Prestige, *God in Patristic Thought* (London: SPCK, 1959), ch. VII: "Subordinationism," pp. 129–56, as well as subsequent chapters on the histo-

ry of the Trinitarian and Christological controversies; T. A. Kopecek, *History of Neo-Arianism* (Philadelphia Patristic Foundation, 1979), vol. I, chs. 1–4.

[5] R. P. Vaggione (ed. and tr.), *Eunomius: The Extant Works* (Oxford: Clarendon Press, 1987), "Liber Apologeticus" [Vaggione prefers this title to "Apologia"], pp. 3–12 and (especially) chs. 7–9 and 23–28 of the "Liber" itself. Also see B. Barmann's ch. I, pp. 13–62 and ch. V, section 4: "*Energeia* and the New Metaphysics," pp. 306–17; T. A. Kopecek, *History of Neo-Arianism* vol. II, chs. 5–7.

[6] This treatise can be divided as follows: introduction (chs. 1–6) culminating in a symbol of faith, Father (chs. 7–11), Son (chs. 12–24) and Spirit (ch. 25), summary and conclusion (chs. 26–27) and appendix (ch. 28). For a textual division which Vaggione considers to give "a more satisfactory understanding of Eunomius' meaning" and which is based on Eunomius' "two methods of doing theology, the one *a priori*...the other *a posteriori*," see Vaggione, *Eunomius: The Extant Works*, pp. 11–12.

For the Greek text and French translation of Eunomius' *Apologia* see B. Sesboüé, G.-M. de Durand and L. Doutreleau, *Basil de Césarée: Contre Eunome* II; Sources Chrétiennes, 305 (Paris: Les Editions du Cerf, 1983), pp. 235–99. For the Greek text and Latin translation see *PG* XXX,835–68.

Eunomius' *Apologia apologiae*, listed below as stage (3), is no longer extant and is known through Gregory's quotations of it in his *Contra Eunomium*. See R. P. Vaggione, *Eunomius: The Extant Works*, pp. 79–127.

[7] For this list of stages and dates, see Barmann, pp. 9–10. The Greek text used will be that established by Werner Jaeger, *Contra Eunomium libri*, cited above. In my paraphrases and translations of *Contra Eunomium* I have consulted the English translation of W. Moore and H. Wilson in *Gregory, Bishop of Nyssa: Select Writings and Letters*, *NPNF* II:V, and the Latin translation in *PG* XLV. For an explanation of why the books of *Contra Eunomium* as found in *PG* are ordered differently from those in Jaeger's volume, see Quasten, *Patrology* III, 257–58.

[8] *Contra Eunomium* I,151: *GNO* I,71,28–72,7: *PG* XLV,297A: *NPNF* II:V,50a. The last portion of the third clause in the quotation from Eunomius is translated in *PG* XLV, 297A, thus: *Sed illi quidem ut causae, huic vero ut operationi qua facta est subjicitur.*

[9] *Contra Eunomium* I,223: *GNO* I,91,20–92,1: *PG* XLV,317C: *NPNF* II:V,56b. For additional information on the Arian position see *Arianism: Historical and Theological Re-Assessments*, ed. R. C. Gregg (Cambridge: Philadelphia Patristic Foundation, 1985).

[10] *Contra Eunomium* I,224: *GNO* I,92,2–11: *PG* XLV,317D: *NPNF* II:V,56b–c.

[11] *Contra Eunomium* I,228: *GNO* I,93,17–21: *PG* XLV,320C: *NPNF* II:V,56d.

[12] Here paragraphs will be marked by bracketed arabic numbers to facilitate references and to distinguish them from paragraphs in the "Context" marked by bracketed lower-case letters.

[13] *GNO* I,94,20–22

[14] See *Contra Eunomium* I,168–70: *GNO* I,77,7–26: *PG* XLV,310D: *NPNF* II:V, 51d–52a.

[15] *Contra Eunomium* I,231–37: *GNO* I,94,15–96,12: *PG* 45,321A–324A: *NPNF* II:V, 57a–c.

[16] *GNO* I,95,15–23; 95,26–96,6.

[17] In this conclusion Gregory anticipates Aquinas, for whom also the divine Being is infinite as free from determination. But even though the Latin author often uses the theory of participation to express other doctrines (for instance, see *Summa theologica* I–I,iii,4 [*Utrum in Deo sit idem essentia et esse*], resp.), he uses act/potency instead of participated perfection/participant to set forth his view on God as infinite. For example, see *Scriptum super libros Sententiarum* I,xliii,1,1 resp.; *De veritate* II,2 ad 5; *De potentia* I,2 resp.; *Summa theologica* I–I,vii,1 resp.; ibid. III,x,3 ad 2; *Summa contra gentiles* I,43, where ten proofs for divine infinity are given, only in the ninth of which participation is mentioned once: *Omne quod habet aliquam perfectionem tanto est perfectius quanto illam perfectionem plenius participat.* On Aquinas' theory of infinity, see my *Divine Infinity in Greek and Medieval Authors* [hereafter: *Divine Infinity*] (New York/Bern: Peter Lang Publishing Co., 1991), chs. XIX and XXIII and my doctoral dissertation, *Divine Infinity in the Writings of Thomas Aquinas* (University of Toronto, 1954), with introductory chapters on infinity in Aristotle, Plotinus, Proclus, Pseudo-Dionysius and the *Liber de Causis*.

On the other hand and as far as I currently know, Gregory shows no awareness of an Aristotelian doctrine of act/potency. True enough, he speaks often of *energeia* (as do Basil and Eunomius) but solely, it seems, as "operation" or "activity" and, often, linked with the *ergon* it produces. So too he mentions *dynamis* frequently but as operative power rather than a constitutive and ontological factor within substance or essence. Moreover, if B. Barmann (pp. 368–70) is right, *hypokeimenon* comes to the Cappadocian from Stoicism and not from Aristotle.

Finally, Gregory apparently does not speak of God as subsistent act, even though he thinks of the divine reality as being, goodness, beauty and other perfections free of any determination which might come from a participant or recipient. In contrast, Thomas constantly conceives and speaks of God as subsistent act of being, and Aristotle in *Metaphysics*, Lambda, ch. 7, of the Unmoved Mover as subsistent act of intellection. Perhaps Gregory's silence is evidence of his not being acquainted fully with Aristotelian metaphysics. All agree that he knows Aristotle's *Categories*—for instance, see D. Balás, *Metousia Theou*, p. 133; E. Mühlenberg, *Die Unendlichkeit Gottes*, pp. 123 and 160; B. Barmann, p. 227.

[18] Whitney J. Oates (ed.), *Basic Works of Saint Augustine* (New York: Random House, 1948), II,666. Also see W. J. Mountain, *Sancti Aurelii Augustini De trinitate* in *CC* L,vii–x.

[19] Oates, *Basic Works*, II,666.

[20] *De trinitate* VI,i,1: *CC* L,228,10.

[21] *De trinitate* VI,i,1: *CC* L,228,15.

[22] *De trinitate* XV,xx,38: *CC* L/A,515,1. Noteworthy too is Augustine's own initial description (*De trinitate* I,i,1: *CC* L,27) of his treatise as a guard "against the sophistries of those who disdain to begin with faith and are deceived by a crude and perverse love of reason" (*aduersus eorum…calumnias qui fidei contemnentes initium immaturo et peruerso rationis amore falluntur*) and he describes three classes of such persons.

[23] For documentation, see Mountain, *passim*.

[24] *De trinitate* I,ii,4: *CC* L,31,4–5: *...unius eiusdemque substantiae uel essentiae....*

[25] *De trinitate* I,iv,7: *CC* L,35,5: *...unius substantiae inseparabili aequalitate diuinam insinuent unitatem....*

[26] *De trinitate* I,vi,9: *CC* L,38,10–11: *declarat non tantum deum esse sed etiam eiusdem cum patre substantiae*; see also VI,iii,4: *CC* L,231,35.

[27] *De trinitate* VII,iv–vi.

[28] *De trinitate* VII,v,10: *CC* L,261,17: *...deum abusiue substantiam uocari....*

[29] *De trinitate* VII,v,10: *CC* L,261,19–22: *...fortasse solum deum dici oporteat essentiam. Est enim uere solus quia incommutabilis est, idque suum nomen famulo suo Moysi enuntiauit cum ait: "Ego sum qui sum," et: "Dices ad eos: Qui est misit me ad uos."*

[30] *De trinitate* VII,v,10: *CC* L,261,1.

[31] *De trinitate* VI,x,11–12: *CC* L,241–43. Line numbers in the text to follow refer to these pages. In Hilary's own *De trinitate* II,i,1: *PL* X,51, the initial noun is *infinitas* and not *aeternitas*—see Mountain, *CC* L,241. On Hilary's position on infinity see my *Divine Infinity*, ch. XV: "Divine Infinity: 1150–1250," paragraphs corresponding to notes 30–44.

[32] What does *species* mean? It is hard to pin down in Hilary and Augustine, as well as in Bonaventure, Aquinas and other medievals, who use it often. In origin it apparently is a translation of *eidos*, which comes from the Greek verb "to see" and thus which first means "that which is seen or appears." The connotation is that what one sees in an object is the beauty it puts across to the viewer. Consequently, *species* can mean "beauty," and Augustine uses it here in this sense.

[33] *De trinitate* VI,x,11: *CC* L,241,21–23: *...ars quaedam omnipotentis atque sapientis dei plena omnium rationum uiuentium incommutabilium....*

[34] *De trinitate* VI,x,12: *CC* L,242,47–50: *In illa enim trinitate summa origo est rerum omnium et perfectissima pulchritudo et beatissima delectatio. Itaque illa tria et a se inuicem determinari uidentur et in se infinita sunt.*

Here *PL* XLII,932 reads *ad se*. But the difference in meaning between *ad se* and *a se* appears slight: *ad se invicem determinari* signifies that the divine persons are distinct with reference to one another; *a se invicem determinari* that they are distinct from one another as persons.

One should note that Augustine uses *ad se* elsewhere. See *De trinitate* VII,vi,11: *CC* L,261–62, where *ad se invicem* expresses relation and person: *Nam si esse ad se dicitur, persona uero relatiue. Sic dicamus tres personas patrem et filium et spiritum sanctum quemadmodum dicuntur aliqui tres amici aut tres propinqui aut tres uicini quod sint ad inuicem, non quod unusquisque eorum sit ad se ipsum.*

[35] *De trinitate* VI,x,12: *CC* L,243,52–54: *...in summa trinitate tantum est una quantum tres simul, nec plus aliquid sunt duae quam una, et in se infinita sunt.*

[36] *De trinitate* VI,x,12: *CC* L,243,54–56: *Ita et singula sunt in singulis et omnia in singulis et singula in omnibus et omnia in omnibus et unum omnia.*

[37] E. Gilson, "L'infinité divine chez saint Augustin," *Augustinus Magister* (Paris: Études Augustiniennes, 1954), I,570: "...des spéculations futures des théologiens sont ici en germe...." Ibid. 572: "En revanche, il est vrai de dire que ce qu'apporta sur ce point saint Augustin est resté dans la théologie chrétienne du Moyen Age comme une acquisition définitive. Saint Thomas d'Aquin construit sa démonstration de l'infinité de grandeur spirituelle en Dieu sur la conclusion préalablement établie que Dieu est incorporel. La même notion d'infinité spirituelle, établie dans la *Summa contra Gentiles*, est reprise dans la *Summa theologiae*, non d'ailleurs sans y être fondée sur des raisons beaucoup plus profondes...."

[38] "Le principe que l'immatériel est par essence soustrait à la limite, se trouve donc clairement dégagé dans ces textes de saint Augustin" (ibid., 570). "Ici [in *Contra Faustum Manichaeum* XXV,1–2] encore l'élimination de la matière ouvre la voie à la notion d'un être infini parce que sans limite" (ibid., 570–71). It is an infinity "qui suit d'une simple absence de limites corporelles" (ibid., 571).

[39] Ibid., 572.

[40] On Lombard's position, see my *Divine Infinity*, ch. XV: "Divine Infinity: 1150–1250," paragraphs corresponding to notes 21–53, and ch. XVII: "Lombard, Augustine and Infinity," upon which the second half of this current paper is based.

[41] "*Infinita et indistincta secundum essentiam*" (*Der Sentenzenkommentar des Kardinals Stephen Langton*, Band 27, Heft 1 of *Beiträge zur Geschichte der Philosophie und Theologie des Mittelalters* [Münster i. W.: Aschendorffsche Verlagsbuchandlung, 1952], p. 40). He bypasses Augustine's other sentence, *Et in se infinitae sunt*, quoted in distinction nineteen, without any comment. See ibid. pp. 21–22.

[42] *Commentarium in I Sententiis*, d. 31 (Cod. Vat. lat. 1098, 29vb). Hugh makes no comment upon Augustine's sentence in distinction 19—see ibid. d. 19, c. 12 (Cod. Vat. lat., 1098, 21r).

[43] *Commentarium in I Sententiis*, d. 31, c. 4 (Cod. Ottob. lat., 294, 57va). Earlier Richard had commented upon two sentences of Augustine in distinction nineteen: *In rebus corporeis non est tantum una quantum tres simul* and *Et in se infinitae sunt*. With regard to the first, he explains that Augustine is not speaking of bodies which can interpenetrate, such as light and air or fire and iron. But even if he were, any two such bodies are more than one both "naturally" and numerically. *Non est tantum una quantum tres simul.* [*Marg.: Quaestio*] *Contra. Posito quod lux sit corpus, eadem est magnitudo infinitorum corporum, quia luminum quotlibet et aeris, eadem est linea longitudinis, latitudinis et spissitudinis. Similiter est de ferro et igne.* [*Marg.: Solutio*] *Sed Augustinus intelligit quod hic dicitur de talibus corporibus quae non possunt esse simul in eodem loco. Item licet sint in eodem loco, tamen duo sunt maius uno naturaliter, quia plus in eis est de natura; et numeraliter, quia maiorem numerum faciunt* (ibid. d. 19, c. 20, 38vb). As regards the second sentence, his comment is that "infinity" there refers to magnitude and not to number: *Et in se infinitae sunt magnitudine non numero* (ibid.).

[44] Actually, as their previously reproduced texts make clear, both Hugh and Richard suggest two interpretations—the one which we have chosen to retain, and the other in

which infinity is equivalent to incomprehensibility and is referred to divine power and magnitude. Our choice seems better suited to Augustine's aim and to the immediate context of his sentences.

[45] *De trinitate* VI,vi,8: *CC* L,236: *Si autem quaeritur quomodo simplex et multiplex sit illa [diuina] substantia....*

[46] *De trinitate* VI,vii,8: *CC* L,237: *Deus uero multipliciter quidem dicitur magnus, bonus, sapiens, beatus, uerus, et quidquid aliud non indigne dici uidetur; sed eadem magnitudo eius est quae sapientia (non enim mole magnus est sed uirtute), et eadem bonitas quae sapientia et magnitudo, et eadem ueritas quae illa omnia; et non est ibi aliud beatum esse et aliud magnum aut sapientem aut uerum aut bonum esse aut omnino ipsum esse.*

[47] *De trinitate* VI,vii,9: *CC* L,237: *Nec quoniam trinitas est ideo triplex putandus est; alioquin minor erit pater solus aut filius solus quam simul pater et filius....*

[48] *De trinitate* VI,viii,9: *CC* L,238: *In ipso igitur deo cum adhaeret aequali patri filius aequalis aut spiritus sanctus patri et filio aequalis, non fit maior deus quam singuli eorum quia non est quo crescat illa perfectio. Perfectus autem siue pater siue filius siue spiritus sanctus, et perfectus deus pater et filius et spiritus sanctus, et ideo trinitas potius quam triplex.*

[49] *De trinitate* VI,ix,10: *CC* L,240: *Nunc autem aequalitas trinitatis et una eademque substantia, quantum breuiter potuimus, demonstrata est ut...nihil impediat quominus fateamur summam aequalitatem patris et filii et spiritus sancti.*

[50] *De trinitate* VI,x,11: *CC* L, 241. See our paragraphs above, [a]–[i].

[51] *Enarratio in Psalmum CXLIV* 5–6: *CC* XL,2091: *Cogita quantum uis. Quando autem potest cogitari, qui capi non potest? "Laudabilis" est "ualde; et magnitudinis eius non est finis."...Verumtamen, quia "magnitudinis eius non est finis," et eum quem non capimus, laudare debemus (si enim capimus, magnitudinis eius est finis; si autem magnitudinis eius non est finis, capere ex eo aliquid possumus; Deum tamen totum capere non possumus); tamquam deficientes in eius magnitudine, ut reficiamur eius bonitate, ad opera respiciamus, et de operibus laudemus operantem, de conditis Conditorem, de creatura Creatorem.* Besides *Epistula CXVIII* 24, quoted below in note 39 see *Enarratio in Psalmum CXLVI* 11: *CC* XL,2124: *"Intelligentiae eius non est numerus." Conticescant humanae uoces, requiescant humanae cogitationes; ad incomprehensibilia non se extendant quasi comprehensuri, sed tamquam participaturi.*

[52] *Epistula CXVIII* 24: *CSEL* XXXIV,687: *Manifestum est enim omnium rerum descriptionem et modum ab illa [divine wisdom and truth] fieri eamque non incongrue dici infinitam non per spatia locorum sed per potentiam, quae cogitatione humana comprehendi non potest.* Augustine immediately excludes infinity in the sense of "nonbeing" or "formlessness" from divine wisdom. Ibid.: *Neque quod informe aliquid sit ipsa sapientia; hoc enim corporum est, ut, quaecumque infinita fuerint, sint et informia.* See also *De natura boni contra Manichaeos* 3: *PL* XLII,553: *Deus itaque supra omnem creaturae modum est, supra omnem speciem, supra omnem ordinem: nec spatiis locorum supra est, sed ineffabili et singulari potentia, a quo omnis modus, omnis species, omnis ordo.*

516 Relations and Comparisons

⁵³ *CSEL* XXXIV,687–88. Line numbers in the text refer to these pages.

⁵⁴ *Tractatus in Euangelium Ioannis* I,8: *CC* XXXVI,5. For an English translation, as well as helpful introduction and notes, see John W. Rettig (tr.), *St. Augustine: Tractates on the Gospel of St. John 1–10*; *FC* 78,3–33 and 48–49.

⁵⁵ On matter in Augustine as good but also as *mutabilitas, nihil aliquid*, and *est non est*, see Eugene TeSelle, *Augustine the Theologian* (New York: Herder and Herder, 1970), pp. 139–44, with helpful references to E. Gilson, Jules Chaix-Ruy, Jean-Marie LeBlond, as well as to *Confessiones* XII.

For Nyssa (and Basil) matter is not physical but is the intersection of purely "intelligible universal forces" and nothing else—see A. H. Armstrong, "The Theology of the Non-Existence of Matter in Plotinus and the Cappadocians," *Studia Patristica* V (Berlin: Academie-Verlag, 1962), pp. 427–49; Balás, *Metousia Theou*, pp. 41–42.

⁵⁶ For texts on "infinity" see Augustine Concordance residing in VAX computer at Villanova University and efficiently administered by Allan Fitzgerald, O.S.A., to whom I express thanks. See also my paper, "Divine Attributes in *De Doctrina Christiana*: Why Does Augustine Not List 'Infinity'?" in *De Doctrina Christiana: A Classic of Western Culture* (Notre Dame: University of Notre Dame Press, 1992).

Augustine's *De trinitate* and Anselm's *Proslogion*: "Exercere Lectorem"

J. F. Worthen

I

The power of speech, Socrates says in the *Phaedrus*, consists in ψυχαγω-γία, which we might translate as "the leading of souls."[1] Plato as an author is interested in discourse not as a neutral medium for the communication of information but as a way of leading—of shaping, transforming—the souls of his readers. Augustine and Anselm are similarly concerned to create texts that will not only transfer knowledge but engage their readers in the process of coming to know, that will not only inform but rather reform the careful reader. Like Plato, they see the power of discourse in its capacity to mould the mind. This claim could be discussed from many perspectives and with attention to many works, but today I wish to focus exclusively on two particular texts: Augustine's *De trinitate* and Anselm's *Proslogion*.[2] The following paper will attempt to outline the ψυχαγωγία, the soul-leading, suggested by each work and to trace the continuity between them.[3] For Anselm was indebted to Augustine as much for a vision of theological reading and writing as for any individual item of theological dogma.

II

Volentes in rebus quae factae sunt ad cognoscendum eum a quo factae sunt exercere lectorem:[4] these are the opening words of the fifteenth book of the *De trinitate*. Reviewing the project in which he has been enmeshed since Book VIII, Augustine sees in it a sustained attempt to exercise the reader, *exercere lectorem*.[5] Note that Augustine distinguishes Books VIII–XIV from the earlier, exegetical part of the *De trinitate* not only by their method—proceeding from created things rather than from the text of Scripture as such—but also by their relationship with the reader. Unlike the first part of the work, the purpose of these books is not so much to inform the reader as to elicit his participation in a journey whose culmination is signalled by the second part of the sentence just quoted: *iam peruenimus ad eius imaginem*.[6]

How do these later books of the *De trinitate* exercise the reader in a way that finds no parallel in Books I–VII and indeed, I would argue, in theological literature generally? Augustine's own verb, *peruenimus*, supplies an initial clue. It is a verb of travelling, and Augustine here and elsewhere is at pains to emphasize the character of these books as a movement, as a journey, both through using the language of travel and quest and through reflecting on the ground that has been traversed and now past.[7] And to describe a journey is to tell a story; that is, it is to construct a narrative.

Now, to begin with, narrative texts make demands on their readers—exercise their readers—in ways that non-narrative texts do not.[8] The later books of the *De trinitate*, however, not only develop a narrative but develop a narrative of a very particular kind—a narrative of internal events. The elements of this story do not concern physical movements or encounters but rather mental operations. Perception, love, mind, memory, intellect, will—these provide the structure of Augustine's interior narrative. And although some of these mental operations have an external aspect either necessarily or potentially, it is their internal aspect that interests Augustine; indeed, the dynamic of the narrative derives from a progressive concentration on the internal aspect of each individual operation and then on the more internally oriented of the operations until in Book XIV we arrive at the pure interiority of *memoria sui, intellectus sui* and *amor sui* which is the *imago dei*.[9] Hence Augustine's mixing of his spatial metaphors in the attempt to describe the journey: *ascendentibus itaque introrsus*.[10] The narrative moves not over space but across the mind and not towards any physical point but towards the point of utter self-consciousness.

Reading such an interior narrative is different from reading a narrative of external events in certain crucial respects. First, as a narrative focusing on the purely interior as the universal and inalienable *imago dei* in humanity it is a narrative about everyone—about every reader. By contrast, for instance, with the *Confessiones* the narrative is as much the reader's as it is the author's, for all external references that might identify it as the author's peculiar property are progressively eliminated.[11] The narrative lies open to the reader for his or her possession. Furthermore, the fact that this narrative is a narrative of the self positively invites the reader's participation, in that the narrative requires an inner self to be about, and the only interiority to which readers have direct access, the only self which for them can be the narrative's subject, is their own.[12]

For Augustine, speech about intellectual truths refers to that which is always present to the mind of the speaker, whereas speech about physical objects refers to that which is always at a distance from it;[13] hence any reader may experience this narrative of universal interiority. But if his or her reading is an attentive reading then the narrative must be undergone, because to conceive of an inner condition is already to be experiencing it.[14] It is not simply that the later books of the *De trinitate* present a spiritual itinerary which the reader has the option of following or ignoring once the book has been replaced on the shelf. For the stages in this narrative are inevitably enacted by the reader *as he or she reads*. Augustine himself makes this clear. He comments explicitly, for example, on the role of memory and will in reading.[15] We cannot read about remembering and willing without ourselves engaging our own memory and will. Similarly, Augustine analyzes the interaction of physical perception and wholly internal reason in the act of reading:[16] as we peruse the page we are necessarily exercising both the outermost and the innermost trinities of this narrative. But the reader's enactment of the represented narrative has a further, more dynamic dimension. If the inward ascent consists in turning our attention progressively away from the mind's external operations towards the simple interiority at its centre, then are we not necessarily engaged in that ascent as we turn over the pages of the *De trinitate*, as we focus ever more inwardly on the functioning of our own mind? "However much the mind extends itself towards that which is eternal, to that degree it is then shaped according to the image of God."[17] In reading Augustine's interior narrative we are enacting it, and in enacting it we are realizing in ourselves the divine trinitarian image through which we may best perceive the everlasting Trinity of God.

The ψυχαγωγία of Books VIII–XIV of the *De trinitate*, then, proceeds by inviting the reader to enact a narrative of the self whose enactment will end in self-reformation and theological knowledge.

III

What Augustine's *De trinitate* contains implicitly, Anselm's *Proslogion* displays openly. The kind of interior narrative that underlies the later books of the *De trinitate* constitutes the immediate form of the *Proslogion*. The *Pros-*

logion is, and does not merely suggest, a meditation. It presents itself as the script of a self alone before its creator, a text written "in the person of someone striving to raise his mind to contemplate God," as Anselm phrases it.[18] The speaker of the *De trinitate* is evidently Augustine, with his magisterial *nos*, and its explicit addressee is its human audience. The *Proslogion* is addressed to no one but God and the speaker's self, while its speaker is a nameless and singular "I." What we have identified as the hidden structure of Books VIII–XIV of the *De trinitate* therefore becomes the overt structure of the *Proslogion*: a narrative about the self, any self, alone with itself before God. How does this affect the ψυχαγωγία developed by St. Anselm?

Augustine's interior narrative exercises the reader in that it both invites him and in a certain sense compels him to undergo the narrative himself. The mechanism of invitation is the absence of the author: the narrative of the *De trinitate* is not about Augustine specifically, does not belong to Augustine rather than to anyone else and in that sense creates a certain community of equality between author and reader.[19] The author as special authority absents himself so that the reader can become present within the narrative through his own interpretative activity. But Anselm is absent from his narrative in a more palpable sense than Augustine. Augustine's interior narrative appears within a text whose overall form is an authoritative exposition by an identifiable historical figure. This expository context, in which the reader would be excluded from interpretative activity, is discarded in the *Proslogion*. The only voice in the text is a voice that we know in advance to be a fiction, dissociated from the abbot of Bec,[20] and a voice moreover which represents itself as ignorant and sinful, incapable of grasping let alone of imparting truth. The text is then necessarily narrative, in that it is bound to recount the successive states of this mind over time, and necessarily open to the reader's participation: the reader may identify his own self with the self of the text, because that self is never anyone definably other and never presents itself as an author/authority. The author is absent not only from the hidden structure but from the overt structure of the text. The invitation to experience the textual narrative is so much the more unavoidable.

But if the way in which the *Proslogion* lies open to the reader's participation is closely parallel to the strategy of the *De trinitate*, it does not demand the reader's participation in quite the same way. Augustine's method of ψυχαγωγία derived from the fact that his narrative was primarily *about* mental operations, and that both the mental operations described and also their successively inward ordering were enacted by the reader precisely by virtue of his or her reading. The *Proslogion* is not primarily about mental operations but about the being and nature of God, and therefore the necessity of enactment that we found in Augustine cannot apply straightforwardly here. Yet that does not mean that it does not apply at all. For example, the so-called ontological argument could be considered as a case of the same essential method transposed into a different key. We are reading not about a general mental operation—willing, remembering, understanding—but about a very specific mental act: the denial that God is.[21] But, as in the *De trinitate*, in reading about this mental event we are necessarily re-presenting it: we echo the speaker's denial of God's existence, just as the speaker—here himself a reader[22] —is echoing the denial of the fool. And Anselm, like Augustine, will use that echo to create in the reader's self a knowledge of theological truth. For he will show that the presence, within the echoed denial, of the name of God has already committed the speaker and in turn the reader to acknowledging the truth of God's existence. The mental event of conceiving God—even in conceiving his non-existence—contains in itself a knowledge that God is, just as the mental event of remembering, understanding and loving oneself contains in itself a knowledge of the Trinity. In both cases, the reader's own performance of a mental event described in the "script" becomes the fulcrum of theological understanding. The ontological argument can then be seen as another example of Anselm moving to the surface of the text a reader strategy implicit in the *De trinitate*.[23]

In Book XIV of the *De trinitate* Augustine discusses the need for some external force to provoke us to an awareness of the self-knowledge we have always possessed. The initial example of such an external force is an interlocutor, but Augustine then continues:

> the same effect is achieved by letters written about those
> things which the reader finds to be true with reason as his
> guide, not which he believes to be true on the authority of
> the person who wrote them in the manner that history is
> read, but which he himself finds to be true either in himself
> or in that very truth that is the mind's guide.[24]

Is not this in essence the ψυχαγωγία of both the *De trinitate* and the *Proslogion*, that the external text provokes a knowledge of the inner self, which in itself contains an understanding of God? In their use of textual narrative to construct interiority, and in their confidence that God can always be found

within the interiority so constructed, the bishop of Hippo and the abbot of
Bec are one.

IV

Before concluding this paper, however, I want to consider in a little
more detail Anselm's refusal to follow directly the route mapped out in the *De
trinitate* as the road to God—the route that traces the trinitarian structures of
the mind.[25] Towards the end of the first chapter of the *Proslogion* the speaker
says:

> I confess, Lord, and I give thanks, that you have created in
> me this image of you, so that remembering you I may think
> of you, I may love you. But it is so destroyed by the wearing
> down caused by my vices, it is so darkened by the smoke of
> my sins, that it cannot do that for which it was made, unless
> you renew and reform it.[26]

Now, there is nothing here to contradict the letter of the Augustinian doctrine
of the *imago Dei* delineated in the *De trinitate*. Yet it is not, I think, insignificant that this is the only indisputable reference to that doctrine in the *Proslogion*:[27] placed at the end of the programmatic opening section, it constitutes
something of a *recusatio*. Anselm is not going to invite the reader to approach
the knowledge of God by exploring the trinitarian structures of his own mind.
Rather, the possibility of exploring that road has been radically jeopardized by
sin, by the speaker's overwhelming sense of an unbreachable chasm between
himself and the divinity.[28] Whereas for the Augustine of the *De trinitate* self-
knowledge is the certain way to God, for the speaker of the *Proslogion* self-
discovery soon precipitates a collapse in confidence that threatens to sub-
merge the whole theological project:

> I was reaching towards God, and I struck against myself. I
> was seeking rest in my solitude, and I 'found trouble and sor-
> row' in my innermost parts.[29]

The interior journey instigated in the first few sentences of the text leads not
to illumination and understanding but to crippling despair.

It may seem—and indeed it seems to the speaker himself[30] —that this despair is lifted in chapters 2–13, as we steadily advance towards a comprehensive grasp of the divine existence and attributes. But the *Proslogion* does not end with chapter 13.[31] Chapter 14 opens with the self-addressed question, *an invenisti, anima mea, quod quaerebas?*[32] And the clear answer is a perhaps surprising negative. The speaker does not yet perceive God, he does not yet see God.[33] His eye is overcast by too much shadow, while God himself is shrouded in the most blinding light. The idea of God's inaccessible light prompts more constructive reflection in chapters 15–17, but chapter 18 restates the sense of failure with such force that we might be back at chapter one: "And again, see how confusion, see how again sorrow and grief stand in the way of the one who is seeking joy and happiness!"[34] *Iterum...iterum*, again and again. We are back at chapter 1—back with the awareness of separation and alienation that tempts us to despair but yet contains the seed of desire. And it is that desire that forces the voice of the text to go on, forbidding it to rest either in despair or in hope.[35]

This continual deferral of satisfaction is a fundamental—perhaps the fundamental—aspect of Anselm's ψυχαγωγία in the *Proslogion*. Even in those passages where it would appear that the speaker does achieve some kind of satisfaction there is always an element of deferral. For instance, in seeking to understand the divine mercy, the speaker is forced to acknowledge that *et videtur unde sis misericors, et non pervidetur.*[36] Similarly, although he thinks he may have grasped why God should save the wicked, he has to admit his inability to penetrate the mystery of why some wicked people should be saved and others should not.[37] Coming to understand, however successfully, some truths about the divine being also opens up vistas of inscrutable shadow. And at the end of the text, where the speaker finally seems to find the joy he has always been seeking,[38] he only finds it in his contemplation of that which of necessity he does not possess: heaven. What satisfaction is here attained inevitably includes the non-satisfaction of being confined to earth. Contemplation of the ultimate eschatological deferral of happiness is the only happiness we can hope to find. But if happiness can only be found in the embrace of hope and desire, it must always carry in itself the marks of absence and exile. Enacting Anselm's narrative, submitting to his ψυχαγωγία, means abandoning rest for a restless journey.

V

I have so far been presuming that the element of deferral in Anselm's ψυχαγωγία is something that differentiates him from Augustine. Yet perhaps that is to state the matter too simply. Perhaps Anselm is, again, placing on the surface of his text a motif that lies implicitly in Augustine, transposing that same motif from the hidden structure to the overt structure.

We might note, for example, Augustine's concern to stress the provisionality of all that he writes in the *De trinitate*. In the opening chapters of Book I he defines his role not as instructing his readers in what he definitively knows but as disclosing to them simply *quantum eiusdem uiae peregerim.*[39] Similarly, the prologues to Books II and III insist on the need for the reader himself to be questioning and searching: if author and reader are truly on the same road, then not only must the author be humble but the reader must be his active partner. And as the narrative of the later books unfolds, it becomes ever more evident that this road stretches on without limit in this life, that neither writing nor reading the *De trinitate* will permit us to abandon the arduous pilgrimage towards truth: "so let us seek as those who are going to find, and let us find as those who are going to seek."[40] Perfection in this life is nothing but a forgetting of what is past and a reaching out to what lies ahead: it is quest, journey, narrative. Complete knowledge, like complete joy for Anselm, is ineluctably deferred to the time of eternity.[41] Even when some glimpse of the eternal is given to us, this vision of something outside the structure of journey and narrative in which we are bound to live does not absorb but rather is absorbed by our journey, our narrative: *et fit rei non transitoriae transitoria cogitatio.*[42]

The theme of movement without arrival also finds expression at the level of form. For although we described the later books of the *De trinitate* as containing a narrative, it might be more accurate to say that they contain several, or at least the same narrative told twice. Books VIII–X, for instance, represent one telling of the story: from the trinity of outward love (Book VIII), to the psychological trinity of *mens-verbum-amor* (IX), to the purely mental trinity that is the image of God, *memoria-intelligentia-voluntas* (X). With the conclusion of Book X, we reach the end of the journey; but then we do not, for the journey commences again, from a different point of departure, the mechanism of perception, in Book XI, to arrive at the same mental trinity in Book XIV. In other words, this is not a journey that can be undertaken, a narrative that can be experienced, once and for all. It must be continually undertaken, continually experienced.

Book XV begins to make more sense as the culmination of the *De trinitate* when seen from this perspective. It might seem somewhat careless of Augustine to have ended his great work with a long series of rather disconnected essays, the burden of which appears to be to play down the immense theological achievements of Books VIII–XIV. And yet if Augustine's ψυχαγωγία includes a systematic thwarting of the reader's desire to have read enough, to have done enough, then surely this lack of an ending is the perfect ending. Augustine does not leave us with the sense of achievement and closure to which we might have been tempted if he had ended the *De trinitate* with Book XIV. He leaves us rather with a sense of having hardly begun, or perhaps of needing to begin again, and again. And he leaves us in the end not with exposition but with a solitary address to his solitary self, weak and sinful,[43] and with a prayer that his desire may be kindled with ever increasing intensity.[44] *Exercere*, we should perhaps remember, means not only to exercise but also to vex, to provoke, to disturb. Augustine ends the *De trinitate* by bringing the reader to a point where she must confront her own sin, her own exile and her own desire. It is the point at which Anselm will begin the *Proslogion*, some seven centuries later.

Notes

[1] *Phaedrus* 271C–D.

[2] For a very brief attempt to describe the *De trinitate* in terms of such a project of soul-leading, see P. Hadot, "Exercises spirituels," *École pratique des hautes études: V^e section—sciences religieuses* 84 (1976–77) 67–68. Augustine "veut faire expérimenter l'âme, par un retour sur elle-même, le fait qu'elle est l'image de la Trinité" (p. 68). The article argues that ancient philosophical texts in general need to be read from the point of view of the ψυχαγωγία they contain, although Hadot himself does not use this term (pp. 59–70).

[3] The idea of relating the two works in the title was suggested by Anselm himself, who tells us that his *Monologion* was based on Augustine's *De trinitate* and that the *Monologion* in turn served as the point of departure for the *Proslogion*. Anselm asserts the dependency of the *Monologion* on the *De trinitate* in *Epistola* 77: III,199,13–26, and in the prologue to the work itself (*Monologion,prologus*: I,8,8–14). For the origin of the *Proslogion* in Anselm's desire to rework the basic themes of the *Monologion*, see his prologue to the *Proslogion* (*Proslogion,prooemium*: I,93,2–10). All references to Anselm's works include the volume, page, and lines in *S. Anselmi Cantuariensis Episcopi opera omnia*, ed. F. S. Schmitt, 6 vols. (Seckau, 1938; repr. Edinburgh: Thomas Nelson, 1946–61).

⁴*De trinitate* XV,i,1: *CC* L/A,460: "Wanting to exercise the reader in the things that were made in order to know him by whom they were made." All translations are my own.

⁵*De trinitate* XI,i,1: *CC* L,333–34 sets out the methodology of "exercising" ourselves in the sensible so that we may come to a comprehension of the spiritual. The verb *exercere*, however, does not appear here. It recurs several times in Book XV: *ut...distinctius in ea lectoris exerceretur intentio*, where Augustine is referring specifically to Book XI (XV,iii,5: *CC* L/A,466); *exercitata in inferioribus intellegentia*, speaking of the whole of Books IX–XIV (XV,vi,10: *CC* L/A,473); and finally, in a passage concerning the obscurities of Scripture rather than Augustine's own methodology, *ut autem nos exerceret sermo diuinus* (XV,xvii,27: *CC* L/A,501). The Bible also has its ψυχαγωγία in Augustine's eyes.

⁶ "Now we have arrived at his image."

⁷ E.g. *De trinitate* X,xii,19: *CC* L,332; XII,xv,25: *CC* L, 379–80; XIV,viii,11: *CC* L/A, 435–38; XV,iii,4–5: *CC* L/A,462–67; XV,vi,10: *CC* L/A,472–74.

⁸ To construe a series of statements as a narrative—as related along a temporal rather than a logical or otherwise static axis—requires a special effort of the imagination, in which the referents of those statements are perceived to possess a coherence that cannot always be reduced to simple implication. Their happening, one after another, is sufficient basis for the validity of the narrative form whether or not they are causally related. Yet to read a text as a narrative is inevitably to seek some relation other than that of brute consecutivity between the events portrayed. Reading a narrative commits us to a search for coherence, while the narrative form—we might say the fact of the temporal axis itself—denies the possibility of ever reducing those events to a simple and static unity and therefore denies that search any straightforward closure. The narrativity of the texts under consideration already contains in itself, then, the tension between projection towards and postponement of closure that is discussed in sections IV and V of the paper.

⁹ *De trinitate* XIV,viii,11: *CC* L/A,436: *Ecce ergo mens meminit sui, intellegit se, diligit se. Hoc si cernimus, cernimus trinitatem, nondum quidem deum sed iam imaginem dei.*

¹⁰ *De trinitate* XII,viii,13: *CC* L,368: "To those thus ascending inwards"; see *De trinitate* XII,xv,25: *CC* L,379: *introrsum ascendere* and *De trinitate* XIV,iii,5: *CC* L/A,426: *ab inferioribus ad superiora ascendentes uel ab exterioribus ad interiora ingredientes.*

¹¹ The specifically "autobiographical" passages that do occur in the *De trinitate* are found at the early stages of the narrative, where the topic is the more externally oriented operations such as perception; so in the analysis of remembering perception Augustine uses the example of an arch he had seen at Carthage; see *De trinitate* IX,vi,11: *CC* L,302–3.

¹² *De trinitate* VIII,vi,9: *CC* L,280: *Animum igitur cuiuslibet ex nostro nouimus, et ex nostro credimus quem non nouimus.* Compare Georges Poulet on the experience of reading generally: "as soon as something is presented as thought, there has to be a thinking subject with whom, at least for the time being, I identify, forgetting myself, alienated from myself" ("Phenomenology of reading," *New Literary History* 1 [1969] 56–57). The use of interior narrative by Augustine and Anselm might then be seen as a textual strategy which foregrounds the process of identification and alienation implied in every act of reading.

[13] *De trinitate* VIII,vi,9: *CC* L,279–84.

[14] Cf. *De trinitate* IX,ix,14: *CC* L,305–6, where Augustine argues that in spiritual things simply to conceive of and to will something is to possess it.

[15] *De trinitate* XI,viii,15: *CC* L,352.

[16] *De trinitate* XIII,i,4: *CC* L/A,383–85.

[17] *De trinitate* XII,vii,10: *CC* L,365: *Quantumcumque se extenderit in id quod aeternum est tanto magis inde formatur ad imaginem dei.*

[18] *Proslogion, prooemium*: I,93,21–94,1: *Sub persona conantis erigere mentem suam ad contemplandum deum.*

[19] The preface to Book III of the *De trinitate* reveals Augustine's awareness of this community: he wants his readers to be actively critical and not merely passively receptive in their reading, while his own writing is as much a way of learning for himself as of instructing others (III,*prooemium*: *CC* L,127–130).

[20] In saying this I am contradicting most of the modern commentators on the *Proslogion*, who unquestioningly consider it to be the transcript of Anselm's personal struggle for theological understanding mentioned in the prologue (*Proslogion,prooemium*: I,93,2–19). This is to ignore the fact that the only connection made by Anselm himself between that experience and the text he is presenting is the inspiration for its central idea, while he explicitly asserts that the work is written *sub persona* (n. 18 above). He therefore equates the status of the text with that of the *Monologion*, which he also describes as written *sub persona* (*Monologion,prologus*: I,8,18–19), and which is patently not autobiographical. For the assumption of autobiography, see for example K. Barth, *Anselm: Fides quaerens intellectum*, tr. W. Robertson (Cleveland and New York: World Publishing, 1962), p. 168; H. de Lubac, "Sur le chapitre XIVe du Proslogion," *Spicilegium Beccense* 1 (1959) 297; and most recently Y. Cattin, "La prière de S. Anselme dans le Proslogion," *Revue des sciences philosophiques et théologiques* 72 (1988) 375–76.

[21] It was Barth who especially stressed the crucial role of the cognitive dimension of the argument, a dimension written into the very definition of God as *id quo maius cogitari nequit* (e.g. *Proslogion* II: I,101,15–16), and who saw in Gaunilo's neglect of that dimension the root of the argument's subsequent misunderstanding; see *Fides quaerens intellectum*, pp. 84–89.

[22] The discussion of God's existence in chapters 2–4 is occasioned by the speaker's recollection of a text from Scripture: *dixit insipiens in corde suo: non est deus* (*Proslogion* II: I,101,6–7). These are the opening words of Psalms 13 and 52.

[23] That Anselm was both aware of the self-enacting aspect of the *De trinitate* and consciously transposing it to perform the specific function of theological proof is suggested by the *Monologion*, a work which is far more obviously modelled on the *De trinitate*. For the speaker—and therefore by implication the reader—of the *Monologion* by reflecting on his own mental operations performed in the text both discovers and validates the trinitarian nature of God (chapters 29–68). See especially *Monologion* XXXIX: I,51,7–18, where the

speaker's own activity of rational reflection becomes a key premise in an argument about the eternity of the Word. Anselm has already departed from Augustine in the *Monologion* by constructing a proof about the nature of God from the mind's reflection on its own textual activity, a road he will pursue to its conclusion in chapters 2–4 of the *Proslogion*.

²⁴ *De trinitate* XIV,vii,9: *CC* L/A,434: *Id agunt et litterae quae de his rebus conscriptae sunt, quas res duce ratione ueras esse inuenit lector, non quas ueras esse credit ei qui scripsit sicut legitur historia, sed quas ueras esse etiam ipse inuenit siue apud se siue in ipsa mentis duce ueritate.*

²⁵ To the objection that Anselm neglects this route because his search for understanding encompasses more than just the Trinity, it might be pointed out that he has little use for Augustine's route even when the speaker does finally consider the three persons of the Godhead in chapter 23.

²⁶ *Proslogion* I: I,100,12–15: *Fateor, domine, et gratias ago, quia creasti in me hanc imaginem tuam, ut tui memor te cogitem, te amem. Sed sic est abolita attritione vitiorum, sic est offuscata fumo peccatorum, ut non possit facere ad quod facta est, nisi tu renoves et reformes eam.*

²⁷ Cf. *Proslogion* XXVI: I,121,14–17, where intellect and love are coupled and contrasted: *cognoscam te, amem te.... Proficiat hic in me notitia tui...crescat amor tuus.* But no third term is added to these two.

²⁸ This mood is firmly established throughout the whole of the opening chapter, from the question of *Proslogion* I: I,98,2–3 onwards: *ubi te quaeram absentem?*

²⁹ *Proslogion* I: I,99,10–12: *Tendebam in deum, et offendi in me ipsum. Requiem quaerebam in secreto meo, et "tribulationem et dolorem inveni" in intimis meis.*

³⁰ E.g. *Proslogion* IV: I,104,5–7.

³¹ This point was brilliantly expounded by De Lubac, in "Sur le chapitre XIVᵉ du *Proslogion*," *Spicilegium Beccense* 1 (1959) 295–312.

³² *Proslogion* XIV: I,111,8: "Have you found, my soul, what you were seeking?"

³³ We might compare Anselm's third meditation, where a successful intellectual exploration of the doctrine of the incarnation similarly fails to satisfy the speaker's desire to know and experience its reality: *Fac precor, domine, me gustare per amorem quod gusto per cognitionem. Sentiam per affectum quod sentio per intellectum (Meditatio III: III,91,196–97).*

³⁴ *Proslogion* XVIII: I,113,18–19: *Et iterum ecce turbatio, ecce iterum obviat maeror et luctus quaerenti gaudium et laetitiam!*

³⁵ Cattin considers desire to be the unifying force in the *Proslogion*; see "La prière de S. Anselme dans le Proslogion" 394–95. In the light of this reading of the whole text of the *Proslogion* it is clear that Barth's denial of crisis or anxiety in Anselm's theology is unacceptable (*Fides quaerens intellectum*, pp. 26 and 151).

[36] *Proslogion* IX: I,107,14–15: "And it is seen whence you are merciful, and it is not seen clearly." My translation does not do justice to the force of the prefix *per* in this context; that *pervidetur* is here to be understood as something like "is seen through" becomes evident from both the sense and the parallel structure of the next sentence in the text (*Cernitur unde flumen manat, et non perspicitur fons unde nascatur*: *Proslogion* IX: I,107,15–16). For a similar use of *pervidere*, though not one with which Anselm was necessarily familiar, see Lucretius, *De rerum natura* I,1114–17.

[37] *Proslogion* XI: I,109,21–24.

[38] *Proslogion* XXVI: I,120,25–121,1: *Inveni namque gaudium quoddam plenum, et plus quam plenum.*

[39] *De trinitate* I,v,8: *CC* L,37: "How much of the same road I have traversed."

[40] *De trinitate* IX,i,1: *CC* L,293: *Sic ergo quaeramus tanquam inuenturi, et sic inueniamus tamquam quaesituri.*

[41] *De trinitate* IX,i,1: *CC* L,293. This is a theme to which Augustine will return again and again, echoing the words of St. Paul that the only knowledge available to us now is *per speculum in aenigmate* (*De trinitate* XIV,xix,25: *CC* L/A,456–57; XV,ix,16: *CC* L/A,482–83). Trinitarian theology is no different from the rest of Christian experience in its ineradicable resistance to completion and to closure.

[42] *De trinitate* XII,xiv,23: *CC* L,376: "And a transitory act of thought about a thing that is not transitory takes place."

[43] *De trinitate* XV,xxvii,50: *CC* L/A,531–33.

[44] *De trinitate* XV,xxviii,51: *CC* L/A,533–35.

A Comment on
Some Questions Relating to *Confessiones* VII:
A Reply to O'Connell

Frederick Van Fleteren

It is not often that an author has the privilege of reviewing what he wrote some twenty years ago and critiquing it in light of his own research and development. It is even more seldom that the occasion of such a review and critique arises from the comments of a distinguished scholar in the same field. And this is precisely my privilege in this forum. Recently, Rev. Professor Robert O'Connell, S.J. published a critique of my work in *Augustinian Studies* (1990). Although I shall take issue with him on several fronts, I should, at the beginning, wish to thank him for the time and effort he has obviously spent on his lengthy critique of my work. It is an honor to be the subject of such a work.

Almost twenty years ago, in a doctoral dissertation written under the friendly guidance of J. J. O'Meara at University College, Dublin, I analyzed Augustine's ascents of the soul to God in Milan as he himself reported them in *Confessiones* VII,x,16; xvii,23; xx,26, on the occasion of his reading the *libri platonicorum*, and the influence of these ascents on the early works of Augustine. I presented some of the fruits—if that they be—of this research in two articles in *Augustinian Studies* in 1974 and 1975 and continued the investigation of this subject in various articles since then.[1] I have reviewed all of these articles recently in some detail in light of Professor O'Connell's comments and find no reason to change the views expressed in them substantially. So various and diffuse are his comments, however, that I cannot hope to deal with all of them in full detail now. Nevertheless, a general comment on our respective positions is in order.

I. General Thesis

Let me iterate my conclusions of some twenty years ago. In the summer of 386 A.D. in Milan, upon the occasion of reading the *libri platonicorum*, Augustine had an experience of God, a mystical experience if you will. The experience of God was instantaneous; there was in all likelihood more than one vision, and Augustine was unable to sustain them. As had been a commonplace in the Western philosophical tradition since the time of *Republic* VII, Augustine thought that such a sustained vision of the *summum bonum* was possible for the human being in this life. He looked for reasons to explain his failure to sustain the intellectual vision of the divine and thought that he had found it in his lack of intellectual and—in some related sense—moral purity. He sought a program to achieve *katharsis*. Augustine's earliest works, the Cassiciacum dialogues, are to be interpreted in light of this project of ascent of the mind to God. The *De beata uita* demonstrates that human happiness, the end for which the ancient philosophers were searching, consists in the permanent possession of God.[2] The *Contra academicos* assumes that this possession of God is equivalent to the possession of truth and demonstrates, to Augustine's satisfaction at least, that it is attainable by the human being in this life. In *De ordine* II, after Augustine, his friends, and students fail to solve the mystery of the problem of evil and divine providence, Augustine presents a program of the liberal arts, the purpose of which is to achieve a mental purification so that they might solve these difficult questions and, at the same time, attain the vision of Beauty.[3] A Neoplatonic ascent of the soul—not to pinpoint its source as yet—takes place by a method of progressive interiority, from external things to the interior man to God himself. This Augustine applies to himself, starting in the *Soliloquia*. His moral purification, so to speak, takes place in *Soliloquia* I. In the second book of that work, Augustine proceeds through a shortened version of the purification provided by the liberal arts. At the end of *Soliloquia* II, he broaches the question of the immortality of the soul. The *De immortalitate animae*, notes for the projected *Soliloquia* III, represents the turning of the ascent inward to the interior man. In both that work and the *De quantitate animae*, Augustine investigates the spiritual nature of the soul as a propaedeutic to the vision of God. The project of the liberal arts, only partially completed and extant in its incipient form solely in the *De musica* and the notes for the *De dialectica*, was to provide a program of intellectual purification leading to the vision of God.[4] The program of ascent to God which dominates the early works ends more or less abruptly after the *De uera religione*, the last work before Augustine's ordination to the priesthood, though in some sense planned in 386 A.D.[5] The ascent motif is present throughout that work and is present in many of the works, letters, and commentaries of the later periods, but, after that work, it no longer occupies the central role in Augustine's works, with the evident exception of the *De trinitate* where the ascent appears in a form much modified from the early works. No doubt through his own experience Augustine came to realize that his project was, by its very nature, doomed to failure. But it was his close readings of the Epistle to the Romans and the Epistle to the Galatians that put the final nail in the coffin of the project of attaining the vision of God is this life.[6]

I would put the following question to Professor O'Connell: Would he agree, at least in broad outline, that the above sketch is the correct, or at least a valid, interpretation of Augustine's early works?

II. Historicity

If we can agree so far, I should like to proceed to the questions of procedure and historicity. At the end of his commentary on my two articles in *Augustinian Studies*, Professor O'Connell calls into question the very validity of a close textual analysis of *Confessiones* VII,x,16; xvii,23; xx,26, the passages in which Augustine reports his "vaines tentatives de l'extase plotinienne," to use Pierre Courcelle's phrase.[7] I believe now, and I believed then, that Professor Courcelle had gone beyond the textual evidence to identify three separate occurrences of attempts at ascent. Further, I believe now, and I believed then, that, while there were many analogies to a general Neoplatonic ascent of the soul and that the influences of both Porphyry and Plotinus on the ascent were present, the ascents could not be called "Plotinian ascents" in any full and technical sense of the term. There were many Christian elements in them which could not be explained solely by reference to Plotinus.

At the time that I wrote those articles, I acknowledged my debt to Pierre Courcelle, though I believe now, and I believed then, that my analyses go well beyond Professor Courcelle's. My analyses, both in form and in general outline, owe much to Professor Mandouze's analysis of mysticism in Milan and Ostia.[8] Others have analyzed these passages for mysticism; there is no doubt that I owe much to the analyses of Madec, Solignac, du Roy, and O'Connell himself. To my knowledge, scholars have generally recognized the legitimacy of Courcelle's and Mandouze's endeavors, not to mention those of others, if not every word of their analyses. Close textual analysis has been the common manner of studying Augustine since the work of Paul Henry. It is true, as Professor O'Connell correctly points out, that these texts (or any texts for that matter) must be taken within their context. I am in strong agreement with Professor O'Connell that context is important in analysis; I believe that I had followed this procedure in my writings. As Professor O'Connell no doubt realizes, publication imposes some space limitations.

But the argument goes beyond merely the issue of context. The more important question is: Do we have in *Confessiones* VII,x,16; xvii,23; xx,26 reports of actual occurrences in Augustine's life? Professor O'Connell thinks not. Rather, according to Professor O'Connell, when taken in conjunction with the immediately adjoining texts, Augustine has given us a summary of his thinking between 386–91, retrojected onto an apparently historical account in the *Confessiones*. I obviously agree that the early works present a project understandable only in relation to *Confessiones* VII; I do not agree, however, that the historicity of these texts should be called into question. Indeed, I believe that Augustine's early works are understandable only when they are seen to be rooted in his own experience.[9] Much ink has been spilled over the question of the historicity of the *Confessiones*. It is apparent that the *Confessiones* is not a biography in any contemporary understanding of the term. Much more is it an anthropology, a philosophy of the human being, based on Augustine's own life. No doubt Augustine pondered his own life and interpreted events in it through his reading of the Scriptures and the writings of Cicero, Plotinus, and Porphyry, among others. Further, there can be no doubt that Augustine selected the events from his life to illustrate his philosophy. But, far from throwing the historicity of the *Confessiones* into question, such speculation supports it. If someone, for example, were to enter religious life, he might later interpret various earlier events in his life in terms of the Scriptures or various readings which he may have done later. But such interpretation does not call into question the historicity of the earlier events. Rather that person has reached a deeper understanding of the meaning of these events as time passed. It is in this sense that, I believe, all events reported in the *Confessiones*, and a fortiori *Confessiones* VII,x,16; xvii,23; xx,26, are historical. We do not have merely a phenomenology of mysticism, though we do have that. We do not have merely the aspirations of Augustine at that time, though we do have that also. And we do not have only a summary of Augustine's project for the next five years, though the connections are apparent. And though the account may be somewhat stylized, as indeed many accounts in the *Confessiones* are, we have no reason to reject the historicity of these passages any more than we have reason to reject the historicity of the *Confessiones* in general.

III. Quellenforschung

While the purpose of my research on *Confessiones* VII,x,16; xvii,23; xx,26 was to show the relationship between Augustine's ascents of the soul in Milan and his early works, the riddle of Augustine's literary and intellectual sources arose secondarily, albeit quite naturally. Once again, much effort has been expended during the past one hundred years on the question of the sources for Augustine's thought. At times, the question has been ill defined. My concern, and the concern of most recent researchers, has not been how much of Plotinus and Porphyry, or other authors for that matter, Augustine read throughout his life. Such a project could perhaps be proved conclusively only in the lifetimes of several scholars. Obviously Augustine had more than a nodding acquaintance with their works, as *De ciuitate dei* VIII–X witnesses. The question which I, and others, would address is: What works are included in the *libri platonicorum* which, Augustine tells us, he read at Milan in 386 A.D.? In the article in question, I mentioned then, and I would mention now, that Plotinus's *Ennead on Beauty* (*Ennead* I,vi) had inspired Augustine's attempted ascents of the mind at Milan. This thesis was not new with me and has been generally accepted by the Augustinian scholarly community since the time of P. Henry. Professor O'Connell raises some interesting questions vis-à-vis *Ennead* V,viii and *Confessiones* VII; it would go far beyond the confines of this response to engage him on this point. Suffice it to say that we should have a great deal of reserve concerning any additions to the list of the "very few books" that Augustine said that he read at the time.

The two major texts in the early works of Augustine dealing with the question of how much Neoplatonism Augustine read appear in the *De beata uita* and the *Contra academicos*. *De beata uita* I,4 reads:

> *Lectis autem Plotini paucissimis libris, cuius te esse studiossimum accepi, conlataque cum eis, quantum potui, etiam illorum auctoritate, qui diuina mysteria tradiderunt, sic exarsi, ut omnes illas uellem ancoras rumpere, nisi me nonnullorum hominum existimatio commoueret.*

The Latin language—it is true—had degenerated in the late Roman Empire and in the time of Augustine the superlative form had been devalued much in the manner of many English expressions in our own time. *Paucissimi* here, and *paucissimas* in the following text, must therefore be taken *cum grano salis*.

Nevertheless, on the face of it, on the basis of this text, the burden of proof must be on those who would add to the list of Plotinian treatises which Augustine, they suppose, had read at the time of his conversion. Even more interesting is the text from the *Contra academicos* II,ii,4:

> *Et quoniam nondum aderat ea flamma, quae summa nos arreptura erat, illam qua lenta aestuabamus arbitrabamur esse uel maximam, cum ecce tibi libri quidam pleni, ut ait Celsinus, bonas res Arabicas ubi exhalarunt in nos, ubi illi flammulae instillarunt pretiosissimi unguenti guttas paucissimas, incredibile, Romaniane, incredibile et ultra quam de me fortasse et tu credis —quid amplius dicam?—etiam mihi ipsi de me ipso incredibile incendium concitarunt.*

From the point of view of Augustine's relation to the Neoplatonists, the important words are the "very few drops of very precious ointment." These *guttas paucissimas*, the Neoplatonic writings, inspired the "incredible fire" which I take to refer to Augustine's ascents at Milan in particular and such aspirations in general. Not only is the superlative diminutive form used (*paucissimas*), but the entire text compares the "incredible fire" with the fewness of the "drops." The aftermath of these readings was out of all proportion to the phenomena. The main import of the text is clear: Augustine read very few Neoplatonic treatises and was inspired out of all proportion to their numbers. It is difficult to see how *paucissimas* could refer to a list of fifteen Plotinian treatises or more. To be sure, Augustine could have read all the *Enneads* of Plotinus and many works of Porphyry between the time of his intellectual conversion in Milan and the retreat at Cassiciacum. But we have no solid evidence that he had done so. Indeed, the Cassiciacum dialogues are best understood as the works of a philosophical and theological neophyte.

Several methodological problems arise in determining precisely which treatises Augustine read at the time of his conversion. Those problems have been ably discussed elsewhere by others and go far beyond the scope of this rejoinder.[10] Not the least of these problems is that *Confessiones* VII deals predominately with Jn 1:1–14 when describing what he learned from the Neoplatonists. Let me be clear, however, with respect to my position concerning which treatises Augustine read at the time of his conversion. Professor O'Connell describes me as being from the Porphyrian wing of Augustinian exegesis. Unlike Professor Theiler, who held that Augustine read only Porphyry, and Professor O'Connell, who holds with regard to this question of Neoplatonism that Augustine was solely under the influence of Plotinus at the time of his conversion, I hold that Augustine had read a very few treatises of both Plotinus and Porphyry in 386. What treatises did he read? Our answer to this question must be guarded. The following are the treatises which I regard as certain that Augustine would include in the list of the *libri platonicorum* and the reasons why I believe so: *Ennead* I,vi (the ascent of the soul; cf. *De ordine* II,xix,51); *Ennead* I,viii (*Confessiones* VII,xvii,23; *regio dissimilitudinis*); *Ennead* III,ii–iii (divine providence and the problem of evil; see *De ordine* I,2); *Ennead* IV,iii (the soul and its spirituality); *Ennead* V,i (the hypostases; cf. *Confessiones* VII,ix,13; *De beata uita* IV,33–35); *Ennead* V,iii (the doctrine of illumination; *Confessiones* VII,ix,13); *Philosophy from Oracles* (mentioned by title in *Contra academicos* I,i,1) and the *De regressu animae* (return of the soul; see *Confessiones* VII,xx,26). This is the list of Neoplatonic treatises which I believe Augustine to have read at the time of his conversion. In my opinion we should add to this list only with conclusive evidence.

Permit me two more comments. Augustine was a Roman, eclectic by temperament, and thus of a more synthetic than analytic mentality. While, early on, he did see some major differences between Neoplatonism and Christianity, especially on the question of the Incarnation and salvation, he was predisposed by the influence of the "Milanese Circle" to find similarities between Plotinus and Porphyry on the one hand and the Scriptures on the other. In many senses, but not in all, he saw Plotinus and Porphyry as his colleagues. It is we who place the question of Plotinus or Christianity, Plotinus or Porphyry. In all likelihood, he would not have distinguished the thought of Plotinus from that of Porphyry as we do. Nevertheless, Augustine's tendency throughout the early period, and indeed throughout his life, is toward the Scriptures and Christianity and, where choice is involved, away from Platonism, Plotinus, and Porphyry. I concur in the opinion of Etienne Gilson that Augustine was more responsible for halting the spread of Platonism in the West than he was for spreading it.

The second observation has to do with the respective roles of Plotinus and Porphyry on Augustine's early period. In my opinion, Plotinus's influence was largely inspirational. This appears to be the correct interpretation of *Contra academicos* II,ii,4. Augustine's reading of *Ennead* I,vi inspired him toward ascents of the soul in Milan in 386 and remained influential on Augustine throughout his entire life. On the other hand, Porphyry influenced Augustine more in the salvationist aspects of his thought. In my opinion, it was Porphyry, in all likelihood in the *De regressu animae*, not Plotinus, who prodded Augustine to a program of purification through the liberal arts. Augustine's understanding of mediatorship and the Incarnation is developed in contradistinction to Porphyry's views on the subjects.

IV. The Fall of the Soul

No discussion of Neoplatonism and the early Augustine with Professor O'Connell could take place without some discussion of the fall and return of the soul in Augustine's early works. Professor O'Connell remarks that I am a "longtime critic" of his. Let me be clear on this point. I regard Professor O'Connell as one of the fine contemporary researchers on St. Augustine. He is a man of great erudition. He has discovered many things in the writings of Augustine which give us all pause in our research. But on the issue of the fall and return of the soul, Professor O'Connell has led us into a *cul de sac*.

The theme of fall and return is a thematic commonplace in ancient philosophy. From Pythagoras through Plato, Middle Platonism, Cicero, Plotinus, and Porphyry, the fall of the soul from some primordial existence and its efforts to return is present. In addition to the *Enneads* of Plotinus and the *De regressu animae* of Porphyry, Augustine should have been familiar with this theme through the philosophical encyclopediae which he had read, the writings of Cicero, the preaching of Ambrose, and the common fund of traditional philosophical knowledge available to him. That Augustine was familiar with the language and motif of fall and return is undeniable. It was the philosophical language of the time, much in the manner that Thomistic terminology dominated Catholic thought some fifty years ago or Heideggerian jargon dominates today. But that this use of fall and return vocabulary shows that Augustine held to the full metaphysical doctrine of fall and return of the soul, that the presence in Augustine of doctrines allied to the theme of the fall of the soul in other authors, but in no way essentially connected to it, proves that Augustine held this doctrine too, that Augustine's knowledge of and use of the language of fall and return, in and of itself, proves that Augustine read *Ennead* IV,vii (or any other Plotinian treatise for that matter), and that the motif of fall and return forms the basic Plotinian matrix for Augustine's early works goes well beyond the evidence. Though I have been on record for over twenty years on this subject, I am not the only voice—nor indeed, sad to relate, the most distinguished voice—in the chorus voiced against Professor

O'Connell on this point. Since the evidence against Professor O'Connell's position on the origin of the soul in Augustine is well known and sketched by myself and many others over a long period of time, I shall here only point out Augustine's own words on the subject in the *Retractationes*:...*nec tunc sciebam, nec adhuc scio.* To use Augustine's oft miscited words in *Sermo CXXXI* X,10 in an accommodated sense, I might add: *causa finita est; utinam aliquando finiatur error.*

I should like to add that no comment of mine should be interpreted as demeaning the prodigious work that Professor O'Connell has performed on the corpus of Augustine or the insights he has allowed us all to gain into the works of both the early and the late Augustine. Unfortunately—*quelle dommage*—he has allowed his thesis on the fall and return to govern his entire project.

Notes

[1] F. Van Fleteren, "Authority and Reason, Faith and Understanding in the Thought of Augustine," *AS* 4 (1973) 33–71; "Augustine's Ascent of the Soul in Book VII of the Confessions: A Reconsideration," *AS* 5 (1974) 29–71; "The Early Works of Augustine and His Ascents at Milan," *Studies in Medieval Culture* 10 (1977) 19–23; "Augustine and the Possibility of the Vision of God in this Life," *Studies in Medieval Culture* 11 (1977) 9–16; "The Cassiciacum Dialogues and Augustine's Ascents at Milan," *Mediaevalia* 4 (1978) 59–82.

[2] *De beata uita* IV,35: *CC* XXIX,84: *Illa est igitur plena satietas animorum, hoc est beata uita, pie perfecteque cognoscere, a quo inducaris in ueritatem, qua ueritate perfruaris, per quid conectaris summo modo. Quae tria unum deum* ....

[3] *De ordine* II,xix,51: *CC* XXIX,135: *Nihil amplius dicam nisi promitti nobis aspectum pulchritudinis, cuius imitatione pulchra, cuius conparatione foeda sunt cetera.*

[4] *Retractationes* I,vi: *BA* 12,296–98: *Per idem tempus quo Mediolani fui baptismum percepturus, etiam disciplinarum libros conatus sum scribere* ...*per corporalia cupiens ad incorporalia quibusdam quasi passibus certis vel pervenire vel ducere.* Ibid. I,xi,1: *BA* 12,332–34: *Deinde ut supra commemoravi, sex libros de musica scripsi, quorum ipse sextus maxime innotuit, quoniam res in eo digna cognitione versatur, quomodo a corporalibus et spiritualibus, sed mutabilibus numeris, perveniatur ad immutabiles numeros, qui iam sum in ipsa immutabili veritate, et sic "invisibilia Dei, per ea quae facta sunt intellecta conspicitur"* (Rm 1:20). See also *De musica* VI,i,1, which is probably part of the *emendatio* which Augustine appends to the work in 412 A.D.

[5] See *Retractationes* I,xiii,1; xiv,1; *Contra academicos* II,iii,8.

[6] See my "Augustine and the Possibility of the Vision of God in this Life," *Studies in Medieval Culture* 11 (1977) 9–16.

[7] P. Courcelle, *Recherches sur les Confessions de saint Augustin* (Paris: de Boccard, nouvelle edition, 1968), pp. 157–67.

[8] A. Mandouze, *Saint Augustin: L'aventure de la raison et de la grâce* (Paris: Études Augustiniennes, 1968), pp. 686ff.

[9] See O. du Roy, *L'intelligence de la foi en la trinité selon saint Augustin* (Paris: Études Augustiniennes, 1966), p. 15, for a discussion of methodology in the works of Augustine. See also J. J. O'Meara, "Research Techniques in Augustinian Studies," *AS* 1 (1970) 277–85.

[10] See A. Solignac, *Les Confessions*, *BA* 13, note 25, pp. 682ff., and du Roy, *L'intelligence*, pp. 69ff.

Scripture Index

Augustine Citations

Citation Index   549

Contra academicos

III,xvii,37:	197, 204 n. 16
III,xviii,41:	204 n. 20
III,xix,42:	197, 198, 204 nn. 17 & 19
III,xx,43:	282, 290 n. 8

Contra Adimantum

VII,4:	78, 89 n. 34
VII,11:	89 n. 34

Contra epistulam Fundamenti

5:	326, 327 n. 14, 329 n. 37

Contra Faustum Manichaeum

XII,14:	378, 383 n. 14
XV,5–6:	233 n. 34
XX,7:	472, 476 nn. 24, 25, 29 & 32

Contra Iulianum

VI,xxii,68:	355 n. 2

Contra litteras Petiliani

II,xxx,69:	412 n. 5

Contra Maximinum

II,x,2:	494 n. 61
II,xx,3:	494 n. 60

Contra secundam Iuliani responsionem opus imperfectum

I,ci:	12, 24 n. 33

Contra sermonem Arianorum

V,5:	480, 490 n. 26, 491 n. 27, 493 n. 53
VII,6:	480, 482, 491 n. 32, 492 nn. 43 & 44, 495 n. 66
VII,6–VIII,6:	494 n. 62
VIII,6:	491 n. 35, 495 n. 66
IX,7:	487, 492 n. 43, 494 n. 63
X,8:	483, 493, nn. 47 & 48
XII,9:	483, 493 n. 50
XV,9	490 n. 21
XV–XVI,9:	490 n. 23
XIV,9:	490 nn. 24 & 25
XXIII,19:	490 n. 24
XXVII,23:	479, 490 n. 22

De agone christiano

XIII,15:	203 n. 9
XVII,19:	203 n. 11
XX,22:	104, 117 n. 16, 493 n. 54

De continentia

I,1–II,5:	10, 24 n. 27

De correptione et gratia

X,28:	15, 25 n. 51

De diuersis quaestionibus ad
Simplicianum

I,ii,21:	433, 441 n. 13
II,praef.:	81, 93 n. 71
II,ii,1:	77, 88 n. 29

De diuersis quaestionibus LXXXIII

XVI:	489 n. 5
XVIII:	471, 475 n. 21
XXIII:	489 n. 5
XXX:	275 n. 39
XXXVII:	489 n. 5
XLV:	274 n. 20
XLV,1:	376–77, 382 nn. 9 & 10
XLVI,2:	108, 118 n. 24
XLVIII:	203 n. 12, 301, 303 n. 23
L:	489 n. 5
LX:	489 n. 5
LXIV,6–7:	360 n. 42
LXIX:	489 n. 5
LXXI,6:	261 n. 32
LXXIII,2:	493 n. 56
LXXX:	489 n. 5

De doctrina christiana

Prooem.,1:	331, 336 n. 1, 337 nn. 2, 3, & 4.
Prooem.,2:	331, 332, 336 nn. 5, 6 & 8
Prooem.,4:	332, 337 n. 9
Prooem.,8:	332, 334, 337 n. 10, 338 n. 19
I,iv,4:	275 n. 39
I,vi,6:	77–78, 83, 88 n. 32, 95 n. 87
I,xiv,13:	134 n. 17
I,xxiii,23:	259 n. 13
I,xxxiv,38:	378, 383 n. 16
I,xxxix,43:	321, 327 n. 13
II,vi,8:	47, 53 n. 20
II,ix,14:	47, 53 n. 20
II,x,15:	363–64, 371 n. 3
II,xxxviii,57:	274 n. 20
III,v,9:	320, 327 nn. 7 & 9
III,x,14:	321, 327 nn. 11 & 12
III,x,15:	321, 327 n. 14
III,xv,23:	321, 328 n. 15
III,xxv,36:	333, 337 nn. 11 & 12
III,xxvi,37:	321, 328 n. 16, 333, 337 n. 13
III,xxvii,38:	333, 337–38 n. 14
III,xxviii,39:	333–34, 338 n. 15
III,xxix,40:	334, 338 n. 16

Enarrationes in Psalmos

XCIX,6:	83, 93 n. 70, 95 n. 88
XCIX,11:	255, 260 n. 23
XCIX,11–13:	20, 27 n. 68
CI,s.II,10:	75, 79, 87 n. 15, 90 n. 44
CI,s.II,14:	79, 91 n. 52
CIII,s.I,3:	89 n. 36
CIII,s.IV,6:	355 n. 2
CIV,3:	82, 94 n. 77
CIV,4:	78, 90 n. 42
CVI,7:	259 n. 17
CX,s.II,10:	91 n. 49
CXVIII:	398 n. 4
CXVIII,s.XVIII,3:	81, 94 n. 74
CXIX,1:	134 n. 16
CXXI,5:	75, 79, 87 n. 17, 90 n. 43, 91 nn. 48, 49 & 50
CXXX,14:	81, 94 n. 73
CXXXIV,4:	75, 76, 87 nn. 14 & 22
CXXXIV,6:	91 n. 49, 96 n. 92
CXXXVIII,8:	78, 89 n. 38
CXXXVIII,9:	89 n. 36
CXLIV,5–6:	515 n. 51
CXLVI,6:	93 n. 66
CXLVI,11:	81, 93 n. 66, 515 n. 51
CXLVIII,4:	232 n. 16

Enchiridion ad Laurentinum

VIII,27:	54 n. 22
XXIII,93:	15, 25 n. 50
XXVIII,104:	54 n. 22
LXXXI,22:	360 n. 47

Epistulae

I*,5:	414 n. 40
II*:	18, 27 n. 63
X:	453 n. 3
XVII,3:	359 n. 25
XX*:	15, 25 n. 48
XX*,4–7:	415 n. 64
XX*,8:	414 n. 37
XX*,12,25,26:	414 n. 41
XXI,3–4:	413 n. 25
XXII,i,1:	413 n. 13
XXII,i,3–II,8:	413 n. 26
XXII,i,4:	414 n. 33
XXII,i,5:	413 nn. 14 & 20
XXII*,5:	414 n. 35
XXII*A,4–5:	414 n. 42
XXIII,2:	422, 428 n. 36
XXIII,6:	415 n. 65
XXIII,7:	413 n. 21
XXIII*A,3:	6, 23 n. 8, 478, 490 n. 16
XXVI*,2:	414 n. 37
XXVI*,8:	414 n. 37
XXIX, 7:	415 n. 65
XXXI,6:	413 n. 15
XXXI,9:	405, 412 n. 3

Sermones

XXI,2:	80, 92 n. 62
XLIII,1:	289, 294 n. 28
XLIII,9:	81, 92 n. 64
LII,i,1:	415 n. 53
LII,vi,16:	80, 92 n. 60
LII,viii,20:	118 n. 23
LII,x,23:	93 n. 66
LVI,i,1:	444 n. 36
LVI,iii,4:	441 n. 18, 444 n. 40
LVI,v,8:	443 n. 28
LXI,vi,7:	435–36, 443 n. 27
LXXI,18:	111, 119 n. 37
LXXX,7:	432, 441 n. 11
LXXX,8:	20, 27 n. 70
XCVIII,5–6:	356 n. 9
CIII,iii,4:	250, 259 n. 6
CXV,i,1:	437, 444 n. 36
CXVII–CXXI:	398 n. 3
CXVII,ii,3:	399–400 n. 17, 400 n. 26
CXVII,iii,4:	395, 398–99 n. 8, 399 n. 10
CXVII,iii,4–5:	400 n. 25
CXVII,iii,5:	80, 92 nn. 59 & 63, 399 n. 13, 400 n. 27

Sermones

CXVII,iv,6:	401 n. 30
CXVII,iv,6–x,17:	490 n. 13
CXVII,v,7:	78, 89 n. 33, 95 n. 86, 399 nn. 9 & 10, 400 n. 19
CXVII,v,8:	81, 93 n. 70
CXVII,vi,9–10:	78, 89 n. 39
CXVII,vi,10:	399 n. 10, 401 nn. 31 & 32
CXVII,viii,11:	401 nn. 29 & 33
CXVII,ix,12:	401 nn. 34 & 35
CXVII,x,15:	76–77, 88 n. 27
CXVII,x,16:	396, 400 nn. 21 & 22
CXVIII,1:	402 n. 39
CXVIII,2:	401 n. 33
CXIX,iii,3:	396, 399 nn. 9, 11 & 14, 401 n. 37
CXIX,iv,4:	399 n. 12
CXIX,vi,6:	400 n. 23, 402 n. 39
CXIX,vii,7:	398 n. 2, 401 n. 36, 493 n. 52, 494 n. 57

Soliloquia

I,ii,7:	296–97, 302 n. 7, 303 n. 12
I,iii,8:	298–99, 303 nn. 16 & 17
I,iv,9:	476 n. 41
I,vi,12:	298, 301, 303 nn. 14, 15 & 22
I,viii,15:	78, 90 n. 41
I,xii,22:	
I,xiii,22:	10, 23, n. 22, 233 n. 32, 361 n. 50
I,x,17:	232 n. 25
I,xv,30:	301, 304 nn. 24 & 25
II,i,1:	53 n. 8, 441 n. 11

Tractatus in Euangelium Ioannis

I–III:	398 n. 3
I,1,4:	399 n. 9
I,7:	402 n. 41
I,8:	509, 515 n. 54
II,2:	79, 90 n. 45, 91 n. 50
II,4:	205 n. 27, 402 n. 42, 415 n. 57
II,8:	398 n. 2, 401 n. 37
II,10:	402 n. 40
II,16:	399 n. 12

Tractatus in Euangelium Ioannis

III,19:	399 n. 9
VII,23:	387, 388, 393 nn. 8, 9 & 10
IX,10:	388, 393 n. 11
X,1:	445 n. 44
XIII,5:	74, 86 n. 7
XVII,1:	391, 394 n. 18
XVII,1–9:	394 n. 20
XVII,5:	391, 394 n. 19
XVIII:	489 n. 12, 494 n. 58
XVIII,7:	90 n. 46
XIX,5:	231 n. 11
XX:	489 n. 12, 494 n. 58
XX,3:	437, 444 n. 41
XXI,14:	88 n. 31
XXIII,9:	80, 91 n. 57
XXIII,11:	79, 90 n. 46, 91 n. 54
XXVI,5–10:	489 n. 12
XXVII,4:	494 n. 60, 495 n. 64
XXVIII,1:	389, 393 n. 13
XXIX,8:	415 n. 54
XXXIV,9:	206 n. 44
XXXVI,5:	359 n. 25
XXXVIII,8:	79, 90 n. 46
XXXVIII,10:	79, 90 n. 47
XLIX,1:	390, 394 nn. 16 & 17
XLIX,3:	356 n. 9
L,6:	389, 393 n. 14
LVIII,3:	494 n. 61
LVIII,4:	415 n. 55

Other Citations

Timaeus

| 29C: | 195 |
| 65B–68D: | 372 n. 13 |

PLAUTUS

Aulularia

| 801: | 382 n. 4 |

Cistellaria

| 648: | 382 n. 4 |

Menaechmi

| 342: | 382 n. 4 |

PLOTINUS

Enneads

I,i,7:	117 n. 14
I,iv,6:	117 n. 9
I,vi:	537
I,vi,8:	205 n. 27
I,viii:	537
II,ii,10:	117 n. 9

Enneads

III,ii,17:	20, 27 n. 66
III,ii–iii:	537
III,vii:	171, 183 n. 49, 184 n. 52
III,vii,1:	178 n. 3, 183 n. 43
III,vii,3:	183 n. 45
III,vii,5:	182 n. 41, 183 n. 43
III,vii,7:	178 n. 3, 179 n. 6, 182 n. 43
III,vii,7–10:	178 n. 3
III,vii,11:	180 n. 11, 183 n. 48
III,vii,12:	180 n. 11, 183 n. 51
III,vii,13:	180 n. 11
IV,iii:	537
IV,iii,11:	358 n. 23
IV,iii,21:	103, 117 n. 11
IV,iii,22:	103, 104, 117 nn. 12 & 13
IV,iii,27:	476 n. 42
IV,vii:	538
V,i:	537
V,i,10:	476 n. 42
V,iii:	537
V,iii,13–14:	85–86 n. 3
V,v,12:	117 n. 9
V,vii,1:	102, 116 n. 7
V,ix,5:	476 n. 42
VI,iv–v:	361 n. 50
VI,iv,14:	117 n. 9
VI,vii,35:	117 n. 8
VI,ix,1:	300
VI,ix,4:	117 n. 9

ZOZIMUS

Epistulae

"Magnum pondus":	29, 37 n. 2 & 3
"Postquam a nobis":	29, 37 n. 2
"Quamvis patrum":	30, 37 n. 4

ROMAN LAW

Codex Theodosianus

XVI,i,2:	67 n. 17
XVI,ii,3:	415 n. 62

CHURCH DOCUMENTS

Collatio Carthaginiensis

III,155, 185–87:	64, 69 n. 41
III,176–220:	69 n. 40
III,216–20:	69 n. 40

Index of Names

DATE DUE